George Washington's Diaries

An Abridgment

George Washington's Diaries

An Abridgment

Dorothy Twohig
Editor

UNIVERSITY PRESS OF VIRGINIA

Charlottesville and London

The six-volume edition of *The Diaries of George Washington* was prepared by the editors and staff of *The Papers of George Washington:* Donald Jackson, W. W. Abbot, Dorothy Twohig, Beverly H. Runge, Philander D. Chase, Frederick Hall Schmidt, Jesse Shelar, and Kathleen Howard.

This one-volume edition of *The Diaries of George Washington* has been prepared with the support of a grant from the National Historical Publications and Records Commission.

Its publication has been supported by a grant from the National Historical Publications and Records Commission.

THE UNIVERSITY PRESS OF VIRGINIA

First published 1999

⊗ The paper used in this publication meets the minimum requirements of the American National Standard for Information Sciences—Permanence of Paper for Printed Library Materials, ANSI Z39.48-1984.

Library of Congress Cataloging-in-Publication Data
Washington, George, 1732–1799.
  George Washington's diaries : an abridgment / Dorothy Twohig, editor.
    p.   cm. — (The papers of George Washington)
  Includes bibliographical references (p.   ) and index.
  ISBN 0-8139-1856-1 (cloth : alk. paper) — ISBN 0-8139-1857-x (paper : alk. paper)
  1. Washington, George, 1732–1799—Diaries.   2. Presidents—United States—Diaries.   I. Twohig, Dorothy.   II. Washington, George, 1732–1799. Diaries of George Washington.   III. Title.   IV. Series: Washington, George, 1732–1799. Papers of George Washington.
  E312.8   1999
  973.4′1′092—dc21
  [B]   98-11681
                                                                                            CIP

Title page art: detail of portrait of George Washington by Charles Willson Peale, 1780. (National Portrait Gallery, Smithsonian Institution; gift of The Barra Foundation)

Contents

Illustrations

Maps

Introduction

George Washington's Diaries: An Abridgment is a one-volume condensed version of the six-volume complete *Diaries of George Washington,* published by the University Press of Virginia between 1976 and 1979.

Washington's diaries are not those of a literary diarist in the conventional sense. There are few of the self-revealing passages that we have come to expect in the diaries of famous men, such as those of Landon Carter, William Byrd, or John Adams. Washington was an intensely private man; none of his contemporaries would have expected that he would reveal the inner Washington even to his diaries. If he was regarded as aloof and enigmatic by his peers, it was an image he deliberately fostered as contributing to his public role. A close examination of his correspondence gives us a different view of Washington, and we find him warmer and more intense than we knew, given to wry humor, compassion, and sometimes towering rage. Nevertheless, we do not find in the pages of his diaries what we have come to expect of that genre.

But we should not be unfair to a man who had his own definition of a diary: "Where & How my Time is Spent." The phrase runs through the whole record. He accounts for his time because, like his lands and his money, his time is a usable resource; it can be tallied and its usefulness appraised. Perhaps it was more than mere convenience that caused Washington to set down his earliest diary entries in interleaved copies of an almanac, for an almanac, too, is an accounting of time.

That his diaries were important to him there is no doubt. When in the spring of 1787 he journeyed to the Constitutional Convention in Philadelphia and discovered that he would be away from Mount Vernon many weeks, he wrote home for the diary he had accidentally left behind. "It will be found, I presume, on my writing table," he wrote to his nephew. "Put it under a good strong paper cover, sealed up as a letter."

We can be unfair to Washington in another way by calling this collection of diaries uneven, mixed, or erratic. That is not his fault but ours, for it is we—his biographers, editors, and archivists—who have brought these items together since his death and given them a common label. It would surprise Washington as often as it does his readers to find between the same covers his "where and how" diaries, weather records, agricultural notations, tours of the North and South during his presidency, together with such documents as a travel journal published in 1754 under the title *The Journal of Major George Washington, Sent by the*

Hon. Robert Dinwiddie, Esq; . . . Commander in Chief of Virginia, to the Commandant of the French Forces on Ohio (Williamsburg, Va., 1754).

Even when his preoccupation with other matters reduces Washington to a mere chronicling of dinner guests, the record is noteworthy, although at times the reader may feel he has gotten hold of an eighteenth-century guest book rather than a diary. What a diarist chooses to set down, and what not to bother with after a busy day, can be worthy of scrutiny: the number of "respectable ladies" who constantly turned out to pay Washington homage during his southern tour in 1791, tallied so precisely that one suspects Washington of counting heads; his passion for fruits and flowers and the resulting diary notes that very nearly constitute a synopsis of eighteenth-century horticulture; his daily horseback rides, necessary to any large-scale Virginia farmer but clearly a ritual with him; his notices of the dalliance, both planned and impromptu, of his male and female foxhounds—a vital record if canine bloodlines were to be kept pure.

The Washington of the diaries is not the Washington who wrote hundreds of letters to neighbors dealing for farm produce and to foreign potentates attending to the affairs of the eighteenth-century world. He is not on guard here, for he seems unaware that any other eyes will see, or need to see, what he is writing.

"At home all day. About five oclock poor Patcy Custis Died Suddenly," runs the entry for 19 June 1773. Good enough for his purposes; it was what happened on that day. His curt entry would serve to remind him of his devotion to his ill-fated stepdaughter, dead in her teens after a life made wretched by epilepsy. The place for sorrow was in communications to friends, not in the unresponsive pages of a memorandum book, and so it was to his brother-in-law Burwell Bassett that he wrote of his grief for the "Sweet Innocent Girl" who had entered into "a more happy, & peaceful abode than any she has met with in the afflicted Path she hitherto has trod."

Except for special occasions, such as his mission to the French commandant and his voyage to Barbados, Washington apparently kept no daily record until 1760. Even then, his diary keeping was erratic until 1768, when he settled down to a program that he was to continue faithfully until he became commander in chief in 1775.

As Washington notes at the beginning of his 1781 diary, he kept no diary during most of the Revolution. The rigor of his activities would have made it difficult to do so, and the full record of the period that accumulated in his official letterbooks and general orders rendered the custom less necessary. He tried to resume his old habit with his diary of the Yorktown campaign in 1781, but it was not until he had resigned his command and returned home that he became a confirmed diarist again.

It is probable that he kept diaries, mostly now missing, for the presidential years 1789–97, and the fact that so few have survived is particularly vexing for historians. *The Journal of the Proceedings of the President, 1793–1797,* a daily account of Washington's official activities and correspondence, written in the first person but kept by his secretaries, has been published as part of *The Papers of George Washington.* An entry for 16 April 1789, recounting his departure from Mount Vernon to assume office, appears only in Jared Sparks's *Writings of Washington,* 1: 441–42. The entry for 23 April 1789, remarking on the enthusiasm with which the public received him, is from Washington Irving's *Life of George Washington,* 4:511. So at least we know that Sparks and Irving had access to material indicating that Washington began his presidency with a determination to continue the record. Diaries are extant for the period covering his tours of the northern and southern states and a brief one kept during the Whiskey Insurrection of 1794. Apart from an unrewarding record for 1795, all else is lost for the presidential years.

The earliest diaries were kept in notebooks of various sizes and shapes, but when Washington began in earnest to make daily entries he chose to make them in interleaved copies of the *Virginia Almanack,* a Williamsburg publication. By the end of the Revolution he had grown accustomed to the blank memorandum books used in the army, and he adopted a similar notebook for his civilian record. By 1795 he had gone back to his interleaved almanacs.

Upon Washington's death in 1799, most of his papers still in his possession became the property of his nephew Bushrod Washington, an associate justice of the United States Supreme Court. Destruction and dispersal of the papers began very early when Mrs. Washington reportedly burned all the correspondence she had exchanged with Washington during his lifetime—apparently overlooking only two letters. There followed long years of careless handling by Bushrod, biographer John Marshall, and editor Jared Sparks. Indeed, what is most important in the story of Washington's papers is not such natural processes as fire, flood, mildew, and the tendency of paper to fall into dust. Rather, there has been an overabundance of stewardship by misguided caretakers, persons who thought they knew what was important and what was trivial, what should be saved and what given away to friends and autograph collectors.

The editor who laments the disappearance of so many Washington diaries can only sink into despondency upon learning that Bushrod gave many away. To diplomat Christopher Hughes, in 1825, he gave the 1797 diary and a sheaf of Washington's notes on agriculture: Hughes dispersed these among his friends in the United States and Europe. Two years later Bushrod gave the diaries for 1795 and 1798 to Margaret and Robert Adams of Philadelphia. Then he presented the 1767 diary to Dr. James W. Wallace of Warrenton. These and certain other diaries once in private hands have been preserved; others apparently have not.

Jared Sparks's turn to mishandle the papers came in 1827, when he persuaded Bushrod to let him take large quantities to Boston, where he was to prepare his twelve-volume edition, *The Writings of George Washington* (Boston, 1837). Sparks, a prominent nineteenth-century editor and historian, apparently decided that carefully excising a Washington signature from a document and sending it to a friend did not really damage the manuscript as a piece of history; that a page torn from a Washington diary or an entire Washington letter could safely be given away if he, Sparks, judged it to be of no historical value. It was Sparks who cut the draft of Washington's first inaugural address into small pieces and so thoroughly disseminated this document of more than seventy pages that the efforts of a number of collectors and editors have failed to reassemble more than a third of it. Even after he had supposedly returned all the papers to the Washington family, Sparks retained a supply to distribute. He was still mailing out snippets to acquaintances in 1861.

The pillage stopped in 1834 when the Washington family sold the basic collection to the United States government. This corpus, together with a later, smaller sale, forms the basis of the principal Washington archive at the Library of Congress. Other acquisitions have been made throughout the years.

The Worlds of Washington

As he rode about Mount Vernon on his daily inspection trips, Washington could turn his eyes frequently to the shipping traffic on the Potomac, his principal link with the great outside world. Vessels with such names as the *Fair American,* the *Betsy,* and the *Charming Polly* plied the river, some trading with the ports of Virginia and Maryland and some bound for far more distant anchorages in North America, the West Indies, or Europe. Most of the schooners, brigs, and ships that Washington watched come upriver were bound for Alexandria's docks and warehouses, and often their cargoes included goods for him: fine clothing and fabrics, bridles and saddles, books and surveying instruments, tools and nails, delicate chinaware and jewelry, fruits and spices, and great wines from France and Madeira. Outward bound, they carried the tobacco—and in later years the wheat or flour—that was sent abroad to pay for his imports.

Now and then his commercial representatives in London, chiefly Robert Cary & Co., would err and place his shipment aboard a vessel bound for another Virginia river, such as the Rappahannock, and he must endure not only the inconvenience of further transportation but also the risk of loss. On one occasion he warned the Cary company never to ship by any vessel not bound for the Potomac, for when a recent cargo via the Rappahannock finally reached him, he found "The Porter entirely Drank out."

Moving along the growing network of roads that ran from New England to Georgia were more goods and the all-important packets of letters and newspapers that kept Washington in touch with an expanding nation in a restless world. Besides the English journals that came to him, he regularly read American newspapers and periodicals from Boston, New York, Philadelphia, Baltimore, Annapolis, and Williamsburg.

There was little isolation from the world at any time during his life. His diary for 1751–52 relates a voyage to Barbados when he was nineteen, with his dying half brother Lawrence. The next two accounts concern the early phases of the French and Indian War, the momentous struggle for control of the North American continent in which he commanded a Virginia regiment. By the 1760s when Washington's diaries resume, young George III was on the British throne, and the American colonists were beginning to feel an ominous sense of discomfort that during the 1770s grew into rebellion and placed Washington in command of a revolutionary army.

After the War of Independence, Washington never again fought on a field of battle, but military matters and political affairs of national and international import continued to engage his attention. In 1787 he journeyed to Philadelphia for the Constitutional Convention, which he chaired. During his two terms as president of the new nation there were no wars, but serious diplomatic problems arose with Great Britain, France, and Spain in 1793 and 1794. Even in retirement near the end of his life, Washington could not escape the turmoil among nations. When in 1798 relations with France deteriorated to the point that a sea war was developing, the aging General Washington was placed at the head of a nominal land force that never took the field.

In such a world, Washington felt happiest within a much smaller region bounded on the south by the James River and on the north by the Potomac. This was his neighborhood, somewhat extended, a world of very different responsibilities and pleasures that is best revealed in his diaries.

At the heart of this world lay Mount Vernon, the Potomac River plantation that Washington's father Augustine had established in the 1730s on an old family patent and his half brother Lawrence had inherited and built up before his death in 1752. It was to Mount Vernon that young Colonel Washington came when, in 1758, his involvement in the French and Indian War was finished, for the plantation was now his home, Lawrence's widow having leased it to him four years earlier. It would become permanently his by right of inheritance when she died in 1761. In the meantime, Washington settled at Mount Vernon, thinking that his military career had ended forever. He was prepared for country living, a bit of local politics, and plenty of riding to the hounds. The good life truly began for him in January 1759 with his marriage to Martha Dandridge Custis, a wealthy young widow with a handsome dowry and two small children nicknamed Patsy and Jacky.

Washington was passionately devoted to Mount Vernon, eagerly extending its borders during the next three decades with numerous purchases of surrounding lands and striving constantly to improve its crops and buildings. But he did not neglect his immediate neighbors in Fairfax County, nor did they disregard him. He became a vestryman of the local parish, a magistrate of the county court, a trustee of Alexandria, and one of Fairfax's two burgesses in Virginia's legislature, a position that he held from 1765 to 1775. In the course of carrying out the duties of those offices and of conducting the daily business of his plantation, he came to know well a host of local merchants, craftsmen, farmers, and planters. But Washington's closest ties, both of friendship and personal interest, were with the Fairfax family at Belvoir only a few miles down the Potomac from Mount Vernon. There until 1773 lived George William Fairfax, member of the governor's council and collector of customs for the South Potomac Naval District. His influence was derived from his father William Fairfax's cousin Thomas Fairfax, sixth Baron Fairfax of Cameron, proprietor of all the land between the Potomac and the Rappahannock rivers, the area known in Washington's time as the Northern Neck of Virginia. Lord Fairfax, who settled permanently in Virginia in 1747, had the exclusive power to grant lands in the Northern Neck and the right to collect annual quitrents of two shillings per one hundred acres on lands that he granted, privileges that he retained until the Revolution.

The proprietor's home was a hunting lodge called Greenway Court, located west of the Blue Ridge Mountains in Frederick County. It too was an area that Washington knew well, for as a youth he surveyed dozens of Lord Fairfax's grants in the Shendandoah Valley and the valleys beyond. He himself acquired lands along Bullskin Run, a tributary of the Shenandoah River, lands which he retained until his death. During the French and Indian War he was charged for a while with the defense of this region, and for seven years before he was elected a burgess from Fairfax, the freeholders of Frederick sent him to Williamsburg as one of their representatives. In the 1770s and 1780s two of Washington's three younger brothers, Samuel and Charles, also found opportunities west of the Blue Ridge, settling on lands of their own within a few miles of Bullskin.

At the other end of the Northern Neck, south and east of Mount Vernon, lay another part of Washington's extended neighborhood, a region of concern to him mainly because of family ties. Westmoreland County, stretching for about forty miles along the Potomac, was the first home of the Washington family in the New World. Washington's half brother Augustine and his favorite younger brother, Jack, lived there, and it was on the banks of Pope's Creek that Washington was born. Farther up the Potomac, about halfway between Westmoreland County and Mount Vernon, was the Chotank area, part of Stafford County until 1776 and then of King George County. In that locality lived a number of Washingtons: Samuel until 1770, and many cousins, some of whom Washington had known from his childhood. Several miles west of Chotank, at Fredericksburg, on the south bank of the Rappahannock, was the home of Fielding Lewis, husband of Washington's sister Betty, and before 1780 the home of his brother Charles. Across the river from Fredericksburg was Ferry Farm, where Washington lived as a boy and where his mother, Mary Ball Washington, resided until old age obliged her in 1771 to retire to a house in Fredericksburg, near her daughter Betty Washington Lewis's home, there to spend the last eighteen years of her life.

At the southern extremity of Washington's extended neighborhood was the provincial capital of Williamsburg, and near it, on the York and Pamunkey rivers, were the principal lands of the Custis family and the homes of their relations, the Dandridges and the Bassetts. For Washington this was an area to which he came to fulfill his duties as a burgess, to settle accounts with merchants, and to see that the affairs of his Custis stepchildren were properly managed. But it was also the place in which he attended the theater and balls, dined with men of note, and began to move into the role of an American leader, which eventually took him away from his beloved neighborhood again. Indeed, the network of interconnecting regions between the Potomac and the James that made up that neighborhood helped to develop in Washington that broad feeling of kinship and responsibility for men of differing experience and outlook which enabled him to enter the larger world beyond with ease.

But seldom was his home on the Potomac far from his thoughts, and never did he fail to return there when he could, for it was at Mount

Vernon that all his worlds came together. From both inside and outside his extended neighborhood came a galaxy of people from all walks of life to visit him. Some were friends and relatives who came for a holiday to play cards, to ride to the hounds, or to shoot ducks. Others came on business, to discuss politics and land transactions, to deal in wheat, flour, fish, and other commodities, to bring their mares for breeding, to call at his mill and, in the last years, at his distillery, or sometimes just to ask for help in solving their problems. After the Revolution he wrote his mother, hoping to discourage her from making her home with him at Mount Vernon, that "in truth it may be compared to a well resorted tavern, as scarcely any strangers who are going from north to south, or from south to north, do not spend a day or two at it." With this endless flow of friends, neighbors, and the idly curious coming to his home, Washington must have thought it an unusual day indeed when on 30 June 1785, at a time when he truly believed that he was done with service to his country, he wrote in his diary that he "dined with only Mrs. Washington which I believe is the first instance of it since my retirement from public life."

Washington and the New Agriculture

No theme appears more frequently in the writings of Washington than his love for the land—more precisely, his own land. From the ordered beauty of the mansion house grounds to the muddiest fields on Bull-skin plantation in the Shenandoah Valley, his estate and those who inhabited it were his constant concern. The diaries are a monument to that concern. Most of Washington's detailed daily entries describing for each plantation crops planted and harvested, the work assigned slaves, and the constant agricultural experimentation in which he engaged have been omitted in the abridged version of the *Diaries*. The six volumes of the unabridged *Diaries,* however, offer what is probably the most complete day-by-day and year-by-year account extant of the agricultural life of an eighteenth-century Virginia plantation.

In his letters Washington referred often, as an expression of this devotion to his estate and its resulting contentment, to an Old Testament passage. After the Revolution, when he had returned to Mount Vernon, he wrote the marquis de Lafayette on 1 February 1784: "At length my Dear Marquis I am become a private citizen on the banks of the Potomac, & under my own Vine & my own Fig-tree." On the occasion of another joyous homecoming after his two terms as president, the phrase came back to him. He wrote to Oliver Wolcott, Jr., 19 May 1797, that if he ever were to see distant friends again, "it must be under my own Vine and Fig tree as I do not think it probable that I shall go beyond the radius of 20 miles from them."

Maintaining and improving the mansion house and its grounds, which required constant attention from carpenters and gardeners, was in part a diversion; farming, on the other hand, was his profession, and one in which he took immense pride. "I shall begrudge no reasonable expence that will contribute to the improvement & neatness of my Farms," he wrote manager William Pearce on 6 October 1793, "for nothing pleases me better than to see them in good order, and every thing trim, handsome, & thriving about them; nor nothing hurts me more than to find them otherwise."

The diaries that deal with agriculture begin in 1760, a year some-times used to denote the beginning of a new agriculture in England. It was also the year of the ascension of George III, a monarch so fond of farming that he maintained experimental plots at Windsor and sub-mitted articles for publication under the name of his farm overseer. The influence of English agriculture on Washington and others in this country—Jefferson included—was indeed great. But the science of agriculture was changing rapidly. In 1760 Washington was a practi-tioner of Jethro Tull's horse-hoeing husbandry. At his death in 1799 he was devoted to the more sophisticated experiments and writings of Arthur Young and practiced a seven-year rotation instead of Tull's three-year plan for the land. In Washington's *Diaries* his preoccupation with the weather is as evident as his concern with agriculture. For the years when he was at Mount Vernon almost every entry begins with an account of the day's weather. In this abridgment of his diaries, most of these entries have been omitted; but to Washington they clearly were an extension of his needs and interests as a farmer and were inextri-cably intertwined with his agricultural records.

The period extending from Washington's return to Mount Vernon after the Revolution until his death was a time of intensive scientific agriculture for Washington. He was faced with the prospect of rebuild-ing his very large farms after the years of neglect they had suffered while he was the commanding general. He also faced the realization, with many of his fellow Virginians, that soil exhaustion and the evils of a one-crop agriculture were, together with slavery, edging them to-ward disaster. A general agricultural depression in the United States added to the problem. Washington wrote to George William Fairfax, 10 November 1785, that he never rode to his plantations "without see-ing something which makes me regret having [continued] so long in the ruinous mode of farming which we are in."

One of Washington's great preoccupations, during his whole career in agriculture, was finding the right crops for the soil, climate, and practical needs of his Mount Vernon establishment. In a set of "Notes & Observations" he kept for 1785–86, he mentions planting barley, potatoes, pumpkins, rye, spelt, turnips, timothy, and wheat. He raised alfalfa. He tried the horsebean and buckwheat, burnet, rye grass, and Jerusalem artichokes. Experimentation with all these many crops was one of Washington's chief delights as a farmer. His experience with tobacco typifies the change in his thinking. Early in the diaries it is his all-important cash crop—the shipment he sends to England every year to exchange for goods he could not obtain in America. By 1766 he was saying that he raised no tobacco at all except at his dower plantations on the York River, although he continued to plant tobacco in a small way on the Mount Vernon farms. Washington was determined to throw off the bondage of single-crop farming; but when he drastically reduced his tobacco production, he became, in the terminology of the day, no longer a planter but a farmer.

The growing shortage of timber with which to make rail fences caused him to turn to live hedges for fencing. He experimented with honey locust, Lombardy poplar, cedar, and some of the hundreds of species of thorned trees and shrubs. Improved cropping calls for improved machinery, as Washington knew, and he shared Jefferson's interest in the mechanical aspects of agriculture. Like most farmers through the ages, Washington was most fascinated by the plow and its potential for advancing agriculture. He ordered a Rotheram patent plow from England in 1765; and years later, at Washington's request, Arthur Young sent two plows with extra shares and coulters, capable of a nine-inch furrow from four to eight inches deep. By 1788 Washington had found another model he liked so well that he told Thomas Snowden on 3 October "I mean to get into the use of them *generally*."

Livestock was another vital interest of Washington's, though it is not so apparent—either in the diaries or the letters—as his preoccupation with crops. He was fully aware of the breeding required to prosper with livestock and equally aware of the shortcomings of American farmers in that regard.

A few days before his death in December 1799, Washington was hard at work on a plan for his future farming operations. He drew up a scheme for each of the farms at Mount Vernon, setting forth in minute detail such matters as crop rotation, the handling of pasturelands and meadows, and the use of manures. His instructions for his manager, written 10 December 1799, closed with a characteristic statement: "There is one thing however I cannot forbear to add—and in strong terms;—it is, that whenever I order a thing to be done, it must be done;

or a reason given at the *time,* or as soon as the impracticability is discovered, why it cannot; which will produce a countermand, or change." Any other course of action was disagreeable to him, he said, "having been accustomed all my life to more regularity, and punctuality, and *know* that nothing but system & method is required to accomplish all reasonable requests."

Four days later he was dead, and system and method began to disappear from the farms of Mount Vernon. It would be more than fifty years before the mansion house, eventually bereft of most outlying farmland, was restored to beauty and order. Meanwhile, time and neglect diminished much of what Washington had longed to improve and preserve.

Although superficially Washington's travel journals of his trips to the frontier in his youth and to distant parts of the new nation during his presidency appear of more interest than his daily diary entries at Mount Vernon, it is in the latter entries that the rich kernel of Washington's life appears. It is hoped that this abridged diary will induce readers to sample the rich mosaic of Washington's life that presents itself in his complete diaries and correspondence. As John C. Fitzpatrick, an earlier editor of Washington's journals, wrote, "Now that I have read every word of these Diaries, from the earliest to the last one, it is impossible to consider them in any other light than that of a most marvelous record. It is absolutely impossible for anyone to arrive at a true understanding or comprehension of George Washington without reading this Diary record."

Editorial Procedures

Transcription of the diaries has remained as faithful as possible to the original manuscript. Because of the nature of Washington's diary entries, absolute consistency in punctuation has been virtually impossible. Where feasible, the punctuation has generally been retained as written. However, in cases where sentences are separated by dashes, a common device in the eighteenth century, the dash has been changed to a period and the following word capitalized. Dashes which appear after periods have been dropped. Periods have been inserted at points which are clearly the ends of sentences. In many of the diaries, entries consist of phrases separated by dashes rather than sentences. Generally, if the phrase appears to stand alone, a period has been substituted for the dash.

Spelling of all words is retained as it appears in the manuscript. Errors in spelling of geographic locations and proper names have been corrected in notes or in brackets only if the spelling in the text makes the word incomprehensible. The ampersand has been retained. The thorn has been transcribed as "th." Capitalization is retained as it appears in the manuscript; if the writer's intention is not clear, modern usage is followed.

Contractions and abbreviations are retained as written; a period is inserted after abbreviations. When an apostrophe has been used in contractions, it is retained. Superscripts have been lowered, and if the word is an abbreviation, a period has been added. Other editorial insertions or corrections in the text also appear in square brackets. Angle brackets ⟨   ⟩ are used to indicated mutilated material. A space left blank by Washington in the diaries is indicated by a square-bracketed gap in the text.

Bibliographical citations have been used as sparingly as possible and are indicated by the author's name and a short title. A short-title list appears at the end of the front matter. Complete bibliographical information for people identified and information supplied in annotation may be found in the unabridged *Diaries*.

In order to compress the six-volume edition of Washington's diaries into one volume, much telescoping has been necessary; not only are many complete entries omitted, but material within sentences is deleted as well. In order to retain as much of the variety of the complete diaries as possible without intrusive editorial apparatus, such omissions have not been indicated.

The Papers of George Washington are being published in five series, the

Colonial Series, the Revolutionary War Series, the Confederation Series, the Presidential Series, and the Retirement Series. Whenever possible, citations to the published volumes are given as the source for manuscripts quoted or cited in the abridged diary. In cases where the document has not yet been published, the manuscript repository owning it has been cited. Many of the documents quoted may also be found in their entirety in such collections as John C. Fitzpatrick's edition of *The Writings of George Washington from the Original Manuscript Sources, 1745–1799* (Washington, D.C., 1931–44), and Stanislaus Murray Hamilton, ed., *Letters to Washington and Accompanying Papers* (Boston and New York, 1898–1902). Virtually all of the letters to and from Washington will also appear in the CD-ROM edition of Washington's papers, in process of preparation by the Papers of George Washington at the University of Virginia and the Packard Humanities Institute.

The editor would like to express appreciation for the able assistance of Pamela J. Grizzard, Robert F. Haggard, Debra B. Kessler in the preparation of this volume.

Short-Title List

Abbott, "James Bloxham."   Wilbur Cortez Abbott. "James Bloxham, Farmer," *Massachusetts Historical Society Proceedings*, 59 (1925–26), 177–203.

Adams, *Diary*.   John Adams. *Diary and Autobiography of John Adams*. Ed. Lyman H. Butterfield. 4 vols. Cambridge, Mass., 1961–62.

Annals of Congress.   Joseph Gales, ed. *The Annals of Congress: The Debates and Proceedings in the Congress of the United States*. 42 vols. Washington, D.C., 1834–56.

ASP, Indian Affairs.   Walter Lowrie and Matthew St. Clair Clarke, eds. *American State Papers*. Washington, D.C., 1832.

Bacon-Foster, *Patomac Route*.   Corra Bacon-Foster. *Early Chapters in the Development of the Patomac Route to the West*. Washington, D.C., 1912.

Bagnall, *Textile Industries*.   William R. Bagnall. *The Textile Industries of the United States*. Cambridge, Mass., 1893.

Baker, *Itinerary*.   William S. Baker. *Itinerary of General Washington from June 15, 1775, to December 23, 1783*. Philadelphia, 1892.

Baker, *Washington after the Revolution*.   William S. Baker. *Washington after the Revolution*. Philadelphia, 1898.

Baurmeister, *Revolution in America*.   Carl Leopold von Baurmeister. *Revolution in America: Confidential Letters and Journals, 1776–1784, of Adjutant General Major Baurmeister of the Hessian Forces*. New Brunswick, N.J., 1957.

Bergh, *Writings of Thomas Jefferson*.   Albert Ellery Bergh, ed. *The Writings of Thomas Jefferson*. Memorial Edition. 20 vols. Washington, D.C., 1903–4.

Boyd, *Jefferson Papers*.   Julian P. Boyd et al., eds. *The Papers of Thomas Jefferson*. 27 vols to date. Princeton, N.J., 1950—.

Brissot, *Travels*.   Jean-Pierre Brissot de Warville. *New Travels in the United States of America, 1788*. Translated from the French by Mara Soceanu Vamos and Durand Echeverria. Ed. Durand Echeverria. Cambridge, Mass., 1964.

Brock, *Dinwiddie*.   R. A. Brock, ed. *The Official Records of Robert Dinwiddie, Lieutenant-Governor of the Colony of Virginia, 1751–1758, Now First Printed from the Manuscript in the Collections of the Virginia Historical Society*. 2 vols. Richmond, 1883–84.

Brown, *Virginia Baron*.   Stuart E. Brown, Jr. *Virginia Baron: The Story of Thomas 6th Lord Fairfax*. Berryville, Va., 1965.

Browne.   Fairfax Harrison, ed. "With Braddock's Army: Mrs. Browne's Diary in Virginia and Maryland." *Virginia Magazine of History and Biography*, 32 (1924), 305–20.

Brumbaugh.   Gaius Marcus Brumbaugh. *Maryland Records: Colonial, Revolutionary, County, and Church from Original Sources.* Vol. 1. Baltimore, 1915.

Butler, "Journal."   Richard Butler. "General Richard Butler's Journal of the Siege of Yorktown," *Historical Magazine,* 8 (1864), 102–12.

Carter, *Diary.*   Landon Carter. *The Diary of Colonel Landon Carter of Sabine Hall, 1752–1778.* Ed. Jack P. Greene. 2 vols. Charlottesville, Va., 1965.

Carter, *Great Britain and the Illinois Country.*   Clarence E. Carter. *Great Britain and the Illinois Country.* Washington, D.C., 1910.

Cartmell, *Shenandoah Valley Pioneers.*   Thomas Kemp Cartmell. *Shenandoah Valley Pioneers and Their Descendants: A History of Frederick County, Virginia.* Winchester, Va., 1909.

Caughey, *McGillivray of the Creeks.*   John Walton Caughey. *McGillivray of the Creeks.* Norman, Okla., 1938.

Chastellux, *Travels.*   Marquis de Chastellux. *Travels in North America in the Years 1780, 1781, and 1782.* 2 vols. Ed. Howard C. Rice, Jr. Chapel Hill, N.C., 1963.

Clinton, *American Rebellion.*   William B. Willcox, ed. *The American Rebellion: Sir Henry Clinton's Narrative of His Campaigns, 1775–1782, with an Appendix of Original Documents.* New Haven, 1954.

Closen, *Journal.*   *The Revolutionary Journal of Baron Ludwig von Closen, 1780–1783.* Ed. Evelyn M. Acomb. Chapel Hill, N.C., 1958.

Clunn, "March on Pittsburgh."   John Hugg Clunn. "March on Pittsburgh, 1794." Ed. Nicholas Wainwright. *Pennsylvania Magazine of History and Biography,* 71 (1947), 44–67.

Coleman, *St. George Tucker.*   Mary Haldane Coleman. *St. George Tucker, Citizen of No Mean City.* Richmond, 1938.

Copeland, *The Five George Masons.*   Pamela C. Copeland and Richard K. Macmaster. *The Five George Masons: Patriots and Planters of Virginia and Maryland.* Charlottesville, Va., 1975.

Cramer, *Navigator.*   Zadok Cramer. *The Navigator: Containing Directions for Navigating the Monongahela, Allegheny, Ohio, and Mississippi Rivers; with an Ample Account of These Much Admired Waters, from the Head of the Former to the Mouth of the Latter; and a Concise Description of Their Towns, Villages, Harbours, Settlements &c.* 7th ed. Pittsburgh, 1811.

Cresswell, *Journal.*   *The Journal of Nicholas Cresswell, 1774–1777.* Ed. Lincoln MacVeagh. New York, 1924.

Crofut, *Connecticut.*   Florence S. Marcy Crofut. *Guide to the History and the Historic Sites of Connecticut.* 2 vols. New Haven, 1937.

Cromont Du Bourg, "Diary."   Marie François Joseph Maxime, Baron Cromot Du Bourg. "Diary of a French Officer, 1781," *Maga-*

zine of American History, 4 (1880), 204–14, 293–308, 376–85, 441–52; 7 (1881) 283–95.

Crumrine, *History of Washington County.*   Boyd Crumrine. *History of Washington County, Pennsylvania, with Biographical Sketches of Many of the Pioneers and Prominent Men.* Philadelphia, 1882.

Curwen, *Journal.*   Samuel Curwen. *The Journal of Samuel Curwen, Loyalist.* Ed. Andrew Oliver. 2 vols. Cambridge, Mass., 1972.

Custis, *Recollections.*   George Washington Parke Custis. *Recollections and Private Memoirs of Washington.* New York, 1860.

Darlington, *Henry Bouquet.*   Mary Carson Darlington, ed. *History of Colonel Henry Bouquet and the Western Frontiers of Pennsylvania, 1747–1764.* N.p., 1920.

Day, "A Summary of the English Period."   Richard E. Day. "A Summary of the English Period," in vol. 3 of Alexander Clarence Flick, ed. *History of the State of New York.* 10 vols. New York, 1933–37.

Decatur, *Private Affairs.*   Stephen Decatur, Jr. *Private Affairs of George Washington, from the Records and Accounts of Tobias Lear, Esquire, His Secretary.* Boston, 1933.

DHFC.   Linda Grant De Pauw et al., eds. *Documentary History of the First Federal Congress of the United States of America.* 13 vols. to date. Baltimore, 1972—.

Diaries.   Donald Jackson and Dorothy Twohig, eds. *The Diaries of George Washington.* 6 vols. Charlottesville, Va., 1976–79.

Dict. Biog. Française.   *Dictionnaire de Biographie Française.* 14 vols. to date. Paris, 1931—.

Doniol, *La participation de la France de l'établissement des Etats-Unis.* Henri Doniol. *Histoire de la participation de la France de l'établissement des Etats-Unis d'Amérique: Correspondance diplomatique et documents.* 5 vols. Paris, 1886–92.

Early, *Family of Early.*   Ruth H. Early. *The Family of Early Which Settled upon the Eastern Shore of Virginia and Its Connection with Other Families.* Lynchburg, Va., 1920.

Eddis, *Letters from America.*   William Eddis. *Letters from America.* Ed. Aubrey C. Land. Cambridge, Mass., 1969.

Eisen, *Portraits of Washington.*   Gustavus A. Eisen. *Portraits of Washington.* 3 vols. New York, 1932.

Enys, *Journal.*   John Enys. *The American Journals of Lt. John Enys.* Ed. Elizabeth Cometti. Syracuse, N.Y., 1976.

Farrand, *Federal Convention.*   Max Farrand, ed. *The Records of the Federal Convention of 1787.* Rev. ed. 4 vols. New Haven and London, 1966.

Fithian, *Journal.*   Philip Vickers Fithian. *Journal and Letters of Philip*

Vickers Fithian, 1773–1774: A Plantation Tutor of the Old Dominion. Ed. Hunter Dickinson Farish. Williamsburg, Va., 1943.

Ford, "Journal."   David Ford. "Journal of an Expedition Made in the Autumn of 1794 . . . into Western Pennsylvania," *New Jersey Historical Society Prodeedings,* 8 (1859), 76–88.

Ford, *A Peculiar Service.*   Corey Ford. *A Peculiar Service.* New York, 1965.

Ford, *Washington and the Theatre.*   Paul Leicester Ford. *Washington and the Theatre.* New York, 1899.

Fries, *Moravian Records.*   Adelaide L. Fries et al., eds. *Records of the Moravians in North Carolina.* 11 vols. Raleigh, N.C., 1922–69.

Gist, *Journals.*   William M. Darlington, ed. *Christopher Gist's Journals with Historical, Geographical, and Ethnological Notes and Biographies of His Contemporaries.* Cleveland, 1893.

Gould, "Journal."   William Gould. "Journal by William Gould during an Expedition into Pennsylvania in 1794," *New Jersey Historical Society Proceedings,* 3 (1848–49), 173–91.

Griswold, *Republican Court.*   Rufus Wilmot Griswold. *The Republican Court or American Society in the Days of Washington.* New York, 1855.

Hamilton, *Letters to Washington.*   Stanislaus Murray Hamilton, ed. *Letters to Washington and Accompanying Papers.* 5 vols. Boston and New York, 1898–1902.

H.B.J.   H. R. McIlwaine, ed. *Journals of the House of Burgesses of Virginia.* 13 vols. Richmond, 1905–15.

Heads of Families, Conn.   *Heads of Families at the First Census of the United States Taken in the Year 1790: Connecticut.* 1908. Reprint. Spartanburg, S.C., 1964.

Heads of Families, Mass.   *Heads of Families at the First Census of the United States Taken in the Year 1790: Massachusetts.* 1908. Reprint. Spartanburg, S.C., 1964.

Heads of Families, Va.   *Heads of Families at the First Census of the United States Taken in the Year 1790: Virginia.* 1908. Reprint. Baltimore, 1970.

Hedges, *Browns of Providence.*   James B. Hedges. *The Browns of Providence Plantations: Colonial Years.* Providence, 1968.

Heitman, *Historical Register.*   Francis Bernard Heitman. *Historical Register of the United States Army.* 2 vols. Washington, D.C., 1903.

Henderson, *Washington's Southern Tour.*   Archibald Henderson. *Washington's Southern Tour, 1791.* Boston and New York, 1923.

Hening.   William Waller Hening, ed. *The Statues at Large; Being a Collection of All the Laws of Virginia from the First Session of the Legislature, in the Year 1619.* 13 vols. 1819–23. Reprint. Charlottesville, Va., 1969.

Honyman, *Journal.*   Robert Honyman. *Colonial Panorama 1775: Dr.*

Robert Honyman's Journal for March and April. Ed. Philip Padelford. San Marino, Calif., 1939.

Hooper, *Lexicon-Medicum.* Robert Hooper. *Lexicon-Medicum or Medical Dictionary: Containing an Explanation of the Terms in Anatomy, Botany, Chemistry, Materia Medica, Midwifery, Mineralogy, Pharmacy, Physiology, Practice of Physic, Surgery, and the Various Branches of Natural Philosophy Connected with Medicine; Selected, Arranged, and Compiled from the Best Authors.* New York, 1826.

Hufeland, *Westchester County.* Otto Hufeland. *Westchester County during the American Revolution, 1775–1783.* White Plains, N.Y., 1926.

"Indian Wars." "Indian Wars in Augusta County, Virginia," *Virginia Magazine of History and Biography,* 2 (1894–95), 397–404.

Irving, *Life of Washington.* Washington Irving, *Life of George Washington.* 5 vols. New York, 1857–59.

Jackson, "Washington in Philadelphia." Joseph Jackson, "Washington in Philadelphia," *Pennsylvania Magazine of History and Biography,* 56 (1932), 110–55.

JCC. Worthington C. Ford et al., eds. *Journals of the Continental Congress, 1774–1789.* 34 vols. Washington, D.C., 1904–37.

Jones, *Finger-Ring Lore.* William Jones. *Finger-Ring Lore: Historical, Legendary, and Anecdotal.* London, 1898.

Kelly, *Medical Biography.* Howard A. Kelly and Walter L. Burrage. *Dictionary of American Medical Biography.* New York and London, 1928.

Kent, *French Invasion.* Donald H. Kent. *The French Invasion of Western Pennsylvania, 1753.* Harrisburg, Pa., 1954.

Ledger A. Manuscript Ledger in George Washington Papers, Library of Congress.

Ledger B. Manuscript Ledger in George Washington Papers, Library of Congress.

Ledger C. Manuscript Ledger in Morristown National Historical Park.

LMCC. Edmund C. Burnett, ed. *Letters of Members of the Continental Congress.* 8 vols. Reprint. Gloucester, Mass., 1963.

Mackenzie, *Diary.* Frederick Mackenzie. *Diary of Frederick Mackenzie, Giving a Daily Narrative of His Military Service as an Officer of the Regiment of Royal Welch Fusiliers during the Years 1775–1781 in Massachusetts, Rhode Island, and New York.* 2 vols. Cambridge, Mass., 1930.

Maclay, *Diary.* Kenneth R. Bowling and Helen E. Veit, eds., *The Diary of William Maclay and Other Notes on Senate Debates.* Baltimore, 1988.

Marshall, *Life of Washington.* John Marshall. *The Life of George Washington, Commander in Chief of the American Forces . . . and First President of the United States.* 5 vols. London, 1804.

Mathews, *Andrew Ellicott.*   Catherine Van Cortlandt Mathews. *Andrew Ellicott, His Life and Letters.* New York, 1908.

Md. Archives.   Archives of Maryland. 72 vols. to date. Baltimore, 1883—.

Meade, "Frederick Parish."   Everard Kidder Meade. "Frederick Parish, Virginia, 1744–1780: Its Churches, Chapels, and Ministers," *Proceedings of the Clarke County Historical Association,* 5 (1945), 18–38.

Memoir.   A Memoir Containing a Summary View of Facts, with Their Authorities. In Answer to the Observations Sent by the English Ministry to the Courts of Europe. Trans. from the French. New York, 1757.

Mitchell, *New Letters of Abigail Adams.*   Stewart Mitchell, ed. *New Letters of Abigail Adams, 1788–1801.* New York, 1947.

Monaghan, *This Was New York.*   Frank Monaghan and Marvin Lowenthal. *This Was New York, the Nation's Capital in 1789.* Garden City, N.Y., 1943.

Niemcewicz, *Vine and Fig Tree.*   Julian Ursyn Niemcewicz. *Under Their Vine and Fig Tree: Travels through America in 1797–1799, 1805, with Some Further Account of Life in New Jersey.* Ed. Metchie J. E. Budka. Elizabeth, N.J., 1965.

Norris, *Lower Shenandoah Valley.*   J. E. Norris, ed. *History of the Lower Shenandoah Valley.* 1890. Reprint. Berryville, Va., 1972.

Nussbaum, *Commercial Policy in the French Revolution.*   Frederick L. Nussbaum. *Commercial Policy in the French Revolution: A Study of the Career of G. J. A. Ducher.* New York, 1970.

Pa. Arch.   Samuel Hazard et al., eds. *Pennsylvania Archives.* 9 ser., 138 vols. Philadelphia and Harrisburg, 1852–1949.

Pa. Arch., Col. Rec.   Colonial Records of Pennsylvania, 1683–1800. 16 vols. Phildelphia, 1852–53.

Papers.   W. W. Abbot et al., eds. *The Papers of George of George Washington.* Charlottesville, Va., 1983—.

Papiers Contrecoeur.   Fernand Grenier, ed. *Papiers Contrecoeur et autres documents concernant le conflit anglo-français sur l'Ohio de 1745 à 1756.* Quebec, 1952.

Pennypacker, *General Washington's Spies.*   Morton Pennypacker. *General Washington's Spies on Long Island and in New York.* Brooklyn, N.Y., 1939.

Pickell, *Potomac Company.*   John Pickell, *A New Chapter in the Early Life of Washington, in Connection with the Narrative History of the Potomac Company.* New York, 1856.

Powell, *Old Alexandria.*   Mary G. Powell. *The History of Old Alexandria, Virginia, from July 13, 1749 to May 24, 1861.* Richmond, 1928.

Pownall, *Topographical Description.*   Thomas Pownall. *A Topographical Description of the Dominions of the United States of America.* Ed. Lois Mulkearn. Pittsburgh, 1949.

Randolph, *Treatise on Gardening.*   John Randolph. *A Treatise on Gardening by a Citizen of Virginia.* Ed. M. F. Warner. Reprint. Richmond, 1924.

Rankin, *Theater in Colonial America.*   Hugh F. Rankin. *The Theater in Colonial America.* Chapel Hill, N.C., 1960.

Rice, *American Campaigns of Rochambeau's Army.*   Howard C. Rice, Jr., and Anne S. K. Brown, eds. *The American Campaigns of Rochambeau's Army, 1780, 1781, 1782, 1783.* 2 vols. Princeton, N.J., and Providence, 1972.

Robitaille, *Washington et Jumonville.*   Georges Robitaille. *Washington et Jumonville.* Montreal, 1933.

Rochambeau, *Mémoires.*   Jean Baptiste Donatien, comte de Rochambeau. *Mémoires militaires, historiques, et politiques de Rochambeau.* 2 vols. Paris, 1809.

Roof, *William Smith.*   Katherine Metcalf Roof. *Colonel William Smith and Lady.* Boston, 1929.

Rosenthal, "Journal."   Gustavus Rosenthal. "Journal of a Volunteer Expedition to Sandusky, from May 24 to June 13, 1782," *Pennsylvania Magazine of History and Biography,* 18 (1894), 129–57, 293–328.

Rutland, *Madison Papers.*   Robert A. Rutland et al., eds. *The Papers of James Madison.* Chicago, 1962–75; Charlottesville, Va., 1977—.

Rutland, *Mason Papers.*   Robert A. Rutland, ed. *The Papers of George Mason, 1725–1792.* 3 vols. Chapel Hill, N.C., 1970.

Scharf, *History of Philadelphia.*   J. Thomas Scharf and Thompson Westcott. *History of Philadelphia, 1609–1884.* 3 vols. Philadelphia, 1884.

Scott, *Gazetteer.*   Joseph Scott. *The United States Gazetteer: Containing an Authentic Description of the Several States. Their Situation, Extent, Boundaries, Soil, Produce, Climate, Population, Trade, and Manufactures, Together with the Extent, Boundaries, and Population of Their Respective Counties, Also, an Exact Account of the Cities, Towns, Harbours, Rivers, Bays, Lakes, Mountains.* Philadelphia, 1795.

Seilhamer, *American Theatre.*   George O. Seilhamer. *History of the American Theatre.* 3 vols. Philadelphia, 1889.

Smyth, *A Tour in the United States of America.*   John Ferdinand Dalziel Smyth. *A Tour in the United States of America, Containing an Account of the Present State of the Country. . . .* 2 vols. London, 1784.

Sparks, *Writings of Washington.*   Jared Sparks, ed. *The Writings of George Washington: Being His Correspondence, Addresses, Messages, and*

Other Papers, Official and Private, Selected and Published from the Original Manuscripts. 12 vols. Boston, 1833–37.

1 Stat. Richard Peters, ed. *The Public Statues at Large of the United States of America.* Vol. 1. Boston, 1845.

Stevens, *Annapolis.* William Oliver Stevens. *Annapolis: Anne Arundel's Town.* New York, 1937.

Thacher, *Military Journal.* James Thacher. *Military Journal of the American Revolution.* Hartford, 1862.

Tilghman, *Memoir.* Tench Tilghman. *Memoir of Lieut. Col. Tench Tilghman, Secretary and Aid to Washington, Together with an Appendix, Containing Revolutionary Journals and Letters, Hitherto Unpublished.* Albany, 1876.

Tousey, *Military History.* Thomas G. Tousey. *Military History of Carlisle and Carlisle Barracks.* Richmond, 1939.

Trumbull, "Minutes." Jonathan Trumbull, Jr. "Minutes of Occurrences Respecting the Siege and Capture of York in Virginia, Extracted from the Journal of Colonel Jonathan Trumbull, Secretary to the General, 1781." *Proceedings of the Massachusetts Historical Society,* 1st ser., 14 (1876), 331–38.

Tucker, "Journal." Edward M. Riley, ed. "St. George Tucker Journal of the Siege of Yorktown, 1781." *William and Mary Quarterly,* 1st ser., 4 (1895–96), 46–52, 95–103, 183–87.

Va. Exec. Jls. *Executive Journals of the Council of Colonial Virginia.* Ed. H. R. McIlwaine, Wilmer L. Hall, and Benjamin Hillman. 6 vols. Richmond, 1925–66.

Van Schreeven, *Revolutionary Virginia.* William J. Van Schreeven et al., eds. *Revolutionary Virginia: The Road to Independence.* 7 vols. Charlottesville, Va., 1973–83.

Van der Kemp, *Autobiography.* Francis Adrian Van der Kemp. *Francis Adrian Van der Kemp, 1752–1829: An Autobiography Together with Extracts from His Correspondence.* Ed. Helen Lincklaen Fairchild. New York, 1903.

Washington and de Grasse. Institut Français de Washington. *Correspondence of General Washington and Comte de Grasse, 1781, Aug. 17–November 4.* Washington, D.C., 1931.

Walpole, *Memoirs.* Horace Walpole. *Memoirs of the Reign of King George the Second.* 3 vols. London, 1847.

Watson, *Men and Times of the Revolution.* Winslow C. Watson, ed. *Men and Times of the Revolution, or Memoirs of Elkanah Watson.* New York, 1856.

Webb, *Correspondence.* Worthington Chauncey Ford, ed. *Correspondence and Journals of Samuel Blachley Webb.* 3 vols. New York, 1893.

Wellford, "Diary." Robert Wellford. "A Diary Kept by Dr. Robert

Wellford, of Fredericksburg, Virginia, during the March of the Virginia Troops to Fort Pitt (Pittsburg) to Suppress the Whiskey Insurrection in 1794," *William and Mary Quarterly,* 1st ser., 11 (1902–3), 1–19.

Westcott, *Life of John Fitch.* Thompson Westcott. *The Life of John Fitch, the Inventor of the Steamboat.* Philadelphia, 1857.

Writings. John C. Fitzpatrick, ed. *The Writings of George Washington from the Original Manuscript Sources, 1745–1799.* Washington, D.C., 1931–44.

George Washington's Diaries

An Abridgment

Surveying for Lord Fairfax
11 March–13 April 1748

During the spring of 1748 the young George Washington undertook a journey that introduced him for the first time to an area which was to play an important part in his career. In March of that year he had an opportunity to join a party engaged by Thomas Fairfax, sixth Baron Fairfax of Cameron, to survey his properties on the South Branch of the Potomac River. Lord Fairfax was the proprietor of the Northern Neck of Virginia, which encompassed the area between the Potomac and Rappahannock rivers from the Chesapeake Bay to the headwaters of the two rivers. The royal grant for the proprietorship of the Northern Neck was originally made in 1649 to a member of Fairfax's family by the exiled Charles II, and by 1719 the region came into the possession of Thomas Fairfax. By the time Fairfax left England and settled in Virginia in 1747, there had been extensive occupation of his lands by settlers. There was considerable uneasiness on the part of the settlers concerning the validity of their claims and an increasing desire on the part of Lord Fairfax to confirm title to his property in the area.

Washington's association with the powerful Fairfax family grew out of the marriage of his half brother Lawrence, owner of Mount Vernon, to Ann Fairfax, daughter of Col. William Fairfax, Lord Fairfax's cousin. Whenever possible, young George escaped from the austerity of his mother's home at Ferry Farm, near Fredericksburg, to the pleasant life of his brother's plantation. While he was staying with Lawrence at Mount Vernon, he was a frequent visitor at Belvoir, the estate of William Fairfax some four miles from Mount Vernon. He soon became an intimate of the family, forming a warm friendship with George William Fairfax, Colonel Fairfax's son. It was natural, therefore, when George William was sent as Lord Fairfax's agent on a surveying trip, that the sixteen-year-old George should be invited to accompany him.

It is uncertain when Washington's interest in surveying as a career began. For a time in 1746 he had considered the possibility of going to sea, but the determined opposition of his mother and her family, partly because of his youth and partly because of discrimination in the British navy against colonials, had compelled him to seek a career closer to home. Surveying in eighteenth-century Virginia promised a respectable and lucrative career to a young man without a large estate. As early as August 1745, in his "School Exercise Book," Washington had made notes on "Surveying or Measuring of Land," including examples of plats with fields, trees, and streams. It is probable that he received some instruction in surveying before the journey over the mountains, but in any case the chance to acquire practical experience under the supervision of a skilled surveyor was not to be missed. On 11 Mar. 1748, with George William Fairfax and the rest of the surveying party, he set out for the South Branch of the Potomac. The group was led by experienced surveyor

James Genn, with Henry Ashby and Richard Taylor as chainmen, Robert Ashby as marker, and William Lindsey as pilot.

Washington's journal of the trip was kept in a small notebook measuring 6 × 3¼ inches. Together with the entries for the "Journey over the Mountains," GW kept in this book accounts of the group's surveying activities for the period.

A Journal of my Journey over the Mountains began Fryday the 11th. of March 1747/8

March

Fryday March 11th. 1747/8. Began my Journey in Company with George Fairfax Esqr.; we travell'd this day 40 Miles to Mr. George Neavels in Prince William County.

> The two dates used by GW are explained by the difference between New Style and Old Style dating. Until 1752 England, Ireland, and the colonies followed the Julian calendar (Old Style). By 1752, when Great Britain adopted the Gregorian calendar, the difference between the two calendars was 11 days.
>
> George Neville (Neavil; d. 1774), a planter and land speculator, had settled on Cedar Run, then in Prince William County (now in Fauquier County), as early as 1730. The location of his house at the juncture of the Carolina Road and a branch of the Dumfries Road made it a convenient stopping place for travelers.

Saturday March 12th. This Morning Mr. James Genn the surveyor came to us. We travel'd over the Blue Ridge to Capt. Ashbys on Shannondoa River. Nothing remarkable happen'd.

> John Ashby (1707–1797) was a member of a prominent frontier family. In 1741 Ashby married Jean Combs of Maryland and moved to the banks of the Shenandoah, where the Ashby Tract lay along the river just below the mouth of Howell's Run. He was widely known as an Indian fighter.

Sunday March 13. Rode to his Lordships Quarter about 4 Miles higher up the River we went through most beautiful Groves of Sugar Trees & spent the best part of the Day in admiring the Trees & richness of the Land.

Monday 14th. We sent our Baggage to Capt. Hites (near Frederick Town) went ourselves down the River about 16 Miles to Capt. Isaac Penningtons (the Land exceeding Rich & Fertile all the way produces abundance of Grain Hemp Tobacco &c.) in order to Lay of some Lands on Cates Marsh & Long Marsh.

> Jost Hite (d. 1760) was born in Strasbourg, Alsace, and immigrated to America about 1710, settling first in New York and moving to Pennsylvania around 1716. In 1732 he moved to his Virginia lands—nearly 40,000 acres in what soon became Frederick County with 16 other families of settlers. Hite

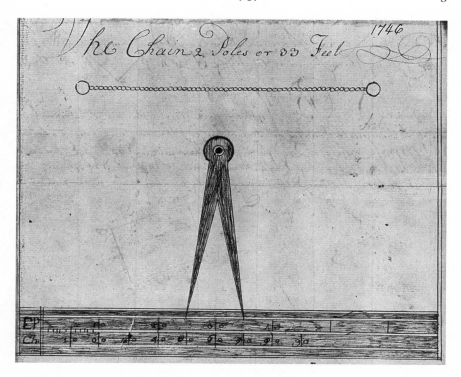

Chain, compass, and scale drawn by the young Washington. (Cornell University)

was one of the leading land speculators and developers in Frederick, eventually settling families on a tract amounting to 94,000 acres. Frederick Town is now Winchester, Va.

Isaac Pennington came to the Shenandoah Valley, probably from New Jersey, about 1734 and settled a tract of some 600 acres on the south bank of Buck Marsh Run, near present-day Berryville, Va.

Tuesday 15th. We set out early with Intent to Run round the sd. Land but being taken in a Rain & it Increasing very fast obliged us to return. It clearing about one oClock & our time being too Precious to Loose we a second time ventured out & Worked hard till Night & then returnd to Penningtons we got our Suppers & was Lighted in to a Room & I not being so good a Woodsman as the rest of my Company striped my self very orderly & went in to the Bed as they call'd it when to my Surprize I found it to be nothing but a Little Straw—Matted together without Sheets or any thing else but only one Thread Bear blanket with double its Weight of Vermin such as Lice Fleas &c. I was glad to get up (as soon as the Light was carried from us) & put on my Cloths & Lay as my Companions. Had we not have been very tired, I am sure we should not have slep'd much that night. I made a Promise not to Sleep so from that time forward chusing rather to sleep in the open Air before a fire as will Appear hereafter.

Wednesday 16th. We set out early & finish'd about one oClock & then Travell'd up to Frederick Town where our Baggage came to us. We cleaned ourselves (to get Rid of the Game we had catched the Night before) & took a Review of the Town & then return'd to our Lodgings where we had a good Dinner prepar'd for us Wine & Rum Punch in Plenty & a good Feather Bed with clean Sheets which was a very agreeable regale.

Thursday 17th. Rain'd till Ten oClock & then clearing we reached as far as Major Campbells one of there Burgesses about 25 Miles from Town. Nothing Remarkable this day nor Night but that we had a Tolerable good Bed [to] lay on.

> Andrew Campbell, who lived northwest of Winchester, was one of Frederick County's most prominent residents, serving as one of the county's first justices, as a member of the House of Burgesses from Frederick in 1745–47, and as the third sheriff of the county. On 2 Jan. 1744 the Frederick County court licensed Campbell and several other residents to keep ordinaries "at their respective houses" and to "furnish lodgings and food and Liquors at prices fixed by the court" (Cartmell, *Shendandoah Valley Pioneers*, 21). Campbell appears to have had a puritanical interest in preserving decorum in Frederick County. The long list of charges laid by him against various citizens range from breaking the Sabbath to "raising a riot" (see Norris, *Lower Shenandoah Valley*, 83, 85). Retribution finally overtook him. He had served as a vestryman for Frederick Parish since 1745, but in the latter part of the decade charges were laid against him for collecting and appropriating for himself the funds collected for the use of the parish. Campbell eventually "had to run away to Carolina" (Meade, "Frederick Parish").

Fryday 18th. We Travell'd up about 35 Miles to Thomas Barwicks on Potomack where we found the River so excessively high by Reason of the Great Rains that had fallen up about the Allegany Mountains as they told us which was then bringing down the melted Snow & that it would not be fordable for severall Days it was then above Six foot Higher than usual & was Rising. We agreed to stay till Monday. We this day call'd to see the Fam'd Warm Springs. We camped out in the field this Night. Nothing Remarkable happen'd till sunday the 20th.

> Thomas Barwick (Berwick) was settled in Frederick County as early as 1744 and served as a juror in the county court in February of that year (Cartmell, *Shenandoah Valley Pioneers*, 23). Warm Springs is now Bath, or Berkeley Springs, Morgan County, W.Va.

Monday 21st. We went over in a Canoe & Travell'd up Maryland side all the Day in a Continued Rain to Collo. Cresaps right against the

Mouth of the South Branch about 40 Miles from Polks I believe the Worst Road that ever was trod by Man or Beast.

> Thomas Cresap (1694–1790) was born at Skipton, Yorkshire, Eng., and immigrated to America about 1719. Around 1736 he moved to the vicinity of Shawnee Old Town (now Oldtown, Md.), where he built a fortified trading post. By 1749, when he was one of the organizers of the Ohio Company, Cresap was widely known throughout the frontier as a trader and land speculator, and Shawnee Old Town had become one of the leading frontier trading posts.

Wednesday 23d. Rain'd till about two oClock & Clear'd when we were agreeably surpris'd at the sight of thirty odd Indians coming from War with only one Scalp. We had some Liquor with us of which we gave them Part it elevating there Spirits put them in the Humour of Dauncing of whom we had a War Daunce. There Manner of Dauncing is as follows Viz. They clear a Large Circle & make a great Fire in the Middle then seats themselves around it the Speaker makes a grand Speech telling them in what Manner they are to Daunce after he has finish'd the best Dauncer Jumps up as one awaked out of a Sleep & Runs & Jumps about the Ring in a most comicle Manner he is followd by the Rest then begins there Musicians to Play the Musick is a Pot half of Water with a Deerskin Streched over it as tight as it can & a goard with some Shott in it to Rattle & a Piece of an horses Tail tied to it to make it look fine the one keeps Rattling and the other Drumming all the While the others is Dauncing.

Fryday 25th. 1784. Nothing Remarkable on thursday but only being with the Indians all day so shall slip it. This day left Cresaps & went up to the Mouth of Patersons Creek & there swum our Horses over got over ourselves in a Canoe & travel'd up the following Part of the Day to Abram Johnstones 15 miles from the Mouth where we camped.

> Abram Johnson received a deed to 309 acres on Patterson's Creek on 26 Oct. 1748 (Northern Neck Deeds and Grants, Book G, 141).

Saterday 26. Travelld up the Creek to Solomon Hedges Esqr. one of his Majestys Justices of the Peace for the County of Frederick where we camped. When we came to Supper there was neither a Cloth upon the Table nor a Knife to eat with but as good luck would have it we had Knives of [our] own.

> Solomon Hedges, usually called Squire Hedges, a justice of the peace for Frederick County, was a member of a Quaker family from Maryland who were early settlers in Frederick County.

Monday 28th. Travell'd up the Branch about 30 Miles to Mr. James Rutlidge's Horse Jockey & about 70 Miles from the Mouth.

James Rutledge acquired 500 acres in Frederick County in May 1748 (Northern Neck Deeds and Grants, Book G, 56). He was presumably a member of the family that had settled on the South Branch as early as 1734 or 1735.

Tuesday 29th. This Morning went out & Survey'd five Hundred Acres of Land & went down to one Michael Stumps on the So. Fork of the Branch. On our way Shot two Wild Turkies.

Michael Stump, Sr. (1709–1768), received a grant for Lot No. 3, on the South Fork of the South Branch of the Potomac, on 8 Sept. 1749 (Northern Neck Deeds and Grants, Book G, 227).

Thursday 31st. Early this Morning one of our Men went out with the Gun & soon Returnd with two Wild Turkies. We then went to our Business. Run of three Lots & returnd to our Camping place at Stumps.

April

Saterday April 2d. Last Night was a blowing & Rainy night. Our Straw catch'd a Fire that we were laying upon & was luckily Preserv'd by one of our Mens awaking when it was in a ⟨   ⟩ We run of four Lots this day which Reached below Stumps.

Sunday 3d. Last Night was a much more blostering night than the former. We had our Tent Carried Quite of with the Wind and was obliged to Lie the Latter part of the Night without covering. There came several Persons to see us this day one of our Men Shot a Wild Turkie.

Monday 4th. This morning Mr. Fairfax left us with Intent to go down to the Mouth of the Branch. We did two Lots & was attended by a great Company of People Men Women & Children that attended us through the Woods as we went shewing there Antick tricks. I really think they seem to be as Ignorant a Set of People as the Indians. They would never speak English but when spoken to they speak all Dutch. This day our Tent was blown down by the Violentness of the Wind.

Tuesday 5th. We went out & did 4 Lots. We were attended by the same Company of People that we had the day before.

Wednesday 6th. Last Night was so Intolerably smoaky that we were obliged all hands to leave the Tent to the Mercy of the Wind and Fire this day was attended by our aforesd. Company untill about 12 oClock when we finish'd we travell'd down the Branch to Henry Vanmetris's. On our Journey was catch'd in a very heavy Rain. We got under a Straw House untill the Worst of it was over & then continued our Journy.

Thursday 7th. Rain'd Successively all Last Night. This Morning one of our men Killed a Wild Turkey that weight 20 Pounds. We went & Surveyd 15 Hundred Acres of Land & Returnd to Vanmetris's about 1 oClock. About two I heard that Mr. Fairfax was come up & at 1 Peter Casseys about 2 Miles of in the same Old Field. I then took my Horse & went up to see him. We eat our Dinners & Walked down to Vanmetris's. We stayed about two Hours & Walked back again and slept in Casseys House which was the first Night I had slept in a House since I came to the Branch.

> Peter Casey acquired 356 acres of land on the South Branch on 14 Aug. 1749 (Northern Neck Deeds and Grants, Book G, 271).

Fryday 8th. We breakfasted at Casseys & Rode down to Vanmetris's to get all our Company together which when we had accomplished we Rode down below the Trough in order to Lay of Lots there. We laid of one this day. The Trough is couple of Ledges of Mountain Impassable running side & side together for above 7 or 8 Miles & the River down between them. You must Ride Round the back of the Mountain for to get below them. We Camped this Night in the Woods near a Wild Meadow where was a Large Stack of Hay. After we had Pitched our Tent & made a very Large Fire we pull'd out our Knapsack in order to Re-cruit ourselves. Every[one] was his own Cook. Our Spits was Forked Sticks our Plates was a Large Chip as for Dishes we had none.

Sunday 10th. We took our farewell of the Branch & travelld over Hills and Mountains to 1 Coddys on Great Cacapehon about 40 Miles.

> James Caudy (Coddy) owned some 98 acres of land in Frederick County.

Monday 11th. We Travell'd from Coddys down to Frederick Town where we Reached about 12 oClock. We dined in Town and then went to Capt. Hites & Lodged.

Tuesday 12th. We set of from Capt. Hites in order to go over Wms. Gap about 20 Miles and after Riding about 20 Miles we had 20 to go for we had lost ourselves & got up as High as Ashbys Bent. We did get over Wms. Gap that Night and as low as Wm. Wests in Fairfax County 18 Miles from the Top of the Ridge. This day see a Rattled Snake the first we had seen in all our Journey.

> Williams' Gap, later known as Snickers' Gap, was a pass through the Blue Ridge Mountains on a line east from Winchester. Ashby's Bent, or Ashby's Gap, is a pass into the Shenandoah Valley through the Blue Ridge Mountains. West's ordinary was at the junction of the Carolina Road and the Colchester Road near Bull Run, slightly east of the beginning of the Bull Run Mountains. It was operated by William West, who died between 1762 and 1765. As early as 1740 West had acquired grants of land in the area (Northern Neck Deeds and Grants, Book E, Vi Microfilm). The ordinary was operated after the Revolution under the name Lacey's and was located at the present site of Aldie, in what is now Loudoun County, Va.

Wednesday the 13th. of April 1748. Mr. Fairfax got safe home and I myself safe to my Brothers which concludes my Journal.

Voyage to Barbados
1751–52

GW's older half brother Lawrence had been in poor health during the decade following his participation in the British assault upon Spanish bases in the Caribbean, an encounter commonly termed the War of Jenkins' Ear. Lawrence had led a Virginia military company in the 1741 attack on Cartagena, becoming so impressed with Vice Admiral Edward Vernon, naval commander of the expedition, that he later named his own home Mount Vernon. Now Lawrence's lung ailment was worse, and his life had been further burdened by the deaths since 1745 of three young children, Janet, Fairfax, and Mildred. In 1751 he decided to sail for Barbados in search of a healing climate, accompanied by his young half brother.

Barbados was a logical destination. Not only were there strong commercial ties between Virginia and the Leeward Islands, but there also were family connections. Gedney Clarke, a prominent Barbados merchant and planter, was the brother of William Fairfax's second wife; he was from Salem, Mass., and owned property along Goose Creek in Virginia. The Clarkes and their Barbadian friends would be the principal hosts of the two Washingtons during their stay on the island.

Lawrence and GW set sail about 28 Sept. 1751. Because the first few pages of GW's diary are missing, we cannot know for certain the date, the port of embarkation, or the vessel upon which the two took passage. If the vessel did sail from the Potomac, it was the Success, *Jeremiah Cranston master, 40 tons, 8 men, carrying a cargo of 4,480 barrel staves, 7,627 feet of plank, 984 bushels of corn, and 31 barrels of herring. Cranston gave bond for his square-sterned sloop at the customs office of the South Potomac district either on 23 Aug. or 23 Sept. — the surviving report is not clear. If August, the delay between the date of clearing the port and leaving the river was not unusual. GW himself remarked in later life that masters of vessels never sail on time.*

Two elements of ocean travel fascinated GW most: the daily progress as indicated in the captain's log and the variable and often violent weather. He kept his own log, now greatly mutilated, as part of his diary, very probably basing it upon the captain's and introducing such nautical acronyms as RMTS, reefed main topsail; DRTS, double-reefed topsail; HFS, hauled foresail. His amazement at the stormy weather seems justified. There had been severe hurricanes in the West Indies in September, resulting in heavy shipping losses. Though the heaviest losses were in the Jamaica area, merchants in the Leewards reported considerable loss in their letters to American shippers, and on *18 Oct.* when *GW was noting in the log the occurrence of heavy seas and high winds, there was a strong earthquake in the Santo Domingo area.*

The Washingtons' arrival at Bridgetown, on Carlisle Bay, is not well documented because pages are missing from the diary at this point. There are no collateral data such as newspaper listings of shipping arrivals, for not a single copy of the Barbados Gazette *for 1751 is known to exist. The first two diary entries after the Washingtons disembarked are supplied by Jared Sparks, who obviously saw them while he was preparing his edition of GW's papers. He may indeed be responsible for the fact that the originals are missing, considering his penchant for distributing sample pages from GW manuscripts to friends and colleagues.*

After dining with the Clarkes and taking up temporary lodging with James Carter, the travelers confronted the matter of prime importance—Lawrence's physical condition. Then, assured by Dr. Hillary that the disease was "not so fixed but that a cure might be effectually made," they looked for a place to live.

Although they thought it extravagant at £15 a month, they chose a house owned by Captain Croftan, or Crofton, overlooking Carlisle Bay.

The brothers had a busy social life, and those who entertained them were prominent in commercial, political, and military circles. GW delighted in the novelty of his surroundings. He developed a taste for the "avagado pair," the "Pine Apple," and other tropical fruits. He indulged his emerging taste for the theater by attending a performance of George Lillo's The London Merchant, or The History of George Barnwell, *which was also playing in Drury Lane that season. Lillo's play may have been the first stage production that GW had ever seen, other than amateur performances.*

While Lawrence's health was still failing, illness struck GW. On 16 Nov. he developed smallpox and Dr. Lanahan was sent for. It may have been fortunate for GW that smallpox caught up with him in Barbados rather than in Virginia. The practice of inoculation—not vaccination—was common in Barbados but frowned upon in Virginia. Rev. Griffith Hughes reported that although the island was seldom free of the disease, the practice of inoculation had lowered the death rate to a very small percentage. It is conceivable that GW had been inoculated sometime before his trip to Barbados, causing his attack to be a relatively mild one. The practice of vaccination with cowpox vaccine did not begin until the end of the century.

It was decided that Lawrence would try Bermuda and that GW would return to Virginia. Lawrence wrote a friend from Bermuda 6 April 1752, despairing over his health and expressing the wish that his wife Anne would come to him—accompanied by GW. As his condition worsened, however, he returned hastily to Mount Vernon and died there 26 July.

By 19 Dec. 1751 GW had booked passage out of Barbados on the Industry. *He spent Christmas at sea, dining on beef and "Irish Goose," and settled*

*down to an uneventful though frequently stormy homeward voyage, content
to maintain a terse diary rather than a ship's log.*

At the end of January the Industry *cleared the Virginia capes and made
a landfall in the lower York River. Proceeding by land to Williamsburg,
GW paid a call on Gov. Robert Dinwiddie, gave him some letters, and was
invited to dine. It may have been a crucial moment in GW's career, providing
Dinwiddie an opportunity to evaluate the young man. The governor, only
recently appointed, had lived in America for several years and may already
have known the Washingtons; certainly he knew the Fairfaxes. Within a few
years, disquieting differences would arise to mar GW's relationship with
Dinwiddie, but the young man's immediate prospects brightened after his dinner with the governor. Later in 1752 when the colony was divided into four
military districts, Dinwiddie appointed him one of the district adjutants; and
in 1753, upon dispatching GW with a message to the French on the Ohio
River, Dinwiddie would refer to him as "a person of distinction."*

*The Barbados diary had deteriorated seriously before it was silked and
mounted at the Library of Congress; there is evidence that some of the prelimi-
nary pages were already missing when Jared Sparks used it in the nineteenth
century.*

1751

November

We were grea⟨tly a⟩larm'd with the cry of Land at 4 A:M: we quitted our
beds with surprise and found the land plainly appearing at ⟨*mutilated*⟩
at 3 leagues distance when by our reckonings we shou'd have been
near 150 Leauges to the Windward we to Leeward.abt the distance
above mention'd and had we been but 3 or 4 leagues more we shou'd
have been out of sight of the Island run down the Latitude and probably not have discover'd ⟨*mutilated*⟩ Error in time to have gain'd ⟨*mutilated*⟩ for 3 Weeks or More.

November 4th 1751. This morning received a card from Major Clarke,
welcoming us to Barbadoes, with an invitation to breakfast and dine
with him. We went,—myself with some reluctance, as the smallpox was
in his family. We were received in the most kind and friendly manner
by him. Mrs. Clarke was much indisposed, insomuch that we had not
the pleasure of her company, but in her place officiated Miss Roberts,
her neice, and an agreeable young lady. After drinking tea we were
again invited to Mr. Carter's and desired to make his house ours till
we could provide lodgings agreeable to our wishes, which offer we
accepted.

*Lawrence Washington, whose poor health took him and his half brother
George to Barbados in the fall of 1751. (Mount Vernon Ladies' Association
of the Union)*

Gedney Clarke (1711–1764) was a member of the council, collector of customs at Barbados, merchant, and planter with holdings in America, including 3,000 acres on Goose Creek in northern Virginia. Clarke's sister Deborah
was William Fairfax's wife and his connection with the Fairfaxes. Because
of this link GW and Lawrence depended much upon Gedney and his wife
Mary Clarke.

James Carter (d. 1753), of St. Thomas Parish, was a member of the Barbados council in the 1740s and served as chief justice of grand sessions in 1749.

Elizabeth Roberts was Mary Clarke's niece.

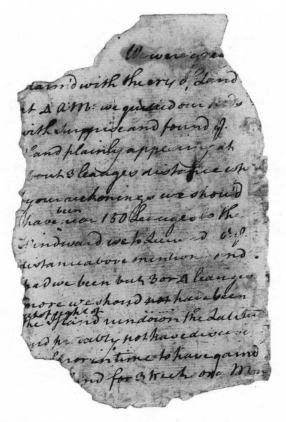

Page from George Washington's Barbados diary. (Library of Congress)

5th,—Early this morning came Dr. Hilary, an eminent physician recommended by Major Clarke, to pass his opinion on my brother's disorder, which he did in a favorable light, giving great assurance, that it
was not so fixed but that a cure might be effectually made. In the cool
of the evening we rode out accompanied by Mr. Carter to seek lodgings
in the country, as the Doctor advised, and was perfectly rap⟨*mutilated*⟩
the beautiful prospects which on every side presented to our view The
fields of Cain, Corn, Fruit Trees &c in a delightful Green. We return'd
without accomplis⟨h⟩ing our intentions.

> Dr. William Hillary (1697–1763) was a physician trained at Leyden and
> newly arrived in Barbados. He became Lawrence's doctor.

⟨*Mutilated*⟩ 7th. Dined at Majr. Clarkes; and by him was introduced to
the Surveyor Genl. & Judges, Finley & Hacket, who likewise din'd there:
in the Evening they complaisantly accompanied us in another excur-

sion in the Country to choose such lodgings as most suited; we pitched on the house of Captn. Croftan commander of James Fort; he was desir'd to come to Town next day to propose his terms. We return'd by way of Needham's fort & was introduced to the Captn. thereof, a Genteel pre⟨*mutilated*⟩ man. Sup'd and spent the Evening at Majr. Clarke with the Gentlemen before mentioned.

> The surveyor general of customs for Barbados was William Patterson. He was succeeded by Gedney Clarke in 1759.
>
> Thomas Finlay was a native of Scotland whose will was recorded in Barbados, 27 May 1762, after his return to his Scottish estate called Balkirsty. He served as clerk of the General Assembly of Barbados in 1743–44.
>
> Othniel Haggatt (d. 1761) was probably the individual GW is referring to as Hacket, although Nathaniel Haggatt was living in Barbados at the same time. One of the plantations on Barbados was called Haggatt Hall.
>
> Captain Croftan (Crofton) was the officer commanding James Fort who rented a house to the Washingtons. He may have been a militia officer. James Fort was a fortification in Holetown in St. James Parish which by 1762 mounted 23 guns and 10 swivels.

Thursday 8th. Came Captn. Croftan with his proposals which tho extravagantly dear my Brother was oblig'd to give, 15 pr Month is his charge exclusive of Liquors & washing which we find.

Fryday 9th. We receiv'd a Card from Marj Clarke inviting us to dine with him at Judge Maynards on the Morrow he had a right to ask being a Member of the Club call'd the Beefstake & tripe instituted by himself. after Dinner was the greatest Collection of Fruits I have yet seen set on the Table there was the Granadella the Sappadilla Pomgranate Sweet Orange Water Lemmon forbidden Fruit apples Guavas &c. &c. &c. We received invitations from every Gentleman there.

> William Maynard, a member of the Barbados General Assembly for many years, owned Black Rock Plantation in St. Thomas Parish.

Sunday 11th. Dressed in order for Church but got to town two Late dined at Majr. Clarkes with the S:G: went to Evening Service and return'd to our Lodgings.

⟨*Mutilated*⟩ 13th. Dined at the Fort with some Ladys its pretty strongly fortifyed and mounts about 36 Gunes within the fortifin., but 2 facine Batterys.

Wednesday 14. At our Lodgings.

Thursday 15. Was treated with a play ticket by Mr. Carter to see the Tragedy of George Barnwell acted: the character of Barnwell and several others was said to be well perform'd there was a Musick a Dapted and regularly conducted by Mr. [   ].

Fryday 16th. Mr. Graeme la⟨*mutilated*⟩ of the Master's of the College of
Virginia paid us a Mornings Visit and invited us to dine with Judge
Graeme his Br. on Sunday: and din'd this Day at Majr. Clarke's.

> John Graeme (d. 1755) had served at one time as professor of natural phi-
> losophy and mathematics at the College of William and Mary, succeeding
> Joshua Fry. He came from England in 1725 to take over the ironworks and
> plantation of Alexander Spotswood, an assignment in which he was not very
> successful. Graeme joined the college faculty in Aug. 1737. Although not an
> experienced surveyor, he apparently was in charge of the licensing of survey-
> ors in Virginia, a privilege assigned to the college by the crown. There is
> nothing in the scant record to connect him with GW before their meeting in
> Barbados, although GW had been surveying for Lord Fairfax and others.
> Graeme's brother was George Graeme (d. 1755), a judge and member of the
> General Assembly representing Christ Church Parish.

Saturday 17th. Was strongly attacked with the small Pox. sent for
Dr. Lanahan whose attendance was very constant till my recovery, and
going out which was not 'till thursday the 12th of December.

> It is not clear why Dr. John Lanahan (1699–1762), a physician and a third-
> generation resident of Barbados, was called to attend GW during his illness
> with smallpox while Lawrence was being treated by Dr. Hillary, unless it was
> because he was a friend of the Clarkes. Gedney was executor of Lanahan's
> estate when he died in 1769.

December

⟨*Mutilated*⟩ December 12th. Went to Town visited Majr. Clarke's Family
(who kindly visited me in my illness and contributed all they cou'd in
sendg. me the necesssary's required in the disorder) and dined with
Majr. Gaskens a half Br. to Mrs. Clarke: on Munday last began the
Grand sessions and this Day brought on the Tryal of Colo. Chaunack a
Man of oppulent fortune and infamous Character he was indicted for
commiting a Rape on his servant Maid and was brought in guiltless and
sav'd by one single Evidence ⟨*mutilated*⟩.

> John Gaskin (d. 1779), of St. Michael's Parish, was a Barbados shipowner.
>   *Chaunack:* perhaps Benjamin Charnock (1698–1783) of St. James Parish.
> At his death Charnock left what remained of his "oppulent fortune" to a
> friend, Dowding Thornhill. There is no surviving record of the criminal pro-
> ceedings against him for "committing a rape on his servant maid."

Wednesday 17th. Dined with Messrs Stephenson's Merchts.

> Thomas Stevenson (d. 1763) owned Pool plantation in St. Johns Parish and
> engaged in mercantile activities with his sons on other islands of the Leeward
> group.

Thursday 18. Provided my Sea Store & dined with Mr. Carter.

Fryday 19th. Got my Clothes Store &c on board the Industry Captn.
John Saunders for Virginia.

Saturday 21st. At my Lodgings ⟨*mutilated*⟩ my Brother—.

Sunday 22d. Took my Leave of my Br. Majr. Clarke &c & Imbar⟨*mutilated*⟩ in the Industry Captn John Saund ⟨*mutilated*⟩ for Virginia wai'd anchor and got out of Carlile Bay abt 12.

The Governor of Barbado's seems to keep a proper State: Lives very retired and at Little expence it is said he is a Gentleman of good Sence As he avoids the Errors of his predecessor he give no handle for complaint but at the same time by declining much familiarity is not over zealously beloved and being deprived of power to ⟨*mutilated*⟩ours meet with ⟨*mutilated*⟩ &ca.

There is several regular Risings in this Island one above another so that scarcely any part is deprived of a beautiful Prospect both of sea & Land and what is contrary to the observation on other Countrys is that each Rising is better than the other below.

There are many delicious Fruits in this but as they are particularly describ'd by the Revd. Mr. Hughs in his Natural histy. of the Island shall say nothing further than that the Pine Apple China Orange is good the Avagado pair is generally most admired tho none pleases my taste as do's the Pine ⟨*mutilated*⟩

The Earth in most parts is extremely rich & as black as our richest Marsh M⟨*mutilated*⟩ common produce of ea⟨*mutilated*⟩ Canes is from 40 to 70 polls of Sugar each poll valued at 20/ out of which a third is deduced for expences unless Rum sells for 2/ and upwards pr Gallon then it is though the Sugar is near clear. There was many Acres last Year that turn'd out from 140 to 170, as I was inform'd by credible authy. tho that was in Ginger & a very extraordinary Year for the Sail thereof. . . .

After a relatively uneventful voyage, GW's vessel reached the mouth of the York River on 29 Jan. 1752. His last very mutilated entries in the Barbados diary indicate that on Monday 3 Feb. he went to Hobbs Hole, now Tappahannock. On Tuesday 4 Feb. he crossed at Layton's ferry on the Rappahannock about 20 miles above Tappahannock. This crossing would have placed him in Westmoreland County, not far from the old family home at Pope's Creek where his brother Augustine then lived.

Journey to the French Commandant
1753-54

In the two years between his return from Barbados and the outbreak of the French and Indian War, GW steadily advanced his position in the Virginia community. Lawrence Washington's marriage into the Fairfax family had introduced his young brother to the most influential segment of Virginia society.

GW was well on his way to becoming a respected member of Virginia's ruling class, and his attention was turning increasingly to public affairs. He already owned some two thousand acres of land in the Shenandoah Valley, with additional holdings at Ferry Farm and Deep Run, and his half brother Lawrence's death in July 1752 brought expectations of more property. In February 1753, when GW was twenty-one, Gov. Robert Dinwiddie appointed him adjutant of the Southern District of Virginia with the rank of major. His military duties were light, leaving him ample time to pursue his flourishing career as a surveyor. It was natural, therefore, that he should offer his services to Dinwiddie when, in the fall of 1753, it became apparent that French forces from Canada were moving into the Ohio Valley and posing a threat to Virginia's ambitions in the area.

Before the early 1750s the contest between England and France in America had been chiefly over control of the Indians in the region. The French based their claims in the Ohio Valley largely on early exploration of the area, and the British contended that not only had the territory been included in the original grant of 1609 but their traders had already established a firm foothold in the region. Settlement beyond the mountains would clearly benefit British ambitions, and the Privy Council regarded favorably a petition to the king by the newly organized Ohio Company of Virginia for a grant of more than a half-million acres in the Ohio Valley. The company offered the further inducement of providing an impetus to the fur trade and instituting a lucrative trade with the Indians. The Ohio Company moved quickly to fulfill the terms of its grant. Wills Creek, near the present site of Cumberland, Md., was selected as the company's headquarters on the frontier, and in the winter of 1749–50 a storehouse was built on the Virginia side. In 1750 the company sent out Thomas Cresap, Hugh Parker, and other traders to locate tentative sites for settlement and commissioned Christopher Gist to make a complete survey of the area. Some 150 families were soon settled on Ohio Company lands.

The French government in Canada was by no means indifferent to British advances. Since the 1720s judicious observers had been urging the establishment of French settlements on the Ohio frontier as a barrier to British encroachment. With substantial support from at least some of the Indian tribes in the area, they proceeded to move south into the Ohio country. Early in 1753 the French developed a plan to send a force of some two thousand men under the command of Pierre Paul de La Malgue, sieur de Marin, to establish an effective occupation of the Ohio frontier. An advance party established a base at Presque Isle portage and by the end of May 1753 was ready to move south from Niagara. From Presque Isle the French constructed a road south to a new post at Le Boeuf, and by midsummer of 1753 a small but effective French army was operating at various sites in the Ohio country. The French thus far had been plagued with bad weather, labor troubles with their Indian workmen, lack of supplies, and dissension among the officers. They had not as yet met any opposition from the British or the Indians in the Ohio Valley. As they moved farther south, however, they confronted the pro-English Seneca chief, the Half-King, who warned them at a council at Presque Isle in September that the Iroquois tribes were in treaty with the English, who had agreed not to occupy the valley. But the Indians were clearly impressed by the French advance, and English traders on the frontier had even more reason to be apprehensive.

During the winter and spring of 1752–53, Dinwiddie and the other colonial governors were in constant correspondence concerning the French threat. In June 1753 Dinwiddie transmitted to the Board of Trade the reports he had received from other colonial governors complaining of French encroachments on the frontier. By mid-November he received orders from the crown to investigate the validity of the reports and, if they were found to be accurate, to expel the intruders. In November he informed the Board of Trade that he had already sent one of the colony's adjutants to the Ohio country to evaluate the situation.

The adjutant sent by Dinwiddie was, of course, GW. An entry for 27 Oct. 1753 in the journals of the council reads: "The Governor acquainted the Board that George Washington Esqr. Adjutant General for the Southern District, had offered himself to go properly commissioned to the Commandant of the French Forces, to learn by what Authority he presumes to make Incroachments on his Majesty's Lands on the Ohio." The council approved the appointment, and a committee of the council prepared a letter to be taken to the French commandant. On 31 Oct. 1753 GW set out for Fredericksburg on the first stage of his journey.

The text for this diary has been taken from a copy in the British Public Record Office.

1753

October–November

On Wednesday the 31st. of October 1753 I was Commission'd & appointed by the Honble. Robert Dinwiddie Esqr. Governor &ca. of Virginia

To visit & deliver a Letter to the Commandant of the French Forces on the Ohio, & set out on the intended Journey the same Day. The next I arriv'd at Fredericksburg, & engag'd Mr. Jacob Vanbraam, Interpreter, & proceeded with him to Alexandria where we provided Necessaries. From thence we went to Winchester & got Baggage Horses &ca. & from there we pursued the new Road to Wills Creek, where we arriv'd the 14th: of November.

Robert Dinwiddie, governor of Virginia from 1751 to 1758. From a minia-
ture by C. Dixon. (Colonial Williamsburg photograph)

Here I engag'd Mr. Gist to Pilot us out, & also hired four others as
Servitors (vizt.) Barnaby Currin, & John McGuier (Indian Traders)
Henry Steward, & William Jenkins; & in Company with those Persons I
left the Inhabitants the Day following. The excessive Rains & vast Quan-
tity of Snow that had fallen prevented our reaching Mr. Frazer's, an
Indian Trader at the Mouth of Turtle Creek, on Monongahela, 'til
Thursday.

In addition to delivering Dinwiddie's letter to the French commandant, GW
was instructed to bring back information concerning "the Numbers & Force
of the French on the Ohio, & the adjacent Country and the number and
garrisoning of the forts the French were constructing." For GW's instructions, passport, and commission, see *Papers, Colonial Series,* 1:56–62. See also
Va. Exec. Jls., 5:444–45.

Robert Dinwiddie (1693–1770) was born in Scotland and, after a brief
career as a merchant, entered the British civil service. His appointment as
lieutenant governor of Virginia came in July 1751, and he arrived in the
colony in November to take up his duties. Dinwiddie served as Virginia's governor from 1751 to Jan. 1758. In spite of numerous conflicts with the House
of Burgesses, he was successful in raising funds and military support for the
defense of the colony during the French and Indian War.

Christopher Gist (c.1706–1759), a prominent figure on the Virginia-Pennsylvania frontier, was born in Maryland. After early experience in surveying and exploration, he was living in northwestern North Carolina when approached in 1750 by the Ohio Company and engaged to explore the Ohio country as far as the mouth of the Scioto River. In 1751 he carried on further explorations as far south as the Great Kanawha, and in 1752 he represented the Ohio Company at the Logstown council. By 1753 he had settled on the frontier near the site of Brownsville, Pa., but soon moved to a new settlement near Mount Braddock, Pa.

Jacob Van Braam, born about 1729 in Bergen op Zoom, Holland, had come to America in 1752, where he solicited employment as a teacher of French (*Md. Gaz.*, 30 July 1752). In 1753 he was living in the vicinity of Fredericksburg.

Barnaby Currin was a Pennsylvania trader. McGuire (McGuier) served as a soldier from Fairfax County in 1754. Jenkins was frequently employed by Governor Dinwiddie as a messenger. John Fraser (Frazier), a Pennsylvania gunsmith and Indian trader, had established a trading post at Venango in the 1740s. Forced to leave by a French force that occupied the post in 1753, he resumed his trading operations at another post he had already established at the mouth of Turtle Creek on the Monongahela about ten miles above the present site of Pittsburgh.

22d: We were inform'd here, that Expresses were sent a few Day's ago to the Traders down the River to acquaint them with the General's Death, & return of Major Part of the French Army into Winter Quarters. The Waters were quite impassable, without Swimming our Horses, which oblig'd us to get the loan of a Canoe from Mr. Frazer, & to send Barnaby Currin & Henry Steward down Monongahela, with our Baggage to meet us at the Forks of Ohio, about 10 Miles to cross Allegany.

As I got down before the Canoe, I spent some Time in viewing the Rivers, & the Land in the Fork, which I think extreamly well situated for a Fort; as it has the absolute Command of both Rivers. The Land at the Point is 20 or 25 Feet above the common Surface of the Water; & a considerable Bottom of flat well timber'd Land all around it, very convenient for Building. The Rivers are each a quarter of a Mile, or more, across. About two Miles from this, on the S: E: Side of the River, at the Place where the Ohio Company intended to erect a Fort; lives Singess, King of the Delawars; We call'd upon him to invite him to Council at the Logstown.

As I had taken a good deal of Notice Yesterday of the Situation at the Forks; my Curiosity led me to examine this more particularly; & my Judgement [is] to think it greatly inferior, either for Defence or Advantages, especially the latter; For a Fort at the Forks wou'd be equally well situated on Ohio, & have the entire Command of Monongahela, which runs up to our Settlements & is extreamly well design'd for Water Carriage, as it is of a deep still Nature; besides a Fort at the Fork might be built at a much less Expence, than at the other Place. Nature has well contriv'd the lower Place for Water Defence, but the Hill whereon it must stand, being a quarter of a Mile in Length, & then descending gradually on the Land Side, will render it difficult & very expensive making a sufficient Fortification there. The whole Flat upon the Hill must be taken in, or the Side next the Descent made extreamly high; or else the Hill cut away: otherwise the Enemy will raise Batteries within that Distance, without being expos'd to a single Shot from the Fort.

Singess attended us to Logstown, where we arriv'd between Sunsetting & Dark, the 25th: Day after I left Williamsburg. We travel'd over some extream good & bad Land to get to this Place. As soon as I came into Town, I went to Monacatoocha (as the Half King was out at his hunting Cabbin on little Bever Creek, about 15 Miles off) & inform'd him, by John Davison Interpreter that I was sent a Messenger to the French General, & was ordered to call upon the Sachems of the Six Nations, to acquaint them with it. I gave him a String of Wampum, & a twist of Tobacco, & desir'd him to send for the Half King; which he promis'd to do by a Runner in the Morning, & for other Sachems. I invited him & the other Great Men present to my Tent, where they stay'd an Hour & return'd.

Pierre Paul de La Malgue, sieur de Marin (1692–1753), commandant of the French army on the Ohio during its advance into the Ohio country in 1753, died at Fort Le Boeuf 29 Oct. 1753. Shortly before his death the major part of the French forces were sent into winter quarters; most returned to Montreal, except for a garrison force in the frontier forts (Kent, *French Invasion,* 64).

Shingas was a principal chief of the Turkey or Unalachtigo tribe of Delawares. At the time of GW's visit to the frontier, Shingas was supporting the British, but he went over to the French after Braddock's Defeat in 1755. Logstown was located about 18 miles below the Forks of the Ohio on the north bank of the river (near present-day Ambridge, Pa.) and was one of the chief Indian trading villages in the Ohio Valley.

Monacatoocha, a pro-English Oneida chief also known as Scarouady, apparently ranked only below the Half-King in authority. He had been sent by the Six Nations to superintend the Shawnee at Logstown. The Half-King, or Tanacharison, a Seneca chief, represented the Onondaga Council of the Six Nations among the Seneca. Considered the most reliable of England's Indian allies, he was one of the most prominent of the Indian chiefs at the Treaty of Logstown in 1752 and accompanied GW on his 1754 expedition.

25th: About 3 o'Clock this Evening the Half King came to Town; I went up & invited him & Davison privately to my Tent, & desir'd him to relate some of the Particulars of his Journey to the French Commandant, & reception there, & to give me an Account of the Way & Distance. He told me that the nearest & levelest Way was now impassable, by reason of the many large miry Savannas; that we must be oblig'd to go by Venango, & shou'd not get to the near Fort under 5 or 6 Nights Sleep, good Traveling. When he went to the Fort he said he was receiv'd in a very stern Manner by the late Commander, who ask'd him very abruptly, what he had come about, & to declare his Business; which he says he did in the following Speech.

> Davison was an experienced Indian interpreter, operating a trading business out of Logstown and generally acting as interpreter for the Half-King in his negotiations with the English and French. Pennsylvania trader George Croghan, not unprejudiced in his views of other traders, observed that he "talks a Little of ye Indian Languidge, and makes a great Deal of Disturbance" (*Pa. Arch.*, 1st ser., 2 : 119).
>
> For the speeches exchanged by GW and the chiefs at this meeting, see *Diaries*, 1 : 136–40.

26th: We met in council at the Long House, about 9 o'Clock. As I had Orders to make all possible Dispatch, & waiting here very contrary to my Inclinations; I thank'd him [the Half-King] in the most suitable Manner I cou'd, & told that my Business requir'd the greatest Expedition, & wou'd not admit of that Delay: He was not well pleas'd that I shou'd offer to go before the Time he had appointed, & told me that he cou'd not consent to our going without a Guard, for fear some Accident shou'd befall us, & draw a reflection upon him—besides says he, this is a Matter of no small Moment, & must not be enter'd into without due Consideration, for I now intend to deliver up the French Speech Belt, & make the Shawnesse & Delawars do the same, & accordingly gave Orders to King Singess, who was present, to attend on Wednesday Night with the Wampum, & two Men of their Nation to be in readiness to set off with us next Morning. As I found it impossible to get off without affronting them in the most egregious Manner, I consented to stay.

27th: Runners were dispatch'd very early for the Shawness Chiefs, the Half King set out himself to fetch the French Speech Belt from his hunting Cabbin.

28th: He return'd this Evening, & came with Monacatoocha & two other Sachems to my Tent, & beg'd (as they had comply'd with his Honour the Governor's Request in providing Men, &ca.) to know what Business we were going to the French about? This was a Question I all along expected, & had provided as satisfactory Answers as I cou'd, which allay'd their Curiosity a little. Monacatoocha Informed me, that an Indian from Venango brought News a few Days ago; that the French had call'd all the Mingo's, Delawar's &ca. together at that Place, & told them that they intended to have been down the River this Fall, but the Waters were geting Cold, & the Winter advancing, which obliged them to go into Quarters; but they might assuredly expect them in the Spring, with a far greater Number; & desired that they might be quite Passive, & not intermeddle, unless they had a mind to draw all their Force upon them; for that they expected to fight the English three Years, (as they suppos'd there would be some Attempts made to stop them) in which Time they shou'd Conquer, but if they shou'd prove equally strong, that they & the English wou'd join to cut them off, & divide the Land between them: that though they had lost their General, & some few of their Soldiers, yet there was Men enough to reinforce, & make them Masters of the Ohio. This Speech, he said, was deliver'd to them by an Captn. Joncaire, their Interpreter in Chief, living at Venango, & a Man of Note in the Army.

> Phillipe Thomas de Joncaire, sieur de Chabert (1707–c.1766), captain of marines in the French army, was a member of a family known in Canada for its influence among the Indians. Joncaire was among the most adroit of French negotiators among the Indians, particularly the Seneca. As one of the leaders in the French advance during the summer of 1753, he had arrived to take up quarters at Venango about 1 Dec. 1753.

29th: The Half King and Monacatoocha came very early & beg'd me to stay one Day more, for notwithstanding they had used all the Diligence in their Power, the Shawnesse Chiefs had not brought the Wampum they order'd, but wou'd certainly be in to Night, if not they wou'd delay me no longer, but send it after us as soon as they arriv'd: When I found them so pressing in their request; & knew that returning of Wampum, was the abolishing of Agreements; & giving this up was shaking of all Dependence upon the French, I consented to stay, as I believ'd an Offence offer'd at this Crisis, might have been attended with greater ill Consequence than another Day's Delay.

They also inform'd me that Singess cou'd not get in his Men, & was prevented from coming himself by His Wife's Sickness, (I believe by fear of the French) but that the Wampum of that Nation was lodg'd with Custaloga, one of their Chiefs at Venango. In the Evening they came again, & acquainted me that the Shawnesse were not yet come, but it shou'd not retard the Prosecution of our Journey. He deliver'd in my Hearing the Speeches that were to be made to the French by Jeskakake, one of their old Chiefs, which was giving up the Belt the late Commandant had ask'd for, & repeating near the same Speech he himself had done before. He also deliver'd a String of Wampum to this Chief, which was sent by King Singess to be given to Custaloga, with Orders to repair to, & deliver up the French Wampum. He likewise gave a very large String of black & white Wampum, which was to be sent immediately up to the Six Nations, if the French refus'd to quit the

Land at this Warning, which was the third & last Time, & was the right of this Jeskakake to deliver.

> Custaloga was a Delaware chief. Custaloga's Town (Meadville, Pa.) was on the west side of French Creek. In July 1753 Pennsylvania trader William Trent noted that Custaloga's people were helping the French move their supplies across the Presque Isle portage (Darlington, *Henry Bouquet,* 18–19). By 1754 the chief was openly supporting the French.
>
> Jeskakake became a supporter of the French and was given for his services a *commission de chef* in June 1754.

30th: Last Night the great Men assembled to their Council House to consult further about this Journey, & who were to go; the result of which was, that only three of their Chiefs, with one of their best Hunters shou'd be our Convoy: the reason they gave for not sending more, after what had been propos'd in Council the 26th. was, that a greater Number might give the French Suspicion of some bad Design, & cause them to be treated rudely; but I rather think they cou'd not get their Hunters in.

We set out about 9 o'Clock, with the Half King, Jeskakake, White Thunder, & the Hunter; & travel'd on the road to Venango, where we arriv'd the 4th: of December, without any Thing remarkably happening, but a continued Series of bad Weather. This is an old Indian Town, situated on the Mouth of French Creek on Ohio, & lies near No. about 60 Miles from the Logstown, but more than 70 the Way we were oblig'd to come. We found the French Colours hoisted at a House where they drove Mr. John Frazer an English Subject from: I immediately repair'd to it, to know where the Commander resided: There was three Officers, one of which, Capt. Joncaire, inform'd me, that he had the Command of the Ohio, but that there was a General Officer at the next Fort, which he advis'd me to for an Answer.

He invited us to Sup with them, & treated with the greatest Complaisance. The Wine, as they dos'd themselves pretty plentifully with it, soon banish'd the restraint which at first appear'd in their Conversation, & gave license to their Tongues to reveal their Sentiments more freely. They told me it was their absolute Design to take Possession of the Ohio, & by G—— they wou'd do it, for tho' they were sensible, that the English cou'd raise two Men for their one; yet they knew their Motions were too slow & dilatory to prevent any Undertaking of theirs. They pretended to have an undoubted right to the river from a Discovery made by one La Sol Years ago, & the use of this Expedition is to prevent our Settling on the River or Waters of it, as they have heard of some Families moving out in order thereto.

From the best Intelligence I cou'd get, there has been 1,500 Men this Side Oswago Lake, but upon the Death of the General, all were recall'd to about 6 or 7 Hundred, which were left to Garrison four Forts, 150 or thereabouts in each, the first of which is on French Creek, near a small Lake, about 60 Miles from Venango near N: N: W: the next lies on Lake Erie, where the greatest Part of their Stores are kept about 15 Miles from the other; from that it is 120 Miles from the Carrying Place, at the Fall of Lake Erie, where there is a small Fort, which they lodge their Goods at, in bringing them from Morail [Montreal], the Place that all their Stores come from; the next Fort lies about 20 Miles from this, on Oswago Lake; between this Fort & Morail there are three others; the first of which is near the English Fort Oswago. From the Fort on Lake Erie to Morail is about 600 Miles, which they say if good Weather, requires no more than 4 Weeks Voyage, if they go in Barks or large Vessells that they can cross the Lake; but if they come in Canoes, it will require five or six Weeks for they are oblig'd to keep under the Shoar.

> White Thunder, or Belt of Wampum, was an Iroquois chief. The Hunter, also known as Guyasuta or Kiasutha, was a Seneca who later became a principal chief of the Six Nations and participated in many of the councils between the Iroquois and the English before the Revolution. After Braddock's Defeat in 1755, Guyasuta went over to the French and led the Indians in the defeat of Maj. James Grant in 1758. GW encountered him again during his journey to the Ohio in 1770.

December

5th: Rain'd successively all Day, which prevented our traveling. Capt. Joncaire sent for the half King, as he had but just heard that he came with me: He affected to be much Concern'd that I did not make free to bring him in before; I excused it in the best Manner I was capable, & told him I did not think their Company agreeable, as I had heard him say a good deal in dispraise of Indians in General. But another Motive prevented my bringing them into his Company: I knew that he was Interpreter, & a Person of very great Influence among the Indians, & had lately used all possible means to draw them over to their Interest; therefore I was desirous of giving no more Opportunity than cou'd be avoided. When they came in there was great Pleasure express'd at seeing them, he wonder'd how they cou'd be so near without coming to visit him, made several trifling Presents, & applied Liquors so fast, that they were soon render'd incapable of the Business they came about notwithstanding the Caution that was given.

6th: The Half King came to my Tent quite Sober, & insisted very much that I shou'd stay & hear what he had to say to the French. I fain wou'd have prevented his speaking any Thing 'til he came to the Commandant, but cou'd not prevail. He told me that at this Place Council Fire was kindled, where all their Business with these People were to be transacted, & that the Management of the Indian Affairs was left solely to Monsieur Joncaire. As I was desirous of knowing the Issue of this, I agreed to stay, but sent our Horses a little Way up French Creek, to raft over & Camp, which I knew wou'd make it near Night.

About 10 oClock they met in Council, the King spoke much the same as he had done to the General, & offer'd the French Speech Belt which had before been demanded, with the Marks of four Towns in it, which Monsieur Joncaire refused to receive; but desired him to carry it to the Fort to the Commander.

7th: Monsieur La Force, Commissary of the French Stores, & three other Soldiers came over to accompany us up. We found it extreamly difficult getting the Indians off to Day; as every Strategem had been used to prevent their going up with me. I had last Night left John Davison (the Indian Interpreter that I brought from Logstown with me) strictly charg'd not to be out of their Company, as I cou'd get them over to my Tent (they having some Business with Custaloga, to know the reason why he did not deliver up the French Belt, which he had in keeping,) but was oblig'd to send Mr. Gist over to Day to fetch them, which he did with great Perswasion.

At 11 o'Clock we set out for the Fort, & was prevented from arriving there 'till the 11th: by excessive rains, Snows, & bad traveling, through many Mires & Swamps, which we were oblig'd to pass to avoid crossing the Creek, which was impassible either by Fording or Rafting, the Water was so high & rapid. We pass'd over much good Land since we left Venango, & through several extensive & very rich Meadows, one of which was near 4 Miles in length, & considerably wide in some Places.

Michel Pepin, called La Force, was captured by the British near Great Meadows in the spring of 1754 and sent to Williamsburg as a hostage after the surrender of Fort Necessity. GW shared the general respect for his ability. Writing to Governor Dinwiddie, 29 May 1754, he observed that La Force "is a Person whose active Spirit, leads him into all parlys, and brought him acquainted with all parts, add to this a perfect use of the Indian Tongue, and gt influence with the Indians" (*Papers, Colonial Series*, 1:111).

12th: I prepar'd early to wait upon the Commander, & was receiv'd & conducted to him by the 2d. Officer in Command; I acquainted him with my Business, & offer'd my Commission & Letter, both of which he desir'd me to keep 'til the Arrival of Monsieur Riparti, Capt. at the next Fort, who was sent for & expected every Hour.

This Commander is a Knight of the Military Order of St: Lewis, &

named Legadieur St. Piere, he is an elderly Gentleman, & has much the Air of a Soldier; he was sent over to take the Command immediately upon the Death of the late General, & arriv'd here about 7 Days before me. At 2 o'Clock the Gentleman that was sent for arriv'd, when I offer'd the Letters &ca. again, which they receiv'd, & adjourn'd into a private Appartment for the Captain to translate, who understood a little English, after he had done it, the Captain desir'd I wou'd walk in & bring my Interpreter to peruse & correct it, which I did.

> The commander was Jacques Le Gardeur, sieur de Saint-Pierre (1701–1755), who had succeeded the sieur de Marin as commandant of the French forces in the Ohio country upon the latter's death. He had been commissioned an ensign in 1732 and served as a lieutenant in the Chickasaw campaign in 1739. Commissioned captain in 1749, he engaged in extensive western exploration. He was killed at Lake George 8 Sept. 1755. "Monsieur Riparti" was Louis Le Gardeur de Repentigny, commandant at Fort Presque Isle and probably a kinsman of Le Gardeur de Saint-Pierre. Repentigny had become commandant of Fort Le Boeuf upon the death of Marin and remained there until he was relieved by Le Gardeur de Saint-Pierre.

13th: The chief Officer retired to hold a Council of War, which gave me an Opportunity of taking the Dimensions of the Fort, & making what Observations I cou'd.

I cou'd get no certain Account of the Number of Men here; but according to the best Judgement I cou'd form, there is an Hundred exclusive of Officers, which are pretty many. I also gave Orders to the People that were with me, to take an exact Account of the Canoes that were haled up, to convey their Forces down in the Spring, which they did, and told 50 of Birch Bark, & 170 of Pine; besides many others that were block'd out, in Readiness to make.

14th: As the Snow increased very fast, & our Horses daily got weaker, I sent them off unloaded, under the Care of Barnaby Currin & two others, to make all convenient Dispatch to Venango, & there wait our Arrival, if there was a Prospect of the Rivers Freezing, if not, then to continue down to Shanapin's Town at the Forks of Ohio, & there wait 'till we came to cross Allegany; intending my Self to go down by Water, as I had the Offer of a Canoe or two.

As I found many Plots concerted to retard the Indians Business, & prevent their returning with me, I endeavour'd all in my Power to frustrate their Schemes, & hurry them on to execute their intended Design. They accordingly pressed for admittance this Evening, which at length was granted them privately with the Commander, & one or two other Officers. The Half King told me that he offer'd the Wampum to the Commander, who evaded taking it, & made many fair Promises of Love & Friendship; said he wanted to live in Peace & trade amicably

with them; as a Proof of which, he wou'd send some Goods immediately down to the Logstown for them, but I rather think the Design of
that is to bring away all of our stragling traders that they may meet with;
as I privately understood they intended to carry an Officer, &ca. with
them; & what rather confirms this Opinion, I was enquiring of the
Commander by what Authority he had taken & made Prisoners of several of our English Subjects. He told me the Country belong'd to them,
that no English Man had a right to trade upon them Waters; & that he
had Orders to make every Person Prisoner that attempted it on the
Ohio or the Waters of it.

I enquir'd of Capt. Riparti about the Boy that was carried by, as it was
done while the Command devolved upon him, between the Death of
the late General & the Arrival of the Present. He acknowledg'd that a
Boy had been carried past, & that the Indians had two or three white
Scalps, (I was told by some of the Indians at Venango) but pretended
to have forgot the Name of the Place that the Boy came from, & all
the Particulars, tho' he Question'd him for some Hours as they were
carrying him past. I likewise enquired where & what they had done with
John Trotter, & James McClocklan, two Pensylvania Traders, which they
had taken with all their Goods; they told me that they had been sent to
Canada, but were now return'd Home.

This Evening I receiv'd an Answer to His Honour the Governor's
Letter from the Commandant.

This letter, signed by Legardeur de Saint-Pierre and dated 15 Dec. "From
the Fort of the Rivière au Beuf," was in reply to Gov. Robert Dinwiddie's
letter of 31 Oct. 1753, warning the French not to invade the Ohio country.
A translation of the letter reads:

"As I have the honor of commanding here in chief, Mr. Washington delivered me the letter which you wrote to the commander of the French troops.

"I should have been glad if you had given him orders, or he had been
inclined, to proceed to Canada to see our General, to whom it belongs,
rather than to me, to set forth the evidence and the reality of the rights of
the King, my master, to the lands situated along the Belle Riviere, and to
contest the pretensions of the King of Great Britain thereto.

"I am going to send your letter to the Marquis Duquesne. His reply will be
a law to me, and, if he should order me to communicate it to you, Sir, I can
assure you that I shall neglect nothing to have it reach you very promptly.

"As to the summons you send me to retire, I do not think myself obliged
to obey it. Whatever may be your instructions, I am here by virtue of the
orders of my General, and I entreat you, Sir, not to doubt for a moment that
I have a firm resolution to follow them with all the exactness and determination which can be expected of the best officer.

"I do not know that anything has happened in the course of this campaign
which can be construed as an act of hostility, or as contrary to the treaties
between the two Crowns; the continuation of which interests and pleases us
as much as it does the English. If you had been pleased, Sir, to go into detail

regarding the deeds which caused your complaints, I should have had the honor of answering you in the most positive manner, and I am sure that you would have had reason to be satisfied.

"I have made it a particular duty to receive Mr. Washington with the distinction owing to your dignity, his position, and his own great merit. I trust that he will do me justice in that regard with you, and that he will make known to you the profound respect with which I am, Sir, Your most humble and most obedient servant" (Kent, *French Invasion,* 75–76).

Le Gardeur de Saint-Pierre forwarded Dinwiddie's letter to Governor Duquesne on 22 Dec. The governor found the claims of the Virginians to be without foundation; the area incontestably belonged to the French (Duquesne to Le Gardeur de Saint-Pierre, 30 Jan. 1754, *Papiers Contrecoeur,* 98–99).

15th: The Commander order'd a plentiful Store of Liquor, Provisions & ca. to be put on board our Canoe, & appear'd to be extreamly complaisant, though he was ploting every Scheme that the Devil & Man cou'd invent, to set our Indians at Variance with us, to prevent their going 'till after our Departure. Presents, rewards, & every Thing that cou'd be suggested by him or his Officers was not neglected to do. I can't say that ever in my Life I suffer'd so much Anxiety as I did in this affair: I saw that every Stratagem that the most fruitful Brain cou'd invent: was practis'd to get the Half King won to their Interest, & that leaving of him here, was giving them the Opportunity they aimed at: I went to the Half King and press'd him in the strongest Terms to go. He told me the Commander wou'd not discharge him 'till the Morning; I then went to the Commander & desired him to do their Business, & complain'd of ill Treatment; for keeping them, as they were Part of my Company was detaining me, which he promis'd not to do, but to forward my Journey as much as he cou'd: He protested he did not keep them but was innocent of the Cause of their Stay; though I soon found it out. He had promis'd them a Present of Guns, &ca. if they wou'd wait 'till the Morning. As I was very much press'd by the Indians to wait this Day for them; I consented on a Promise that Nothing shou'd hinder them in the Morning.

16th: The French were not slack in their Inventions to keep the Indians this Day also; but as they were obligated, according to promise, to give the Present: they then endeavour'd to try the Power of Liquor; which I doubt not wou'd have prevail'd at any other Time than this, but I tax'd the King so close upon his Word that he refrain'd, & set off with us as he had engag'd. We had a tedious & very fatiguing Passage down the Creek, several Times we had like to have stove against Rocks, & many Times were oblig'd all Hands to get out, & remain in the Water Half an Hour or more, getting her over the Shoals: on one Place the Ice had lodg'd & made it impassable by Water; therefore we were oblig'd to carry our Canoe across a neck Land a quarter of a Mile over. We did not reach Venango 'till the 22d: where we met with our Horses. This Creek is extreamly crooked, I dare say the Distance between the Fort & Venango can't be less than 130 Miles to follow the Meanders.

23d: When I got Things ready to set off I sent for the Half King, to know whether they intended to go with us, or by Water. He told me that the White Thunder had hurt himself much, & was Sick & unable to walk, therefore he was oblig'd to carry him down in a Canoe: As I found he intended to stay a Day or two here, & knew that Monsieur Joncaire wou'd employ every Scheme to set him against the English, as he had before done; I told him I hoped he wou'd guard against his Flattery, & let no fine Speeches Influence Him in their Favour: He desired I might not be concern'd, for he knew the French too well, for any Thing to engage him in their Behalf, & though he cou'd not go down with us, he wou'd endeavour to meet at the Forks with Joseph Campbell, to deliver a Speech for me to carry to his Honour the Governor. He told me he wou'd order the young Hunter to attend us, & get Provision &ca. if wanted. Our Horses were now so weak & feeble, & the Baggage heavy; as we were oblig'd to provide all the Necessaries the Journey wou'd require, that we doubted much their performing it; therefore my Self & others (except the Drivers which were oblig'd to ride) gave up our Horses for Packs, to assist along with the Baggage; & put my Self into an Indian walking Dress, & continue'd with them three Day's, 'till I found there was no Probability of their getting in, in any reasonable Time; the Horses grew less able to travel every Day. The Cold increas'd very fast, & the Roads were geting much worse by a deep Snow continually Freezing; And as I was uneasy to get back to make a report of my Proceedings to his Honour the Governor; I determin'd to prosecute my Journey the nearest way through the Woods on Foot. Accordingly I left Mr. Vanbraam in Charge of our Baggage, with Money and Directions to provide Necessaries from Place to Place for themselves & Horses & to make the most convenient Dispatch in. I took my necessary Papers, pull'd off my Cloths; tied My Self up in a Match Coat; & with my Pack at my back, with my Papers & Provisions in it, & a Gun, set out with Mr. Gist, fitted in the same Manner, on Wednesday the 26th.

> Joseph Campbell was an unlicensed Pennsylvania trader in 1747 and 1748, employed by Alexander Moorhead. He was represented by George Croghan to be "a bad man, and corrupted by the French" (*Pa. Arch. Col. Rec.*, 5:693). Campbell was killed by an Indian of the Six Nations at Parnell's Knob in Sept. 1754.

The Day following, just after we pass'd a Place call'd the Murdering Town where we intended to quit the Path & steer across the Country for Shanapins Town, we fell in with a Party of French Indians, which had laid in wait for us, one of them fired at Mr. Gist or me, not 15 Steps, but fortunately missed. We took this Fellow into Custody, & kept him 'till about 9 o'Clock at Night, & then let him go, & then walked all the remaining Part of the Night without making any Stop; that we might get the start, so far as to be out of the reach of their Pursuit next Day, as were well assur'd they wou'd follow upon our Tract as soon as it was Light: The next Day we continued traveling 'till it was quite Dark, & got to the River about two Miles above Shanapins; we expected to have found the River Froze, but it was not, only about 50 Yards from each Shoar; the Ice I suppose had broke up above, for it was driving in vast Quantities.

> Murdering Town, or Murthering Town, was a Delaware village on Conoque-
> nessing Creek, a subsidiary of Beaver Creek.

There was no way for us to get over but upon a Raft, which we set about with but one poor Hatchet, & got finish'd just after Sunsetting, after a whole days Work: We got it launch'd, & on board of it, & sett off; but before we got half over, we were jamed in the Ice in such a Manner, that we expected every Moment our Raft wou'd sink, & we Perish; I put out my seting Pole, to try to stop the Raft, that the Ice might pass by, when the Rapidity of the Stream through it with so much Violence against the Pole, that it Jirk'd me into 10 Feet Water, but I fortunately saved my Self by catching hold of one of the Raft Logs. Notwithstanding all our Efforts we cou'd not get the Raft to either Shoar, but were oblig'd, as we were pretty near an Island, to quit our Raft & wade to it. The Cold was so extream severe, that Mr. Gist got all his Fingers, & some of his Toes Froze, & the Water was shut up so hard, that We found no Difficulty in getting off the Island on the Ice in the Morning, & went to Mr. Frazers. We met here with 20 Warriors that had been going to the Southward to War, but coming to a Place upon the Head of the Great Cunnaway, where they found People kill'd & Scalpt, all but one Woman with very Light Hair, they turn'd about; & ran back, for fear of the Inhabitants rising & takeing them as the Authors of the Murder: They report that the People were lying about the House, & some of them much torn & eat by Hogs; by the Marks that were left, they say they were French Indians of the Ottaway Nation, &ca. that did it.

As we intended to take Horse here, & it requir'd some Time to hunt them; I went up about 3 Miles to the Mouth of Yaughyaughgane to visit Queen Aliquippa, who had express'd great Concern that we pass'd her in going to the Fort. I made her a Present of a Match Coat; & a Bottle of rum, which was thought much the best Present of the two.

The report probably refers to the massacre of the family of Robert Foyles, "his wife & 5 children," who were killed on the Monongahela rather than the Great Kanawha ("Indian Wars," 399). In Mar. 1754 Dinwiddie in writing to Gov. James Hamilton noted that "the Incursions of these People with their Ind's on our present Settlem'ts, will be constantly, and attended with Robberies and Murders, w'ch was the Case last Year w'n some of their Ind's Came to our Frontiers, Murder'd a Man, his Wife and five Children, Robbed them of all they had, and left their Bodies to be tore in Pieces by the wild Beasts" (Brock, *Dinwiddie*, 1:119).

Queen Alliquippa (Allaquippa), who died about 1754, was frequently described as a Delaware. Conrad Weiser, Pennsylvania's leading Indian negotiator, who met her at Logstown in 1748, described her as the old Seneca queen.

1754

January

Tuesday 1st: Day of Jany: We left Mr. Frazers House, & arriv'd at Mr. Gists at Monangahela the 2d. where I bought Horse Saddle &ca.

The 6th: We met 17 Horses loaded with Materials & Stores for a Fort at the Forks; & the Day after, a Family or two going out to settle; this Day we arriv'd at Wills Creek, after as fatiguing a Journey as it is possible to conceive, rendered so by excessive bad Weather: From the first Day of December 'till the 15th. there was but one Day, but what it rain'd or snow'd incessantly & throughout the whole Journey we met with nothing but one continued Series of cold wet Weather; which occasioned very uncumfortable Lodgings, especially after we had left our Tent; which was some Screen from the Inclemency of it.

On the 11th. I got to Belvoir, where I stop'd one Day to take necessary rest; & then set out for, & arrived at Williamsburg, the 16th. & waited upon His Honour the Governor with the Letter I had brought from the French Commandant, & to give an Account of the Proceedures of my Journey. Which I beg leave to do by offering the Foregoing, as it contains the most remarkable Occurrences that happen'd to me.

I hope it will be sufficient to satisfy your Honour with my Proceedings; for that was my Aim in undertaking the Journey: & chief Study throughout the Prosecution of it.

With the Assurance, & Hope of doing it, I with infinite Pleasure subscribe my Self Yr. Honour's most Obedt. & very Hble. Servant.

Go: Washington

Belvoir was the estate of Col. William Fairfax on the southern shore of the Potomac, near Mount Vernon.

Upon GW's arrival in Williamsburg, he presented the French comman- dant's letter and this journal of the expedition to the governor. His verbal account of French activities was accorded equal attention by Dinwiddie. The governor informed the council and the House of Burgesses that "Major Washington further reports that he ask'd why they [the French] had seized the Goods of our Traders, and sent their Persons Prisoners to Canada, to w'ch the Com'dt answer'd; That his Orders from their Gen'l, the Governor of Canada, were, Not to permit any English Subjects to trade on the Waters of the Ohio, but to seize their Goods and send them Prisoners to Quebeck" (Brock, *Dinwiddie*, 1:73–74). A further account of GW's comments was forwarded by the governor to the Board of Trade, together with his journal, his map of the frontier, and his plan of Fort Le Boeuf, on 29 Jan. 1754: "Mr. Washington had my Orders to make what Observations he cou'd on his Journey, & to take a Plan of their Fort, which I now enclose You, & from these Directions his Journal becomes so large. He assures me that they had begun another Fort at the Mouth of the Creek, which he thinks will be finish'd by the Month of March. There were in the Fort where the Commander resided, about 300 regular Forces; & nine hundred more were gone to Winter Quar- ters (in order to save their Provisions) to some Forts on Lake Erie &ca. but that they were to return by the Month of March; then they fully determin'd with all the Forces they cou'd collect, which he understood wou'd be fifteen hundred regulars, besides Indians, to go down the River Ohio, & propose building many other Forts, & that their chief residence wou'd be at the Logs- town; & that they had near three hundred Canoes to transport their Soldiers, Provisions & Ammunition &ca." (Great Britain, Public Record Office).

Almost immediately upon GW's return to Williamsburg, Dinwiddie or- dered publication of his journal. It appeared as *The Journal of Major George Washington, Sent by the Hon. Robert Dinwiddie, Esq; His Majesty's Lieutenant- Governor, and Commander in Chief of Virginia, to the Commandant of the French Forces on Ohio. To Which Are Added, the Governor's Letter, and a Translation of the French Officer's Answer* (Williamsburg, Va.: William Hunter, 1754). GW pref- aced the publication with the following "Advertisement":

"As it was thought adviseable by his Honour the Governor to have the following Account of my Proceedings to and from the French on Ohio, com- mitted to Print; I think I can do no less than apologize, in some Measure, for the numberless Imperfections of it.

"There intervened but one Day between my Arrival in Williamsburg, and the Time for the Council's Meeting, for me to prepare and transcribe, from the rough Minutes I had taken in my Travels, this Journal; the writing of which only was sufficient to employ me closely the whole Time, consequently admitted of no Leisure to consult of a new and proper Form to offer it in, or to correct or amend the Diction of the old; neither was I apprised, or did in the least conceive, when I wrote this for his Honour's Perusal, that it ever would be published, or even have more than a cursory Reading; till I was informed, at the Meeting of the present General Assembly, that it was already in the Press.

"There is nothing can recommend it to the Public, but this. Those Things which came under the Notice of my own Observation, I have been explicit and just in a Recital of:— Those which I have gathered from Report, I have been particularly cautious, not to augment, but collected the Opinions of the several Intelligencers, and selected from the whole, the most probable and consistent Account.

                                                                    G. Washington."

The journal was printed in various colonial newspapers (see, for example, *Md. Gazette.*, 21 and 28 Mar. 1754; *Boston Gazette.*, 16 April–21 May 1754). On 15 Feb. 1754 the journal was delivered to the House of Burgesses, and on 21 Feb. the burgesses voted the sum of £50 to GW "to testify our Approbation of his Proceedings on his Journey to the *Ohio*" (*H.B.J.*, 1752–58, 182, 185).

Expedition to the Ohio
1754

In the weeks after GW's return from his journey to the French commandant, reports of further French infiltration into the Ohio Valley continued to reach Williamsburg, and Virginia's governor Robert Dinwiddie made preparations to resist. He appealed to other colonial governors for aid in repelling the French, and a small force was ordered to the Ohio to construct a fort at the Forks (now Pittsburgh). Dinwiddie had already sent ten cannon and a supply of ammunition to Alexandria for transportation to the Ohio. GW, as adjutant of the Northern Neck of Virginia, was instructed to raise 50 men from Frederick County and 50 men from Augusta County and march them to the Forks to aid in the construction of the fort. However, neither Augusta nor Frederick complied with the request for men, and in mid-February GW returned to Williamsburg. To encourage enlistments Dinwiddie issued a proclamation on 19 Feb. promising that a grant of 200,000 acres of land on the east side of the Ohio would be distributed among those who volunteered for service in the army.

When the House of Burgesses met in February, Dinwiddie immediately informed it of the French threat. The burgesses proved less cooperative than he had hoped. An inadequate grant of £10,000 for protecting the frontier was hedged with restrictions as to the terms under which the money could be spent. By this time Dinwiddie realized the futility of relying on the counties to raise enough militia for the campaign and decided to use the funds voted by the assembly to raise a force of six companies composed of 50 men each. Both New York and South Carolina were to send independent companies of regular troops, and it was hoped that contributions would be forthcoming from the other colonies.

GW was definitely interested in a command for the campaign against the French. In a letter written sometime between February and March 1754 to Richard Corbin, a member of the council, he stated: "In a conversation with you at Green Spring, you gave me some room to hope for a commission above

*that of a major, and to be ranked among the chief officers of this expedition.
The command of the whole forces is what I neither look for, expect, nor desire;
for I must be impartial enough to confess, it is a charge too great for my youth
and inexperience to be entrusted with. . . . But if I could entertain hopes, that
you thought me worthy of the post of Lieutenant-colonel, and would favour
me so far as to mention it at the appointment of officers, I could not but entertain a true sense of the kindness." Corbin, and probably others, apparently
spoke for GW, since he did indeed receive the appointment he sought. General
command of the Virginia forces was given to Joshua Fry, who was ordered to
march first to Alexandria and then on to Wills Creek to aid in construction of
the fort at the Forks of the Ohio. Even before the receipt of his commission as
lieutenant colonel, GW had established headquarters at Alexandria and was
actively engaged in recruiting and making preparations for the campaign.
The French were moving down the Ohio more rapidly than expected. GW's
diary of the campaign begins 31 Mar. 1754 and includes the march from
Alexandria to the frontier, the defeat of a party of French troops under the
command of Joseph Coulon de Villiers, sieur de Jumonville, and the construction of Fort Necessity at the Great Meadows. The last entry is for 27 June
1754, with GW's force planning to move to erect a fort on Red Stone Creek.*

*On 28 June word was received from Chief Monacatoocha that the French
at the Forks were preparing to send out eight hundred of their own troops and
four hundred Indians under the command of Louis Coulon de Villiers, brother
of the defeated Jumonville. It was clear that the Indians with GW's troops
would leave unless he returned to Great Meadows. Accordingly, the retreat
was ordered, and after a backbreaking march over a mountainous terrain, the
Virginia troops and Capt. James Mackay's Independent Company of regulars
from South Carolina arrived at little Fort Necessity on Great Meadows on
1 July. There they found almost no provisions; but the exhausted men were in
no condition to retreat farther. GW ordered them to dig in. Their Indian allies
quietly disappeared. On 1 July scouts informed GW that the French had advanced as far as Red Stone, and about 11:00 A.M. on 3 July the French
command approached the fort. After a day of fighting, faced by a greatly superior force, GW was compelled to surrender. On 3 July he and Captain
Mackay signed the articles of capitulation including the controversial admis-
sion that they had "assassinated" Jumonville.*

*The diary was among the papers lost by GW at the surrender of Fort Neces-
sity. Retrieved by the French, it became part of a pamphlet published in Paris
in 1756 under the title* Mémoire contenant le précis des faits, avec
leurs pièces justificatives pour servir de réponse aux observations en-
voyées par les ministres d'Angleterre, dans les cours de l'Europe.

*In addition to GW's journal, numerous other letters and journals were in-
cluded with editorial notes justifying French activities in the Ohio Valley. In
1757 a copy of the pamphlet was captured on board a French ship taken as a*

prize and was translated and published by printer Hugh Gaine in New York under the title A Memorial Containing a Summary View of Facts with Their Authorities, in Answer to the Observations Sent by the English Ministry to the Courts of Europe. *This translation has been used in the abridged diary as the source for the text of the 1754 diary. Two additional printings, one by J. Parker in New York and one by James Chattin in Philadelphia, appeared also in 1757. Two English editions were also published.*

As the original of GW's journal has not been found, the accuracy of the version published in the Memoir *must remain questionable; it was indeed challenged by contemporaries, including GW. Discovery in the twentieth century of a contemporary copy of GW's diary in the Contrecoeur Papers, Archives du Seminaire de Quebec, Université Laval, indicates that the amount of deliberate French "editing" of the journal was probably less than historians have believed and was probably confined to critical annotation and comments. Aside from variations in spelling of places and proper names, the French translator probably closely followed GW's original diary.*

1754

March–April

On the 31st of *March,* I received from his Honour a Lieutenant Colonel's Commission, of the *Virginia* Regiment, whereof *Joshua Fry,* Esq; was Colonel, dated the 15th; with Orders to take the Troops, which were at that Time quartered at *Alexandria,* under my Command, and to march with them towards the *Ohio,* there to help Captain *Trent* to build Forts, and to defend the Possessions of his Majesty against the Attempts and Hostilities of the *French.*

William Trent (1715–1787), a native of Lancaster, Pa., was an experienced frontiersman who had acted for the Pennsylvania assembly in carrying messages and gifts to the Indians. In the 1740s he had built up a considerable Indian trade and formed a partnership with George Croghan. He was an agent for the Ohio Company in the construction of storehouses and a fort. During the French and Indian War he served with both the Pennsylvania and Virginia forces. Trent lost much of his holdings during Pontiac's rebellion in 1763 and became a leader of the "Suffering Traders," who perennially requested restitution of their losses from the crown.

Joshua Fry (c.1700–1754) was born in Crewkerne, Somerset, Eng., and educated at Oxford. Sometime before 1720 he immigrated to Virginia and in 1729 became master of the grammar school at the College of William and Mary and in 1731 professor of mathematics and natural philosophy. After the formation of Albemarle County in 1744, he filled a variety of posts, including county surveyor, and represented Albemarle County in the House of Burgesses from 1745 until his death. Fry collaborated with Peter Jefferson in 1751 to produce the "Map of the Inhabited Parts of Virginia," one of the most famous of colonial maps. He received a commission as colonel of the

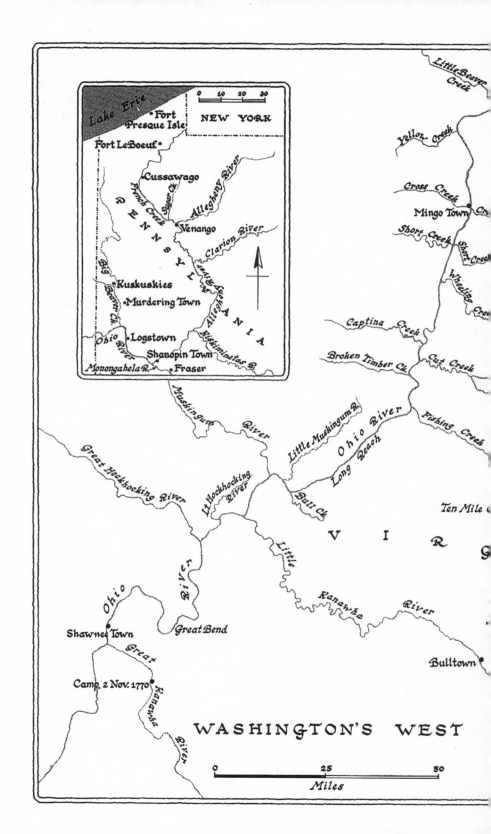

WASHINGTON'S WEST

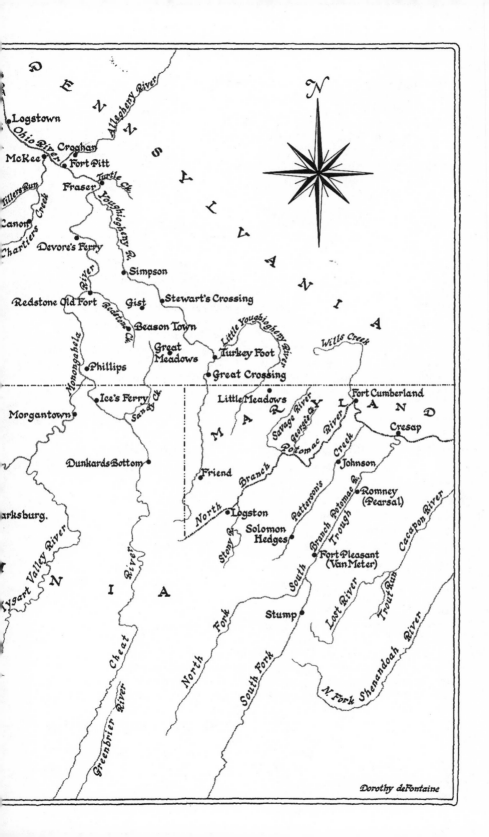

Dorothy deFontaine

Virginia Regiment in 1754 and was put in command of the campaign to drive the French from the Ohio. On his way to Wills Creek, Fry fell from his horse and died of his injuries 31 May, leaving the command of the regiment to devolve on GW.

The date of the commission's receipt as given here is in error. Dinwiddie wrote to GW 15 Mar. enclosing the commission as lieutenant colonel of the Virginia Regiment, "pay, 12s. 6d. per day," and GW acknowledged its receipt 20 Mar.

In Alexandria, GW was facing the perennial problems of recruiting and supply. On 9 Mar. he wrote to Dinwiddie: "I have increased my number of Men to abt. 25, and dare venture to say, I should have had several more if the excessive bad weather did not prevent their meeting agreeable to their Officer's Commands. We daily Experience the great necessity for Cloathing the Men, as we find the generallity of those, who are to be Enlisted, are of those loose, Idle Persons, that are quite destitute of House, and Home, and, I may truly say many of them of Cloaths; which last, render's them very incapable of the necessary Service, as they must unavoidably be expos'd to inclement weather in their Marches &c.; and can expect no other, than to encounter almost every difficulty, that's incident to a Soldiers Life[.] There is many of them without Shoes, others want Stockings, some are without Shirts, and not a few that have Scarce a Coat, or Waistcoat to their Backs; in short, they are as illy provided as can be well conceiv'd" (*Papers, Colonial Series,* 1:73–75).

April the 2d, Every Thing being ready, we began our march according to our Orders, the 2d of *April,* with two Companies of Foot, commanded by Captain *Peter Hog,* and Lieutenant *Jacob Vambraam,* five Subalterns, two Serjeants, six Corporals, one Drummer, and one Hundred and twenty Soldiers, one Surgeon, one *Swedish* Gentleman, who was a Volunteer, two Waggons, guarded by one Lieutenant, Serjeant, Corporal, and Twenty-five Soldiers.

We left *Alexandria* on Tuesday Noon, and pitched our Tents about four miles from *Cameron,* having travelled six Miles.

Peter Hog (1703–1782), a native of Edinburgh, settled in Augusta County about 1745. He was commissioned a captain in the Virginia Regiment 9 Mar. 1754. During the French and Indian War he served in GW's Virginia Regiment.

Jacob Van Braam had accompanied GW on his journey to the French commandant in 1753. He was made hostage by the French at Fort Necessity and remained in captivity in Canada for several years. Van Braam's role in translating the articles of capitulation of Fort Necessity aroused so much criticism in Virginia that his name was omitted from the list of officers thanked by the assembly for their participation in the campaign. By 1761, however, tempers had cooled, and Van Braam was specifically recommended by Gov. Francis Fauquier for a commission in the British army. He subsequently received a commission in the Royal American Regiment.

The surgeon who accompanied the expedition was Dr. James Craik (1730–1814), a native of Arbigland, Scot. Educated at the University of Edinburgh, Craik immigrated in 1750, first to the West Indies and then to

Virginia, opening a practice in Norfolk, where he was living when commissioned in the Virginia Regiment 7 Mar. 1754. During the French and Indian War he was stationed at Winchester and served in the Braddock campaign. At the close of the war he settled on a plantation at Port Tobacco, Charles County, Md. During the Revolution, Craik held, among other posts, that of chief physician and surgeon of the Continental Army. He was a frequent visitor to Mount Vernon, especially when there was illness in the family and among the slaves, accompanied GW on his journey to the Ohio and Kanawha rivers in 1770 and 1784, and attended him in his last illness.

The Swedish gentleman was Carolus Gustavus de Spiltdorf, commissioned an ensign in the Virginia Regiment 21 July 1754 and promoted to lieutenant 29 Oct. 1754. He was killed during Braddock's Defeat 9 July 1755.

Cameron was located at the head of Hunting Creek, Fairfax County.

At this point the Gaine edition of the 1754 diary apparently omitted a number of entries "From the 3d of April, to the 19th of said Month, this Journal only contains the March of the Troops, and how they were joined by a Detachment which was brought by Captain Stevens." Although the printed diary does not indicate the route taken by the expedition from Cameron, it can be partially reconstructed from the account of GW's expenses submitted to the colony of Virginia in October 1754. See *Papers, Colonial Series*, 1:221–23. It appears likely that after leaving Cameron, GW probably proceeded through Loudoun County to the establishment of the Quaker Edward Thompson at the later site of Hillsboro. The regiment crossed the Blue Ridge at Vestal's Gap 8 April and proceeded across the Shenandoah by ferry and on to Winchester. The next stage was to Joseph Edwards's fort on Cacapon Creek, then to Job Pearsal's on the right of the South Branch of the Potomac, then to Thomas Cresap's establishment near the mouth of the South Branch, and on to Wills Creek.

The Captain Stevens who joined GW's troops was Adam Stephen (c.1718–1791) who was born in Scotland and studied medicine at the University of Edinburgh. After briefly pursuing a career in the British navy, Stephen settled down to the practice of medicine in Virginia. He joined the Virginia Regiment in 1754 as a captain and was later promoted to lieutenant colonel, taking part in the Braddock campaign in 1755 and in 1756 was in the campaign against the Creeks in South Carolina. He served with the Virginia troops until 1758.

The 19th, Met an Express who had Letters from Captain *Trent,* at the *Ohio,* demanding a Reinforcement with all Speed, as he hourly expected a Body of Eight Hundred *French.* I tarried at *Job Pearsall's* for the Arrival of the Troops, where they came the next Day. When I received the above Express, I dispatched a Courier to Colonel *Fry,* to give him Notice of it.

Job Pearsal's cabin was on the south branch of the Potomac.

The 20th, Came down to Colonel *Cresap,* to order the Detachment, and on my Rout, had Notice that the Fort was taken by the *French.* That News was confirmed by Mr. *Wart,* the Ensign of Captain *Trent,* who had been obliged to surrender to a Body of One Thousand *French* and up-

wards, under the Command of Captain *Contrecoeur,* who was come from
Venango (in *French,* the Peninsula) with Sixty Battoes, and Three Hundred Canoes, and who having planted eighteen Pieces of Cannon
against the Fort, afterwards had sent him a Summons to depart.

Mr. *Wart* also informed me, that the *Indians* kept stedfastly attached
to our Interest. He brought two young *Indian* Men with him, who were
Mingoes, that they might have the Satisfaction to see that we were
marching with our Troops to their Succour.

> *Wart:* Trent left Ens. Edward Ward in charge of the construction of the fort
> at the mouth of the Monongahela while he returned to Wills Creek for pro-
> visions. Shortly after Trent's departure, Ward received word that a body of
> French were marching on the fort. Upon the advice of the Half-King, Ward
> hastily threw up a stockade at the Forks. On 17 April the French forces ap-
> peared, and he was forced to surrender.
>
> Claude Pierre Pécaudy, sieur de Contrecoeur (1706–1775), began his
> military career in the French army as an ensign in 1729. He was a captain in
> 1754 when he was ordered to construct a fort at the Forks of the Ohio and
> put in command of French forces in the Ohio country.
>
> Venango (now Franklin, Pa.) was at the junction of the Allegheny River
> and French Creek. "Peninsula" is a translation, not of Venango, but of
> Presque Isle (Erie, Pa.), on Lake Erie.
>
> Ward noted in his deposition the strong support given to his detachment
> by the Half-King, who had helped him to erect the fort. The chief "stormed
> greatly at the French at the Time they were oblieged to march out of the Fort
> and told them it was he Order'd that Fort and laid the first Log of it himself,
> but the French paid no Regard to what he said" (Gist, *Journals,* 278).

April 23d. A Council of War held at *Wills-Creek,* in order to consult upon
what must be done on Account of the News brought by Mr. *Wart,*

The News brought by Ensign *Wart,* having been examined into, as
also the Summons sent by Captain *Contrecoeur,* Commander of the
French Troops, and the Speeches of the *Half-King,* and of the other
Chiefs of the *Six-Nations;* it appears, that Mr. *Wart,* was forced to surrender the said Fort, the 17th of this Instant, to the *French,* who were above
One Thousand strong, and had eighteen Artillery Pieces, some of
which were nine Pounders, and also that the Detachment of the *Virginia* Regiment, amounting to One Hundred and Fifty Men, commanded by Colonel *Washington* had Orders to reinforce the Company
of Captain *Trent,* and that the aforesaid Garrison consisted only of
Thirty-three effective Men.

It was thought a Thing impracticable to march towards the Fort without sufficient Strength; however, being strongly invited by the *Indians,*
and particularly by the Speeches of the *Half-King,* the President gave
his Opinion, that it would be proper to advance as far as *Red-Stone-Creek,*
on *Monaungahela,* about Thirty-seven Miles on this Side of the Fort,
and there to raise a Fortification, clearing a Road broad enough to pass

with all our Artillery and our Baggage, and there to wait for fresh Orders.

Whereupon, I sent Mr. *Wart* to the Governor, with one of the young *Indians* and an Interpreter: I thought it proper also to acquaint the Governors of *Maryland* and *Pennsylvania* of the News; and I sent away the other *Indian* to the *Half-King*, with the Speeches inclosed in the following Letter.

To the Honourable Robert Dinwiddie, *Esq; Governor, &c.*

Sir,

Mr. *Wart*, an Ensign of Captain *Trent's* Company, is this Day come from *Monaungahela*, and has brought the sorrowful News of the Reduction of the Fort, on the 17th of this Instant; having been summoned by Captain *Contrecoeur* to surrender to a Body of *French* Troops who were a Thousand strong, who came from *Venango*, with eighteen Pieces of Cannon, sixty Battoes, and Three Hundred Canoes; they permitted all our Men to retire, and take with them their Working-Tools out of the Fort, which was done the same Day.

Upon receiving this News, I called a Council of War, in order to consult what was best to be done in such Circumstances; and have sent you a particular Account of every Thing agreed upon at the said Council by the same Express, that you may know Things yet more particularly. I hope you will find it necessary, to send us our Forces as soon as they are raised, as also a sufficient Number of Canoes, and other Boats with Decks; send us also some Mortar-Pieces, that we may be in a Condition to attack the *French* with equal Forces. And as we are informed that the *Indians* of the *Six Nations,* and the *Outawas,* are coming down *Sciodo-Creek,* in order to join the *French* who are to meet at the *Ohio;* so I think it would not be amiss to invite the *Cherokees, Catawbas,* and the *Chickasaws* to come to our Assistance; and as I have received Intelligence, that there is no good Understanding between them and the *Indians* of the *Six Nations* aforesaid, it would be well to perswade them to make a Peace with them; otherwise if they should meet at the *Ohio,* it might cause great Disorder, and turn out to our Disadvantage.

We find the great Advantage there is in Water-Carriage, wherefore, I would remind you to provide a Number of Boats for that Purpose.

This Day, arrived the Men belonging to Captain *Trent,* who by your Orders had been inlisted as Militia-Troops; the Officers having imprudently promised them *Two Shillings* per Day, they now refuse to serve for less Pay; *Wart* shall receive your Orders on that Head.

To his Excellency Horatio Sharpe, *Governor* of Maryland.

Sir,

I am here arrived with a Detachment of One Hundred and Fifty Men: We daily expect Colonel *Fry* with the remaining Part of the Regiment

and the Artillery; however, we shall march gently a-cross the Mountains, clearing the Roads as we go, that our Cannon may with the
greater Ease be sent after us; we propose to go as far as *Red-Stone River,*
which falls into *Monaungahela,* about Thirty-seven Miles this Side of the
Fort which the *French* have taken, from thence all our heavy Luggage
may be carried as far as the *Ohio.* A Store is built there by the *Ohio*
Company, wherein may be placed our Ammunition and Provisions.

Besides the *French* Forces above mentioned, we have Reason to believe, according to the Accounts we have heard, that another Party is
coming to the Ohio; we have also learnt that Six Hundred of the *Chip-
powais* and *Ollowais Indians,* are coming down to the River *Sciodo,* in
order to join them.

> The letters and following speeches to the Half-King were inserted by GW in
> the journal. For his letter to Gov. Horatio Sharpe of Maryland, 25 April, and
> to James Hamilton, of Pennsylvania, c.24 April, see *Papers, Colonial Series,* 1 :
> 85–87, 83–85. The letter to Dinwiddie, 25 April, is in ibid., 87–91.
>
> In recruiting men to construct the fort at the Forks, Trent apparently had
> promised them pay of 2s. per day, the amount commonly allowed volun-
> teers; however, he had enlisted the men in the militia, where the rate allowed
> private soldiers was 8d. per day. GW had additional reason to fear unrest
> among his men since four of them had been detected in a plan to desert
> when the company had arrived in Winchester. An entry in his account book
> for 10 April indicates that £1 4s. had been paid to one B. Hamilton for "dis-
> covering the Plot of 4 Soldrs. To Desert" (Washington Papers, Library of
> Congress). GW continued to have trouble with Trent's soldiers until, against
> his orders, they finally dispersed (GW to Dinwiddie, 18 May 1754, *Papers,
> Colonial Series,* 1:96–100).

April 28. Came to us some Pieces of Cannon, which were taken up to
the Mouth of *Patterson's* River.

> Entries from 29 April to 11 May are omitted from the translation, which
> states that the journal for these days "only contains Marches, and Things of
> little Consequence." Some of GW's activities for the missing period can be
> reconstructed from his letter written from the Little Meadows to Robert
> Dinwiddie, 9 May 1754. During these days his command began the slow push
> from Wills Creek. The initial problem was transportation. William Trent had
> been ordered to have packhorses waiting at Wills Creek to convey troops and
> supplies, but when GW arrived "there was none in readiness, nor any in ex-
> pectation, that I could perceive." The troops therefore were compelled to
> wait until wagons could be procured from the South Branch of the Potomac
> some 40 miles away. The wagons probably did not arrive until 29 April. For
> the party to reach the Ohio Company's new store at Red Stone Creek, it was
> necessary to improve and widen the existing road; GW detached a body of
> 60 men for the work, "which party since the 25th of Apl., and the main body
> since the 1st Instt. have been laboriously employ'd, and have got no further
> than these Meadows abt. 20 Miles from the new Store, where we have been
> two Days making a bridge across and are not done yet." The pace slowed to

as little as four miles a day, and reports poured into camp that the French were on the march.

May

May the 11th, Detached a Party of Twenty-five Men, commanded by Captain *Stevens* and Ensign *Peronie,* with Orders to go to Mr. *Gist's,* to enquire where *La Force,* and his Party were; and in case they were in the Neighbourhood, to cease pursuing and to take care of themselves. I also ordered them to examine closely all the Woods round about, and if they should find any *Frenchman* apart from the rest, to seize him and bring him to us, that we might learn what we could from him: We were exceedingly desirous to know, if there was any Possibility of sending down any Thing by Water, as also to find out some convenient Place about the Mouth of *Red-Stone-Creek,* where we could build a Fort, it being my Design to salute the *Half-King,* and to send him back under a small Guard; we were also desirous to enquire what were the Views of the *French,* what they had done, and what they intended to do, and to collect every Thing, which could give us the least Intelligence.

> William La Peronie (Peyroney), a native of France who settled in Virginia about 1750, apparently had had previous military experience and was appointed an ensign in the Virginia Regiment. He was wounded in the engagement at Fort Necessity. In a letter of 12 June 1754 to Dinwiddie, GW warmly recommended him for promotion to adjutant. He received the appointment but was killed at Braddock's Defeat the next year.
>
> Christopher Gist's new settlement was in central Fayette County, Pa., near present-day Mount Braddock.

The 12th, Marched away, and went on a rising Ground, where we halted to dry ourselves, for we had been obliged to ford a deep River, where our shortest Men had Water up to their Arm-pits.

There came an Express to us with Letters, acquainting us, that Col. *Fry,* with a Detachment of One Hundred Men and upwards, was at *Winchester,* and was to set out in a few Days to join us; as also, that Col. *Innis* was marching with Three Hundred and Fifty Men, raised in *Carolina;* that it was expected *Maryland* would raise Two Hundred Men, and that *Pennsylvania* had raised *Ten T[h]ousand Pounds* (equal to about *Fifty-two Thousand Five Hundred Livres*) to pay the Soldiers raised in other Colonies, as that Province furnisheth no Recruits, as also that Governor *Shirley* had sent 600 Men to harass the *French* in *Canada;* I hope that will give them some Work to do, and will slacken their sending so many Men to the *Ohio* as they have done.

> James Innes (d. 1759) was born in Scotland and immigrated to North Carolina sometime after 1733. He settled in Wilmington and in 1740–41 commanded the Cape Fear Company in the campaign against Cartagena. At the

outbreak of the French and Indian War, Innes was named commander of the North Carolina forces and, after Joshua Fry's death, was appointed by his friend Governor Dinwiddie to overall command of the combined colonial forces for the expedition against the French in the Ohio Valley.

The 16th, Met two Traders, who told us they fled for Fear of the *French*, as Parties of them were often seen towards Mr. *Gist's*. These Traders are of Opinion, as well as many others, that it is not possible to clear a Road for any Carriage to go from hence to *Red-Stone-Creek*.

The 17th, This Night Mr. *Wart* arrived with the young *Indian* from *Williamsburg*, and delivered me a Letter, wherein the Governor is so good as to approve of my Proceedings, but is much displeased with Captain *Trent*, and has ordered him to be tried, for leaving his Men at the *Ohio:* The Governor also informs me, that Capt. *Mackay*, with an Independant Company of 100 Men, excluding the Officers, were arrived, and that we might expect them daily; and that the Men from *New-York* would join us within ten Days.

This Night also came two *Indians* from the *Ohio*, who left the *French* Fort five Days ago: They relate that the *French* Forces are all employed in building their Fort, that it is already Breast-high, and the Thickness of twelve Feet, and filled up with Earth and Stone, *&c*. They have cut down and burnt up all the Trees which were about it, and sown Grain instead thereof. The *Indians* believe there were only 600 in Number; though they say themselves they are 800: They expect a greater Number in a few Days, which may amount to 1600, then they say they can defy the *English*.

Dinwiddie's letter to GW is dated 4 May 1754 (*Papers, Colonial Series*, 1:91–93). Capt. James Mackay and his company from South Carolina did not catch up with the Virginians until 14 June. The South Carolina force and its captain were part of the regular British army establishment, a fact which raised the delicate question of rank between Mackay, who held the king's commission, and GW, whose commission was provincial. James Mackay (d. 1785) had been appointed an ensign in a Georgia independent company of foot in 1737 and had served at Fort Diego, Fla., where he was promoted to lieutenant in May 1740. In Feb. 1741/42 he was promoted to captain lieutenant and in July 1745 to captain in Oglethorpe's Regiment. After the disbandment of this regiment in 1749, he became captain of one of the newly organized independent companies in South Carolina. Mackay apparently resigned his commission in 1755 and returned to Georgia, where he was an active politician and extensive landowner.

The 18th, The Waters being yet very high, hindred me from advancing on Account of my Baggage, wherefore I determined to set myself in a Posture of Defence against any immediate Attack from the Enemy, and went down to observe the River.

The question of the discrepancy between the pay of British officers and that of provincial officers had rankled with GW's troops throughout the campaign. By 18 May the irritation of GW and the officers of his command reached the boiling point. At the beginning of the campaign the estimate was 15s. per day for a lieutenant colonel and 12s. 6d. for a major. GW had objected to the sums at the time as being lower than the pay of corresponding ranks in the British regular army (GW to Dinwiddie, 29 May 1754). Dinwiddie, however, had assured him that subsistence for the officers would be provided. When GW's commission was sent to him, the pay had been reduced to 12s. 6d. for a lieutenant colonel and 10s. for a major, with a corresponding reduction for lesser ranks. Ward presumably had brought word to GW's camp that the committee of the General Assembly overseeing expenditure had refused an increase. GW wrote to Dinwiddie 18 May, transmitting a written memorial from his officers protesting pay and rations. Although GW claimed he was reluctant to surrender his commission, "I would rather prefer the great toil of a daily laborer, and dig for a maintenance . . . than serve upon such ignoble terms; for I really do not see why the lives of his Majesty's subjects in Virginia should be of less value, than of those in other parts of his American dominions. . . . Upon the whole, I find so many clogs upon the expedition, that I quite despair of success." Dinwiddie responded angrily 25 May, expressing surprise at "Such ill timed Complaints. . . . The Gent. very well knew the Terms on w'ch they were to serve. . . . Thus much, in answer to the paper signed by Capt. Stephen and others. Now, Colo. W., I shall more particularly answer w't relates to Y'rself, and I must begin with expressing both Concern and Surprize to find a Gent. . . . from whom I had so great Expectat's and Hopes . . . concuring with Complaints in general so ill-founded." The importance of this pay issue to GW and his officers during the campaign is indicated by the fact that before giving Dinwiddie on 29 May a detailed account of his defeat of Jumonville's forces, he prefaced his report with a lengthy refutation of the governor's letter of 25 May.

The 19th, I dispatched the young *Indian* which was returned with Mr. *Wart,* to the *Half King,* with the following Speech.

To *the* Half King, *&c.*

My Brethren,

It gives me great Pleasure, to learn that you are marching to assist me with your Counsels; be of good Courage, my Brethren, and march vigorously towards your Brethren the *English;* for fresh Forces will soon join them, who will protect you against your treacherous Enemy the *French.* My Friends whom I send to you, will acquaint you of an agreeable Speech which the Governor of *Virginia* addresses to you: He is very sorry for the bad Usage you have received. The great Waters do not permit us to make such Haste towards you as we would do; for that Reason I have sent the young Men to invite you to come and meet us: They can tell you many Things which they have seen in *Virginia,* and also how well they were received by the most Part of our Grandees; they did not use them as the *French* do your People who go to their Fort:

they refuse them Provisions; this Man has had given him, all that his Heart could wish: For the Confirmation of all this, I here give you a Belt of *Wampum.*

The 20th, Embarked in a Canoe with Lieut. *West,* three Soldiers, and one *Indian;* and having followed the River along about Half a Mile, were obliged to come ashore, where I met *Peter Suver,* a Trader, who seemed to discourage me from seeking a Passage by Water; that made me alter my Mind of causing Canoes to be made; I ordered my People to wade, as the Waters were shallow enough; and continued myself going down the River in the Canoe: Now finding that our Canoe was too small for six Men, we stopped to make some Sort of a Bark; with which, together with our Canoe, we gained *Turkey-Foot,* by the Beginning of the Night. We underwent several Difficulties about eight or ten Miles from thence, though of no great Consequence, finding the Waters sometimes deep enough for Canoes to pass, and at other times more shallow.

John West, Jr. (d. 1777), of Fairfax County was commissioned a lieutenant in the Virginia Regiment 27 Feb. 1754 and served until August, when he resigned.

The Indian who accompanied the party refused to proceed beyond the Forks until GW "promised him a ruffled shirt, which I must take from my own, and a match-coat" (GW to Joshua Fry, 23 May 1754).

Peter Suver was probably Peter Shaver (Shafer), a licensed trader in Pennsylvania. Shaver was killed by Indians in the fall of 1755.

Turkey Foot, present-day Confluence, Pa., is at the junction of Laurel Creek, Casselman's River, and the Youghiogheny.

The 21st, Tarried there some Time to examine the Place, which we found very convenient to build a Fort, not only because it was gravelly, but also for its being at the Mouth of three Branches of small Rivers: The Plan thereof, which may be seen here, is as exact as could be done, without Mathematical Instruments.

We went about two Miles to observe the Course of the River, which is very strait, has many Currents, is full of Rocks, and rapid; we waded it, though the Water was pretty high, which made me think it would not be difficult to pass it with Canoes.

We also found other Places where the Water was rapid, but not so deep, and the Current smoother; we easily passed over them; but afterwards we found little or scarce any Bottom: There are Mountains on both Sides of the River. We went down the River about ten Miles, when at last it became so rapid as to oblige us to come ashore.

The translation of the diary notes that "From the 22d to the 24th, the Journal contains only a Decription of the County."

The 24th, This Morning arrived an *Indian*, in Company with him I had sent to the *Half King*, and brought me the following Letter from him.

To any of his Majesty's Officers whom these may concern.

As 'tis reported that the *French* Army is set out to meet M. *George Washington*, I exhort you, my Brethren, to guard against them; for they intend to fall on the first *English* they meet; they have been on their March these two Days; the *Half King*, and the other Chiefs, will join you within five Days, to hold a Council, though we know not the Number we shall be. I shall say no more; but remember me to my Brethren the *English*.

                          Signed, The Half-King.

I Examined those two young *Indians* in the best Manner I could, concerning every Circumstance, but was not much the better satisfied.

They say there are Parties of them often out, but they do not know of any considerable Number coming this Way. The *French* continue raising their Fort, that Part next to the Land is very well inclosed, but that next to the Water is much neglected, at least without any Defence: They have only nine Pieces of Cannon, and some of them very small, and not one mounted. There are two on the Point, and the others some Distance from the Fort next to the Land.

They relate that there are many sick among them, that they cannot find any *Indians* to guide their small Parties towards our Camp, these *Indians* having refused them.

The same Day at Two o'Clock, we arrived at the Meadows, where we saw a Trader, who told us that he came this Morning from Mr. *Gist's*, where he had seen two *Frenchmen* the Night before; and that he knew there was a strong Detachment out, which confirmed the Account we had received from the *Half King:* Wherefore I placed Troops behind two natural Intrenchments, where our Waggons also entered.

> *Meadows:* GW is referring to Great Meadows, near Laurel Hill (approximately 11 miles southeast of present-day Uniontown, Pa.). It was here that he erected Fort Necessity. In 1769 GW acquired ownership of more than 200 acres at Great Meadows, including the site of Fort Necessity.
>
> On the evening of 24 May, GW received a report that the French were at the crossing of the Youghiogheny some 18 miles away; he decided upon Great Meadows as a convenient place to make a stand. "We have, with Natures assistance made a good Intrenchment and by clearing the Bushes out of these Meadows prepar'd a charming field for an Encounter" (GW to Dinwiddie, 27 May 1754).

The 25th, Detached a Party to go along the Roads, and other small Parties to the Woods, to see if they could make any Discovery. I gave the Horse-men Orders to examine the Country well, and endeavour to get some News of the *French*, of their Forces, and of their Motions, *&c.*

At Night all these Parties returned, without having discovered any thing, though they had been a great way towards the Place from whence it was said the Party was coming.

The 26th, Arrived *William Jenkins;* Col. *Fry* had sent him with a Letter from Col. *Fairfax,* which informed me, that the Governor himself, as also Colonels *Corbin* and *Ludwell,* were arrived at *Winchester, Half King* and were desirous to see the Half King there, whereupon I sent him an Account thereof.

> William Fairfax was at this time lieutenant colonel of the Fairfax County mi-
> litia. The letter has not been found.
>
> Dinwiddie was preparing for a conference at Winchester with chiefs of
> both northern and southern tribes. He hoped to settle the differences be-
> tween these traditional enemies and to hold them to the British interest.
> Richard Corbin and Philip Ludwell, both members of the governor's council,
> accompanied Dinwiddie to the Winchester council.
>
> Upon GW's arrival at Great Meadows he had sent out "small light partys of
> Horse (Wagn. Horses) to reconnoitre the Enemy, and discover their strength
> & motion, who return'd Yesterday with't seeing any thing of them never-
> theless, we were alarm'd at Night and remaind under Arms from two oClock
> till near Sun rise. We conceive it was our own Men, as 6 of them Deserted,
> but can't be certain whether it was them or other Enemy's. Be it as it will,
> they were fired at by the Centrys, but I believe without damage" (GW to
> Dinwiddie, 27 May 1754).

The 27th, Arrived Mr. *Gist,* early in the Morning, who told us, that Mr. *la Force,* with fifty Men, whose Tracks he had seen five Miles off, had been at his Plantation the Day before, towards Noon; and would have killed a Cow, and broken every Thing in the House, if two *Indians,* whom he had left in the House, had not persuaded them from their Design: I immediately detached 65 Men, under the Command of Captain *Hog,* Lieut. *Mercer,* Ensign *Peronie,* three Sergeants, and three Corporals, with Instructions.

The *French* enquired at Mr. *Gist's,* what was become of the *Half King?* I did not fail to let the young *Indians* who were in our Camp know, that the *French* wanted to kill the *Half King;* and that had its desired Effect. They thereupon offered to accompany our People to go after the *French,* and if they found it true that he had been killed, or even insulted by them, one of them would presently carry the News thereof to the *Mingoes,* in order to incite their Warriors to fall upon them. One of these young Men was detached towards Mr. *Gist's;* that if he should not find the *Half King* there, he was to send a Message by a *Delaware.*

About eight at Night, received an Express from the *Half King,* which informed me, that, as he was coming to join us, he had seen along the Road, the Tracts of two Men, which he had followed, till he was brought thereby to a low obscure Place; that he was of Opinion the whole Party of the *French* was hidden there. That very Moment I sent out Forty Men, and ordered my Ammunition to be put in a Place of Safety, under a strong Guard to defend it, fearing it to be a Stratagem of the *French* to attack our Camp; and with the rest of my Men, set out in a heavy Rain, and in a Night as dark as Pitch, along a Path scarce broad enough for one Man; we were sometimes fifteen or twenty Minutes out of the Path, before we could come to it again, and so dark, that we would often strike one against another: All Night long we continued our Rout, and the 28th, about Sun-rise, we arrived at the *Indian* Camp, where, after having held a Council with the *Half King*, it was concluded we should fall on them together; so we sent out two Men to discover where they were, as also their Posture, and what Sort of Ground was thereabout; after which, we formed ourselves for an Engagement, marching one after the other, in the *Indian* Manner: We were advanced pretty near to them, as we thought, when they discovered us; whereupon I ordered my Company to fire; mine was supported by that of Mr. *Wager's*, and my Company and his received the whole Fire of the *French,* during the greatest Part of the Action, which only lasted a Quarter of an Hour, before the Enemy was routed.

We killed Mr. *de Jumonville,* the Commander of that Party, as also nine others; we wounded one, and made Twenty-one Prisoners, among whom were M. *la Force,* M. *Drouillon,* and two Cadets. The *Indians* scalped the Dead, and took away the most Part of their Arms, after which we marched on with the Prisoners and the Guard, to the *Indian* Camp, where again I held a Council with the *Half-King;* and there informed him, that the Governor was desirous to see him, and was wait-ing for him at *Winchester;* he answered that, he could not go just then, as his People were in too eminent a Danger from the *French,* whom they had fallen upon; that he must send Messengers to all the allied Nations, in order to invite them to take up the Hatchet. He sent a young *Dela-ware Indian* to the *Delaware* Nation, and gave him also a *French* Scalp to carry to them. This young Man desired to have a Part of the Presents which were allotted for them, but that the remaining Part might be kept for another Opportunity: He said he would go to his own Family, and to several others, and would wait on them at Mr. *Gist's,* where he desired Men and Horses should be sent ready to bring them up to our Camp. After this I marched on with the Prisoners; *They informed me that they had been sent with a Summons to order me to depart.* A plausible Pre-tence to discover our Camp, and to obtain the Knowledge of our Forces and our Situation! It was so clear that they were come to reconnoitre what we were, that I admired at their Assurance, when they told me they were come as an Embassy; for their Instructions mentioned that they should get what Knowledge they could of the Roads, Rivers, and of all the Country as far as *Potowmack:* And instead of coming as an Embassador, publickly, and in an open Manner, they came secretly, and sought after the most hidden Retreats, more like Deserters than Embassadors in such Retreat they incamped, and remained hid for whole Days together, and that, no more than five Miles from us; From thence they sent Spies to reconnoitre our Camp; after this was done, they went back two Miles, from whence they sent the two Messengers spoken of in the Instruction, to acquaint M. *de Contrecour* of the Place we were at, and of our Disposition, that he might send his Detachments to inforce the Summons as soon as it should be given.

Besides, an Embassador has princely Attendants; whereas this was only a simple petty *French* Officer; an Embassador has no Need of Spies, his Character being always sacred: And seeing their Intention was so good, why did they tarry two Days, at five Miles distance from us, without acquainting me with the Summons, or, at least, with something that related to the Embassy? That alone would be sufficient to raise the greatest Suspicions, and we ought to do them the Justice to say, that, as they wanted to hide themselves, they could not pick out better Places than they had done.

The Summons was so insolent, and savoured the Gasconnade so much, that if it had been brought openly by two Men, it would have been an immediate Indulgence, to have suffered them to return.

It was the Opinion of the *Half-King* in this Case, that their Intentions were evil, and that it was a pure Pretence; that they never intended to come to us but as Enemies; and if we had been such Fools as to let them go, they would never help us any more to take other *Frenchmen.*

They say they called to us as soon as they had discovered us; which is an absolute Falshood, for I was then marching at the Head of the Company going towards them, and can positively affirm, that, when they first saw us, they ran to their Arms, without calling; as I must have heard them, had they so done.

George Mercer (1733–1784) was educated at the College of William and Mary and served in the 1st and 2d Virginia regiments from 1754 to 1760. For a period he was GW's aide. When the Ohio Company renewed its activities after the French and Indian War, Mercer was an active promoter of its interests, serving as the company's London agent. He returned to Virginia in the autumn of 1765 for a brief but stormy career as stamp officer for the colony under the Stamp Act and went back to London at the end of the year.

Wager: Thomas Waggoner held the rank of lieutenant in Jacob Van Braam's company and was slightly wounded during the skirmish with Jumonville.

The site of the French camp is present-day Jumonville's Rocks, three miles north of Summit, Pa. The officers were Michel Pépin, called La Force, and Pierre Jacques Drouillon de Macé (b. 1725). Drouillon had been commissioned in 1750 and had served with Marin in constructing forts in the Ohio country.

The historical controversy over this engagement has continued to recent times. The French claimed that Jumonville's mission was that of an ambassador, similar to GW's own journey to the French forts a few months earlier, and that the English opened fire on the French without warning. The young commander of the French force, Joseph Coulon de Villiers, sieur de Jumonville (1718–1754), had joined the French army in 1738 and served in the French campaign against the Chickasaw in 1739. After further service in Canada he was appointed in 1754 by Contrecoeur to carry an ultimatum to the English forces to leave the Ohio country. According to the French, he was on this peaceful mission when he was attacked by the English early on the morning of 28 May 1754. What was to become the French version of the engagement is contained in a letter from Contrecoeur to Duquesne, 2 June 1754: "I expected Mr. *de Jumonville,* within four Days; the *Indians* have just now informed me, that that Party is taken and defeated; they were Eight in Number, one whereof was Mr. *de Jumonville.* One of that Party, *Monceau* by Name, a *Canadian,* made his Escape, and tells us that they had built themselves Cabbins, in a low Bottom, where they sheltered themselves, as it rained hard. About seven o'Clock the next Morning, they saw themselves surrounded by the *English* on one Side and the *Indians* on the Other. The *English* gave them two Volleys, but the *Indians* did not fire. Mr. *de Jumonville,* by his Interpreter, told them to desist, that he had something to tell them. Upon which they ceased firing. Then Mr. *de Jumonville* ordered the Summons which I had sent them to retire, to be read. . . . The aforesaid *Monceau,* saw all our *Frenchmen* coming up close Mr. *de Jumonville,* whilst they were reading the Summons, so that they were all in Platoons, between the *English* and the *Indians,* during which Time, said *Monceau* made the best of his Way to us, partly by Land through the Woods, and partly along the River *Monaungahela,* in a small Canoe.

"This is all, Sir, I could learn from said *Monceau.* The Misfortune is, that our People were surprized; the *English* had incircled them, and came upon them unseen. . . .

"The *Indians* who were present when the Thing was done, say, that Mr. *de Jumonville* was killed by a Musket-Shot in the Head, whilst they were reading the Summons; and that the *English* would afterwards have killed all our Men, had not the *Indians* who were present, by rushing in between them and the *English,* prevented their Design" (*Memoir,* 69; see also Robitaille, *Washington et Jumonville*).

The British version of the engagement follows closely GW's own account sent to Dinwiddie on 29 May: "I set out with 40 Men before 10, and was from that time till near Sun rise before we reach'd the Indian's Camp, hav'g March'd in [a] small path, & heavy Rain, and a Night as Dark as it is possible to concieve—we were frequently tumbling one over another, and often so lost, that 15 or 20 Minutes' search would not find the path again.

"When we came to the Half-King, I council'd with him, and got his assent to go hand in hand and strike the French. Accordingly, himself, Monacatoocha, and a few other Indians set out with us, and when we came to the place where the Tracts were, the Half King sent Two Indians to follow their Tract, and discover their lodgment which they did abt half a mile from the Road in a very obscure place surrounded with Rocks. I thereupon in conjunction with the Half King & Monacatoocha, formd a disposi[ti]on to attack them on all sides, which we accordingly did and after an Engagement of abt 15 Minutes we killd 10, wounded one, and took 21 Prisoner's, amongst those that were killd was Monsieur De Jumonville the Commander. . . . [The] Officers pretend they were coming on an Embassy, but the absurdity of this pretext is too glaring as your Honour will see by the Instructions and summons inclos'd. . . . These Enterpriseing Men were purposely choose out to get intelligence. . . . This with several other Reasons induc'd all the Officers to beleive firmly that they were sent as spys, rather than any thing else, and has occasiond my sending them as prisoners, tho they expected (or at least had some faint hope, of being continued as ambassadors)" (*Papers, Colonial Series,* 1 : 107–15).

In a letter to his brother, John Augustine, 31 May 1754, GW wrote a brief description of the engagement and its aftermath, which was printed in the *London Magazine,* Aug. 1754. According to this letter there were 12 Frenchmen killed. "We had but one man killed, and 2 or 3 wounded. . . . We expect every hour to be attacked by a superior Force, but shall if they stay one day longer be prepared for them; We have already got Intrenchments, & are about a Pallisado'd fort which will I hope be finished today. . . . I fortunately escaped without a wound, tho' the right Wing where I stood, was exposed to & received all the Enemy's fire. . . . I heard Bullets whistle and believe me, there was something charming in the sound" (*Papers, Colonial Series,* 1 : 118–19). It was the latter observation which prompted George II's wry remark: "He would not say so, if he had been used to hear many" (Walpole, *Memoirs,* 1 : 400).

The 29th, Dispached Ensign *Latour* to the *Half-King,* with about Twenty-five Men, and almost as many Horses; and as I expected some *French* Parties would continually follow that which we had defeated, I sent an Express to Colonel *Fry* for a Reinforcement.

After this the *French* Prisoners desired to speak with me, and asked me in what Manner I looked upon them, whether as the Attendants of an Embassador, or as Prisoners of War: I answered them it was in Quality of the Latter, and gave them my Reasons for it, as above.

Ens. James Towers, of Capt. Peter Hog's company, resigned from the Virginia Regiment at the end of 1754.

The 30th, Detached Lieutenant *West,* and Mr. *Spindorph,* to take the Prisoners to *Winchester,* with a Guard of Twenty Men. Began to raise a Fort with small Pallisadoes, fearing that when the *French* should hear the News of that Defeat, we might be attacked by considerable Forces.

June

June the 1st, Arrived here an *Indian* Trader with the *Half-King:* They said that when Mr. *de Jumonville* was sent here, another Party had been detached towards the lower Part of the River, in order to take and kill all the *English* they should meet.

We are finishing our Fort.

Towards Night arrived Ensign *Towers,* with the *Half-King,* Queen *Alguipa,* and about Twenty-five or Thirty Families, making in all about Eighty or One Hundred Persons, including Women and Children. The old King being invited to come into our Tents, told me that he had sent *Monakatoocha* to *Log's Town,* with Wampum, and four *French* Scalps, which were to be sent to the *Six Nations,* to the *Wiendots, &c.* to inform them, that they had fallen upon the *French,* and to demand their Assistance.

He also told me he had something to say at the Council, but would stay till the Arrival of the *Shawanese,* whom we expected next Morning.

The 2d, Arrived two or three Families of the *Shawanese:* We had Prayers in the Fort.

The 3d, The *Half-King* assembled the Council, and informed me that he had received a Speech from *Grand-Chaudiere,* in Answer to the one he had sent him.

> Big Kettle (Canajachera) was a Seneca chief living in the Ohio country. The Pennsylvanians referred to him as Broken Kettle.

The 5th, Arrived an *Indian* from the *Ohio,* who had lately been at the *French* Fort: This *Indian* confirms the News of two Traders being taken by the *French,* and sent to *Canada;* he saith they have set up their Pallisadoes, and enclosed their Fort with exceeding large Trees.

There are eight *Indian* Families on this side the River, coming to join us: He met a *Frenchman* who had made his Escape in the Time of M. *de Jumonville's* Action, he was without either Shoes or Stockings, and scarce able to walk; however he let him pass, not knowing we had fallen upon them.

The 6th, Mr. *Gist* is returned, and acquaints me of the safe Arrival of the *French* Prisoners at *Winchester,* and of the Death of poor Colonel *Fry.*

It gave the Governor great Satisfaction to see the *French* Prisoners safely arrived at *Winchester.*

I am also informed that Mr. *Montour,* is coming with a Commission to command Two Hundred *Indians.*

Mr. *Gist* met a *French* Deserter, who assured him, that they were only Five Hundred Men, when they took Mr. *Wart's* Fort, that they were now less, having sent Fifteen Men to *Canada,* to acquaint the Governor of their Success: That there were yet Two Hundred Soldiers who only waited for a favourable Opportunity to come and join us.

> Fry died on 31 May. On 4 June Dinwiddie wrote to GW, giving him the command of the Virginia Regiment (*Papers, Colonial Series,* 1:126–28).
>
> Andrew Montour, a French and Indian fur trader, was the son of Madam Montour, a prominent frontier figure who frequently acted as interpreter,

and of Roland Montour, a Seneca. He was at various times Indian agent and interpreter for both Virginia and Pennsylvania. For his service he received a grant of land on Sherman's Creek in Perry County, Pa. In 1754 Montour held a commission from Dinwiddie to organize scouts for the English forces. GW had requested that Montour join him since "he would be of singular use to me here at this present, in conversing with the Indians" (GW to Dinwiddie, 3 June 1754).

The 9th, Arrived the last Body of the *Virginia* Regiment, under the Command of Colonel *Must,* and we learnt that the Independent company of *Carolina* was arrived at *Wills-Creek.*

> *Colonel Must:* George Muse (1720–1790) was born in England, had served in the campaign against Cartagena, and in 1752 was appointed adjutant of the Middle Neck in Virginia. He served in the Virginia Regiment of 1754 as captain, major, and lieutenant colonel. Muse apparently behaved badly at the Fort Necessity engagement during the 1754 campaign. According to Landon Carter, "instead of bringing up the 2d division to make the Attack with the first, he marched them or rather frightened them back into the trenches" (Carter, *Diary,* 1:110). His name was intentionally omitted from the list of officers thanked by the House of Burgesses after the campaign. Criticized for the way he conducted himself in the confrontation with the French, he resigned his commission. Reporting this to James Innes on 20 July, Dinwiddie wrote: "as he is not very agreeable to the other Officers, I am well pleased at his resignation."

The 10th. I received the Regiment, and at Night had Notice, that some *French* were advancing towards us; whereupon I sent a Party of *Indians* upon the Scout towards *Gist's,* in order to discover them, and to know their Number: Just before Night we had an Alarm, but it proved false.

The 12th, Returned two of the Men, whom we had sent out Yesterday upon the Scout; they discovered a small Party of *French;* the others went on as far as *Stuart's.* Upon this Advice, I thought it necessary to march with the major Part of the Regiment, to find out those Ninety Men, of whom we had Intelligence. Accordingly I gave Orders to Colonel *Must,* to put away all our Baggage and Ammunition, and to place them in the Fort, and set a good Guard there till my Return; after which I marched at the Head of One Hundred and Thirty Men, and about Thirty *Indians;* but at the Distance of half a Mile, I met the other *Indians,* who told me, there were only nine Deserters; whereupon I sent Mr. *Montour,* with some few *Indians,* in order to bring them safe to me; I caused them to be drest, and they confirmed us in our Opinion, of the Intention of M. *de Jumonville's* Party; that more than One Hundred Soldiers were only waiting for a favourable Opportunity to come and join us; that M. *de Contrecour* expected a Reinforcement of Four Hundred Men; that the Fort was compleated; and its Artillery a shelter to its Front and Gates; that there was a double Pallisadoe next to the Water; that they have only eight small Pieces of Cannon; and know what Number of Men we are.

They also informed us, that the *Delaware* and *Shawanese* had taken up the Hatchet against us; whereupon, resolved to invite those two Nations to come to a Council at Mr. *Gist's*. Sent for that Purpose Messengers and Wampum.

> *Stuarts:* Stewart's Crossing was on the Youghiogheny River below present-day Connellsville in Fayette County, Pa.

The 13th, Perswaded the Deserters to write the following Letter, to those of their Companions who had an Inclination to Desert.

> The translation notes that this letter was omitted from the published diary, and no copy has been found. However, GW apparently dispatched a Delaware carrying the letter into Contrecoeur's headquarters at the Forks.

The 15th, Set about clearing the Roads.

16th. Set out for *Red-Stone-Creek,* and were extremely perplexed, our Waggons breaking very often.

17th, Dispatched an Express to the *Half-King,* in order to perswade him to send a Message to the *Loups* [Delawares]; which he did.

18th, Arrived eight *Mingoes* from *Loiston* [Logstown], who at their Arrival told me of a Commission they had, and that a Council must be held. When we assembled, they told us very shortly, that they had often desired to see their Brethren out in the Field with Forces, and begged us not to take it amiss, that they were amongst the *French,* and that they complied with some of their Customs; notwithstanding which they were naturally inclined to fall upon them, and other Words to that Purport: After which they said, they had brought a Speech with them; and desired to deliver it with Speed. These, and other Discourses to the same Purpose, made us suspect that their Intentions towards us were evil; wherefore I delayed giving them Audience until the Arrival of the *Half-King,* and desired also the *Delawares* to have Patience till then, as I only waited their Arrival to hold a Council, which I expected would be that same Day. After the eight *Mingoes* had conferred a while together, they sent me some Strings of Wampum, desiring me to excuse their insisting on the Delivery of their Speech so speedily, that they now perceived it necessary to wait the Arrival of the *Half King.*

When the *Half-King* arrived, I consented to give them Audience.

A Council was held in the Camp for that Purpose, where the *Half-King,* and several of the *Six Nations, Loups* and *Shawanese,* to the Number of Forty, were present.

> The council was held from 18 to 21 June.

After this, the Council broke up, and those treacherous Devils, who had been sent by the *French* as Spies, returned, though not without some Tale ready prepared to amuse the *French,* which may be of Service to make our own Designs succeed.

As they had told me there were Sixteen Hundred *French,* and Seven Hundred *Indians* on their March, to reinforce those at the Garrison, I perswaded the *Half King* to send three of his Men to inquire into the Truth of it; though I imagined this News to be only Soldiers Discourse; these *Indians* were accordingly sent in a secret Manner, before the Council broke up, and had Orders to go to the Fort, and get what Information they could from all the *Indians* they should meet, and if there was any News worth while, one of them should return, and the other two continue their Rout as far as *Venango,* and about the *Lake,* in order to obtain a perfect Knowledge of every Thing.

I also perswaded King *Shingas,* to send out Rangers towards the River, to bring us News, in Case any *French* should come; I gave him also a Letter, which he was to send back again by an Express, to prevent my being imposed upon by a false Alarm.

Though King *Shingas,* and others of the *Delawares,* could not be persuaded to retire to our Camp with their Families, through the Fear they were in of *Onondago's* Council, they nevertheless gave us strong Assurances of their Assistance, and directed us in what Manner to act, in order to obtain our Desire: the Method was this; we were to prepare a great War-Belt, to invite all those Warriors who would receive it, to act independantly from their King and Council; and King *Shingas* promised to take privately the most subtil Methods to make the Affair succeed, though he did not dare to do it openly.

[21 June] The very Day the Council broke up, I perswaded *Kaquehuston,* a trusty *Delaware,* to carry that Letter to the Fort which the *French* Deserters had written to their Comrades, and gave him Instructions how he should behave in his Observations, upon several Articles of which I had spoken to him; for I am certain the Fort may be surprized, as the *French* are encamped outside, and cannot keep a strict Guard, by Reason of the Works they are about.

I also perswaded *George,* another trusty *Delaware,* to go and take a View of the Fort, a little after *Kaquehuston,* and gave him proper Instructions recommending him particularly to return with Speed, that we might have fresh News.

Presently after the Council was over, notwithstanding all that Mr. *Montour* could do to disswade them, the *Delawares,* as also the *Half-King,* and all the other *Indians,* returned to the Great Meadows; but though we had lost them, I still had Spies of our own People, to prevent being surprised.

As it had been told me, that if I sent a Belt of *Wampum* and a Speech, that might bring us back both the *Half-King* and his young Men; accordingly I sent the following Speech by Mr. *Croghan.*

'Tis but lately since we were assembled together; we were sent here by your Brother the Governor of Virginia, *at your own Request, in Order to succour you, and fight for your Cause; wherefore my Brethren, I must require that you and your young Men come to join and encamp with us, that we may be ready to recieve our Brother* Monacotocha, *whom I daily expect: That this Request may have its desired Effect, and make a suitable Impression upon your Minds, I present you with this String of* Wampum.

As those *Indians,* who were Spies sent by the *French,* were very inquisitive, and asked us many Questions in order to know by what Way we proposed to go to the Fort, and what Time we expected to arrive there; I left off working any further at the Road, and told them we intended to keep on across the Woods as far as the Fort, falling the Trees, *&c.* That we were waiting here for the Reinforcement which was coming to us, our Artillery, and our Waggons to accompany us there; but, as soon as they were gone, I set about marking out and clearing a Road towards *Red-Stone.*

> *Kaquehuston:* This is probably a reference to Kekeuscung, "the healer," who later became a Delaware chief. Like most of his tribe, he eventually supported the French.
>
> Delaware George later became a chief and went over to the French.
>
> George Croghan (d. 1782) was the best-known Indian trader on the Pennsylvania frontier. He was born in Ireland and immigrated to Pennsylvania around 1741, settling near Carlisle. In the years before the French and Indian War he established a network of trading posts on the frontier and became Pennsylvania's chief agent to the Indians. During the war he served with GW and Braddock in their campaigns and in 1756 was appointed deputy superintendent of Indian affairs by Sir William Johnson. Like most of the traders, his business had been destroyed by the war, and after 1763 he turned his attention to western lands. From Croghan Hall, his estate near Pittsburgh, where he had moved in 1758, he engaged in extensive speculations in Ohio and Illinois lands, participating in the Illinois Company and the Grand Ohio Company. The Revolution wrecked most of these western land schemes, and Croghan died near Philadelphia in comparative poverty.

The 25th, Towards Night came three Men from the Great Meadows, amongst whom was the Son of Queen *Aliguipa.*

He brought me a Letter from Mr. *Croghan,* informing me what Pains he was at to perswade any *Indians* to come to us; that the *Half-King* was inclined, and was preparing to join us, but had received a Blow which was a Hindrance to it. I thought it proper to send Captain *Montour* to

Fort-Necessity, in order to try if he could, possibly, gain the *Indians* to come to us.

> *Son of Queen Aliguipa:* This was probably Canachquasy, also known as Captain New Castle (d. 1756), an important agent of the Pennsylvania government in its relations with the Indians.

The 26th, Arrived an *Indian,* bringing News that *Monacotoocha,* had burnt his Village (*Loiston*) and was gone by Water with his People to *Red-Stone,* and may be expected there in two Days. This *Indian* passed close by the Fort, and assures us, that the *French* had received no Reinforcement, except a small Number of *Indians,* who had killed, as he said, two or three of the *Delawares.* I did not fail to relate that Piece of News to the *Indians* in its proper Colours, and particularly to two of the *Delawares* who are here.

The 27th, Detached Captain *Lewis,* Lieutenant *Wagghener,* and Ensign *Mercer,* two Serjeants, two Corporals, one Drummer, and Sixty Men, in order to endeavour to clear a Road, to the Mouth of *Red-Stone Creek* on *Monaungahela.*

> Andrew Lewis (1720–1781) was a native of Ulster, Ireland, came to Virginia in 1732, and settled in what is now Augusta County. He served in the Augusta militia, received a commission as captain in the Virginia Regiment in 1754, and was present at the capitulation of Fort Necessity. During the French and Indian War Lewis served in Braddock's campaign and as commissioner to the Cherokee and to the Six Nations. After the war he held a number of public offices. In 1774 he led the Virginia forces that defeated the Indians under Cornstalk at the Battle of Point Pleasant. During the Revolution he held the rank of brigadier general and took part in the campaign against Dunmore.
>
> John Fenton Mercer (1735–1756), a son of John Mercer (1704–1768), served successively as ensign, lieutenant, and captain in the Virginia Regiment. He was killed by Indians while on scouting duty for GW in Apr. 1756.

GW served with the Virginia Regiment until early January 1759. The French and Indian War was winding down in Virginia. Wearied of the difficulties of military life and eager to advance his position in Virginia society, GW submitted his resignation to Gov. Francis Fauquier. GW was now the proprietor of Mount Vernon. His half brother Lawrence died in 1752, and Lawrence's widow, Ann Fairfax Washington Lee, from whom GW had rented the plantation after his brother's death, died in 1761; by the terms of Lawrence's will Mount Vernon passed to GW. On 6 April 1759 GW married Martha Dandridge Custis, widow of the wealthy Virginia landowner Daniel Parke Custis and the mother of two small children, five-year-old John Parke Custis (1754–1781) and three-year-old Martha Parke Custis (1756–1773). Following their marriage in New Kent County, Va., GW took Martha and the two Custis children to their new home at Mount Vernon. With his marriage, GW was now in control of one of Virginia's largest and most profitable estates, including property in six counties amounting to nearly 8,000 acres, slaves valued at nearly £9,000 Virginia currency, and accounts current and other liquid assets in England of about £10,000. Until they reached their majority, GW was guardian for the extensive estates of Martha's two children and submitted an accounting of his stewardship each year to Virginia's General Court. During the first years after his return to Mount Vernon, GW faced a struggle to make it a paying plantation. In a letter to one of his former officers in the regiment he described "under what terrible management and disadvantages I found my Estate when I retired from the Publick Service of this Colony; and that besides some purchases of Lands and Negroes I was necessitated to make adjoining me — (in order to support the Expences of a large Family) — I had Provision's of all kinds to buy for the first two or three years, and my Plantations to Stock — in short with every thing — Buildings to make, and other matters, which swallowed up before I well knew where I was, all the money I got by Marriage nay more, brought me in Debt" (GW to Robert Stewart, 27 April 1763, Papers, Colonial Series, 7:205–7). As the years passed, however, with the farming of his own plantations and additional business enterprises, in addition to the financial resources he had acquired through his marriage, GW and his new family were able to become part of the comfortable and pleasant plantation life of Fairfax County.

1760

January

January 1 Tuesday. Visited my Plantations and receivd an Instance of Mr. French's great Love of Money in disappointing me of some Pork because the price had risen to 22/6 after he had engagd to let me have it at 20/.

Calld at Mr. Possey's in my way home and desird him to engage me 100 Barl. of Corn upon the best terms he coud in Maryland.

And found Mrs. Washington upon my arrival broke out with the Meazles.

Daniel French (1733–1771), a wealthy Fairfax County planter, lived at Rose Hill, about five miles west of Alexandria. Although his main plantation lay in the vicinity of his house, he also owned a plantation on Dogue Creek a short distance west of Mount Vernon.

John Posey, whose home, Rover's Delight, stood near the Potomac River about a mile southwest of Mount Vernon, was a member of GW's social circle in the 1760s, often joining him in fox hunts. Posey farmed a plantation of about 400 acres and operated a public ferry from a landing near his house across the Potomac to Maryland, where he had many personal contacts.

Mrs. Washington, born Martha Dandridge (1731–1802), first married (1749) Daniel Parke Custis (1711–1757), of the White House, New Kent County. They had two children who survived infancy, John Parke Custis

The Custis children, Jacky and Patsy, in a painting by John Wollaston. (Washington and Lee University, Washington-Custis-Lee Collection)

(1754–1781) and Martha Parke Custis (1756–1773). Following Martha's wedding to GW 6 Jan. 1759 in her home county of New Kent, GW took Martha and the two Custis children to their new home at Mount Vernon.

Jany. 2d. Wednesy. Mrs. Barnes who came to visit Mrs. Washington yesterday returnd home in my Chariot the Weather being too bad to

Travel in an open Carriage—which together with Mrs. Washington's Indisposition confind me to the House and gave me an oppertunity of Posting my Books and putting them in good Order.

Fearing a disappointment elsewhere in Pork I was fein to take Mr. French upon his own terms & engagd them to be delivd. at my House on Monday next.

> Sarah Barnes was the daughter of Col. William Ball of Northampton County and thus a distant relation to GW. After the death in 1743 of her first husband, Dennis McCarty, of Prince William County, she married Abraham (Abram) Barnes, of Truro Parish, Fairfax County.

Thursday Jany. 3d. The Weather continuing Bad & the same causes subsisting I confind myself to the House.

Morris who went to work Yesterday caught cold, and was laid up bad again—and several of the Family were taken with the Measles, but no bad Symptoms seemd to attend any of them.

Hauled the Sein and got some fish, but was near being disappointd of my Boat by means of an Oyste⟨r⟩ Man who had lain at my Landing and plagud me a good deal by his disorderly behaviour.

> *Morris:* Because Mrs. Washington's first husband died without a will, his property was divided according to English common law, which allowed the widow one-third of the property for her life only (called her right of dower), after which it would revert to their children or their descendants. Upon her marriage to GW, all of Martha's property came under his control during her lifetime, including her share of the slaves from the Custis estate. One of her "dower slaves" who was transferred to Mount Vernon by GW was Morris (born c.1730), who worked as a carpenter 1760–63, a tradesman 1764–65, and overseer of GW's Dogue Run plantation 1766–94. Morris's wife was Hannah, who, with a child, had been purchased by GW from William Cloptan 16 June 1759 for £80 (Ledger A, 56). Morris and Hannah were married c.1765 when both were transferred to the Dogue Run plantation. Like most large planters, GW referred to his plantation workers collectively either as his "people" or his "family."

Friday Jany. 4th. The Weather continud Drisling and Warm, and I kept the House all day. Mrs. Washington seemg. to be very ill ⟨I⟩ wrote to Mr. Green this afternoon desiring his Company to visit her in the Morng.

> Rev. Charles Green (c.1710–1765) was the first permanent rector of Truro Parish, recommended to that post in 1736 by GW's father. He also practiced medicine.

Saturday Jany. 5th. Mrs. Washington appeard to be something better. Mr. Green however came to see her abt. 11 Oclock and in an hour Mrs. Fairfax arrivd. Mr. Green prescribd the needful and just as we were going to Dinnr Captn. Walter Stuart appeard with Doctr. Laurie.

The Evening being very cold, and the wind high Mrs. Fairfax went

*A portrait of Sally Cary Fairfax, done by Duncan Smith from a copy of the lost
original by an unknown artist. (Owned by Mrs. Charles Baird, Jr.)*

home in the Chariot & soon afterwards Mulatto Jack arrivd from Fredk.
with 4 Beeves.

Mrs. Fairfax is Sarah (Sally) Cary Fairfax (c.1730–1811), wife of George
William Fairfax. Walter Stuart (Stewart) served with GW in the Virginia Regi-
ment and in 1755 was wounded in Braddock's Defeat. Dr. James Laurie
(Lowrie), a physician of Alexandria, may have come that day to tend those in
GW's "family" who were down with measles. Mulatto Jack, a dower Negro
from the Custis estate, was regularly used by GW as a courier, often to and

from his Bullskin plantation in the Shenandoah Valley, which at this time was part of Frederick County (later Berkeley County and now Jefferson County, W.Va.).

Sunday Jany. 6th. The Chariot not returng. time enought from Colo. Fairfax's we were prevented from Church.

> Mount Vernon was in Truro Parish, which in 1760 served all but the upper edge of Fairfax County. In the 1760s "Church" for GW was the old wooden Pohick Church, built sometime before 1724 in Mason's Neck, about a seven-mile ride from Mount Vernon. Originally called Occoquan Church, it became the main church for Truro Parish when that parish was formed in 1732 and was renamed Pohick Church the following year.

Wednesday. Jany. 9. Killd and dressd Mr. French's Hogs which weighd 751 lbs. neat.

Colo. West leaving me in doubt about his Pork yesterday obligd me to send to him again to day, and now no definitive answr was receivd— he purposing to send his Overseer down tomorrow to agree abt. it.

Colo. Bassetts Abram arrivd with Letters from his Master appointing Port Royal, & Monday next as a time and place to meet him. He brought some things from me that Lay in Mr. Norton's Ware house in York Town.

> Burwell Bassett (1734–1793), husband of Mrs. Washington's sister Anna Maria, lived at Eltham on the Pamunkey River, where the Washingtons usually stayed when visiting Williamsburg. The two families were close, particularly before the death of Mrs. Bassett in 1777. Port Royal, a small port town on the Rappahannock River, was a convenient rendezvous almost equidistant between Eltham and Mount Vernon.

Thursday Jany. 10th. Accompanied Mrs. Bassett in a Visit to Belvoir.

She this day determind on setting of for Port Royal on Saturday.

Colo. West wrote me word that he had engag'd his Pork.

Killd the Beeves that Jack brought down two of which were tolerable good.

> Belvoir, located on a bluff overlooking the Potomac on the next "neck" downriver from Mount Vernon, was the first seat of the Fairfax family of Virginia, built around 1741 by William Fairfax (1691–1757), cousin and agent of Thomas, Lord Fairfax. GW first visited there while in his early teens, during stays with his brother Lawrence at Mount Vernon. It was then that the long friendship began between GW and William Fairfax's son George William. From 1757 to 1773, when Belvoir was the permanent home of George William and Sarah Cary Fairfax, the Washingtons often visited it. Years later, in reflecting on his days at Belvoir, GW observed that "the happiest days of my life had been spent there" (GW to George William Fairfax, 27 Feb. 1785, *Papers, Confederation Series*, 2:386–87).

Saturday Jany. 12th. Sett out with Mrs. Bassett on her journey to Port Royal. The morning was clear and fine but soon clouded and promisd much Rain or other falling weather wch. is generally the case after remarkable white Frosts—as it was to day. We past Occoquan witht. any great difficulty notwithstanding the Wind was something high and Lodgd at Mr. McCraes in Dumfries—sending the Horses to the Tavern.

Here I was informd that Colo. Cocke was disgusted at my House, and left it because he see an old Negroe there resembling his own Image.

> The ferry at Occoquan Creek, about ten miles south of Mount Vernon, was owned by George Mason of Gunston Hall and run by one of his slaves. Allan Macrae (d. 1766), who had come to Virginia about 1750, was one of the Scottish merchants who contributed to the development of Dumfries in lower Prince William County as a tobacco port. Catesby Cocke (b. 1702) served successively as clerk of Stafford, Prince William, and Fairfax counties. In 1746 he retired and lived in Dumfries near his daughter Elizabeth, who had married John Graham (1711–1787), founder of Dumfries.

Sunday Jany. 13th. We reachd Mr. Seldons abt. 3 Oclock and met with a certain Captn. Dives there a Man who, as I have been informd is pretty well known for some of his Exploits and suspected to be an instrument in carrying Dickenson whose Character and Memory are too well established to need any Commentaries.

> Samuel Selden lived at Selvington on the south side of the mouth of Potomac Creek in Stafford (now King George) County. Dickenson is probably William Dickenson, who came to Virginia with two partners about 1754. They opened a store in Williamsburg and began buying up tobacco at advanced prices. In the spring of 1759, when they were unable to pay their creditors, Dickenson and his partners fled the colony, leaving debts of over £20,000 and taking their profits with them.

Monday Jany. 14th. The Wind at No. West, and the Morning being clear and cold but otherwise fine we set out—Mr. Seldon obligingly accompanying us a few Miles to prevent any misapprehensions of the Road. We arrivd about 2 Oclock to the Plantation late Colo. Turners but now Inhabited by an Overseer directly opposite to Port Royal (at this place also Mr. Giberne lodges) and here we were disagreably disappointed of meeting him for a few hours but at length he arrivd almost at the same Instant that Colo. Bassett did. From hence we moved over to Port Royal and spent the Evening at Fox's with Mr. & Mrs. Bassett.

Mr. Bassett brought me a letter from Captn. Langbourn Inclosing a Bill of Lading for 20 Hhds. pr. the Deliverance Captn. Wm. Whyte. One other was sent by the Ship neither of which signifying to whom the Tobo. was Consignd which is not less strange than that only two Bills shd. be given when 4 and never less than three is customary in War time.

Thomas Turner, owner of Walsingham, a plantation in King George County, was an old family friend from the days of GW's youth. At the age of 16 GW had won 1s. 3d. from Turner in a game of billiards. Rev. Isaac William Giberne was licensed in 1758 and came to Virginia the next year to find a parish, settling eventually at Lunenburg Parish in Richmond County. A hard drinker, an avid cardplayer, and an active Whig, Giberne was generally considered to be the most popular preacher in the colony. The original Roy's tavern at Port Royal was bought in 1755 by Capt. William Fox (d. 1772) and was run by his wife Ann during the captain's sailing trips between England and Virginia. Capt. William Langbourne (Langborn) (1723–1766) was a ship captain who sailed between Virginia and Bristol, England. Langbourne's home, in King William County, was about three miles up the Pamunkey River from Williams's ferry. The bill of lading, for tobacco from a Custis estate in York County, was directed to the Hanbury firm of London. In 1754 Capt. William Whyte was commanding the *Deliverance* between Virginia and Barbados.

Tuesday Jany. 15th. Mr. Gibourne and I, leaving Mr. Bassett Just ready to set out recrossd the River and proceeded to Colo. Carters where we dind and in the Evening reachd Colo. Champes.

Several Gentlemen dind with us at Colo. Carters (neighbours of his) but we spent a very lonesome Evening at Colo. Champes not any Body favouring us with their Company but himself.

Charles Carter (1707–1764), of Cleve, King George County, was the third son of Robert "King" Carter. In 1760 Charles was one of the most powerful members of the House of Burgesses. Col. John Champe (d. 1765), of Lamb's Creek, King George County, served variously as sheriff, coroner, and justice of the peace. Champe's daughter Jane became the first wife of GW's younger brother Samuel.

During the previous summer GW, Colonel Carter, Colonel Champe, and 15 other men had been commissioned justices for King George County by the governor and council. GW was entitled to be a King George justice by virtue of owning Ferry Farm and other property in the county, but he declined to serve, apparently finding the distance from Mount Vernon to the King George courthouse too great to attend the frequent court sessions. Like several others named in the commission, he did not take the required oaths of office, and his name was explicitly deleted from the county's next commission of the peace, which was issued in 1770.

Wednesday Jany. 16. I parted with Mr. Gibourne, leaving Colo. Champes before the Family was Stirring and abt. 10 reachd my Mothers where I breakfasted and then went to Fredericksburg with my Brothr. Saml. who I found there.

Abt. Noon it began Snowing, the Wind at So. West but not Cold; was disappointed of seeing my Sister Lewis & getting a few things which I wanted out of the Stores returnd in the Evening to Mother's—all alone with her.

My Mothers: the Ferry Farm of GW's youth. When GW was about three years old, the Washingtons moved from his birthplace at Pope's Creek, Westmoreland County, about 60 miles up the Potomac River to a new home near Little Hunting Creek. There the family lived for three years on the plantation that later became Mount Vernon in Prince William (after 1741, Fairfax) County. In Nov. 1738 GW's father bought 260 acres on the north bank of the Rappahannock River just below the new town of Fredericksburg, and the next month he moved his family to this new home. Although GW, by his father's will, inherited the farm upon reaching his majority in 1753, his mother remained there until the early 1770s.

Samuel Washington (1734–1781), the eldest of GW's three younger brothers, left Ferry Farm in the mid-1750s and settled on a 600-acre plantation in the Chotank district of Stafford County that he had inherited from his father. GW's sister was Betty Washington (1733–1797), born at Pope's Creek and raised at Ferry Farm. In 1750 she married Fielding Lewis (1725–1782), a widower and the son of John and Frances Fielding Lewis, of Warner Hall in Gloucester County. Fielding Lewis was a second cousin to GW and Betty. The Lewises, who had seven children that survived to adulthood, lived in Fredericksburg at Kenmore, a house built for Lewis in 1752.

Thursday Jany. 17th. Abt. Noon I set out from my Mother's & Just at Dusk arrivd at Dumfries.

Friday Jany. 18th. Continued my Journey home, the Misling continuing till Noon when the Wind got Southerly and being very warm occasiond a great thaw. I however found Potomk. River quite coverd with Ice & Doctr Craik at my House.

Saturday Jany. 19. Recd. a Letter from my Overseer Hardwick, informing me that the Small Pox was surrounding the Plantation's he overlookd—& requiring sundry Working Tools.

During the surveying trips of his early years GW discovered the rich lands in the lower Shenandoah Valley. The first real property GW owned was several tracts of land along Bullskin Run in Frederick County, which he bought in 1750. These lands he named the Bullskin plantation and on them were raised crops of corn, wheat, and tobacco. In 1756 GW hired Christopher Hardwick to be resident overseer. The smallpox epidemic in Frederick County was, by Jan. 1760, in its seventh month. It had already become so general by Oct. 1759 that the county court had closed down for the duration of the epidemic, thus bringing all legal and much other business to a standstill.

Wednesday Jany. 23d. Doctr. Craik left this for Alexandria and I visited my Quarter's & the Mill. According to Custom found young Stephen's absent.

GW's gristmill at this time was on the east side of Dogue Run, about 2 miles northwest of Mount Vernon. Lawrence Washington, acting on behalf of his father, Augustine, had apparently obtained this mill for the family in 1738, when he bought a 56-acre tract of land on the run from William Spencer.

This property was transferred to Augustine and remained his until his death in 1743, when Lawrence was bequeathed the Mount Vernon tract and the mill and in 1750 and 1751 bought additional land adjoining the "Mill Tract." Thus, there were now 172 acres around GW's mill, land which he later called his mill plantation.

Robert Stephens, son of Richard Stephens, worked on GW's Williamson farm in 1760. He apparently left before the harvest, for GW directed the 1760 Williamson farm harvest himself.

Friday Jany. 25th. Went to Alexandria and saw my Tobo. wch. came from the Mountns. lying in an open shed with the ends of the Hhds out and in very bad order. Engagd the Inspection of it on Monday. Wrote to Doctr. Ross to purchase me a Joiner, Bricklayer, and Gardner if any Ship of Servants was in.

Also wrote to my old Servt. Bishop to return to me again if he was not otherwise engagd. Directed for him at Phila. but no certainty of his being there.

Saw my Tobo.: Nicotiana tabacum, tobacco, was GW's main cash crop during this period but less important to him later. Tobacco was inspected in tobacco warehouses, established in compliance with the acts of 1730 and 1732 of the General Assembly to prevent the exportation of "bad, unsound, and unmerchantable tobacco" (Hening, 4:247, 331).

Mountns.: The tobacco was from GW's Bullskin plantation in Frederick County.

Dr. David Ross (d. 1778) was a merchant in Bladensburg, Md. GW had dealt with him during the French and Indian War, when Ross was a commissary for the Maryland troops. The servants were undoubtedly indentured servants emigrating from the British Isles.

Thomas Bishop (c.1705–c.1795) came to America with General Braddock in the spring of 1755. Soon after GW was appointed colonel of the new Virginia Regiment, he hired Bishop as his personal servant, paying him £10 per year. Seven months after GW retired from military life, Bishop resigned from GW's service, apparently with the intention of rejoining a unit of the British army. Philadelphia had been since 1757 the eastern headquarters for the frontier expeditions in which GW and Bishop had served. Bishop finally appeared at Mount Vernon in Sept. 1761, resuming his service with GW which continued until Bishop's death 33 years later.

Saturday Jany. 26th. Rode to Williamsons Quarter—the Overseer not there—a very remarkable Circle round the Moon—another Indication of falling Weather.

In 1756 Benjamin Williamson rented a farm from GW near Mount Vernon on Little Hunting Creek. During the next four years he slowly slipped behind in his rent. The rental was not renewed for 1760, and in that year GW turned Williamson's farm (possibly combined with the farm of Thomas Petit) into a Mount Vernon quarter called Williamson's. He assigned six hands to it and hired Robert Stephens as overseer. By 1761 Stephens was replaced by Josias Cook and the quarter was renamed the Creek plantation.

Monday Jany. 28th. Visited my Plantation. Severely reprimanded young Stephens for his Indolence, & his father for suffering of it.

Found the new Negroe Cupid ill of a pleurisy at Dogue Run Quarter & had him brot. home in a Cart for better care of him.

> Cupid was a dower Negro, and hence new to the plantation. In 1760 he was one of four slaves assigned to the Dogue Run quarter, which was divided into tracts and was still being planted in tobacco. Through various land acquisitions this farm came by 1793 to comprise close to 649 working acres.

Thursday Jany. 31st. He was somewhat better.

February

Friday Feby. 1st. 1760. Visited my Plantation's. Found Foster had been absent from his charge since the 28th. Ulto. Left Order's for him to come immediately to me upon his return & reprehended him severely.

> John Foster was overseer of the Dogue Run Farm on the Mount Vernon plantation.

Sunday Feby. 3d. Breechy was laid up this Morning with pains in his breast & head attended with a fever.

Mrs. Possey went home and we to Church at Alexandria. Dind at Colo. Carlyles and returnd in the Evening.

One Newell offerd himself to me to be Overseer. Put him of to another day.

> Breechy, a dower slave, was a house servant. *Mrs. Possey:* Martha Posey was the wife of Capt. John Posey of Rover's Delight. Mrs. Posey and two of her children had arrived at Mount Vernon on 3 Feb. (*Diaries*, 1:231). She bore Posey at least four children: John Price, Hanson, St. Lawrence, and Amelia (Milly), all of whom were frequent visitors to Mount Vernon.
>
> Episcopal services in Alexandria at this time were held in a small building furnished jointly by local subscription and by Truro Parish. The Rev. Mr. Green preached there every third Sunday from 1753 until 1765, when Fairfax Parish was formed. John Carlyle (1720–1780), of Dumfrieshire, Scot., was a merchant and a founder of Alexandria. In 1745 he married Sarah Fairfax (1728–1761), of Belvoir, a sister-in-law of GW's brother Lawrence. During the French and Indian War, Carlyle was a supplier of GW's troops.

Monday Feby. 4th. Dispatchd Foster to Occoquan, to proceed from thence in Bailey's Vessell to Portobacco for 100 Barrls. of Corn wch. Captn. Possey purchased of Mr. Hunter the Priest for my use. Sent money to pay for the Corn viz.—37 pistoles and a Shilling, each pistole weighing 4 d[ram]s 8 gr.

Breechy's pains Increasd and he appeard extreamely ill all the day. In Suspence whither to send for Doctr. Laurie or not.

Visited my Plantations and found two Negroes Sick at Williamson's

Quarter viz. Greg and Lucy—orderd them to be Blooded. Stepns. at Wk.

> Father George Hunter (1713–1779) was one of the handful of Roman Catholic priests—all Jesuits—who served the small Catholic populace living in colonial Maryland. As there was no official support (in the form of taxes or glebe land) to provide a living for the Jesuits, the Roman Catholic community of Maryland made use of Maryland's manor system of land tenure by establishing several manors that were held in trust by the community's leaders in the name of one or more of the Jesuits residing in the colony. Each manor, like St. Thomas Manor, in Charles County, had a chapel and usually slaves to work the manor's fields. Port Tobacco, founded in 1728 as the county seat (1728–1895) of Charles County, Md., was literally a small tobacco port on Port Tobacco Creek, which joined the Potomac opposite the Chotank district of King George County in Virginia. Roman Catholic priests in this period were commonly addressed as "Mister." In 1760 Father Hunter was the superior for the Maryland Mission.

Tuesday Feby. 5th. Breechy's pains Increasg. & he appearing worse in other Respects inducd me to send for Dr. Laurie. Wrote to Mr. Ramsay Begging the favour of him to enquire in to the price of Mr. Barnes Sugar Land Tract & he informd me that the value set on it by Mr. Barnes was £400.

Visited my Plantation and found to my great surprise Stephens constt. at Work. Greg and Lucy nothing better.

Passing by my Carpenters that were hughing I found that four of [them] viz. George, Tom, Mike & young Billy had only hughd 120 Foot Yesterday from 10 Oclock. Sat down therefore and observd.

Tom and Mike in a less space than 30 Minutes cleard the Bushes from abt. a Poplar Stock-lind it 10 Foot long and hughd each their side 12 Inches deep.

Then, letting them proceed their own way—they spent 25 Minutes more in getting the cross cut saw standing to consider what to do—sawing the Stock of it in two places—putting it on the Blocks for hughing it square lining it &ca. and from this time till they had finishd the Stock entirely; requird 20 Minutes more, so that in the Spaces of one hour and a quarter they each of them from the Stump finishd 20 Feet of hughing: from hence it appears very clear that allowing they work only from Sun to Sun and require two hour's at Breakfast they ought to yield each his 125 feet while the days are at their present length and more in proportion as they Increase.

While this was doing George and Billy sawd 30 Foot of Plank so that it appears as clear making the same allowance as before (but not for the time requird in pilling the Stock) that they ought to Saw 180 Feet of Plank.

It is to be observd here, that this hughing, & Sawing likewise was of

Poplr. What may be the difference therefore between the working of this Wood and other some future observations must make known.

> William Ramsay (1716–1785) migrated to Virginia from the Galloway district of Scotland and became a founder and merchant of Alexandria. During the French and Indian War, Ramsay, then in financial straits, was appointed a commissary of British troops on GW's recommendation. The land of Abraham Barnes was part of an area full of sugar-bearing maple trees and hence called the Sugar Lands which lay along Sugar Land Run.
>
> *Stock-lind it:* cut it into sections before hewing it into square timbers.

Sunday Feby. 10th. Orderd all the Fellows from the different Quarter's to Assembly at Williamson's Quarter in the Morning to move Petits House.

> Thomas Petit rented a Mount Vernon quarter from GW in 1759 and 1760, after which he disappears from GW's records.

Monday Feby. 11th. Went out early myself and continued with my People till 1 Oclock in which time we got the house abt. 250 yards. Was informd then that Mr. Digges was at my House upon which I retd. finding him & Doctr Laurie there.

The Ground being soft and Deep we found it no easy matter with 20 hands and 8 Horses & 6 Oxen to get this House along.

> The Digges family of Virginia and Maryland descended from Edward Digges, who settled in Virginia in the mid–seventeenth century and served as governor of Virginia 1655–57. His eldest son, William, later moved north of the Potomac River and founded the Maryland branch of the Digges family. The Mr. Digges who appears here is William Digges (1713–1783), a grandson of the elder William. This William, a prominent layman in the Roman Catholic church in Maryland, married Ann Atwood and lived at his plantation, Warburton Manor, across the Potomac River within sight of Mount Vernon. For many years the families of Warburton Manor and Mount Vernon exchanged visits across the Potomac.

Tuesday Feby. 12th. Visited at the Glebe the day being very fine clear & still.

Sett Kate & Doll to heaping the Dung abt. the Stable.

Recd. a Letter & Acct. Currt. from Messrs. Hanbury the former dated Octr. 1–1759 the other Septr. 1st. same yr.

> The Truro Parish glebe, which grew from 176 acres in 1752 to 385 in 1767, included a house and outbuildings for the Rev. Charles Green and his wife. The house, begun in 1752 by Green and Thomas Waite, had been newly completed in 1760 by William Buckland (1734–1774), a talented joiner previously imported from England for the construction of George Mason's Gunston Hall.
>
> The Hanbury firm, a powerful London merchant house, had served the Custis plantations for a number of years. On 12 June 1759 GW had written to the firm, then known as Capel & Osgood Hanbury, informing them of his

marriage to Martha Custis and stating: "I must now desire that you will please to address all your Letters which relate to the Affairs of the Deceas'd Colo. Custis to me as by Marriage I am entitled to a third part of that Estate, and invested with the care of the other two thirds by a Decree of our Genl Court which I obtain in order to strengthen the power I before had in Consequence of my Wifes Administration" (*Papers, Colonial Series,* 6:322–23).

Thursday Feby. 14th. Mr. Clifton came here and we conditiond for his Land viz., if he is not bound by some prior engagemt. I am to have all his Land in the Neck (500 Acres about his house excepted) and the Land commonly calld Brents for 1600 £ Curr[enc]y. He getting Messrs. Digges &ca. to join in making me a good & Sufft. Title. But Note I am not bound to Ratifie this bargain unless Colo. Carlyle will let me have his Land adjoining Brents at half a Pistole an Acre.

Visited my Quarters and saw a plant patch burnt at the Mill.

Brought home 4003 lbs. of Hay from Mr. Digges's.

William Clifton (died c.1770) was descended from an English Roman Catholic family, several branches of which began leaving England for Maryland and Virginia in the mid–seventeenth century. William left England in the early eighteenth century and settled in Truro Parish, where he was living in 1739 when he bought 500 acres of the Neck land from his brother-in-law George Brent (d. 1778) of Stafford County. By 1760 Clifton's land was a plantation of about 1,806 acres in Clifton's Neck, which lay on the east side of Little Hunting Creek, facing the Potomac River, across which Clifton ran a ferry often used by GW.

Brents: George Brent's remaining land in the Neck, 238 acres lying between Little Hunting Creek and Clifton's plantation.

Friday Feby. 15th. Went to a Ball at Alexandria—where Musick and Dancing was the chief Entertainment. However in a convenient Room detachd for the purpose abounded great plenty of Bread and Butter, some Biscuets with Tea, & Coffee which the Drinkers of coud not Distinguish from Hot water sweetned. Be it remembered that pocket handkerchiefs servd the purposes of Table Cloths & Napkins and that no Apologies were made for either. I shall therefore distinguish this Ball by the Stile & title of the Bread & Butter Ball.

The Proprietors of this Ball were Messrs. Carlyle Laurie & Robt. Wilson, but the Doctr. not getting it conducted agreeable to his own taste woud claim no share of the merit of it.

We lodgd at Colo. Carlyles.

A man named Robert Wilson voted for GW in the 1758 Frederick County election for the House of Burgesses. GW apparently played cards at the ball, because on the following day he recorded the loss of 7s. "By Cards" (Ledger A, 63).

Sunday Feby. 17th. Went to Church & Dind at Belvoir.

Sent 4 Yews & Lambs to be fatted.

Tuesday Feby. 19th. Went to Court, and Administerd upon Nations Effects. Got Mr. Smiths Lease to me recorded and Mr. Johnston not having Darrels Deeds ready I was obligd to get the acknowledging of them postpond.

Recd. a Letter from my Brothr. Austin by Mr. Lane & answerd it.

William Nations, who died in late January, had rented a quarter from GW since 1755, paying a rent of 1,000 pounds of tobacco per year.

GW's first expansion of the Mount Vernon property occurred in Dec. 1757, when he bought two pieces of land on the plantation's northern boundary from Sampson Darrell (d. 1777) of Fairfax County: a tract of 200 acres on Dogue Run and an adjoining tract of 300 acres on Little Hunting Creek. The total price of these two tracts was £350, which GW paid with £260 in cash and a bond for £90 due in two years, and in return he received Darrell's bond guaranteeing him title to the land. For details of the transaction, see *Papers, Colonial Series,* 5:74–75, 78–79. The official deeds were not immediately signed and recorded in court because the property was held under right of dower by Darrell's mother, Ann, for her lifetime; only after her death would it revert to Darrell as a surviving son. Thus, although GW owned Darrell's right to the land, he could not obtain the deeds until Ann died or rented the land to him. GW did not have to await her death, because on 20 Sept. 1759 he signed a lease with her and her present husband, Thomas Smith (d. 1764) of Fairfax County, agreeing thereby to pay them 1,030 pounds of tobacco a year until Ann died (lease of Thomas and Ann Smith to GW, Gratz Collection, Historical Society of Pennsylvania; Ledger A, 111). Having recorded the lease on this day, GW was eager to get and record Darrell's deeds, but he was obliged to wait for the May court session.

Augustine Washington (1720–1762), half brother of GW by his father's first wife, Jane Butler, married Anne Aylett (d. 1773) and lived at Pope's Creek in Westmoreland County. GW usually called him "Austin." Mr. Lane was probably one of the three sons of William Lane (1690–1760) of Nomini Forest, Westmoreland County: James Lane (d. 1777), William Carr Lane (d. 1770), and Joseph Lane (d. 1796).

Thursday Feby. 21. Visited at Mr. Clifton's and rode over his Lands— but in an especial manner view'd that tract called Brents, which wd. have pleas'd me exceedingly at the price he offerd it at viz., half a pistole an Acre provided Colo. Carlyle's 300 Acres just below it coud be annexd at the same price and this but a few Months ago he offerd it at but now seeming to set a higher value upon it, and at the same time putting on an air of indifference inducd me to make Clifton another for his Land—namely £1700 Cury. for all his Lands in the Neck Including his own Plantn. &ca. which offer he readily accepted upon Condition of getting his wife to acknowledge her Right of Dower to it and of his success in this he was to inform me in a few days.

Clifton's wife was his cousin Elizabeth Brent (d. 1773), a daughter of Robert Brent of Woodstock, Stafford County, whose seventeenth-century ancestor Giles Brent had originally patented most of the land in what was now called Clifton's Neck. Mrs. Clifton's "Right of Dower" referred to that portion of

Clifton's Neck which, although controlled by her husband under the law of martial right, could only be alienated (given or sold) by Mrs. Clifton, the legal owner.

Friday Feby. 22. Upon my return found one of my best Waggon Horses (namely Jolly) with his right foreleg Mashd to pieces which I suppose happend in the Storm last Night by Means of a Limb of a tree or something of that sort falling upon him.

Did it up as well as I coud this Night.

This was GW's birthday according to the Gregorian calendar, but there is no indication that he took note of it either on this day or 11 Feb., the Old Style date on which he actually was born. In 1798 and 1799 the citizens of Alexandria celebrated his birthday on or near the old date.

Saturday Feby. 23. Had the Horse slung upon Canvas and his leg fresh set—following Markhams directions as near as I coud.

Captn. Bullet came here from Alexandria, and engagd to secure me some Lands on the Ohio being lately appointed Surveyor of a District there.

Markhams directions: Gervase Markham (1568–1637) wrote many treatises on diseases of cattle and horses. In 1759 GW purchased a much more current work, William Gibson's *Treatise on the Diseases of Horses* (London, 1751).

Thomas Bullitt, son of Benjamin Bullitt (d. 1766) of Fauquier County, served with GW in the Virginia Regiment, rising to captain. He was with GW at Fort Necessity and at Braddock's Defeat and held his Virginians in a bloody skirmish at Grant's Defeat.

Sunday Feby. 24th. Captn. Bullet dined here to day also. So did Mr. Clifton but the latter was able to give me no determinate answer in regard to his Land.

Monday Feby. 25th. Lord Fairfax, Colo. F[airfa]x & his Lady, Colo. Martin, Mr. B. F[airfa]x, Colo. Carlyle, & Mr. Green & Mrs. Green dind here.

The Broken Legd. horse fell out of his Sling and by that means and struling together hurt himself so much that I orderd him to be killd.

Thomas Bryan Martin (1731–1798), a nephew of Lord Fairfax, came to Virginia in 1751 and the next year was appointed land agent for the Fairfax Grant, taking up residence with Lord Fairfax at Greenway Court in the Shenandoah Valley. In 1758 Martin and GW were elected burgesses for Frederick County. Bryan Fairfax (1737–1802) was a half brother of George William Fairfax. After an erratic youth Bryan married Elizabeth Cary, a sister of Sarah Cary Fairfax, and settled in Fairfax County, making his home at Towlston Grange on Difficult Run. Before the Revolution he was one of GW's frequent fox-hunting companions.

Tuesday Feby. 26th. Made an absolute agreement with Mr. Clifton for his Land (so far as depended upon him) on the following terms—to wit, I am to give him £1150 Sterling for his Neck Lands, containg. 1806 Acres, and to allow him the use of this Plantn. he lives on till fall twelve months.

He on his part is to procure the Gentlemen of Maryland to whom his Lands are under Mortgage to join in a Conveyance and is to put me into possession of the Land so soon as this can be done. He is not to cut down any Timber, nor clear any Ground nor to use more Wood than what shall be absolutely necessary for Fences and firing. Neither is he to assent to any alterations of Tenants transferring of Leases &ca. but on the contrary is to discourage every practice that has a tendancy to lessen the value of the Land.

N.B. He is also to bring Mr. Mercers opinion concerning the validity of a private sale made by himself.

Went down to Occoquan, by appointment to look at Colo. Cockes Cattle, but Mr. Peakes being from home I made no agreemt. for them not caring to give the price he askd for them.

Bottled 35 dozn. of Cyder, the weather very warm, & Cloudy with some Rain last Night.

The "Gentlemen of Maryland" who held mortgages from Clifton were Charles Carroll (1702–1782) of Annapolis, Benjamin Tasker (1690–1768) of Anne Arundel County, and William Digges, Ignatius Digges, and John Addison, all of Prince George's County. The Carroll and Digges families of Maryland had married into the Brent family of Maryland and Virginia, and all of these parties were now in the fifteenth year of a struggle over Clifton's Neck, producing a maze of lawsuits involving leases, inheritances, mortgages, injunctions, and ejectments. Clifton's suit for a final settlement in Virginia's General Court (sitting in chancery) was now awaiting the report of court-appointed commissioners, one of whom was GW. Since the court case was still pending, the validity of such a "private sale" was a moot point, and GW wisely advised Clifton to seek a legal opinion. Mr. Mercer is probably John Mercer (1704–1768), who emigrated from Ireland to Virginia in 1720 and made his home near the Potomac River at Marlborough, Stafford County. As a lawyer Mercer became so aggressive in the courtroom that in 1734 he was barred from practice. He then turned to legal scholarship, spending the next few years preparing a compliation of Virginia laws. Mercer himself was later appointed a justice of Stafford County. GW had known John Mercer for years. Mercer's home of Marlborough, on the neck between Aquia and Potomac creeks, was only a few miles up the Potomac from the Chotank neighborhood, so well known to GW from youth and later so thickly populated with his cousins. As early as 1754 GW had asked for Mercer's legal advice regarding the disposition of Mount Vernon after Lawrence Washington's death. Mercer had also served the Custis family for 16 years during a major legal battle in which GW took an interest following his marriage to Martha Custis in 1759.

Three of John Mercer's sons served with GW in the Virginia Regiment, one of whom, John Fenton Mercer (1735–1756), was killed in battle. The other two sons, George Mercer (1733–1784) and James Mercer (1735/36–1793), appear in the diaries along with other members of the family.

William Peake (d. 1761), of Fairfax County, lived at Willow Spring in the fork of Little Hunting Creek and was hence GW's closest neighbor. William was a Truro Parish vestryman for many years, and upon his death GW was chosen by the vestry to take his place. .

March

Sunday Mar. 2. Mr. Clifton came here to day, & under pretence of his Wife not consenting to acknowledge her Right of Dower wanted to disengage himself of the Bargain he had made with me for his Land on the 26th. past and by his shuffling behaviour on the occasion convinced me of his being the trifling body represented.

Monday Mar. 10th. Rode to my Plantation and the Mill, & there partly agreed with Jerry Mitchell to rebuild my Mill when She runs dry in the Summer.

Dispatchd Mulatto Jack to Frederick for some Mares from thence to Plow.

Jeremiah Mitchell, an independent artisan, contracted to do this repair work for 4s. 6d. a day. He put in 97 days in all, finishing the job by 1 Dec. 1760 (Ledger A, 102).

Tuesday Mar. 11th. Visited at Colo. Fairfax and was informd that Clifton had sold his Land to Mr. Thompsons Mason for 1200 £ Sterlg. which fully unravelled his Conduct on the 2d. and convincd me that he was nothing less than a thorough pacd Rascall—disregardful of any Engagements of Words or Oaths not bound by Penalities.

George William Fairfax was one of GW's fellow commissioners in the Clifton case. Thomson Mason (1733–1785), of Raspberry Plain in Loudoun County and a younger brother of George Mason of Gunston Hall, studied law in England at the Middle Temple and in 1760 was a member of the House of Burgesses for Stafford County.

Thursday Mar. 13th. Mr. Carlyle (who came here from Port Tobo. court last Night) and Mrs. Carlyle were confind here all day.

Mulatto Jack returnd home with the Mares he was sent for, but so poor were they, and so much abusd had they been by my Rascally Overseer Hardwick that they were scarce able to go highlone, much less to assist in the business of the Plantations.

Highlone: alone, without support.

Friday Mar. 14th. Mr. Carlyle & his Wife still remain here. We talkd a good deal of a Scheme of setting up an Iron Work on Colo. Fairfax's Land on Shannondoah. Mr. Chapman who was proposd as a partner being a perfect Judge of these matters was to go up and view the Conveniences and determine the Scheme.

> Colonel Fairfax's land on the Shenandoah River included the east bank of
> the crossing for Vestal's ferry. Carlyle and his brother-in-law George William
> Fairfax went ahead with the ironworks project. Nathaniel Chapman, who
> died later this year, had iron experience both with the Principio Company
> of Maryland and the Accokeek works in Stafford County. Chapman had also
> served as an executor for the estates of Augustine and Lawrence Washington,
> both of whom had had interests in ironworks.

Tuesday Mar. 18th. Went to Court partly on my own private Business and partly on Cliftons Affair but the Commissioners not meeting nothing was done in regard to the Latter. Much discourse happend between him and I con⟨cer⟩ning his ungenerous treatment of me. The whole turning to little Acct. tis not worth reciting here the result of which was that for £50 more than Mr. Mason offerd him he undertook if possible to disengage himself from that Gentleman & to let me have his Land. I did not think Myself restraind by any Rules of Honour, Conscience or &ca. from makeg. him this offer as his Lands were first engagd to me by the most Solemn assurances that any Man coud give.

> The following month this move by GW in the Clifton affair was criticized by
> the Virginia General Court sitting in chancery. GW was putting himself into
> a potentially awkward situation, for as a commissioner he was responsible for
> giving a disinterested report to the chancery court on how the Clifton case
> should be settled.
>
> GW dined today at Mrs. Chew's tavern (Ledger A, 89).

Wednesday Mar. 19. Peter (my Smith) and I after several efforts to make a plow after a new model—partly of my own contriving—was fiegn to give it out, at least for the present.

Thursday Mar. 20th. Colo. F[airfa]x and I set out to Alexa. by appointmt. to Settle & adjust (with the other Comrs.) Cliftons & Carrols accts. conformable to a decree of our Genl. Court but not being able to accomplish it then the 28th. was a further day appointed to meet and my house the place resolvd upon.

> The other commissioners were Rev. Charles Green and John West, Jr., now
> sheriff of Fairfax County. It was the common practice in such cases for the
> court to appoint four commissioners, any three of whom could act as a
> quorum.

Sunday Mar. 23d. Miss Fairfax & Miss Dent came here.

> Hannah Fairfax was a younger sister of George William Fairfax. Miss Dent
> was possibly Elizabeth Dent (1727–1796) or one of her younger sisters, all
> daughters of Peter Dent (c.1694–1757), of Whitehaven, on Mattawoman
> Creek in the Piscataway region of Prince George's County, Md.

Thursday Mar. 27. Agreed to give Mr. William Triplet £18 to build the two houses in the Front of my House (plastering them also) and running Walls for Pallisades to them from the Great house & from the Great House to the Wash House and Kitchen also.

> William Triplett (d. 1803) of Truro Parish lived with his wife Sarah Massey Triplett at Round Hill about four miles northwest of Mount Vernon. He had participated in a recent remodeling of GW's mansion house, doing brickwork on the foundation and chimneys and plastering the interior of the house. His bill for those jobs, which totaled £52 8s. 4d., had been discharged by GW on 26 Feb. 1760 (Ledger A, 72).

Friday Mar. 28. According to appointment, Colo. F⟨airfa⟩x & Mr. Green met here upon Clifton's Affair, he being present as was Mr. Thompson Mason (as Council for him). Mr. Digges and Mr. Addison were also here and after examining all the Papers and Accts. on both sides, and stating them in the manner wch. seemd most equitable to Us, the debt due from Mr. Clifton according to that Settlement amounted to £[   ] that is to say—to Mr. Carroll £[243 13s 1d.] to Mr. Tasker pr. Mr. Digges [£304 15s.3d.] to Do. pr. Mr. Addison [£364 19s.].

We also agreed to report several things which appeard necessary, as well, in behalf of Mr. Clifton as the other party.

The Gentlemen from Maryland, Mr. Mason & Clifton left this; but Colo. Fairfax and Mr. Green stayd the Night.

Abt. Noon Mulatto Jack finishd plowing the Field below the Garden and went into the lower Pasture to work.

> The Addison family of Maryland descended from John Addison, who emigrated from England in 1677. His son Thomas Addison (1679–1727) built Oxon Hill in Prince George's County, Md., across the Potomac from Alexandria. By his second wife, Eleanor Smith Addison, Thomas had one daughter and four sons, one of whom was John Addison (1713–1764) of Oxon Hill, who appears here.
>
> The gross amounts filled in here are taken from the Virginia General Court decree of 12 April 1760. They are probably the amounts decided upon at this meeting but left blank by GW because interest and court costs were still to be figured into the final totals.

Monday Mar. 31st. Went to Belvoir (according to Appointment on the 28th. past) and drew up and Signd a Report of our Proceedings in Clifton's affair to be sent with the Accts. to the Genl. Court.

Finishd plowing the Fallowd Ground abt. Sun Setting.

Wrote to Lieutt. Smith to try if possible to get me a Careful Man to Overlook my Carpenters. Wrote also to Harwick ordering down two Mares from thence & desiring him to engage me a Ditcher. Inclosd a Letter from my Brother Jno. to his Overseer Farrell Littleton and directed him what to do if the Small pox shd. come amongst them.

Lt. Charles Smith, who was given command of Fort Loudoun at Winchester in 1758, had been recommended to that post by GW as an officer both "diligent" and "exceedingly industrious" (GW to John Blair, 28 May 1758). Having lost an arm in the service, Smith received a life pension from the House of Burgesses on the recommendation of a committee which included GW (*H.B.J.*, 1761–65, 179, 185).

Ditcher: an employee to supervise the construction of drainage ditches, along field boundaries and elsewhere. The customary boundaries delineating GW's fields consisted of two parallel ditches with a row of defense hedge along the center ridge. They served the dual purpose of draining wet lands and making it more difficult for livestock to pass through the hedge.

GW's younger brother John Augustine Washington (1736–1787), who lived at Bushfield in Westmoreland County, had inherited land in Frederick County which lay near GW's Bullskin plantation. "Jack," as GW called him, had managed Mount Vernon for GW during the latter's absence in the French and Indian wars, bringing his bride, Hannah Bushrod Washington, to Mount Vernon in 1756 and living there until 1758. It was partly in acknowledgment of Jack's help and loyalty that GW in his will left part of the Mount Vernon estate to Jack's older son, Bushrod Washington.

April

Tuesday April 1—1760. Recd. a Letter from Mr. Digges, Inclosing a Packet for Messrs. Nichos. & Withe wch. he desird I woud send under Cover to some Friend of mine in Williamsburg as it was to go by Clifton suspecting that Gentleman woud not deal fairly by it.

Began to prepare a Small piece of Ground of abt. [   ] Yards Square at the lower Corner of my Garden to put Trefoil in—a little Seed given me by Colo. F[airfa]x Yesterday.

On 2 April GW wrote a covering letter to accompany the packet. In the letter, addressed to Benjamin Waller of the General Court, GW recited his differences with Clifton and Thomson Mason and argued strongly for his own position, which was that the court should "confirm the Opinion of the Commissioners" (*Papers, Colonial Series,* 6:407–11.) Of the two interested parties named Digges, this reference is probably to William, since Ignatius, as an agent for Charles Carroll of Carrollton, consistently refused to cooperate in the Clifton proceedings (GW to Carroll, 31 July 1791, Washington Papers, Library of Congress). In 1760 Robert Carter Nicholas (1728–1780), a burgess for York County, and George Wythe (1726–1806), the burgess for the College of William and Mary, were already recognized as having two of Virginia's most talented legal minds.

Friday Apl. 4th. Apprehending the Herrings were come Hauled the Sein but catchd only a few of them tho a good many of other sorts. Majr. Stewart and Doctr. Johnston came here in the Afternoon and at Night Mr. Ritchie attended by Mr. Ross solliciting Freight—promisd none.

Herring came up the rivers of tidewater Virginia and Maryland every spring to spawn near the falls.

Robert Stewart entered the Virginia Regiment in 1754. He was soon made captain and was with GW at Fort Necessity and Braddock's Defeat, becoming one of GW's favorite officers. In the fall of 1758 he became brigade major of the Virginia troops on GW's recommendation, and in 1760 he was still in the service, stationed at Winchester. Dr. Johnston is probably Robert Johnston (Johnson), originally of James City County, who served as the surgeon in Col. William Byrd's Virginia Regiment; he may have been attending the Virginia troops in Winchester at this time. Johnston, who voted for GW in the lively 1758 burgesses election in Frederick County, died in that county in 1763.

Archibald Ritchie (d. 1784) was a Scottish merchant in Hobbs Hole or Tappahannock, on the Rappahannock River, Essex County, Va. Hector Ross, a merchant at Colchester, Fairfax County, bought tobacco and Indian corn from GW, and his establishment served as a local source for clothing and minor necessities for GW's white servants, his tenants, and his slaves.

Tuesday April 8th. What time it began Raining in the Night I cant say, but at day break it was pouring very hard, and continued so, till 7 oclock when a Messenger came to inform me that my Mill was in great danger of blowing. I immediately hurried off all hands with Shovels &ca. to her assistance and got there myself just time enough to give here a reprieve for this time by Wheeling dirt into the place which the Water had Washd.

While I was here a very heavy Thunder Shower came on which lasted upwards of an hour.

Here also, I tried what time the Mill requird to grind a Bushel of Corn and to my Surprize found She was within 5 Minutes of an hour about. This old Anthony attributed to the low head of Water (but Whether it was so or not I cant say—her Works all decayd and out of Order wch. I rather take to be the cause).

The mill was probably a small, one- or two-story wooden structure with an overshot or breast wheel and a single set of grinding stones. GW's assessment of the mill's machinery must have been correct, but Anthony recognized an equally important problem. The head of water was not high enough to generate much force when the water fell on the wheel, and without more power, better machinery could not be used to its full capacity. Some work was done on the millrace by Hosea Bazell during the late summer, but any improvement made in the head of water was probably minimal (Ledger A, 102). Jerry Mitchell apparently confined his efforts this year to rebuilding the mill's internal works.

The slave carpenter Anthony was in his middle fifties when he was brought to Mount Vernon in 1759 as part of Martha Custis's dower. GW made him his miller but the next year reassigned him to the crew of carpenters, where by 1762 he had become head slave carpenter. He may have died by 1763 when he disappears from GW's tithable lists.

Wednesday Apl. 9th. Doctr. Laurie came here. I may add Drunk.

Thursday Apl. 10th. Mrs. Washington was blooded by Doctr. Laurie who stayd all Night.

Sunday April 13th. My Negroes askd the lent of the Sein to day but caught little or no Fish. Note the Wind blew upon the shore to day.

Tuesday April 15th. Being informd that French, Triplet and others were about buying (in conjunction) a piece of Land of Simon Piarson lying not far from my Dogue Run Quarter I engagd him to give me the first offer of it so soon as he shoud determine upon selling it.

> Simon Pearson (c.1738–1797) owned 558 acres of land which lay on the main road from Alexandria to Colchester, northwest of the land on Dogue Run that GW had bought from Sampson Darrell in 1757. On 14 Feb. 1769 GW bought 178 acres of Pearson's land for £191 7s. The remainder went to William Triplett and George Johnston.

Wednesday Apl. 16. Mr. Triplet & his Brother came this day to Work. Abt. 10 Oclock they began, and got the Wall between the House and Dairy finishd.

Thursday April 17th. By 3 Oclock in the afternoon Mr. Triplet finishd the Wall between the Dairy and Kitchen. The Rain from that time prevented his Working.

Friday April 18th. Mr. Barnes's Davy brot. home my Negroe fellow Boson who Ran away on Monday last.

> Davy was one of Abraham Barnes's slaves. In 1760 Boson was assigned to the Mount Vernon quarter called Williamson's. GW today paid Davy 10s. for capturing Boson (Ledger A, 89).

Saturday Apl. 19th. Crossd at Mr. Possey's Ferry and began my journey to Williamsburg about 9 Oclock. Abt. 11 I broke my Chair and had to Walk to Port Tobo. where I was detaind the whole day getting my Chair mended—no Smith being with 6 Miles. Lodgd at Doctr. Halkerson's.

> John Posey's ferry crossed the Potomac River from the lower point of the Mount Vernon neck to Marshall Hall in Charles County, Md., home of Capt. Thomas Hanson Marshall (1731–1801). Robert Halkerston had lived in Fredericksburg during GW's youth, where he was a founding member of the Masonic Lodge in 1752 and probably was present at the 1758 lodge meetings in which the young GW was initiated, passed, and raised into Masonry.

Sunday Apl. 20th. Set out early, and crossd at Cedar point by 10; the day being very calm & fine, Dind and lodgd at my Brother's.

> The lower of the two Cedar Points in Maryland was about a 13-mile ride south from Port Tobacco, a small tobacco port and county seat of Charles County, Maryland. His brother Samuel's plantation in the Chotank area of

Stafford County (now King George County) was originally one of their father's quarters, inherited by Samuel when he came of age in 1755.

Monday Apl. 21st. Crossd at Southern's and Tods Bridge and lodgd at Major Gaines's.

After leaving his brother's home GW rode about three miles below Leedstown to Southern's ferry on the Rappahannock River, whose owner lived on the far side of the river in Essex County. GW then rode southwest through Essex and King and Queen counties to arrive at Todd's Bridge, where he crossed the Mattaponi River into King William County a short way upriver from Aylett's Warehouse (later the village of Aylett, Va.). In 1760 William Todd, who lived on the King and Queen side of the bridge, also had a warehouse and an ordinary at this crossing. Maj. Harry Gaines (d. 1766), a local planter, was elected a burgess for King William County in 1758.

Tuesday April 22d. Crossd Pamunky at Williams's Ferry, and visited all the Plantations in New Kent. Found the Overseers much behind hand in their Business. Went to Mrs. Dandridges and lodgd.

From Major Gaines's, GW rode south through King William County to cross the Pamunkey River into New Kent County at Williams's ferry. The crossing brought him very near the Custis plantations in the vicinity of the White House, which had been the home of Martha Dandridge Custis when GW met her. Mrs. Frances Jones Dandridge (1710–1785), widow of John Dandridge (1700–1756), was GW's mother-in-law. She lived at Chestnut Grove in New Kent County, about midway along the Pamunkey River between the White House and the Bassetts' home, Eltham. GW was obviously fond of her. In June 1773 he wrote another of her sons-in-law Burwell Bassett from Mount Vernon that he wished "that I was Master of Arguments powerful enough to prevail upon Mrs. Dandridge to make this place her entire & absolute home. I should think, as she lives a lonesome life . . . it might suit her well, & be agreeable, both to herself & my wife, to me most assuredly it would" (*Papers, Colonial Series*, 9:243–44).

Wednesday Apl. 23d. Went to Colo. Bassetts and remaind there the whole day.

Burwell Bassett's home, Eltham, in New Kent County, was less than a mile up the Pamunkey River from West Point, where the Pamunkey joins the Mattaponi to form the York River.

Thursday April 24th. Visited my Quarters at Claibornes and found their business in tolerable forwardness. Dind at Mr. Bassetts and went in the Evening to Williamsburg.

Claibornes: This Custis plantation, containing about 3,080 acres, lay in King William County on the neck of land the Pamunkey River forms just above Eltham. When the Custis estate was apportioned among Martha and the two children, Claiborne's was one of the plantations assigned to her by right of dower. As her second husband, GW was entitled to use the dower plantations as if they were his own, except that he could not sell them or encumber them, for on Martha's death the dower plantations were to go to John Parke Custis.

At this time 19 dower slaves worked at Claiborne's, getting tobacco, wheat, and corn under the direction of the plantation's overseer John Roan.

Friday Apl. 25th. Waited upon the Govr.

In 1760 the governor of Virginia was Sir Jeffery Amherst, and the lieutenant governor Francis Fauquier resided in Virginia and administered the colony. It was Lieutenant Governor Fauquier whom GW visited on this date; he was following the common practice of Virginians in referring to him as the governor.

Saturday Apl. 26th. Visited all the Estates and my own Quarters about Williamsburg. Found these also in pretty good forwardness.

Receivd Letters from Winchester informing me that the Small Pox had got among my Quarter's in Frederick; determind therefore to leave Town as soon as possible and proceed up to them.

Estates: John Parke Custis's plantations in York County. Young Custis had also inherited the Custis lands in New Kent, Hanover, and Northampton counties as well as lots in Williamsburg and Jamestown. *My own Quarters:* Martha Washington's dower plantations in York County—Bridge Quarter and the Ship Landing, both of which lay near the Capitol Landing on Queen's Creek about two miles north of Williamsburg. Together they contained about 1,000 acres, of which "100 or more" were "firm hard marsh, supporting a numerous flock of cattle winter and summer," and 10 to 12 were swamp (*Va. Gaz.*, P&D, 2 April 1767).

Sunday Apl. 27th. Went to Church.

Church: probably Bruton Parish Church on Duke of Gloucester Street in Williamsburg.

Tuesday Apl. 29th. Reachd Port Royal by Sunset.

GW crossed the Pamunkey River at Thomas Dansie's ferry and dined at Todd's ordinary on his way to Port Royal (Ledger A, 89).

Wednesday 30th. Came to Hooes Ferry by 10 Oclock but the wind blew too fresh to cross; detained there all Night.

Hooe's ferry, running from Mathias Point in Virginia to lower Cedar Point in Maryland, was established in 1715 by Col. Rice Hooe (Hoe, Howe). At Colonel Hooe's death (1726), the ferry was inherited and run by his son John (1704–1766), and following John's death by John's widow, Ann Alexander Hooe, and their son Gerard Hooe (1733–1786).

From Hooe's ferry, GW probably retraced his steps home but entered no expense in his ledger for recrossing the Potomac to reach Mount Vernon.

May

Friday May 2d. My English Horse Coverd the great bay Mare.

GW had bought an English colt from Col. Bernard or Thomas Moore in Mar. 1759 for £17 10s. (Ledger A, 55).

Saturday May 3d. The Stallion coverd Ranken—and afterwards breaking out of his pasture Coverd the great bay Mare again.

Sunday May 4th. Warm and fine. Set out for Frederick to see my Negroes that lay Ill of the Small Pox.

Monday May 5th. Reach'd Mr. Stephenson in Frederick abt. 4 Oclock. Here I was informd that Harry & Kit, the two first of my Negroes that took the Small Pox were Dead and Roger & Phillis the only two down with it were recovering from it.

Wednesday May 7. After taking the Doctrs. Direction's in regard to my People I set out for my Quarters and got there abt. 12 Oclock—time enough to go over them and find every thing in the utmost confusion, disorder, & backwardness my Overseer lying upon his Back of a broken Leg, and not half a Crop especially of Corn Ground prepard.
    Engagd. Vale. Crawford to go in pursuit of a Nurse to be ready in case more of my People shd. be seizd with the same disorder.

> Valentine Crawford (d. 1777) lived near GW's Bullskin plantation in Frederick County and was regularly hired to bring down GW's mountain tobacco from those quarters.

Thursday May 8th. Got Blankets and every other requisite from Winchester & settld things upon the best footing I coud to prevt. the Small Pox from Spreading—and in case of its spreading for the care of the Negroes. Mr. Vale. Crawford agreeing in case any more of the People at the lower Quarter getting it to take them home to his House—& if any of those at the upper Quarter gets it to have them removd into my Room and the Nurse sent for.

Friday May 9th. Set out on my return Home. The Morning drizzling a little. Calld at the Bloomery and got Mr. Wm. Crawford to shew me the place that has been so often talkd of for erecting an Iron Work upon.

> William Crawford (1732–1782), brother of Valentine Crawford, entered the Virginia Regiment in 1755 as an ensign and scout and later served with GW on the Forbes Expedition in 1758. He lived in Frederick County until 1765, when he moved to the Youghiogheny country in western Pennsylvania. During the 1770s he acted as GW's land agent. Despite Crawford's approval of this site for an ironworks, GW did not join in the venture.

Saturday May 10. Arrivd at home abt 10 Oclock where I found my Brother Jno. And was told that my great Chesnut folded a Horse Colt on the 6 Instt. and that my Young Peach trees were Wed according to Order.

Sunday May 11th. Mrs. Washington we[nt] to Church.
    My black pacing Mare was twice Coverd.

Proposd a purchase of some Lands which Col. F[airfa]x has at the Mouth of the Warm Spring Run joing. Barwicks bottom. He promisd me the preference if he shd. sell but is not inclind to do it at prest.

Wednesday May 14th. Visited at Belvoir.
People & Plows at Muddy Hole.

Thursday May 15th. Drying Winds—People at Muddy hole again.

Saturday May 17th. Brought a Pipe of Wine from there [Alexandria] wch. Captn. McKie brought from Madeira also a Chest of Lemons and some other trifles.
The Great Bay was coverd. Got an Acct. that the Assembly was to meet on Monday. Resolvd to set of to Morrow.

> McKie is possibly Capt. William Macky, who entered his ship into the York River Naval District records, 1 April 1760, as having come from South Carolina, a common port of call in the trade between Chesapeake Bay and the wine islands (Public Record Office, Great Britain: C.O.5/1448, f. 25).
> GW was a burgess for Frederick County 1758–65. The House of Burgesses met 19–24 May 1760 to consider an urgent message from Governor Fauquier for men and money to relieve Fort Loudoun on the Little Tennessee River, which was in danger of falling to the Cherokees (*H.B.J.,* 1758–61, 171–79).

Sunday May 18th. Set out in Company with Mr. George Johnston. At Colchester was informd by Colo. Thornton and Chissel that the Assembly wd. be broke up before I could get down. Turnd back therefore & found Colo. Fairfax and his Family and that Lightning wch. had attended a good deal of Rain had struck my Quarter & near 10 Negroes in it some very bad but with letting Blood they recoverd.

> George Johnston, of Belvale, was a burgess for Fairfax County 1758–65. Colchester, a small settlement of Scottish merchants, lay on Occoquan Creek about eight miles below Mount Vernon. Colonels Thornton and Chissel may have been Col. Presley Thornton, burgess for Northumberland County, and John Chiswell, of Hanover County.

Monday May 19th. Went to Alexandria to see Captn. Littledales Ship Launchd wch. went of extreamely well.

> In 1760 Isaac Littledale was establishing his trade between his home in Whitehaven, Eng., and the Potomac River valley. For this trade the *Hero,* a 200-ton ship which required 14 hands, was built in the Alexandria shipyard in 1760. Littledale was her captain on the maiden voyage.

Tuesday May 20th. Being Court day Mr. Clifton's Land in the Neck was exposd to Sale and I bought it for £1210 Sterlg. & under many threats and disadvantages paid the Money into the Comrs. hands and returnd home at Night with Colo. Fairfax & Famy. Captn. Dalton's Dun Mare again Covd.

The final decree of Virginia's General Court in chancery ordered that the commissioners on 20 May at Alexandria sell at public auction to the highest bidder the lands in Clifton's Neck and that Clifton's creditors then be paid off. The "threats and disadvantages" to GW came from all sides. Thomson Mason threatened to appeal the sale decree; Ignatius Digges and Charles Carroll refused to show up at all to deliver their mortgages, thus barring GW from a clear title; and Carroll had already decided to appeal the case to the Privy Council in London. Finally, Clifton declared he would not vacate the land until 1762, which, among other problems, threatened GW with a two-year loss of rent from the Clifton's Neck tenant farmers (Robert Carter Nicholas and George Wythe to GW, 27 May 1760).

1761

May

May 24th. Betty from Riverside Quarter came home Sick & did not again in a Condition to work till the 13th. July fol[lowing].

Riverside Quarter, or River Quarter, a newly developed part of the Mount Vernon cropland, was in the 1,806 acres of land GW had bought from William Clifton in 1760. Most of the remaining cleared land in the Neck owned by GW was, in 1760, being worked by tenants. Riverside Quarter became the basis for the larger River plantation (later River Farm) that GW developed in subsequent years.

GW went to Frederick County early in May to campaign for reelection to the House of Burgesses. He and George Mercer won the county's two seats in the assembly despite a determined campaign by GW's former lieutenant colonel in the Virginia Regiment, Adam Stephen (see *Papers, Colonial Series,* 7:44–45).

GW contracted a bad cold during the election campaign in Frederick County in May 1761, which turned into a long, serious illness during the summer and fall of 1761. In August he went to Berkeley Springs to try to recover his health. Although he felt an improvement after a few weeks at the warm springs, he had a slight relapse while attending the House of Burgesses in October and missed some of the meetings. (On GW's illness, see *Papers, Colonial Series,* 7:60, 97, 98).

October

Octr. 22d. Began Captn. Posey's Barn with Turner Crump & Six Carpenters.

GW hired Turner Crump in Dec. 1760 at a wage of £30 per year to oversee his slave carpenters.

1762

February

20. Rented George Ashfords Plantn. to Nelson Kelly for 1000 lbs. Tobo. & Cash.

Sowed a good deal of Tobo. Seed at all my Quarters.

George Ashford of Fairfax County sold GW 135 acres of land on the west side of Dogue Run 13–14 Jan. 1762 for £165 (Fairfax County Deeds, Book E-1, 22–30). Adjoining this land on the north was another 135-acre tract that GW had bought from Ashford's brother John 29–30 Jan. 1761 for £150 (Fairfax County Deeds, Book D-1, 822–27). Both tracts lay on the east side of the land that GW purchased from Simon Pearson 14 Feb. of this year, giving him a solid 448-acre section between Dogue Run and the main road from Alexandria to Colchester. Kelly later in the year became overseer of the Dogue Run plantation.

March

2. There having fallen a Snow of abt. 2 Inches depth the Night before—I sowed thereupon, at the Meadow at Fosters, where the grass was entirely destroyd by the Winter's Frosts, Six pecks of Ray grass Seed & three quarts of Timothy Seed mixed well in Ashes.

Also Sowed, from the North Side of the Inclosure by the Quarter, to the Quarter with Ray grass, hop Clover, & Lucerne Mixed—viz. for the whole Inclosure 8 Pecks of Ray seed, 3 ditto of the Clovr., & 1 ditto of the Lucerne—but the Snow dissolving & the Wind coming out very fresh at No. West I was obligd to desist and a prodigious severe frost happeng. that Night 'tis to be fear'd the Seed all perished.

18th. Agreed to give Turner Crump one Sixth part of what he can make by my Carpenters this Year, which is to commense the 22d. day of Octr. being the time when he began Captn. Poseys Work, and to give him the Seventh of what he can make by them the Year after.

In March GW's half brother Augustine Washington died and GW went to Westmoreland County to attend the funeral. He undoubtedly gave advice and help to Augustine's family, but he refused to act as executor, probably because of the distance involved and the press of his own affairs. After his trip to Augustine's home, GW traveled to Williamsburg to attend a meeting of the House of Burgesses which began on 30 Mar.

April

5. Sowed Timothy Seed in the old Apple Orchard below the Hill.

7. Sowed—or rather sprinkled a little of Ditto on the Oats.

8. to the 10th. Getting Swamp Mud, & laying it in heaps—also got a little of the Creek Mud—Both for tryal as Manures.

14. Inspected 20 Hhds. [hogsheads] Tobo.

15. John Foster run away.

21. Sent Jno. Alton to take charge of Plantation.

> John Alton, a white servant, worked faithfully for GW for more than 30 years, accompanying him as his body servant in the Braddock campaign and later serving in various capacities at Mount Vernon. When John Foster ran away from Mount Vernon, GW sent Alton to take over the overseer's duties at the Dogue Run farm. Later in the year he transferred him to Muddy Hole to succeed Edward Violette, who was overseer at that plantation until he moved to Bullskin in 1762. At the time of his death in 1785 Alton was overseer at River Farm.

22. Attachts. in my hands for Fosters effects.

24. Had the Plantn. viewed. Herrings run in gt. quantity's. Planted new gd. at Williamson's.

26. Began to plant Corn at all my Plantation's.

May

13. Got a Cask of Leith Ale from Mr. Marshall Piscatwy. Agreed to do Mr. Bells Work for £59.

> Marshall is probably James Marshall, who owned or managed a "Public House of Entertainment" in 1761 in Piscataway, on Piscataway Creek in Prince George's County, Md., almost directly across the Potomac from Mount Vernon. At this time the thriving town was made up largely of Scottish merchants engaged in the tobacco trade. *Mr. Bells Work:* On 15 Aug. 1763 GW received £41 15s. 8d. from "Mr. Josias Bell for Carpenters w[ork]" (Ledger A, 166). Most of GW's carpenters were involved in this work during the summer of 1762. Bell was probably Josias Beall (born c.1725) of Prince George's County, Md.

28. Planted abt. 50, or 60,000—being the first—Tobo. put in. Roan's bay & sorrel covered by Mr. Rozers Traveller. English bay & black covered by Aeriel.

> Roan may have been John Roan, overseer of Claiborne's, the Custis dower plantation in King William County.
>   Ariel was a thoroughbred black stallion from the famous Belair stables in Prince George's County, Md. In 1762 he was standing at William Digges's plantation.
>   Henry Rozer or Rozier (born c.1725), of Prince George's County, Md., lived at Notley Hall, nearly opposite Alexandria (*Browne,* 309; *Brumbaugh,* 1: 85). The previous spring he had advertised in the *Maryland Gazette,* 2 April

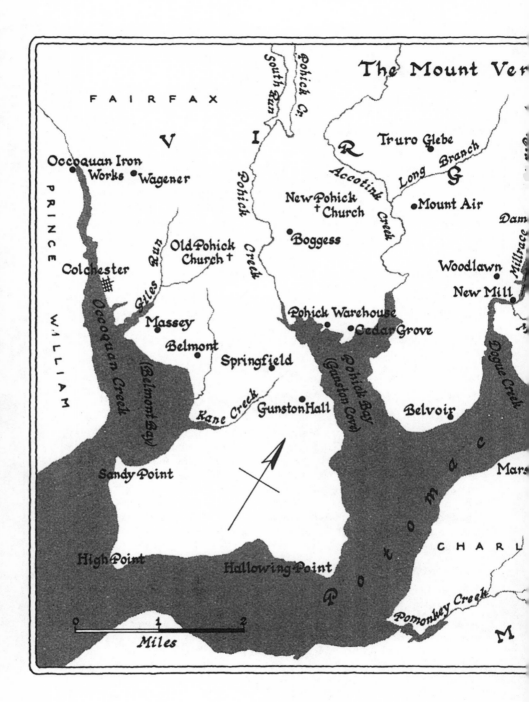

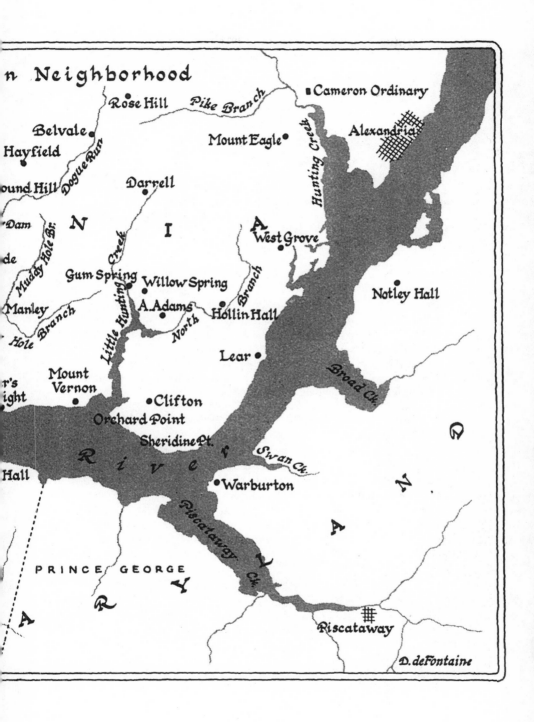

n Neighborhood

Cameron Ordinary

Rose Hill   Pike Branch

Belvale

Hayfield   Mount Eagle

Alexandria

ound Hill   Dogue Run

Darrell

Dam   N   I   A   Hunting Creek

de

Muddy Hole Br.   Little Hunting Creek

Gum Spring   West Grove

Manley   Willow Spring   North Branch   Notley Hall

Hole Branch   A. Adams

Hollin Hall

Lear   Broad Ck.

Mount
Vernon   Clifton

r's
ight   Orchard Point

Sheridine Pt.   River   Swan Ck.   D

Hall   Warburton   A

Piscataway Ck.   Y

PRINCE   GEORGE

R

A   Piscataway

D. deFontaine

1761, "Young Traveller, now in the Possession of Mr. *Henry Rozer,* in *Prince-George's* County, Covers Mares at Two Guineas. He is Five Years old, full Sixteen Hands and an Inch high, was bred by Col. *Tasker,* got by Mr. *Moreton's* Traveller in *Virginia,* and came out of Miss Colvill."

June

4. Jno. Askew came to Work.

In 1759 GW hired John Askew (Askin), a local joiner, for £25 per year plus housing. In Oct. 1761 they changed the agreement, GW now paying Askew a per diem wage that amounted to the same £25-per-year rate. For a 5-day week with 11 holidays per year Askew's pay would come to 2s. per day. Hence, as Askew was paid by the day, GW kept track of any absence or return to work by Askew.

July

15. Nancy Gist left this.

Nancy Gist, daughter of Christopher and Sarah Howard Gist, went to live with William Fairfax's family at Belvoir in 1757 while her father was on the frontier, first as a captain with the Virginia Regiment, then as deputy to Edmund Atkins, superintendent for Indian affairs in the southern colonies (William Fairfax to GW, 17 July 1757; GW to Sally Fairfax, 25 Sept. 1758, *Papers, Colonial Series,* 4:309–11, 6:41–43). She never married and after her father's death in 1759 lived with one of her brothers.

20. Recd. my Goods from the Unity—Captn. Robson. Bot. Frederick & Judy of Mr. Lewis.

Capt. William Robson of the *Unity* carried a large shipment of goods which GW had ordered from Robert Cary & Co. on behalf of himself and the two Custis children. The complete order amounted to £463 15s. 8d. and included such items as a new still, clothing, china, food, farm equipment, and books. GW wrote Cary & Co. on 18 Sept. 1762 that everything had arrived except some shoes. "There must likewise have been a mistake in Shipping the Plows, for many of the most material parts being wanting, the rest, according to the Bill of Parcells, is entirely useless, and lye upon my hands a dead charge" (*Papers, Colonial Series,* 7:153–55).

Frederick & Judy: On this date GW paid £115 to Col. Fielding Lewis for two slaves (Ledger A, 146).

27. Crump went over to Bells to work.

29. Tom also went over.

31. B. Mitchell went away.

GW employed Burgess Mitchell of Maryland 1 May 1762 as overseer of the Home House plantation, the farm on which the mansion house was located. He was to work until the end of October, for which GW was to pay him £6 plus his levy and tax and to provide him with laundry services, lodging, and food. According to the terms of the agreement, if Mitchell did not fulfill his obligations satisfactorily he could be "turned of at any season between this" and the last of October and would forfeit his wages (*Papers, Colonial Series*, 7: 131–32). He left before the six months were up.

August

2. Philip Fletcher came to making Bricks.

GW paid Philip Fletcher £14 10s. for making 78,000 nine-inch bricks, 2,125 tiles for the garden wall, and 1,080 nine-inch square flooring tiles (Ledger A, 130).

September

8. Carried the last of my Tobo. to H[untin]g C[reek] W[arehouse]. Finished sowing Wheat at Muddy hole 15 [   ].

13. Began getting Fodder at Muddy hole.

October

4. Put up 4 Hogs for forwd. Bacon at R[iver] Side.

GW left Mount Vernon for Frederick County 3 Oct. and did not return until eight days later (*Papers, Colonial Series*, 7:158).

12. Sowed Rye at Muddy hole.

18. Planted 4 Nuts of the Medateranean Pine in Garden close by the Brick Ho[use].

23. At Night set fire to brick Kiln.

27. Stopd Kiln holes about 2 oclock. Ned Violette moved off for Frederick & John Alton to Muddy hole.

Edward Violette (d. 1773) was overseer at Muddy Hole until he moved to the Bullskin plantation in 1762.

30. Sowed 3 pints of Timothy Seed below my Meadow at Ashfords.

Note—A small part on the So. West Side not broke up, but very light notwithstanding.

November

10. Set of for Williamsburg & returnd Decr. 1st.

GW apparently repeated his practice of visiting the Custis plantations on his way to Williamsburg and probably arrived in that city on 15 Nov., when he took his seat in the House of Burgesses. The fourth session of the 1761–65 assembly had begin on 2 Nov. 1762 and was a busy one, passing 44 acts before its prorogation on 23 Dec. As the assembly tended to do most of its major work in the middle half of a session, GW was present for consideration of most of the major bills, including some which must have been of particular interest to him. Among the bills passed were four that concerned military affairs; one for encouraging local manufactures; one for enlarging the growing town of Alexandria; and one for enlarging the boundaries of Truro Parish, to whose vestry he had just been elected in October. While in Williamsburg, GW stayed at Christiana Campbell's tavern on Duke of Gloucester Street near the Capitol. He also tended to some personal and financial matters; he paid Anthony Walke for the sugar and rum delivered the previous August, collected some of his burgess's allowances which allowed him 15s. per diem plus £7 10s. travel expenses per session, and visited his barber.

December

4. Finished Measg. & Lofting Corn.

6. 94 Barrls. Corn in great Corn Ho[use] at Muddy hole—when they began to use it. Mr. Adams 8 Sheep from Mudy. hole.

> GW records this delivery to Robert Adam of Alexandria in his Ledger A, 133, as "8 Fat Sheep."

1763

June

24. Began to cut Timothy at Ashfords.

30. Finished Do.—2 days Rain in the time.

> On 3 June 1763 GW attended the initial meeting, probably at Stafford Court House, of a group of Potomac Valley men who were interested in developing western lands. This meeting followed by only four months the Treaty of Paris, in which France renounced all claim to lands west of the Appalachian Mountains, thus opening these lands to settlement by the American colonists. To this end a number of colonial land companies were formed, and one of the first was the Mississippi Company, organized at this meeting. The regulations agreed upon provided for a limit of 50 members (there were never more than 40), each of whom was to get 50,000 acres, and none of whom could transfer his interest without approval of the company, thus protecting the company from infiltration by members of rival land companies. Assessments were to be provided for as needed. The company would be run by a ten-member executive committee, which was to execute the decisions of the annual meeting of the full company. For GW's involvement in the company, see *Papers, Colonial Series,* 7:219–25, 242–50, 415–17, 8:62–65, 149–53.

September

8. Agreed with Thomas Nichols a farmer to Overlook my people at Home & work wt. them for £20.

9. Began to sow wheat at C[ree]k Qrs.

On this day GW attended the first annual meeting of the Mississippi Company, held at Thomas Ludwell Lee's home, Belleview, on the south side of Potomac Creek in Stafford County. At the meeting the company agreed on a formal memorial to be submitted to the crown, appointed William Lee treasurer-secretary, and chose its ten-member executive committee, which was to meet semiannually at Westmoreland Court House. GW was not one of the ten. He paid his company quota of £8 5s. for hiring an agent in England who was to present the memorial and also invite into the company not more than nine English members "of such influence and fortune as may be likely to promote its success" (Carter, *Great Britain and the Illinois Country*, 170).

Four weeks after this meeting the crown promulgated the Proclamation Line of 1763, which prohibited any settlement west of the Appalachian Mountains. Although GW later observed to William Crawford (21 Sept. 1767) that he could "never look upon that Proclamation in any other light . . . than as a temporary expedient to quiet the Minds of the Indians and must fall of course in a few years," the presence of the Line, coupled with the instability of British ministries during the 1760s and the claims of competing land companies, caused the Mississippi Company's petition to remain dormant for the next four years.

To the Great Dismal Swamp
October 1763

The following entry, recording details of GW's visit to the Dismal Swamp south of the James River in tidewater Virginia, appears faintly in pencil on the front of the 1763 diary and is repeated, in ink, in the diary for 1764. Variations between the two texts are minor. Although the entry is dated 15 Oct., it covers his first visit to the swamp in May, while he was attending meetings of the General Assembly in Williamsburg. The notes apparently were prompted by his second visit to the area in October, during which he did not enter the swamp.

The Dismal Swamp, in southeast Virginia and northeast North Carolina, is a coastal swamp about twenty miles long which at one time extended over some two thousand square miles. It is geologically unusual in that it is higher than the surrounding land, and water drains out of it rather than into it. At its center is Lake Drummond, about three miles across, which GW calls "the Pond."

In 1763 GW and several partners including Fielding Lewis and Burwell Bassett formed a company, "Adventurers for Draining the Dismal Swamp," and the General Assembly of Virginia empowered them to construct canals and causeways through private land without being subject to suits for damages (Hening, 8:18). The purpose of the undertaking was to harvest lumber while the swamp was draining and to farm the land once it became dry. Although GW acquired land in the area and helped to finance some draining, his

Stylized artist's view of the Dismal Swamp. (Library of Congress)

*interest waned about twenty years after the following memorandum was writ-
ten. For GW's participation in the company, see* Papers, Colonial Series, *7:
269–74.*

*In these entries GW documents a trip from Suffolk, down the west side of
the swamp, across the Perquimans River to a site near present-day Elizabeth
City, N.C., then back along the eastern side of the swamp to Suffolk. Among
the landowners named by GW were some from the prominent Nansemond
County families of Riddick, Sumner, and Norfleet. Willis Riddick, from whom
GW later bought land, was a member of the House of Burgesses for many
years.*

15 Octobr. 1763

Memm. From Suffolk to Pocoson Swamp is reckoned about 6 Miles,
and something better than 4 perhaps 5 Miles from Collo. Reddicks Mill
run (where the Road x's it). The land within this distance especially
after passing Willis Reddicks is Level & not bad. The banks down to this
(Pocoson) Swamp declines gradually, and the Swamp appears to be
near 75 yds. over, but no Water in it at present. Note—Mills Riddicks
Plantn. seems to be a good one the land being level and stiff. So does
Henry Riddicks above.

From Pocoson Swamp to Cyprus Swamp (which conducts more
Water into the great Dismal than any one of the many that leads into
it) is about 2½ Miles. This also is dry at present, but appears to be 60
or 65 yards across in the wettest part.

The next Swamp to this is called Mossey Swamp and distant about
3 Miles. Near this place lives Jno. Reddick on good Land, but hitherto
from Pocoson Swamp, the land lyes flat, wet, & poor. This Swamp is
60 yards over and dry.

Between Cyprus Swamp, and the last mentioned one, we went on
horse back not less than ½ a Mile into the great Swamp (Dismal) without any sort of difficulty, the horse not sinking over the fetlocks—the
first quarter however abounding in Pine and Gallbury bushes, the soil
being much intermixed with Sand but afterwards it grew blacker and
richer with many young Reeds & few pines and this it may be observed
here is the nature of the Swamp in general.

From Mossey Swamp to a branch and a large one it is, of Oropeak
(not less than 80 yards over) is reckoned 4 Miles—two Miles short of
which is a large Plantation belonging to one Brindle near to which (on
the South side) passes the Carolina line.

The Main Swamp of Oropeak is about ½ a Mile onwards from this,
where stands the Widow Norflets Mi⟨ll⟩ & luke Sumners Plantations.

This Sw⟨amp⟩ cannot be less than 200 yards across but does not nevertheless discharge as much Water as Cyprus Swamp.

At the Mouth of this Swamp is a very large Meadow of 2 or 3000 Acr⟨es⟩ held by Sumner, Widow Norflet, Marmaduke Norflet, Powel & others & valuable ground it is.

From Oropeak Swamp to loosing Swamp is about 2 Miles, and this 70 yards across.

From hence again to Bassey Swamp the lower Road may be allowed 2 Miles More but this Swamp seems trifling.

And from Bassey Swamp to Horse Pool (which is the last, & including Swamp running into the Dismal) is about 2 Miles more & 35 yards across only.

The whole Land from Pocoson Swamp to this place and indeed all the way to Pequemen Bridge is in a manner a dead level—wet & cold in some places—sandy in others and generally poor.

This last named Swamp—viz. the Horse pool, is called 9 Miles from the upper Bridge on Pequemin River; within a Mile of which lives one Elias Stallens, and within 5 Miles is the lower Bridge—from whence to the bridge, or Ferry over little River is 15 measured Miles the course nearly due South as it likewise is from Suffolk to the said Bridge the Dismal running that course from that place.

From little River Bridge (or Ferry) to Ralphs Ferry on Paspetank is (I think we were told) abt. 16 Miles, the course East or No. East; and from thence if the ferry is not crossed along up the West Side of the River to the Rivr. Bridge of the said Paspetank is reckoned —— Miles and about a No. Wt. course the Dismal bordering close upon the left all the way.

Note—the above Acct. is from Information only, for instead of taking that Rout, we crossed from Elias Stallens (one Miles above the upper bridge on Pequemin) across to a set of People which Inhabit a small slipe of Land between the said River Pequemen & the Dismal Swamp and from thence along a new cut path through the Main Swamp a Northerly course for 5 Miles to the Inhabitants of what they call new found land which is thick settled, very rich Land, and about 6 Miles from the aforesaid River Bridge of Paspetank. The Arm of the Dismal which we passed through to get to this New land (as it is called) is 3¼ Miles Measured—Little or no timber in it, but very full of Reeds & excessive Rich. Thro. this we carried horses—without any great difficulty.

This Land was formerly esteemed part of the Dismal but being higher tho' full of Reeds People ventured to settle upon it and as it became more open, it became more dry & is now prodigeous fine land but subject to wets & unhealthiness.

It is to be observed here that the tide, or still Water that comes out of the sound up Pequemen River flows up as high as Stallens, and the River does not widen much untill it passes the lower Bridge some little distance. At Ralphs ferry upon Paspetank the River is said to be 2 Miles over, and decreases in width gradually to the bridge called River bridge, where it is about 30 yards across and affords sufficient Water for New England Vessels to come up and Load.

From what observations we were capable of making it appeared, as if the swamp had very little fall (I mean the Waters out of the great Swp.) into the heads of these Rivers which seems to be a demonstration that the Swamp is much lower on the South & East Sides because it is well known that there is a pretty considerable fall on the West side through all the drains that make into Nansemond River & the Western Branch of Elizabeth at the North End of the Dismal.

From the River Bridge of Paspetank to an Arm of the Dismal at a place called 2 Miles Bridge is reckoned 7 Miles, & a branch of Paspetank twice crossed in the distance.

This Arm of the Dismal is equally good & Rich like the rest & runs (as we were informed) 15 or 20 Miles Easterly, and has an outlet (as some say) into Curratuck Inlet by No. West River, or Tulls C[ree]k but these accts. were given so indistinctly as not to be relied upon. However it is certain I believe that the Water does drain of at the East end somewhere, in which case a common causay through at the crossing place woud most certainly lay all that Arm dry.

From this place wch. is 2 Miles over to the Carolina line is about 4 Miles, and from thence to No. West landing on No. West Rivr. a branch of Curratuck, is 3 Miles more.

Note—the Carolina line crosses the Swamp in a West direction, and is 15 Miles from the place where it enters to its coming out of the same near Brindles Plantation. Flats and small Craft load at No. West landing.

To the great Bridge from No. West landing is accounted 12 Miles the Lands good, as they are on all this (East) side and highly esteemed valued in general according to the Propretors own Accts. from 20/. to £3. pr. acre but we were told they were to be had for less. This gt. Bridge is upon the South Branch of Elizabeth River & abt. 10 Miles from Norfolk and heads in the Dismal as does likewise No. West River Paspetank little River & Pequemen.

From the Great Bridge to Collo. Tuckers Mills is about 8 Miles within which distance several small Creeks making out of South Rivr. head up in the Dismal.

Farleys Plantation at the Forks of the Road is reckoned 5 Miles from the aforesaid Mills near to which the dismal runs.

From hence to Roberts's Ord[inar]y is 6 Miles and from thence to Suffolk 10 more. The lands from the Great bridge to within a Mile or two of Roberts's is generally sandy & indifferent. From hence to Cowpers Mill they are good & from thence to Collo. Reddicks Mean again.

Note—from the River B. on Paspetank to the Great Bridge on South River the Road runs nearly North and from thence to Farleys Plantation it seems to be about West from this again to Collo. Reddicks (or Suffolk) So. Wt. and from thence to Pequemen B. & little Rivr. South as beforemend. the Swamp bordering near to the Road all the way round—in some place close adjoining & in others 2 and 3 Miles distant.

1764

June

11. Finishd (with two Plows) the Gd. behind the Garden wch. was begun the 4th.

12. Began to cut Meadow (Creek).

13. Meazured of 64 Gallons & put undr. Bishops care for Harvest &ca.

1765

March

5th. March 1765. Grafted 15 English Mulberrys on wild Mulberry Stocks on the side of the Hill near the Spring Path. Note the Stocks were very Milkey.

May

30. Peter Green came to me [as] a Gardener.

> Apparently Peter Green was on a yearly wage contract of £5. In 1771 GW was trying to find a good "Kitchen Gardener" on a four- or five-year indenture at a moderate wage, and even inquired in Scotland. He hired David Cowan, "late of Fredericksburg," as a gardener for the year 1773. According to the articles of agreement signed 11 Jan. 1773, Cowan agreed to serve "in the capacity of a Gardener; & that he will work duely & truely, during that time, at the business; and also when need be, or when thereunto required, employ himself in Grafting, Budding, & pruning of Fruit Trees and Vines—likewise in Saving, at proper Seasons, and due order, Seeds of all kinds." His salary was £25, plus lodging and food for his family.
>
> The diary entries for the month of May are taken from a loose sheet in the Dreer Collection, Historical Society of Pennsylvania, Philadelphia.

September

28. This Week my Carpenters workd 22 day's upon my Schooner. And John Askew 3 days upon her.

> GW revised his contract with his joiner Askew in April 1764, now paying him per diem at the rate of £4 per month. In Dec. 1765 Askew agreed to supervise GW's slave carpenters for an annual salary of £35 per year plus some provisions and to pay GW £7 10s. per year for rent. Askew's employment ended in the spring of 1767.

1767

February

13th. Vestry to meet by 2d. appointmt.

> Some of GW's diary entries, such as these three in February, are appointment reminders rather than a record of occurrences. The vestry of Truro Parish met on 23 Feb.

16th. Vestry to meet at Pohick.

26. Sale of Colo. Colvills Negroes.

> Thomas Colvill died in 1766, and these slaves apparently were sold to pay some of his debts. On his deathbed Colvill had persuaded GW to be one of his executors by assuring him that he would be expected only to give his good name to the administration of the will and to check occasionally on its progress, while the actual work was done by the other executors: Colvill's wife Frances (d. 1773) and John West, Jr., husband of Colvill's niece Catherine. As it happened, the estate was so troublesome and Mrs. Colvill and West proved to be so unequal to their task that GW had to take an active part in the matter, which was to plague him until 1797 (GW to Bushrod Washington, 10 Feb. 1796, Washington Papers, Library of Congress). For details of GW's involvement in the Colvill estate, see *Papers, Presidential Series*, 1:63–66. One difficulty was that Colvill had left legacies to English relatives who could not be easily identified and whose confusing claims were almost impossible to authenticate. A second problem was that in May 1765 Colvill, as executor for his brother John, had sold Merryland, a 6,300-acre tract in Frederick County, Md., to John Semple of Prince William County, Va., for £2,500 sterling. That sum was to have paid John's debts, including £742 owed to Thomas, but Semple gave a bond for the £2,500, which he was later unwilling or unable to honor. Thus, neither Colvill estate could be settled until some agreement could be reached with the contentious Semple.

1768

January

Jany. 1st. Fox huntg. in my own Neck with Mr. Robt. Alexander and Mr. Colvill—catchd nothing. Captn. Posey with us.

Although GW's friend John Posey joined in the chase today and on other occasions during the next few months, he was now, in GW's opinion, a man "reduced to the last Shifts," for he was being destroyed financially by enormous debts that he had acquired over the past several years. See *Papers, Colonial Series,* 8:34–37. GW was one of Posey's principal creditors, holding mortgages on his lands and slaves for a total of £820 Virginia currency. With interest accumulating at the rate of £41 a year and miscellaneous charges against him, Posey now owed GW nearly £1,000 (Ledger A, 168, 256). But Posey was strongly opposed to selling his property to clear his books and had begged GW several times to lend him more money in order to avoid that end. GW had agreed not to press Posey for repayment of his previous loans and was willing to act as his security for a £200 sterling loan from George Mason, but he refused to advance Posey any more cash (GW to Posey, 24 June and 24 Sept. 1767, *Papers, Colonial Series,* 8:1–4, 34–37).

2. Surveying some Lines of my Mt. Vernon Tract of Land.

The Mount Vernon tract was the original Washington family land on Little Hunting Creek, part of a grant for 5,000 acres between Little Hunting and Dogue creeks that the proprietors of the Northern Neck had made 1 Mar. 1674 to Col. Nicholas Spencer (d. 1689) of Albany, Westmoreland County, and GW's great-grandfather, Lt. Col. John Washington (1632–1677) of Bridges Creek, Westmoreland County (Northern Neck Deeds and Grants, Book 5, 207–8). The Spencer-Washington grant was divided in 1690 between Colonel Spencer's widow, Frances Mottram Spencer (died c.1727), and John Washington's son Lawrence Washington (1659-1697/98). Mrs. Spencer chose the western half of the grant which bordered on Dogue Creek, or Epsewasson Creek as the Indians had called it, and Lawrence Washington took the eastern half on Little Hunting Creek. The Little Hunting Creek tract was inherited by Lawrence's daughter Mildred Washington (1696–c.1745), who, after her marriage to Roger Gregory of King and Queen County, sold it for £180 to her brother Augustine Washington, GW's father (deed of Roger and Mildred Gregory to Augustine Washington, 19 Oct. 1726, owned by Mount Vernon). From Augustine the tract passed to GW's half brother Lawrence, who during the 1740s named it Mount Vernon. After Lawrence's death in 1752, his widow Ann and her second husband, George Lee (1714–1761) of Westmoreland County, rented the tract and 18 slaves to GW for her lifetime at the rate of 15,000 pounds of tobacco or £93 15s. Virginia currency a year, and upon Ann's death in 1761, it became GW's outright by virtue of a provision in Lawrence's will. Although the tract was originally supposed to contain about 2,500 acres, it now contained only about 2,126 acres because of a change in the northern boundary that had been made about 1741.

3. At Home with Doctr. Rumney.

Dr. William Rumney (d. 1783), who was born and trained in England, served as a surgeon with the British army in the French and Indian War and settled in Alexandria in 1763.

11. Running some Lines between me and Mr. Willm. Triplet.

Triplett's land bordered on part of GW's Dogue Run farm.

12. Attempted to go into the Neck on the Ice but it wd. not bear. In the Evening Mr. Chs. Dick Mr. Muse & my Brother Charles came here.

> Charles Dick (b. 1715), of Caroline and Spotsylvania counties, supplied GW's troops in 1754–55 as a Virginia commissary for the British forces. By 1768 Dick's mercantile business was centered in Fredericksburg. George Muse of Caroline County married Elizabeth Battaile (d. 1786) in 1749 and had a son, Battaile Muse (1751–1803), who also appears in the diaries.

13. At Home with them—Col. Fairfax, Lady, &[   ]

14. Ditto—Do. Colo. Fx. & famy. went home in the Evening.

15. At Home with the above Gentlemen and Shooting together.

16. At home all day at Cards—it snowing.

> GW lost 3s. 6d. in playing cards with his friends (Ledger A, 269).

18. Went to Court & sold Colo. Colvils Ld. Returned again at Night.

> As an executor for Thomas Colvill's estate, GW signed an advertisement in Rind's *Virginia Gazette* (24 Dec. 1767) announcing that "upwards of six hundred acres of valuable Land . . . will be sold to the highest bidder, at the courthouse of *Fairfax* county, on the 3d *Monday* in next month (being court day)."
> GW today recorded losing 11s. 3d. at cards (Ledger A, 269).

21. Surveyd the Water courses of my Mt. Vernon Tract of Land—taking advant. of the Ice.

> The freezing over of the Potomac River and Little Hunting Creek enabled GW to survey their shorelines on this day more easily than usual.

22. Fox hunting with Captn. Posey, started but catchd nothing.

27. Went out again—started a Fox abt. 10. Run him till 3 and lost him.

30. Dined at Belvoir and returnd in the Afternoon. Borrowd a hound from Mr. Whiting—as I did 2 from Mr. Alexr. the 28th.

> GW was connected with the Whiting family of Gloucester County through his uncle John Washington (1692–1743), who had married Catherine Whiting (1694–1734), daughter of Henry and Elizabeth Whiting of Gloucester County. The Mr. Whiting who loaned GW the dog today may be Catherine's nephew Francis Whiting (d. 1775), who was born in Gloucester County and moved to the Shenandoah Valley later in his life. Francis's older brother Beverley Whiting (c.1707–1755), burgess of Gloucester County, may have been the Beverley Whiting who was one of GW's godfathers.

31. At Home alone all day.

Observations

Jany. 1st. Neck People clearing a piece of ground which was begun the 23d. of Decr.

Doeg Run People working in the Swamp which they began to clear this Fall.

Muddy hole People (except two threshing) clearing the Skirt of woods within the fence 4 Men & 2 Women from Doeg Run assisting.

Mill People also clearing.

6. Doeg Run People finishd grubbing the Swamp they were in and proceeded to another adjacent.

12. Threshing Wheat at all Plantations Ground being too hard froze to Grub to any advantage.

16. Finishd my Smiths shop—that is the Carpenters work of it.

18. Carpenters went to Saw Plank at Doeg Run for finishing the Barn there.

Will put new girders into my Mill where they had Sunk.

19. Mike, Tom, & Sam went abt. the Overseers House at Muddy hole.

20. Plantations chiefly employd in getting out Wheat.

22. Davy, George, Jupiter and Ned, finishd Sawing at Doeg Run & Joind Mike &ca. abt. Overseers House at Muddy hole.

February

Where & how—my time is Spent.

1st. Rid round into the Neck and directed the running of a Fence there.

2. Rid to Muddy hole—Doeg Run & Mill.

3. Fox hunting with Captn. Posey & Ld. Washington. Started but catchd nothg.

> Lund Washington (1737–1796), a distant cousin of GW, was the son of Townshend and Elizabeth Lund Washington, of the Chotank area, where GW spent part of his youth. In 1765 GW hired him as manager for his Mount Vernon plantations, and he remained in charge of Mount Vernon when GW assumed command of the Continental Army in 1775.

6. Fox hunting with Mr. Alexander & Captn. Posey. Started but catchd nothing.

12. Fox hunting with Colo. Fairfax, Captn. McCarty, Mr. Chichester, Posey, Ellzey & Manley who dined here with Mrs. Fairfax & Miss Nicholas. Catchd two foxes.

Richard Chichester (c.1736–1796) was a distant relation of GW. He was living at this time in Fauquier County, marrying Sarah McCarty (d. 1826), daughter of his cousin Capt. Daniel McCarty of Mount Air, here mentioned. In 1774 Chichester bought land on Accotink Creek in Fairfax County, near McCarty's home and settled there with his family for the rest of his life.

Harrison Manley (d. 1773), was one of GW's closest neighbors. Manley occasionally sold wheat to GW and used the services of GW's mill, blacksmith shop, and weaving shop as part payment in return (Ledger B, 9).

Two daughters of Wilson and Sarah Cary—Sarah and Elizabeth—married the brothers George William and Bryan Fairfax. A third daughter, Anne Cary (b. 1733), married Robert Carter Nicholas (1728–1780) of James City County and had four daughters, one of whom, probably either Sarah Nicholas (b. 1752) or Elizabeth Nicholas (1753–1810), is the Miss Nicholas who appears here.

13. Hunting in the same Company. Catchd 2 More foxes. None dined at Mt. Vernon.

GW today lent Ellzey £10 (Ledger A, 269).

16. Went up to Alexa. and returnd in the Eveng.

While GW was in town today he received £75 cash as part payment for wheat sold to the Alexandria firm of John Carlyle & Robert Adam. During the late 1760s GW sold most of his wheat to the firm and regularly drew on his account with it for his cash needs (Ledger A, 180, 271, 280, 310, 326).

17. Rid to Muddy hole, Doeg Run, & the Mill. Returnd to Dinner and alone.

18. Went a ducking between breakfast & dinner. In the Afternoon Mr. Thruston Mr. Alexander, & Mr. Carter from Gloster came in.

Charles Mynn Thruston (1738–1812), originally of Gloucester County, raised a body of volunteers in 1758 and joined William Byrd's Virginia Regiment as a lieutenant. In the fall of 1764 Thruston, having been chosen minister of Petsworth Parish, Gloucester County, went to England to take orders and was licensed for Virginia in Aug. 1765. The Alexander family of Gloucester County had been headed by David Alexander (d. 1750), who immigrated to Virginia from England. This Mr. Alexander may have been David's son Morgan Alexander (b. 1746), who, like Thruston, was now looking for land, in either Loudoun or Frederick County, where he could settle. There were several Carter families in Gloucester County at this time.

19. After dinner the above Gentlemen went to Belvoier.

20. Fox hunting with Captn. Posey. Catchd a Fox.

22. Rid to Muddy hole, Doeg Run and the Mill before Dinner and went out with my Gun after it.

23. Fox hunting with Captn. Posey. Catchd a Fox we suppose, but being dark coud not find it.

On this day, while ordering a butt of Madeira wine from a dealer in the Madeira Islands, GW asked for some cuttings of the grape. As if suspecting that the request would run counter to the policy of the vintners, he wrote, "but if in requiring this last Article there be any sort of Impropriety I beg that no notice may be taken of it" (GW to Scott, Pringle, Cheape & Co., 23 Feb. 1768).

24. Went a ducking between breakfast & dinner & killd 2 Mallards & 5 bald faces. Found Doctr. Rumney here at Dinner who staid all Night.

Rumney had come to see GW's stepdaughter, Martha Parke Custis, who was known as Patsy (Patcy) to her family and friends. Now 11 or 12 years old, Patsy had suffered from epilepsy at least since the age of 6, and with the beginning of her adolescence, the malady showed no signs of abating (receipt from James Carter, 12 April 1762, Custis Papers, Virginia Historical Society). On this occasion Rumney prescribed 12 powders of unidentified composition, "a vial of Nervous Drops," and a package of valerian, a drug that was thought to be useful in controlling epileptic spasms (receipt from William Rumney, 18 Feb. 1769, Custis Papers, Virginia Historical Society; Hooper, *Lexicon-Medicum,* 981). But these medicines, and the many others that would be tried in the future, could not relieve Patsy's condition. She was beyond the help of eighteenth-century physicians, and much to the dismay of her family, epileptic attacks would plague her at frequent intervals until one caused her death in July 1773.

26. Laid of a Road from Mt. Vernon to the Lain by Mr. Manleys.

27. Went on the Road, clearing between Mt. Vernon, and the Mill. In the Evening Mr. Stedlar came.

In 1765 GW hired John Stedlar, a local music teacher, for the purpose of "teaching Mrs. Washington & two Childn Musick" (Ledger A, 231). During the next six years Stedlar frequently visited Mount Vernon to give lessons, mostly to the children. Patsy was learning to play the spinet, and her brother, John Parke Custis, the fiddle (GW to Robert Cary & Co., 12 Oct. 1761 and 20 July).

28. In the Afternoon went up to Mr. Robt. Alexanders in order to meet Mr. B. Fairfax & others a fox Huntg. None came this day but Captn. Posey.

Robert Alexander lived just north of Four Mile Run. He had inherited the house and 904 acres of land from his father, Gerard Alexander (will of Gerard Alexander, 9 Aug. 1760, Fairfax County Wills, Book B-1, 327–29).

Observations

Feby. 1st. Carpenters all (except Will) Went to Sawing Pailing for a Goose yard.

18. Rais'd Overseers House at Muddy hole. Finishd Threshing & cleaning my Wheat at Doeg Run Plantn. [   ] Bushl.

26. Began to deliver my Wheat to Mr. Kirk.

Carpenters not having quite finishd the Overseers Ho[use] at Muddy hole for want of some Plank went abt. a Corn Ho[use] there.

Much abt. this time a Hound Bitch Mopsey of Mr. R. Alexanders (now with me) was proud, & shut up chiefly with a black dog Taster who lind her several times as did Tipler once, that is known of. The little Bitch Cloe in the House was also proud at the same time—but whether lined or not cannot be known. See how long they go with Pup—and whether both the sametime—being very difft. in size.

> James Kirk, an emigrant from England, established himself as a wheat merchant and also invested heavily in western lands. He kept a store and office in Alexandria and maintained a country residence across the Potomac in Maryland. GW's wheat is today being loaded on a ship owned by Kirk for Carlyle & Adam, the purchasers.

March

Where & how my time is Spent.

Mar. 1st. Went a fox hunting with the two Alexrs. and Posey. Was during the chase (in which nothing was catchd) joind by Mr. Fairfax, Jno. Alexander & Muir.

> John Alexander (1735–1775), of King George and Stafford counties, was a burgess from Stafford County 1765–75. John Muir (c.1731–1791), of Dumfries, Scot., settled as a merchant in Alexandria; in 1758 he was chosen a town trustee.

2. Hunting again, & catchd a fox with a bobd Tail & cut Ears, after 7 hours chase in wch. most of the Dogs were worsted.

3. Returnd home much disordered by a Lax, Griping and violent straining.

4. At Home, worse with the above complaints. Sent for Doctr. Rumney, who came in the Afternn.

5. Very bad the Doctr. staying with me.

6. Something better—Doctr. still here—& Mr. Ramsay came down to see me.

7. Rather better. Doctr. went home after breakfast. Mr. Ramsay staid to Dinner.

8. Mending fast. Colo. Thos. Moore calld here on his way from Alexa. Home, but made no stay. Colo. Fairfax, & Mr. Gilbt. Campbell (Comptroller) Dined here.

Thomas Moore, who was heavily indebted to the estate of the late Speaker of the House of Burgesses, John Robinson (d. 1766) of King and Queen County, was now trying to renew his bond to GW for his debt to the Custis estate, which GW had been carrying, with interest, for eight years (Ledger A, 204).

Gilbert Campbell, of Westmoreland County, was comptroller of the South Potomac Naval District. Campbell was a signer of the Westmoreland County association to prevent the execution of the Stamp Act in the colony, 27 Feb. 1766, and was still serving as comptroller in 1776.

11. At home alone all day.

12. Rid to the new Road—Mill, Doeg Run & Muddy hole Plantns. & found Doctr. Rumney upon my return, who dind & stayd all Night.

During this visit Rumney treated Patsy Custis with valerian and powders and applied some type of plaster (receipt from William Rumney, 18 Feb. 1769, Custis Papers, Virginia Historical Society). GW today paid him £5 in cash (Ledger A, 269).

13. At Home alone all day.

14. With the people working upon the New Road between breakfast and Dinner.

15. At home alone all day.

16. Hunting with Captn. Posey & L[un]d W. Started and catchd a fox in abt. three hours.

25. Went into the Neck. Grafted some Cherries & began to manure the ground for my Grapevines.

26. Went Fox huntg.—but started nothing. Mr. Lawe. Washington came here & Miss Ramsay in the Afternoon.

Mr. Lawe. Washington: probably Lawrence Washington (1728–c.1809), usually called "of Chotank," the son of John and Mary Massey Washington and first cousin to Lund Washington. His home was on a bluff of the Potomac River near Chotank Creek. This Lawrence was one of the two Chotank cousins remembered in GW's will as "acquaintances and friends of my Juvenile years." Lund Washington also had a brother named Lawrence (1740–1799), who may be the one referred to here.

William Ramsay (1716–1785) and his wife Ann McCarty Ramsay (c.1730–1785) had two sons and five daughters. "Miss Ramsay" is probably the eldest daughter, Elizabeth, who appears in the diaries variously as "Betsy," "Betcy," and "Betty."

29. Fox hunting—with Jacky Custis & Ld. Washington. Catchd a fox after 3 hrs. chase.

Jacky: GW's stepson, John Parke Custis, who was described by GW in May of this year as "a boy of good genius, about 14 yrs. of age, untainted in his Morals, & of innocent Manners. Two yrs. and upwards he has been reading of Virgil, and was . . . entered upon the Greek Testament" (GW to Jonathan Boucher, 30 May 1768).

30. Rid to Muddy hole—Doeg Run & Mill Plantation's.

Observations

12. Large parts of my Wheat Field at Doeg Run—the same I believe at the Mill—were found to be exceedingly Injurd by the Frost (and I apprehend by the last frost abt. the 7 & 8th. Instt.). Upon examining the Wheat which appeard to be so much hurt, I found the Roots for the most part were entirely out of the ground. Some indeed had a small fibre or so left in, & here perhaps a green blade might be found in a bunch, but where the Root was quite Out the whole bunch seemd perishd & Perishing.

Note. Watch the Progess of this Wheat, & see if there be any possibility of its taking Root again (as it lyes thick on the gd.). Near a stake in the 18 Inch Cut and abt. 100 yds. from the Barracks is a spot of an Acre or so of this kind. Observe this place—being poor gd. also.

Carpenters returnd from the Road abt. Muddy hole Corn House.

16. Began to list Corn Ground at Muddy hole. Recd. my Goods from Mr. Cary by Captn. Johnston. Sent my Vessel abt. 4 Oclock in the Afternoon to Mr. Kirk agreeable to his Letter.

John Johnstoun, captain of the *Lord Cambden,* was delivering GW's major spring shipment of supplies from England; the shipment comprised a great variety of goods collected from 39 different London shops, including a set of surveyor's instruments for John Parke Custis and some harpsichord music for Patsy. These were all gathered together and shipped by Robert Cary & Co., which was the major London merchant house for the Custis estates and subsequently was retained by GW after his marriage to Martha Dandridge Custis.

18. Began to lay of my Corn ground in the Neck.

19. Sent Chaunter (a Hound Bitch) up to Toulston; to go to Mr. Fairfax's Dog Forester—or Rockwood—She appearg. to be going Proud. Forrester not beg. at Home she went to Rockwood.

26. My Vessel returnd from Mr. Kirks employ abt. sundown—being 10 days gone.

Memms.

If Ewes & Lambs are restraind from Wheat Fields, & no green food sowd to support them in the Spring—contrive that no more fall after this year till the last of March.

April

Where & how—my time is Spent

April 1st. At home with Mr. Crawford.

William Crawford's visit was not purely social. By the fall of 1767 GW had concluded that because the survey of the Pennsylvania-Maryland boundary line (Mason and Dixon's Line) would soon be completed, and because western expansion (temporarily barred by the Royal Proclamation of Oct. 1763) would soon be at least partially opened up by a treaty with the Indians, the time was ripe for acquiring tracts of choice land in western Pennsylvania and the Ohio Valley. GW made a major effort between 1769 and 1773 to acquire for himself and other Virginians land promised to those who had fought in the French and Indian War. At the outbreak of that war, Robert Dinwiddie, lieutenant governor of Virginia, signed a proclamation dated 11 Feb. 1754 setting aside 200,000 acres on the Ohio River for the officers and men who voluntarily served in the upcoming campaign against the French. Nine years later, in 1763, a royal proclamation rewarded the officers and men who had served in America during the French and Indian War with tracts of western land, ranging from 50 acres for privates to 5,000 acres for field officers. Because the Proclamation of 1763 had closed the transmontane west to settlement, the Virginia veterans were not able to acquire their bounty lands under either proclamation for nearly a decade after the war. On 15 Dec. 1769, however, GW petitioned the Virginia governor and council on behalf of the officers and men of the Virginia Regiment of 1754 for the 200,000 acres of land promised them by Dinwiddie. The council agreed that 200,000 acres would be surveyed along the Great Kanawha and Ohio rivers for the benefit of the 1754 veterans (*Va. Exec. Jls.*, 6:337–38). William Crawford, who often served as GW's agent in the west, made the first survey in 1771. GW received four tracts of land surveyed by Crawford, three on the Ohio River between the Little Kanawha and Great Kanawha rivers totaling 9,157 acres and one tract of 10,990 acres along the Great Kanawha. In the second bounty allotment under the Proclamation of 1754, made in November 1773, he secured a tract of 7,276 acres on the Great Kanawha, 3,953 acres in his own right and the rest by a trade with George Muse (ibid., 513–14, 548–49).

On 6 Nov. 1773, after gaining the Virginia council's approval for the second allotment of land under the Proclamation of 1754, GW persuaded the governor and council to authorize warrants of survey on the "western waters" for those entitled to land under the Royal Proclamation of 1763 (Hening, 7:663–69). Under the second proclamation GW was entitled to 5,000 acres for his own service as colonel of the Virginia Regiment. In addition, he already had purchased shares entitling him to an additional 5,000 acres from other officers, and in 1774 he obtained the right to purchase 3,000 more acres through his purchase of a warrant of survey from a former captain in the 2d Virginia Regiment.

Crawford's appearance today at Mount Vernon, allowing land discussions that were spread over a six-day period, was GW's first opportunity to confer personally with his man in the field.

2. Rid to Muddy hole—Doeg Run & the Mill. Mr. Crawford went to Alexandria.

3. Went to Pohick Church & returnd to Dinner. Mr. Crawford returnd in the Afternoon.

6. Mr. Crawford set of home, and we (together w. Miss Betcy Ramsay) went up to Alexa. to a Ball.

7. We returnd from Alexandria thro Snow.

17. Went to a Church & returnd to Dinner.

18. Went to Court and returnd in the Evening.

24. Mr. & Mrs. Peake & their daughter dined here as also did Mr. Stedlar.

> Humphrey Peake of Willow Spring married Mary Stonestreet, daughter of Butler Stonestreet (d. 1755) of Prince George's County, Md. Of the two daughters of Humphrey and Mary Peake, this is probably the elder, Ann Peake (d. 1827), often referred to in the diaries as "Nancy."

26. Set of for Williamsburg with Mrs. Washington, Jacky & Patcy Custis & Billy Bassett. Lodgd. at Mr. Lawsons.

> GW may have originally planned to combine this visit to Eltham and Williamsburg with attendance at a session of the House of Burgesses, which although scheduled to open on 1 May, had met from 31 Mar. to 16 April. Billy is William Bassett (1760–1775), eldest son of Mrs. Washington's sister Anna Maria Dandridge Bassett and Col. Burwell Bassett of Eltham. The Washingtons probably stayed at the home of Thomas Lawson, who ran John Tayloe's ironworks on Neabsco Creek, Prince William County, from which GW bought bar iron in 1761.

27. Reachd Fredericksburg.

28. Stayed there all day at Colo. Lewis.

30. Breakfasted at Todds Bridge—dind at Claibornes & came to Colo. Bassetts.

> From Todd's Bridge on the Mattaponi River, GW's party followed his regular route through King William County to a fork in the road just beyond King William Court House. About nine miles beyond Sweet Hall was Col. Burwell Bassett's home, Eltham, which he inherited as the eldest surviving son of his father, William Bassett (1709–c.1743).
>
> GW today paid a Dr. Lee, possibly Arthur Lee, £2 3s. 9d. for treatment of Patsy Custis (Ledger A, 269).

May

Where & how—my time is Spent.

2. Went to Williamsburg with Colo. Bassett, Colo. Lewis & Mr. Dick. Dind with Mrs. Dawson & went to the Play.

Mrs. Dawson was born Elizabeth Churchill (c.1709–1779), daughter of Col. William and Elizabeth Churchill of Middlesex County. In 1729 she married Col. William Bassett (1709–c.1743) of Eltham, by whom she had at least five children, one of whom was Col. Burwell Bassett. After the death of her first husband, Elizabeth Churchill Bassett moved to the Bassett family town house in Williamsburg, two blocks south of the market square. In 1752 she married Rev. William Dawson, then commissary of the Church of England in Virginia, who died within a fortnight after the wedding.

The play was given in Williamsburg's second theater, built by local subscription in 1751 behind the Capitol on Waller Street. In 1768 a group of players—male and female—was formed by David Verling, their actor-manager, into the Virginia Company. After opening in Norfolk they moved to Williamsburg, where they opened their run on 31 March, coinciding with the meeting of the Burgesses. Which play GW saw is not known; the Virginia Company had a broad repertory, including Restoration comedy, eighteenth-century satire such as the popular *Beggar's Opera* by John Gay, and many of the plays of William Shakespeare, who was being "rediscovered" by the eighteenth-century English theater (see Rankin, *Theater in Colonial America*).

3. Dined with the Speaker.

The Speaker: Peyton Randolph (c.1721–1775), son of Sir John and Susanna Beverley Randolph, was king's attorney and burgess for Williamsburg. From Nov. 1766 until the Revolution, Randolph served as Speaker of the House of Burgesses.

4. Dined with Mrs. Dawson, & suppd at Charlton's.

Richard Charlton (d. 1779) had announced in June 1767 that he had opened "the Coffee-House" in Williamsburg "as a Tavern," and GW had supped there on a visit to the city the previous fall (*Va. Gaz.*, P&D, 25 June 1767; Ledger A, 262).

5. Dined at Mrs. Campbells.

Christiana Campbell's tavern was GW's habitual lodging place in Williamsburg from 1761 to 1771. On this visit to the city, he paid Mrs. Campbell £2 10s. "for Board," which included his lodgings as well as the daily breakfasts and other occasional meals that he ate at the tavern (Ledger A, 274). Mrs. Campbell (1722–1792) was described by a young Scottish merchant in 1783 as "a little old Woman, about four feet high; & equally thick, a little turn up Pug nose, a mouth screw'd up to one side" (Macaulay, "Journal," 187–88). The daughter of a Williamsburg innkeeper named John Burdett (d. 1746), she had married Dr. Ebenezer Campbell, an apothecary in Bland-ford, and had lived there with him until his death about 1752. Returning to Williamsburg a short time later, she had by 1760 begun to operate her tavern on Duke of Gloucester Street in the second block from the Capitol.

9. Went a Fox hunting and catched a Fox after 35 Minutes chace; returnd to Dinner & found the Attorney his Lady & daughter there.

> John Randolph (c.1728–1784), of Williamsburg, succeeded his older brother
> Peyton Randolph as attorney general of Virginia in 1766. John married
> Ariana Jennings (1730–1801) of Maryland, who bore him a son, Edmund,
> and two daughters, Susanna and Ariana. Like GW, John Randolph was an
> avid gardener, and he wrote a book on vegetable gardening (probably dur-
> ing the 1760s) which became the first gardening book published in the
> American colonies (see Randolph, *Treatise on Gardening*). At the outbreak of
> the American Revolution Randolph supported the crown and fled to En-
> gland in 1775.

10. Rid to the Brick House & returnd to Dinner—after which went a
dragging for Sturgeon.

> The phrase "the Brick House" referred originally (in the seventeenth cen-
> tury) to a particular house built of brick, indicating how unusual such a
> building was in the early years of the colony. The original house lay about
> three miles east of Eltham on the south side of the York River across from
> West Point; after 1738 it was also the location of the Brick House tobacco
> warehouse. By the mid–eighteenth century the Brick House lent its name to
> its immediate surrounding neighborhood, which is the sense in which GW
> refers to it here.

21. Reachd my Brothr. John's who & his wife were up the Country.
Crossd over to Mr. Booths.

22. Went to Church (nomony) & returnd to Mr. Booths to Dinner who
was also from home in Glousester. Mr. Smith the Parson dind with us.

> Nomini Church was on the east bank of Nomini Creek about 3½ miles up-
> stream from William Booth's home. Rev. Thomas Smith (1738–1789) was
> the rector of Cople Parish, which comprised the lower end of Westmoreland
> County, including both Nomini and Yeocomico churches.

23. At Mr. Booths all day with Revd. Mr. Smith.

> Pope's Creek was an addition to the Bridges Creek plantation, the original
> seat of GW's family in Virginia. In the 1720s GW's father, Augustine, built a
> house on the site lying on the west side of Pope's Creek about three-quarters
> of a mile from the Potomac River, and it was there that GW was born. On the
> death of GW's father, the plantation was inherited by GW's half brother Au-
> gustine Washington. It was now the home of Augustine's widow, Anne Aylett
> Washington, and their four children, including their only son, William Au-
> gustine Washington (1757–1810), who inherited the plantation upon his
> mother's death in 1773 and renamed it Wakefield. The present house, con-
> structed in the 1930s, is a memorial house near the site of the original one.

31. Returnd home crossing at Hooes Ferry through Port Tobacco.

Observations

May 3. The hound bitch Mopsey brought 8 Puppys, distinguishd by the following Names—viz.—Tarter—Jupiter—Trueman—& Tipler (being Dogs)—and Truelove, Juno, Dutchess, & Lady being the Bitches—in all eight.

29. The bitch Chanter brought five Dog Puppies & 3 Bitch Ditto which were named as follow—viz.—Forrester—Sancho—Ringwood—Drunkard—and Sentwell. And Chanter—Singer—& Busy.

June

13. Went to Belvoir where Mr. Seldon his Lady &ca. were.

Mary Cary (1704–1775), an aunt of Sarah Cary Fairfax, married Joseph Selden (d. 1727) of Elizabeth City County and had three sons: Col. Cary Selden of Buckroe, Elizabeth City County; Col. Samuel Selden of Selvington, Stafford County; and Rev. Miles Selden (d. 1785) of Henrico County.

14. Sent for Doctr. Rumney to Patcy Custis who was seized with fitts. Mr. M. Campbell lodgd here.

Rumney treated this outbreak of epileptic convulsions by bleeding Patsy and prescribing some of the same medicines that he had given her earlier: valerian, "nervous drops," and ingredients for another medicinal brew (receipt from William Rumney, 18 Feb. 1769, Custis Papers, Virginia Historical Society).

18. At home all day prepg. Invoices and Letters for England.

The "Invoices and Letters" were all dated 20 June 1768, the "Invoices" listing personal and plantation items needed from England for Mount Vernon and the Custis estates. To Charles Lawrence of London, GW wrote for a "Suit of handsome Cloth Cloaths," reminding the tailor that his long-legged correspondent stood a "full Six feet high" and was "not at all inclind to be corpulent." GW also ordered new clothes, including a green riding outfit for "Mastr. Custis . . . now 15 Yrs. of age & growing fast" and "a Suit of blew Livery" for Jacky's body servant (*Papers, Colonial Series,* 8:98–99). From John Didsbury of London, GW ordered 32 pairs of shoes and boots for the Washington family, including 2 pairs of satin pumps, one in black and one in white, for Patsy Custis; also ordered were 4 pairs of coarse, strong shoes for Jacky's body servant (ibid., 97–98). In his cover letter to Robert Cary & Co., GW complained that for "four years out of five" he had made less profit by consigning his tobacco to Cary to sell in England than he would have made if he had sold it in Virginia.

28. Set of for, and Reachd Fredericksburg.

GW was taking Jacky Custis to a boarding school in St. Mary's Parish, Caroline County, which the parish rector, Rev. Jonathan Boucher, ran in his home on a small plantation about 11 miles from the parish church. The two Custis

Jonathan Boucher, schoolmaster and clergyman, ran a boarding school below Fredericksburg which Jacky Custis attended. (Yale University Art Gallery, Mabel Brady Garvan Collection)

children had been tutored since the fall of 1761 by Walter Magowan (d. 1784), an emigrant from Scotland who had been hired by GW at a wage of £35 a year. Magowan left the position in the late fall of 1767 and applied for the rectorship of Frederick Parish in Frederick County. Jacky had received no instruction since Christmas when Magowan had ceased tutoring him, and GW was now anxious to have the boy resume his education. To school Jacky took his luggage, a body servant, and two horses (GW to Boucher, 30 May 1768, *Papers, Colonial Series*, 8:89–91).

30. Went to Mr. Bouchers. Dined there and left Jackey Custis. Returnd to Fredericksburg in the Afternn.

Jonathan Boucher (1737/38–1804), son of a poor English schoolmaster, came to Port Royal in 1759 to earn his living by tutoring gentlemen's sons. He soon began incurring heavy debts, a habit that would plague him for most of his life, but his fortune took a turn for the better in 1761 when he was offered the rectorship of neighboring Hanover Parish in King George County. During the following year he took holy orders in England and, returning to Virginia, was confirmed as Hanover's rector. He later moved to his current position as rector of St. Mary's Parish in Caroline County, where he had a busy bachelor existence, preaching, working his plantation, and running the school for boys that Jacky had come to attend.

Observations

June 1st. Upon looking over my Wheat, I found all those places which had been injurd by the March frosts extreamely thin, low & backwards, having branchd but little, & looking puny—indeed in many places the Ground was entirely naked and where it was not, there was but too much cause to apprehend that the Wheat woud be choaked with Weeds.

8th. Carpenters went to getting the frame for my Barn at the House.

[1]5. The Maryland hound Bitch Lady took Forrester & was also servd by Captn., & refusd the Dogs on the 11th. Finishd breaking up Corn Ground at Doeg Run.

22. About this time Captn. Posey's Bitch Countess was discoverd Lind to Dabster & was immediately shut up & none but Sterling sufferd to go to her. Musick was also in heat & servd promiscuously by all the Dogs, intending to drown her Puppy's.

25. The Carpenters finishd getting the Frame for the Barn at my Ho. House.

28. Began to cut the upper part of my Timothy Meadow.

July

Where & how—my time is Spent.

July 1st. Went over to Stafford Court House to a meeting of the Missisipi. Dined and lodged there.

> During the first four years of its existence the Mississippi Company had made such a small impression in England that many contemporaries and most early authorities did not even know it had existed before 1767. With another change of the ministry in England, and because of the new Indian treaties in progress that opened large parts of trans-Appalachian land to white settlement, the company's hopes were quickening. Dr. Arthur Lee, brother of the company's treasurer, William Lee, was taken into the company and chosen as the agent to be sent to England. He probably received his instructions at this meeting. Although the Lee family—the original movers for the company—maintained their hopes up to the outbreak of the Revolution, GW was not so sanguine. While transferring his accounts to a new ledger in Jan. 1772, GW wrote off his £27 13s. 5d. investment in the company as a total loss (Ledger A, 169).

6. Rid to Muddy hole and Doeg Run after Doctr. Rumney went away. When I returnd found Mr. Wm. Lee & Doctr. Lee here.

Arthur Lee (1740–1792) was the youngest of the six surviving sons of Thomas Lee (1690–1750), builder of Stratford Hall, Westmoreland County, Va., and his wife, Hannah Ludwell Lee (1701-1749/50). He attended Eton and the University of Edinburgh, where he took a medical degree in 1764, and then returned to Virginia to practice medicine in Williamsburg. Arthur and his elder brother William (1739–1795) were now preparing for a visit to England where Arthur would take up the study of law and William would enter the tobacco trade in London. During this visit to Mount Vernon the brothers probably discussed with GW the prospects for the Mississippi Land Company, in which both were deeply involved.

9. Rid to Muddy hole, the Mill, and Doeg Run before Dinner & to the Mill afterwards—where my People was harvesting.

10. Went to Church and returnd to Dinner.

16. Went by Muddy hole & Doeg Run to the Vestry at Pohick Church. Stayd there till half after 3 Oclock & only 4 Members coming returned by Captn. McCartys & dined there.

24. Went to Pohick Church.

25. Went to Alexandria & bought a Bricklayer from Mr. Piper & re- turnd to Dinner. In the Afternoon Mr. R. Alexander came.

Michael Tracy (Treacy), probably an Irish indentured servant, was bought by GW for £18 4s., a good price if Tracy was an apt bricklayer (Ledger A, 277).

31. Went to Alexa. Church. Dind at Colo. Carlyles & returnd in the Afternoon.

The Fairfax vestry decided 27 Nov. 1766 to replace the parish's two church buildings with new brick structures, one near Four Mile Run called Falls Church, and one at Alexandria, later called Christ Church.

Memm. On the 30th. Of this Month I agreed with Jonathan Palmer to come and Work with my Carpenters; either at their Trade—Cowper- ing—or, in short at any thing that he may be set about—In considera- tion of which, I am to pay him £40 pr. Ann. allow him 400 lbs. Of Meat & 20 Bushels of Indian Corn. I am also to allow him to keep two Milch Cows (one half of whose Increase I am to have) and to have Wheat for which he is to pay. He is to be allowed a Garden & I am to get the old dwelling House at Muddy hole repaird for him. I am also to take his Waggon at £17. If he brings it free from damage and it is no older than he says—that is about a 12 Month. Note he is to be here as early as possible in April—if not in March.

On this day GW paid Edmund Palmer 17 shillings for 1 day of cradling and 4 days of mowing. He also settled accounts with his head harvester, Jonathan Palmer, who was paid £6 for 18 days of cradling and 4 days of mowing, plus a bonus of £1 4s. "In considn. Of his g[oo]d behaviour" (Ledger A, 277).

The contract with Palmer is typical of the time; while the form is standard, the content, being the product of bargaining by both sides, reflects the particular strengths and needs of each party. Such contracts were usually annual, and their renegotiation tended to reflect the changed circumstances of one or both parties.

Cowpering: an older spelling of coopering.

August

Where and how my time is Spent.

19. At home—settled & paid the Sheriff.

The Virginia county sheriff was more an administrator than a law officer, having the major responsibility for running elections, serving summonses, and collecting the annual levies in his county, which included those laid by the county and the parishes within the county as well as public levies set for the entire colony by the General Assembly. Much of this collecting was done by sub-sheriffs; in 1768 Sampson Darrell was sheriff of Fairfax County and Pierce Baily was the sub-sheriff who appears here to collect the balance owed by GW for this year, £1 15s. 3d. (Ledger A, 277). For the Fairfax County levy this year GW paid for 85 tithables at 14 pounds of tobacco each. Sixty-seven of these tithables lived in Truro Parish and thus came under that parish's levy of 41 pounds of tobacco per tithable. GW also paid the public tax of £1 10s. on his chariot and his chair as well as some minor fees he owed for government services. The total of the levies paid by GW in 1768 was 3,937 pounds of tobacco and £3 14s. 4d. cash. Because GW no longer grew tobacco at Mount Vernon, he paid his tobacco levies in local tobacco warehouse, or transfer, notes, mostly on tobacco paid him by his local Mount Vernon renters. With tobacco worth 2d. a pound, these notes were equivalent to £32 16s. 2d. in currency (Ledger A, 236; Washington Papers, Library of Congress, Truro Vestry Book, 128, 130).

20. Set of for my Brother Sam's & Nomony. Crossd at the Mouth of Nangamy & went to my Brothers.

Mrs. Washington and Patsy Custis accompanied GW on this trip, and Jacky Custis, taking a vacation from his studies, met them today at Samuel Washington's house (GW to Jonathan Boucher, 19 Aug. 1768, *Papers, Colonial Series,* 8:127).

26. Reachd my Brother John's at Night.

While the Washingtons were in Westmoreland County, Jacky Custis became "much disorder'd by an intermitting fever, attended with billeous vomittings," and Dr. Charles Mortimer of Fredericksburg was called to treat him. Jacky was soon better, but he remained so "very weak & low" that "his Mamma" insisted on taking him to Mount Vernon until he was fully recovered (GW to Jonathan Boucher, 4 Sept. 1768, *Papers, Colonial Series,* 8:128–29).

September

Where & how my time is spent.

Septr. 1. Set out from Nomony in my return to Chotanck.

6. Went in the Forenoon to the Mill—Doeg Run & Muddy hole. In the Afternoon paid a visit to Majr. Fairfax (Brother to Lord Fx.) at Belvoir.

Maj. Robert Fairfax (1707–1793), of Leeds Castle, Yorkshire, Eng., was the younger brother of Thomas Fairfax, sixth Baron Fairfax of Cameron. Robert had recently arrived from England to visit his relatives, dividing his time between Belvoir and Lord Fairfax's home, Greenway Court, in the Shenandoah Valley. Robert preferred Belvoir, finding that Valley living placed him "quite beyond the gentry . . . among the woods, with nothing but buckskins, viz., back-woodsmen and brutes . . . it is almost past description" (quoted in Brown, *Virginia Baron,* 160).

7. Dined at Belvoir with Mrs. W——n &ca.

8. Went to a Ball in Alexandria.

19. Went to Court with Colo. Burwell &ca.

On this day the Fairfax County court formally received a new commission of the peace from the governor and the council. Dated 29 July 1768, it authorized 23 justices for the county, including all the current justices but one and adding three new members to the court: GW, Daniel French, and Edward Payne (*Va. Exec. Jls.,* 6:345). In court today several of the old justices renewed their oaths of office according to law, but GW did not take his oaths until 21 Sept. (Fairfax County Order Book for 1768–70, 36–55).

20. Colo. Burwell &ca. went away to Belvoir—& Mrs. Washington & the two Childn. went up to Alexandria to see the Inconstant, or way to Win him Acted.

The Inconstant, or The Way to Win Him, by the Irish playwright George Farquhar (1677–1707), was first produced in London in 1702. Although not one of Farquhar's better farces, it became highly popular later in the century, enjoying long runs at Covent Garden and Drury Lane. GW, who accompanied his family to town today, paid £3 12s. 6d. for tickets to this play and the one seen on the following day, both of which were performed by David Verling's Virginia Company (Ledger A, 277).

21. Stayd in Town all day & saw the Tragedy of Douglas Playd.

Douglas, written by John Home (1722–1808), a Presbyterian clergyman of Edinburgh, was produced first in Edinburgh in Dec. 1756 and opened in London at Covent Garden the following year. The play was considered one of the finest British tragedies of the period and with its medieval Scottish setting probably drew well in Alexandria, a town founded and still heavily populated by Scots.

22. Came home in the forenoon.

24. At Home all day. Colo. Henry Lee & Lady, & Miss Ballendine came to dinner & stayd all Night.

> Col. Henry Lee (1729–1787) of Leesylvania, Prince William County, was a younger son of Henry Lee (1691–1747) of Lee Hall, Westmoreland County, and a cousin of William and Arthur Lee. Miss Ballendine is probably Frances Ballendine (d. 1793) of Dumfries, sister of John Ballendine.

29. Went to a Purse Race at Accatinck & returnd with Messrs. Robt. and George Alexander.

> GW spent 12s. 6d. at the race and also paid Robert Sanford 12s. "for Pacing my Horse" (Ledger A, 277). George Dent Alexander (d. 1780), of Fairfax County, was a younger brother of Robert Alexander.

Observations—in—Septembr.

14. Finishd Sowing the Second cut of Wheat in the Neck which compleated the half of the Corn Ground there.

16. Anointed all my Hounds (as well old Dogs as Puppies) which appeard to have the Mange with Hogs Lard & Brimstone.

17. Got done Sowing Wheat at Doeg Run. Sowed 92½ Bushels.

18. My Schooner Saild for Suffolk for a load of Shingles.

October

Where & how—my time is—Spent.

Octr. 1. Fox huntg. back of Mr. Barry's with Mr. Robt. Alexander Mr. Manley & Captn. Posey.

5. Went to Alexandria, after an early dinner to see a Ship (the Jenny) Launched but was disappointed & came home.

6. Went up again. Saw the Ship Launchd. Stayd all night to a Ball, & set up all Night.

> On this date GW lost 19s. at cards and paid 5s. for a play ticket for Jacky Custis (Ledger A, 277).

19. Set of on my Journey to Williamsburg & reachd Colo. Henry Lees to Dinner.

> GW is beginning a multipurpose trip. Although the assembly was not scheduled to meet, the General Court, Virginia's principal judicial body, had begun its 24-day fall session, which would draw most of the merchants and many lawyers and planters to Williamsburg for both their public and private affairs. Virginia was also expecting the arrival in Williamsburg of a new governor; Norborne Berkeley, baron de Botetourt (c.1718–1770), was ap-

pointed 12 Aug. 1768 to be the royal governor of Virginia. Rather than sending a deputy to the colony, Botetourt chose to reside in Virginia and govern directly, thus becoming the first peer in 80 years to reside as governor in the colony.

Jacky Custis accompanied GW on this trip as far as Boucher's school where he resumed his studies.

Col. Henry Lee's home, Leesylvania, was on the south side of Neabsco Creek near the Potomac River. Henry and his wife Lucy had eight children who lived to maturity, all of whom appear in the diaries.

24. Dined at Josh. Valentine's sent Chair's & Horses over James River & lodgd in Wmsburg. ourselves.

Lower down the James River the 50-gun ship of the line of the Royal Navy, H.M.S. *Rippon,* was dropping anchor. On board was Virginia's new governor.

30. Set out early, breakfasted at Hog Island and dined in Wms.

GW returned to a capital in thrall over the presence of a peer of the realm: Lord Botetourt had arrived in the city four days before. GW lodged at Mrs. Campbell's tavern.

November

Where & how—my time is—Spent

Novr. 1. In Williamsburg Dined at the Speakers—with many Gentlemen.

2. In Ditto. Dined at the Attorney Genls. with Lord Botetourt (the Govr.) & many other Gentlemen.

4. In Ditto. Dined with several Gentlemen at Ayscoughs. Colo. Byrds Lottery began drawing.

Christopher Ayscough and his wife Anne (both died c.1772) had recently opened a tavern on Francis Street about 100 yards south of the Capitol. Col. William Byrd III, in a desperate attempt to pay his debts, was raffling off much of his property, including "the intire Towns of Rocky Ridge and Shockoe, lying at the Falls of James river," valued at over £50,000, at £5 per ticket (*Va. Gaz.*, R, 23 July 1767). Besides owing gambling losses, Byrd was the largest single debtor to the estate of the late Speaker-Treasurer John Robinson. Upon Robinson's death it was discovered that he had loaned out personally over £100,000 worth of retired notes which had been issued by the Virginia government to finance the French and Indian War. To settle Robinson's estate and satisfy his creditors (mainly the government), his administrators had to force the sale of the land and slaves of a number of Robinson's debtors. Some debtors, like William Byrd, turned to lotteries. Besides causing financial confusion, the "Robinson affair" had an unsettling effect on the political life and social fabric of Virginia in the late years of the colonial period.

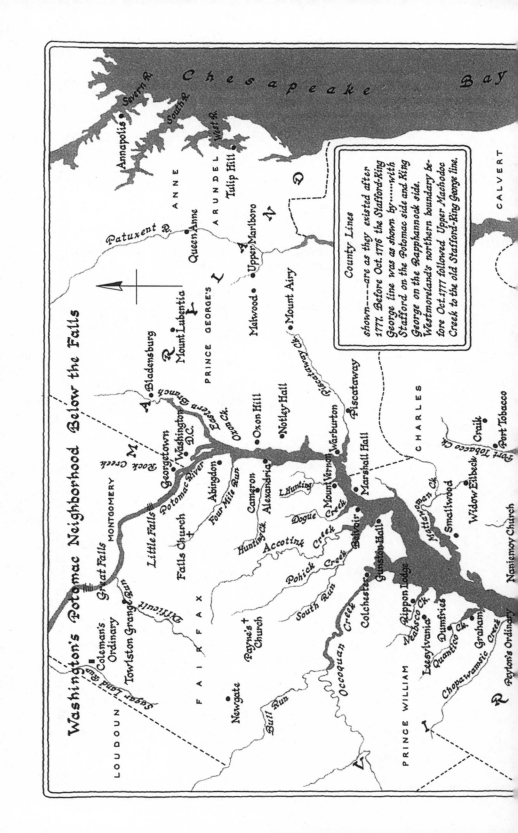

Washington's Potomac Neighborhood Below the Falls

Chesapeake Bay

Severn R.
South R.
Annapolis
Patuxent R.
Queen Anne
ANNE ARUNDEL
West R.
Tulip Hill
CALVERT

County Lines
shown‑‑‑are as they existed after
1777. Before Oct. 1776 the Stafford-King
George line was as shown by‑‑‑‑‑with
Stafford on the Potomac side and King
George on the Rappahannock side.
Westmoreland's northern boundary be‑
fore Oct. 1777 followed Upper Machodoc
Creek to the old Stafford-King George line.

Mount Lubentia
Bladensburg
Mahwood
Upper Marlboro
Mount Airy
PRINCE GEORGES

Eastern Branch
Rock Creek
Georgetown
Washington D.C.
MONTGOMERY
Oxon Ck.
Oxon Hill
Notley Hall
Piscataway Ck.
Piscataway
Warburton
CHARLES

Potomac River
Little Falls
Falls Church
Four Mile Run
Abingdon
Cameron Cameron Ck.
Alexandria
L. Hunting
Dogue Creek
Mount Vernon
Marshall Hall
Mattawoman Ck.
Smallwood
Widow Eilbeck
Craik
Fort Tobacco
Port Tobacco

Great Falls
Coleman's Ordinary
Towlston Grange
Difficult Run
Sugar Land Run
LOUDOUN
FAIRFAX
Hunting Ck.
Accotink
Pohick Creek
South Run
Belvoir
Gunston Hall
Colchester
Occoquan Creek
Bull Run
Newgate
Payne's Church
Rippon Lodge
Neabsco Ck.
Leesylvania
Dumfries
Quantico Ck.
PRINCE WILLIAM
Chopawamsic Creek
Graham
Peyton's Ordinary
Naniemoy Church
Fort Tobacco Ck.

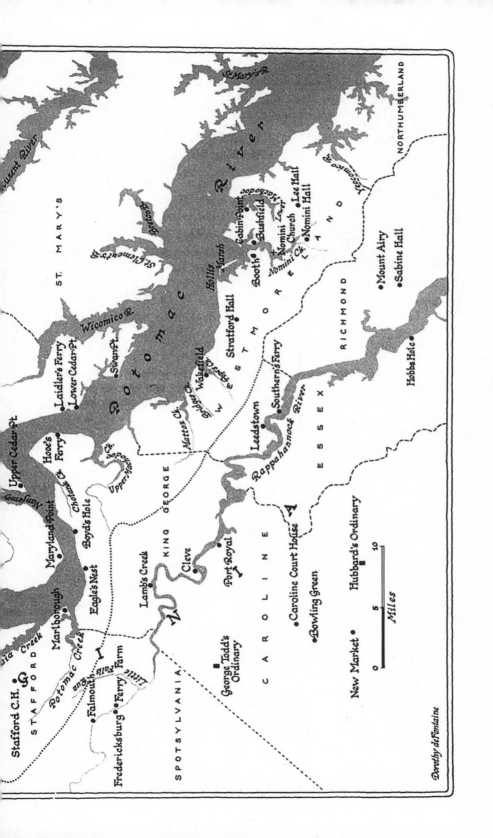

Dorothy deFontaine

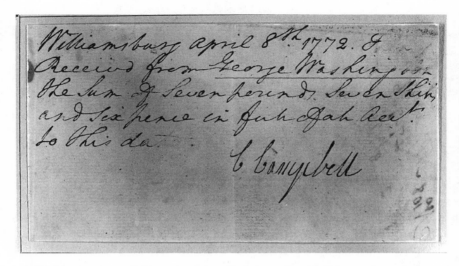

Washington pays a bill owed to Mrs. Christiana Campbell for service at her tavern. (Colonial Williamsburg photograph)

21. Went up to Court and returnd in the Evening with my Brothr. John.

GW was attending the Fairfax County court as a justice for the first time since taking his oaths of office 21 Sept. GW was present only today (Fairfax County Order Book for 1768–70, 56–75). Like most Virginia county justices of the time, GW attended court primarily at his convenience, coming when his affairs allowed or when a matter of special concern was to be heard.

December

Where & how—my time is—Spent.

Decr. 1. Went to the Election of Burgesses for this County, & was there, with Colo. West chosen. Stayd all Night to a Ball wch. I had given.

The election, held at the county courthouse in Alexandria, had been called by the Virginia's new governor Lord Botetourt. White adult males who owned a minimal amount of real property were allowed to vote. In accordance with the English belief that secrecy bred corruption, all voting was done in public. The election proceedings were the responsibility of the county sheriff. As the clerks (one provided by each candidate) sat together at a table, each voter would step forward and announce his two choices, which were then marked down by the clerks on their respective poll sheets. As each vote was given and recorded, the candidate chosen often would thank the voter, and toward the end of a close election, when every vote would elicit a round of cheering, the crowd sometimes became unruly.

During the voting in the 1755 Fairfax County burgess poll, GW got into a violent argument over the candidacy of his friend George William Fairfax. See *Papers, Colonial Series,* 2:226, 227–28.

In this election GW and Col. John West were standing for reelection. A third candidate was GW's neighbor and fox-hunting companion Capt. John Posey, who was trying for the second time to unseat West. The final poll this day was: GW, 205; John West, 175; John Posey, 132. GW spent about £25 on his election, including cakes and drink (unspecified) and £1 each for his clerk, John Orr, and his "fidler [at] the ball" (Posey to GW, 25 May 1771; Ledger A, 281, 287; Hening, 4:476, 7:518). See also *Papers, Colonial Series,* 8:145–49.

17. Rid out with my Gun but killd nothg. Mary Wilson came to live here as a Ho[use]keeper a[t] 15/. pr. Month.

Mrs. Mary Wilson was probably a widow. She left her position at Mount Vernon in June 1769 (Ledger A, 288).

1769

January

Where & how—my time—is Spent

3. Came home again. Colo. Carlyle & Mr. Ramsay returnd with us.

The visit may have been more than social. About three weeks later, on 29 Jan., GW wrote William Ramsay to say that it was "out of my power . . . to furnish you & Mr. Fairfax with the sum asked." Then shifting to a subject closer to his heart, GW continued: "Having once or twice of late heard you speak highly in praise of the [New] Jersey College, as if you had a desire of sending your Son William there (who I am told is a youth fond of study & instruction, & disposed to a sedentary studious Life; in following of which he may not only promote his own happiness, but the future welfare of others) I shou'd be glad, if you have no other objection to it than what may arise from the expence, if you wou'd send him there as soon as it is convenient & depend upon me for Twenty five pounds this [Virginia] Currency a year for his support so long as it may be necessary for the completion of his Education. . . . No other return is expected or wished for, for this offer than that you will accept it with the same freedom & good will with which it is made, & that you may not even consider it in the ⟨light⟩ of an obligation, or mention it as such; for be assur'd that from me it never will be known" (*Papers, Colonial Series,* 8:167–68)

30. At home all day, Mr. Campbell the Comptroller dind here & in the afternoon Doctr. Mercer came.

Hugh Mercer (c.1725–1777), born in Aberdeenshire, Scot., studied medicine at the University of Aberdeen from 1740 to 1744. Around 1746 Mercer immigrated to America, settling on the Pennsylvania frontier. There he practiced medicine until the outbreak of the French and Indian War, when he joined the Pennsylvania forces as an officer. During this service he became acquainted with GW. After retiring from the military, he settled in Fredericksburg, where he opened an apothecary shop and practiced medicine.

31. Doctr. Rumney dind and lodged here.

Rumney and Mercer apparently consulted with one another today about Patsy Custis's case and decided on a new way of treating her epilepsy, because four days later Rumney recorded giving her mercurial pills, purging pills, and ingredients for a decotion (receipt from William Rumney, 18 Feb. 1769, Custis Papers, Virginia Historical Society). Unfortunately, those medicines, like the others tried previously, would give Patsy no relief from her fits.

February

Where & how—my time is—Spent

16. At home all day, Joshua Evans who came here last Night put an Iron Ring upon Patcy (for Fits) and went away after Breakfast.

Joshua Evans is probably the blacksmith of that name who was living in Loudoun County at this time and died there in 1773 (Loudoun County Wills, Book B, 71–79, Vi Microfilm). According to an English folk tradition dating from the fourteenth century, certain rings called cramp rings could relieve or cure epileptic convulsions when worn on a finger. These rings, varying in design and composition, depended on a particular blessing, inscription, or material for their supposed efficacy (Jones, *Finger-Ring Lore,* 154–55, 162–65, 522–26). GW today paid Evans £1 10s. for his service (Ledger A, 287).

March

Where & how—my time is Spent—

6. Set out with Fieldg. Lewis for Fredg. where we reachd after dinner at Peyton's on Acquia—i.e. reachd my Mother's.

Peyton's ordinary, on Aquia Creek in Stafford County, was about 16 miles above Fredericksburg on the main road from Alexandria. While GW was at Ferry Farm he gave his mother £3 cash (Ledger A, 287).

8. Still there, dind at the same place, spending the Evening at Weedon's at the Club.

George Weedon (c.1734–1793) kept a "large and commodious" tavern on the main street of Fredericksburg (now Caroline Street) "nearly opposite" the town hall and public market. Frequented "by the first gentlemen" of Virginia and "neighboring colonies," it contained "a well accustomed billiard room" and was the place where local horse races were arranged (*Va. Gaz.*, P&D, 12 Sept. 1766, and P, 15 Sept. 1775; Fredericksburg *Va. Herald,* 23 Oct. 1788).

The Club: It was a common practice among Virginia gentlemen of this time, when dining or supping at a tavern, to do so in groups either at a private table or, at a large tavern like Weedon's, in a private room. They would be served as a unit by the innkeeper and then would *club* for the cost of the food, drink, and room; that is, they would divide the total bill equally. On this evening GW paid 2s. 6d. as his share of the club and lost 1s. 6d. at cards (Ledger A, 287).

9. Set of for Robt. Ashbys, and after dining by the way, reachd it a little after dark.

Capt. Robert Ashby (c.1707–1792) was the second son of Thomas Ashby. Robert had worked as a marker for GW during the survey of the Fairfax lands in 1748 and was now living at Yew Hill, Fauquier County, about eight miles south of Ashby's Gap on the southern road to Winchester.

10. Went out to run out the bounds of the Land I bot. of Carters Estate but the Weathr. being very cold & windy was obligd to return.

George Carter, the youngest son of Robert "King" Carter, died intestate in England c.1742. To settle his estate the Virginia Assembly passed an act in 1744 directing trustees to sell Carter's vast holdings of more than 20,000 acres of land in Prince William, Fairfax, and Frederick counties (Hening, 5:300). Twenty years later less than half of the lands had been sold, and Carter's heirs petitioned the assembly to name a new set of trustees to sell the remaining acreage. An act was passed in 1766 naming Robert Burwell, Fielding Lewis, and GW as the new trustees (Hening, 8:215). In Nov. 1767 they met at Capt. Robert Ashby's home in Fauquier County to sell the remaining lands, and GW bought 2,682 acres "of Geo Carter's Estate" for himself (*Va. Gaz.*, P&D, 19 Nov. 1767; Ledger A, 257).

17. Executing Leases to those who had taken Lotts—being at Captn. Ashbys.

GW had cut up his purchase of Carter's land into lots of about 100 acres each and was leasing them on a long-term basis to local farmers for about £4 Virginia currency per lot. On this day GW made at least 11 leases, some of which were for more than one lot.

18. Went up to Greenway Court where I dined and stayd all Night. Met Colo. Lewis here.

Greenway Court was not only the residence of Lord Fairfax but also the permanent location of the proprietor's land office. There GW and Fielding Lewis, in their capacity as trustees for the sale of George Carter's estate, paid Fairfax the balance of quitrents owed by the estate since 1746.

21. Went & laid of 4 Lots at the head of Bullskin for several Tenents.

24. Reachd home before dinner.

Remarks & Observations—in Mar[ch]

26. The Bitch Musick brought five Puppies one of which being thought not true was drownd immediately. The others being somewhat like the Dog (Rockwood of Mr. Fairfaxs) which got them were saved.

April

Where & how—my time is—Spent

11. Went a fox hunting & took a fox alive after running him to a Tree. Brot him home.

12. Chased the above fox an Hour & 45 Minutes when he treed again after which we lost him.

17. Went up to Court & lodged at Mr. Jno. Wests at Night.

> The court met two days in April. GW was present from the beginning today, but he came late the next day, arriving after five items of business were finished (Fairfax County Order Book for 1768–70, 120–27). John West, Jr., and his wife Catherine Colvill West lived near Cameron. GW today lost £2 15s. 6d. at cards and apparently lost £1 1s. more on the following day (Ledger A, 290).

21. At home with Colo. Mason who went away in the Afternoon.

> Mason today signed an agreement promising to sell GW a strip of 100 acres on Little Hunting Creek, adjoining the Darrell tract, for £100 (Rutland, *Mason Papers,* 1 : 102; Ledger A, 61).

22. Surveying in the Woods all day.

24. Measuring the Road to Poseys ferry and seeing how a new one coud be laid out.

29. Went up to Alexandria and Mr. Jno. Wests & returnd to Dinner.

> John West, Jr., today agreed in writing to sell GW about 200 acres of land lying on the Potomac River next to the Mount Vernon tract for 43s. an acre. This land had been part of John Posey's plantation by virtue of his wife Martha's inheritance from her first husband, George Harrison. She had been given use of it for her lifetime only, and she had died during the past year. According to the terms of Harrison's will, the land then automatically passed to John West, Jr., who as Harrison's nephew was his nearest male descendant (Harrison's will, 21 Nov. 1748, Fairfax County Wills, Book A-1, 260–61). However, West was prevented from deeding the property to GW at this time because of a bitter dispute between West and Posey over the ownership of a thin strip along the Potomac. West had recently brought suit to force Posey off the strip, and GW was obliged to await the outcome of that case so that there would be no further confusion over titles or acreages.

30. Set of for Williamsburg.

> GW was going to Williamsburg to attend the House of Burgesses, scheduled to convene 8 May. This session promised to be a stormy one because of the deepening crisis in the American colonies over the Townshend Acts, which remained in effect despite American demands for their repeal. Leaders in several colonies north of Virginia had begun to organize nonimportation associations to boycott British goods until Parliament rescinded the offensive

duties, and GW, who had heard of those endeavors, was convinced that some kind of nonimportation association was now needed in Virginia. "Addresses to the Throne, and remonstrances to parliament," he wrote to George Mason on 5 April 1769, "we have already . . . proved the inefficacy of; how far then their attention to our rights & priviledges is to be awakened or alarmed by starving their Trade & manufactures, remains to be tryd" (*Papers, Colonial Series,* 8:177–81).

May

Where & how—my time is—Spent

May 1. Set out from Peytons & passing thro Fredericksburg reachd Hubbards Ordy.

2. Got to Eltham—after foundg. my Horse.

3. Went into Williamsburg and dined with the Council & spent the Evening in the Daphne.

> The Daphne was a room in the Raleigh Tavern, on Duke of Gloucester Street about half a block from the Capitol. Owned at this time by Anthony Hay (d. 1770), a former cabinetmaker, the Raleigh was a center of social, political, and business activities in Williamsburg. Public auctions were often held in front of it, and many important meetings and fashionable balls took place inside its elegant rooms. While GW was at the Raleigh on this date, he bought subscriptions to three Williamsburg purse races from Hay (Ledger A, 290).
>
> GW also amused himself frequently at the card table during this visit to Williamsburg, winning £4 17s. 6d. this day but losing £1 the next (Ledger A, 290). He did not lodge at the Raleigh but stayed as usual at Mrs. Campbell's place (Ledger A, 291).

5. Dined at the Governors and supped at Mr. Carters.

> Robert Carter (1728–1804) of Nomini Hall in Westmoreland County, a grandson of Robert "King" Carter, became a member of the council in 1758 and now lived in a handsome town house next to the Governor's Palace.

8. Dined at Anthony Hays and Supped at Mrs. Campbells.

> The House of Burgesses sat today as scheduled. Governor Botetourt gave a brief address, and various committees were appointed. GW was placed on the committee of propositions and grievances and the committee of privileges and elections (*H.B.J.,* 1766–69, 187–92). Later this day he lost £1 at cards but won £1 5s. the next (Ledger A, 290).

9. Dined at the Palace, & spent the Evening in my own Room.

11. Again dined at Mrs. Campbell's, and spent the Evening at Hays.

12. Dined with Mr. Wythe and Supped at Hays.

> George Wythe (1726–1806) was at this time clerk of the House of Burgesses and a prominent Williamsburg lawyer. He lived in a brick mansion on the Palace green.

13. Dined at Mrs. Campbells and went over to Gloucester to Colo. W. Lewis's afterwards.

> Col. Warner Lewis (b. 1720), son of Col. John and Frances Fielding Lewis and the elder brother of Fielding Lewis, GW's sister Betty's husband, lived at Warner Hall in Gloucester County.
>
> Today being Friday, the burgesses adjourned for the weekend after attending to a few items of routine business.

16. Rid over my dower Land in York, to shew that, and the mill, to the Gentlemen appointed by the Genl. Court to value & report thereon. Came in to Breakfast. Dined at the Speakers and spent the Evening at Hays.

> GW had been trying for at least the last two years to rent out the dower property in York County, because it was too far from Mount Vernon for him to inspect as often as he thought he should (*Va. Gaz.*, P&D, 2 April 1767). "Middling Land under a Mans own eye," he later remarked, "is more profitable than rich Land at a distance" (GW to John Parke Custis, 24 July 1776, *Papers, Revolutionary War Series*, 5:441–42). He had now decided to rent the property to Jacky Custis and thus consolidate all the Custis lands in York County under his name, if a place could be found near Mount Vernon to which the dower slaves on the York plantations could be moved and if the General Court, to which GW was responsible for the administration of Jacky's estate, approved the transaction (GW to John Posey, 11 June 1769). Both conditions were fulfilled by 1771 when GW began to charge Jacky's account £150 a year for the use of the "Land and Mill in York County as settled with the Genl. Court" (Custis Account Book).
>
> The burgesses on this date passed the Virginia Resolves, claiming, among other matters, that they, with the consent of the governor and the council, had the sole right to impose taxes on the inhabitants of Virginia. Before adjournment, the resolves were ordered to be sent to the assemblies of the other colonies, and a committee was appointed to write the petition to the king (*H.B.J.*, 1766–69, 214–15).

17. Dined at the Treasurers and was upon a Committee at Hays till 10 oclock.

> The address to the king was presented to the burgesses today and accepted without dissent. The house then turned to other business, but about noon Speaker Randolph received a message from Governor Botetourt commanding the burgesses to come immediately to the council chamber. When they were assembled there, Botetourt spoke: "Mr. Speaker, and Gentlemen of the House of Burgesses, I have heard of your Resolves, and augur ill of their Effect. You have made it my Duty to dissolve you; and you are dissolved accordingly" (*H.B.J.*, 1766–69, 215–18). With that statement this session of the house came to an abrupt end, but most of the dissolved burgesses, including GW, promptly reassembled a few doors down the street at Hay's Raleigh Tavern, meeting unofficially in the Apollo Room to consider "their distressed Situation." Peyton Randolph was elected moderator of the group,

and a committee was appointed to prepare a plan for a Virginia nonimportation association (*H.B.J.*, 1766–69, xxxix-xl).

18. Dined at Mrs. Dawsons & went to Bed by 8 Oclock.

Another meeting of the dissolved burgesses was held in the Apollo Room today beginning at 10:00 A.M. The committee appointed on the previous day presented a nonimportation plan, and after being "read, seriously considered, and approved," it was signed by 88 "of the principal Gentlemen of the Colony," including GW. No member of the association was henceforth to import directly or indirectly any article taxed by Parliament for the purpose of raising a revenue in America (except inexpensive paper) or any untaxed article appearing on a long detailed list of European agricultural and manufactured goods. These agreements were to remain in effect until one month after the repeal of the Townshend Acts or until the members of the association decided to dissolve it (*H.B.J.*, 1766–69, xl-xliii).

GW today bought a copy of John Dickinson's recent pamphlet *Letters from a Farmer in Pennsylvania to the Inhabitants of the British Colonies*. He also purchased a pair of gloves, medicines, and coffee and paid his bill at Hay's: £2 12s. 9d. (Ledger A, 290).

19. Dined again at Mrs. Dawson's and went to the Queens Birth Night at the Palace.

Today "being the QUEEN's birthday, the flag was displayed on the Capitol; and in the evening . . . the Governour gave a splendid ball and entertainment at the Palace to a very numerous and polite company of Ladies and Gentlemen" (*Va. Gaz.*, P&D, 25 May 1769).

20. Left Williamsburg on my return home. Dined at Colo. Bassetts & stayd the rest of the day there.

22. Reached home.

30. Rid to Muddy hole about 11 Oclock and returnd to Dinner.

31. Set of with Mrs. Washington & Patcy . . . for Towlston in order to stand for Mr. B. Fairfax's 3d. Son which I did together with my Wife, Mr. W[arne]r Washington & his Lady.

Mr. B. Fairfax's 3d. Son: Ferdinando Fairfax (1769–1820), who is here becoming a godson of GW, married Elizabeth Cary, was the heir of George William Fairfax, and was a principal mourner at GW's funeral.

Remarks & Occurances in May

22. Returnd home from Williamsburg and found my Wheat much better in general; than ever it was at this Season before—being Ranker, better spread over the ground & broader in the Blade than usual. It was also observable that in general the head was shot out, and in many places in Blossom.

29. Mopsy the Hound Bitch and Truelove another Hound brought 12 Puppies—that is Mopsy had five and the other seven.

June

Where & how—my time is—Spent

14. Rid to Muddy hole, Doeg Run, and Mill & from thence went to Belvoir to pay my respects to Lord Fairfax. Dind there & returnd in the Afternoon.

17th. Rid to Muddy hole, Doeg Run, & Mill Plantation.

19. Went up to Court & returnd in the Evening.

> In Alexandria today GW settled with Pierce Baily for this year's taxes. His personal bill was £1 10s. cash for the public tax on his chariot and chair, £2 2s. cash for miscellaneous fees, and 4,754 pounds of tobacco for the county and parish levies: 534 pounds to Fairfax County for 89 tithables at 6 pounds each, 1,140 pounds to Fairfax Parish for 19 tithables at 60 pounds each, and 3,080 to Truro Parish for 70 tithables at 44 pounds each (Ledger A, 291, 293).

20. Went up to Court again & returnd in the Evening with Colo. Mason, Mr. Scott and Mr. Bryan Fairfax.

26. At home all day—Measuring salt from a Bermudian.

> *A Bermudian:* GW is here receiving salt from a Bermudian vessel, which likely came from Turks Islands in the British West Indies.

Remarks & Occurances in June

June 2d. Finishd breaking up my Corn gd. with the Plows at Muddy hole.

3d. Finishd going over the field abt. the Overseers House at the Mill with the Hoes.

6. Went over my plowed Corn at Doeg Run a 2d. time with the Plows.

7. Rid into the Neck, and went all ovr. my Wheat there, which in general I think very good; and at this time free from any appearance of Rust. I think it is observable that the Wheat on the River side appeard to be better head than the other tho not superior in look in any other respect to many other parts of the field.

12. Went over all my Wheat at Muddy hole and at Doeg Run & found it at both places good and promising, and entirely clear from every appearance of Rust. I also found that the Straw at the lower joints was turnd, & turning yellow—that the blade was putting on a yellowish

Hue—and that the head was in general grey—& turning yellowish the grain being mostly plump and the departments strutting with the Ripening Corn.

24. Finishd going over my Corn in the Neck with the Hoes as also with the Plows the second time. Worked over all the Swamps (North of the Meadow) at Doeg Run with the Hoes. Jonathan Palmer who came to the House that was provided for him last Night began Working with my People this day.

> On this day GW debited Jonathan Palmer, his newly hired master carpenter, "2 Barrels of Herrings delivered per your order to the Waggoner that brought his [Palmer's] family down" (Ledger A, 294). The house, although not recorded by GW in their contract, was provided rent-free.

27. James Cleveland spaed the three hound Bitches Musick, Tipsey, & Maidien as also two hound puppies which came from Musick & Rockwood. Note—the Bitch Tipsey was going into heat but had not been lind. Began in the Afternoon to cut my wheat at Doeg Run Quarter with Jonathan Palmer and 6 other Cradlers.

> James Cleveland was employed by GW as the overseer of the River Farm on Clifton's Neck from 1765 to 1775, when he was put in charge of an expedition of workers to GW's lands on the Ohio.

28. Elijah Houghton joind the above at the same place. The whole made but a bad days work. They complaind of the Straw cutting very hard. Note. The wheat this year appeard different from what it did last year the Straw being quite changd (even the Knots and joints nearly so) when the Grain was not hard. On the Contrary last year—the grain was tolerably hard whilst part of the Straw retaind a good deal of green.

> Elijah Houghton was retained by GW as a harvester and paid at the rate of 5s. per day, with an allowance of three Spanish dollars for travel. Ledger A, 292, shows that on 13 July 1769 he was paid £3 13s.

29. Eliab Roberts, William Acres, Joseph Wilson & Azel Martin set into work today—& I think workd but indifferently. The Wheat on the other side the Run was not cut down. Michael Davy Schomberg & Ned Holt were left with Morris's People to finish it.

> Eliab Robert, William Acres, Joseph Wilson, and Azel Martin were retained by GW as harvesters at the rate of 5s. per day, with an allowance of three Spanish dollars each for travel. The men were paid £4 13s., £3 16s. 4d., £1 15s., and £4 13s., respectively, for their work (Ledger A, 292). Besides these men and Elijah Houghton, GW also retained Thomas Williams, Thomas Pursel (Pursley), John Pursel, and "Young Palmer" (Ledger A, 292). Michael, Davy, and Schomberg were GW's slaves. Michael was a carpenter and tradesman; Davy, a mulatto, was a servant at the Home House plantation 1762–64, a field hand on the Mill plantation 1765–69, and subsequently served for

many years as overseer of various Mount Vernon farms; Schomberg was a field hand on River Farm. Ned Holt, who appears in GW's tithable list for 1761 as being at the home plantation, was probably one of GW's slaves.

July

Where & how—my time is—Spent

2. At home all day—the Captn. of the Burmudian dining here.

> *The Captn. of the Burmudian:* Captain Burch, from whom GW bought 562 barrels of salt, a cotton line, and 40 yards of nautical rope, totaling £35 7s. 6d. (Ledger A, 291).

3. Rid round to my Harvest field in the Neck with Mrs. Washington, Patcy & Mill[y] Posey. Returnd to Dinner.

19. Again went up to Court and returnd in the Afternoon.

23. Went to Pohick Church and returnd to Dinner. Mr. Magowan w[ith] us.

25. At home all day writing Letters & Invoices for England.

> GW today ordered goods for Mount Vernon and the Custis plantations from Robert Cary & Co. and Capel & Osgood Hanbury. In his letter to Cary & Co., he requested that if any items on the invoices, except paper, "are Taxd by Act of Parliament for the purpose of Raising a Revenue in America, it is my express desire and request, that they may not be sent, as I have very heartily enterd into an Association . . . not to import any Article which now is or hereafter shall be Taxed for this purpose until the said Act or Acts are re-peal⟨d⟩. I am therefore particular in mentioning this matter as I am fully determined to adhere religiously to it, and may perhaps have wrote for some things unwittingly which may be under these Circumstances" (*Papers, Colonial Series,* 8:229–31).

26. Rid to my Meadow at the Mill & to Doeg Run after Dinner.

29. At home all day posting my Books.

30. At Home all day preparing for my journey to the Springs.

31. Set out with Mrs. Washington & Patcy Custis for the Frederick Springs.

> The family was going to Warm Springs in order to test the efficacy of the waters in relieving Patsy's epileptic fits (GW to John Armstrong, 18 Aug. 1769, *Papers, Colonial Series,* 8:241–43). GW had intended to leave on 27 July but had been delayed by other matters (GW to Jonathan Boucher, 13 July 1769, ibid., 226).

August

Where & how—my time is—spent—

Augt. 1st. Set out from Chs. Wests. Dined at Snickers and got to Mr. W[arne]r Washington's abt. 5 Oclock.

> Edward Snickers (d. 1791) settled at a site near Buck Marsh Run in Frederick (now Clarke) County, where he later built his home, Springfield. Snickers' Gap in the Blue Ridge Mountains was named after him. Warner Washington was living in Frederick (now Clarke) County, probably on the 3,000-acre plot he purchased in 1770 from his brother-in-law, George William Fairfax. On this land was built Warner's home, Fairfield, a few miles northwest of Snickers's ordinary.

5. Prosecuted our Journey to the springs (by Jacob Hites). Bated at Opeekon and lodged at Joshua Hedges.

> Jacob Hite, son of Jost Hite, was a resident of Frederick County. In 1772 he became a justice of the peace of newly formed Berkeley County.

6. Arrivd at the Springs about One Oclock & dind w. Colo. F[airfa]x.

19. Rid with Mrs. Washington & others to the Cacapehon Mountain— to see the prospect from thence.

20. Went to Church in the fore and Afternoon. Mr. Jno. Lewis dind here. Lord Fairfax the two Colo. Fairfaxs & others drank Tea here.

23. Dined alone—Patcy unwell.

> Patsy had "found little benefit" from taking the waters, but the Washingtons had decided to continue the experiment for another week or two in order to be sure there was no help for her here. The springs at this time were crowded with people from all walks of life seeking to restore their health. The waters, GW wrote to a friend, "are applied . . . in all cases, altho there be a moral certainty of their hurting in some. Many poor, miserable objects are now attending here, which I hope will receive the desired benefit, as I dare say they are deprivd of the means of obtaining any other relief, from their Indigent Circumstances" (GW to John Armstrong, 18 Aug. 1769, *Papers, Colonial Series,* 8:240–41).

September

Where & how—my time is—Spent

9. Set out on my return home about 8 Oclock but broke the Chariot & made it 11. before we got a Mile. Reachd Joshua Hedges.

11. Continued my Journey and reached Chas. Wests Ordinary after baiting under the Ridge at the blacksmiths shop.

12. Breakfasted at Wm. Carr Lanes & arrived at home about 3 Oclock in the Afternoon.

14. Went to Alexandria to the Election of Burgesses for Fairfax & was chosen together with Colo. West without a Poll, their being no opposition.

> This election was called in consequence of Governor Botetourt's dissolution of the last House of Burgesses in May 1769. When there was no opposition in a burgess election (which was seldom) the sheriff took the vote "by view," although it is not clear whether GW was reelected by voice vote or by a show of hands.

18. Went to court at Alexandria and returnd home in the Evening.

22. Went a huntg. & killd a bitch fox in abt. an hour. Returnd home with an Ague upon me. Mr. Montgomery came to dinner.

> Thomas Montgomerie was a prominent merchant in Dumfries. The purpose of his visit today apparently was to discuss the troubled affairs of Mrs. Margaret Savage, the elderly wife of Dr. William Savage, formerly of Dumfries. Mrs. Savage's first husband, the Rev. Charles Green, had established a trusteeship for her, and after his death in 1765, GW and George William Fairfax became her trustees, giving the Fairfax County court a bond to guarantee that they would pay her an annuity out of the estate's proceeds. Sometime before 25 April 1767, she married Dr. Savage, who subsequently took control of Green's estate and assumed responsibility for paying his wife's annuity, giving a bond for that purpose to GW and Bryan Fairfax, who were to be her trustees henceforth. By the terms of the doctor's bond, Mrs. Savage was to receive £100 at the beginning of each year (GW to Margaret Savage, 28 June 1768, and to William Savage, 28 June 1768, *Papers, Colonial Series*, 8:107–11). However, since 1767, neither of the annuities that had come due had been paid, and during the latter half of 1768, Dr. Savage had taken his wife to Ireland to live, leaving his affairs in Virginia to the care of Thomas Montgomerie (GW to William Ellzey, 3 Oct. 1769, ibid., 251–52; *Va. Gaz.*, R, 13 Oct. 1768). Although Mrs. Savage had repeatedly told both GW and Fairfax in private that she wanted her money, the doctor insisted that she was willing to give up her annuities and apparently had given instructions not to pay them. The dispute, which was complicated by Mrs. Savage's vacillation in the matter and her absence from the colony, would continue in and out of court, plaguing GW and the other executors for many years to come.

23. Went a huntg. again with the Compy. aforesaid & suppose we killd a fox but coud not find it. Returnd with my Ague again.

28. I rid to Alexandria to see how my House went on. Returnd to Dinr.

> GW had paid £48 10s. in 1764 for two lots on Pitt Street in Alexandria: No. 112 at the corner of Prince Street and No. 118 at the corner of Cameron Street (Ledger A, 180). The lot at the corner of Prince Street would remain vacant for most of GW's lifetime, but during the spring of this year he had engaged to have a small town house built on the other one. Construction of the

house, which would continue until sometime in 1771, was primarily the responsibility of two Alexandria men: Edward Rigdon (d. 1772), a joiner, and Richard Lake—variously spelled Leak and Leake—(d. 1775).

October

Where & how—my time—is Spent

Octr. 1. Dined at Belvoir with Mrs. Washington and Patcy Custis. Returnd in the Evening.

4. Rid to Alexandria to see how my Carpenters went on with my Ho. Returnd to Dinr.

5. Went after Blew Wings with Humphrey Peake. Killd 3 & returnd by Muddy hole.

12. Rid to Muddy hole Doeg Run and Mill.

13. Captn. Marshall came over here & dined & I rid with him round his Land.

> Thomas Hanson Marshall owned 4,802 acres that bordered the Mount Vernon tract on the west, lying on both sides of the road that ran from Gum Spring to Dogue Creek. GW had long wished to acquire that land, but Marshall, who was in no great want of money, had been reluctant to let it go unless he could make an exchange for land adjoining his Maryland plantation. Consequently, GW persuaded his fellow fox hunter Robert Alexander to promise to sell him, at £2 Maryland currency an acre, 300 to 400 acres of a tract next to Marshall's plantation that Alexander's wife, Mariamne Stoddert Alexander, had inherited. It was the offer of Mrs. Alexander's land that today brought Marshall to Mount Vernon, where he agreed to give GW that part of his land lying south of the Gum Spring road in return for an equal acreage from the Alexander tract, provided that he could obtain immediate use of the Alexander land (Ledger A, 96; Marshall to GW, 18 June 1769 and 8 Mar. 1770).

16. Went up to Court and returnd at Night.

30. Set out on my Journey to Williamsburg & reachd Colo. Henry Lees to a Late Dinner.

> Governor Botetourt had summond the burgesses to a new session beginning 7 Nov. On this trip GW took Mrs. Washington and Patsy with him, traveling in a handsome green chariot trimmed with gold that had arrived from England sometime during the past 12 months (invoice of goods shipped to GW, Sept. 1768).

November

Where & how—my time is—Spent

6. Came to Williamsburg.

7. Dined at the Governors & supped at Anthony Hayes.

> The burgesses convened today. A moderate tone was set for this session by Governor Botetourt's opening remarks to the house, pledging his support for repeal of England's revenue taxes on the colonies, except for the one on tea. The burgesses were not fully appeased by his speech, continuing to object to the tea tax, and no steps were taken to dissolve or modify the association. But Botetourt was personally popular with the burgesses, and they chose not to make an issue of the remaining tax at this time. The session would be a long one devoted to the colony's normal business. GW was today appointed to the same three committees on which he had served during the last session: religion, privileges and elections, and propositions and grievances (*H.B.J.,* 1766–69, 225–30).

21. Came to Town with Mrs. Washington P & Jacky Custis. I dind at Mrs. Campbells. Mrs W &ca. dined at Mrs. Dawsons. I spent the Eveng. (without suppg.) at Mrs. Campbells.

> Patsy and Jacky lodged with GW at Mrs. Campbell's place (Custis Account Book). Mrs. Washington may have stayed there also since GW apparently had a private room, or she may have been the guest of Mrs. Dawson or some other acquaintance in the town.

23. Dined with Mrs. Washington &ca. at the Speakers by Candlelight & spent the Evg. there also.

24. J.P. Custis and I dined with others at the Govrs. I spent the Evening at Hayes.

> GW and Thomas Nelson, Jr., of York County were today ordered by the burgesses to prepare "a Bill for laying a Tax upon Dogs." Nelson presented the bill to the house 1 Dec., but it was defeated (*H.B.J.,* 1766–69, 289, 309).

December

Where & how—my time is—Spent

2. Mrs. Washington & children, myself, Colo. Basset, Mrs. Basset & Betcy Bassett all Eat Oysters at Mrs. Campbells abt. One oclock and afterwards went up to Eltham.

> The burgesses once more adjourned until 11:00 A.M. Monday. Before the family left town, GW paid Miss P. Davenport £3 3s. 8d. for clothing furnished Patsy and Mrs. Washington. He also paid 3s. for postage and gave Jacky £1 in cash. Mrs. Washington and Patsy had received spending money earlier in the week (*H.B.J.,* 1766–69, 311–12; Ledger A, 299).

22. Sett of for home. Dined at Todds Bridge and lodgd at Hubbards.

Jacky Custis apparently had returned to Boucher's school before this date and was not with the family today.

23. Breakfasted at Caroline Ct. House and reachd Fredericksburg abt. 4 Oclock in the Aftern. ding. at Colo. Lewis.

Caroline Court House was about halfway between Todd's Bridge and Fredericksburg but lay a few miles east of the main road.

24. Went to Prayers, & dined afterwds. at Colo. Lewis. Spent the Evening with Mr. Jones at Julians.

Edward Jones was Mary Ball Washington's overseer at the Ferry Farm. Mrs. Julian kept a tavern on the main street of Fredericksburg until about 1777.

28. Reached home to Dinner with Mr. Boucher &ca.

29. At Home all day.

30. Mr. Boucher went away. I Rid to My Mill with [   ] Ball and agreed with [him] to Build here.

GW had decided in the spring to replace his small plantation mill with a merchant mill which could manufacture large quantities of high-grade flour suitable for sale in the colony or for export to lucrative markets abroad (GW to Charles West, 6 June 1769). The new mill was to be built downstream from GW's old mill, near the point where narrow, shallow Dogue Run widened into navigable Dogue Creek, a convenient location for water transportion. But the exact site would not be determined until the terrain in the area had been thoroughly studied.

The millwright was John Ball of Frederick County.

1770

January

Where & how my time is Spent

6. The two Colo. Fairfaxs and Mrs. Fairfax dind here as did Mr. R. Alexander & the two Gentn. that came the day before. The Belvoir Family returnd after Dinner.

23. Went a hunting after breakfast & found a Fox at Muddy hole & killd her (it being a Bitch) after a chace of better than two hours & after treeing her twice the last of which times she fell dead out of the Tree after being therein sevl. minutes apparently we[ll]. Rid to the Mill afterwards.

February

Where & how my time is Spent

7. Rid to Alexandria to a Meeting of the Trustees. Returnd in the Evening & found Captn. McCarty here.

> GW had been appointed a trustee of Alexandria on 16 Dec. 1766. However, there is no record in the trustees' minutes of his ever officially attending one of their meetings, even on this day, nor is there any record of his formally resigning the office or being replaced.

9. Went a hunting—found a fox and lost it.

10. Jacky Custis returnd to Mr. Bouchers to School. Mr. Ballendine and myself leveled Doeg Run in ordr. to fix on a Mill seat.

> Jacky's departure had been delayed for several weeks, first by the freezing over of the fords between Mount Vernon and Caroline County, then by the heavy snowfall of 4 Feb. (GW to Jonathan Boucher, 3–10 Feb. 1770, *Papers, Colonial Series,* 8:305–6).

18. Went to Pohick Church and returnd to Dinner.

22. Went up to Court again. Mr. Ross returnd to Colchester. Returnd in the Evening and found my Brothers Saml. & John & the latters wife & Daughter Mr. Lawe. Washington & Daughter & the Revd. Mr. Smith here.

> John Augustine and Hannah Bushrod Washington had two daughters: Jane Washington (1759–1791) and Mildred Washington (born c.1760). The daughter of Lawrence Washington of Chotank who came with him on this day is apparently Mary Townshend Washington, who married Robert Stith of King George County in 1773. The Rev. Mr. Smith is Thomas Smith of Cople Parish, Westmoreland County.

Remarks & Occurs. in Feby.

Feby. 2d. Agreed with Joseph Goart, to come down and raise Stone out of my Quarry for my Mill at the Rate of Three pounds pr. Month 26 days to the Month and lost time to be made up.

> The walls of the new mill were to be built with local sandstone, which the residents of the area called freestone because of its abundance and the ease with which it could be cut and carved. GW's quarry may have been on the banks of the Potomac River west of his mansion house, where a large bed of freestone was located. Goart, whose name GW variously spelled Gort, Goord, Goort, and Gourt, began his work on 6 Mar. (Ledger A, 314, 333, 340).

3. Agreed with Mr. Robt. Adam for the Fish catchd at the Fishing Landing I bought of Posey, on the following terms—to wit

He is obligd to take all I catch at that place provided the quantity does not exceed 500 Barls. and will take more than this qty. if he can get Cask to put them in. He is to take them as fast as they are catchd with out giving any interruption to my people; and is to have the use of the Fish House for his Salt, fish, &ca. taking care to have the House clear at least before the next Fishing Season.

In consideration of which he is to pay me Ten pounds for the use of the House, give 3/ a thousd. for the Herrings (Virg. Money) and 8/4 a hundred (Maryland Curry.) for the whitefish. Mr. Piper and Lund Washington present.

> The fishery was on the 200-acre tract of land GW had acquired at the sale of John Posey's effects the previous October (*Va. Gaz.*, R, 19 Oct. 1769). Taken by seining in the Potomac, the fish were packed with salt in large barrels to be sold to local planters for their slaves or to be shipped abroad, often to the West Indies.

March

Where & how my time is Spent

Mar. 1. My Brothers and the Company with them went away about 10 O clock. I went to level the Ground on the other side of Doeg Run. Mr. Magowan & Captn. Wm. Crawford came here this afternoon.

> GW was taking elevations west of Dogue Run to determine the best route for a millrace to his new mill. William Crawford came today to report on his surveys for GW in western Pennsylvania.

22. Rid to the Mill and laid of with the Millwright the foundation for the New Mill House. Upon my return found Captn. Crawford here.

> The site selected for the new mill was about one-third of a mile down Dogue Run, on the opposite bank, from the old mill. There, as planned, the tidal waters of the navigable portion of the stream, Dogue Creek, would flow up to the tailrace, enabling flat-bottom boats to deliver grain to the mill's door. The same boats would carry flour down to the mouth of the creek, where a brig or schooner would take the cargo aboard and transport it to the markets at Alexandria, Norfolk, or elsewhere. The foundations of the building, as laid off on this day, measured roughly 40 by 50 feet (Burson, "George Washington Grist Mill," blueprint no. 2). When finished, the mill would be 2 2 stories high, equipped with a breast wheel 16 feet in diameter and two sets of millstones, one to be used exclusively for merchant work and the other for custom work, that is, grinding local farmers' grain in return for one-eighth of the amount brought in, the legal toll at this time (Hening, 6:58). This custom business would be still another source of income provided by the new mill.

Remarks & Occurans. in Mar.

26. Countess a hound Bitch after being confind sometime got loose and was lined before it was discovered by my Water dog once and a small foist looking yellow cur twice.

GW had paid £1 16s. for a spaniel on 5 Feb. (Ledger A, 302).

28. She was lined by Ranger a dog I had from Mr. Fairfax. I planted three french Walnuts in the New Garden, & on that side next the work House.

April

Where & how my time is Spent

16. Went up to Alexandria to Court & stayed all Night.

17. Returnd home in the Afternoon with Mr. Josh. Gallaway, & Colo. R. Lee.

> In court today Thomas Montgomerie of Dumfries recorded a letter from Margaret Savage (see entry for 22 Sept. 1769) which granted him power of attorney in her affairs (Fairfax County Order Book for 1770–72). Mrs. Savage's husband apparently had coerced or coaxed her into taking this step, which put her trustees, GW and Bryan Fairfax, in the awkward position of having to demand payment of her annuity from Montgomerie as Dr. Savage's agent and then giving the money to him as Mrs. Savage's legal representative. Knowing that Montgomerie had no obligation to send Mrs. Savage her money, GW and Fairfax tried to postpone dealing with him until they could get some clarification of the matter from Mrs. Savage.
> Joseph Galloway (c.1731–1803) of Philadelphia was a rich and powerful lawyer with scholarly tastes. At this time he was speaker of the Pennsylvania Assembly and vice-president of the American Philosophical Society. He also had a great interest in western lands and was a member of the Grand Ohio Company, commonly known as the Walpole Company.

18. The above Gentlemen went away after breakfast. Patsy Custis, & Milly Posey went to Colo. Mason's to the Dancing School. Mr. Magowan who I found here yesterday stayed. Mr. Ball & one of his People set in to Work today—as did the Mason's to raising stone yesterday.

> Francis Christian, a dancing master from Richmond County, was holding a series of dancing classes for the young people of the neighborhood. Some of the classes would meet at George Mason's Gunston Hall, some at Mount Vernon, and some possibly at other nearby houses. GW today paid Christian £2 to admit Patsy and Milly to his school (Ledger A, 314). Christian's dancing classes often lasted several days in each home, and the days were usually long. In a class which he held in Westmoreland County in 1773, "the Scholars" began soon after breakfast by having "their Lesson singly round." Then, "there were several Minuets danced with great ease and propriety; after

which the whole company Joined in countrydances." The class continued until 7:30 P.M. with breaks for dinner and candle lighting. Christian was observed to be "punctual, and rigid in his discipline, so strict indeed that he struck two of the young misses for a fault in the course of their performance" (Fithian, *Journal*, 44–45).

May

Where & how my time is Spent

3. Went the above rounds before dinner—but did not go out afterwards.

4. Rid to the Masons & Ditchers before dinner.

5. Rid to the Mill Rights—Masons & Ditchers before dinner, & to Doeg Run Qr.

8. Went the same rounds again and promised the ditchers 18d. a Rod if they woud be brisk and stick to it.

19. Set of for Williamsburg—dind at Dumfries—calld at My Mothers and lodgd at Colo. Lewis's in Fredericksbg.

The burgesses were to begin meeting again on 21 May.

20. Breakfasted at Mr. Bouchers—dind at Coleman's & lodgd at Todds bridge.

Jonathan Boucher had been trying for several years to obtain the rectorate of St. Anne's Parish in Annapolis, Md., which offered a better livelihood than he had in Caroline County. At breakfast on this day, he and GW apparently discussed the matter and agreed that, if the move was made, Jacky would go to Annapolis also and continue his schooling under Boucher, provided that Mrs. Washington approved. But GW was unwilling to agree with the tutor on another point. Boucher had been recently urging the Washingtons to allow him to take Jacky on an extended tour of Europe beginning about 1772. GW did not dispute the educational advantages of such a tour, but he was concerned that its cost would be more than Jacky's estate could afford. Any decision about the trip, he told Boucher, would have to wait until he consulted friends in Williamsburg (Boucher to GW, 9 and 21 May 1770; GW to Boucher, 2–9 June 1770; *Papers, Colonial Series*, 8:332–33, 336–41, 348–49).

Coleman tavern was probably at Bowling Green, on the main road from Fredericksburg to Williamsburg.

21. Breakfasted at King Wm. Ct. House & dind & lodgd at Eltham.

22. Reached Williamsburg to Breakfast & dined at the Club at Mrs. Campb[ells] and supped at the Raleigh.

GW lodged at Mrs. Campbell's tavern for his stay in town. The House of Burgesses, which had convened the previous day as scheduled, dealt mostly with private bills during this session and transacted relatively "little business of a public nature" (GW to George W. Fairfax, 27 June 1770, *Papers, Colonial Series*, 8:353–55).

25. Dined at the Palace & attended a Committee of the Association at Hayes. Spent the Eveng. there.

A general meeting of the Virginia nonimportation association had been held in Williamsburg 22 May, and a committee of 20 gentlemen, including GW, had been appointed to revise the agreement that the associators had signed the previous year (*Va. Gaz.*, R, 3 May 1770; Carter, *Diary*, 1:418).

June

Where & how my time is Spent

June 1st. Dined at the Club at Mrs. Campbells (Williamsburg) and attended a Meeting of the Association at the Capitol at 6 Oclock & contd. there till Eleven Oclock.

At this general meeting, it was resolved "that a friendly Invitation be given to all Gentlemen Merchants, Traders, and others, to meet the associators, in *Williamsburg*, on *Friday* the 15th Instant, in order to consult and advise touching an association, and to accede thereto in such Manner as may best answer the Purposes of the same" (*Va. Gaz.*, R, 31 May 1770).

4. Dined at the Club and spent the Evening at the Councills Ball at the Capitol.

The council's ball was held this evening in honor of the king's birthday. Attending, besides the members of the council, were the governor, the burgesses, and "the magistrates and other principal inhabitants" of Williamsburg (*Va. Gaz.*, P&D, 7 June 1770).

11. Went over to Colo. Thos. Moores Sale & purchasd two Negroes— to Wit Frank & James & returnd to Eltham again at Night.

All of Moore's estate, including 26 slaves and about 1,000 acres of land on the Mattaponi River, was offered for sale at West Point today in order to pay some of his many debts (*Va. Gaz.*, R, 31 May 1770). The Negro Frank cost £31 and James, a boy, cost £55. GW also bought a bay mare at the sale for £8 5s. All sums were credited against Moore's debt to the Custis estate (Ledger A, 204).

16. Dined at the Club at Mrs. Campbells and went to the Play in the Evening.

The American Company of Comedians had arrived in town from Philadelphia on 13 June and today opened the theater with *The Beggar's Opera* and "other entertainments" (*Va. Gaz.*, P&D, 14 June 1770). While the Washingtons were in Williamsburg, GW recorded paying £1 10s. for a pair of gold earrings for Patsy Custis and 3s. 7½d. for a tortoiseshell comb (Ledger A, 318; receipt from James Craig, Custis Papers, Virginia Historical Society).

22. Dined at the Club and went to the Play after meeting the Associates at the Capitol.

> On this day a new nonimportation agreement was signed by 164 persons, including GW, and a copy was sent to Governor Botetourt. The new association, GW wrote to George W. Fairfax on 27 June, "is form'd, much upon the old plan, but more relax'd." Previously prohibited items now to be allowed included barley, pork, sugar, pewter, trinkets and jewelry, plate and gold, bridles, and cheap hats, shoes, boots, and saddles. Price limitations on several types of cheap cloth were eased somewhat, but horses were added to the list of prohibited imports. Committees in each county would enforce the regulations. GW, like many Virginians, was not entirely pleased with this compromise plan, but he was satisfied that "it was the best that the friends to the cause coud obtain" (GW to Jonathan Boucher, 30 July 1770, *Papers, Colonial Series,* 8:361–62).

23. Dined at Mrs. Campbells & set off homewards after it—reaching Colo. Bassetts.

26. Dined at home before three Oclock.

28. Rid into the Neck between breakfast and Dinner. Mr. Addison and Mr. Boucher, who came yesterday in the Afternoon went away today after Breakfast.

> Jonathan Boucher had been installed as rector of St. Anne's Parish in Annapolis, 12 June, and now, accompanied by his sponsor Rev. Henry Addison, he was returning to Caroline County to settle his affairs there. Mrs. Washington by this time had given her permission for Jacky to go with him to Annapolis, and GW today paid Boucher £75 on the boy's account (Ledger A, 318).

July

Where & how my time is Spent

8. Went to Pohick Church & returnd to Dinner. Mr. Stedlar went away after Breakft.

> GW had paid Stedlar £21 10s. on the previous day for music lessons given to Jacky and Patsy Custis. Today he let Patsy have £2 2s. pocket money and her friend Milly Posey 7s. 6d. (Ledger A, 319).

26. Jackey Custis went away after Breakfast to Annapolis to School.

28. Went up to Alexandria with the Association Papers. Dined at Mr. Ramsays calld at Mr. Jno. Wests and returnd home in the Evening.

> GW apparently was taking printed copies of the nonimportation agreement to Alexandria to be circulated and signed. At least 333 signatures eventually were obtained, and sometime before 11 Oct. an association committee was elected for the county. Its members were GW, George Mason, John West, Peter Wagener, and John Dalton (*Va. Gaz.*, R, 11 Oct. 1770).

30. After an Early Dinner we set of for Fredericksburg that is Mrs. Washington, P. Custis & myself. Reachd Mr. Lawson's.

> GW had asked the original officers of the Virginia Regiment to meet him at Fredericksburg 1 Aug. to discuss matters relating to bounty lands in the Ohio Valley that Gov. Robert Dinwiddie had promised members of the regiment in 1754 to encourage enlistment during the French and Indian War (*Va. Gaz.*, P&D, 21 June 1770). Surveying and distribution of the lands had been delayed first by war and then by the Royal Proclamation of 1763, which prohibited settlement west of the Appalachian Mountains. However, much of the territory was opened by treaties signed with the Indians at Hard Labour and Fort Stanwix in 1768. In Dec. 1769 GW brought the Virginia soldiers' claims to the attention of the current Virginia governor, Lord Botetourt, and in the same month presented the governor and council a petition requesting that the grant be implemented.
>
> The council agreed to the petition, specifying that the grant should be limited to veterans who had entered the service before the battle at Great Meadows in July 1754 and that the 200,000 acres should be "taken up in one or more Surveys, not exceeding twenty, on the great Canhawa [Kanawha] and the other places particularized in their Petition so as not to interfere with prior Settlements or surveys actually and legally made." It was also suggested that GW should arrange for a surveyor and insert a notice in the *Virginia Gazette* requiring eligible officers and soldiers to present their claims to him (*Va. Exec. Jls.*, 6:338). GW advertised for the claims in various issues of the *Virginia Gazette,* Dec. 1769 to Apr. 1770. However, he decided that before beginning the expensive and troublesome business of surveying, he must assemble the officers "to consert measures how we shall proceed" (Andrew Lewis to GW, 1 Mar. 1770, *Papers, Colonial Series,* 8:307–9). The meeting at Fredericksburg was the result of that decision.

31. Got to my Mothers to Dinner and staid there all Night.

> Patsy Custis became gravely ill today, suffering not only from "her old complaint" of epilepsy but also "ague and fever" (GW to Jonathan Boucher, 15 Aug. 1770, *Papers, Colonial Series,* 8:365). Dr. Hugh Mercer of Fredericksburg was promptly summoned to Ferry Farm, where he bled the patient and gave her medicines. Patsy remained under his care until the family returned home nine days later. The grip that epilepsy now had on Patsy is documented by a record of her seizures that GW kept 29 June–22 Sept. 1770 on the margins of the printed calendar pages in his almanac. Of the 86 days included in that period, Patsy had "fits" on 26, often two a day. For 31 July GW entered the notation "1 very bad Do.," indicating the exceptional severity of this day's attack.

August

Where & how my time is Spent

Augt. 1. Dined at my Mother's. Went over to Fredericksburg afterwards & returnd in the Evening back again.

2. Met the Officers of the first Virga. Troops at Captn. Weedens where we dined & did not finish till abt. Sun set. Mrs. Washington & Patcy dind at Colo. Lewis's where we lodgd.

> Meeting a day later than scheduled, the officers and representatives of officers who were present accepted William Crawford as surveyor for the veterans' bounty lands and resolved that GW should make a journey to the Ohio Valley with Crawford and Dr. James Craik to locate the best areas for the surveys (minutes of the officers of the Virginia Regiment, 5 Mar. 1771, Washington Papers, Library of Congress; Ledger A, 322).

3. Dined at my Brother Charles's—spent the Evening there & lodgd at Colo. Lew[is].

> Charles Washington was now a leading citizen of Fredericksburg, being both a vestryman of St. George's Parish and a Spotsylvania County justice. He owned a considerable amount of land in Fredericksburg and its vicinity and according to popular tradition operated the Rising Sun Tavern, located on Fauquier Street between Princess Ann and Caroline streets.

6. Dined with Mr. James Mercer.

> James Mercer (1735–1793), a younger brother of Lt. Col. George Mercer but no relation of Hugh Mercer, was a prominent Fredericksburg lawyer. Educated at the College of William and Mary, he held the rank of captain during the French and Indian War and served from 1762 to 1776 as a burgess from Hampshire County, where he owned land.

9. Breakfasted at my Mothers—dined at Dumfries & came home by Night.

14. At home all day writing Invoices and Letters.

September

Where & how my time is Spent

Septr. 1st. In the Evening my Brothr. Saml. & his wife & children came hither from Fredericksburg in their way to Frederick.

> Samuel Washington moved his family about this time to Harewood in Frederick County, where he lived until his death in 1781. His present wife was his fourth, Anne Steptoe Washington. The children who came today were probably Thornton Washington (c.1760–1787), Samuel's son by his second wife, Mildred Thornton Washington, and Ferdinand Washington (1767–1788), his eldest surviving son by Anne Steptoe Washington.

3. Went in the Evening a fishing with my Brothers Saml. & Charles.

23. At Home all day Mr. Campbell and Captn. Sanford dind here.

> Matthew Campbell was an agent for the Alexandria merchant firm of Carlyle & Adam. Capt. Lawrence Sanford, a shipmaster who had been sailing out of Alexandria for the past six years, currently commanded the brig *Swift* of Al-

exandria owned by Joseph Thompson & Company. He had taken a shipment of fish to the West Indies for GW during the previous year and today was arranging to take some herring jointly owned by GW and Matthew Campbell to Jamaica for sale. On 29 Sept. GW instructed Sanford by letter to bring him some West Indian goods on the return voyage: a hogshead of rum, a "Barrel of good Sprits," 200 pounds of coffee, 200 pounds of sugar, and 100 or 200 oranges "if to be had good." Those items were to be paid for out of GW's share of the herring sales, his balance to be rendered in cash. The *Swift* returned with GW's goods a few months later, but GW received no cash balance, because the costs of his goods, £50 10s. 1d., exceeded his eventual proceeds from the deal, £40 15s. 9d. (GW to Sanford, 26 Sept. 1769, Robert McMickan to GW, 7 Dec. 1770, *Papers, Colonial Series*, 8:249, 407–8, Robert McMickan & Co.'s account with GW, 6 Dec 1770–16 Feb. 1771, Mount Vernon Ladies' Association of the Union).

October

Where & how my time is Spent

2. At home all day. John Savage formerly a Lieutt. in the Virga. Service & one Wm. Carnes came here to enter their claim to a share in the 200,000 acres of Land. W[arne]r. Washington & Doctr. Rumney here.

Carnes (Carns) was a private in the Virginia Regiment as early as 9 July 1754.

Several factors induced GW to undertake an arduous journey through western Pennsylvania and the Ohio country in the fall of 1770. Among the most pressing was the question of locating bounty lands on the Kanawha and Ohio rivers for the officers and soldiers of the Virginia Regiment (see main entry for 30 July 1770). GW felt a special sense of urgency about this business because rumors had recently reached Virginia of a newly established land company in England whose proposed claims appeared to overlap those of the Virginia veterans (see *Diaries*, 2:287–88). Furthermore, GW noted, "any considerable delay in the prosecution of our Plan would amount to an absolute defeat of the Grant inasmuch as Emigrants are daily Sealing the choice Spots of Land and waiting for the oppertunity . . . of solliciting a legal Title under the advantages of Possession & Improvement—two powerful Plea's in an Infant Country" (GW to Lord Botetourt, 9 Sept. 1770, *Papers, Colonial Series*, 8:378–80). The movement of settlers into the area also made action imperative. GW's own land interests also induced him to make a firsthand investigation of conditions in western Pennsylvania. In Sept. 1767 GW had instructed William Crawford, his western land agent, to "look ⟨me⟩ out a Tract of about 1500, 2000, or more acres somewhere in your Neighbourhood. . . . Any Person . . . who neglects the present oppertunity of hunting ou⟨t⟩ good Lands & in some measure Marking & distinguishing them for their own (in order to keep others from settling them) will never regain it." Crawford proceeded to have a considerable tract of land surveyed for GW in the area of Chartier's Creek. "When you come up," he informed GW, "you will see the hole of your tract finisht" (GW to Crawford, 21 Sept. 1767, and Crawford to GW, 5 May 1770, *Papers, Colonial Series*, 8:26–32, 330–32).

There are two sets of diary entries for those portions of Oct. and Nov. 1770 covering GW's trip to the Ohio country. Selections from the first set of entries are printed here. The second set describes in great detail the quality of the land the party passed through. It is printed in its entirety in *Diaries*, 2:277–328. Substantive comments relating to GW's trip in the second set of entries have been printed here in the notes to the appropriate date.

5. Set out in Company with Doctr. Craik for the Settlement on Redstone &ca. dind at Mr. Bryan Fairfax's & lodged at Leesburg.

6. Bated at old Codleys. Dind and lodgd at my Brother Sam's.

GW's expenses at Codley's (Caudley's) were £6 (Ledger A, 329). Codley's was located at Williams' (later Snickers') Gap in the Blue Ridge.

7. Dind at Rinkers and lodgd at Saml. Pritchards.

Casper (Jasper) Rinker's house was located approximately ten miles from Winchester on the Winchester-Cumberland road. Samuel Pritchard resided on the Cacapon River some 40 miles from Samuel Washington's establishment.

8. Vale. Crawford joind us, & he and I went to Colo. Cresaps leaving the Doctr. at Pritchards with my boy Billy who was taken sick.

Thomas Cresap's establishment was at Shawnee Old Town (now Oldtown, Md.). Billy is GW's mulatto body servant William, whom he had bought in 1768 from Mrs. Mary Lee of Westmoreland County, the widow of Col. John Lee, for £61 15s. (Ledger A, 261). Billy had assumed the surname Lee, and was also referred to by GW as Will or William. He was to accompany his master throughout the Revolutionary War.

The second set of entries for this day notes that GW, Craik, and Valentine Crawford proceeded to Cresap's in order "to learn from him (being just arrived from England) the particulars of the grant said to be lately sold to Walpole & others, for a certain Tract of Country on the Ohio." Undoubtedly one of the factors that prompted GW's trip to the Ohio in the fall of 1770 to examine western lands was information concerning a new land scheme being promoted in England. While Cresap was in England, he had made particularly inquiry into the affairs of the new company. The project grew out of negotiations between Thomas Walpole, a prominent British politician, and Samuel Wharton, Philadelphia merchant and land speculator. The plan called for the acquisition of over 20,000,000 acres, which would have encompassed much of the area of Kentucky, southwestern Pennsylvania, and the western part of what is now West Virginia. The proposal included a plan to establish a new colony to be called Vandalia. In Dec. 1769 the Grand Ohio Company was formed to further the scheme. In the fall of 1770 GW wrote to Lord Botetourt pointing out the conflict between the Walpole associates' plans and the interests of Virginia. See *Papers, Colonial Series*, 8:378–380, 388–93. It had soon become evident that the boundaries of the new grant would overlap the claims of the Mississippi Company (of which GW was a member) and those of the Ohio Company of Virginia and would encroach on the bounty lands claimed by veterans of the Virginia Regiment.

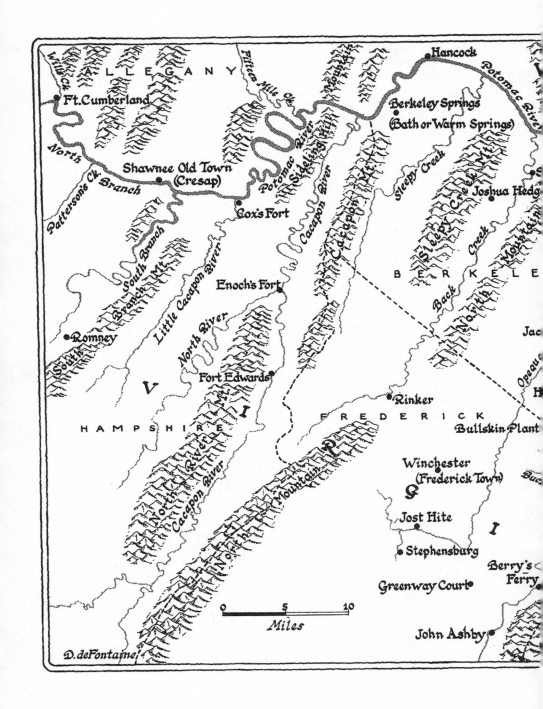

ALLEGANY

Wills Ck.

Ft. Cumberland

North

Patterson's Ck. Branch

Shawnee Old Town (Cresap)

Cox's Fort

Fifteen Mile Ck.

Sideling Hill

Potomac River

Cacapon River

Enoch's Fort

South Branch Mt.

Little Cacapon River

North River

Romney

Fort Edwards

North River

Cacapon River

HAMPSHIRE

V   I

North Mountain

Hancock

Potomac River

Berkeley Springs (Bath or Warm Springs)

Sleepy Creek

Joshua Hedg

Cacapon Mt.

Sleepy Creek Mt.

Back Creek

North Mountain

BERKELE

Jac

Opequ

H

Rinker

FREDERICK

Bullskin Plant

Winchester (Frederick Town)

Bu

G

Jost Hite

I

Stephensburg

Berry's Ferry

Greenway Court

0   5   10

Miles

John Ashby

D. de Fontaine

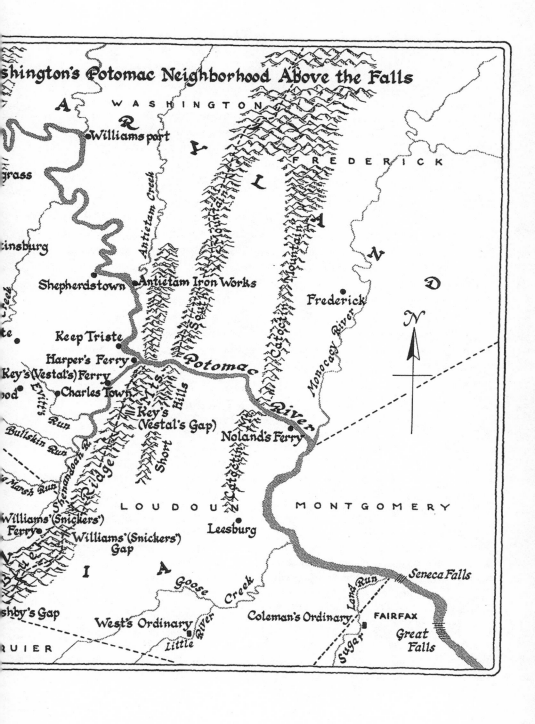

Washington's Potomac Neighborhood Above the Falls

WASHINGTON

•Williams port

MARYLAND

FREDERICK

grass

tinsburg

Antietam Creek

•Shepherdstown •Antietam Iron Works

•Frederick

•Keep Triste

Catoctin Mountain

Monocacy River

te •

•Harper's Ferry

Potomac River

Key's (Vestal's) Ferry

•Charles Town

Evitt's Run

Bullskin Run

Key's (Vestal's) Gap

Short Hills

Noland's Ferry

ood•

Shenandoah R.

Marsh Run

Blue Ridge

LOUDOUN

MONTGOMERY

•Williams'(Snickers') Ferry

Williams'(Snickers') Gap

•Leesburg

N

V I A

Goose Creek

Seneca Falls

shby's Gap

West's Ordinary

Little River

Coleman's Ordinary

Sugar Land Run

FAIRFAX

Great Falls

RUIER

9. Went from Colo. Cresaps to Rumney where in the afternoon the Doctr. & my Servant & Baggage arrivd.

> The town of Romney on the South Branch of the Potomac River was established in 1762 (Hening, 7:598–600).

12. Started from Gillams between Sunrising & Day Break and arrivd at the Great crossing of Yaugha. about Sun set or before.

> *Gillams:* probably Joseph Gillam who lived on a branch of George's Creek, a little more than ten miles from the North Branch of the Potomac River. Fort Cumberland is now Cumberland, Md. The Great Crossing of the Youghiogheny is near present-day Addison, Pa.

13. Left this place early in the Morning and arrivd at Captn. Crawfords (known by the name of Stewarts crossing) abt. ½ after four Oclock.

> Stewart's Crossing was on the Youghiogheny River below present-day Connellsville, Pa. The site was named for William Stewart, who settled there in 1753.

14. At Captn. Crawfords all day.

> The entry for this day in the second set of diary entries indicates that GW "Went to see a Coal Mine not far from his [William Crawford's] house on the Banks of the River. The Coal seemd to be of the very best kind, burning freely & abundance of it."

15. Rid to see the Land he got for me & my Brother's.

> This land, which William and Valentine Crawford had surveyed for the Washingtons in 1769, is in the vicinity of Perryopolis, Pa., in what is now Fayette County, Pa.

17. Arrivd at Fort—dining at one Widow Miers at Turtle Creek.

> GW had arrived at Fort Pitt. The Widow Myers's tavern was probably at Sycamore and Sixth streets within the boundaries of present-day Pittsburgh. It frequently served as a rallying point for frontier militia and was still operating in the 1790s. GW spent 3s. 9d. at the tavern. Turtle Creek enters the Monongahela above the site of Fort Pitt.
> The entry describing GW's stay at Fort Pitt in the second diary indicates that the party "lodgd in what is calld the Town—distant abt. 300 yards from the Fort at one Mr. Semples who keeps a very good House of Publick Entertainment. These Houses which are built of Loghs, & rangd into Streets are on the Monongahela, & I suppose may be abt. 20 in Number and inhabited by Indian Traders &ca." GW is referring to the tavern kept by Samuel Semple in Baynton, Wharton, & Morgan's former storehouse. The house stood at what is now the corner of Water and Ferry streets in Pittsburgh. GW's total expenses for the party at Semple's were £26 1s. 10d., which he paid 21 Nov. on his return to Fort Pitt.

18. Dined in the Fort at the Officers Club.

The entry for this day in the second diary notes that GW dined with Colo. Croghan & the Officers of the Garrison. "Supped there also meeting with great Civility from the Gentlemen, & engaged to dine with Colo. Croghan the next day at his Seat abt. 4 Miles up the Alligany."

19. Dined at Colo. Croghans abt. 4 Miles from Pittsburg & returnd.

George Croghan and GW were old acquaintances from the 1754 campaign against the French, in which Croghan had agreed to provision the Virginia troops. At that time GW had been highly critical of his efforts. After the French and Indian War, Croghan became one of the frontier's leading land speculators. For his attempt to entice GW into his land schemes, see *Diaries*, 2:281–82.

This day's entry in the second diary notes that GW "Recd. A Message from Colo. Croghan that the White Mingo & other Chiefs of the 6 Nations had something to say to me, & desiring that I woud be at his House abt. 11. (Where they were to meet) I went up and receivd a Speech with a String of wampum from the White Mingo to the following effect.

"That as I was a Person who some of them remember to have seen when I was sent on an Embassy to the French, and most of them had heard of: they were come to bid me welcome to the Country, and to desire that the People of Virginia woud consider them as friends & Brothers linked together in one chain—that I wd. Inform the Governor, that it was their wish to live in peace and harmy, with the white People, & that tho their had been some unhappy differences between them and the People upon our Froniers, it was all made up, and they hopd forgotten; and concluded with saying, that, their Brothers of Virginia did not come among them and Trade as the Inhabitants of the other Provences did, from whence they were affraid that we did not look upon them with so friendly an Eye as they coud wish.

"To this I answered (after thanking them for their friendly welcome) that all the Injuries & Affronts that had passd on either side was not totally forgotten, and that I was sure nothing was more wishd and desird by the People of Virginia than to live in the strictest friendship with them. That the Virginians were a People not so much engagd in Trade as the Pensylvanians, &ca., wch. was the Reason of their not being so frequently among them; but that it was possible they might for the time to come have stricter connections with them, and that I woud acquaint the Govr. with their desires."

The White Mingo (Conengayote) was a Six Nations chief of some importance in this area.

The second diary entry for this day also notes that "After dining at Colo. Croghan we returnd to Pittsburg—Colo. Croghan with us, who intended to accompany us part of the Way down the River, having engaged an Indian calld the Pheasant & one Joseph Nicholson an Interpreter to attend us the whole Voyage. Also a young Indn. Warrior." The Pheasant had attended the Indian congress at Fort Stanwix in 1768 with a delegation of 16 warriors. He may have been an Oneida. GW paid the Pheasant and the young warrior £10 13s. for their services on the trip to the Ohio (Ledger A, 329).

20. Set out for the Big Kanhawa with Dr. Craik Captn. Crawford & others. Incampd abt. 14 Miles off.

> The second diary entry for this day indicates that the party "Imbarkd in a large Canoe with sufficient Stores of Provision & Necessaries" accompanied by GW's party "& the Indians who went in a Canoe by themselves. From Fort Pitt we sent our Horses & boys back to Captn. Crawford wt. orders to meet us there again the 14th. Day of November."

21. Got abt. 32 Miles further and Incampd abt. 3 Miles below little Bever Ck.

> The second diary's entry states that the party "Left Our Incampment abt. 6 Oclock & breakfasted at the Logs Town, where we parted with Colo. Croghan &ca. Abt. 9 Oclock."
>
> Little Beaver Creek empties into the Ohio from the north, about 42 miles from Fort Pitt (Pownall, *Topographical Description,* 166).

22. Reachd the Mingo Town abt. 29 Miles by my Computation.

> Mingo Town (now Mingo Junction, Ohio) was an Indian village several miles below Steubenville, Ohio. In 1766 it was apparently the only Indian village on the banks of the Ohio between its location and Fort Pitt; it contained some 60 families (Cramer, *Navigator,* 25n). The entry for this date in the second diary notes that "Upon our arrival at the Mingo Town we receivd the disagreeable News of two Traders being killd at a Town calld the Grape Vine Town, 38 Miles below this; which causd us to hesitate whether we shoud proceed or not, & wait for further Intelligence."

23. Stayd at this place till One Clock in the Afternoon & padled abt. 12 Miles down the River & Incamped.

> GW noted in his second diary that "Several imperfect Accts. Coming in agreeing that only one Person was killd, & the Indians not supposing it to be done by their people, we resolvd to pursue our passage, till we coud get some more distinct Acct. Of this Transaction. Accordingly abt. 2 Oclock we set out with the two Indians which was to accompany us, in our Canoe."

24. We reachd the Mouth of a Creek calld Fox Grape vine Creek (10 Miles up which is a Town of Delawares calld Franks Town) abt. 3 Oclock in the afternoon—distant from our last Camp abt. 26 Miles.

> Fox Grape Vine Creek, also called Captina Creek, flows into the Ohio from the west. Frank's Town was a well-known Delaware village about six miles from the Juniata River. Originally called Assunepachla, it was referred to as Frank's Town, for the Pennsylvania trader Frank Stevens, as early as 1734.

25. Incampd in the long reach abt. 30 Miles from our last lodge according to my Computation.

> The "long reach" of the Ohio is a section of the river with relatively few curves stretching approximately from Paden City to Raven Rock, W.Va. Its length is 18 to 20 miles. According to the second diary, on 24 Oct. GW had sent Nicholson and one of the Indians to investigate the rumored death of

the trader. They returned on 25 Oct. reporting "they found no body at the Town but two Old Indian women (the Men being a Hunting). From these they learnt that the Trader was not killd, but drownd in attempting to Ford the Ohio; and that only one boy, belonging to the Trader, was in these parts; the Trader (fathr. To him) being gone for Horses to take hom their Skins."

26. Incampd at the Mouth of a Creek about 4 Miles above the Mouth of Muskingham distant abt. 32 Miles.

27. Incampd at the Mouth of great Hockhocking distant from our last Incampment abt. 32 Miles.

28. Meeting with Kiashuta & other Indian Hunters we proceeded only 10 Miles to day, & Incampd below the Mouth of a Ck. on the west the name of wch. I know not.

GW met Guyasuta during his journey to the French commandant in 1753. After joining the French in 1755, Guyasuta had actively engaged in hostilities against the British during the French and Indian War and was a leader in Pontiac's rebellion. Changing his allegiance after the war, he again supported the English and aided the firm of Baynton, Wharton, & Morgan in opening up the Illinois trade. He continued to support the British during the Revolution and participated in the attack against Hannastown, Pa., in 1782. After the Revolution he settled in the area of Pittsburgh and died there about 1800. In his second diary GW describes the meeting: "In the Person of Kiashuta I found an old acquaintance. He being one of the Indians that went with me to the French in 1753. He expressd a satisfaction in seeing me and treated us with great kindness, giving us a Quarter of very fine Buffalo. He insisted upon our spending that Night with him, and in order to retard us as little as possible movd his camp down the River about 3 Miles just below the Mouth of a Creek the name of which I could not learn (it not being large). At this place we all Incampd. After much Councelling the overnight they all came to my fire the next Morning, with great formality; when Kiashuta rehearsing what had passd between me & the Sachems at Colo. Croghan's, thankd me for saying that Peace & friendship was the wish of the People of Virginia (with them) & for recommending it to the Traders to deal with them upon a fair & equitable footing; and then again expressd their desire of having a Trade opend with Virginia, & that the Governor thereof might not only be made acquainted therewith, but of their friendly disposition towards the white People. This I promised to do."

29. Went round what is calld the Great Bent & Campd two Miles below it distant from our last Incampment abt. 29 Miles.

The Great Bend of the Ohio is in the region of Meigs County, Ohio.

30. Incampd Early Just by the old Shawna Town distant from our last no more than 15 Miles.

Shawnee Town appears on Lewis Evans's 1766 map of the middle colonies just north of the confluence of the Ohio and the Great Kanawha rivers.

31. Went out a Hunting & met the Canoe at the Mouth of the big Kanhawa distant only 5 Miles makg. the whole distance from Fort Pitt accordg. to my Acct. 266 Miles.

> GW's calculations on the distance from Fort Pitt to the mouth of the Great Kanawha at present-day Point Pleasant, W.Va., agree substantially with those of Capt. Harry Gordon, chief engineer of the Northern Department in North America. In Gordon's table of distances it is logged as 266¼ miles (Pownall, *Topographical Description,* 166).

November

where & how my time is Spent

1. Went up the Great Kanhawa abt. 10 Miles with the People that were with me.

2. Hunting the most part of the day. The Canoe went up abt. 5 Miles further.

3. Returnd down the River again and Incampd at the Mouth.

4. Proceeded up the Ohio on our return to Fort Pitt. Incampd abt. 9 Miles below the rapid at the Grt. Bent.

6. In about 5 Miles we came to Kiashutas Camp & there Halted.

> In his second set of entries, GW noted for this date that "We left our Incampment a little after daylight, & in about 5 Miles we came to Kiashutes Hunting Camp. . . . By the kindness, and Idle ceremony of the Indians, I was detaind at Kiashuta Camp all the remaing. Part of this day; and having a good deal of conversation with him on the Subject of Land."

7. Reachd the Mouth of the Hockhocking—distant abt. 20 Miles.

8. Came within a Mile of the Mouth of Muskingham 27 Miles.

9. Got to the 3 Islands in the 2d. long reach about 17 Miles.

12. Got only about 5 Miles the Currt. being very strong against us.

15. Reachd Weeling (on the West) where there had been an Indian Town & where some of the Shawnes are going to settle in the Spring distant from our last Incampment 12 Miles.

16. Got within 13 Miles of the lower cross Creeks—13 Miles.

17. Reachd the Mingo Town about 13 Miles more.

18. At this place all day waiting for Horses which did not arrive.

19. At the same place, & in the same Situation as yesterday.

20. Our Horses arriving about One Oclock at 2 we set out for Fort Pitt & got about 10 Miles.

21. Reachd Fort Pitt in the Afternoon & lodged at Samples.

22. Invited the Officers of the Fort and other Gentlemen to dine with me at Samples.

23. Left Fort Pitt and reachd Mr. John Stephensons.

24. Got to Captn. Crawfords—the Rivr. Youghyaughgane being very high.

> In a section headed "Remark & Occurs, in Novr." GW noted under this day's date that "When we came to Stewards Crossing at Crawfords, the River was too high to Ford and [the] Canoe gone a Drift. However after waiting there 2 or 3 hours a Canoe was got in which we passd and Swam our Horses. The remainder of this day I spent at Captn. Crawfords it eiher Raining or Snowing hard all day."

26. Came to Killams on Georges Creek.

> In the second set of entries, GW noted that at Killams (Gillam's) the party met "several Families going over the Mountains to live—some witht. Having any places provided. The Snow upon the Alligany Mountains was near knee deep."

27. Got to Old Town to Colo. Cresaps distant from Killams about 25 Miles.

28. Reachd Jasper Rinkers about 38 Miles from Cresaps & 30 Miles from Cox's—not long ones.

29. Came to my Brothers (distant about 25 miles) to Dinner.

30. Reachd Charles Wests 35 Miles from My Brother's.

> West's ordinary was located at the junction of the Colchester and Carolina roads in Loudoun County, near present-day Aldie, Va. By 1765 Charles West had taken over management of the inn from his father, William West.

December

Where & how my time is Spent.

Decr. 1st. Reachd home from Wests after an absence of 9 Weeks and one Day.

3. Rid to the Mill in the forenoon, and returnd to Dinner.

4. Rid by Posey's to the Mill, and to the Ditchers. Mr. Boucher and Jacky Custis came here in the Afternoon.

Boucher had not given up the idea of taking Jacky to Europe. At this time he was urging the Washingtons to prepare the boy for travel by having him inoculated for smallpox in Baltimore, where Dr. Henry Stevenson ran a popular inoculation clinic, free of legal restrictions that the burgesses had recently imposed on inoculators in Virginia. GW favored the inoculation, thinking that Jacky should be protected against smallpox whether he went abroad or not (GW to Boucher, 13 May 1770, *Papers, Colonial Series,* 8:333–35). Mrs. Washington agreed that the benefits were very desirable but feared exposing her son to the inoculating process, which brought on a fatal case of the disease in 1 of every 50 to 60 inoculations (GW to Boucher, 20 April 1771, ibid., 448–49). The decision on this matter, like the one on the tour, was postponed.

17. Jacky Custis went to Annapolis & I to Court. Returnd in the afternoon.

Jacky was not eager to return to school. "His mind," GW warned Jonathan Boucher, is "a good deal relaxed from Study, & more than ever turnd to Dogs Horses & Guns" (16 Dec. 1770, *Papers, Colonial Series,* 8:411–12).

18. Rid to my Mill and to the Ditchers in the Fore and Afternoon.

25. Went to Pohick Church and returnd to Dinner.

27. Went a fox Hunting and killd a fox in Company with the two Mr. Triplets and Mr. Peake who dined here.

30. My Miller & his wife and Mr. Ball dind here.

GW's miller was William Roberts, a Pennsylvanian whom he engaged in Oct. 1770 to run the new mill at Mount Vernon for £80 a year plus the privilege of feeding a cow and raising domestic fowl at GW's expense. Roberts was highly skilled in the business of grinding grain, a delicate art requiring great judgment in fixing the speed and interval of the millstones to produce good-quality flour with minimum waste. He was also, like John Ball, a capable millwright who could keep the mill in proper working order, and when he was not grinding grain, he could work in the nearby cooper's shop making barrels needed for flour and other products. Aided by an apprentice miller whom he had brought with him, Roberts worked diligently and honestly for GW for several years, but an addiction to liquor eventually proved to be his undoing (GW to Robert Lewis & Sons, 6 Sept. 1783, Washington Papers, Library of Congress, and 12 April 1785, *Papers, Confederation Series,* 2:493–94).

31. I rid to My Mill in the forenoon and Afternoon.

1771

January

Where & how my time is Spent

Jany. 1st. Rid to my Mill in the forenoon and afternoon.

2. Did the same thing again. Met Colo. Robt. Fairfax there, & upon my return home found Mr. Piper, Mr. Muir, and Doctr. Rumney here who dined & lodged.

> Robert Fairfax was preparing at this time to return to his home in England, Leeds Castle, where he lived until his death in 1793. He became the seventh Baron Fairfax when his brother Thomas died in 1781.
>   Rumney apparently brought a quantity of the "Best Bark" for Patsy Custis. Peruvian bark, also called cinchona, was one of the popular eighteenth-century remedies for epilepsy as well as for malaria. Before Rumney left Mount Vernon, he also furnished Patsy with a fresh assortment of pills, powders, and drops (receipt from William Rumney, 24 June 1772, Custis Papers, Virginia Historical Society).

13. Mrs. Washington Patcy Custis & myself Dined and lodged at Belvoir.

17. Rid to the Mill &ca. in the Afternn. and went up to Alexa. with Mrs. Washington & Patcy Custis in the Afternoon.

20. Went to Pohick Church with Mrs. Washington and returnd to Dinr. Mr. Ball dined here.

31. Returnd home by my Mill & the Dam where my People were attempting to stop water.

> The Dogue Run dam at the head of the millrace apparently was under construction, but the heavy rain that fell 29–30 Jan. had swollen the stream, making the job more difficult.

February

Where and how my time is Spent

Feby. 1st. At the Mill in the forenoon and afternoon. Doctr. Rumney came here before Dinner & stayd all Night.

2. At the Mill and where my People was at Work on the Race in the forenoon & afternoon. Mr. Rutherford & Price Posey came here in the Evening.

> Robert Rutherford (1728–1803) was a prominent landowner and burgess from Frederick County. During the French and Indian War he had served for a time as a deputy commissary for the Virginia Regiment and in the fall

of 1757, on the recommendation of GW, raised a partisan company called Rutherford's Rangers. After the war he settled on Flowing Springs farm near Evitt's Run.

John Price Posey (d. 1788), a son of Capt. John Posey, began working about this time in Thomas Lawson's iron and flour business on Neabsco Creek. Young Posey was able to obtain the job because GW persuaded Lawson to hire him (Posey to GW, 25 May 1771, *Papers, Colonial Series,* 8: 470–73). GW had cause to regret his magnanimity. By the mid-1780s Posey had several brushes with the law, including attempts to defraud Jacky Custis and Bartholomew Dandridge. In the summer of 1787 he was arrested for an attack on the sheriff of New Kent County. He escaped from jail but retaliated for his arrest by burning down the county jail and the clerk's office. Convicted of arson by Virginia's General Court, Posey was hanged in Richmond on 25 Jan. 1788.

3. Val. Crawford came this Afternoon & Price Posey went away in the Morng.

Posey was going to Annapolis and apparently carried a letter from GW to Jonathan Boucher, in which GW asked the tutor on behalf of Mrs. Washington to buy two ounces of ether for Patsy Custis, "if such a thing is to be had in Annapolis," and to send it by Price Posey on his return to Virginia (3 Feb. 1771). Ether, like valerian and musk, was thought to be a strong antispasmodic, useful in treating epilepsy when taken internally in small doses (Hooper, *Lexicon-Medicum,* 383). It was not employed as an anesthetic until the next century.

6. Rid to my Mill by the Ferry in the forenoon, & afternoon. Price Posey came here this Evening.

The Ferry: Capt. John Posey's ferry which GW had begun to rent 23 April 1770.

9. Attempted to go a hunting, but prevented by Rain. Rid to the Mill in the fore and Afternoon.

23. I rid to the Mill before breakfast and returnd to Dinner. Doctor Rumney went away after breakfast.

On the following day Rumney charged a package of valerian and "a vial of drops" to Patsy Custis's account (receipt from William Rumney, 24 June 1772, Custis Papers, Virginia Historical Society).

March

Where & how my time is disposed of

Mar. 1. I rid to my Mill and Ditchers in the forenoon. In the Afternoon Doctr. Craik came.

2. The Doctr. & I set of for Winchester. Dined at Triplets and lodgd at Wests.

GW had called a meeting of the officers of the Virginia Regiment at Winchester on 4 Mar. to report on the trip down the Ohio River that he had made the previous fall (*Va. Gaz.*, P&D, 31 Jan., 7 Feb., and 14 Feb. 1771).

Triplets: the ordinary of James and William Carr Lane at Newgate (now Centreville), Va.

3. Dined at Barry's (on Shanondoah) and reached Greenway Court in the Afternoon where we stayd all Night.

Berry's ferry was on the Shenandoah River about eight miles east of Greenway Court.

4. Reachd Winchester to Dinner according to Appointment with the Officers &ca. claimg. part of the 200,000 Acs. of L[an]d.

Before GW left Greenway Court, he obtained a grant from Lord Fairfax for the unclaimed land on Dogue Run he had surveyed on 24 Mar. 1770, a total of 202 acres (Lord Fairfax's grant to GW, 4 Mar. 1771, Northern Neck Deeds and Grants, Book I, 187). This land gave him control of most of the area around his new dams and upper millrace.

5. At Winchester all day. Dined with Lord Fairfax.

Although scheduled for 4 Mar., the officers' meeting was actually held today. Besides GW and Dr. James Craik, only four officers or their representatives were present. After hearing GW's report and learning that William Crawford had begun to survey along the Great Kanawha River, the meeting unanimously agreed that he should be instructed to finish his work there and then proceed as soon as possible to survey lands on the Tygart Valley River, a branch of the Monongahela.

6. Dined at my Lodging which was at Mr. Philp. Bushes and went home with my Br. Mr. Saml. Washington in the Eveng.

Philip Bush (1732–1812) reputedly offered the best accommodations in Winchester at his Golden Buck Inn, a handsome two-story stone building on Cameron Street.

7. At my Brothers all day writing Instructions & dispatches for Captn. Crawford the Surveyor of our 200,000 Acs. of Land.

11. Set of from my Brother's for Mr. Warnr. Washington's on my return Home.

12. Left Mr. Washingtons, & crossing at Snickers's (where I eat an early Dinner) reach'd Leesburg betwn. 4 & 5 Oclock in the Afternoon.

Leesburg, founded in 1758, was the county seat of Loudoun County.

13. Reachd home, after being obliged to Ferry over goose Creek at Houghs Mill & coming Round by Ellzeys. Found Doctr. Craik here.

Hough's mill was owned by John Hough (d. 1797), of Loudoun County, a well-known surveyor who had settled in the area about 1744.

Ellzeys: probably the home of Lewis Ellzey, who was the first sheriff of Fairfax County and served as a Truro Parish vestryman from 1744 to 1748.

19. At Court all day. In the Afternoon came home, and found Majr. Jenefir, Mr. Boucher, & Jacky Custis here.

> Jacky and his tutor had come at Robert Fairfax's request to see him before he returned to England. Fairfax shared Boucher's opinion that Jacky should tour Europe, and he had invited him to vacation at Leeds Castle during his stay abroad. No definite decision about the trip had yet been made (GW to Jonathan Boucher, 3 Feb. 1771, *Papers, Colonial Series,* 8:432–33).

26. Rid to My Mill and Mill dam at the head of the Race in the forenoon (after going a hunting in the Morning). In the Afternoon Rid to Posey's.

> GW today provided Jacky Custis with £5 10s. for traveling expenses to Annapolis and Baltimore. GW had decided to allow Jacky to go to Baltimore to be inoculated, but upon his departure sometime within the next few days, he had "so many doubts and difficulties" about the matter that GW and Mrs. Washington "concluded nothing was more foreign from his Intention" (GW to Jonathan Boucher, 20 April 1771, *Papers, Colonial Series,* 8:448–49).

April

15. Went to Alexandria to Court. Stayd all Night. Mr. Magowan w[en]t.

16. Came home to Dinner. Mr. Magowan & Mr. Pierce Baily came with me the latter went away afterwds.

> Before returning to Mount Vernon, GW attended a meeting of the Fairfax nonimportation committee. At the request of two merchants the committee examined the invoices for cargoes that had recently arrived from Glasgow and ruled that the merchants could properly accept them (*Va. Gaz.*, R, 18 July 1771).

27. Set out with Mrs. Washington & Patcy Custis on my journey to Williamsburg. Dined at Colchester & Suppd & lodgd in Dumfries.

> The family traveled south in GW's chariot. The burgesses were not meeting this spring because they had no pressing business to consider. But GW had to go to Williamsburg to give the General Court his annual report on the administration of Jacky and Patsy Custis's affairs and to collect interest on various Custis bonds (Custis Account Book).

28. Dined at my Mother's and lodgd at Colo. Lewis's. Supped at my Brother Charles's.

29. Dined at Caroline Court House and lodgd at Hubbards Ordinary.

> GW today recorded paying 2s. 6d. for repair of his chariot (Ledger A, 335).

30. Breakfasted at Todds Ordinary and after making some considerable stop at Ruffins Ferry, occasioned by a Sick Horse—reachd Colo. Bassetts a little in the Night.

May

2. Set out with Colo. Bassett for Williamsburg and reachd Town about 12 Oclock. Dined at Mrs. Dawson's & went to the Play.

> At the theater GW saw a performance by the American Company of Comedians, which had been in Williamsburg for more than a month (Ledger A, 335; Rankin, *Theater in Colonial America,* 159). Mrs. Campbell, with whom he lodged as usual, had by this time moved down Duke of Gloucester Street to "the coffee-house . . . next the Capitol."

3. Dined at the Speaker's and went to the Play—after wch. Drank a Bowl or two of Punch at Mrs. Campbells.

4. Dined at Mrs. Campbells (& paid for Dinner & Club) and went up to Eltham with Colos. Bassett & Lewis.

30. Reachd home—crossing at Boyd's hole. Found Jacky Custis there.

> Jacky's presence at Mount Vernon was an occasion for rejoicing. Without informing his mother or GW he had changed his mind about smallpox inoculation, had been inoculated in Baltimore 8 April, and was now fully recovered "without hardly one Mark to tell that He ever had it" (Jonathan Boucher to GW, 9 May 1771, *Papers, Colonial Series,* 8:464–67).

31. Rid to Muddy hole—Doeg Run & the Mill before Dinner. In the Afternoon Vale. Crawford came here & went away again in the Morning.

June

18. Went up to Alexandria & returnd in the Afternoon Mr. Magowan with me. My Brothr. went in the Morning.

> GW went to Alexandria for a meeting of the Fairfax nonimportation committee, which had just examined two new shipments of goods. Only 12 hats sent by mistake of the manufacturer were found to be unacceptable, and the committee was convinced that the importing merchants had "strictly adhered to the spirit and intention of the association" for their part. But the two merchants complained "that they found so little regard paid to the association by others . . . that they should think themselves obliged for the future" to protect their business by sending "their orders in the same manner with other importers; restraining themselves only from importing tea, and other taxed articles" (*Va. Gaz.,* R, 18 July 1771).

Remarks & Occurs. in June

6. Sold all the Flour I have left to Robt. Adam & Co. at the following Rates—fine flour at 12/6 Midlings at 10/. & Shipstuff at 8/4 pr. Ct. £300 of the Money, to be paid in Octr.—the residue in April with Int[eres]t from Octr.

In May the company had bought about 13,500 pounds of GW's flour for £60 7s. 10d., and during June it bought about 128,000 pounds more for £765 3s. 7d. (Ledger A, 326, 341). Over three-fourths of this flour was of fine quality, that is, finely ground and relatively free of bran and impurities. The rest consisted of middlings, a coarse medium-grade flour containing some bran, and ship stuff, the lowest quality of flour, containing much bran. Adam & Co. may have used some of GW's flour for local sale or for making bread at the company's bakery, but much of it, especially the fine flour, must have been exported as it was.

During the spring GW also sold flour to two Norfolk merchants. Philip Carberry, a baker, bought 1,432 pounds of ship stuff for £5 19s. 4d., and William Chisholm, who traded with the West Indies, purchased 36,997 pounds of fine flour for £236 19s. 8d. (Ledger A, 336, 338; Lund Washington to GW, 12 May 1771).

7. Agreed with Mr. Pendleton of Frederick for all the Land to be Included by a Line to be run from the No. West C[orne]r of Owen Thomas's Patent to a Corner of the Land on which James McCarmick lives in my Line supposd to contain abt. 180 Acres for £400 the Money to be paid in two years with Int[eres]t from the 25th. of next Decr. This years Rent to be paid to me & only a special Warrantee to be given with the Land. Got done breaking up my Corn Ground at the Mill.

GW is agreeing to sell Philip Pendleton (1752–1802) a small part of his Bullskin plantation. A contract was not signed until 7 Dec. 1771, but the terms remained unchanged. Owen Thomas's patent for 400 acres, which GW had surveyed 3 April 1750, adjoined GW's land on the south and east. Pendleton had previously bought all or part of this patent from Thomas (Northern Neck Grants and Deeds, Book H, 88).

July

4. At home all day with Mr. Smith. In the Afternoon Jno. Custis came.

Jacky probably brought GW the letter that Jonathan Boucher wrote to him on this date, asking for a final decision about Jacky Custis's proposed European tour. GW replied five days later that he thought that Mrs. Washington was so reluctant to part with her son for a long period and Jacky was so indifferent about the trip that "it will soon be declared he has no inclination to go" (9 July 1771, *Papers, Colonial Series*, 8:494–98). Boucher did not again raise the subject.

8. Went to a Vestry held at the New Church at Pohick.

12. I set of for Williamsburg & crossing at Laidlers lodged at Mr. Lawe. Washingtons.

GW was going to attend the House of Burgesses, which had convened 11 July to deal with problems resulting from a great flood that had come down the James, Rappahannock, and Roanoke rivers in late May, causing about 150 deaths and much property damage. The calamity had not affected Mount Vernon or the Custis lands, but many Virginia planters had lost both their recently planted tobacco crop and the harvested tobacco they had stored in public warehouses for shipment to England. Prompt financial relief was needed to save the planters from bankruptcy. Laidler's ferry landing on the Potomac River was about 14 miles below Port Tobacco, Md.

15. Came to Williamsburg abt. 10 Oclock. Dined at Mrs. Campbells— spent the Evening in my own Room.

GW may have arrived too late to attend the House of Burgesses today; during this session the burgesses were sitting at 9:00 A.M. to avoid the midday heat, and this day's meeting apparently was brief. The flood relief bill was presented to the burgesses on 19 July, and after several amendments it was ordered to be engrossed for a final reading. The bill as amended authorized the issuance of up to £30,000 in treasury notes for payment of planters' claims, which were to be examined and approved by a commission appointed for that purpose (*H.B.J.*, 1770–72, 136–38; Hening, 8:493–503).

Later this day at the Capitol there was a general meeting of the Virginia association, at which GW was probably present. Responding to complaints from Fairfax and Fauquier counties about unequal enforcement of the current agreements, the associators decided in the future to prohibit the importation of only "Tea, Paper, Glass, and Painters Colours of foreign Manufacture, upon which a Duty is laid for the Purpose of raising a Revenue in America" (*Va. Gaz.*, P&D, 18 July 1771). GW lodged with Mrs. Campbell.

16. Dined at the Speakers spent the Evening in my own Room.

17. Dined at the Treasurers. Supd at Mrs. Campbell's.

18. Dined and Supped at Mrs. Campbell's.

19. Dined at Mrs. Campbells & Spent the Evening at Southalls.

23. Breakfasted at the Caroline Court House & Reachd Fredericksburg before two Oclock & dined and lodgd at Colo. Lewis's.

25. Dined at Colo. Lewis's & went to the Play.

The American Company of Comedians had been performing in Fredericksburg every Tuesday, Wednesday, and Thursday since late May, when it had come to take advantage of the crowds at the town's annual June fair (*Va. Gaz.*, P&D, 16 May 1771). The plays may have been staged in the county courtroom, a warehouse, or the 44-by-25-foot billiard room of George Weedon's tavern.

26. Breakfasted at my Mother's. Dined at Dumfries & lodged at Home.

September

10. In the Afternoon set of for Fredericksburg and lodgd at Colo. Harry Lees.

The purpose of this trip was to make final arrangements for GW's mother, Mary Ball Washington, now about 63 years old, to move from the Ferry Farm plantation to a house in Fredericksburg, where she could live in comfort, free from the cares of the plantation. GW had previously discussed the matter with her, and in May, at her request and his expense, he made a down payment of £75 on a house of her choice: a commodious white frame residence on Charles Street near the home of her daughter Betty Lewis (GW to Benjamin Harrison, 21 Mar. 1781, Washington Papers, Library of Congress; Ledger A, 336). Now, in further preparation for his mother's move to town, GW was ready to begin settling her affairs at Ferry Farm and at Little Falls Quarter, a tract of land about two miles farther down the Rappahannock which she had inherited from her father in 1711.

12. Rid all over the Plantn. at the Ho[me] House, & then went to the Quarter and rid all over that & returnd to Dinner Colo. Lewis & my Brothr. Charles being there. In the Afternoon went over to Fredg.

The Plantn. at the Ho[me] House: Ferry Farm. At this time it consisted of about 600 acres of land, and by the terms of Augustine Washington's will, it was legally GW's to do with what he wished.

The Quarter: the plantation at Little Falls, which apparently contained about 400 acres. During this visit GW agreed to take over the quarter at the beginning of 1772, paying his mother an annual rent for it thereafter. Because the livestock and slaves at both Ferry Farm and the quarter were hers, he further agreed to buy her livestock and to rent her slaves. The price of the livestock and the rents for the land and slaves were to be determined within the next few weeks by Fielding Lewis and Charles Washington.

21. Set out with Mr. Wormeley for the Annapolis Races. Dind at Mr. Willm. Digges's & lodgd at Mr. Ignatis Digges's.

The fall racing at Annapolis was an annual highlight of both the sporting and social seasons for the Chesapeake gentry, being an occasion not only for indulging in "the pleasures of the turf" but for going to dinners, balls, and plays in the city (Eddis, *Letters from America*, xxv-xxvi, 54–55). Sponsored by the prestigious Annapolis Jockey Club, the races attracted the finest thoroughbreds in the region to run for purses of up to 100 guineas. This year the jockey club had announced four days of racing to begin at 11:00 A.M. each day from 24 to 27 Sept. and three balls to be held on the nights of 24, 25, and 27 Sept. (*Md. Gaz.*, 12 Sept. 1771).

22. Dind at Mr. Sam Gallaway's & lodged with Mr. Boucher in Annapolis.

Jonathan Boucher and Jacky Custis were living in the St. Anne's Parish parsonage on Hanover Street. Jacky had written to GW on 18 Aug., extending an invitation on behalf of Boucher to stay at his house, as it would be "almost impossible to get a Room at any of the ordinaries, the Rooms being pre-engaged to their [regular] customers" (*Papers, Colonial Series*, 8:518–19).

23. Dined with Mr. Loyd Dulany & Spent the Evening at the Coffee Ho[use].

Lloyd Dulany (1742–1782), son of Daniel Dulany the elder and his third wife, Henrietta Maria Dulany, had recently returned to Annapolis after studying law at the Inns of Court in London. The Coffeehouse, a popular tavern run by a Mrs. Howard, was on Main (now Church) Street near the State House.

24. Dined with the Govr. and went to the Play & Ball afterwards.

GW probably attended the races before dinner on this and the following three days. The track adjoined the town on the west, and because of the beautiful autumn weather "there was a prodigious concourse of spectators and considerable sums were depending on the contest of each day" (Eddis, *Letters from America,* 54). Gov. Robert Eden's home stood on a small peninsula extending into the Severn River.

The play was performed by the American Company of Comedians, which had begun a run in town on 9 Sept., when a new theater was opened on West Street near St. Anne's Church (ibid., 55). The balls were held at the Assembly House on Duke of Gloucester Street. There was a room for dancing in the front of the building, and in a chamber at the back gentlemen gathered to play cards and to drink wine (Stevens, *Annapolis,* 111). GW recorded losing £13 4s. 3d. "By cards—[at] different times" (Ledger A, 344).

27. Dined at Mr. Carrolls and went to the Ball.

Charles Carroll of Annapolis lived in a comfortable brick mansion on Spa Creek. His son Charles Carroll of Carrollton also resided there, and GW probably saw both of them on this occasion.

28. Dined at Mr. Bouchers and went from thence to the Play and afterwards to the Coffee Ho[use].

30. Left Annapolis, & Dind and suppd with Mr. Saml. Gallaway.

October

Octr. [1]. Dined at Upper Marlborough & reachd home in the Afternoon. Mr. Wormley—Mr. Fitzhugh, Mr. Randolph, Mr. Burwell, & Jack Custis came with me. Found Mr. Pendleton here.

Upper Marlboro was a small tobacco town on the western branch of the Patuxent River in Prince George's County, Md., about halfway between Annapolis and Mount Vernon. In 1775 it was described by a visitor as "a very pleasant" place, "containing about a Dozen very neat houses & 3 or 4 stores" (Honyman, *Journal,* 4).

Atty. Gen. John Randolph of Williamsburg and Edmund Pendleton (1721–1803) of Caroline County were retained by GW about this time to act with James Mercer of Fredericksburg as attorneys for the Custis estate in a suit that apparently was to be heard in the General Court at Williamsburg between 10 and 15 Oct. See *Diaries,* 3:60.

2. Mr. Pendleton went away after Breakfast. The other Gentlemen Stayd all day.

10. At home all day. Captn. Crawford came here in the Afternoon.

William Crawford had surveyed the lands between the Great and Little Kanawha rivers for the Virginia Regiment, and he was now bringing in his rough field notes from which finished drafts were to be made with GW's help (Crawford to GW, 2 Aug. 1771). See *Diaries,* 3:61–62.

11. Still at home all day Plotting & Measuring the Surveys which Captn. Crawford made for the Officers & Soldiers.

23. After dinner set of for Williamsburg.

> GW was going to Williamsburg to give the council a list of 81 members of the Virginia Regiment who had presented him with claims under the Proclamation of 1754 and to petition the councillors to devise a system for distributing the 200,000 acres among the claimants (*Va. Exec. Jls.,* 6:438–39)

29. Reach'd Williamsburg before Dinner. And went to the Play in the Afternoon.

> About four weeks before GW arrived in town, Christiana Campbell had moved again, this time to Waller Street behind the Capitol, and in a newspaper advertisement she had announced that "I shall reserve Rooms for the Gentlemen who formerly lodged with me" (*Va. Gaz.,* P&D, 3 Oct. 1771). But for the first time in ten years, GW did not stay with her. He chose, instead, to lodge with John Carter, a well-established merchant who ran a general store next door to the Raleigh Tavern and who at this time lived in a house directly across the street from the Raleigh (*Va. Gaz.,* P&D, 6 Feb. 1772). The play was performed by the American Company of Comedians, which had again returned to Williamsburg from Annapolis.

31. Dined at the Governors & went to the Play.

> John Murray, earl of Dunmore (1732–1809), successor to Lord Botetourt as governor of Virginia, had taken his oath of office before the council 25 Sept. 1771. A Scottish peer, he had sat in Parliament for several years and for 11 months before coming to Virginia had been governor of New York.

November

Novr. 1st. Dined at Mrs. Dawson's. Went to the Fireworks in the Afternoon and to the Play at Night.

2. Dined with the Council and Spent the Evening in my own Room a writing.

> GW was probably preparing his petition to the council on behalf of the Virginia Regiment.

6. Dined at Mrs. Dawsons and Spent the Evening at Mrs. Campbells.

> On this date GW and James Mercer appeared before the council to argue in favor of the petition presented two days earlier. The councillors allotted 170,000 acres to the officers and men of the Virginia Regiment. The remaining 30,000 acres, after being used to satisfy the claims of any more private soldiers who might apply, were to "be divided among those who have hitherto born the whole Expense, & who in all Probability must continue to do so till the full Quantity is surveyed" (*Va. Exec. Jls.,* 6:438–41). The council's

answer to the petition did not please GW, but he remained determined to pursue the business regardless of the difficulties and expense involved.

7. Left Williamsburg on my return home, dined & lodged at Colo. Bassetts.

GW arrived at Mount Vernon on 11 Nov. "about Dark."

29. Went to the Vestry at Pohick Church & reachd home in the Evening. Found Mr. Johnson here.

The Truro Parish vestry today set the parish levy for the year—70 pounds of tobacco per tithable—and appointed various parish officials (Truro Vestry Book, 150–52, Library of Congress). Dr. John Johnson was continuing to treat Patsy Custis for her epilepsy. Although Patsy still had not improved in any way under his care, the Washingtons continued to consult him about her health for several more months (Johnson to Martha Washington, 21 Mar. 1772, Hamilton, *Letters to Washington*, 4:119, n.2).

December

4. Went up to the Election & the Ball I had given at Alexa. Mr. Crawford & Jno. P. Custis with me. Stayd all Night.

On 12 Oct. 1771 Governor Dunmore had dissolved the General Assembly, which necessitated new elections to the House of Burgesses (*H.B.J.*, 1770–72, 145). GW and Col. John West were again chosen to represent Fairfax County. GW's election expenses included £4 7s. 8d. to tavern keeper John Lomax (d. 1787) of Alexandria for "getting a Supper" at the ball, £4 1s. 9d. to William Shaw, also of Alexandria, for "Sundries &ca. for the Election & Ball & his own Trouble," 12s. to Harry Piper for his slave Charles playing the fiddle, and £1 9s. 8d. to a Mr. Young for cakes (Ledger A, 347; Ledger B, 50).

9. Went to meet Govr. Eden at Mr. Willm. Digges's where we dined. In the Afternoon the Govr. Mr. Calvert, Majr. Fleming Mr. Boucher, Mr. Geo. Digges and Doctr. Digges came over with me.

Benedict Calvert (c.1724–1788), an illegitimate son of Charles Calvert, fifth Baron Baltimore, lived at Mount Airy (later called Dower House) in Prince George's County, Md., near present-day Rosaryville. Born in England, he was known in his early years as Benedict Swingate, but Lord Baltimore, while refusing to identify Benedict's mother, acknowledged him as his son and provided well for him. Benedict took the Calvert name and at the age of 18 went to Maryland, where in 1745 he was appointed collector of customs at Patuxent and in the following year became a member of the provincial council.

Maj. William Fleming of the British army, currently acting commander of the 64th Regiment of Foot stationed at Halifax, Nova Scotia, was visiting the southern provinces for his health.

Dr. Joseph Digges, son of William Digges and younger brother of George Digges, had studied at the University of Edinburgh but had not received a degree.

11. The Govr. and all the Compy. dined at Colo. Fairfaxs & returned in the Afternoon.

12. The foregoing Gentlemen still here.

13. The Governor, and other Gentlemen cross'd over to Mr. Digges on their return home. I dined with them there & came back in the Aftern.

14. Went a fox hunting with John Parke Custis Lund Washington & Mr. Manley—killed a Fox.

15. At home all day alone, in the Evening the same.

23. At home all day writing and alone.

25. Went to Pohick Church with Mrs. Washington and returned to Dinner.

31. Went up to Alexandria at the request of Messrs. Montgomerie Wilson and Steward, to settle with them along with Mr. John (as Exr. of Colo. Thoms. Colvil) for the Maryland Tract of Land which they had Purchasd of Mr. Semple. Staid all Night.

> John Semple, plagued by many debts and unable to pay off the purchase bond for the Merryland tract that he had bought from Thomas Colvill, had assigned his rights to the land to three merchants: Thomas Montgomerie and Cumberland Wilson of Dumfries and Adam Stewart of Georgetown, Md. The Colvill executors—Frances Colvill, John West, Jr., and GW—had been empowered by the Maryland General Assembly on 23 Nov. 1771 to deed the Merryland tract to Semple, his heirs, or his assignees, provided that the balance due on the original contract was paid by 20 April 1773. If it were not paid, the executors could sell the land at public auction to the highest bidder (*Md. Archives*, 63:293–95). The purpose of the meetings on this and subsequent days was to determine exactly what balance was owed for Merryland and to arrange for payment of it by the merchants.
>
> *Mr. John:* either John West, Jr., or John Semple.

1772

January

Where & how my time is Spent

Jany 1st. Upon the same business this day as brought me to Alexandria yesterday. Came home in the Afternoon and found Mr. Ramsay and his daughter here.

2. At home all day. Mr. Montgomerie Mr. Piper and Mr. Harrison came to dinner & staid all Night.

4. Went a Hunting with the above Gentlemen. Found both a Bear & Fox but got neither. Went up to Alexandria with these Gentlemen to finish the business with Montgomerie &ca. which was accordg. done.

6. Went a Hunting in the Neck with Mr. Fairfax. Found a fox & run him into a hole near Night, without Killing him. Found Doctr. Rumney & Mr. Magowan here when we returnd.

7. The above Gentlemen continued here all day and Night. Mr. Fairfax & myself rid to my Mill before Dinner.

8th. At home all day. Mr. Fairfax and Doctr. Rumney went away after Breakfast.

14. Went to Belvoir with Mrs. Washington, Miss Custis & Mr. Gowan [Magowan] dind and stayed all Night.

23. Went up to George Town to convey Deeds to Messrs. Montgomerie Stewart & Wilson for the Marryland Tract of Land wch. was accordingly done Mrs. Colvil being carried up in my Chariot returnd to Mr. Jno. Wests at Night.

> As arranged at previous meetings, the three merchants today gave the Colvill executors £816 13s. 7d. in bills of exchange drawn on Glasgow firms. Although the Merryland tract was not formally deeded to the merchants until this day, they had begun to advertise in the *Maryland Gazette* on 16 Jan. that they would offer it for sale to the public on 28 May "in separate Lots or all together, for Sterling or Current Money." Merryland eventually was sold to several purchasers. However, money was still being collected from the merchants in Nov. 1790, and their obligations to the Colvill estate were not fully discharged until May 1795 (Thomas Montgomerie to GW, 17 Nov. 1790; Ledger C, 16).

February

7. Attempted to ride to the Mill, but the Snow was so deep & crusty, even in the Tract that had been made that I chose to Tye my Horse half way & walk there.

25. Set of for Williamsburg but not being able to cross Accatinck (which was much Swelled by the late Rains) I was obliged to return home again.

> The first session of the new Virginia General Assembly, after several prorogations, was scheduled to begin on 6 Feb. but did not obtain a quorum until four days later due to the bad weather and poor roads (*H.B.J.*, 1770–72, 145–53).

26. Sett off again and reachd Colchester by nine Oclock where I was detaind all day by high Winds & low tide.

March

Mar. 1st. Reachd Colo. Bassetts from Todds Bridge by 12 Oclock. Stayd there the remainder of the day.

2. Set out for Williamsburg and got in about 12 Oclock. Dined at the Speakers and supd at the Treasurers.

> This session of the assembly had already met for three weeks and was to continue for another six.
>
> GW lodged with Edward Charlton, whose two-story frame house stood almost directly across Duke of Gloucester Street from the Raleigh Tavern. A wigmaker in Williamsburg for many years, Charlton had not advertised himself as a tavern keeper and apparently was renting private rooms in his house only during public times.

3. Dined and Supd at the Governors.

> GW today was reappointed to the standing committees of privileges and elections, propositions and grievances, and religion and was one of a committee of three appointed to review a petition for financial relief from John Robinson, a disabled veteran of the Virginia Regiment (*H.B.J.*, 1770–72, 204).

4. Dined at the Attorneys and Spent the Evening at the Governors.

10. Dined and Spent the Evening at the Palace.

12. Dined at the Club and went to the Play.

> The play was presented by David Douglass's American Company, which came to Williamsburg for the spring season, from the convening of the General Assembly in early February through the April session of the General Court (Rankin, *Theater in Colonial America*, 165).

13. Dined at the Club and Spent the Evening at Southalls.

14. Dined at the Club & Spent the Evening there also.

15. Dined at the Speakers & Spent the Evening at my own lodgings.

16. Dined at the Club, & spent the Evening there also.

17. Dined at the Club and went to the Play in the Afternoon.

18. Dined at the Club and Spent the Evening at the Burgesses Ball in the Capitol.

19. Dined at Mrs. Dawsons & went to the Play in the Evening.

20. Dined at Mrs. Amblers and Spent the Evening at Southalls.

> Mary Cary Ambler had a town house in Williamsburg, where GW apparently dined with her on this day, but her principal residence was at her plantation about seven miles away on Jamestown Island.

21. Dined at the Club & Spent the Evening there also.

22. Went over to Colo. Warner Lewis's in Gloucester. Dined & Lodged there.

26. Dined at the Club and went to the Play.

GW is here attending the local premiere of the "new Comedy . . . *A Word to the Wise*" by Hugh Kelly (1739–1777). It was received, reported Purdie and Dixon's *Virginia Gazette* a week later, "with the warmest Marks of Approbation."

31. Dined at Mrs. Campbells & spent the Evening there also.

April

2. Dined and Spent the Evening at Mrs. Campbells.

On this day GW was appointed to a committee of three to consider a proposed amendment to the act regarding deer hunting and the control of hounds.

3. Dined at Mrs. Campbells and went to the Play—then to Mrs. Campbells again.

On this day GW was appointed to two committees, one to write a Potomac navigation bill and one to amend the colony's flour inspection regulations.

6. Returnd to Williamsburg. Dined at Mrs. Campbells—went to the Concert & then to Mrs. Campbells again.

Today Thomson Mason, burgess for Stafford County, presented the Potomac navigation bill to the house on behalf of the committee. The bill, which authorized a public subscription to finance the project, was received, read, and ordered to be engrossed for final action (*H.B.J.*, 1770–72, 297; Hening, 8:570–79).

9. Took an early Dinner at Southalls and set of for Eltham on my return home.

GW left Williamsburg two days before Governor Dunmore prorogued the General Assembly (*H.B.J.*, 1770–72, 317). Before GW left, he finished paying his personal accounts in town: £5 12s. 6d. for various play tickets for himself and others during his stay, £2 12s. 6d. for his and his servant's expenses at the Raleigh Tavern, and 5s. to a blacksmith for shoeing his horses.

11. Breakfasted at Hubbards and dined at Colo. Lewis's in Fredericksburg where Colo. Bassett &ca. lodged. I lodged at my Mothers.

12. Dined in Dumfries and reachd home in the Afternoon.

20. Went up to Court, Colo. Bassett & Jno. Custis with me. Returnd in the Afternoon.

23. Dined at Belvoir with Colo. Bassett & Lady & Daughter, Mrs. Washington & Patcy. Returnd in the Evening. J.P. Custis dind also.

24. Rid to Muddy hole Doeg Run and Mill with Colo. Bassett before Dinner.

25. Went a Hunting with Colo. Bassett. Found nothing.

May

May 1st. Went a Hunting with Mr. Jno. Custis. Found nothing. Returnd to Dinner.

12. Went up to Alexandria with Mrs. Washington & Miss Custis to see Captn. Woods Ship Launched. Returnd in the afternoon.

18. Went up to Court and stayed all Night. In the Evening Mr. Peale & J.P. Custis came to Mount Vernon.

> Charles Willson Peale (1741–1827), a resident of Annapolis, came to Mount Vernon with a letter of introduction from Jonathan Boucher. Peale had forsaken his saddlery business, to which he had been apprenticed as a youth, to take up painting. He was now making his living painting miniatures, and on occasion larger portraits, of gentry and merchants in Pennsylvania, Maryland, and Virginia.

20. I sat to have my Picture drawn.

> On 21 May, GW wrote to Jonathan Boucher: "Inclination having yielded to Importunity, I am now, contrary to all expectations under the hands of Mr. Peale; but in so grave—so sullen a mood—and now and then under the influence of Morpheus, when some critical strokes are making, that I fancy the skill of this Gentleman's Pencil, will be put to it, in describing to the World what manner of man I am" (*Papers, Colonial Series*, 9:49–50).

21. Captn. Posey who came here the 19th. went up to Alexandria this day. I set again to take the Drapery.

> Peale's practice was to sketch the painting out in one neutral color, show the sketch to the subject for his approval, and then paint the portrait, thus demanding a minimum of time and patience of the subject. On this day Peale had GW wear the "Drapery" (clothing) chosen for the painting, which was GW's colonel's uniform from his service in the Virginia Regiment.

22. Set for Mr. Peale to finish my Face.

24. Set out after Dinner for Loud[ou]n &ca. Reachd Mr. Fairfax's and lodged there.

> Peale remained at Mount Vernon to paint miniatures of Patsy and Jacky Custis. Jacky also paid Peale for a miniature of his mother, Martha Washington, probably for Jacky's own use (Ledger B, 50; Custis Account Book, 30 May 1772).

*Charles Willson Peale visited Mount Vernon to make portraits of the Wash-
ington family, including these miniatures of Jacky and Patsy Custis. (Mount
Vernon Ladies' Association of the Union)*

June

4. Set of on my return home.

8. Rid to the Ferry Plantan. and Mill.

GW today gave John Posey £50 in cash and a horse and saddle worth £10 for
a deed to the six-acre strip of land where Posey's house and ferry were located
(Ledger B, 50).

28. Went after Dinner in my Whale Boat to the Spring at Johnson's
Place.

In a letter dated 5 Mar., Jonathan Boucher told GW that Governor Eden of
Maryland "has got You a very handsome . . . Whale Boat, for £20, which, I
fancy is by this Time at Mount [Vernon]." On 22 May, Boucher invited GW
to visit him in Maryland and added: "Shou'd . . . your Whale Boat be arriv'd,
perhaps You may be tempted to try her." Since GW paid 18s. for "Freight of
my Whale Boat from Patux[ent]" on 17 June, this excursion may have been
his first in it (Ledger B, 50).

July

22. At home all day with the Company that remain yesterday. Mr. Jenifer Adams Dined here.

Daniel Jenifer Adams (b. 1751) was currently involved in a trading partnership with GW and Samuel Brodie. GW had consigned to Adams 273 barrels
of flour to be shipped to the West Indies on board the brig *Fairfax*, owned
and captained by Brodie. Adams was to be the supercargo, or agent, who

would accompany the flour and decide on which island and at what price it should be sold. For the voyage GW also sold on credit 115 barrels of herring to Adams. Adams wrote GW from Jamaica on 3 Oct. that he had disposed of 220 barrels of GW's flour for 20s. per hundredweight. Receiving disturbing reports about Adams's activities and concerned about his investment, GW wrote him on 12 Jan. 1773, severing business ties with him (*Papers, Colonial Series,* 10:157). See also entry for 28 Mar. 1774.

25. Went a fishing and dined at the Fish House at the Ferry Plantation.

August

17. Went up to Alexandria to Court. Stayd all Night. Dind with Mr. Adam.

18. In Town all day and Night. Din'd & Supd at Arrells.

September

4. Set out with Mrs. Washington & Miss Custis (attended by Mr. Custis) on a Visit to Mr. Boucher &ca. Breakfasted at Mr. Wm. Digges's (the Horses & carriage being got over the day before) and dined at Mr. Bouchers with Govr. Eden and Mr. Calvert & his two Daughters.

In June, Jonathan Boucher had married Eleanor Addison (1739–1784) of Oxon Hill, niece of his benefactor the Rev. Henry Addison. The Washingtons had intended to pay their respects to the newlyweds earlier in the summer but had been prevented by "Harvest, Company, and one thing or another" (GW to Boucher, 18 Aug. 1772). Benedict Calvert's two eldest daughters were Elizabeth (Betsey) Calvert (born c.1752) and Eleanor (Nelly) Calvert (1754–1811). Unknown to the Washingtons or the Bouchers, Jacky Custis was at this time courting Nelly Calvert. When their romance did become known several months later, Boucher was shocked: "Never . . . had I the most distant Suspicion of any such Thing's being in Agitation," he wrote GW. "You will remember, I always thought, that He was enamoured of Miss Betsey [Calvert]; tho' even in that, I suspected not, that there was any Likelihood of its be coming so serious, without my first knowing more of it" (8 April 1773).

6. Went to Church with Govr. Eden in his Phaeton.

St. Barnabas Church, located several miles southeast of Mount Lubentia, was the parish church for Jonathan Boucher's parish of Queen Anne. GW returned home on 11 Sept.

14. Set out for Fredericksburg about 7 Oclock; Dined & Fed my Horses at Peytons on Acquia & reachd Fredericksburg abt. Dusk. Lodgd at my Mothers.

GW's purpose in going to Fredericksburg at this time was to meet with other veteran officers of the French and Indian War "to consider of a proper method to obtain the Lands granted" by the king's Proclamation of 1763.

15. Rid to my two Plantations on the River & returnd to Mr. Lewis's to Dinner. Spent the Eveng. at Weedons.

> GW was preparing to advertise Ferry Farm in the *Virginia Gazette* "To be sold, rented, *or* Exchanged, *for back lands in any of the northern counties*" of Virginia (5 Nov. 1772). Fielding Lewis agreed to act as GW's Fredericksburg agent in this business.
>
> Weedon's tavern was probably the scene of today's meeting of the veteran officers. Fourteen officers, including GW, were present and agreed to organize in order to assert their claims. Each man was to be assessed £3 for every thousand acres claimed, and five officers living in the Fredericksburg neighborhood were appointed to disburse the collected money for surveying and other expenses.

22. In Alexandria Still. Dined and Supped at Arrels.

> GW went to Alexandria on 21 Sept. to attend court.

October

4. Set of for the Annapolis Races. Dined and lodged at Mr. Boucher's.

> Jacky Custis accompanied GW on this trip to the races (Ledger B, 60).

6. Dined at Majr. Jenifers—went to the Ball and Suppd at the Govrs.

> The four days of racing began this morning at 11:00. The *Maryland Gazette* expected "good Sport, as a great Number of Horses are already come from the Northward and Southward, to start for the different Purses." GW lost £1 6d. on this year's races (Ledger B, 60). The ball was held at the Assembly House, "Tickets for Gentlemen [priced] at a Dollar each (without which they cannot possibly be admitted)" (*Md. Gaz.*, 1 Oct. 1772).

7. Dined at the Govrs. and went to the Play afterwards.

> The plays attended by GW this week were part of the fall season of David Douglass's American Company, which opened in Annapolis 1 Sept. (Rankin, *Theater in Colonial America,* 166–67).

9. Dined at Mr. Ridouts. Went to the Play & to the Govrs. to Supper.

> Playing at the theater today were a new comedy, *The West Indian,* and a new comic opera, *The Padlock* (*Md. Gaz.*, 8 Oct. 1772; Rankin, *Theater in Colonial America,* 132, 164).

10th. Dined with Mr. Carroll of Carrollton & set out for Mr. Bouchers which place I arrivd abt. 8 Oclock.

11. Got home to a late Dinner. Jno. Parke Custis came with me.

18. Dined at Belvoir & returnd.

19. Went up to Court at Alexa. Returned in the Afternoon.

20. Rid to the Ferry, Mill, Doeg Run & Muddy hole Plantns.

21st. Set of for Williamsburg. Dined at Colchester & lodgd in Dumfries. Mrs. Washington Mr. & Miss Custis with me.

22. Reachd Fredericksburg to Dinner. Lodgd at Colo. Lewis's.

24. Reachd Todds Bridge to Breakfast & Colo. Bassets in the Evening. Captn. Crawford came there to Dinner.

25. Assisting Crawford with his Surveys.

> William Crawford had returned from the Ohio country with 13 surveys total-ing 127,899 acres out of the 200,000 acres of bounty land promised in 1754 by Governor Dinwiddie to soldiers and officers of the Virginia Regiment. Crawford and GW were now preparing to enter the surveys and have patents issued to the various officers and men, or to their survivors.

November

2. Went to Williamsburg in Company with Captn. Crawford. Dined at Southalls & went to Mr. Baylor's Ball in the Evening.

> In town GW lodged with Edward Charlton, while the rest of the family re-mained at Eltham (Ledger B, 62; Custis Account Book). John Baylor (1750–1808) was the eldest son of Col. John Baylor (1705–1772), of Newmarket, Caroline County.

4. Dined at the Speakers and Supped at Mrs. Vobes.

> In the council today was presented a petition that GW had prepared on behalf of himself and veterans of the Virginia Regiment concerning the sur-veys of their 200,000 acres and asking the councillors "to direct in what manner Patents ought to issue for the Lands already surveyed" (*Va. Exec. Jls.*, 6:510, petition of GW and Virginia Regiment to Lord Dunmore and Virginia council, 4 Nov. 1772).
>
> GW had stayed earlier with Jane Vobe (died c.1789) when she operated a well-furnished tavern on Waller Street near the theater. She was in business as early as May 1757, when GW first patronized her tavern, and she remained at this location until 1771. At that time she considered leaving Williamsburg but changed her mind and by Feb. 1771 opened a tavern called the King's Arms, across the street from the Raleigh (*Va. Gaz.*, P&D, 6 Feb. 1772). She remained in business there until about 1785.

6. Took a Cold Cut at Southalls & went up to Colo. Bassetts.

> On this day GW appeared before the council and presented a plan that he had devised for apportioning the 127,899 acres of veterans' bounty lands already surveyed. Although the council had set the quantity of each claim-ant's land the previous year, there remained the more complex problem of giving everyone equal quality of land. The council accepted GW's solution to the problem, authorizing the issuance of patents for the land according to his plan. But before the council rose, GW promised that if objections about the equity of distributions were raised at a meeting of veterans scheduled for

The Capitol at Williamsburg that was standing when Washington visited the town. The building was finished in 1753 and burned in 1832. From a painting c.1830. (Valentine Museum, Richmond, Virginia)

Fredericksburg on 23 Nov. or "any Reasonable time after," he would "give up all *his* Interest" in the 20,147 acres allotted as his share "and submit to such Regulations" as the council might think proper (*Va. Exec. Jls.*, 6:513–14).

16. Dined at Mrs. Amblers & Spent the Evening there also after setting a while with Colo. Bassett at Mrs. Dawsons.

Among the expenses that GW recorded in his ledger under this date were 7s. 6d. for "seeing Wax work" and 11s. 6d. for a "Puppit Shew" (Ledger B, 61).

21. Left Colo. Bassetts on my return home.

23. At Fredericksburg—attending the Intended meeting of Officers at Captn. Weedens.

Besides GW, six officers were present or represented at this meeting. Learning of GW's recent actions on behalf of the veterans, they warmly thanked him for his efforts and approved his distribution of the surveyed lands as an equitable one. He should, they recommended, be excused from his offer to sacrifice his own bounty lands in case of a redivision (resolves and statement of officers of the Virginia Regiment, 23 Nov. 1772). The Virginia council considered this recommendation on 9 Dec. and agreed that if no complaints were received by June, GW would be released from his promise (*Va. Exec. Jls.*, 6:516).

27. Set of from Fredericksburg & reachd Colo. Henry Lees where we lodged.

> GW today recorded paying his mother £15 cash in the presence of his sister Betty (Ledger B, 45, 62).

28. Stayed at Colo. Lees all day.

29. Reachd home to Dinner.

1773

January

2. Lord Sterling & Captn. Foy with Colo. Fairfax came to Dinner. The latter went away afterwards. The other Gentlemen stayd.

> Capt. Edward Foy was secretary to Lord Dunmore. William Alexander (1726–1783) of New Jersey called himself Lord Stirling, although his claim to a Scottish earldom was disallowed by the House of Commons. In the coming Revolution he was to serve through most of the war as a major general in the Continental Army. Although Stirling was a man of wealth and social prominence, for several years past he had overextended himself and was currently attempting to solve his financial difficulties by holding a lottery. It was to promote this "Delaware Lottery" that he visited Mount Vernon. He put 60 tickets into GW's hands, 6 of which GW kept himself. The venture, however, was a failure, and Stirling eventually refunded the money to those who had bought tickets.

6. The 4 Mr. Digges's came to Dinner also Colo. Fairfax, Colo. Burwell Messrs. Tilghman, Brown, Piper, Adam, Muir, Herbert, Peake, and Doctr. Rumney all of whom stay'd all Night except Mr. Peake.

> The four Mr. Diggeses were probably Ignatius Digges of Melwood, William Digges of Warburton, and William's two sons, George and Dr. Joseph Digges. Mr. Brown may be Bennett Browne (Brown) There was a merchant of this name in Urbanna, near the Rappahannock River (*Va. Gaz.*, P&D, 9 June 1775). William Herbert (1743–1818), merchant of Alexandria, emigrated from Ireland to Virginia c.1770. Herbert married Sarah Carlyle, eldest daughter of John Carlyle. The host of dinner and house guests who descended upon Mount Vernon this day may have been celebrating Twelfth Night and Twelfth Day.

April

3. Colo. Thornton & Son went away after Breakfast. Mr. Custis also returnd to Maryld.

> Col. Francis Thornton (d. 1784) of Society Hill, King George County, had arrived at Mount Vernon with his son on 1 April. Jacky Custis probably carried with him a letter which GW wrote to Benedict Calvert on this date. Having just been apprised that Jacky had contracted a secret engagement to Calvert's daughter Eleanor (Nelly), GW wrote Calvert his feelings on the mat-

ter: "I am now set down to write to you on a Subject of Importance, & of no small embarrassment to me. My Son in Law [stepson] & Ward, Mr Custis, has, as I have been informd, paid his Addresses to your Second Daughter, & having made some progress in her Affections required her in Marriage." He then expressed his approval of Nelly but added firmly that Jacky was too young and inexperienced for marriage and needed to complete his education. "Delivering my Sentiments thus, will not, I hope, lead you into a belief that I am desirous of breaking of the Match—to postpone it, is all I have in view; for I shall recommend it to the young Gentleman with the warmth that becomes a Man of honour (notwithstanding he did not vouchsafe to consult either his Mother, or me, on the occasion) to consider himself as much engaged to your Daughter as if the indissoluble Knot was tied; and as the surest means of effecting this, to stick close to his Studies (in which I flatter myself you will join me) by which he will, in a great measure, avoid those little Flirtation's with other Girls which may, by dividing the attention, contribute not a little to divide the affection" (*Papers, Colonial Series,* 9:209–11).

10. At home all day alone. Mr. Custis came in the afternoon.

John Parke Custis was probably returning from the Calvert home of Mount Airy with Benedict Calvert's reply, 8 April 1773, to GW's letter, 3 April 1773, regarding Custis's betrothal to Calvert's daughter Nelly. Calvert agreed with GW that the match, which met with his approval, should be postponed while Custis studied at King's College in New York City (*Papers, Colonial Series,* 9:215–16).

11. Went to Pohick Church with Mrs. Washington & Mr. Custis & returnd to Dinner.

12. Set of for Annapolis with Mr. Custis. Dined & lodgd at Mr. Bouchers with Govr. Eden & others.

Jonathan Boucher had written to GW 8 April: "I am told, You have Business to our Provincial Court, the next week; I hope to see You either agoing, or returning. The Govr., Mr. Calvert, the chief Justice, & Mr. Dulany dine here on Monday: shou'd You set out on that Day, You know, You can be here in Time to Dinner" (*Papers, Colonial Series,* 9:211–15). GW's business at the Maryland court was to submit a proved account against Daniel Jenifer Adams for £106 14s. 6d. Virginia currency. Adams, who had taken some of GW's flour to the West Indies to be sold (see entry for 22 July 1772), had perpetrated what GW feared was a swindle, and GW feared he would be able to get no money from Adams for his cargo.

GW's visit to Jonathan Boucher's home is his last contact with Boucher recorded in the diaries. In the fall of 1774 Boucher, coming under increasing attack for his personal resistance to the rising activism of local Whigs, moved to The Lodge, a plantation near Oxon Hill, across the Potomac from Alexandria. On 6 Aug. 1775, a month before he and his wife sailed for England, Boucher wrote GW a long letter regarding GW's apparent lack of sympathy toward his sufferings, which concluded: "You are no longer worthy of my friendship; a man of honour can no longer without dishonour be connected with you. With your cause I renounce you" (*Papers, Revolutionary War Series,* 1:252–55).

May

8. Mr. Custis, set of for Mr. Calverts on his way to New York. I rid to the Plantations in the Neck.

> Jacky Custis was on his way to enroll at King's College, now Columbia University. GW had been dissatisfied with his young stepson's progress under Jonathan Boucher, and his desire to settle Jacky in college was further strengthened by the young man's engagement to Nelly Calvert. GW's first choice was the College of Philadelphia, but Boucher persuaded him to enroll his stepson in King's College where Dr. Myles Cooper, president of the college, had introduced extensive reforms in curriculum and discipline. Although GW planned to leave for New York on 10 May to place Jacky in school, young Custis left two days early to spend some time at his fiancée's home in Maryland.

14. Stopd at George Town, on Sasafras, & dind & lodgd at Mr. Dl. Heaths.

> GW left Mount Vernon on 10 May. Georgetown, Kent County, Md., is on the Sassafras River about 16 miles northeast of Chestertown. Daniel Charles Heath was the son of James Paul and Rebecca Dulany Heath, a sister of Daniel Dulany the younger.

15. Dined at Newcastle & lodgd at Wilmington.

16. Breakfasted at Chester & Dined at Govr. Penns in Philadelphia.

> Richard Penn (1735–1811) was appointed lieutenant governor of Pennsylvania in 1771 to replace his brother John, who returned to England. The governor's house, later owned by Robert Morris, was occupied by GW during his presidency.

23. Set out for New York with Lord Sterling, Majr. Bayard & Mr. Custis after Breakfasting with Govr. Penn. Dind with Govr. Franklin at Burlington & lodgd at Trenton.

> Major Bayard is probably Maj. Robert Bayard, a member of the Jockey Club. Lord Stirling had been a guest at the 17 May meeting of the Jockey Club (Jackson, "Washington in Philadelphia," facing p. 118). William Franklin (1731–1813), son of Benjamin Franklin, became the last royal governor of New Jersey in 1763. His championship of the rights of the crown led to an estrangement between father and son. During the Revolution the younger Franklin was held prisoner for two years by the Americans and went to England shortly after his exchange.

26. Din'd at Elizabeth Town, & reachd New York in the Evening wch. I spent at Hull's Tavern. Lodg'd at a Mr. Farmers.

> Hull's tavern, run by Robert Hull, was located "in the Broadway" (*N.Y. Gazette & Weekly Mercury,* 8 Nov. 1773). In 1774, according to John Adams, Hull's tavern was at "the Sign [of] the Bunch of Grapes" (Adams, *Diary,* 2:102).

27. Din'd at the Entertainment given by the Citicens of New York to Genl. Gage.

Gen. Thomas Gage (1721–1787) had been for ten years commander in chief of British troops in North America with headquarters at New York. He was at this time relinquishing his post and returning to England for a brief visit. The entertainment GW attended was a farewell from the merchants of New York to General Gage held at Hull's tavern (*Rivington's N.Y. Gazetteer,* 3 June 1773).

28. Dined with Mr. James Dillancey & went to the Play & Hulls Tavern in the Evening.

> *James Dillancey:* James De Lancey (1732–1800), the eldest son of Lt. Gov. James De Lancey (1703–1760) of New York, was a merchant and landowner and the owner of New York's largest racing stable. The plays GW saw this evening were *Hamlet* and a new farce by William O'Brien called *Cross Purposes,* performed for the first time. The playhouse was a large, red, wooden building on the north side of John Street (Monoghan, *This Was New York,* 123; Day, "A Summary of the British Period," 127).

31. Set out on my return home.

June

11. Cloudy & exceeding Cold Wind fresh from the No. West, & Snowing.

> A memorandum in the Fairfax County Order Book for 1772–74 reads: "Be it remembered that on the eleventh day of June one thousand seven hundred and seventy three It rain'd Hail'd snow'd and was very cold."

19. At home all day. About five oclock poor Patcy Custis Died Suddenly.

> GW wrote to Burwell Bassett, 20 June, that "It is an easier matter to conceive, than to describe, the distress of this Family; especially that of the unhappy Parent of our Dear Patcy Custis, when I inform you that yesterday removd the Sweet Innocent Girl into a more happy, & peaceful abode than any she has met with in the afflicted Path she hitherto has trod. She rose from Dinner about four Oclock, in better health and spirits than she appeared to have been in for some time; soon after which she was siezd with one of her usual Fits, & expir'd in it, in less than two Minutes without uttering a Word, a groan, or scarce a Sigh. This Sudden, and unexpected blow, I scarce need add has almost reduced my poor Wife to the lowest ebb of Misery" (*Papers, Colonial Series,* 9:243–44).

20. Colo. Fairfax & Lady as also Mr. Massey dind here—Patcy Custis being buried—the first went away. Mr. Massey stayd.

> Patsy was laid to rest in the family vault, about 200 yards south of the main house. The Rev. Lee Massey read the funeral service, and GW paid him £2 6s. 3d., about normal compensation (Ledger B, 90). The coffin, which had been bought from James Connell of Alexandria, was draped with a black pall belonging to GW (Ledger B, 90; Robert Adam to GW, 16 Sept. 1773).

21. Mr. Massey went away after Breakfast. I continued at home all day.

22. My Brother, his Wife, Miss Reed & Nelly Calvert Dind at Belvoir & returnd in the Afternn. I contd. at home all day.

> Miss Mary Read, evidently a sort of retainer in Benedict Calvert's family, was left in his will a legacy for service to the family.

July

8. At home all day. Colo. Fairfax & Mrs. Fairfax came in the Aftern. to take leave of us & returnd again. Doctr. Craik also came & stayd all Night.

> The inheritance of an estate in England necessitated George William Fairfax's presence there for an indefinite period. GW was to take over the management of his affairs during his and his wife's absence, with the help of Francis Willis, Jr., and Craven Peyton. On this day GW was given Fairfax's power of attorney. On 5 Aug., Fairfax wrote GW that their ship was still at Yorktown, where it had been delayed by sickness among the crew. GW retained his power of attorney and continued to supervise the Fairfax properties until the Revolution, when he wrote Fairfax, 26 July 1775, that he could no longer continue to do so. See *Papers, Revolutionary War Series*, 1:176–77.

August

4. At home all day. Captn. Posey here—he came on Sunday last.

> Posey's visit lasted for a week and was for the purpose of extracting more money from GW. His nerve failed, however, and it was not until he was on his way back to Maryland that he wrote GW, 9 Aug. 1773, concerning the purpose of his visit: "You have grant'd me many Favours since I have been Acquaint'd with you—I am now Reduc'd Very Low—and Advanc'd in years—I have noe Person in the world to Apply to, for Assistance—and Really am not Able to work—Pray would you be kind Enough to Let me have the Some [of] About £50 Maryland Currancy I think with that some I could fix my self for Life, and not to want Again. . . . I want'd to mention'd this Affaire to you when I was at Your house but I could not have the Face to Doe" (*Papers, Colonial Series*, 9:301). GW did not let Posey have the £50 but continued to supply him with small amounts of money from time to time. His ledger records £4 "By Charity to Captn. Posey" on 15 Oct. 1773 and, in April 1774, £12 (Ledger B, 93, 106).

23. At home all day. In the Afternoon came David Allan, & James Whitelaw, two Scotchmen empowerd by a Number of Familys about Glasgow to look out Land for two hundred Familys who had a Mind to settle in America.

> Although there had been a large emigration from Scotland for a number of years, after 1763 it greatly increased, and between 1763 and 1775 about 25,000 Scots immigrated to America. David Allen and James Whiteland were commissioners sent by the Glasgow-based American Company of Farmers to find a large tract of land, 16,000–20,000 acres in size, upon which to settle the 200 Lowland families waiting in Scotland. Although they promised to

view GW's Ohio lands, they were concerned that the frontier area would be too far from markets or landing places.

24. The above person's prosecuted their journey towards Carolina in pursuit of this scheme purposing also to view the Lands on Ohio, & to see Mine there before they returnd with their Report to Scotland. I rid to the Ferry Doeg Run and Mill Plantations.

> GW had decided to lease his 20,000 acres of bounty land on the Ohio and Great Kanawha rivers (*Pa. Gaz.*, 22 Sept. 1773, supplement). He felt that these lands, leased to tenants who would settle and develop them for their own use, would prosper more than lands placed under the management of an overseer. Nothing ever came of this scheme. Perhaps, as one prospective tenant claimed, GW's terms were unrealistic (Richard Thompson to GW, 30 Sept. 1773, *Papers, Colonial Series*, 9:337–40).

December

17. Rid to Muddy hole, & into the Neck. Mr. George Mason Dined here.

> During much of GW's lifetime there were three George Masons living within eight miles of Mount Vernon. Col. George Mason of Gunston Hall, who appears regularly in the diaries as "Col. Mason," had a son named George Mason (1753–1796), who lived near his father in Mason's Neck at Lexington. This George was called George Mason of Lexington, and sometimes George Mason, Jr. A third George Mason, first cousin of Col. George Mason of Gunston Hall, lived near Pohick Creek, where in 1782 he owned one tithable slave (*Heads of Families, Va.*, 18). This George was called George Mason of Pohick and, to distinguish him from his elder cousin and neighbor Col. George Mason, was also sometimes called George Mason, Jr. (Copeland, *The Five George Masons*, 88).

20. Went up to Alexandria to Court. Returnd in the Eveng.

22. Went out after Breakfast with the Dogs. Dragd a fox for an hour or two, but never found. Returnd to Dinner & found Mrs. Slaughter here.

> Anne Clifton Slaughter (d. 1798), only child of William and Elizabeth Brent Clifton (d. 1773) of Clifton's Neck, was married to Thomas Slaughter. She borrowed £6 from GW on this day—the loan was not repaid until 1788 (Ledger B, 98).

28. At home all day Mr. Digges & Custis continuing here.

> It was probably during this week at Mount Vernon that Benjamin Dulany, George Digges, Jacky Custis, and Charles Willson Peale participated in an event which Peale later related: "One afternoon several young gentlemen, visiters at Mount Vernon, and myself were engaged in pitching the bar, one of the athletic sports common in those days, when suddenly the colonel appeared among us. He requested to be shown the pegs that marked the bounds of our efforts; then, smiling, and without putting off his coat, held out his hand for the missile. No sooner . . . did the heavy iron bar feel the

grasp of his mighty hand than it lost the power of gravitation, and whizzed through the air, striking the ground far, very far, beyond our utmost limits. We were indeed amazed, as we stood around, all stripped to the buff, with shirt sleeves rolled up, and having thought ourselves very clever fellows, while the colonel, on retiring, pleasantly observed, 'When you beat my pitch, young gentlemen, I'll try again' " (Custis, *Recollections,* 519).

1774

January

10. At home all day. A Mr. Young recommended by Mr. Adams came here and dind—going away afterwards.

> *Mr. Young:* GW was facing a deadline for establishing his rights to the Kanawha land in the Ohio Valley that he received under Governor Dinwiddie's 1754 Proclamation. Having been unable to attract settlers either from the colonies or from Ireland, Scotland, or Germany, GW was now planning at least to "seat" the lands within the three-year period provided by law. This "seating" involved making minimal improvements on the land that had been granted and surveyed, including constructing buildings and clearing and planting at least one out of every 500 acres (Hening, 3:313–14). For this job GW was buying white indentured servants and hiring carpenters. George Young had been recommended to GW to be the leader of his Kanawha expedition.

13. Dind here no body but Captn. Posey. I walked out with my Gun. In the Afternoon Mr. Geo. Young came here to live.

> GW hired Young at £25 for one year to accompany the Kanawha expedition (Ledger B, 107).

28. At home all day. Majr. Chas. Smith & Andw. Wagener came here to dinner. The last went away after it—the other stayd all Night.

> Smith and Andrew Wagener (Wagoner, Wagner), both veterans of the 1754 campaign against the French, probably were at Mount Vernon to discuss their shares of the bounty land promised to all such veterans. Wagener had made no effort heretofore to cooperate with GW in obtaining the grant for the veterans. On this visit GW presented Wagener with a bill of £9 5s. 3d. for his share of the expenses already incurred.

February

3. Set out after an early Dinner (with Lund Washington) for Mr. Calverts, to Mr. Custis's Wedding who was this Eveng. married to Miss Nelly Calvert.

> On 15 Dec. 1773 GW had written to Rev. Myles Cooper, president of King's College, N.Y., that his hopes of Jacky's continuing his education were "at an end; & at length, I have yielded, contrary to my judgment, & much against my wishes, to his quitting College; in order that he may enter soon into a new

scene of Life, which I think he would be much fitter for some years hence, than now; but having his own inclination—the desires of his mother—& the acquiescence of almost all his relatives, to encounter, I did not care, as he is the last of the family, to push my opposition too far; & therefore have submitted to a Kind of necessity" (*Papers, Colonial Series,* 9:406–7).

4. At Mr. Calverts all day. With much other company.

March

28. Doctr. Craik went away after Breakfast. I went up to Alexandria to the Sale of the Anne & Elizabeth which I bought myself at the price of £175. Returnd home in the Afternoon.

This purchase was in consequence of the voyage of John Carlyle's brigantine the *Fairfax* to the West Indies in the summer of 1772, carrying a cargo of herring and flour which GW had placed in the care of Daniel Jenifer Adams (see entry for 22 July 1772). After selling the cargo, Adams bought the *Fairfax* from the captain and owner Samuel Brodie, renamed it the *Anne and Elizabeth* (in honor, apparently, of his sisters), and proceeded to sail and trade about the West Indies and along the Atlantic coast without ever paying GW for the cargo. It was not until the fall of 1773 that GW was, by court order (at a cost of more than £200), finally able to get the brig to Alexandria, where the vessel was offered for sale to pay Adams's obligations. When no offers were made for the vessel, GW "was compelled to buy it in myself . . . much against my Inclination, as I had no desire of being concernd in Shipping." GW renamed the brig the *Farmer,* and it proved a valuable investment for him (GW to Robert McMickan, 10 May 1774, *Papers, Colonial Series,* 10: 55–58; Ledger B, 57, 99, 117). In 1775 GW finally settled his accounts with Adams, receiving land in Charles County amounting to 5,522 acres.

30. Walk in the Evening over my three Plantations in the Neck.

31. Mr. George Johnston dind here. I rid as [far as] the Gumsp[rin]g with my People and Vale. Crawford who were moving to the Ohio.

George Johnston, Jr. (1750–1777), of Fairfax County was appointed a captain in the 2d Virginia Regiment in 1775. In Jan. 1777, with the rank of lieutenant colonel, he became an aide-de-camp to GW, serving until his death in the fall of 1777.

Before Crawford could get his "People" to GW's lands, Dunmore's War broke out between settlers and Indians along the Ohio frontier. Less than two months after leaving Mount Vernon, Crawford gave up in the face of the hostilities and sold the servants to frontier buyers, including two to himself (Crawford to GW, 27 July 1774, *Papers, Colonial Series,* 10:133–36).

April

11. At home all day. Mr. Milner & a Mr. Marle dined here.

William Milnor, merchant of Philadelphia, had come to Mount Vernon to buy fish taken from GW's fishing grounds along the Potomac (Ledger B, 123). *Mr. Marle:* may be Richard Marley, merchant of Philadelphia.

24. Mr. Tilghman & Mr. Stewart came here to Dinner. The first stayed all Night the other returnd.

25. Mr. Lanphire came to W[or]k.

Mr. Lanphire: Going Lanphier (1727–1813), a house joiner and carpenter from Alexandria, had first done interior carpentry for GW in 1758, when the Mount Vernon mansion house was "raised" from 1½ to 2½ stories (Ledger A, 58). GW had now hired Lanphier to work on extending both ends of the house, which would add a downstairs library and upstairs master bedroom on the south end and a two-story room on the north end later referred to as the Banquet Hall. The south end, built first, was not completed until after GW had left Mount Vernon to serve in the Revolution. On 10 Dec. 1775 Lund Washington wrote to GW that the south addition was almost done. Because of his service in the Revolutionary War, GW did not see the south end or the unfinished north end until the fall of 1781.

May

16. Came to Wmsburg., dind at the Governors & spent the Evening at Mrs. Campbells.

The current session of the House of Burgesses opened on 4 May and achieved a quorum the next day.

21st. Dined at the Speakers & went up to Colo. Bassetts in the afternoon.

During this week news reached Williamsburg of the passage of an act by the British Parliament closing the port of Boston on 1 June until it paid reparations for the tea destroyed in the Boston Tea Party the previous December.

23. Came to Williamsburg with Mrs. Washington. Dined at the Attorneys, & spent the Evening there.

While the Washingtons were dining at the home of John Randolph, a handful of younger burgesses, led by Thomas Jefferson, Patrick Henry, and Richard Henry Lee, "cooked up a resolution," as Jefferson later recalled, "for appointing the 1st day of June, on which the [Boston] port-bill was to commence, for a day of fasting, humiliation, and prayer" (Bergh, *Writings of Thomas Jefferson*, 1:9–10).

26. Rid out with the Govr. to his Farm and Breakfasted with him there. Dined at Mrs. Dawson's, & spent the Evening at my lodgings.

Today's House of Burgesses session did not begin until 11:00 A.M., giving GW ample time to return the few miles from Governor Dunmore's farm. When the governor returned to town this day, he dissolved the assembly, ostensibly because of the resolution for a fast day. GW later discussed Dunmore's action in a letter to George William Fairfax, 10 June 1774: "this Dissolution was as sudden as unexpected for th[e]re were other resolves of a much more spirited Nature ready to be offerd to the House wch would have been adopted respecting the Boston Port Bill as it is call'd but were withheld till the Important business of the Country could be gone through. As the case stands the assembly sat the 22 day's for nothing—not a Bill being ⟨passed⟩" *(Papers, Colonial Series,* 10:94–101).

27. Dined at the Treasurers and went to the Ball given by the House of Burgesses to Lady Dunmore.

In the issue of this date the *Virginia Gazette* had some political news: "This Day, at ten o'Clock, the Honourable Members of the late House of Burgesses met, by Agreement, at the long Room in the Raleigh Tavern, in this City, called the Apollo," where an "Agreement was unanimously entered into by that patriotick Assembly, in Support of the constitutional Liberties of America, against the late oppressive Act of the British Parliament respecting the Town of Boston, which, in the End, must affect all the other Colonies" (*Va. Gaz.,* P&D, 26 May 1774).

The meeting agreed to boycott tea and other goods of the East India Company and then directed the House of Burgesses' committee of correspondence to write to other colonies "on the expediency of appointing deputies from the several colonies of British America, to meet in general congress" (*H.B.J.* 1773–76, xiv). GW joined the other burgesses and a number of local leaders in signing the statement. The "Ball and Entertainment at the Capitol" was given "to welcome Lady Dunmore and the rest of our Governour's Family to Virginia" (*Va. Gaz.,* P&D, 26 May 1774).

29. Went to Church in the fore, & afternoon. Dined at Mrs. Dawsons & spent the Eveng. at my Lodgings.

On this Sunday afternoon letters from Boston to the Virginia committee of correspondence arrived in Williamsburg asking for a nonimport and nonexport association by all of the colonies, to reopen the port of Boston.

30. Dined at Mr. Southalls. Spent the Evening in my own Room.

Peyton Randolph called together the 25 burgesses who remained in town to discuss what action Virginia should take on the circular letters from Boston. The meeting agreed that Virginia should act in concert as much as possible with the other colonies, voting to call a meeting of the burgesses in 90 days to decide on steps to be taken (*H.B.J.,* 1773–76, 139–40).

GW commented that "the Ministry may rely on it that Americans will never be tax'd without their own consent that the cause of Boston . . . is and ever will be considerd as the cause of America (not that we approve their cond[uc]t in destroyg. the Tea) & that we shall not suffer ourselves to be sacrificed by piecemeal though god only knows what is to be become of us" (GW to George William Fairfax, 10 June 1774, *Papers, Colonial Series,* 10: 94–101).

31. Dined at Mr. Charltons & spent the Evening in my Room.

Although by law only the governor could summon the burgesses into session, the members remaining in Williamsburg today called for a convention of all their colleagues on 1 Aug.

June

June 1st. Went to Church & fasted all day.

> This service was pursuant to the resolution passed on 24 May for a day of fasting, humiliation, and prayer to symbolize Virginia's solidarity with the people of Boston.

15. Dined at Mrs. Dawson's & Spent the Evening at the Capitol at a Meeting of the Society for promoting useful Kn[owledge].

> The Philosophical Society for the Advancement of Useful Knowledge was formed in May 1773 in Williamsburg. This 1774 meeting, held "at the Capitol . . . at four o'Clock in the Afternoon," was the first attended by GW, and he paid his dues of £1 (*Va. Gaz.*, P&D, 9 June 1774; Ledger B, 115).

16. Dined at the Governors & Spent the Evening at Anderson's.

19. At Colo. Bassetts all day.

20. Set of from thence on my return home.

July

July 1st. Rid to Dogue Run, Mill, Mill Plantation & the Ferry at Posey's, before Dinner.

2. At home all day. Mr. Wm. Waite dind here.

> William Waite (died c.1787), of Fauquier County, was a stonemason who owned his own quarry. On this day GW made his first payment to Waite for an order of over 700 feet of stone (Ledger B, 111).

3. Went to Pohick Church & returnd home to Dinner.

4. At home all day. Mr. & Mrs. Custis came here from Maryland.

5. Went up to Alexandria to a Meeting of the Inhabitts. of this County. Dined at Arrells & lodgd at my own Ho[use].

> The date for the convention in Williamsburg had been set as late as 1 Aug., so that each burgess might test opinion in his respective county, and it was for this purpose that GW attended this Fairfax County meeting of inhabitants, probably held at the courthouse.

6. Dined at Doctr. Brown's & returnd home in the Eveng.

> The meeting of inhabitants, held the previous day, chose a committee to draft resolutions to instruct their two burgesses, who would represent them in the August convention, on nonimportation, nonexportation, aid to Boston, a continental congress to give the 13 colonies one voice, and general views on English liberty and American rights. GW was chosen chairman of the committee, which was probably meeting in Alexandria on this day.

14. Went up to Alexandria to the Election where I was Chosen, together with Majr. Broadwater, Burgess. Staid all Night to a Ball.

Governor Dunmore, who had dissolved the assembly upon its protest of the Boston Port Bill in May 1774, had issued the writs for new elections on 16 June (*Va. Gaz.*, P&D, 16 June 1774, supp.).

Maj. Charles Broadwater (d. 1806) lived at Springfield, in northern Fairfax County. He served for a number of years as a vestryman in Truro Parish and was elected to the vestry of newly created Fairfax Parish in 1765. He was a member of the last session of the Virginia House of Burgesses and of the first four Virginia conventions of 1774–75.

An English visitor in Alexandria, who was present for the election, recorded in his diary: "*Thursday, July 14th, 1774*. An Election for Burgesses in town. . . . There were three Candidates, the Poll was over in about two hours and conducted with great order and regularity. The Members Col. George Washington and Major Bedwater. The Candidates gave the populace a Hogshead of Toddy (what we call Punch in England). In the evening the returned Member [GW] gave a Ball to the Freeholders and Gentlemen of the town. This was conducted with great harmony. Coffee and Chocolate, but no Tea. This Herb is in disgrace amongst them at present" (Cresswell, *Journal*, 27–28).

In his accounts GW entered £8 5s. 6d. for "my p[ar]t of the Electn. Ball" (Ledger B, 126).

17. Went to Pohick Church & returnd to Dinner. Colo. Mason came in the Afternoon & stayed all Night.

George Mason of Gunston Hall was a member of the Fairfax resolutions committee that GW chaired. He and GW probably spent this Sunday afternoon and evening perfecting a draft, probably Mason's, of resolutions to be presented the following day. The final draft submitted to the committee contained 24 separate resolutions regarding English liberty, American rights, taxation and representation, the boycotting of most British imports (including slaves), and "a Congress [that] shou'd be appointed, to consist of Deputies from all the Colonies, to concert a general and uniform Plan for the Defence and Preservation of our common Rights" (Rutland, *Mason Papers*, 1:205).

18. Went up to Alexandria to a Meeting of the County. Returnd in the Evening—Mr. Magowan with me.

On GW's arrival in Alexandria he first attended a meeting wherein "the Resolution's (which were adjudg'd advisable for this county to come to) [were] revis'd, alterd, & corrected in the Committee" (GW to Bryan Fairfax, 20 July 1774, *Papers, Colonial Series*, 10:128–31). Then the whole committee went "into a general Meeting in the Court House," where GW found an almost "perfect satisfaction & acquiescence to the measures propos'd," though his friend Bryan Fairfax thought otherwise (see Fairfax to GW, 5 Aug. 1774). These resolutions, approved on this day by the "General Meeting of the Freeholders and other Inhabitants of the County of Fairfax, at the Court House," thereafter were commonly known as the Fairfax Resolves. The meeting also chose a 25-man committee, headed by GW, which would "have power to call a General Meeting, and to Concert and Adopt such Measures as may be thought most expedient and Necessary" (Van Schreeven, *Revolutionary Virginia*, 1:127–33).

August

Augt. 1st. Went from Colo. Bassetts to Williamsburg to the Meeting of the Convention. Dined at Mrs. Campbells. Spent the Evening in my Lodgings.

> After he arrived at the convention, GW wrote to Thomas Johnson, 5 Aug. 1774: "We never before had so full a Meeting . . . as on the present Occasion." At least 108 delegates, most of whom were also burgesses, were present at some time during the convention, which met in the Capitol (see Van Schreeven, *Revolutionary Virginia*, 1:109, 219–22).

5. Dined at Mrs. Dawson's & Spent the Evening at my own Lodgings.

> The *Virginia Gazette* reported: "Friday, *August 5.* This Day the Commissioners on Behalf of this Colony, to attend the General Congress at Philadelphia the 5th of next Month, were appointed by Ballot." GW was one of the commissioners (*Va. Gaz.*, P&D, 4 Aug. 1774). The convention voted to ask for a contribution of £15 from each of the 61 counties. GW's "proportion of the Sum voted" was £90 13s. 9d., which he received on the day he entered Philadelphia (Ledger B, 30).

6. Dined at Mrs. Campbells & Spent the Evening at my own Lodgings.

> On this day the convention adjourned, after a nonimportation/nonexportation association had been "unanimously resolved upon and agreed to" (Van Schreeven, *Revolutionary Virginia*, 1:231–35). Unless Britain repealed its new laws applying to Boston and Massachusetts, Virginia would stop all British imports, including slaves (but excluding medicines), beginning 1 Nov. 1774, and would end all export of tobacco to Britain beginning 1 Aug. 1775. The associators also agreed to foster county enforcement committees, encourage all merchants to sign the association and boycott those who would not, prevent inflated prices, support Boston with contributions, refrain from drinking tea, and empower the moderator to reconvene the convention when he thought necessary. These articles became the basis for those adopted for all of the colonies by the First Continental Congress in Oct. 1774.

7. Left Williamsburg abt. 9 Oclock.

> On his way back to Mount Vernon, GW visited his lands in King William County and Jacky Custis's property in King and Queen County and spent the night of 9 Aug. with Betty and Fielding Lewis in Fredericksburg. He arrived home on 10 Aug. For the rest of the month he resumed his normal activities on the plantation and made preparations for his journey to Philadelphia to attend the First Continental Congress.

15. Went . . . to Colo. Fairfax's Sale.

> Since it seemed unlikely that George William and Sally Fairfax would return to Virginia, a sale of their household and kitchen furniture and other effects was advertised for this day. Belvoir itself and its 2,000 acres and several fisheries were offered for rent (*Va. Gaz.*, P&D, 2 June 1774). GW acquired several items from the sale: a card table for £4 and a Wilton carpet for £8.

31. with Colo. Pendleton, & Mr. Henry I set out on my journey for Phila. & reachd uppr. Marlbro.

September

Septr. 1. Breakfasted at Queen Anne. Dined in Annapolis, & lodged at Rock Hall.

Queen Anne was a small village on the Patuxent River in Prince George's County, Md., nine miles northeast of Upper Marlboro. In 1783 it consisted of only a few houses and a tobacco warehouse. *Rock Hall:* GW lists expenses "at Hodges" as 16s. 9d. (GW's Cash Memoranda, 24 Mar.–25 Oct. 1774, Huntington Library, San Marino, Calif.). A 30 Nov. 1775 advertisement in the *Maryland Gazette* for the rental of the "White Rock-Hall ferry" describes James Hodges as currently living on the ferry plantation. He probably ran the ferry house where GW stayed.

2. Din'd at Rock Hall (waiting for my Horses) & lodg'd at New Town on Chester.

3. Breakfasted at Down's. Dind at the Buck Tavern (Carsons) & lodg'd at Newcastle.

Down's: a tavern operated by William Down at Down's Cross Roads, now Galena, Md., 12 miles south of Georgetown. The Buck Tavern was in New Castle County, Del., 11 miles south of the present city of Newark, Del. William Carson, a tavern keeper in New Castle County in 1778, was probably the proprietor at this time.

4. Breakfasted at Christeen Ferry. Dined at Chester & lodged at Doctr. Shippens's in Phila. after Supping at the New Tavern.

William Shippen, Jr. (1736–1808), was a Philadelphia physician and surgeon, educated at Edinburgh. In 1765 he was appointed professor of surgery and anatomy at the new medical school connected with the College of Philadelphia, and during the Revolution he was chief physician and director general of the military hospital of the Continental Army.

5. Breakfasted and Dined at Doctr. Shippen's. Spent the Eveng. at Tavern.

On this day the delegates to Congress met at City Tavern. The credentials of the various members were read, and Peyton Randolph of Virginia was elected chairman, or president, and Charles Thomson of Pennsylvania secretary. Carpenters' Hall, which had been offered by the Carpenters' Guild of Philadelphia, was chosen as the meeting place for Congress (*JCC*, 1:13–14). GW rarely mentions in his diaries anything concerning his presence in Congress, but he seems to have attended the sessions regularly.

6. Dined at the New Tavern—after being in Congress all day.

On this day GW spent 15s. for shoes, etc., for William Lee, his body servant, who accompanied him to Philadelphia (Cash Memoranda, 24 Mar.–

25 Oct. 1774, Huntington Library, San Marino, Calif.). In Congress today the decision was made to keep secret the proceedings of the Congress (*JCC,* 1:25–26).

8. Dined at Mr. Andw. Allan's & spent the Evening in my own Lodgings.

Andrew Allen (1740–1825), a son of William Allen, chief justice of Pennsylvania until 1774, and Margaret Hamilton Allen, graduated from the College of Philadelphia and studied law in England as well as Philadelphia. He was at this time an influential Patriot active in opposing British policies. Allen was attorney general of Pennsylvania and a member of the provincial council. In 1775 he was elected to the Continental Congress. However, after the move toward independence seemed inevitable, he resigned from Congress and fled behind British lines.

My own Lodgings: The location of GW's lodgings during his attendance at the First Continental Congress is uncertain. A mutilated entry in his cash memoranda book for 24 Oct., two days before he left Philadelphia, shows a payment of £34 2s. 6d. "at Carsons" (Huntington Library). The size of this expenditure would be commensurate with the cost of lodgings for himself and his servant, William, during his stay in the city. William Carson (b. 1728), an Irish emigrant, at this time ran a tavern called the Harp and Crown, on North Third Street just below Arch Street.

October

26. Dined at Bevans's, and Spent the Evening at the New Tavern.

After approving an address to be printed for distribution among the inhabitants of Quebec, the First Continental Congress adjourned (*JCC,* 1:113–14). GW and Richard Henry Lee were the only members of the Virginia delegation still remaining in Philadelphia at the time of the adjournment. The other Virginia delegates left on 23 Oct. for Virginia, where the House of Burgesses was due to meet on the first Thursday in November.

27. Set out on my return home.

30. Breakfasted at Mr. Calverts & reachd home abt. 3 Oclock.

November

10. At home all day. Doctr. Craik came here in the Evening and stayed all Night.

11. At home all day. Mr. Bryan Fairfax came here & stayed all Night.

12. I went up to George Town To an intended meeting of Trustees for openg. Potomack River. None Met. Returnd home at Night.

After inspecting canal works in England, John Ballendine had returned to the Potomac Valley in the late summer of 1774 with a plan for opening navigation of the Potomac River "at and above the Lower Falls" to boats that could carry wheat and iron downriver to the ports of Georgetown and Alexandria (*Md. Gaz.,* 8 Sept. 1774). At a meeting held in the early fall, probably at Georgetown, 37 trustees were chosen from the subscribers to Ballendine's project, among whom was GW.

13. Went up to Alexandria Church. In the Evening Colo. Blackburn Mr. Lee, & Mr. Richd. Graham came here as a Committee from the Prince Wm. Independ. Compy.

> Mr. Lee was Philip Richard Francis Lee (died c.1834), son of Squire Richard Lee of Blenheim, Charles County, Md. Philip Richard, a merchant in Dumfries, was a captain in the Prince William Independent Company, which was absorbed into the 3d Virginia Regiment early in 1776.
>
> *Prince Wm. Independ. Compy.:* On 21 Sept. 1774 a meeting of local men in Alexandria formed an agreement to organize the Fairfax Independent Company of Volunteers, which was probably the first "Independent Company" so organized in a Virginia county. On 11 Nov. 1774 the Independent Company of Cadets of Prince William County appointed the three men who appeared here today as a delegation to "wait upon Collonel George Washington, and request of him to take the command of this Company as their Field Officer, and that he will be pleas'd to direct the fashion of their uniform," which request GW accepted (Hamilton, *Letters to Washington,* 5:68–69). By the late spring of 1775 GW had also accepted the commands of the independent companies of Fairfax, Fauquier, Richmond, and Spotsylvania counties.

1775

January

Where, how, or with whom, my time is Spent

16. Went up to Alexandria to a review of the Independant Company & to choose a Com[mitt]ee for the County of Fairfax.

> When first organized in Sept. 1774, the company agreed to limit its number to 100 men, to elect its own officers, to drill from time to time, and to supply its own ammunition. Each volunteer was to carry "a good Fire-lock and Bayonet, Sling Cartouch-Box, and Tomahawk" and to dress in "a regular Uniform of Blue, turn'd up with Buff" (Rutland, *Mason Papers,* 1:211).

17. Under Arms this day also and in Committee in the Eveng.

> Today the committee, chaired by GW, passed resolutions to assess 3s. for every tithable in the county to pay for powder, to keep a list "of such persons as shall refuse to pay the same," and to organize a countywide militia system of 68-man companies (Rutland, *Mason Papers,* 1:212–13).

18. In Committee all day.

> No contemporary reference has been found during the period covered by GW's diaries to any county committee in Virginia being called a committee of safety, each committee usually referring to itself merely as "the committee" for the county.

22. At home all day. Danl. Jenifer Adams came here abt. 11 Oclock, & went away. Price Posey came—Dined and stayd all Night.

> Adams was still trying to settle his debts to GW growing out of his role in the 1772 voyage of the brig *Fairfax* to the West Indies (see entries for 22 July 1772 and 28 Mar. 1774). GW was pressing "that worthless young Fellow" Adams for possession of about 550 acres of Adams family lands in Charles County, Md., which GW accepted later in the year as "all I am likely to get for my debt" (GW to Thomas Pollock, 29 Nov. 1773, and to Robert McMickan, 10 May 1774, Daniel Jenifer Adams to GW, 4 Feb. 1775, *Papers, Colonial Series*, 9:387–88, 10:55–58, 253–54; Ledger B, 99).

February

8. Mr. Willm. Milner came to Dinner & went over to Mr. Digges's in the Aftern.

> William Milnor continued to do business with GW, although there is no record of his buying fish after May 1774. Milnor was a Quaker, but he was an ardent supporter of the colonists against the British ministry and, on GW's orders, furnished drums, fifes, and colors for the Fairfax and Prince William Independent companies, as well as a number of muskets. He also furnished GW with an officer's sash, gorget, epaulets, and sword knots, a treatise on military discipline, and several political pamphlets (Ledger B, 123; Milnor to GW, 29 Nov. 1774, *Papers, Colonial Series*, 10:189–91).

20. Went up to Alexandria to the Choosing of Delegates to go to Richmond.

> Pursuant to a resolution by the First Virginia Convention (1–6 Aug. 1774) authorizing the moderator, Peyton Randolph, to call another convention when he thought necessary, Randolph issued a call on 19 Jan. 1775 for each county to choose two delegates to a convention to be convened in Richmond on 20 Mar. (Van Schreeven, *Revolutionary Virginia*, 2:245–54).

March

7. I set my People off for the Ohio under the care of Willm. Stevens. Captn. Wood went away and Doctr. Craik went up with Lund Washington to see Jas. Cleveland.

> GW was making his second attempt in two years to seat his frontier lands on the Ohio and Kanawha rivers, for which he had gathered, through purchase and hire, a collection of black and white artisans and laborers. He was now sending them west under the temporary direction of William Stevens, who had replaced the ailing James Cleveland.

15. Set of for Richmond. Dind in Colchester with Mr. Wagener & lodgd at Colo. Blackburns.

16. Went to Dumfries to review the Independant Company there.

20. Reach'd Richmond abt. 11 Oclock. Dind at Mr. Richd. Adam's. Went to Col. Archy Carys abt. 7 Miles in the Aftern.

> The Second Virginia Convention was called to order at the Henrico Parish Church in Richmond, built in the 1740s on Indian Town Hill. The house of Richard Adams (c.1726–1800) was about a block from the church. Col. Archibald Cary (1720–1787) lived at Ampthill, on the south side of the James River in Chesterfield County, the county he represented in the House of Burgesses 1756–75 and in the Virginia conventions.
>
> The convention spent this day's session hearing reports from their seven delegates to the First Continental Congress and discussing the proceedings of that congress (Van Schreeven, *Revolutionary Virginia*, 2:353).

22. Dined at Galts Tavern & lodgd at a House of his providing.

> The convention concluded the day's deliberations by voting unanimous approval to "the proceedings and Resolutions of the American Continental Congress" and unanimous thanks to their seven delegates (Van Schreeven, *Revolutionary Virginia*, 2:361). Gabriel Galt (1748–1788) ran the City Tavern, on the northwest corner of Nineteenth and Main streets.

23. Dined at Mr. Patrick Cootes & lodgd where I had done the Night before.

> At this day's session Patrick Henry proposed resolutions "that this Colony be immediately put into a posture of Defence." After much debate, in the course of which Henry gave his "liberty or death" speech, the resolutions passed by a close vote. GW was appointed to a committee to "prepare a Plan for embodying, arming and disciplining" such an armed force, after which the convention adjourned for the day (Van Schreeven, *Revolutionary Virginia*, 2:366–69).
>
> At this time Patrick Coutts (d. 1776), a Richmond merchant, was living on Shockoe Hill, later the site of the state Capitol.

24. Dined at Galts & spent the Evening & lodgd at Mr. Saml. Duvals.

> The convention decided on this day to send seven delegates to the Second Continental Congress (Van Schreeven, *Revolutionary Virginia*, 2:371). Samuel Du Val (1714–1784) lived near Shockoe Creek at Mount Comfort.

25. Returnd to the Convention in Richmond. Dined at Galts.

> Today the convention accepted an amended report of the defense committee, which recommended that each county "form one or more voluntier Companies of Infantry and Troops of Horse" and that every infantryman have a rifle or firelock and a tomahawk and "be cloathed in a hunting Shirt by Way of Uniform." The convention also appointed a committee to report on manufactures, to which GW was appointed, and then chose the same seven delegates who had attended the First Continental Congress to attend the second Congress set for May. In the polling GW stood second to Peyton Randolph (Van Schreeven, *Revolutionary Virginia*, 2:376).

28. Left Richmond.

29. Got to Fredericksburg abt. 11 Oclock. Dined at Colo. Lewis's & spent the Evening at Weedons.

> George Weedon was described by an English traveler who stopped at his tavern about this time as "very active and zealous in blowing the flames of sedition" (Smyth, *A Tour in the United States of America,* 2 : 151).

April

17. Colo. Mason & myself went up to Alexa. to a Committee & to a New choice of Delegates. I returnd at Night.

> This meeting was called in Alexandria for election of delegates to the Virginia Convention from Fairfax County. GW and Charles Broadwater were again elected. By early May GW and the other Virginia delegates to the Second Continental Congress, all of whom were also Virginia Convention delegates, had advised their Virginia constituents to replace them in the convention "during their necessary Absence" at the Congress in Philadelphia (*Va. Gaz.,* D&H, 13 May 1775).

25. At home all day. A Mr. Johnson—a Muster Master dind here & went away afterwds. Thos. Davis came Express & returnd.

> William Johnson was sent by the Fairfax County Independent Company to consult GW on its new uniform. The members wrote GW to ask if they could "take the fashion of the Hunting shirt Cap and Gaiters from you" and inquired "whether you Intend to send yours up that we may get the fashion" (Fairfax County Independent Company to GW, 25 April 1775). Thomas Davis (Davies) was sent from Fredericksburg to GW with £4 16s. to buy gunpowder for the Spotsylvania Independent Company (Ledger B, 192).

May

2. Messrs. Hendks. Dalton & others Breakfasted here & Majr. Gates & Mr. B. Fairfax dind & lodgd here.

> James Hendricks, an Alexandria merchant, was one of ten Alexandrians who formed a town committee of correspondence in May 1774; he later served in the Revolution as a major and colonel with the Virginia troops (Van Schreeven, *Revolutionary Virginia,* 2 : 88; Heitman, *Historical Register,* 217).
>
> Horatio Gates (1727–1806) had been a captain in the British army in 1755 when he was wounded in Braddock's Defeat. After serving in the French and Indian War he returned to Great Britain, where he subsequently retired on half pay with the rank of major. In 1772 he and his family moved to America and settled on a farm near Opequon Creek, about six miles northwest of Charles Town in the Shenandoah Valley. This home, which he named Traveller's Rest, was situated in newly formed Berkeley County (now in Jefferson County, W.Va.) where he served with GW's brother Samuel Washington as a county justice of the peace. Gates probably used this visit at Mount Vernon to discuss with GW the recent battles of Lexington and Concord, the current siege of Boston by New England troops, and the prospects for the two serving in an American army against Lt. Gen. Thomas Gage, with

whom they had both served in Braddock's campaign, and who was now commander of the British troops in Boston.

4. Set out for the Congress at Phila. Dind in Alexa. & lodgd at Marlborough.

GW left Mount Vernon in his chariot, probably accompanied by Richard Henry Lee who was already at Mount Vernon. He may have met several of the other delegates on the road between Mount Vernon and Baltimore.

5. Breakfasted at Mrs. Ramsays & Lodged at Baltimore.

9th. Breakfasted at Chester, & dined at the City Tavern Phila. Supped at Mr. Jos. Reads.

Samuel Curwen, a Loyalist, also spent this evening at Joseph Reed's house "in company with Colonel Washington a fine figure, and of a most easy and agreeable address," Richard Henry Lee, Benjamin Harrison, and others, "I staid till 12 o'clock, the conversation being chiefly on the most feasible and prudent method of stopping up the Channel of Delaware to prevent the coming up of any large King's ships to the City. I could not perceive the least disposition to accomodate matters or even risk" (Curwen, *Journal,* 1:7–8).

19. Dined at Mr. Allans. Spent the Evening in my own lodgings.

The committee of Congress to consider the defense of New York, which had occupied much of GW's time for two days past, brought in its report. The report was read and referred to the committee of the whole, which made its resolutions regarding New York's defense on 25 May (see *JCC,* 2:57).

27. Dined at the City Tavern & spent the Evening at my own Lodgings.

GW, Philip Schuyler, Thomas Mifflin, Silas Deane, Lewis Morris, and Samuel Adams were named a committee "to consider of ways and means to supply these colonies with Ammunition and military stores and to report immediately" (*JCC,* 2:67). Congress appointed a number of committees, including one composed of GW, Philip Schuyler, Silas Deane, Thomas Cushing, and Joseph Hewes "to bring in an estimate of the money necessary to be raised" (*JCC,* 2:79–80).

June

4. Dined at Mr. Robt. Morris's on the Banks of Schoolkill & Spent the Eveng. at the City Tavn.

Robert Morris (1734–1806), born in England, came in his youth to Maryland where his father was engaged in the tobacco export business. The younger Morris settled in Philadelphia and as a partner in the firm of Willing, Morris & Co. eventually became one of America's wealthiest merchants. Morris signed the nonimportation agreement in 1765 and in 1775 was a member of the council of safety. He was a member of the Continental Congress Nov. 1775–78, and he served as superintendent of finance 1781–84. Morris and his wife, Mary White Morris of Maryland, became close friends of the Washingtons.

7. Dined at the City Tavern and spent the Evening at home.

GW's committee to estimate the amount of money to be raised today gave its report, which was referred to the committee of the whole (*JCC*, 2:81). GW made a number of purchases on this day, including "5 Books—Military" (Cash Memoranda).

15. Dined at Burns's in the Field. Spent the Eveng. on a Committee.

Congress resolved today "that a General be appointed to command all the continental forces, raised, or to be raised, for the defence of American liberty" (*JCC*, 2:91). GW, nominated by Thomas Johnson of Maryland, was unanimously elected. For GW's election, see *Papers, Revolutionary War Series*, 1:1–5.

The committee which occupied GW all the evening was the one on drafting army regulations.

16. Dined at Doctr. Cadwaladers. Spent the Evening at my lodgings.

GW was informed officially in Congress of his appointment as general and commander in chief, and he read his acceptance speech "standing in his place." Although, GW stated, he was "truly sensible of the high Honour done me in this Appointment, yet I feel great distress, from a consciousness that my abilities & Military experience may not be equal to the exensive & important Trust: However, as the Congress desire i⟨t⟩ I will enter upon the momentous duty, & exert every power I Possess In their service & for the Support of the glorious Cause: I beg they will accept my most cordial thanks fore this distinguished testimony of their Approbation. But lest some unlucky event should happen unfavourable to my reputation, I beg it may be rememberd by every Gentn in the room, that I this day declare with the utmost sincerity, I do not think my self equal to the Command I ⟨am⟩ honoured with." He refused the salary which Congress had voted, asking only that his expenses be paid (*Papers, Revolutionary War Series*, 1:1–3). Other resolutions on this day set up an establishment of major generals, brigadiers, aides, secretaries, and so forth (*JCC*, 2:92–94).

On 18 June, perhaps while he was alone in his room during the evening, GW wrote to Mrs. Washington: "My Dearest: I am now set down to write to you on a subject which fills me with inexpressible concern. . . . You may Beleive me my dear Patcy, when I assure you, in the most solemn manner, that, so far from seeking this appointment I have used every endeavour in my power to avoid it, not only from unwillingness to part with you and the Family, but from a consciousness of its being a trust too great for my Capacity and that I should enjoy more real happiness and felicity in one month with you, at home, than I have the most distant prospect of reaping abroad, if my stay was to be Seven times Seven years. But, as it has been a kind of destiny that has thrown me upon this Service, I shall hope that my undertaking of it, is designed to answer some good purpose. . . . i was utterly out of my power to refuse this appoinment without exposing my Character to such censures as would have reflected dishonour upon myself, and given pain to my friends. . . . I shall rely therefore, confidently, on That Providence which has heretofore preserved, & been bountiful to me, not doubting but that I shall return safe to you in the fall—I shall feel no pain from the Toil of the danger of the Campaign—My unhappiness will flow, from the uneasiness I know you

On 23 June 1775, as he was leaving Philadelphia to take command of the American army at Boston, Washington wrote a farewell to Martha. (Mount Vernon Ladies' Association of the Union)

will feel at being left alone" (*Papers, Revolutionary War Series,* 1:3–6)." In the letter GW enclosed his will.

On 19 June, John Hancock, president of the Continental Congress, signed GW's commission as "General and Commander in Chief of the army of the United Colonies." Meanwhile, GW was writing more letters home to Virginia, including one to his closest brother, John Augustine, 20 June, wherein he "bid adieu to you, & to every kind of domestick ease, for a while. I am

Imbarked on a wide Ocean, boundless in its prospect & from whence, perhaps, no safe harbour is to be foun[d]. I have been called upon by the
unanimous Voice of the Colonies to take the Command of the Continental
Army. An honour I neither sought after, nor desired, as I am thoroughly
convinced, that it requires greater Abilities, and much more experience,
than I am Master of" (ibid., 19–20).

During this week, while Congress was choosing 13 new generals, drafting
GW's initial instructions, and deciding how to finance the campaign, GW
was preparing for his trip to Massachusetts to form the thousands of citizen-
soldiers surrounding Boston into an army of the united colonies. He chose
Joseph Reed as his secretary and Thomas Mifflin as his first aide-de-camp. He
queried the Massachusetts delegates about what arrangements their government had made for supporting the army and whom he would be dealing
with. And he sent his chariot home.

On 23 June the new commander in chief left Philadelphia, accompanied
by Generals Charles Lee and Philip Schuyler and their aides. While he was
but "a few Minutes of leaving this City" and "surrounded with Company to
take leave of me," GW wrote again to Mrs. Washington: "My Dearest. . . . I go
fully trusting in that Providence, which has been more bountiful to me than
I deserve, & in full confidence of a happy meeting with you some time in the
fall. . . .I retain an unalterable affection for you, which neither time or distance can change" (ibid., 27–28). He then rode off to a campaign that would
last for more than seven years, during which he saw Mount Vernon only in
his 1781 visits during the Yorktown campaign.

*For the period between 19 June 1775 and January 1780, except for one
weather diary, no journals of GW's have been found; his opening remarks in
his 1781 Yorktown diary indicate that no other war journals were kept.*

*When GW began his entries for 1781 he was writing from his headquarters
at New Windsor, N.Y.*

1781

May

I begin, at this Epoch, a concise Journal of Military transactions &ca. I
lament not having attempted it from the commencement of the War,
in aid of my memory and wish the multiplicity of matter which continually surround me and the embarrassed State of our affairs which is
momently calling the attention to perplexities of one kind or another,
may not defeat altogether or so interrupt my present intention, & plan,
as to render it of little avail.

To have the clearer understanding of the entries which may follow,
it would be proper to recite, in detail, our wants and our prospects but
this alone would be a Work of much time, and great magnitude. It may
suffice to give the sum of them—wch., I shall do in a few words—viz.—

Instead of having Magazines filled with provisions, we have a scanty

pittance scattered here & there in the different States. Instead of having our Arsenals well supplied with Military Stores, they are poorly provided, & the Workmen all leaving them. Instead of having the various
articles of Field equipage in readiness to deliver, the Quarter Master
General (as the denier resort, according to his acct.) is but now applying to the several States to provide these things for their Troops respectively. Instead of having a regular System of transportation established
upon credit or funds in the Qr. Masters hands to defray the contingent
Expences of it, we have neither the one nor the other and all that business, or a great part of it, being done by Military Impress, we are daily
& hourly oppressing the people—souring their tempers and alienating
their affection. Instead of having the Regiments compleated to the
New establishment (and which ought to have been So by the [   ] of
[   ] agreeably to the requisitions of Congress, scarce any State in the
Union has, at this hour, an eighth part of its quota in the field and little
prospect, that I can see, of ever getting more than half. In a word—
instead of having everything in readiness to take the Field, we have
nothing—and instead of having the prospect of a glorious offensive
campaign before us, we have a bewildered, and gloomy defensive
one—unless we should receive a powerful aid of Ships—Land Troops
and Money from our generous allies & these, at present, are too contingent to build upon.

May 1st. Induced by pressing necessity—the inefficacy, & bad tendency
of pushing Military Impresses too far and the impracticability of keeping the Army supplied without *it,* or *money,* to pay the transportation I
drew for 9000 dollars of the Sum sent on by the State of Massachusetts
for payment of their Troops; and placed it in the hands of the QM
General [1] with the most positive orders to apply it solely to this purpose.

Fixed with Ezekiel Cornell Esqr. a member of the Board of War (then
on a tour to the Eastward to inspect some of the Armoury's &ca.) on
certain articles of Cloathing—arms and Military Stores which might be
sent from hence to supply the wants of the Southern Army.[2]

Major Talmadge was requested to press the C——s Senr. & Junr. to
continue their correspondence and was authorized to assure the elder
C—— that he should be repaid the Sum of 100 Guineas, or more, with
interest; provided he advanced the same for the purpose of defraying
the expence of the correspondence, as he had offered to do.[3]

Colo. [Jonathan] Dayton was also written to, and pressed to establish
a correspondence with New York, by way of Elizabeth Town for the purpose of obtaining intelligence of the Enemys movemts. and designs;
that by a comparison of Accts. proper & just conclusions may be drawn.

1. Timothy Pickering (1745–1829) had been appointed quartermaster

general in Aug. 1780.

2. Ezekiel Cornell (1733–1800) was a delegate to the Continental Congress from Rhode Island 1780–83 and member of the Board of War. In the spring of 1781 he had received leave from Congress "for visiting the military Magazines, Laboratories, etc., and causing some necessary reforms" (*LMCC,* 6:65). Cornell reported back to GW on 24 May 1781.

3. Maj. Benjamin Tallmadge (1754–1835), a native of Brookhaven, N.Y., conducted secret service operations for GW in the New York area, operating under the name of John Bolton, from 1778 to the end of the war.

Samuel Culper was the name used by two New York intelligence agents who furnished information on British troops and naval movements in the area of New York and Long Island. Samuel Culper, Sr., was Abrahan Woodhull (c.1750–1826) of Setauket, Long Island. Samuel Culper, Jr., was Robert Townsend (1753–1838) of Oyster Bay, Long Island. From 1778 to the end of the war, both, usually reporting to GW through Benjamin Tallmadge, gave invaluable information on British activities. For the operation of this intelligence ring, see Pennypacker, *General Washington's Spies,* and Ford, *A Peculiar Service.*

4th. A Letter of the Baron de Steuben's from Chesterfield Court House Virga. dated the 21st. Ulto. informs that 12 of the Enemys Vessels but with what Troops he knew not, had advanced up James River as high as Jamestown—that few Militia were in arms and few arms to put into their hands—that he had moved the public Stores from Richmond &ca. into the interior Country.[1]

A Letter from the Marqs. de la Fayette, dated at Alexandria on the 23d., mentioned his having commenced his march that day for Fredericksburg—that desertion had ceased, & that his detachment were in good Spirits.[2]

1. Friedrich Wilhelm Augustus von Steuben (1730–1794), after an extensive military career in Europe, came to the United States bearing somewhat inflated European references in Dec. 1777. Joining GW at Valley Forge in Feb. 1778, he quickly proved his value to the Continental forces as an instructor in discipline and tactics, his "blue book"—*Orders and Discipline of the Troops of the United States*—becoming the manual of instruction in the U.S. Army for many years. On 5 May 1778 he was appointed inspector general of the army with the rank of major general (*JCC,* 11:465). In Oct. 1780, when Maj. Gen. Nathanael Greene replaced Horatio Gates as commander of the Southern Department, Steuben accompanied Greene in order to aid in the restoration of the army in the South. Setting up headquarters at Chesterfield Court House, Va., about 12 miles south of Richmond, he attempted to organize Virginia's defenses and arrange for men and supplies for Greene in the Carolinas. In Dec. 1780 Sir Henry Clinton dispatched to Virginia from New York a fleet and over 1,500 British soldiers under the command of Benedict Arnold, now a brigadier general in the British army. The force landed at Hampton Roads 30 Dec. 1780 and, moving up the James River, took Richmond 5–7 Jan. 1781, then withdrawing to Westover. Steuben participated in the attempt to halt the British in Virginia in the spring of 1781. In mid-April, Arnold and Maj. Gen. William Phillips, now in command of British forces in

Virginia, moved against the Continental troops in Richmond and Chester-field Court House. Lafayette arrived at Richmond 29 April with reinforce-ments in time to force Phillips's withdrawal to the area of Jamestown Island.

2. The marquis de Lafayette (1757–1834) had been selected by GW in Feb. 1781 to lead a force of 1,200 light infantry to Virginia to halt Arnold's advance. Lafayette was to cooperate with a French fleet under Admiral Des-touches. The plan to capture Arnold's forces failed, partly because the dam-age inflicted on Destouches's fleet by a British naval force under Admiral Marriot Arbuthnot in an engagement on 16 Mar. had sent the French back to Newport, R.I. Arnold himself had been substantially reinforced by the ar-rival of British transports. Lafayette and his troops remained in Virginia, and on 6 April 1781 GW ordered him to march south to reinforce Greene. On 21 April he reached Alexandria.

6th. Colo. Menonville,[1] one of the Adjutt. Generals in the French Army came to Head Quarters by order of Count de Rochambeau to make arrangements for supplying the Troops of His Most Christian Majesty with certain provisions contracted for by Doctr. Franklin. This demand, tho' the immediate compliance with it, was not insisted upon, com-ports illy with our circumstances; & is exceedingly embarrassing.[2]

That the States might not only know our Wants, which my repeated & pressing letters had recently, & often communicated, but, if possible, be impressed with them and adopt some mode of Transporting it to the Army, I resolved to send Genl. Heath (2d. Offr. in Commd.)[3] to make to the respective legislatures East of York State, pointed repre-sentations; & to declare explicitly that unless measures are adopted to supply transportation, it will be impossible to subsist & keep the Troops together.

1. François Louis Arthur Thibaut, comte de Ménonville (1740–1816), was appointed lieutenant colonel in the French army in 1772 and came to America as aide to the French general staff.

2. The French army at Newport, R.I., was encountering the same prob-lems in obtaining supplies as the American army. Although the French army usually had paid for its supplies—some estimates of expenditures run as high as $6 million—locating adequate provisions remained a problem. From France, Benjamin Franklin reported to Congress in Dec. 1780 that he had made an arrangement with the French ministry to have provisions delivered at current prices for the use of the French troops in America. On the assump-tion that Franklin had signed the contract as a form of payment to the French government for funds furnished him by France to discharge bills of exchange drawn on him by Congress, that body confirmed the contract and agreed to provide the supplies (*JCC,* 19:373–73, 20:528).

GW's interview with Ménonville lasted several days, after which the com-mander in chief referred him to Congress for a decision. Ménonville then conferred with Robert Morris, superintendent of finance, who informed him that the prospects for supplying the French army were not promising. By late July, however, Morris wrote Franklin that he would endeavor to carry out the commitment to France (Morris to Franklin, 21 July 1781, Robert Morris

Papers, Library of Congress).

    3. Maj. Gen. William Heath (1737–1814) was at this time in command of the area of the lower Hudson.

11th. Major Genl. Heath set out this day for the Eastn. States, provided with Instructions, and letters couched in strong terms—representing the distresses of the Army for want of provisions and the indispensable necessity of keeping up regular supplies by the adoption of a plan, which will have system & permanency in't.[1]

This day also I received advice from Colo. Dayton that 10 Ships of the line, and 3 or 4000 Troops had sailed from New York. The intelligence was immediately communicated to Congress, and to the French Genl. & Admiral at R. Isld.

    1. See entry for 6 May 1781.

    2. The information was sent to the comte de Rochambeau, in command of the French forces at Newport, 11 May 1781, with a request that it be transmitted to Charles René Dominique Sochet, chevalier Destouches (1727–1794), temporarily commanding the French fleet at Newport.

13th. Received Letters from Count de Rochambeau advising me of the arrival of his Son[1] & from Count de Barras[2] informing me of his appointment to the Command of the French Squadron at Rhode Island—both solliciting an Interview with me as soon as possible. Appointed, in answer, Monday the 21st. Inst. & Wethersfield, as the time & place of Meeting.

    1. Rochambeau's letter is dated 11 May 1781 (Washington Papers, Library of Congress). Rochambeau's son, Donatien Marie Joseph de Vimeur, vicomte de Rochambeau (1755–1813), served with his father in America as *mestre de camp en second* of the Régiment de Bourbonnais, commanding a battalion of grenadiers at the Battle of Yorktown. In May 1781 the younger Rochambeau had just returned from France, where he had gone in Oct. 1780 in the hope of obtaining additional supplies for the American campaign. The French frigate *Concorde* brought the comte de Rochambeau dispatches from the minister of war and the minister of marine informing him that the anticipated reinforcement of troops would not be available for the campaign and that the present army under Rochambeau would serve under GW's orders. A sum of six million livres tournois had been granted for the supply of the American army (Doniol, *La participation de la France de l'établissement des Etats-Unis,* 5:466–70). In addition, he learned that Admiral de Grasse's fleet had been ordered to the West Indies and would be available to support the upcoming summer campaign. In light of this new information, Rochambeau urgently requested a conference with GW. GW agreed to meet with Rochambeau and Admiral Barras at Wethersfield, Conn., on 21 May (GW to Ralph Pomeroy, 14 May 1781, Washington Papers, Library of Congress).

    2. Jacques Melchior Saint-Laurent, comte de Barras, had replaced Admiral de Ternay as commander of the French naval squadron at Newport.

14th. About Noon, intelligence was recd. from Genl. Patterson at West point, that the Enemy were on the No. side of Croton in force—that Colo. Green, Majr. Flag, & some other officers with 40 or 50 Men were surprized & cut off at the Bri⟨dg⟩e & that Colo. Scammell with the New Hampshire Troops had Marched to their assistance. I ordered the Connecticut Troops to move in & support those of New Hampshire.[1]

In the evening, information was brot. that the enemy (consisting of about 60 horse, & 140 Infantry) had retreated precipitately & that several of our Soldiers had been inhumanly murdered.

1. John Patterson (1744–1808) was in command of the 2d Massachusetts brigade, operating around West Point. Col. Christopher Greene, commanding the 1st Rhode Island Regiment, and Maj. Ebenezer Flagg, of the same regiment, were part of a small force guarding a ford on the Croton River in Westchester County, N.Y. Both men were killed in a surprise attack just after sunrise on 13 May by a troop of James De Lancey's Tories. The Americans were particularly incensed by rumors that Greene, wounded in the first attack, was "carried into the woods and barbarously murdered" by the Tories (Thacher, *Military Journal,* 262). By mid-May De Lancey's force had withdrawn.

Alexander Scammell (1747–1781) was adjutant general on GW's staff Jan. 1778–Jan. 1781. He was mortally wounded during the siege of Yorktown under conditions of considerable controversy, the Americans charging that he had been shot after surrendering to a party of British soldiers. At this time he was in command of the 1st New Hampshire Regiment.

15th. Information, dated 12 oclock yesterday reports 15 Sail of Vessels & a number of Flatboats to be off Fort Lee.[1] Ordered a detachment of 200 Men to March immediately to support the Post at Dobbs's. ferry—countenance the Militia, & cover the Country in that Neighbourhood.

Intelligence from C—— Senr., dated 729[2]—a detachment is expected to Sail tomorrow from New York to be conveyed by 7 Ships of the line, 2 fifties, & 3 forty fours which are to cruize of the Capes of Virginia. He gives it as the opinion of C—— Junr. that the above detachmt. does not exceed 2000 Men—that not more than 4000 remain—wch. is only (he adds) to be accounted for on the supposition of their expecting a reinforcement immediately from Europe.

1. Fort Lee was on the New Jersey side of the Hudson River, opposite Fort Washington.

2. "729" was the cipher for Setauket, Long Island, where Samuel Culper, Sr., was operating (see entry for 1 May 1781).

16th. Went to the Posts at West point. Received a particular acct. of the surprize of Colo. Green & the loss we sustained which consisted of himself & Major (Flag) killed—three officers & a Surgeon taken prisoners (the latter & two of the former wounded)—a Sergeant & 5 R[ank] &

F[ile] killed—5 left wounded & 33 made Prisoners & missing—in all 44 besides Officers.

The report of the number of Shipping &ca. at Fort Lee was this day contradicted in part—the number of Vessels being reduced, & said to be no higher than Bulls ferry.[1] In consequence of this intelligence Lt. Colo. Badlam who marked with the detachment of 200 Men pursuant to the order of Yesterday & had reached Stony point halted—but was directed not to return till the designs of the enemy were better understood.[2]

1. Bull's Ferry was approximately two miles below Fort Lee.
2. Ezra Badlam (d. 1788) was lieutenant colonel of the 8th Massachusetts Regiment.

17th. Received a letter from Captn. Lawrence, near Dobbss ferry, informing me that abt. 200 Refugees were building a block house & raising other works at Fort Lee.[1] Order'd the detachment which had halted at Kings Ferry[2] & another forming under Colo. Scammel to advance down & endeavour to annoy, if they could not prevent them.

A Letter from Genl. Foreman of Monmouth (dated the 14th. Instt.) informs me that the British fleet from New York consisting of Seven Ships of 60 Guns & upwards—12 large Transport Vessels, & 10 topsail Schooners & Sloops made Sail from Sandy hook the 12th., with the wind at So. East. but veering round to the Southward, & Westward, it returned within the hook & lay there till 10 o'clock next day when it again Sailed. By two oclock it was clear of the hook and steering Southard.[3]

1. Jonathan Lawrence, Jr. (d. 1802), was a captain in the Corps of Sappers and Miners. On receipt of Forman's letter, GW ordered Alexander Scammell to incorporate Lawrence's New York Levies and any available New Jersey militia in his command and, if possible, attack the British party of refugees at Fort Lee. The British received intelligence reports of GW's plans, and Sir Henry Clinton ordered the refugees to withdraw from the post (Mackenzie, *Diary*, 2:526–27).
2. King's Ferry was the Hudson River crossing between Verplanck's Point and Stony Point.
3. David Forman (1745–1797) was a brigadier general in the New Jersey militia.

18th. Set out this day for the Interview at Weathersfield with the Count de Rochambeau & Admiral Barras. Reached Morgans Tavern 43 Miles from Fishkill Landing after dining at Colo. Vandebergs.[1]

1. The Connecticut assembly was meeting at Hartford, so the conference with the French was held at nearby Wethersfield. Morgan's Tavern was probably the establishment kept by Gideon Morgan, who was licensed in 1781 as a tavern keeper in Washington, Litchfield County, Conn. (Crofut, *Connecticut*, 1:442). Also in GW's party were Brig. Gen. Henry Knox (1750–1806),

chief of artillery for the Continental Army, and the French engineer Brig. Gen. Louis Le Bègue Duportail, who had been serving with the American forces since 1777.

19th. Breakfasted at Litchfield—dined at Farmington & lodged at Weathersfield at the House of Joseph Webb Esqr. (the Quarters wch. were taken for me & my Suit).[1]

> 1. GW may have breakfasted at Samuel Sheldon's tavern in Litchfield. In Wethersfield, GW and his suite lodged at Webb House, owned at this time by Col. Joseph Webb (1749–1815) and his wife, Abigail Chester Webb. Webb's brother, Samuel Blachley Webb (1753–1807), had served as GW's aide-de-camp from June 1776 to Jan. 1777. The officers in the French party lodged at Stillman's tavern.

20th. Had a good deal of private conversation with Govr. Trumbull who gave it to me as his opinion that if any important offensive operation should be undertaken he had little doubt of our obtaining Men & Provision adequate to our wants.[1]

> 1. Jonathan Trumbull, Sr. (1710–1785), served as governor of Connecticut from 1769 to 1784.

21st. The Count de Rochambeau with the Chevr. de Chastellux arrived about Noon.[1] The appearance of the British Fleet (under Adml. Arbuthnot) off Block Island prevented the attendance of the Count de Barras.[2]

> 1. François Jean le Beauvoir, chevalier de Chastellux (1734–1788), served with some distinction in the Seven Years' War. After 1763, while he retained his position in the army, his literary activities earned him a place among the Encyclopedists and philosophes. In 1780 Chastellux was promoted to *maréchal de camp* and named a major general in Rochambeau's army. He arived in America in July 1780 with Admiral de Ternay's fleet, served in the Yorktown campaign, and remained in America until Jan. 1783. His relations with GW were excellent, and they remained in correspondence after the war.
>
> 2. Marriot Arbuthnot (c.1711–1794) was an admiral in the British navy and commander of the American station. Barras was reluctant to leave Newport for Wethersfield after the arrival of the British fleet, partly because the French were in daily expectation of the arrival of a convoy from France and he hoped to sail to meet the French ships.

22nd. Fixed with Count de Rochambeau upon a plan of Campaign—in Substance as follows. That the French Land force (except 200 Men) should March so soon as the Squadron could Sail for Boston—to the North River & there, in conjunction with the American, to commence an operation against New York (which in the present reduced State of the Garrison it was thought would fall, unless relieved; the doing which wd. enfeeble their Southern operations, and in either case be productive of capital advantages) or to extend our views to the Southward as circumstances and a Naval superiority might render more necessary &

eligable. The aid which would be given to such an operation in this quarter—the tardiness with which the Regiments would be filled for any other—the insurmountable difficulty & expence of Land transportation—the waste of Men in long marches (especially where there is a disinclination to the Service—objections to the climate &ca.) with other reasons too numerous to detail, induced to this opinion. The heavy Stores & Baggage of the French Army were to be deposited at Providence under Guard of 200 Men (before mentioned) & Newport Harbour & Works were to be secured by 500 Militia.[1]

1. The Wethersfield Conference was held in the Webb House. Rochambeau informed GW of the probability that the combined French and American forces would be able to count on the arrival of de Grasse's fleet in American waters later in the summer. The main question to be considered at Wethersfield was where the summer campaign should take place. Rochambeau contended that Virginia offered the best hope for a successful campaign, while GW stressed the advantages of an attack on the British in New York. In Mar. 1781 GW and Rochambeau had determined at a conference at Hartford that the French fleet would remain at Newport, a decision that conflicted with Admiral Barras's orders which had stipulated that after Rochambeau marched to join GW the fleet would sail for Boston. In light of the possible transfer of the fleet, it was decided at the meeting that the extensive stores and munitions which had been collected at Providence for the use of the fleet at Newport would remain there under the guard of French troops. Later, however, a council of war of French officers at Newport decided that Barras's fleet would stay at Newport rather than move operations to Boston (Rochambeau to GW, 31 May 1781; Doniol, *La participation de la France de l'établissement des Etats-Unis*, 5:477–86.

24th. Set out on my return to New Windsor.

26th. Received a Letter from the Honble. Jno. Laurens Minister from the United States of America at the Court of Versailles—informing me that the Sum of 6,000,000 of Livres was granted as a donation to this Country—to be applied in part to the purchase of Arms—Cloaths &ca. for the American Troops and the ballance to my orders, & draughts at long sight and that a Fleet of 20 Sail of the Line was on its departure for the West Indies 12 of which were to proceed to this Coast where it was probable they might arrive in the Month of July.[1] He also added that the Courts of Petersbg. & Vienna had offered their Mediation in settling the present troubles wch. the King of France, tho' personally pleas'd with, could not accept without consulting his Allies.

1. John Laurens (1754–1782), of South Carolina, son of Henry Laurens, former president of the Continental Congress, was appointed aide-de-camp to GW in 1777. In Dec. 1780 Congress appointed the younger Laurens a special envoy to France to obtain additional aid for the United States. When he returned from his mission to France, he rejoined the army, participated in the Yorktown campaign, and was killed in a minor skirmish with the Brit-

ish at Combahee Ferry, S.C., in Aug. 1782. Laurens's letter to GW, written from Paris, is dated 24 Mar. 1781 (Washington Papers, Library of Congress).

31st. A Letter from Count de Rochambeau informed me that the British fleet had left Block Island—that Adml. de Barras would Sail with the first fair Wind for Boston (having 900 of his Soldiers on Board to Man his fleet) and that he should commence his March as soon as possible, but would be under the necessity of Halting a few days at Providence.[1]

A Letter from Major Talmage, inclosing one from C—— Senr. & another from S. G. dated the 27th. were totally silent on the subject of an evacuation of New York;[2] but speak of an order for Marching the Troops from Long Island and the Countermand of it after they had commenced their March; the cause for either they could not assign. Neither C. Senr. nor S. G. estimate the Enemys regular force at New York or its dependencies at more than 4500 men including the New Levies; but C—— says it is reported that they can command five & some add 6,000 Militia & refugees.

    1. Rochambeau's letter to GW, partly in cipher, is dated 29 May 1781 (Washington Papers, Library of Congress).

    2. Benjamin Tallmadge to GW, 29 May 1781 (Washington Papers, Library of Congress). *C—— Senr.* (Samuel Culper, Sr.) was an alias for Abraham Woodhull (see entry for 1 May 1781). *S. G.* was the code name for another American spy, George Smith of Nissequogue, Long Island, who before he joined the Culper spy ring had served in a Suffolk County militia regiment as a lieutenant.

    On 31 May 1781 GW wrote to the marquis de Lafayette in Virginia that "Upon a full consideration of our affairs in every point of view, an attempt upon New York with its present Garrison . . . was deemed preferable to a Southern operation as we had not the Command of the Water." The letter contained considerable detail on the proposed campaign, including the vital information that "above all, it was thought that we had a tolerable prospect of expelling the enemy or obliging them to withdraw part of their force from the Southward, which last would give the most effectual relief to those States." This letter was among a number of others, including some of GW's dispatches to Congress and correspondence of the French command, which were captured by the British on 3 June. British ensign John Moody arrived at Clinton's headquarters in New York City with the captured mail and was rewarded by the elated Clinton with 200 guineas. "The Capture of this Mail is extremely consequential, and gives the Commander in Chief the most perfect knowledge of the designs of the Enemy" (Mackenzie, *Diary*, 2:536; Clinton, *American Rebellion*, 305–6).

June

4th. Letters from the Marquis de la Fayette of the 25th Ulto. informs that Lord Cornwallis had formed a junction with Arnold at Peters-bourg—that with their United force he had Marched to City point on James River and that the detachment which sailed from New York the 13th of May had arrived in James River and were debarking at Westover and that he himself had removed from Wilton to Richmond.[1]

The Duke de Lauzen arrived this afternoon with Letters from Count de Rochambeau & Admiral Count de Barras, with the proceedings of a Council of War held on Board the Duke de Burgoyne proposing to continue the Fleet at Rhode Island under the protection of 400 French Troops & 1000 Militia in preference to the plan adopted at Weathersfield; requiring my opinion thereon which was given to the effect— that I conceived the first plan gave a more perfect security to the Kings fleet than the latter, & consequently left the Land force more at liberty to act, for which reason I could not change my former opinion but shou'd readily acquiesce to theirs if upon a re-consideration of the matter they adhered to it. Accordingly, that delay might be avoided, I inclosed letters (under flying Seals) to the Governors of Rd. Island & Massachusetts, to be made use of or not, requesting the Militia; & pressed the March of the Land Troops as soon as circumstances would admit of it.[2]

1. Wilton was an estate on the north side of the James River, six miles south of Richmond. Lafayette had established his headquarters there in May 1781. Westover was the estate of Col. William Byrd III.

2. Armand Louis de Gontaut Biron, duc de Lauzun (1747–1793), served in the French guards and in 1767 in the French campaign in Corsica. In 1780 he was appointed brigadier general in command of the legion of horse which bore his name and in July 1780 arrived with his troops at Newport, R.I. He was in the Yorktown campaign in 1781 and carried the news of the capitulation at Yorktown to Paris.

The council of war was held on board Barras's flagship, the *Duc-de-Bourgogne*, 31 May 1781. A second council of war, held on board the *Neptune* 8 June 1781, confirmed the decision to hold the fleet at Newport.

5th. Governor Rutlidge of South Carolina came to Head Qrs. with representations of the situation of Southern affairs, & to sollicit aids. I communicated the plan of Campaign to him & candidly exposed the true State of our Circumstances which convinced him—or seemed to do so—that no relief cd. be given from this army till we had acquired a Naval Superiority and cd. transport Troops by Water.[1]

1. At this time John Rutledge was governor of South Carolina. Rutledge had left Philadelphia 23 May to visit headquarters at New Windsor, N.Y., before returning to South Carolina (*LMCC*, 6:96). Presumably his mission was to relay to GW the hopes of the southern delegates in the Continental Congress for a summer campaign in the South rather than an attack on New York.

7th. A Letter from the Govr. of Virginia dated at Charlottesville the 28th. Ulto. representing the distressed State of Virginia & pressing my repairng thither, was received[1]—other letters (but not official) speak of Lord Cornwallis's advance to Hanover Court House—that the Marquis was retreating before him towards Fredericksburg and that General Leslie[2] was embarked in James River with about 1200 Men destined, as was supposed, to Alexandria whither it was conjectured by the letter writers Lord Cornwallis was pointing his March.

1. Gov. Thomas Jefferson joined other southerners in pressing for a summer campaign in the South. In May 1781 Cornwallis had moved north from the Carolinas to reinforce Gen. William Phillips and Benedict Arnold in Virginia. Jefferson now informed GW that Cornwallis's army had joined forces with troops under Arnold at Petersburg, Va. The combined force had evacuated Petersburg and, with reinforcements sent by Sir Henry Clinton from New York, marched on Richmond, then held by Lafayette with 3,000 regulars and militia. Jefferson's intelligence reports estimated that some 7,000 British troops were operating in Virginia. On 8 June, GW wrote to Jefferson, giving his reasons for remaining in the North to direct an attack on New York City, in expectation that such an attack would compel the British to recall at least part of their forces in the South (Gratz Collection, Pennsylvania Historical Society).

In mid-June, after some weeks of skirmishing with Lafayette and Anthony Wayne, Cornwallis moved toward Williamsburg in what was less a retreat than a planned withdrawal, although Lafayette harassed the British forces all the way. Reaching the town on 25 June, he waited orders from Sir Henry Clinton in New York and by 26 June received directions from him to establish a base in Virginia for operations against the Americans. In the midst of a confusion of orders and counterorders from Clinton in New York and Lord George Germain in England, Cornwallis in August selected Yorktown as his headquarters. Entrenchments were also established at Gloucester, across the York River from Yorktown.

2. Maj. Gen. Alexander Leslie (1740–1794) was active in British campaigns in the South in 1780 and 1781 and was in command at Charleston at the end of the war.

14th. Received agreeable ac[coun]ts. from General Greene, of his Successes in South Carolina[1]—viz.—that Lord Rawden[2] had abandoned Cambden with precipitation, leaving all our wounded taken in the action of the 25th. of April last, together with 58 of his own too bad to remove—that he had destroy'd his own Stores—burnt many buildings and in short left the Town little better than a heap of Rubbish—That Orangeburg, Forts Mott. & Granby, had surrendered;[3] their Garrisons including officers consisting of near 700 Men—That Ninety Six & Fort Augusta were invested[4]—that he was preparing to March to the Former and that, Lord Rawden was at Nelsons ferry[5] removing the Stores from that place which indicated an Evacuation thereof.

1. News of Greene's victories was relayed to the army in General Orders, 15 June 1781 (Washington Papers, Library of Congress).

2. Francis, Lord Rawdon (1754–1826), commanded a company at Bunker Hill and served on the staffs of Burgoyne and Cornwallis. In 1778 he was promoted to lieutenant colonel and in 1780 was ordered south for the campaign against Charleston, S.C. By Jan. 1781 Rawdon was left in virtual command of some 8,000 troops to face Greene's army in South Carolina and Georgia while Cornwallis moved into North Carolina. On 25 April 1781 Rawdon defeated Greene at the Battle of Hobkirk's Hill, S.C., suffering heavy casualties. He then moved on to capture Camden, but finding it impossible to hold, he withdrew to Monck's Corner, S.C.

3. These forts were in South Carolina: Orangeburg in Orange County, taken by Brig. Gen. Thomas Sumter 11 May; Fort Motte on the Congaree River in Orange County, captured 12 May by Lt. Col. Henry ("Light Horse Harry") Lee and Brig. Gen. Francis Marion; Fort Granby, on the Congaree River, taken by Lee on 15 May.

4. Ninety Six, Greenwood County, S.C., was under siege from 22 May to 19 June 1781. Rawdon ordered the fort abandoned, but his instructions miscarried. Ninety Six was on the verge of surrender to the Americans when Rawdon mustered 2,000 men and marched to its relief. On 20 June, Greene pulled back from the fort and was briefly pursued by the British. Rawdon then ordered Ninety Six abandoned, and the evacuation was completed by 3 July.

Fort Augusta on the Savannah River, Richmond County, Ga., was under siege by Henry Lee and Andrew Pickens 22 May–5 June 1781. The fort surrendered on 5 June.

5. Nelson's Ferry was on the Santee River about five miles from Eutaw Springs, S.C.

16th. Directed that no more Invalids be transferred till further Orders[1]—that a detachment be formed of the weakliest Men for garrisoning of West point & that a Camp be marked out by the Chief Engineer & Q. M. Genl. near Peekskill to assemble the Troops on.

1. The Corps of Invalids had been established on 16 July 1777 for the utilization of veterans who were not fit for active service but were still able to perform such assignments as garrison duty (*JCC,* 8:554–56).

18th. Brigaded the Troops, and made an arrangement of the Army, which is to March for the New Camp in three divisions.[1] To strengthen the detachment intended for the Garrison of West point, I had previously called upon the State of Connecticut for 800 Militia.

1. Headquarters was being moved from New Windsor, N.Y., to Peekskill, N.Y. (General Orders, 19 June, Washington Papers, Library of Congress).

24th. A Letter from the Count de Rochambeau dated at Windham the 20th. advises me of his having reached that Town, that day, with the first division of his army—that the other 3 divisions were following in regular succession—that he expected to Halt the Troops two days at

Hartford, but would come on to my Camp from that place after the arrival of the division with which he was.[1]

1. The main body of the French army left Newport between 10 and 12 June 1781 and arrived in the vicinity of White Plains 6 July (Rice, *American Campaigns of Rochambeau's Army,* 1:27, 32, 246).

25th. Joined the Army at its Encampment at Peekskill. Mrs. Washington set out at the same time towards Virginia but with an intention to Halt at Philadelphia if from information & circumstances it was not likely she should remain quietly at Mt. Vernon.[1]

Recd. a Letter from the Minister of France advising me of the arrival of between 3 & 4000 Troops abt. the 4th. Inst. at Charles Town[2]—that 2000 of them had debarked & that the rest were said to be destined for St. Augustine & New York—that George Town was evacuated & the Enemy in Charles town weak (not exceeding 450 Men before the reinforcement arrived—which latter must be a mistake, as the Ministers informant added, that Lord Rawden had got there after a precipitate retreat from a Post above and that the American parties were within 5 Miles of the Town. Lord Rawdens Troops alone amounted to more than the Number here mentioned).

Having suggested to the Count de Rochambeau the advantages which might be derived to the common cause in general and the Southern States in particular, if by arming the Fantasque & bringing the 50 gun ship to Rhode Isld. (which then lay at Boston) the fleet of his most Christian Majesty at Newport could appear in Chesapeak bay.[3] I received an answer from the French Admiral through the General that he was disposed to the measure provided he could obtain a loan of the French Guard (of 400 Men which were left at Newport & which were granted) and 4 pieces of heavy artillery at Brentons point[4] which the Count could not spare but that the fleet could not be ready to Sail under 20 days from the date of his letter (the 21st.)—thus uncertain, the matter stands.

1. Mrs. Washington had joined GW in winter quarters at New Windsor in late November 1780. She planned to return to Virginia before the summer campaign started. On 17 June 1781 GW wrote Joseph Webb that "Upon my return from Weathersfield I found Mrs. Washington extremely unwell, she still continues low & weak, but will set out for the Southward as soon as she can bear the fatigue of the journey" (Washington Papers, Library of Congress). By 21 June she had "so perfectly recovered, as to be able to set out for Virginia in a day or two" (GW to Martha Mortier, 21 June 1781, Clinton Papers, Clements Library, University of Michigan). Although she was well enough to start south on 25 June, GW wrote Fielding Lewis on 28 June that she "left me on Monday last in a very low and weak state having been sick for more than a Month with a kind of Jaundice" (Armstrong Photostats, University of Pennsylvania).

2. Anne César, chevalier de La Luzerne (1741–1791), served as French minister plenipotentiary to the United States 1779–84.

3. Rochambeau had already informed GW that the French admiral François Joseph Paul, comte de Grasse, had confirmed his intention of bringing his fleet north from the West Indies during the summer to aid the French and American armies in an attack against the British and had estimated the fleet would arrive in American waters around 15 July at the earliest (Rochambeau to GW, 10 June 1781, Washington Papers, Library of Congress). In addition to urging Rochambeau to march as rapidly as possible to join the American army at White Plains, GW requested that Rochambeau persuade de Grasse not only to use his fleet to support the attack on New York but to bring a substantial body of troops with him. A similar request was made to La Luzerne, the French minister in the United States (GW to La Luzerne, 13 June 1781, Archives du Ministère des Affaires Etrangères [photostats and microfilm at Library of Congress]). Rochambeau replied, 20 June, that de Grasse had been informed "that Your Excellency preferred that he should make his first appearance at New York . . . that I submitted, as I ought, my opinion to yours" (Washington Papers, Library of Congress). In expressing his own views to de Grasse, however, Rochambeau was not as submissive as his letter to GW would indicate. He had not given up his preference for a Virginia campaign and clearly hoped that his apprehensions for the success of operations against the British in New York City would influence de Grasse to make the Chesapeake his destination (Doniol, *La participation de la France de l'établissement des Etats-Unis,* 5:395).

4. Brenton's Point is at the entrance of Newport harbor.

28th. Having determined to attempt to surprize the Enemys Posts at the No. end of Yk. Island, if the prospt. of success continued favourable, & having fixed upon the Night of the 2d. of July for this purpose[1] and having moreover combined with it an attempt to cut off Delancy's[2] And other light Corps without Kingsbridge and fixed upon Genl. Lincoln to Commd. the first detachment & the Duke de Lauzen the 2d. every thing was put in train for it and the Count de Rochambeau requested to file of from Ridgebury to Bedford & hasten his March— while the Duke de Lauzen was to do the same & to assemble his command (which was to consist of abt. 3 or 400 Connecticut State Troops under the Command of Genl. Waterbury[3]—abt. 100 York Troops under Captn. Sacket[4]—Sheldons Legion[5] of 200, & his own proper Corps). Genl. Lincolns command was to consist of Scammells light Troops and other detachments to the amt. of 800 Rank & file properly officerd—150 watermen and 60 artillerists.

1. As the British had detached troops into Monmouth County, N.J., to forage for horses and cattle, GW thought it a propitious moment to launch an attack on the relatively unprotected posts at the northern end of Manhattan Island. Maj. Gen. Benjamin Lincoln was to bring his two regiments and a detachment of artillery from Peekskill to attack Fort Tryon, Fort Knyphausen, and Fort George (GW to Lincoln, 1 July 1781). If this plan proved un-

successful, he was to move across the river and support the duc de Lauzun's cavalry in an attack on James De Lancey's Loyalists at Morrisania. Rochambeau was to begin marching his troops toward Kingsbridge. Although GW's later report to Congress on the affair puts it in the most favorable light, it is evident that the attack was anything but successful in spite of the cooperation of the French. The forts along the Hudson were unexpectedly reinforced by the return of British foraging parties from New Jersey, one of which encountered Lincoln's men, costing the Americans the element of surprise. Lauzun's forces arrived too late, and most of the outlying British posts were withdrawn across the Harlem River to safety. The only material result of the raid was the opportunity of "reconnoitring the works upon the north end of the Island and making observations which may be of very great advantage in future" (GW to Samuel Huntington, 6 July 1781, Papers of the Continental Congress, item 152, National Archives).

2. Lt. Col. James De Lancey (1746–1804) commanded a Loyalist partisan corps operating in the vicinity of New York from 1776 to the end of the war. The corps was generally known as De Lancey's Refugees or Westchester Refugees.

3. David Waterbury (d. 1801) was brigadier general of Connecticut state troops.

4. William Sackett, a captain of New York state levies, was in command of three companies of New York state troops at Bedford.

5. Elisha Sheldon was colonel of the 2d Continental Light Dragoons.

29th. Recd. a letter from the Marqs. de la Fayette informing me that Lord Cornwallis after having attempted to surprise the Virginia Assembly at Charlottesville and destroy some Stores at the Forks of James River in which he succeeded partially had returned to Richmond without having effected any valuable purpose by his manoeuvers in Virginia.[1] In a private letter he complains heavily of the conduct of the Baron de Steuben whom he observes has rendered himself extremely obnoxious in Virga.[2]

1. Lafayette was referring to the raid by British cavalry leader Banastre Tarleton on Charlottesville, Va., 4 June 1781, and the attack by Lt. Col. John Graves Simcoe on Point of Fork, at the confluence of the James and Rivanna rivers in Virginia, 5 June 1781. At this time the Virginia legislature was meeting in Charlottesville, and Thomas Jefferson and the members of the legislature whom he was entertaining at Monticello barely escaped capture. Aside from a few prisoners taken, including seven members of the legislature, the principal result of the raids was the capture by the British of a considerable store of arms and ammunition at Point of Fork and the destruction of a similar store at Charlottesville.

2. Lafayette contended that Steuben's military tactics during the British raids on Point of Fork and Charlottesville had come under so much criticism that "Every man woman and Child in Virginia is Roused against him. They dispute even on his Courage" (Lafayette to GW, 18 June 1781, Washington Papers, Library of Congress).

July

July 2d. Genl. Lincoln's detachment embarked last Night after dark, at or near Tellers point;[1] and as his operations were to be the movement of two Nights he was desired to repair to Fort Lee this day & reconnoitre the enemy's Works—Position and strength as well as he possibly could & take his ultimate determination from appearances—that is to attempt the surprize if the prospect was favourable or to relinquish it if it was not, and in the latter case to land above the Mouth of Spikendevil[2] & cover the Duke in his operation on Delancys Corps.

At three o'clock this Morning I commenced my March with the Continental Army in order to cover the detached Troops and improve any advantages which might be gained by them. Made a small halt at the New bridge over Croton abt. 9 Miles from Peekskill—another at the Church by Tarry Town till Dusk (9 Miles more) and compleated the remaining part of the March in the Night—arriving at Valentines Hill[3] (at Mile square) about Sun rise.

Our Baggage & Tents were left standing at the Camp at Peekskill.

    1. Teller's Point (Croton Point) is on the Hudson River below Verplanck's Point.

    2. Spuyten Duyvil, a creek connecting the Hudson River with the Harlem River.

    3. Valentine's Hill, north of Spuyten Duyvil in present-day Yonkers.

3d. The length of Duke Lauzens March & the fatiegue of his Corps, prevented his coming to the point of Action at the hour appointed. In the meantime Genl. Lincolns Party who were ordered to prevent the retreat of Delancy's Corps by the way of Kg. Bridge & prevent succour by that Rout were attacked by the Yagers and others but on the March of the Army from Valentines Hill retired to the Island. Being disappointed in both objects from the Causes mentioned I did not care to fatiegue the Troops any more but suffered them to remain on their Arms while I spent good part of the day in reconnoitering the Enemys works.

In the afternoon we retired to Valentines Hill & Lay upon our Arms. Duke Lauzen & Waterbury lay on the East side of the Brunxs [Bronx] river on the East Chester road.

4th. Marched & took a position a little to the left of Dobbes ferry & marked a Camp for the French Army upon our left. Duke Lauzen Marched to the Whitepl[ai]n & Waterbury to Horseneck.[1]

    1. The area called Horseneck is now the borough of Greenwich, Fairfield County, Conn.

5th. Visited the French Army which had arrived at Northcastle.[1]

1. The French army had arrived at North Castle on 3 July, finding few amenities. GW left immediately for North Castle. On his arrival he inspected the French troops and spent some five hours in conference with Rochambeau. He dined with the French officers, who then escorted him for several miles on his return to the American camp at Philipsburg (Cromut du Bourg, "Diary," 296).

6th. The French Army formed the junction with the American on the Grounds marked out.[1] The Legion of Lauzen took a position advanced of the plains on Chittendens hill[2] west of the River Brunx [Bronx]. This day also the Minister of France arrived in Camp from Philadelphia.

1. The French reached Philipsburg about six o'clock on the evening of 6 July and camped about a quarter of a mile from the American camp (Closen, *Journal,* 91–92). GW's Headquarters was at the house of Joseph Appleby, "on the cross-road from Dobbs' Ferry to White Plains, and about three and a half miles from the ferry" (Baker, *Itinerary,* 226). Rochambeau's headquarters was at the Odell house, about 12 miles east of the Appleby house.

On 8 July, GW reviewed the French and American armies. This was the first glimpse for many of the French officers of the American forces. One of them, Jean François Louis, comte de Clermont-Crèvecoeur, noted in his journal: "In beholding this army I was struck, not by its smart appearance, but by its destitution: the men were without uniforms and covered with rags; most of them were barefoot. They were of all sizes, down to children who could not have been over fourteen. There were many negroes, mulattoes, etc. Only their artillerymen were wearing uniforms. These are the elite of the country and are actually very good troops, well schooled in their profession" (Rice, *American Campaigns of Rochambeau's Army,* 1:33).

2. Chatterton's Hill was at White Plains, Westchester County, N.Y.

13th. The Jersey Troops arrived at Dobbs's Ferry agreeable to orders. Some French Frigates made an attempt on the Enemy's Post at Loyds Neck but without success not being able to Land in the Night.[1]

1. The raid on the British fort at Lloyd's Neck (also called Fort Franklin), on the Cold Spring Harbor side of Huntington Bay, had been discussed as early as April 1781. GW had pointed out to the French commanders that possession of the post would cut off communication between the British army on Long Island and Loyalists on the mainland (GW to Rochambeau and Destouches, 8 April 1781; Francis Warrington Dawson Papers, Duke University). The plan was revived in early July, and on the evening of 10 July the French vessel *Romulus* and three frigates left Newport for the Lloyd's Neck post. The French were unable to land their troops at night as had originally been planned, and when the attack was launched against the fort at daybreak, it was easily repulsed by the British, who had already been warned of the French enterprise.

14th. Near 5000 Men being ordered to March for Kings bridge, to cover and secure a reconnoitre of the Enemys Works on the No. end of York Island, Harlaem river, & the Sound were prevented doing so by incessant rain.[1]

    1. These troops were being held in readiness for a reconnaissance by French and American forces of the New York defenses.

15th. The Savage Sloop of War of 16 Guns—the Ship Genl. Washington, lately taken by the Enemy—a row Galley and two other small armed Vessels passed our post at Dobbs Ferry (which was not in a condition to oppose them).[1] At the same time three or four river Vessels with 4 Eighteen pounders—stores &ca. had just arrivd at Tarry town and with infinite difficulty, & by great exertion of Colo. Sheldon, Captn. Hurlbut, (who got wounded)[2]—Captn. Lieutt. Miles[3] of the artillery & Lt. Shayler[4] were prevented falling into the hands of the Enemy as they got a ground 100 yards from the Dock and were set fire to by the Enemy but extinguished by the extraordinary activity & spirit of the above Gentn. Two of the Carriages however were a good deal damaged by the fire. The Enemy however by sending their armed Boats up the River took the Vessel of a Captn. Dobbs laden with Bread for the French Army—Cloathing for Sheldons Regiment & some passengers. This was done in the Night—it being after Sunset before the Vessels passed the Post at Dobs ferry.

    1. These British vessels were dispatched to attack American supply depots at West Point and Tarrytown and American supply boats plying the Hudson River. The British captured 1,000 rations of bread on board a small vessel commanded by William Dobbs of Fishkill and a negligible amount of military supplies.
    2. George Hurlbut (d. 1783) of Connecticut was a captain in the 2d Continental Dragoons.
    3. John Miles of New York was a captain lieutenant in the 2d Continental Artillery.
    4. Joseph Shaylor (d. 1816) of Connecticut was a lieutenant in the 4th Continental Regiment. These officers were thanked for their actions by GW in General Orders, 17 July 1781.

16th. The Cannon & Stores were got out of the Vessels & every thing being removed from Tarry town, two french twelve pounders, & one of our 18 prs. wer[e] brought to bear upon the Ships which lay of Tarry town, distant about a Mile, and obliged them to remove lower down & move over to the West shore.

18th. I passed the North River with Count de Rochambeau Genl. de Beville[1] his Qr. Mr. Genl. & Genl. Duportail in order to reconnoitre the Enemy Posts and Encampments at the North end of York Island. Took an Escort of 150 Men from the Jersey Troops on the other side.

1. Pierre François, chevalier de Béville, was quartermaster general to the French army during its American tour. Jean Nicolas, vicomte Desandrouins (1729–1792), commander of Rochambeau's corps of engineers, also accompanied the party, which left camp at daybreak and returned in the evening.

19th. The Enemys Shipping rundown the river, and left the Navigation of it above once more free for us.[1]

1. The British ships involved included the *General Monk,* the *Savage,* and several other vessels. As the British ships passed the American batteries at Dobbs Ferry, the Americans fired red-hot shot from the New Jersey shore, hitting the masts and rigging of both vessels and blowing up an arms chest on board the *Savage,* killing several men.

20th. Count de Rochambeau having called upon me, in the name of Count de Barras, for a definitive plan of Campaign, that he might communicate it to the Count de Grasse[1]—I could not but acknowledge, that the uncertainties under which we labour—the few Men who have joined (either as recruits for the Continental Battns. or Militia) & the ignorance in which I am kept by some of the States on whom I mostly depended. . . . rendered it impracticable for me to do more than to prepare, first, for the enterprize against New York as agreed to at Weathersfield[2] and secondly for the relief of the Southern States if after all my efforts, & earnest application to these States it should be found at the arrivl. of Count de Grasse that I had neither men, nor means adequate to the first object. To give this opinion I was further induced from the uncertainty with respect to the time of the arrival of the French Fleet & whether Land Troops would come in it or not as had been earnestly requested by me & inforced by the Minister of France.

The uncertainty of sufficient aids, of Men & Means from the States to whom application had been made, and the discouraging prospects before me of having my requisitions complied with—added to an unwillingness to incur any expence that could be avoided induced me to desire Genl. Knox to suspend the Transport of the heavy Cannon & Stores from Philadelphia lest we should have them to carry back again or be encumbd. with them in the field.

1. Rochambeau had written to GW, 19 July, relaying Barras's request and inviting GW to confer with him. On the same day the commanders met at Dobbs Ferry, and Rochambeau posed a series of questions concerning plans for the coming campaign. GW replied that in case the comte de Grasse should delay in joining the American and French forces in the North or should bring few land troops with him, the allies should leave a garrison at West Point and a small force in the New York area and march the remainder of their troops to Virginia for a late summer or early fall campaign. "But should the Fleet arrive in Season, not be limited to a short Stay; should be able to force the Harbour of N York, and in addition to all these, should find

the British Force in a divided State, I am of Opinion that the Enterprize against N York & its Dependencies shou'd be our primary Object."

2. See entry for 22 May 1781.

21st. Again ordered abt. 5000 Men to be ready to March at 8 oclock, for the purpose of reconnoitering the enemys Posts at Kings bridge and to cut off, if possible, such of Delancys Corps as should be found without their lines.[1]

At the hour appointed the March commenced in 4 Columns, on different roads. Majr. Genl. Parsons[2] with the Connecticut Troops & 25 of Sheldon's horse formed the right column (with two field pieces) on the No. River road. The other Two divisions of the Army, under the Majr. Generals Lincoln & Howe,[3] together with the Corps of Sappers and Miners, and 4 field pieces, formed the next column on the Sawmill river road.[4] The right column of the French (on our left) consisted of the Brigade of Bourbonnis, with the Battn. of Grenadiers and Choissairs, 2 field pieces & 2 twelve pounders. Their left column was composed of the Legion of Lauzen—one Battn. of Grenadiers, & Choissairs of Soussonnis,[5] 2 field pieces & 2 Howitzers. General Waterbury with the Militia and State Troops of Connecticut, were to March on the East chester Road and to be joined at that place by the Cavalry of Sheldon, for the purpose of Scouring Frogs Neck.[6] Sheldons Infantry was to join the Legion of Lauzen for the purpose of Scouring Morrissania,[7] and to be covered by Scammells light Infantry who were to advance thro' the fields & way lay the Roads—stop all communication & prevent Intelligence getting to the Enemy.

At Mile Square (Valentine's hill) The left column of the American Troops, and right of the french formed their junction, as did the left of the French also, by *mistake* as it was intended it should cross the Brunx by Garrineaus,[8] & recross it at Williams's bridge.[9]

The whole Army (Parson's division first) arrived at Kingsbridge about day light & formed on the heights back of Fort Independance[10]— extending towards delancy's Mills[11]—While the Legion of Lauzen & Waterbury proceeded to scour the Necks of Morrissania & throgs to little effect, as most of the Refugees were fled, & hid in such obscure places as not to be discovered; & by stealth got over to the Islands adjacent, & to the enemys shipping which lay in the East River. A few however were caught and some cattle & Horses brought off.

1. Although a definite decision had not yet been reached to implement the earlier plans for the attack on New York, both GW and Rochambeau carried on extensive reconnaissance of British defenses in the area. A reconnaissance in force by the French and American armies of the British posts had been scheduled for the evening of 13 July but was delayed by bad weather.

2. Samuel Holden Parsons (1737–1789) was in command of the Connecticut divisions.

3. Maj. Gen. Robert Howe (1732–1786) of North Carolina.

4. The Sawmill River Road paralleled the Sawmill or Nepperhan River on the east, turning east north of Philipse's toward Valentine's Hill.

5. The French regiments referred to by GW in this entry were the Bourbonnais and the Soissonnais, both of which were sent to America in 1780. Chasseurs were light cavalry trained for rapid maneuvering. Lauzun's Legion was composed of infantry and cavalry units under the command of the duc de Lauzun. The legion had arrived at Newport, R.I., in July 1780.

6. Frog's (Throg's or Throck's) Neck is a peninsula extending into the East River from the Westchester shore.

7. Morrisania, the estate of the Morris family, in southern Westchester County.

8. Garineau's was about 16 miles north of the mouth of the Bronx River.

9. Williams's Bridge crossed the Bronx River in southern Westchester.

10. Fort Independence, later called Fort No. 4 by the British, "was located between the old Boston and the Albany Post Roads . . . just within the old line of Yonkers" (Hufeland, *Westchester County,* 104).

11. De Lancey's Mills was on the Bronx River near West Farms in Westchester County.

22d. The enemy did not appear to have had the least intelligence of our movement or to know we were upon the height opposite to them till the whole Army were ready to display.[1]

After having fixed upon the ground, & formed our line, I began, with General Rochambeau and the Engineers, to reconnoitre the enemy's position and Works first from Tippets hill[2] opposite to their left and from hence it was evident that the small redoubt (Fort Charles)[3] near Kings bridge would be absolutely at the command of a battery which might be erected thereon. It also appeared equally evident that the Fort on Cox's hill was in bad repair, & little dependence placed in it. There is a house on this side under Tippets hill but out of view, I conceive of the crossing place most favourable to a partizan stroke. From this view, and every other I could get of Forts Tryon, Knyphausen & Laurel hill the Works are formidable.

There is no Barracks or huts on the East side of the Hill on which Fort Tryon and Knyphausen stands—nor are there any on the hill opposite except those by Fort George. Near the Blew bell[4] there is a number of Houses but they have more the appearance of Stables than Barracks. In the hollow, near the Barrier gate, are about 14 or 15 Tents; which is the only Encampment I could see without the line of Pallisading as the large one discovered on the 18th. through the brake of the Hill betwn. Fort Tryon & Coxss hill was not to be seen from any view I had.

1. The appearance of the Americans at Morrisania was so unexpected that the Loyalist troops there were forced to pull back hurriedly to the British lines "but had not time to bring off their stock, which the Rebels sezied upon and drove off" (Mackenzie, *Diary*, 2:570).

2. Tippett's Hill, on the bank of Tippett's Brook, a tributary of Spuyten Duyvil Creek.

3. Fort Charles, or Fort Prince Charles, was located on the top of Marble Hill, overlooking King's Bridge.

4. The Blue Bell Tavern was on the west side of the road from New York City to King's Bridge.

23d. Went upon Frogs Neck, to see what communication could be had with Long Isld. The Engineers attending with Instrumts. to measure the distance across found it to be [   ] Yards.[1]

Having finished the reconnoitre without damage—a few harmless shot only being fired at us—we Marched back about Six o'clock by the same routs we went down & a reversed order of March and arrived in Camp about Midnight.

1. Rochambeau described this incident in his memoirs: "While our engineers carried out this geometrical operation, we slept, worn out by fatigue, at the foot of a hedge, under fire from the cannon of the enemy's ships, who wished to hinder the work. Waking first, I called General Washington, and remarked to him that we had forgotten the hour of the tide. We hurried to the causeway of the mill on which we had crossed this small arm of the sea which separated us from the mainland; we found it covered with water. We were brought two little boats, in which we embarked, with the saddles and trappings of the horses; they then sent back two American dragoons, who drew by the bridle two horses, good swimmers. These were followed by all the others, urged on by the lashes of some dragoons remaining on the other shore, and for whom we sent back the boats. This maneuver was made in less than an hour, but happily our embarrassment was unnoticed by the enemy" (Rochambeau, *Mémoires*, 1:283–84).

30th. Received a Letter from the Count de Barras, refering me to one written by him to Genl. Rochambeau in Cypher; pointing, in stronger terms than heretofore, his disinclination to leave Newport till the arrival of Adml. de Grass. This induced me to desist from further representing the advantages which would result from preventing a junction of the enemy's force at New York; & blocking up those which are now in Virginia, lest in the Attempt any disaster should happen, & the loss of, or damage to his fleet, should be ascribed to my obstinacy in urging a measure to which his own judgment was oppos'd, & the execution of which might impede his junction with the West India fleet, & thwart the views of the Count de Grasse upon this Coast—especially as he gave it as a clear opinion, that the West India fleet might be expected by the 10th. of Next Month.

August

1st. By this date all my Boats were ready—viz.—One hundred New ones at Albany (constructed under the direction of Genel. Schuyler) and the like number at Wappings Creek by the Qr. Mr. Genl.; besides old ones which have been repaired. My heavy ordnance & Stores from the Eastward had also come on to the North Rivr. and every thing would have been in perfect readiness to commense the operation against New York, if the States had furnished their quotas of men agreeably to my requisitions but so far have they been from complying with these that of the first, not more than half the number asked of them have joined the Army; and of 6200 of the latter pointedly & timously called for to be with the Army by the 15th. of last Month, only 176 had arrived from Connecticut, independant of abt. 300 State Troops under the Command of Genl. Waterbury, which had been on the lines before we took the field, & two Companies of York levies (abt. 80 Men) under similar circumstances.

Thus circumstanced, and having little more than general assurances of getting the succours called for and energetic Laws & resolves or Laws & resolves energetically executed, to depend upon—with little appearance of their fulfillment, I could scarce see a ground upon wch. to continue my preparations against New York—especially as there was much reason to believe that part (at least) of the Troops in Virginia were recalled to reinforce New York and therefore I turned my views more seriously (than I had before done) to an operation to the Southward and, in consequence, sent to make enquiry, indirectly, of the principal Merchants to the Eastward what number, & in what time, Transports could be provided to convey a force to the Southward if it should be found necessary to change our plan & similar application was made in a direct way to Mr. [Robert] Morris (Financier) to discover what number cd. be had by the 20th. of this Month at Philadelphia or in Chesapeak bay. At the sametime General Knox was requested to turn his thoughts to this business and make every necessary arrangement for it in his own Mind—estimating the ordnance & Stores which would be wanting & how many of them could be obtained without a transport of them from the North River. Measures were also taken to deposit the Salt provisions in such places as to be Water born. More than these, while there remained a hope of Count de Grasses bringing a land force with him, & that the States might yet put us in circumstances to prosecute the original plan could not be done without unfolding matters too plainly to the enemy & enabling them thereby to Counteract our Schemes.

4th. Fresh representations of the defenceless State of the Northern frontier, for want of the Militia so long called for and expected from Massachusets bay; accompanied by a strong expression of the fears of the People that they should be under the necessity of abandoning that part of the Country & an application that the Second York Regiment (Courtlandts)[1] at *least* should be left for their protection induced me to send Major Genl. [Benjamin] Lincoln (whose influence in his own State was great) into the Counties of Berkshire & Hampshire to enquire into the causes of these delays & to hasten on the Militia. I wrote at the same time to the Governor of this State consenting to suffer the 4 Companies of Courtlandts Regiment (now at Albany) to remain in that Quarter till the Militia did come in, but observed that if the States instead of filling their Battalions & sending forth their Militia were to be calling upon, & expecting me to dissipate the sml. operating force under my command for local defences that all offensive operations must be relinquished and we must content ourselves (in case of compliance) to spend an inactive and injurious Campaign which might— at this critical moment—be ruinous to the common cause of America.

1. Col. Philip Van Cortlandt (1749–1831) commanded the 2d New York Regiment from Nov. 1776 to the end of the war.

7th. Urged Governor Greene of Rhode Island to keep up the number of Militia required of that State at Newport & to have such arrangements made of the rest as to give instant & effectual support to the Post, & the Shipping in the harbour, in case any thing should be enterprized against the latter upon the arrival of Rodney; who, with the British fleet, is said to be expected at New York, & in conjunction with the Troops which are Embarked in Virginia & their own Marines are sufficient to create alarms.[1]

1. GW wrote William Greene, 7 Aug., that "It is reported in New York, perhaps not without foundation, that Rodney's Fleet may be expected upon this Coast. In such case we may suppose that the Count de Grasse would follow him: But can we say which would arrive first" (Washington Papers, Library of Congress). At this time Admiral Sir George Rodney (1719–1792) was in command of the British fleet in the West Indies. Although British intelligence reports indicated that the French fleet was about to sail for the Chesapeake, Rodney gambled on the assumption that de Grasse would divide his fleet, taking part to the Chesapeake and leaving the remaining ships to guard the French West Indies. When de Grasse left the West Indies (6 Aug.) taking with him his entire fleet, Rodney had already (1 Aug.) sailed for England, leaving command of the fleet in southern waters to Rear Admiral Sir Samuel Hood.

8th. The light Company of the 2d. York Regiment (the first having been down some days) having joined the Army, were formed with two

Companies of Yk. levies into a Battn. under the Command of Lieutt. Colo. Hamilton[1] & Major Fish[2] & placed under the orders of Colo. Scammell as part of the light Troops of the Army.

> 1. Lt. Col. Alexander Hamilton (1755–1804) had resigned as GW's aide-de-camp in Feb. 1781 after a dispute with the commander in chief, and in July 1781 he was successful in securing command of a battalion composed of New York levies.
>
> 2. Nicholas Fish (1758–1833), of New York City, was at this time a major in the 2d New York Regiment and during the Yorktown campaign served as Alexander Hamilton's second-in-command.

10th. Ordered the first York, and Hazens Regiments immediately to this place from West point—The Invalids[1] having got in both from Philadelphia & Boston and more Militia got in from Connecticut, as also some from Massachusetts bay giving with 4 Companies of Court-landts Regiment in addition to the detachment left there upon the March of the Army perfect security to the Posts.

> 1. That is, troops from the Corps of Invalids (see entry for 16 June 1781).

11th. A Fleet consisting of about 20 Sail, including 2 frigates & one or two prizes, arrived within the harbour of New York with German recruits.[1]

> 1. In the evening of 11 Aug., Brig. Gen. David Forman wrote GW from Freehold, N.J., that his observers had sighted a British fleet of 20 sail off Sandy Hook but weather conditions prevented identification of the vessels. At first it was conjectured that the fleet was carrying part of Cornwallis's troops from Virginia to reinforce Clinton in New York. The fleet observed by Forman, however, consisted of 2 British armed ships and 23 transports carrying 2,750 German recruits.

14th. Received dispatches from the Count de Barras announcing the intended departure of the Count de Grasse from Cape FranHois with between 25 & 29 Sail of the line & 3200 land Troops on the 3d. Instant for Chesapeake bay and the anxiety of the latter to have every thing in the most perfect readiness to commence our operations in the moment of his arrival as he should be under a necessity from particular engagements with the Spaniards to be in the West Indies by the Middle of October[1]—Matters having now come to a crisis and a decisive plan to be determined on—I was obliged, from the Shortness of Count de Grasses premised stay on this Coast—the apparent disinclination in their Naval Officers to force the harbour of New York and the feeble compliance of the States to my requisitions for Men, hitherto, & little prospect of greater exertion in future, to give up all idea of attacking New York; & instead thereof to remove the French Troops & a detachment from the American Army to the Head of Elk[2] to be transported to Virginia for the purpose of cooperating with the force from the West Indies against the Troops in that State.[3]

1. Barras's squadron left Newport for the Chesapeake on 23 Aug. with the French siege artillery and most of the troops that had been left at Newport under the command of the marquis de Choisy.

2. Now Elkton, Md.

3. "In consequence of the dispatches received from your Excellency by the Frigate La Concorde," GW wrote de Grasse, 17 Aug., "it has been judged expedient to give up for the present the enterprise against New York and to turn our attention towards the South, with a view, if we should not be able [to] attempt Charles town itself, to recover and secure the States of Virginia, North Carolina and the Country of South Carolina and Georgia. We may add a further inducement for giving up the first mentioned enterprise, which is the arrival of a reinforcemt. of near 3000 Hessian Recruits. For this purpose we have determined to remove the whole of the French Army and as large a detachment of the American as can be spared to Chesapeake, to meet Your Excellency."

15. Dispatched a Courier to the Marquis de la Fayette with information of this matter—requesting him to be in perfect readiness to second my views & to prevent if possible the retreat of Cornwallis toward Carolina.

16th. Letters from the Marqs. de la Fayette & others, inform that Lord Cornwallis with the Troops from Hampton Road, had proceeded up York River & landed at York & Gloucester Towns where they were throwing up Works on the 6th. Inst.[1]

1. See entry for 7 June 1781, n.1.

19th. The want of Horses, or bad condition of them in the French army delayed the March till this day. The same causes, it is to be feared, will occasion a slow and disagreeable March to Elk if fresh horses cannot be procured & better management of them adopted.

The detachment from the American [army] is composed of the light Infantry under Scammell—two light companies of York to be joined by the like Number from the Connecticut line—the remainder of the Jersey line—two Regiments of York—Hazens Regiment & the Regiment of Rhode Island—together with Lambs regiment of Artillery with Cannon and other Ordnance for the field & Siege.[1]

Hazens regiment being thrown over at Dobbs's ferry was ordered with the Jersey Troops to March & take Post on the heights between Spring field & Chatham & Cover a french Battery at the latter place to veil our real movement & create apprehensions for Staten Island.[2] The Quarter Master Genl. was dispatched to Kings ferry—the only secure passage—to prepare for the speedy transportation of the Troops across the River.

Passed Singsing[3] with the American column. The French column marched by the way of Northcastle, Crompond & Pinesbridge being near ten miles further.

1. GW's General Orders for 31 July 1781 had stated that the light infantry companies "of the first and second regiments of New York (upon their arrival in Camp) with the two companies of [New] York Levies under command of Captains [William] Sackett and [Daniel] Williams will form a Battalion under command of Lieutenant Colonel [Alexander] Hamilton and Major [Nicholas] Fish. After the formation of the Battalion Lieutenant Colonel Hamilton will join the Advanced Corps under the Orders of Colonel [Alexander] Scammell" (Washington Papers, Library of Congress). At this time Hazen's 2d Canadian Regiment was acting as the 4th Battalion of Lafayette's Light Division under the command of Lt. Col. Edward Antil. Col. John Lamb's Regiment was the 2d Battalion of Continental Artillery, organized in 1777 and composed of companies from New York, Connecticut, New Hampshire, and Rhode Island.

2. Elaborate plans were made to deceive the British concerning the army's movements. Thirty boats were mounted on carriages and taken with the troops to give the appearance of preparations for an attack on Staten Island. Clinton apparently was not completely deceived about GW's intentions toward New York; but as long as de Grasse's destination was uncertain, he believed that the allies would probably not move their entire force south. It was not until 6 Sept., when Clinton received Cornwallis's letter of 4 Sept. announcing de Grasse's arrival off the Capes, that "Mr. Washington's design in marching to the Southward remained no longer an object of doubt" (Clinton, *American Rebellion*, 327–29).

3. Ossining, N.Y.

20th. The head of the Americans arrived at Kings ferry about ten O'clock & immediately began to cross.

21st. In the course of this day the whole of the American Troop, all their baggage, artillery & Stores, crossed the river. During the passing of the French Army I mounted 30 flat Boats (able to carry about 40 Men each) upon carriages—as well with a design to deceive the enemy as to our real movement, as to be useful to me in Virginia when I get there.[1]

1. Both the French and American armies left camp at Philipsburg on 19 Aug. but took different routes to King's Ferry.

22d. 23d. 24th. & 25th. Employed in transporting the French Army, its baggage & Stores over the river.[1]

1. On 23 Aug. GW and Rochambeau visited West Point (Cromot Du Bourg, "Diary," 307).

[25th.] The 25th. the American Troops marched in two Columns— Genl. Lincoln with the light Infantry & first York Regiment pursuing the rout by Peramus to Springfield—while Colo. Lamb with his Regiment of Artillery—the Parke[1]—Stores and Baggage of the Army covered by the Rhode Island Regt. proceeded to Chatham by the way of Pompton & the two bridges.

The Legion of Lauzen & the Regiments of Bourbonne & Duponts[2] with the heavy Parke of the French Army also Marched for percipony[3] by Suffrans Pompton & [   ].

1. That is, gun or artillery park.

2. The Deux-Ponts Regiment was composed primarily of officers and men from the duchy of Deux-Ponts on the Franco-German border. Its colonel was Christian, comte de Deux-Ponts, with Guillaume, comte de Deux-Ponts, as lieutenant colonel. The regiment came to America with Admiral de Ternay's fleet in the spring of 1780.

3. Parsippany, Morris County, N.Y., is six miles northeast of Morristown.

28th. The American columns and 1st. division of the French Army arrived at the places assigned them.

29th. The Second division of French joined the first. The whole halted—as well for the purpose of bringing up our rear—as because we had heard not of the arrival of Count de Grasse & was unwilling to discover our real object to the enemy.

30th. As our intentions could be concealed one March more (under the idea of Marching to Sandy hook to facilitate the entrance of the French fleet within the Bay), the whole Army was put in motion in three columns—the left consisted of the light Infantry, first York Regiment, and the Regiment of Rhode Island—the Middle column consisted of the Parke Stores & Baggage—Lambs Regt. of Artillery—Hazens & the Corps of Sappers & Miners—the right column consisted of the whole French army, Baggage Stores &ca. This last was to march by the rout of Morristown—Bullions Tavern[1]—Somerset C[our]t House[2] & Princeton. The middl. was to go by Bound brooke[3] to Somerset &ca. and the left to proceed by the way of Brunswick to Trenton, to which place the whole were to March Transports being ordered to meet them there.

I set out myself for Philadelphia to arrange matters there—provide Vessels & hasten the transportation of the Ordnance Stores, &ca.—directing before I set out, the secd. York Regiment (which had not all arrived from Albany before we left Kings ferry) to follow with the Boats—Intrenching Tools &ca. the French Rear to Trenton.

1. Bullion's Tavern was at Liberty Corner, N.J.

2. Somerset Court House is now Millstone, Somerset County, N.J., eight miles west of New Brunswick.

3. Bound Brook is on the Raritan River, Somerset County, N.J., six miles northwest of New Brunswick.

31st. Arrived at Philadelphia to dinner and immediately hastened up all the Vessels that could be procured—but finding them inadequate

to the purpose of transporting both Troops & Stores, Count de Rochambeau & myself concluded it would be best to let the Troops March
by land to the head of Elk, & gave directions accordingly to all but the
2d. York Regiment which was ordered (with its baggage) to come down
in the Batteaux they had in charge to Christiana bridge.[1]

1. The *Pa. Packet,* 2 Sept. 1781, Trumbull, "Minutes," 332, and Closen,
Journal, 116, all give 30 Aug. as the date of arrival in Philadelphia where GW,
Rochambeau, and their entourage were "received by crowds of people with
shouts and acclamations" (Trumbull, "Minutes," 332). On 28 Aug., Robert
Morris had offered GW his house for the commander in chief's stay in Philadelphia since the city was "filled with Strangers" and private lodgings were
almost impossible to acquire. The French officers lodged at the residence of
the chevalier de La Luzerne, "where M. de Rochambeau and his staff were
housed like princes." In the evening they dined with Robert Morris (Closen,
Journal, 116). GW's main purpose in visiting Philadelphia was to arrange for
supplies and transport for the march to Virginia.

September

5th. The rear of the French army having reached Philadelphia and the
Americans having passed it—the Stores having got up & every thing in
a tolerable train here; I left this City for the head of Elk to hasten the
Embarkation at that place and on my way—(at Chester)—received the
agreeable news of the safe arrival of the Count de Grasse in the Bay of
Chesapeake with 28 Sail of the line & four frigates—with 3000 land
Troops which were to be immediately debarked at James town & form
a junction with the American Army under the command of the Marqs.
de la Fayette.[1]

Finding upon my arrival at the head of Elk a great deficiency of
Transports, I wrote many letters to Gentn. of Influence on the Eastern
shore, beseeching them to exert themselves in drawing forth every
kind of Vessel which would answer for this purpose and agreed with
the Count de Rochambeau that about 1000 American Troops (including the Artillery Regiment) and the Grenadiers & Chasseurs of the Brigade of Bourbonne with the Infantry of Lauzen's legion should be the
first to Embark and that the rest of the Troops should continue their
march to Baltimore proceeding thence by Land, or Water according to
circumstances. The Cavalry of Lauzen, with the Saddle horses & such
teams of both armies as the Qr. Masters thereof might judge necessary
to go round by Land to the place of operation.

Judging it highly expedient to be with the army in Virginia as soon
as possible, to make the necessary arrangements for the Siege, & to get
the Materials prepared for it, I determined to set out for the Camp of
the Marqs. de la Fayette without loss of time and accordingly in Com-

*Comte de Rochambeau, the French commander in chief, in a painting by
Charles Willson Peale. (Independence National Historical Park Collection)*

pany with the Count de Rochambeau who requested to attend me, and
the Chevr. de Chastellux set out on the [6th.]

1. On 31 Aug., Brig. Gen. David Forman wrote GW from his observation
post in Freehold, N.J., that two British squadrons under Admirals Graves and
Hood were in process of setting sail from New York City. Barras's fleet had
sailed from Newport, R.I., on 23 Aug. carrying siege guns and provisions for
Yorktown, and no word had since been received from him. If he were inter-
cepted by the British fleet before he joined de Grasse in the Chesapeake, the
results could be disastrous to the allied campaign in the South.

On 5 Sept., GW informed the president of Congress that he had received
a letter from Brig. Gen. Mordecai Gist announcing the arrival of de Grasse's

fleet. By 7 Sept., GW was able to report that the French fleet from Rhode Island was "hourly expected" to join de Grasse's fleet. According to Jonathan Trumbull's journal, GW had left Philadelphia with his suite and about three miles below Chester met the express from de Grasse. He then returned to Chester to inform Rochambeau and Congress of the French fleet's arrival (Trumbull, "Minutes," 332). Rochambeau had decided to come from Philadelphia to Chester by water. As the ship approached Chester, "We discerned in the distance General Washington, standing on the shore and waving his hat and a white handkerchief joyfully. . . . MM. de Rochambeau and Washington embraced *warmly* on the shore" (Closen, *Journal,* 123).

8th. and reached Baltimore.[1]

    1. While GW and his party were in Baltimore they stayed at Daniel Grant's Fountain Inn.

9th. I reached my own Seat at Mount Vernon (distant 120 Miles from the Hd. of Elk) where I staid till the 12th. and in three days afterwards that is on the 14th. reached Williamsburg. The necessity of seeing, & agreeing upon a proper plan of cooperation with the Count de Grasse induced me to make him a visit at Cape Henry where he lay with his fleet after a partial engagement with the British Squadron off the Capes under the Command of Admiral Graves whom he had driven back to Sandy hook.[1]

    1. GW, who had not seen his home since his departure in May 1775, was accompanied to Mount Vernon by Lt. Col. David Humphreys, one of his staff, while the "rest of the family jogg on easily" (Trumbull, "Minutes," 333). GW's aides arrived at midday on 10 Sept., and Rochambeau and his staff in the evening; Chastellux and his aides came the next day. Trumbull noted: "A numerous family now present. All accommodated. An elegant seat and situation, great appearance of oppulence and real exhibitions of hospitality & princely entertainment." On 13 Sept. the party left Mount Vernon for Williamsburg and "between Colchester and Dumphries meet letters giving an account of an action between the two Fleets, & that the French were gone out from the Bay in pursuit of the English. The event not known. Much agitated" (Trumbull, "Minutes," 333). In light of the news from the Capes, troops moving south were temporarily halted.

    After Rodney's departure from the West Indies for England, Sir Samuel Hood had sailed for New York, joining Graves there on 28 Aug. The combined fleets of Graves and Hood, consisting of 19 ships of the line, did not sail from New York until 31 Aug. Both admirals underestimated de Grasse's strength. Still unaware of the arrival of de Grasse, the British fleet reached the Chesapeake on 5 Sept. and virtually stumbled into the French fleet anchored just inside the bay. The two fleets met on 5 Sept. off the Chesapeake in a 2½-hour action. The results were inconclusive, but the two fleets remained in contact, 6–7 Sept., drifting south to the vicinity of Cape Hatteras, which allowed Barras's fleet from Newport to sail into Chesapeake Bay unmolested. By 11 Sept. the French fleet was back in the Chesapeake, and on 14 Sept. the British fleet sailed for New York.

    On the way to Williamburg, Trumbull noted that the party heard "rumours of the return of the French Fleet, with some advantage, which relieved our fears" (Trumbull, "Minutes," 333). Both GW and Trumbull mistakenly date the party's arrival in Williamsburg as 15 Sept. rather than 14 Sept. St. George Tucker states that GW reached the city about four o'clock in the afternoon. "He had passed our camp which is now in the rear of the whole army, before we had time to parade the militia. The French line had just time to form. The Continentals had more leisure. He approached without any pomp or parade attended only by a few horsemen and his own servants. The Count de Rochambeau and Gen. Hand with one or two more officers were with him. . . . The Marquis [de Lafayette] rode up with precipitation, clasped the General in his arms and embraced him with an ardor not easily described. The whole army and all the town were presently in motion. The General—at the request of the Marquis de St. Simon—rode through the French lines. The troops were paraded for the purpose and cut a most splendid figure. He then visited the Continental line" (St. George Tucker to Frances Tucker, 15 Sept. 1781, Coleman, *St. George Tucker,* 70–71). In Williamsburg, GW lodged at George Wythe's house. In the evening "an elegant supper was served up" and "an elegant band of music played an introductive part of a French Opera" (Butler, "Journal," 106).

On 15 Sept., GW wrote to de Grasse, expressing his desire for a conference aboard the admiral's flagship, the *Ville de Paris,* and requesting de Grasse to send some form of conveyance for GW and his officers. In the evening he dined with Lafayette and on 16 Sept. with Baron von Steuben (ibid.).

17th. In company with the Count de Rochambeau—the Chevr. Chastellux—Genls. Knox & Duportail, I set out for the Interview with the Admiral & arrived on board the Ville de Paris (off Cape Henry) the next day by Noon and having settled most points with him to my satisfaction except not obtaining an assurance of sending Ships above York and one that he could not continue his fleet on this Station longer than the first of November I embarked on board the Queen Charlotte (the Vessell I went down in) but by hard blowing; & contrary Winds, did not reach Williamsburg again till the 22d.[1]

1. On 17 Sept. de Grasse sent a small vessel, the *Queen Charlotte,* captured from the British, to convey GW and his party to the *Ville de Paris* for the conference. Also accompanying GW were aides David Cobb and Jonathan Trumbull, Jr. (Trumbull, "Minutes," 333).

De Grasse had already warned Rochambeau and GW that the stay on the Chesapeake of his fleet and Saint Simon's troops would be limited, probably not extending beyond mid-October. The question uppermost in GW's mind was whether de Grasse would be able to remain until the British could be forced to surrender, particularly if the siege of Yorktown proved to be protracted.

22d. Upon my arrival in Camp I found that the 3d. Maryland Regiment had got in (under the Command of Colo. Adam)[1] and that all except a few missing Vessels with the Troops from the head of Elk were arrived, & landing at the upper point of the College Creek[2]—where

Genl. Choisy[3] with 600 Fr. Troops who had from R. Isld. had arrived in the Squadron of Count de Barras.

1. Lt. Col. Peter Adams was in command of the 3d Maryland Regiment.

2. College Creek is a branch of the James River.

3. Claude Gabriel, marquis de Choisy (b. 1723), a brigadier general in the French army, had commanded the French troops left behind in Newport to guard Barras's fleet and the French artillery. In Aug. he sailed with Barras's fleet to the Chesapeake and was now ordered to "take command of the Troops ordered to besiege the village of Gloucester, a post opposite the town of York held by the English, in which they had 1,100 men in addition to their hospitals and stores. The troops under M. de Choisy included the Lauzun Legion, 800 men from the garrisons of our ships, and 1,500 militia" (Clermont-Crèvecoeur's journal in Rice, *American Campaigns of Rochambeau's Army*, 1:56).

25th. Admiral de Barras having Joined the Count de Grasse with the Squadron and Transports from Rhode Island, & the latter with some Frigates being sent to Baltimore for the remr. of the French army arrived this day at the usual port of debarkation above the College Creek and began to land the Troops from them.

28th. Having debarked all the Troops and their Baggage—Marched and Encamped them in Front of the City and having with some difficulty obtained horses & Waggons sufficient to move our field Artillery—Intrenching Tools & such other articles as were indispensably necessary—we commenced our March for the Investiture of the Enemy at York.

The American Continental, and French Troops formed one column on the left—the first in advance—the Militia composed the right column & marched by the way of Harwoods Mill.[1]

1. The American forces moved toward Yorktown; the French marched to the left to Murford's Bridge where they were to join the militia. About noon both forces arrived in the Yorktown area. Some of the British pickets and horse were forced to withdraw, and the Americans and French dug in for the night.

29th. Moved the American Troops more to the right, and Encamped on the East side of Bever dam Creek,[1] with a Morass in front, about Cannon shot from the enemys lines. Spent this day in reconnoitering the enemys position, & determining upon a plan of attack & approach.

1. Beaver Dam Creek, or Great Run, is about halfway between Yorktown and Wormley Creek. The creek and its branches formed a marsh about the middle of the allied lines which stretched from the edge of the York River above Yorktown to Wormley Creek.

30th. The Enemy abandoned all their exterior works, & the position they had taken without the Town; & retired within their Interior works of defence in the course of last Night—immediately upon which we

George Washington, in an oil painting by Charles Willson Peale. (Fogg Art Museum, Harvard University, Grenville L. Winthrop Bequest)

possessed them, & made those on our left (with a little alteration) very serviceable to us. We also began two inclosed Works on the right of Pidgeon Hill[1]—between that & the ravine above Mores Mill.[2]

From this time till the 6th. of October nothing occurred of Importance.

The Teams which were sent round from the head of Elk, having arrived about this time, we were enabled to bring forward our heavy Artillery & Stores with more convenience and dispatch and every thing being prepared for opening Trenches 1500 Fatiegue men & 2800 to cover them, were ordered for this Service.[3]

> 1. Among the other defenses, the British had abandoned the redoubts at Pigeon Quarter and Pigeon Hill approximately two miles southwest of the town.
>
> 2. Moore's Mill was on Wormley's Pond at the head of Wormley Creek.
>
> 3. On 27 Sept., GW had received welcome news from de Grasse, suggesting that he had abandoned the prospect of cruising to intercept British Admirals Digby and Hood and was willing to commit his fleet to the investiture of Yorktown (de Grasse to GW, 25 Sept. 1781, *Washington and de Grasse*, 51–52). GW also requested and received 600 to 800 marines from the French ships. On the 27th de Grasse had reluctantly agreed to GW's request for the French troops, but added "I earnestly beseech Your Excellency to dispense in future with the necessity of demanding men from my vessels. I am mortified that I can not do all that I would wish, but there is no doing impossibilities" (*Washington and de Grasse*, 56–57).
>
> During this period GW also ordered construction and fortification of a trench commanding the main British defenses. He personally inspected the ground selected for this first parallel on 1 Oct., narrowly escaping fire from the British defenses 300 yards away. The parallel was not occupied until the siege guns could be transported from Trebell's Landing on the James River six or seven miles from Yorktown. A minor contretemps was presented to GW by Lafayette when he requested command of the right wing of the siege army in place of Benjamin Lincoln, who held the position by right of seniority. GW refused as tactfully as possible. On 3 Oct. the marquis de Choisy moved his troops in tighter formation about Gloucester Point. In the process the duc de Lauzun, one of his officers, encountered Banastre Tarleton's Dragoons, resulting in an action also involving the Virginia militia which GW described somewhat excessively in General Orders as a "brilliant success." On 5 Oct. the army rejoiced at the news of Nathanael Greene's victory at Eutaw Springs, S.C. Jonathan Trumbull, Jr., notes that during these days there was almost no fire from the British on the Americans busily digging in on the Yorktown perimeter.

October

6th. Before Morning the Trenches were in such forwardness as to cover the Men from the enemys fire.[1] The work was executed with so much secresy & dispatch that the enemy were, I believe, totally ignorant of our labor till the light of the Morning discovered it to them. Our loss on this occasion was extremely inconsiderable.

> 1. The trenches were opened between 500 and 600 yards from the British works, and the first parallel, supported by four redoubts (two on American ground, two on French), ran from the center of the enemy's works to the York River (Tilghman, *Memoir*, 104).

7th & 8th. Was employed in compleating our Parallel—finishing the redoubts in them and establishing Batteries.

9th. About 3 o'clock P.M. the French opened a battery on our extreme left, of 4 Sixteen pounders, and Six Morters & Hawitzers and at 5 oclock an American battery of Six 18s & 24s; four Morters & 2 Hawitzers, began to play from the extremity of our right—both with good effect as they compelled the Enemy to withdraw from their ambrazures the Pieces which had previously kept up a constant firing.[1]

> 1. According to Dr. James Thacher, "his Excellency General Washington put the match to the first gun, and a furious discharge of cannon and mortars immediately followed, and Earl Cornwallis has received his first salutation" (Thacher, *Military Journal*, 283).

12th. Began our second parallel within abt. 300 yards (& in some places less) of the enemys lines and got it so well advanced in the course of the Night as to cover the Men before morning.[1]

> 1. The second parallel was opened "1152 feet from the main fortifications" (Closen, *Journal*, 147).

13th. The fire of the enemy this Night became brisk—both from their Cannon and royals[1] and more injurious to us than it had been; several Men being killed and many wounded in the Trenches, but the works were not in the smallest degree retarded by it. Our Batteries were begun in the course of the Night and a good deal advanced.

> 1. A royal was a small mortar carrying a shell with a diameter of 5.5 inches.

14th. The day was spent in compleating our parallel, and maturing the Batteries of the second parallel. The old batteries were principally directed against the abattis & salient angles of the enemys advanced redoubts on their extreme right & left to prepare them for the intended assault for which the necessary dispositions were made for attacking the two on the left and,

At half after Six in the Evening both were carried—that on their left (on the Bank of the river) by the Americans and the other by the French Troops. The Baron Viominel commanded the left attack & the Marqs. de la fayette the right on which the light Infantry were employed.[1]

In the left redoubt (assaulted by the Americans) there were abt.

45 men under the command of a Major Campbell;[2] of which the Major a Captn. & Ensign, with 17 Men were made Prisoners—But few were killed on the part of the Enemy & the remainder of the Garrison escaped. The right Redoubt attacked by the French, consisted of abt. 120 Men, commanded by a Lieutenant Colo.—of these 18 were killed, & 42 taken Prisoners—among the Prisoners were a Captain and two Lieutenants. The bravery exhibited by the attacking Troops was emulous and praiseworthy—few cases have exhibited stronger proofs of Intripidity coolness and firmness than were shown upon this occasion.

1. Antoine Charles du Houx, baron de Vioménil (1728–1792), was at this time Rochambeau's second-in-command in America. Ever since the épaulement had been started on 12 Oct., American and French guns had been pounding at the advanced British redoubts. By the evening of the 14th the engineers reported that the two British works had been sufficiently damaged by the shelling to make an assault practicable. It was decided that the redoubt on the extreme left would be attacked by American light infantry under the command of the marquis de Lafayette and the other by French grenadiers and chasseurs under Vioménil. In the midst of preparations for the attack, GW was forced to settle a squabble between Lafayette's two ranking subordinates, Alexander Hamilton and the chevalier de Gimat, as to which was to command the attack on the extreme left redoubt. GW decided in Hamilton's favor on grounds of seniority. Diversionary fire was ordered from Gloucester and from Saint Simon's troops on the left flank.

2. Maj. James Campbell was an officer in the 71st Regiment.

15th. Busily employed in getting the Batteries of the Second parallel compleated, and fixing on New ones contiguous to the Redoubts which were taken last Night. Placed two Hawitzers in each of the Captured Redoubts wch. were opened upon the enemy about 5 oclock in the Afternoon.

16th. About four O'clock this Morning the enemy made a Sortee upon our Second parallel and spiked four French pieces of Artillery & two of ours—but the guards of the Trenches advancing quickly upon them they retreated precipitately. The Sally being made upon that part of the parallel which was guarded by the French Troops they lost an officer & 12 Men killed and 1 Officer taken prisoner. The American loss was one Sergeant of Artillery (in the American battery) Wounded. The Enemy, it is said, left 10 dead and lost 3 Prisoners.[1]

About 4 Oclock this afternoon the French opened two Batteries of 2. 24s. & four 16s. each. 3 pieces from the American grand battery were also opened—the others not being ready.

1. The British sortie, about 4:00 A.M., against the second parallel was led by Lt. Col. Robert Abercrombie with 350 men of the light infantry and Guards. Although the British attackers succeeded in spiking the guns in two allied batteries, the spikes were quickly removed by the defenders. On the

16th, after the failure of Abercrombie's sortie had become apparent, Cornwallis made a last desperate attempt to escape the siege. He planned an attack on Choisy on Gloucester, hoping to break through his lines and march his troops north. Tarleton, already entrenched on Gloucester, sent 16 large boats across the river to ferry the British forces to Gloucester, since Cornwallis, "hoped to pass the infantry during the night, abandoning our baggage and leaving a detachment to capitulate for the townspeople and for the sick and wounded, on which subject a letter was ready to be delivered to General Washington." At this point a violent storm broke, driving the boats down the river. When the American batteries opened fire at daybreak, a substantial portion of Cornwallis's troops were marooned at Gloucester; he was not able to get them back across the river until just before noon (Cornwallis to Clinton, 20 Oct. 1781, Clinton, *American Rebellion*, 583–87).

17th. About ten Oclock the Enemy beat a parley and Lord Cornwallis proposed a cessation of Hostilities for 24 hours, that Commissioners might meet at the house of a Mr. Moore (in the rear of our first parallel) to settle terms for the surrender of the Posts of York and Gloucester.[1] To this he was answered, that a desire to spare the further effusion of Blood would readily incline me to treat of the surrender of the above Posts but previous to the meeting of Commissioners I wished to have his proposals in writing and for this purpose would grant a cessation of hostilities two hours—Within which time he sent out A letter with such proposals (tho' some of them were inadmissable) as led me to believe that there would be no great difficulty in fixing the terms.[2] Accordingly hostilities were suspended for the Night & I proposed my own terms to which if he agreed Commissioners were to meet to digest them into form.

1. GW is referring to the Moore House, 1½ miles below Yorktown on Temple Farm. At this time the house was owned by Augustine Moore (d. 1788), a leading York County landowner.
2. In his reply GW agreed that the garrisons of Yorktown and Gloucester should be considered prisoners of war, but Cornwallis's suggestion that the British and German troops should be returned to Europe was clearly inadmissible; instead the troops would be marched to whatever section of the country was best prepared to receive them. British shipping in the area was to be delivered to an officer of the navy and all British armament except officers' small arms was to be surrendered.

18th. The Commissioners met accordingly; but the business was so procrastinated by those on their side (a Colo. Dundas & a Majr. Ross) that Colo. Laurens & the Viscount De Noailles who were appointed on our part could do no more than make the rough draft of the Articles which were to be submitted for Lord Cornwallis's consideration.[1]

1. The British commissioners were Lt. Col. Thomas Dundas of the 80th Regiment of Foot (Royal Edinburgh Volunteers) and Maj. Alexander Ross, Cornwallis's aide-de-camp. The American commissioners wre Lt. Col. John

CHARLES EARL CORNWALLIS. 1783.

Charles Cornwallis, second Earl Cornwallis, the general defeated by the Americans and French at Yorktown, sat for this Thomas Gainsborough portrait in 1783. (National Portrait Gallery, London)

Laurens and the vicomte de Noailles, *mestre de camp en second* of the Soissonnais Regiment and brother-in-law of Lafayette. The discussions dragged on through the day, and in late evening the commissioners reported that negotiations had been so protracted that an extension of the truce until 9:00 the next morning had been necessary.

19th. In the Morning early I had them copied and sent word to Lord Cornwallis that I expected to have them signed at 11 Oclock and that the Garrison would March out at two O'clock—both of which were accordingly done.[1] Two redoubts on the Enemys left being possessed (the one by a detachment of French Grenadiers, & the other by American Infantry) with orders to prevent all intercourse between the army & Country and the Town—while Officers in the several departments were employed in taking acct. of the public Stores &ca.

1. The final articles of capitulation, signed 19 Oct. by GW, Rochambeau, and Barras (signing for himself and de Grasse) for the allies and Cornwallis and Thomas Symonds for the British, contained customary conditions of honorable surrender. In addition, British officers were permitted to return to Europe or to any British-held American port on parole. Land troops were to be considered prisoners of the United States; naval prisoners would be in the custody of the French. British soldiers were "to be kept in Virginia, Maryland or Pennsylvania, and as much by Regiments as possible, and supplied with the same Rations of provisions as are allowed to Soldiers in the service of America." On this day GW wrote to Congress announcing the British surrender and enclosing his correspondence with Cornwallis and commissioned his aide Lt. Col. Tench Tilghman to carry the victory dispatch to Congress.

At 2:00 P.M. French and American troops began to move into British positions at the east end of the town. With American troops lined up on the right and French on the left, the British began their march through the lines, "their Drums in Front beating a slow March. Their Colours furl'd and Cased . . . General Lincoln with his Aids conducted them—Having passed thro' our whole Army they grounded their Arms & march'd back again thro' the Army a second Time into the Town—The sight was too pleasing to an American to admit of Description" (Tucker, "Journal," 392–93). French army officer baron von Closen noted that in passing through the lines the British showed "the greatest scorn for the Americans, who, to tell the truth, were eclipsed by our army in splendor of appearance and dress, for most of these unfortunate persons were clad in small jackets of white cloth, dirty and ragged, and a number of them were almost barefoot" (Closen, *Journal,* 153). Cornwallis, claiming illness, did not accompany his troops, and the surrender was carried out by Brig. Gen. Charles O'Hara, who had accompanied Cornwallis through the Carolina campaign. The British officer's sword was accepted by Maj. Gen. Benjamin Lincoln.

On the evening of the 19th Cornwallis was invited to dine at Headquarters "but excuses himself on account of health. Keeps his Quarters." O'Hara came in his place "very social and easy" (Trumbull, "Minutes," 337).

20th. Winchester & Fort Frederick in Maryland, being the places destined for the reception of the Prisoners they were to have commenced their March accordingly this day, but were prevented by the Commissary of Prisoners not having compleated his Accounts of them & taken the Paroles of the Officers.[1]

1. On 20 Oct., GW was informed by the marquis de Choisy that the surrender of Gloucester by Tarleton was progressing smoothly.

21st. The prisoners began their March & set out for the Fleet to pay my respects, & offer my thanks to the Admiral for his important Services and to see if he could not be induced to further co-operations before

A mezzotint of the marquis de Lafayette after Charles Willson Peale. (Mount Vernon Ladies' Association of the Union)

his final departure from this Coast. Despairing from the purport of my former conferences with him, & the tenor of all his letters, of obtaining more than a Convoy, I contented myself with representing the import, consequences and certain prospect of an attempt upon Charles town and requesting if his orders or other Engagements would not allow him to attend to that great object, that he would nevertheless transport a detachment of Troops to, & cover their debarkation at Wilmington that by reducing the enemy's post there we might give peace to another State with the Troops that would afterwards join the Southern army under the Command of Majr. Genl. Greene.[1]

1. De Grasse agreed in principle to the attack on Wilmington but on further reflection decided that it would be impossible for him to transport American troops, supplies, and ammunition for the Wilmington expedition and still be certain of keeping his other engagements, although he was still willing to provide a convoy. GW left Lafayette, to whom GW had promised

command of the Wilmington campaign, on board the *Ville de Paris* in the hope he could change de Grasse's mind.

23d. The Marqs. returned with assurances from the Admiral, that he would countenance, & protect with his fleet, the Expedition against Wilmington. Preparations were immediately [begun] for Embarking Wayne's & Gists[1] Brigades with a sufficiency of Artillery, Stores, & provisions for this purpose.

> 1. Mordecai Gist (1743–1792) served as brigadier general in the Maryland Line, 9 Jan. 1779 to 3 Nov. 1783.

24th. Received advice, by Express from General Forman, of the British Fleet in the Harbour of New York consisting of 26 Sail of the line, some 50s. & 44s.—Many frigates—fire Ships & Transports mounting in the whole to 99 Sail had passed the Narrows for the hook, & were as he supposd, upon the point of Sailing for Chesapeak.[1] Notice was immediately communicated to the Count de grasse.

From this time to the 28th. was employed in collecting and taking an acct. of the different species of Stores which were much dispersed and in great disorder.

All the Vessels in public employ in the James River were ordered round for the purpose of receiving and transporting Stores &ca. to the Head of Elk.

> 1. In New York, Clinton and Graves, increasingly alarmed by Cornwallis's reports from Yorktown, had since mid-October been in the midst of preparations to send a fleet to his relief. Vessels of the British navy and transports carrying British troops began straggling out of New York on 17 Oct., but it was the 19th before the fleet was completely under way. By the 24th, when Graves had arrived at the Chesapeake, "he found Comte de Grasse's superior fleet of thirty-three ships of the line and two fifty-gun ships at anchor in a position of defense. Since they were so stationed that he could not attack them without first running past a formidable land battery, he thought it foolhardy to stake everything" (Baurmeister, *Revolution in America,* 475–76). The fleet was back in New York by 3 Nov.

28th. Began to Embark the Ordnance and Stores for the above purpose.

Received a Letter from the Count de Grasse, declining the Convoy he had engaged to give the detachment for Wilmington & assigning his reasons for it. This after a suspence & consequent delay of 6 or 7 days obliged me to prepare to March the Troops by Land under the command of M. Genl. St. Clair.

In the Evening of this day Intilligence was received from the Count de Grasse that the British fleet was off the Capes, & consisted of 36 Ships 25 of which were of the line & that he had hove out the Signal for all his People to come on board & prepare to Sail—but many of his Boats & hands being on Shore it could not be effected.

29th. The British Fleet still appeared in the offing without the Capes, but the Wind being unfavourable, and other causes preventing, the French Fleet kept to their Moorings within. In the Evening of this day the former fleet disappeared, & Count de Grasse engaged to remain a few days in the Bay to cover the Water transport of our Stores & Troops up the Bay to the River Elk.

From this time to the 5th. of Novr. was employed in embarking the ordnance & Stores, & the Troops which were returning to the Northward—preparing the detachment for the Southward—providing Cloathing & Stores for the Army commanded by Majr. Genl. Greene—depositing a Magazine at Westham for the use of the Southern States and making other necessary arrangements previous to the division of the army and my return to the North river—also in marching off 467 Convalescents from the British Hospital under escort of Courtlandts York Regiment for Fredericksburg on their way to join their respective Regiments at Winchester & Fort Frederick in Maryland.

November

5th. The detachment for the Southward, consisting as has been before observed, of Waynes & Gists Brigades (excepting such Men of the Maryland & Virginia lines whose terms of Service would expire before the first of Jany.). Began their March and were to be joined by all the Cavalry that could be equiped of the first—third & fourth Regiments at

At this point GW's 1781 diary abruptly ends. By 3 Nov. most of the American troops and supplies which GW was moving north were on their way to Head of Elk. The main body of Rochambeau's army was to go into winter quarters in Virginia. Cornwallis and those British officers who were going to New York and directly to Europe left Yorktown on 4 Nov.

As GW was preparing to leave his Headquarters at Yorktown, he was called to Burwell Bassett's home, Eltham, to the bedside of his stepson, Jacky (John Parke Custis), who had been taken seriously ill. In the fall of 1781 Jacky had left Mount Vernon for a stay in the area of Pamunkey, and by 12 Oct. he had written his mother from the "Camp before York" that his health had improved and "the general tho in constant Fatigue looks very well." He apparently served briefly as a civilian aide during the Yorktown siege. While at Yorktown he was stricken with what appears to have been camp fever and was moved to the Bassett estate of Eltham, some 30 miles from Yorktown, and his mother and wife were summoned. On 6 Nov., GW wrote his aide Jonathan Trumbull,

Jr., from Eltham: "I came here in time to see Mr. Custis breathe his last. About Eight o'clock yesterday Evening he expired. The deep and solemn distress of the Mother, and affliction of the Wife of this amiable young Man, requires every comfort in my power to afford them; the last rights of the deceased I must also see performed; these will take me three or four days; when I shall proceed with Mrs. Washington and Mrs. Custis to Mount Vernon."

GW probably left Eltham on 11 Nov. or possibly early on the 12th, stopping briefly at Fredericksburg to visit his mother, who proved to be away from home. By 13 Nov. he was at Mount Vernon and remained there until he left for Philadelphia, probably on 20 Nov., to concert with Congress plans for a 1782 campaign.

There are no diaries extant for the remaining years of the Revolution or for the months after Washington returned to Mount Vernon in time for Christmas 1783. Upon his return he immediately took up the duties of planter, devoting himself to the restoration of the household buildings and small industries and resuming the Virginia relationships that had been decimated by the war. Either he did not immediately resume his prewar habit of keeping journals, or the diaries have disappeared. In any case he began again to record his daily activities with his journey west in the autumn of 1784. As he notes in his diary, he undertook the trip to examine his western lands which had been neglected during the war years and to investigate the activities of Gilbert Simpson, who managed GW's land on the west bank of the Youghiogheny River in Pennsylvania. Besides settling the partnership with Simpson, GW was going west to inspect his vacant bounty lands on the Ohio and Kanawha rivers. A third main purpose of the trip was to learn about the possibilities of a convenient water transportation between the Ohio Valley and the eastern seaboard, especially by way of the Potomac River. He also hoped to settle a troublesome legal dispute with a group of squatters who had occupied his land on Chartiers Creek in Washington County, Pa.

1784

September

Having found it indispensably necessary to visit my Landed property west of the Apalacheon Mountains, and more especially that part of it which I held in Co-partnership with Mr. Gilbert Simpson[1]—Having determined upon a tour into that Country, and having made the necessary preparations for it, I did, on the first day of this month (September) set out on my journey.

Having dispatched my equipage about 9 Oclock A.M., consisting of 3 Servants & 6 horses, three of which carried my Baggage, I set out myself in company with Docter James Craik;[2] and after dining at Mr. Sampson

Trammells (abt. 2 Miles above the Falls Church) we proceeded to Difficult Bridge, and lodged at one Shepherds Tavern 25 Miles.

1. Gilbert Simpson, Jr., son of the Gilbert Simpson who for many years leased part of Clifton's Neck from GW, had since 1773 been manager of Washington's Bottom, a 1,644-acre tract that GW owned on the west bank of the Youghiogheny River about 35 miles southeast of Fort Pitt. This land, now the site of Perryopolis, Pa., was the first claimed by GW west of the Appalachians, having been surveyed for him in 1768. GW provided the land; Simpson his personal services as manager; and both an equal amount of slaves, livestock, and supplies. GW soon had reason to regret the arrangement, for the partnership almost from the start proved to be more troublesome than profitable to him. Simpson did clear some land, build a cabin and outbuildings, plant crops, and eventually secure several tenants for various parts of the tract. Nevertheless, he sent to Mount Vernon not profits but a flood of excuses: bad weather, bad health, bad times, and a shrewish wife. Simpson was, in truth, a fickle and careless manager who knew only one art well, that of ingratiating himself with a studied humility and professions of good intentions while feathering his own nest. After GW's return from the war, Simpson's fecklessness was soon apparent, and arrangements were made to dissolve the partnership. On 24 June 1784 GW wrote an advertisement announcing that on 15 Sept. at Washington's Bottom, Simpson's farm would be leased to the highest bidder and GW's part of the partnership's effects, including livestock, would be sold. Simpson was allowed to do as he wished with his share of the effects (*Va. Journal,* 15 July 1784; GW to Simpson, 10 July 1784, *Papers, Confederation Series,* 1:496–98).

2. Besides Dr. Craik and servants, GW was accompanied on this trip only by his nephew Bushrod Washington and Craik's son William, both of whom joined the party at Berkeley Springs.

Sep. 2. About 5 Oclock we set out from Shepperds; and leaving the Baggage to follow slowly on, we arrived about 11 Oclock ourselves at Leesburgh, where we Dined.[1] The Baggage having joined we proceeded to Mr. Israel Thompsons & lodged makg. abt. 36 M.[2]

1. Dinner was at Thomas Roper's ordinary (Cash Memoranda, Washington Papers, Library of Congress).

2. Israel Thompson (d. 1795), a Quaker, lived on a 700-acre plantation in the vicinity of Catoctin Creek in Loudoun County.

3d. Having business to transact with my Tenants in Berkeley;[1] & others, who were directed to meet me at my Brother's (Colo. Charles Washington's),[2] I left Doctr. Craik and the Baggage to follow slowly, and set out myself about Sun rise for that place—where after Breakfasting at Keys's ferry[3] I arrived about 11 Oclock—distant abt. 17 Miles.

Colo. Warner Washington, Mr. Wormeley,[4] Genl. Morgan,[5] Mr. Snickers[6] and many other Gentlemen came here to see me & one object of my journey being to obtain information of the nearest and best communication between the Eastern & Western Waters; & to facilitate as much as in me lay the Inland Navigation of the Potomack; I con-

Bushrod Washington was a law student in Philadelphia when Henry Benbridge painted this 1783 portrait. (Mount Vernon Ladies' Association of the Union)

versed a good deal with Genel. Morgan on this subject, who said, a plan was in contemplation to extend a road from Winchester to the Western Waters, to avoid if possible an interference with any other State but I could not discover that Either himself, or others, were able to point it out with precision. He seemed to have no doubt but that the Counties of Frederk., Berkeley & Hampshire would contribute freely towards the extension of the Navigation of Potomack; as well as towards opening a Road from East to West.

1. In the late 1760s and early 1770s GW leased the lands he owned on Bullskin and Evitt's runs to ten tenants. Collection of rents from those tenants, as well as from ones in Loudoun and Fauquier counties, was much neglected during the war years, and what rents were received were paid mostly in badly depreciated currency. GW could do little about this last circumstance, having given lifetime leases that specified particular cash payments with no allowance for inflation. Nevertheless, he could collect the considerable balances still due and, being in need of ready cash, was determined to do so.

2. Charles Washington had moved to the Shenandoah Valley from Fredericksburg in 1780, settling on land on Evitt's Run which he had inherited from his half brother Lawrence. Charles's new house, Happy Retreat, stood on a hill overlooking the run, near the southern edge of present-day Charles Town, W.Va. The town, named for him, was laid out on his property in 1786.

3. Key's (Keyes') ferry was on the Shenandoah River, about four miles east of Happy Retreat.

4. Ralph Wormeley, Sr., of Rosegill, Middlesex County, was staying at his hunting lodge on the Shenandoah River, Berkeley Rocks, also known simply as The Rocks.

5. Daniel Morgan (c.1735–1802), a rough-and-tumble frontiersman during his youth, had emerged during the Revolution as an American military hero and was now one of the most prominent men in Frederick County. Forced to retire from military service in 1781 because of the ill health that frequently plagued him in his later years, Morgan went home to Frederick County and finished building his house, Saratoga, on his farm between Winchester and Berry's ferry, near present-day Boyce, Va. Morgan shared GW's interest in western lands, east-west transportation, and flour manufacturing.

4th. Having finished my Business with my Tenants (so far at least as partial payments could put a close to it)[1] and provided a waggon for the transportation of my Baggage to the Warm springs (or Town of Bath)[2].

1. While at Happy Retreat, GW collected rent from at least some of his tenants. None of the sums fully discharged the accounts on which they were paid.

2. The small settlement at Warm Springs was officially established as the town of Bath in 1776 but continued to be known also as Warm Springs and Berkeley Springs. GW left Happy Retreat "after dinner" and stayed the night at a farm near Martinsburg.

5th. Dispatched my Waggon (with the Baggage) at day light; and at 7 Oclock followed it. About 5 Oclock P.M. we arrived at the Springs, or Town of Bath—after travelling the whole day through a drizling rain, 30 Miles.

6th. Remained at Bath all day and was shewed the Model of a Boat constructed by the ingenious Mr. Rumsey, for ascending rapid currents by mechanism; the principles of this were not only shewn, & fully explained to me, but to my very great satisfaction, exhibited in practice in private, under the injunction of Secresy, untill he saw the effect of an application he was about to make to the assembly of this State, for a reward.

The model, & its operation upon the water, which had been made to run pretty swift, not only convinced me of what I before thought next to, if not quite impracticable, but that it might be turned to the greatest possibile utility in inland Navigation; and in rapid currents; that are shallow. And what adds vastly to the value of the discovery, is the simplicity of its works; as they may be made by a common boat builder or carpenter, and kept in order as easy as a plow, or any common implement of husbandry on a farm.[1]

Having obtained a Plan of this Town (Bath) and ascertained the situation of my lots therein, which I examined; it appears that the disposition of a dwelling House; Kitchen & Stable cannot be more advantageously placed than they are marked in the copy I have taken from the plan of the Town; to which I refer for recollection, of my design; & Mr. Rumsey being willing to undertake those Buildings, I have agreed with him to have them finished by the 10th. of next July.[2]

Having hired three Pack horses—to give my own greater relief—I sent my Baggage of this day about one oclock, and ordered those who had charge of it, to proceed to one Headricks at 15 Miles Creek, distant abt. ten miles, to Night, and to the old Town next day.

1. James Rumsey (1743–1792) of Bath was a handsome and engaging jack-of-all-trades. Born in Cecil County, Md., he moved to the Warm Springs area from Baltimore about 1782, and although a man of relatively limited means and education, he soon had become owner of a sawmill and bloomery, partner in a store, contractor for building new bathhouses, and operator with Robert Throckmorton (Throgmorton) of a new boardinghouse "at the Sign of the Liberty Pole and Flag" (*Md. Journal,* 15, 25 June 1784).

GW lodged at the boardinghouse and there probably met Rumsey, whose chief interest, he found, was not business but mechanical invention. The small model of the mechanical boat that GW saw today was designed somewhat paradoxically to be propelled foward by the force of the current against which it was to move. The "boat" actually consisted of two boats with a paddle wheel mounted between them. As the wheel turned with the current, it operated poles that were supposed to push against the river bottom, making the vessel "walk" upstream. Before leaving Bath, GW gave Rumsey a certificate attesting to the potential value of the invention and his faith in its ultimate success (*Papers, Confederation Series,* 1:69).

2. In 1777 Fielding Lewis had secured lots 58 and 59 in the new town of Bath for GW at a cost of £100 15s. Virginia money. To maintain title to these lots, GW was now obliged by law to build "a dwelling-house twelve feet square at least" on each one by 1 Nov. 1785 (Hening, 9:247–49, 460, 10:108–9, 11:26).

8th. Set out about 7 oclock with the Doctr. (Craik) his Son William, and my Nephew Bushrod Washington;[1] who were to make the tour with us. About ten I parted with them at 15 Miles Creek, & recrossed the Potomack (having passed it abt. 3 Miles from the Springs before) to a tract of mine on the Virginia side which I find exceedingly rich, & must be very valuable. . . . After having reviewed this Land I again recrossed the river & getting into the Waggon road pursued my journey to the old Town where I overtook my Company & baggage. Lodged at Colo. Cresaps—abt. 35 Miles this day.[2]

1. William Craik (b. 1761) studied law and began practice, probably about this time, in Charles and St. Mary's counties, Md. Bushrod Washington (1762–1829), eldest son of John Augustine and Hannah Bushrod Washington, was long a favorite of GW. After attending the College of William and Mary, Bushrod served briefly as a volunteer cavalryman during the Virginia campaign of 1781 and early the following year went to Philadelphia, where with the help of a recommendation and 100 guineas from GW, he began studying law under politically prominent James Wilson. His studies were now finished, and he was on the verge of setting up practice in Virginia.

2. Col. Thomas Cresap, now about 90 years old, had been blind for several months, but a visitor to Oldtown in May 1785 reported, "his other faculties are yet unimpaired his sense Strong and Manly and his Ideas flow with ease" (Mathews, *Andrew Ellicott*, 34).

10th. Set off a litle after 5 Oclock altho' the morning was very unpromising. Finding from the rains that had fallen, and description of the Roads, part of which between the old Town & this place (old Fort Cumberland)[1] we had passed, that the progress of my Baggage would be tedeous, I resolved (it being Necessary) to leave it to follow; and proceed on myself to Gilbert Simpson's, to prepare for the Sale which I had advertised of my moiety of the property in co-partnership with him and to make arrangements for my trip to the Kanhawa, if the temper & disposition of the Indians should render it advisable to proceed. Accordingly, leaving Doctr. Craik, his Son, and my Nephew with it, I set out with one Servant only.

1. Abandoned since 1765, the fort lay in ruins. The town of Cumberland, Md., was laid out here in 1785 and was established officially by act of the General Assembly 20 Jan. 1787.

11th. Set out at half after 5 oclock[1] & in about 1½ Miles came to what is called the little crossing of Yohiogany—the road not bad.[2] This is a pretty considerable water and, as it is said to have no fall in it, may, I conceive, be improved into a valuable navigation. Bated at the great crossing [of the Youghiogheny], which is a large Water, distant from Mounts's 9 Miles.[3]

1. GW spent the previous night at the Red House tavern at Little Meadows. In 1784 it was operated by Jesse Tomlinson.

2. Little Crossing was a ford of the Little Youghiogheny (now Casselman) River about a mile east of present-day Grantsville, Md.

3. Joseph Mountain kept a tavern on the eastern slope of Negro Mountain in Washington (now Garrett) County, Md. "Mr. Mountain," reported a traveler in November of this year, "has a Sufficiency of Liquors and Provisions but falls short in the Article of Bedding—he has but three one Occupied by himself and Wife one by the small Children and the Other by the Bar-Maid" (Mathews, *Andrew Ellicott,* 27). Another traveler ten years later referred to the place as "Mountain's hovel" (Wellford, "Diary," 11).

12th. Left Daughertys about 6 Oclock, stopped a while at the Great Meadows, and viewed a tenament I have there,[1] which appears to have been but little improved, tho capable of being turned to great advantage, as the whole of the ground called the Meadows may be reclaimed at an easy comparative expence & is a very good stand for a Tavern. Much Hay may be cut here when the ground is laid down in Grass & the upland, East of the Meadow, is good for grain.

Dined at Mr. Thomas Gists at the Foot of Laurel [Hill], distant from the Meadows 12 Miles, and arrived at Gilbert Simpsons about 5 oclock 12 Miles further. Crossing the Mountains, I found tedeous and fatieguing. In passing over the Mountains, I met numbers of Persons & Pack horses going in with Ginsang;[2] & for salt & other articles at the Markets below; from most of whom I made enquiries of the Nature of the Country between the little Kanhawa and ten Miles Creek. I also endeavoured to get the best acct. I could of the Navigation of Cheat River, & find that the line which divides the States of Virginia & Pensylvania crosses the Monongahela above the Mouth of it; wch. gives the Command thereof to Pensylvania—that where this River (Cheat) goes through the Laurel hill, the Navigation is difficult; not from shallow, or rapid water, but from an immense quantity of large Stones, which stand so thick as to render the passage even of a short Canoe impracticable— but I could meet with no person who seemed to have any accurate knowledge of the Country between the navigable, or such part as could be made so, of this River & the No. Branch of Potomack. All seem to agree however that it is rought & a good way not to be found.

The Accts. given by those Whom I met of the late Murders, & general dissatisfaction of the Indians, occasioned by the attempt of our people to settle on the No. West side of the Ohio, which they claim as their territory; and our delay to hold a treaty with them, which they say is indicative of a hostile temper on our part, makes it rather improper for me to proceed to the Kanhawa agreeably to my original intention, especially as I learnt from some of them (one in particular) who lately left the Settlement of Kentucke that the Indians were generally in arms, & gone, or going, to attack some of our Settlements below and that a Party Who had drove Cattle to Detroit had one of their Company & several of their Cattle killed by the Indians—but as these Accts. will either be contradicted or confirmed by some whom I may meet at my Sale the 15th. Instt. my final determination shall be postponed 'till then.

1. GW spent the night of 11 Oct. at James Daugherty's house, "a mile & half short of the Great Meadows—a tolerable good House" (*Diaries*, 4:18). GW's 234½ acres at Great Meadows were offered for lease on a ten-year term to the highest bidder at Washington's Bottom 15 Sept. (GW's advertisement, in *Va. Journal*, 15 July 1784). Writing to Thomas Freeman about the Great Meadows tract on 23 Sept. 1784, GW noted that "there is a house on the premises, arable land in culture, and meadow inclosed."

2. North American ginseng, *Panax quinquefolius*, was a staple of the China trade, being a common substitute for the oriental variety, *P. schinseng*, roots of which the Chinese used extensively in medicines.

13th. I visited my Mill, and the several tenements on this Tract (on which Simpson lives). I do not find the Land in *general* equal to my expectation of it. Some part indeed is as rich as can be, some other part is but indifferent.

The Tenements, with respect to buildings, are but indifferently improved—each have Meadow and arable [land], but in no great quantity. The Mill was quite destitute of Water. The works & House appear to be in very bad condition and no reservoir of Water—the stream as it runs, is all the resource it has. . . . In a word, little rent, or good is to be expected from the present aspect of her.[1]

1. GW had spared little expense in making this large stone gristmill as fine as possible. Its construction, which had taken nearly two years, cost him between £1,000 and £1,200. Equipped with two pairs of millstones made of local rock, which the alcoholic but skilled millwright Dennis Stephens deemed "equal to English burr," the mill was supposed to grind "incredibly fast" when working (GW's advertisement, in *Va. Journal*, 15 July 1784). The shambles that GW found today in his first view of the mill should not have surprised him knowing what he did of his partner and manager Gilbert Simpson. "I never hear of the Mill under the direction of Simpson," he wrote Lund Washington 20 Aug. 1775, "without a degree of warmth & vexation at his extreame stupidity."

14th. Remained at Mr. Gilbert Simpsons all day. Before Noon Colo. Willm. Butler[1] and the Officer Commanding the Garrison at Fort Pitt, a Captn. Lucket[2] came here. As they confirmed the reports of the discontented temper of the Indians and the Mischiefs done by some parties of them and the former advised me not to prosecute my intended trip to the Great Kanhawa, I resolved to decline it.[3]

This day also, the people who lives on my land on Millers run came here to set forth their pretensions to it; & to enquire into my right. After much conversation, & attempts in them to discover all the flaws they could in my Deed, &ca.; & to establish a fair and upright intention in themselves; and after much Councelling which proceeded from a division of opinion among themselves—they resolved (as all who live on the Land were not here) to give me their definitive determination when I should come to the Land, which I told them would probably happen on Friday or Saturday next.[4]

1. William Butler (1745–1789), of Pittsburgh, was an Indian trader in the Ohio Valley.

2. David Luckett of Maryland had very recently assumed command of the small detachment of underpaid and ill-clad Marylanders who currently occupied Fort Pitt.

3. The danger was real, according to Thomas Freeman. "Had you Proceded on you[r] Tour down the River," Freeman wrote GW 9 June 1785, "I believe it would have been attended with the most dreadfull Consequences. The Indians by what means I can't say had Intelligence of your Journey and Laid wait for you. Genl. [James] Wilkinson fell in their Hands and was taken for you and with much difficulty of Persuasion & Gifts got away. This is the Common Report & I believe the Truth."

4. GW's 2,813-acre tract on Millers Run, a branch of Chartier's Creek, lay in Washington County about eight miles northwest of present-day Canonsburg, Pa. William Crawford surveyed this tract for GW in 1771, but almost from the start Crawford was hard put to keep unauthorized settlers off it. To protect GW's claim he built four cabins on the tract in 1772 and engaged a man to stay there (Crawford to GW, 1 May 1772). Ten or twelve persons occupied the tract in the fall of 1773 without purchasing or leasing from GW.

On 5 July 1774 GW obtained a patent for his Millers Run land from Virginia, which was then disputing Pennsylvania's jurisdiction over what is now southwestern Pennsylvania. Although Virginia gave up its rights to the area six years later, its grants there remained valid, being recognized by Pennsylvania as the price for Virginia's concession. Nevertheless, the people on Millers Run questioned GW's title on grounds that Crawford was not a Virginia county surveyor in 1771; that his survey was registered and the patent granted after they moved on the land; and that the tract was deserted when they occupied it. For a detailed account of GW's difficulties with the squatters on his Millers Run land and the legal aftermath, see *Papers, Confederation Series,* 2:338–58.

15th. This being the day appointed for the Sale of my moiety of the Co-partnership stock—Many People were gathered (more out of curiosity I believe than from other motives) but no great Sale made. My Mill I could obtain no bid for, altho I offered an exemption from the payment of Rent 15 Months. The Plantation on which Mr. Simpson lives rented well—Viz. for 500 Bushels of Wheat payable at any place with in the County that I, or my Agent should direct. The little chance of getting a good offer in money, for Rent, induced me to set it up to be bid for in Wheat.

Not meeting with any person who could give me a satisfactory acct. of the Navigation of the Cheat River . . . I gave up the intention of returning home that way—resolving after settling matters with those Persons who had seated my Lands on Millers run, to return by the way I came; or by what is commonly called the Turkey foot Road.[1]

    1. Turkey Foot Road, a relatively new alternative to much of Braddock's Road, offered travelers a more direct route between Fort Cumberland and Fort Pitt than had previously been available.

16th. Continued at Simpsons all day—in order to finish the business which was begun yesterday. Gave leases to some of my Ten[an]ts on the Land whereon I now am.[1]

    1. GW's tract at Washington's Bottom contained, besides Simpson's 600-acre plantation and the mill tract, five small farms leased to tenants. Some of the tenants were much behind in their rent, and as there was evidently some confusion, real or feigned, about the terms under which they were leasing, GW today took the opportunity to explain his terms in person and to make new and apparently more stringent leases with them.

17th. Detained here by a settled Rain the whole day—which gave me time to close my accts. with Gilbert Simpson, & put a final end to my Partnership with him. Agreed this day with a Major Thomas Freeman to superintend my business over the Mountains, upon terms to be inserted in his Instructions.[1]

    1. Thomas Freeman of Red Stone served as GW's western agent until the spring of 1787, when he moved to Kentucky.

18th. Set out with Doctr. Craik for my Land on Millers run (a branch of Shurtees [Chartier's] Creek). . . .

19th. Being Sunday, and the People living on my Land, *apparently* very religious, it was thought best to postpone going among them till tomorrow.[1]

    1. These settlers were members of the Associate Presbyterian Church, commonly called the Seceders' Church, a Presbyterian sect that had broken with the main church in 1733 in a dispute over lay control, especially in the calling of ministers.

20th. Went early this Morning to view my Land, & to receive the final determination of those who live upon it.

Dined at David Reeds, after which Mr. James Scot & Squire [John] Reed began to enquire whether I would part with the Land, & upon what terms; adding, that tho' they did not conceive they could be dispossed, yet to avoid contention, they would buy, if my terms were moderate. I told them I had no inclination to sell; however, after hearing a great deal of their hardships, their religious principles (which had brought them together as a society of Ceceders) and unwilling-

ness to seperate or remove; I told them I would make them a last offer
and this was—the whole tract at 25/. pr. Acre, the money to be paid at
3 annual payments with Interest; or to become Tenants upon leases of
999 years, at the annual Rent of Ten pounds pr. ct. pr. Ann. The former
they had a long consultation upon, & asked if I wd. take that price at
a longer credit, without Interest, and being answered in the negative
they then determined to stand suit for the Land; but it having been
suggested that there were among them some who were disposed to
relinquish their claim, I told them I would receive their answers individually; and accordingly calling upon them as they stood.

They severally answered, that they meant to stand suit, & abide the
Issue of the Law.[1]

This business being thus finished, I returned to Colo. Cannons[2] in
company with himself, Colo. Nevil,[3] Captn. Swearingen (high Sherif)[4]
& a Captn. Richie,[5] who had accompanied me to the Land.

1. According to a Reed family tradition, GW today replied to James Scott
and the Reeds "with dignity and some warmth, asserting that they had been
forewarned by his agent, and the nature of his claim fully made known; that
there could be no doubt of its validity, and rising from his seat and holding
a red silk handkerchief by one corner, he said, 'Gentlemen, I will have this
land just as surely as I now have this handkerchief'" (Crumrine, *History of
Washington County*, 858–59).

The unexpected unity with which the Millers Run people stood against
GW today was attributed by GW and his Pennsylvania lawyer Thomas Smith
to the influence of James Scott, Jr., whom Smith viewed as "the ringleader or
director of the rest" (Smith to GW, 7 Nov. 1786, *Papers, Confederation Series,*
4:339–43). GW's suit apparently was considered to be somewhat of a test
case: "I have . . . been told," GW wrote Edmund Randolph 13 Aug. 1785,
"that the decision of this case will be interesting to numbers whose rights
are disputed on similar grounds" (ibid., 3:179–81). Nevertheless, all of the
defendants fought GW to the last in court (Smith to GW, 7 Nov. 1786, ibid.,
4:339–43).

2. John Cannon (d. 1799), of Washington County, owned about 800 acres
on Chartier's Creek, site of present-day Canonsburg, Pa. Cannon acted as
GW's western agent 1786–94 but proved unsatisfactory in his attention to
GW's business.

3. Presley Neville (1756–1818), a well-to-do young man, lived on Chartier's Creek about six miles west of Pittsburgh in a house known as Woodville.
Nearby on the opposite side of the creek stood Bower Hill, home of his father, John Neville (1731–1803).

4. Van Swearingen (died c.1793) was high sheriff of Washington County
from Nov. 1781 to Nov. 1784. He and his brother Andrew Swearingen apparently moved to this area from Virginia in the early 1770s.

5. Matthew Ritchie (d. 1798), of Washington County, was a well-to-do
bachelor who over a period of years acquired large landholdings in southwestern Pennsylvania. He was a county representative to the General Assembly 1782–84 and became a judge of the county court of common pleas

in 1784. Ritchie bought all of GW's land on Millers Run 1 June 1796 for $12,000.

21st. Colo. Cannon, Captn. Sweringin & Captn. Richie all promised to hunt up the Evidences which could prove my possession & improvement of the Land before any of the present Occupiers ever saw it.

22d. After giving instructions to Major Thomas Freeman respecting his conduct in my business, and disposing of my Baggage which was left under the care of Mr. Gilbert Simpson—consisting of two leather & one linnen Valeses with my Marquee & horseman's Tent Tent Poles & Pins—all my bedding except Sheets (which I take home with me)— the equipage Trunk containing all that was put into it except the Silver Cups and Spoons—Canteens—two Kegs of Spirits—Horse Shoes &ca.[1] I set out for Beason Town,[2] in order to meet with & engage Mr. Thos. Smith to bring Ejectments, & to prosecute my Suit for the Land in Washington County, on which those, whose names are herein inserted, are settled.[3] Reached Beason Town about dusk about (the way I came) 18 Miles.

Note. In my equipage Trunk and the Canteens—were Madeira and Port Wine—Cherry bounce[4]—Oyl, Mustard—Vinegar and Spices of all sorts—Tea, and Sugar in the Camp Kettles (a whole loaf of white sugar broke up, about 7 lbs. weight). The Camp Kettles are under a lock, as the Canteens & Trunk also are. My fishing lines are in the Canteens.

At Beason Town I met with Captn. Hardin[5] who informed me, as I had before been informed by others, that the West fork of Monongahela communicates very nearly with the waters of the little Kanhawa. From this information I resolved to return home that way; & My baggage under the care of Doctr. Craik and Son, having, from Simpsons, taken the rout by the New (or Turkey foot) road as it is called (which is said to be 20 Miles near than Braddocks) with a view to make a more minute enquiry into the Navigation of the Yohiggany Waters—my Nephew and I set out about Noon, with one Colo. Philips for Cheat River;[6] after I had engaged Mr. Smith to undertake my business, & had given him such information As I was able to do.

1. GW obviously anticipated returning to this area at some future date, possibly as early as the next spring. He could not know that he would never again come so far west.

2. Beeson's Town (now Uniontown) was laid out on the upper reaches of Red Stone Creek in 1776.

3. Thomas Smith, whom GW had known in Philadelphia before the war, had recently established a law practice in Carlisle, Pa., from whence he made regular circuits of the western courts. At Uniontown he and GW agreed on a basic strategy for prosecuting the people on Millers Run: the cases would be

removed as soon as possible from the relatively hostile Washington County court to the friendlier Pennsylvania Supreme Court, members of which periodically rode circuit across the mountains from Philadelphia to hold sessions in the western counties. Although the cases in either court would be tried before a jury of western Pennsylvanians, the Supreme Court justices could be expected to make out a less hostile jury list and to rule much more favorably on points of law. GW's suits were tried before Supreme Court justice Thomas McKean in Washington County 24–26 Oct. 1786, with Hugh Henry Brackenridge defending the squatters. See *Papers, Confederation Series*, 2: 338–58. In each instance the jury returned a verdict for GW, and the settlers vacated his land soon afterwards.

4. A drink "made by steeping cherries in brandy with sugar."

5. John Hardin (1753–1792), a miller and experienced Indian fighter, lived on George's Creek in southwestern Fayette County. Hardin moved his wife and children to Kentucky in 1786 and participated in several more Indian campaigns before his death at the hands of Indians while acting as an emissary from the United States to the western tribes.

6. GW and Bushrod Washington were to meet the Craiks at Warner Washington's house in Frederick County, Va.

Theophilus Phillips (died c.1789), of Fayette County, lived about 22 miles north of the mouth of the Cheat River near present-day New Geneva, Pa. He came to this area in 1767, apparently from New Jersey.

23d. Arrived at Colo. Philips abt. five oclock in the afternoon 16 Miles from Beason Town & near the Mouth of Cheat Rivr. Finding by enquiries that the Cheat River had been passed with Canoes thro' those parts which had been represented as impassable and that a Captn. Hanway—the Surveyor of Monongahela County lived within two or three Miles of it, Southside thereof;[1] I resolved to pass it to obtain further information, & accordingly (accompanied by Colo. Philips) set of in the Morning of the

1. Samuel Hanway (1743–1834) became surveyor of Monongalia County 3 June 1783. He apparently moved to Monongalia County about the time of his appointment.

24th. And crossed it at the Mouth, as it was thought the river was too much swelled to attempt the ford a little higher up. From the Fork to the Surveyors Office, which is at the house of one Pierpoint, is about 8 Miles along the dividing ridge.[1] At this Office I could obtain no information of any Surveys or Entries made for me by Captn. Wm. Crawford; but from an examination of his books it appeared pretty evident that the 2500 acres which he (Crawford) had surveyed for & offered to me on the little Kanhawa (adjoining the large Survey under the proclamation of 1754) he had entered for Mr. Robert Rutherford and that the other tract in the fork between the Ohio & little Kanhawa had been entered by Doctr. Briscoe & Sons.[2]

1. John Pierpont (d. 1795) settled here before the War of Independence and married Ann (Nancy) Morgan, daughter of Col. Zackquill Morgan.

2. For an account of this land and the holdings of Robert Rutherford and Dr. John Biscoe, see *Diaries*, 4:41–42.

25th. Having obtained the foregoing information, and being indeed some what discouraged from the acct. given of the passage of the Cheat river through the Laurel hill and also from attempting to return by the way of the Dunkers bottom, as the path it is said is very blind, & exceedingly grown up with briers, I resolved to try the other rout, along the New road to Sandy Creek; & thence by McCullochs path to Logstons; and accordingly set of before Sunrise. From Lemons[1] to the entrance of the Yohiogany glades which is estimated 9 Miles more thro a deep rich Soil in some places, and a very rocky one in others, with steep hills & what is called the briery Mountain to cross is intolerable[2] but these [ascents] might be eased, & a much better way found if a little pains was taken to slant them.

At the entrance of the above glades I lodged this night, with no other shelter or cover than my cloak; & was unlucky enough to have a heavy shower of Rain. Our horses were also turned loose to cator for themselves having nothing to give them. From this place my guide (Lemon) informed me that the Dunkers bottom was not more than 8 Miles from us.

It may not be amiss to observe, that Sandy Creek has a fall within a few miles of its mouth of 40 feet, & being rapid besides, affords no navigation at all.

1. George Lemon appears in the 1782 Monongalia County census as refusing to give the number of persons in his household. In 1785 he was granted 355 acres on Crab Orchard Creek in the county (*Heads of Families, Va.,* 36).

2. Briery Mountain stretches across the eastern half of present-day Preston County, W.Va., running from the Cheat River near Rowlesburg northeast toward Cranesville, in the vicinity of which GW crossed today.

26th. Having found our Horses readily (for they nevr. lost sight of our fire) we started at the dawning of day, and passing along a small path much enclosed with weeds and bushes, loaded with water from the overnights rain, & the showers which were continually falling, we had an uncomfortable travel to one Charles friends, about 10 Miles; where we could get nothing for our horses, and only boiled Corn for ourselves.[1]

A Mile before I came to Friends, I crossed the Great branch of Yohiogany, which is about 25 or 30 yards over; and impassable, according to his Acct., between that [crossing] and Braddocks road [at the Great Crossing] on acct. of the rapidity of the Water, quantity of stone, & Falls therein—but these difficulties, in the eyes of a proper examiner might be found altogether imaginary; and if so, the Navigation of the Yohiogany & No. Branch of Potomack may be brought within 10 Miles, & a good Waggon road betwn.; but then, the Yohiogany lyes altogether in the State of Pensylvania, whose inclination (regardless of the interest of that part which lyes west of the Laurel hill) would be opposed to the extension of their navigation; as it would be the inevitable means of withdrawing from them the trade of all their western territory.

The little Yohiogany[2] from Braddocks road [at the Little Crossing] to the Falls [of the Youghiogheny River] below the Turkey foot, or 3 forks, may, in the opinion of Friend, who is a great Hunter, & well acquainted with all the Waters, as well as hills, having lived in that Country and followed no other occupation for nine years, be made navigable and this, were it not for the reason just assigned, being within 22 Miles of Fort Cumberland, would open a very important door to the trade of that Country.

1. Charles Friend, a squatter on a 5,025-acre glades tract called Small Meadows, lived about 1½ miles southwest of present-day Oakland, Md.

2. GW is referring to the Little Youghiogheny River (now Casselman River) that flows into the Youghiogheny at present-day Confluence, Pa. Another Little Youghiogheny flows into the Youghiogheny near the point where GW crossed it today.

27th. I left Mr. Logston's a little after day-break.[1] At 4 Miles thro' bad road, occasioned by Stone, I crossed the Stony River; which, as hath been before observed, appears larger than the No. Branch. My intention when I set out from Logstons, was to take the Road to Rumney by one Parkers;[2] but learning from my guide (Joseph Logston) when I came to the parting paths at the foot of the Alligany (abt. 12 Miles) that it was very little further to go by Fort pleasant, I resolved to take that Rout as it might be more in my power on that part of the Branch to get information of the extent of its navigation than I should be able to do at Rumney.

1. Thomas Logston lived in Hampshire County, Va. (now Grant County, W.Va.) about halfway between McCullough's crossing (near present-day Gormania, W.Va.) and the Stony River, a tributary of the North Branch of the Potomac.

2. Several Parkers lived west of Romney at this time on Mill, Patterson's, and New creeks.

28th. Remained at Colo. Hite's[1] all day to refresh myslf and rest my Horses, having had a very fatieguing journey thro' the Mountains, occasioned not more from the want of accomodation & the real necessaries of life than the showers of Rain which were continually falling &

wetting the bushes—the passing of which, under these circumstances was very little better than swimming of rivulets.

From Colo. Hite, Colo. Josh. Neville[2] & others, I understood that the navigation of the South Branch in its present State, is made use of from Fort pleasant to its Mouth—that the most difficult part in it, and that would not take £100 to remove the obstruction (it being only a single rift of rocks across in one place) is 2 Miles below the old Fort. That this [distance to the mouth of the river], as the road goes, is 40 Miles; by water more and that, from any thing they knew, or believe to the contrary, it might at this moment be used 50 Miles higher, if any benefits were to result from it.

1. Abraham Hite (1729–1790), a son of Jost Hite, settled in this part of Hampshire County (now Hardy County, W.Va.) about 1762 when he obtained two grants in the area. He apparently became county lieutenant of Hampshire about 1765 and represented the county in the House of Burgesses 1769–71. After service in the Revolution, Hite moved to Jefferson County, Ky., about 1788. GW had reached Hite's a little before sunset on 27 Oct. (*Diaries*, 4:50).

2. Joseph Neville (1740–1819) of Hampshire County became a justice of the county in 1772, served as one of its burgesses 1773–75, and represented it in the Virginia Convention that met 1 Dec. 1775. A military contractor and recruiter for the state during the early part of the War of Independence, he was appointed county lieutenant for Hampshire in 1781.

October

October 1st. Dined at Mr. Gabriel Jones's,[1] not half a mile from Mr. Lewis's, but seperated by the South fork of Shannondoah; which is between 80 and a hundred yards wide, & makes a respectable appearance altho' little short of 150 Miles from its confluence with Potomack River; and only impeded in its navigation by the rapid water & rocks which are between the old bloomery[2] and Keys's ferry; and a few other ripples; all of which might be easily removed and the navigation according to Mr. Lewis's account, extended at least 30 Miles higher than where he lives.

I had a good deal of conversation with this Gentleman on the Waters, and trade of the Western Country; and particularly with respect to the navigation of the Great Kanhawa and it's communication with James, & Roanoke Rivers.

1. From Abraham Hite's GW had traveled to Thomas Lewis's house near Staunton, Va., because Lewis had in his possession papers pertinent to GW's Millers Run suit. Lewis (1718–1790) was a brother of GW's deceased friend Andrew Lewis and was now surveyor of Rockingham County. Gabriel Jones (1724–1806), a competent but hot-tempered lawyer given to outbursts of profanity, had long been prominent in Shenandoah Valley affairs. To his con-

Gabriel Jones, "the Valley Lawyer," by Edward C. Bruce, after a painting by Gilbert Stuart. (Owned by Miss Louisa Morrow Crawford, Kernstown, Virginia)

temporaries he became known as "the Valley Lawyer." It was due in part to Jones's influence and activity that GW was first elected to the House of Burgesses from Frederick County in 1758.

2. Bloomery, W.Va.

2d. I set off very early from Mr. Lewis's who accompanied me to the foot of the blew ridge at Swift run gap,[1] 10 Miles, where I bated and proceeded over the Mountain. Dined at a pitiful house 14 Miles further where the roads to Fredericksburgh (by Orange C[our]t House) & that to Culpeper Court House fork.[2] Took the latter, tho in my judgment Culpeper Court House was too much upon my right for a direct

Course. Lodged at a Widow Yearlys 12 Miles further where I was hospitably entertained.[3]

1. Swift Run Gap, located about seven miles southeast of present-day Elkton, Va., long provided settlers and traders a convenient route across the Blue Ridge Mountains.

2. Traveling southeast from Swift Run Gap, GW passed through the western part of Orange County (now Greene County) and then turned northeast to cross the Rapidan River into the western part of Culpeper County (now Madison County). The Orange County Court House was at the site of the present-day county seat, Orange, Va., and the Culpeper County Court House was at the site of its present-day seat, Culpeper, Va.

3. *Widow Yearlys:* probably Jane Paschal Early, widow of Joseph Early (c.1740–1783) of Culpeper County, an active Baptist who served as a lieutenant in the 5th Virginia Regiment during the Revolution. She lived with her seven children about four miles southwest of present-day Madison, Va. According to a family tradition, GW gave a watch to one of the children during his stay (Early, *Family of Early*, 205–6).

3d. Left Quarters before day, and breakfasted at Culpeper Court house which was estimated 21 Miles, but by bad direction I must have travelled 25, at least.[1] Crossed Normans ford[2] 10 Miles from the Court Ho[use] and lodged at Captn. John Ashbys[3] occasioned by other bad directions, which took me out of the proper road, which ought to have been by Elk run Church[4] 3 or 4 Miles to the right.

1. GW took his breakfast at "Kemps" (Ledger B, 200).

2. Norman's ford on the Rappahannock River lay between Culpeper and Fauquier counties, about two miles south of present-day Remington.

3. John Ashby, whom GW had visited on the Shenandoah River in March 1748, bought land on Licking Run in southern Fauquier County in 1757 and moved there about 1760.

4. Elk Run Church, located on the headwaters of Elk Run in southern Fauquier County, was a handsome brick building finished in 1769.

4th. Notwithstanding a good deal of rain fell in the night and the continuance of it this morning (which lasted till about 10 Oclock) I breakfasted by Candlelight, and Mounted my horse soon after day break; and having Captn. Ashby for a guide thro' the intricate part of the Road (which ought, tho' I missed it, to have been by Prince William old Court Ho[use])[1] I arrived at Colchester, 30 Miles, to Dinner; and reached home before Sun down; having travelled on the same horses since the first day of September by the computed distances 680 Miles.

And tho' I was disappointed in one of the objects which induced me to undertake this journey namely to examine into the situation quality and advantages of the Land which I hold upon the Ohio and Great Kanhawa to take measures for rescuing them from the hands of Land Jobbers & Speculators—who I had been informed regardless of my legal & equitable rights, Patents, &ca.; had enclosed them within other

Surveys & were offering them for Sale at Philadelphia and in Europe. I say notwithstanding this disappointment, I am well pleased with my journey, as it has been the means of my obtaining a knowledge of facts—coming at the temper & disposition of the Western Inhabitants and making reflections thereon, which, otherwise, must have been as wild, incoher[ent], & perhaps as foreign from the truth, as the inconsistencys of the reports which I had received even from those to whom most credit seemed due, generally were.

These reflections remain to be summed up.

The more then the Navigation of Potomack is investigated, & duely considered, the greater the advantages arising from them appear.

The South, or principal branch of Shannondoah at Mr. Lewis's is, to traverse the river, at least 150 Miles from its mouth; all of which, except the rapids between the Bloomery and Keys's ferry, now is, or very easily may be made navigable for inland Craft, and extended 30 Miles higher. The South Branch of Potomack is already navigated from its Mouth to Fort Pleasant; which, as the road goes, is 40 computed Miles; & the only difficulty in the way (and that is a very trifling one) is just below the latter, where the River is hemmed in by the hills or Mountains on each side. From hence, in the opinion of Colo. Joseph Neville and others, it may, at the most trifling expense imaginable, be made navigable 50 Miles higher.

To say nothing then of the smaller Waters, [of the Potomac River], such as Pattersons Creek, Cacapehon [Cacapon River], Opeckon [Opequon Creek] &ca.; which are more or less Navigable; and of the branches on the Maryland side, these two alone (that is the South Branch & Shannondoah) would afford water transportation for all that fertile Country between the blew ridge and the Alligany Mountains; which is immense, but how trifling when viewed upon that immeasurable scale which is inviting our attention!

The Ohio River embraces this Commonwealth [Virginia] from its Northern, almost to its Southern limits. It is now, our western boundary & lyes nearly parallel to our exterior, & thickest settled Country.

Into this river French Creek, big bever Creek, Muskingham, Hockhocking, Scioto, and the two Miames (in its upper region) and many others (in the lower) pour themselves from the westward through one of the most fertile Country's of the Globe; by a long inland navigation; which, in its present state, is passable for Canoes and such other small craft as has, hitherto, been made use of for the Indian trade.

French Creek, down whh. I have myself come to Venango, from a lake near its source, is 15 Miles from Prisque Isle on lake Erie; and the Country betwn. quite level.[2] Both big bever Creek and Muskingham, communicate very nearly with Cayahoga; which runs into lake Erie; the portage with the latter (I mean Muskingham) as appears by the maps, is only one mile; and by many other accts. very little further; and so level between, that the Indians and Traders, as is affirmed, always drag their Canoes from one river to the other when they go to War—to hunt, or trade.[3] The great Miame, which runs into the Ohio, communicates with a river of the same name, as also with Sandusky, which empty themselves into lake Erie, by short and easy Portages.[4] And all of these are so many channels through which not only the produce of the New States, contemplated by Congress, but the trade of *all* the lakes, quite to that of the Wood,[5] may be conducted according to my information, and judgment—at least by one of the routs, thro' a shorter, easier, and less expensive communication than either of those which are now, or have been used with Canada, New Y[or]k or New Orleans.

That this may not appear an assertion, or even an opinion unsupported, I will examine matters impartially, and endeavor to state facts.

Detroit is a point, thro which the Trade of the Lakes Huron, & all those above it, must pass, if it centres in any State of the Union; or goes to Canada; unless it should pass by the River Outawais, which disgorge's itself into the St. Lawrence at Montreal and which necessity only can compel; as it is, from all accts., longer and of more difficult Navigation than the St. Lawrence itself.[6]

To do this, the Waters which empty into the Ohio on the East side, & which communicate nearest & best with those which run into the Atlantic, must also be delineated.

These are Monongahela and its branches viz., Yohiogany & Cheat and the little and great Kanhawas; and Greenbrier which emptys into the latter.

The first (unfortunately for us)[7] is within the jurisdiction of Pensylvania from its mouth to the fork of Cheat indeed 2 Miles higher—as (which is more to be regreted) the Yohiogany also is, till it crosses the line of Maryland; these Rivers, I am perswaded, afford *much* the shortest routs from the Lakes to the tide water of the Atlantic but are not under our controul; being subject to a power whose interest is opposed to the extension of their navigation, as it would be the inevitable means of withdrawing from Philadelphia all the trade of that part of its western territory, which lyes beyond the Laurel hill—Though any attempt of that Government to restrain it I am equally well perswaded, w[oul]d cause a seperation of their territory; there being sensible men among them who have it in contemplation at this moment—but this by the by. The little Kanhawa, which stands next in order, & by Hutchins's table of distances (between Fort Pit and the Mouth of the River Ohio)[8] is 184½ Miles below the Monongahela, is navigable between 40 and 50 Miles up, to a place called Bulls Town. Thence there is a Portage of

9½ Miles to the West fork of Monongahela. Thence along the same to the Mouth of Cheat River, and up it to the Dunker bottom; from whence a portage may be had to the No. branch of Potomack.

Next to the little is the great Kanhawa; which by the above Table is 98½ Miles still lower down the Ohio. This is a fine Navigable river to the Falls; the practicability of opening which, seems to be little understood; but most assuredly ought to be investigated.

These then are the ways by which the produce of that Country; & the peltry & fur trade of the Lakes may be introduced into this State [Virginia]; & into Maryld.; which stands upon similar ground. There are ways, more difficult & expenceve indeed by which they can also be carried to Philadelphia—all of which, with the rout to Albany, & Montreal, and the distances by Land, and Water, from place to place as far as can be ascertained by the best Maps now extant—by actual Surveys made since the publication of them and the information of intelligent persons—will appear as follow—from Detroit—which is a point as has been observed as unfavorable for us to compute from (being upon the North Western extremity of the United [States] territory) as any beyond Lake Erie can be:[9]

Admitting the preceding Statement, which as has been observed is given from the best and most authentic Maps and papers in my possession—from information and partly from observation, to be tolerably just, it would be nugatory to go about to prove that the Country within, and bordering upon the Lake Erie, Huron, & Michigan would be more convenient when they come to be settled—or that they would embrace with avidity our Markets, if we should remove the obstructions which are at present in the way to them.

It may be said, because it has been said, & because there are some examples of it in proof, that the Country of Kentucke, about the Falls, and even much higher up the Ohio, have carried flour and other Articles to New Orleans—but from whence has it proceeded? Will any one who has ever calculated the difference between Water & Land transportation wonder at this? Especially in an infant settlement where the people are poor and weak handed and pay more regard to their ease than to loss of time, or any other circumstance?

Hitherto, the people of the Western Country having had no excitements to Industry, labour very little; the luxuriency of the Soil, with very little culture, produces provisions in abundance. These supplies the wants of the encreasing population and the Spaniards, when pressed by want have given high prices for flour. Other articles they reject: & at times (contrary I think to sound policy) shut their ports against them altogether—but let us open a good communication with the Settlemts. west of us—extend the inland Navigation as far as it can be done with convenience and shew them by this means, how easy it is to bring the produce of their Lands to our Markets, and see how astonishingly our exports will be encreased; and these States benefitted in a commercial point of view—wch. alone, is an object of such Magnitude as to claim our closest attention—but when the subject is considered in a political point of view, it appears of much greater importance.

No well informed Mind need be told, that the flanks and rear of the United territory are possessed by other powers, and formidable ones too—nor how necessary it is to apply the cement of interest to bind all parts of it together, by one indissolvable band—particularly the Middle States with the Country immediately back of them. For what ties let me ask, should we have upon those people; and how entirely unconnected shod. we be with them if the Spaniards on their right, or Great Britain on their left, instead of throwing stumbling blocks in their way as they now do, should envite their trade and seek alliances with them? What, when they get strength which will be sooner than is generally imagined (from the emigration of Foreigners who can have no predeliction for us, as well as from the removal of our own Citizens) may be the consequence of their having formed such connections and alliances, requires no uncommon foresight to predict.

The Western Settlers—from my own observation—stand as it were on a pivet—the touch of a feather would almost incline them any way. They looked down the Mississipi until the Spaniards (very impoliticly I think for themselves) threw difficulties in the way, and for no other reason that I can conceive than because they glided gently down the stream, without considering perhaps the tedeousness of the voyage back, & the time necessary to perform it in; and because they have no other means of coming to us but by a long land transportation, & unimproved roads.

A combination of circumstances make the present conjecture more favorable than any other to fix the trade of the Western Country to our Markets. The jealous & untoward disposition of the Spaniards on one side, and the private views of some individuals, coinciding with the policy of the Court of G. Britain on the other, to retain the Posts of Oswego, Niagara, Detroit &ca. (which tho' done under the letter of the treaty is certainly an infraction of the Spirit of it, & injurious to the Union) may be improved to the greatest advantage by this State [Virginia] if she would open her Arms, & embrace the means which are necessary to establish it. The way is plain & the expence, comparitively speaking deserves not a thought, so great would be the prize. The Western Inhabitants would do their part towards accomplishing it. Weak as they now are, they would, I am perswaded, meet us half way rather than be *driven* into the arms of, or be in any wise dependent upon, foreigners; the consequence of which would be, a seperation, or a War.

The way to avoid both, happily for us, is easy, and dictated by our clearest interests. It is to open a wide door, and make a smooth way for the produce of that Country to pass to our Markets before the trade may get into another channel. This, in my judgment, would dry up the other sources; or, if any part should flow down the Mississipi, from the Falls of the Ohio, in Vessels which may be built—fitted, for Sea & sold with their cargoes the proceeds I have no manner of doubt, will return this way; & that it is better to prevent an evil than to rectify a mistake none can deny; commercial connections, of all others, are most difficult to dissolve—if we wanted proof of this look to the avidity with which we are renewing, after a *total* suspension of Eight years our corrispondence with Great Britain; So, if we [Virginians] are supine; and suffer without a struggle the Settlers of the Western Country to form commercial connections with the Spaniards, Britons, or with any of the States in the Union we shall find it a difficult matter to dissolve them altho a better communication should, thereafter, be presented to them. Time only could effect it; such is the force of habit!

Rumseys discovery of working Boats against stream by mechanical powers principally, may not only be considered as a fortunate invention for these States in general but as one of those circumstances which have combined to render the present epocha favorable above all others for securing (if we are disposed to avail ourselves of them) a large portion of the produce of the Western Settlements, and of the Fur and Peltry of the Lakes, also—the importance of which alone, if there were no political considerations in the way, is immense.

It may be said perhaps, that as the most direct routs from the Lakes to the Navigation of Potomack are through the State of Pensylvania and the inter[es]t of that State opposed to the extension of the Waters of Monongahela, that a communication cannot be had either by the Yohiogany or Cheat River; but herein I differ. An application to this purpose would, in my opinion, place the Legislature of that Commonwealth in a very delicate situation. That it would not be pleasing I can readily conceive, but that they would refuse their assent, I am by no means clear in. There is, in that State, at least 100,000 Souls West of the Laurel hill, who are groaning under the inconveniences of a long land transportation. They are wishing, indeed looking, for the extension of inland navigation; and if this can not be made easy for them to Philadelphia—at any rate it must be lengthy—they will seek a mart elsewhere; and none is so convenient as that which offers itself through Yohiogany or Cheat River. The certain consequence therefore of an attempt to restrain the extension of the navigation of these rivers (so consonant with the interest of these people) or to impose any extra duties upon the exports, or imports, to, or from another State, would be a seperation of the Western Settlers from the old & more interior government; towards which there is not wanting a disposition at this moment in the former.

1. This Prince William County courthouse, which served the county from c.1743 to c.1760, stood near a branch of Cedar Run about three miles southwest of present-day Independent Hill, Va.

2. GW traveled down French Creek from Fort Le Boeuf (now Waterford, Pa.) to Venango (now Franklin, Pa.) 16–22 Dec. 1753. Lake Le Boeuf, near which the fort stood, lay south of Presque Isle (now Erie, Pa.).

3. The headwaters of the Cuyahoga River, the Tuscarawas River (a major branch of the Muskingum River), and the Mahoning River (a major branch of the Beaver River) all lie near one another in the vicinity of present-day Akron, Ohio. The mouth of the Cuyahoga is at present-day Cleveland, Ohio.

4. The Miami River flowing into Lake Erie is now called the Maumee, a corruption of its earlier name. It is the Auglaize River, one of the Maumee's main branches, that runs close to the Great Miami River, the two rivers having headwaters near one another in the area southeast of present-day Lima, Ohio.

The Sandusky River comes within about 35 miles of the source of the Great Miami near present-day Upper Sandusky, Ohio, but it lies much closer there to the headwaters of the Scioto River, another tributary of the Ohio.

5. The Lake of the Woods lies on the border between the United States and Canada west of the Great Lakes.

6. The Ottawa (Outauais) River flows for most of its length along the border between the Canadian provinces of Quebec and Ontario, entering the St. Lawrence River a few miles west of Montreal.

7. Virginians.

8. This table is an appendix to Thomas Hutchins, *A Topographical Description of Virginia, Pennsylvania, Maryland and North Carolina* (London, 1778).

9. At this point in the diary GW inserted a table of distances, probably based on Hutchins's *Topographical Description*. See *Diaries*, 4:62–65.

1785

January

First Monday. Colo. Bassett, who brought his daughter Fanny to this place to remain on the 24th. of last Month set off on his return to the Assembly now sitting at Richmond.

I took a ride to my Plantations in the Neck, & called to see my neighbour Humphrey Peake who has been long afflicted with ill health and appears to be in the last stage of life & very near his end.

Frances (Fanny) Bassett's mother, Anna Maria Dandridge Bassett, had died in 1777, and since then Fanny seems to have spent much time visiting various

Martha Washington's grand-
daughter Eliza Parke Custis,
painted by Robert Edge Pine.
(Washington and Lee University,
Washington-Custis-Lee Collection)

Martha Washington's grand-
daughter Martha Parke Custis,
painted by Robert Edge Pine.
(Mount Vernon Ladies' Associa-
tion of the Union)

relatives. She came to Mount Vernon in Dec. 1784 to make her permanent home with her aunt and uncle.

Monday 3d. Doctr. Stuart—his wife Betcy & Patcy Custis who had been here since the 27th. ulto. returned home.

> Dr. David Stuart (1753–c.1814) had, late in 1783, married John Parke Custis's widow, Eleanor Calvert Custis. Stuart attended the College of William and Mary and graduated from the University of Edinburgh in 1777. He practiced medicine in Alexandria and at this time was living four miles above the city. Elizabeth Parke (Betsy) Custis (1776–1832) and Martha Parke (Patsy) Custis (1777–1854), the two eldest children of John Parke Custis, lived with their mother and stepfather. The two youngest children, who were informally adopted by GW and Mrs. Washington, lived at Mount Vernon. Stuart was a member of the Virginia Assembly 1785–88 and of the Virginia ratifying convention of 1788 and was one of the first three commissioners appointed by GW for the District of Columbia. About 1792 he moved his family to his Hope Park farm and, in later life, to Ossian Hall, both in Fairfax County. In the 1780s Stuart served as translator for the many French letters that GW received, and during the presidency he helped to keep GW informed of public sentiments in Virginia.

Friday 7th. Preparing my dry well, and the Well in my New Cellar for the reception of Ice.

> The well in the new cellar was to prove unsatisfactory. The dry well that GW used as an icehouse was first mentioned in 1773, when it was being repaired

Eleanor ("Nelly") Parke Custis, Martha Washington's grand-daughter, as painted by Robert Edge Pine. (Mount Vernon Ladies' Association of the Union)

George Washington Parke Custis, Martha Washington's grandson, as painted by Robert Edge Pine. (Washington and Lee University, Washington-Custis-Lee Collection)

(Ledger B, 140). It was located at the southeast corner of the river lawn. In 1784 GW had considered building a new icehouse but decided instead to repair and improve the old one. On 2 June he wrote Robert Morris that the snow with which he had packed his icehouse was already gone and requested advice and a description of Morris's icehouse. Morris suggested, among other things, that GW not use snow but pound ice into small pieces so it would freeze into a mass (Morris to GW, 15 June 1784, *Papers, Confederation Series*, 1:450–52).

Wednesday 12th. Road to my Mill Swamp, where my Dogue run hands were at work & to other places in search of the sort of Trees I shall want for my walks, groves, & Wildernesses.

At the Sein Landing & between that & the point at the old Brick kiln I found about half a dozn. young Elm trees, but not very promising ones. Many thriving ash trees on high (at least dry) ground of proper size for transplanting and a great abundance of the red-bud of all sizes. About Sundown Lewis Lemart—one of my Tenants in Fauquier & Collector of the Rents arising from the Tract on which he lives came in with some money & stayed all Night.

Walks, groves, & Wildernesses: Before the Revolution, GW designed a formal English landscape for the western front of Mount Vernon. Little work was done on it, however, until after the war. The design called for a small circular courtyard, bounded by a carriage road. Beyond this was to be a bowling green with a serpentine drive bordering both sides down to a gate at the road. On the outer edges of this serpentine drive, between the drive and the north and south gardens, were what GW called his shrubberies and wildernesses. The shrubberies extended from each side of the courtyard to a point just beyond the gardens, while the wildernesses, more thickly planted areas, stretched from the shrubberies to the road. At the north and south ends of the mansion were to be thick plantings of trees which GW called his groves.

Monday 17th. Went to and returned from Alexandria to day. At my return found dispatches from the assembly respecting the Potomack Navigation.

The "dispatches" were sent by William Grayson. See *Diaries*, 4:77. Also included in today's dispatches from Grayson was a letter to GW from James Madison (1751–1836), member of the Virginia House of Delegates for Orange County (*Papers, Confederation Series*, 2:260–61). Madison had visited Mount Vernon just before the fall 1784 session of the Virginia General Assembly in which he shepherded the Potomac and James River navigation bills through the lower house. In his letter to GW he enclosed three resolutions regarding internal improvements passed in that session.

Tuesday 18th. Sent the dispatches which came to me yesterday to Messrs. Fitzgerald and Hartshorne (managers named in the act for improving & extending the Navigation of Potomack and) who are appointed to receive Subscriptions—that they might get copies of the Act printed and act under them.

William Hartshorne, a Pennsylvania Quaker, was a merchant in Alexandria. He was elected treasurer of the Potomac Company on 17 May 1785 and served until Jan. 1800.

Wednesday 19th. Just as we had done dinner a Mr. Watson—late of the House of Watson & Cossoul of Nantes—and a Mr. Swift Merchant in Alexandria came in, and stayed all Night.

Elkanah Watson (1758–1842), born in Massachusetts, was apprenticed just before the Revolution to John Brown, of Providence, a merchant who became active in importing gunpowder and other supplies for the army. In 1779 Watson went to France as agent for Brown and others. He opened a mercantile business in Nantes in partnership first with Benjamin Franklin's grandnephew, Jonathan Williams, and later with François Cassoul (Cossoul). The business failed in 1783, and Watson returned to the United States in 1784 (Hedges, *Browns of Providence*, 245–54). He came to Mount Vernon bearing a gift for GW from Granville Sharp, the British philanthropist and founder of the colony of Sierra Leone in Africa. Sharp had entrusted to Watson two bundles of books for GW, "embracing his entire publications on emancipation and other congenial topics" (Watson, *Men and Times of the Revolution*, 233). During his visit to Mount Vernon, Watson and GW discussed canals at great length, and particularly the Potomac Company and its plans for navigation of that river (ibid., 244–45).

Jonathan Swift (d. 1824) was a merchant who had moved to Alexandria from New England sometime before 1785.

Thursday 27th. Made Mr. & Mrs. Lund Washington a mornings visit—from thence I went to Belvoir and viewed the ruined Buildings of that place.

> In 1779 Lund Washington married his cousin Elizabeth Foote, daughter of Richard Foote of Prince William County. The couple lived at Mount Vernon until 1784 when they moved into their newly built home, Hayfield, located on the Alexandria Road five miles south of Alexandria.
> *Ruined Buildings:* Belvoir had been badly damaged by fire in 1783. GW wrote George William Fairfax, 27 Feb. 1785, of this visit to Fairfax's former home: "I took a ride there the other day to visit the ruins—& ruins indeed they are. The dwelling house & the two brick buildings in front, underwent the ravages of the fire; the walls of which are very much injured: the other Houses are sinking under the depredation of time & inattention, & I believe are now scarcely worth repairing. In a word, the whole are, or very soon will be a heap of ruin. When I viewed them—when I considered that the happiest moments of my life had been spent there—when I could not trace a room in the house (now all rubbish) that did not bring to my mind the recollection of pleasing scenes; I was obliged to fly from them; & came home with painful sensations, & sorrowing for the contrast" (*Papers, Confederation Series*, 2:386–90). In 1814 the remaining walls of Belvoir were leveled by shells from British ships.

Monday 31st. About one oclock Mr. Wm. Hunter of Alexa. with a Mr. Hadfield (a Manchester Mercht.) recommended by Colo. Sam Smith of Baltimore & Colo. Fitzgerald & a Mr. Dawson came in. Dined & returned to Alexandria.

> William Hunter, Jr. (1731–1792), a Scottish-born merchant of Alexandria, carried on extensive trade with London and Liverpool. He was a member of GW's Masonic lodge and mayor of the city 1788–90.
> Joseph Hadfield (1759–1851), a member of the Manchester firm of Hadfield & Co., was one of a host of British agents who came to America after the Revolution to try to collect pre-Revolutionary debts owed to their firms by American merchants.
> Samuel Smith (1752–1839) served in the Continental Army 1775–79 and after the war returned to his father's mercantile house in Baltimore, becoming a prosperous trader and land speculator.
> *Mr. Dawson* was possibly George Dawson, a friend of Hadfield who had served under Banastre Tarleton during the Revolution as a captain in the King's Orange Rangers, a Loyalist company. He accompanied Hadfield on some of his travels through the colonies.

February

Wednesday 2d. The Snow this morning is about 9 Inches deep & pretty well compressed. Employed myself (as there could be no stirring without) in writing Letters by the Post and in Signing 83 Diplomas for the members of the Society of the Cincinnati.

The Society of the Cincinnati, founded in 1783, was open to American officers who had served for three years in the army or were in the army at the
end of the Revolution and to French officers of the rank of colonel and
above. Later, naval officers were also included. The hereditary nature of the
new society in particular aroused much bitter opposition. GW was the society's first president. It was usual practice for GW to sign blank diplomas and
send them to the state secretaries to be completed and issued to members.

Sunday 6th. Doctr. Brown was sent for to Frank (waiter in the House)
who had been seized in the Night, with a bleeding of the Mouth from
an Orifice made by a Doctr. Dick who some days before attempted in
vain to extract a broken tooth & coming about 11 Oclock stayed to
Dinner & returned afterwards.

Elisha Cullen Dick (1762–1825), of Alexandria, was a Pennsylvanian who
had received his medical degree from the University of Pennsylvania in 1782.
He settled in Alexandria after taking his degree and soon became a popular
member of Alexandria society.

Tuesday 8th. Finding that I should be very late in preparing my Walks
& Shrubberies if I waited till the ground should be uncovered by the
dissolution of the Snow—I had it removed Where necessary & began
to Wheel dirt into the Ha! Haws &ca.—tho' it was it exceeding miry &
bad working.

Ha! Haws, &ca.: A ha-ha wall was a sunken wall which prevented cattle from
approaching the house but left an uninterrupted view of the landscape.

Wednesday 9th. Transplanted an English Walnut tree from the Corner
near where the old School house stood to the opposite side wch. with
the one that was moved in the fall were intended to answer the two
remaining ones—but from their size and age I have little expectation
of their living. Also moved the Apricots & Peach Trees which stood in
the borders of the grass plats which from the same causes little expectation is entertained of their living. These were placed under the
Wall in the North Garden on each side of the Green House and an old
pair tree was movd at the same time into the lowr. Square of the South
Garden from which less hopes of its living were entertained than of any
of the others.

The schoolhouse was a small building at the west end of Mount Vernon's
north garden. The greenhouse was located at the north end of the north
garden and at this time was incomplete. GW had undertaken the construction of the greenhouse soon after his return from the war. On 11 Aug. 1784
he wrote his former aide, Tench Tilghman, for the dimensions and other
details of a greenhouse at Mrs. Margaret Tilghman Carroll's plantation in
Maryland. Tilghman replied on 18 Aug. sending details and sketches. Completion of the building was delayed, and not until 1787 were the roofing and
flooring finished.

Friday 11th. In the Evening a Mr. Andrews, Jeweller in Philadelphia, called to shew me an Eagle medal, which he had made, & was about to offer as Specimen of his Workmanship to the Members of the Society of Cincinnati in hopes of being employed by them in that way. He was accompanied by a Mr. [   ] name not known.

> *Eagle medal:* Maj. Pierre Charles L'Enfant, a French engineer who served in the Continental Army, designed the badges and diplomas for the Society of the Cincinnati and had them produced in France. He returned to America with a supply in time for the May 1784 meeting. The medal was a gold eagle, with an enameled medallion on its breast bearing a motto and a representation of Lucius Quintus Cincinnatus, the Roman general-farmer after which the society was named. It was suspended from a sky-blue ribbon edged in white. Andrews seems not to have been successful in making the gold eagles.

Saturday 12th. Received an Invitation to the Funeral of Willm. Ramsay Esqr. of Alexandria—the oldest Inhabitt. of the Town; & went up. Walked in a procession as a free mason—Mr. Ramsay in his life time being one & now buried with the Ceremony & honors due to one.

Saturday 19th. My Nephew George Steptoe Washington came here to Dinnr. from the Acadamy at George Town.

> George Steptoe Washington (c.1773–1808) was the second of the three sons of GW's youngest brother Samuel Washington and his fourth wife, Anne Steptoe Washington. He and his younger brother, Lawrence Augustine Washington (1775–1824), were being educated under GW's supervision and largely at his expense. Samuel Washington had left his estate badly encumbered by debts, and its proceeds were not enough to provide for his children. GW placed George and Lawrence in Rev. Stephen Bloomer Balch's academy at Georgetown in 1784, but their extravagances led him to remove them in November to the Alexandria Academy. The two boys were to cause problems for GW for several years. See *Papers, Presidential Series,* 1:28–29, 240–41, 321–22. During his presidency GW sent them to the University of Pennsylvania, and in 1792 both went to study law with Attorney General Edmund Randolph, then living in Philadelphia. The money that GW expended on behalf of the two nephews was never recovered, but by the terms of his will the debt, amounting to nearly £450, was erased.

March

Saturday 12th. Went to Abingden to see Mr. John Lewis who lay sick there. Returned in the Afternoon and brot. Betcy Custis home with me.

Planted two Hemlock trees in a line with the East end of my Kitchen, & Servants Hall; & 10 feet from the corner of the Post & rail fence at each.

Laid the borders of the gravel walk to the No. Necessary—from the circle in the Court yard.

Abingdon, the home of Jacky Custis's widow, Nelly, and her second husband, David Stuart, was situated on the Potomac River just north of Four Mile Run. Jacky and Nelly Custis, who had lived at the Custis White House on Pamunkey River after their marriage, had both wanted to return to the Mount Vernon–Mount Airy neighborhood. In 1778 Jacky bought this house and about 900 acres of land from Robert Alexander, agreeing to pay him £12 per acre, the principal and compound interest to be paid in 24 years. GW was horrified at this latest example of his stepson's fecklessness and reminded him that "£12,000 at compound Interest, [amounts] to upwards of £48,000 in twenty four Years. . . . No Virginia estate . . . can stand simple Interest; how then can they bear compound Interest"? (GW to John Parke Custis, 3 Aug. 1778, Washington Papers, Library of Congress). The Stuarts lived at Abingdon until about 1792.

Friday 18th. I went to my Dogue run Plantation to make choice of the size, & to direct the taking up of Pine trees, for my two wildernesses. Brought 3 waggon load of them home, and planted every other hole round the Walks in them.

Saturday 19th. Wind at No. Et. all day; and more or less rain mixed in sml. degree with Snow; which with what fell in the Night made the ground so wet that I could plant no trees to day. Many of those planted yesterday yielded to the Wind & Wet, and required propping.

Received a Swan, 4 Wild Geese, & two Barrels of Holly Berries (in Sand) from my Brother John and a Barrel of the early Corn from New York.

Wednesday 30th. Doctr. Stuart went away after breakfast & carried the three Children Betcy, Nelly, & Washington Custis with him to Abingdon. Arthur Lee Esqr. came to Dinner.

Eleanor Parke (Nelly) Custis (1779–1852) and George Washington Parke Custis (1781–1857), usually called Washington, were the two youngest children of David Stuart's wife Nelly and her first husband, John Parke Custis. Little Nelly had been brought to Mount Vernon soon after her birth for her mother was too ill to take care of her. Washington, too, had lived with his grandparents most of his life. Although there seem to have been no legal documents drawn up, GW spoke of these two youngest children as "adopted" by him and Mrs. Washington (GW to Lawrence Lewis, 20 Sept. 1799, Washington Papers, Library of Congress).

Arthur Lee (1740–1792), of Virginia's prominent Lee family, served abroad as a diplomat for the Continental Congress during the Revolution and was a member of the Virginia House of Delegates 1781–83 and the Continental Congress 1781–84.

April

Sunday 3d. After Dinner Mr. George Lewis & his wife & Mr. Chas. Carter and his wife and Child came here having been detained on the Road by the Weather.

George Lewis (1757–1821) was a son of Fielding Lewis and GW's sister Betty Washington Lewis. At the beginning of the Revolution, he had been captain of an independent troop of cavalry which acted as part of GW's personal bodyguard. He was now living in Fredericksburg.

Charles Carter (1765–1829), son of Edward and Sarah Champe Carter of Blenheim, was married in 1781 to GW's niece, Betty Lewis (1765–1830), daughter of Fielding and Betty Washington Lewis.

Wednesday 6th. Planted in a Nursery in my Vineyard 17 Live Oaks sent me by Colo. Parker of Norfolk 13 of one, and 7 of another kind of what I suppose to be the wild Honeysuckle, they being in different Bundles, and he having been written to for the wild Honey Suckle.

Sent my Shad Sein and Hands to the Ferry to commen⟨ce⟩ Fishing for Mssrs. Douglas & Smith who had engaged to take all the Shad & Herring I can catch in the Season—the first at 15/. a hundred, and the other at 4/. a thousand.

A Mr. Vidler, to whom I had written (an Undertaker at Annapolis) came here and opened the cases wch. contained my Marble chimney piece—but for want of Workmen could not undertake to finish my New room.

Mr. Carter, & Mr. Geo. Lewis returned here this afternoon.

Nursery in my Vineyard: This was one of several experimental or nursery areas GW had on his Mount Vernon farms. The vineyard was behind the stables, south of the mansion house. *Douglas & Smith:* Smith & Douglass of Alexandria also bought the shad and herring for the 1786 season, paying GW a slightly increased rate (Ledger B, 225). The firm partnership was dissolved late in 1786 (*Va. Journal,* 26 Oct. 1786).

There was an Edward Vidler living in Annapolis in 1785 (*Va. Journal,* 25 Aug. 1785). *An Undertaker:* a contractor or subcontractor.

My Marble chimney piece: Samuel Vaughan, a London merchant in the colonial trade, had enthusiastically supported the colonies during the Revolution and had immigrated with his family to Philadelphia in 1783. He was a great admirer of GW and wrote to him on 8 April 1784 offering to send a marble chimneypiece for his New Room at Mount Vernon (Washington Papers, Library of Congress). The chimneypiece, packed in ten cases, arrived in Alexandria in Feb. 1785 aboard Capt. W. Haskell's brig *May.* GW wrote Vaughan's son Benjamin that "by the number of cases . . . I greatly fear it is too elegant & costly for my room, & republican stile of living" (GW to Benjamin Vaughan, 5 Feb. 1785, Washington Papers, Library of Congress).

New room: the large room at the north end of the mansion, now called the Banquet Hall but always referred to by GW as the New Room. Construction on this room was begun during the Revolution by Going Lanphier under Lund Washington's supervision, but Lanphier had left before the interior of the room was completed. After GW's return to Mount Vernon after the war he was anxious to have work resumed on the unfinished structure.

Monday 11th. Rid to Muddy hole & Neck Plantations.

After breakfast Mr. Carter, Wife & Child—Mr. Lewis & his wife, Mr. Craik & the youngest Doctr. Jenifer went away. Soon after which a Mr. Duchi a french Gentleman recommended by the Marquis de la Fayette to me, came in.

Youngest Doctr. Jenifer: Dr. Daniel Jenifer, Jr. (1756–c.1809).

Gaspard Joseph Armand Ducher was a Parisian lawyer who came to America to study the commercial laws of the states. In a shipwreck on the Long Island coast he lost a large part of his personal fortune and suffered badly from exposure (Nussbaum, *Commercial Policy in the French Revolution,* 14). Lafayette's letter of introduction, 15 Sept. 1784, asked GW's advice and patronage for him. GW replied that there was nothing he could do to help Ducher, since he was a foreigner and spoke no English. Many states, he added, demanded a period of residence and study as a prerequisite to practice in the courts. His suggestion was that Ducher's friends procure him a consular post (GW to Lafayette, 12 April 1785, *Papers, Confederation Series,* 2: 492–93). On 1 Sept. 1785 Ducher was appointed vice-consul ad interim at Portsmouth, N.H., and in 1787 he was transferred to Wilmington, N.C. His extensive reports and writings were influential in forming French commercial policies, including the Navigation Act of 21 Sept. 1793.

Saturday 23d. Wind fresh all day from the South West & weather clear and warm. Vegetation much quickened.

Sowed all the Orchard grass Seed I had remaining of my first Stock on part of the ground which was sowed on thursday with Barley. Rolled it. Sent to Alexandria for another parcel which had just arrived for me from Philadelphia, and brought it home [   ] Bushels.

Sowed three Rows of the Holly Berries next the row of shell bark Hickory Nutt; leaving 2 feet space between the Nutts and the Berries, & 18 Inches betwn. the rows of Berries—sticking a stake down at both ends of each row.

Rid to the Fishing Landing at the Ferry, and all over my Wheat field there. Found the Wheat in general good—in places greatly destroyed by the Winters frost, but some of it, by fibres wch. had retained a little footing in the ground, beginning to vegetate feebly. Whether it can recover so much as to produce Wheat remains to be tried. From here rid to my Plantation on Dogue run, & examined that Wheat, & perceived that it had sustained greater injury than that at the Ferry had done—being in places *entirely* destroyed & the ground generally, not so well covered.

No appearances of any of the Clover, or Orchard grass seed of the first sowing (now the 9th. day) coming up—which affords cause to apprehend defect in them—especially the first.

The Sassafras buds had perfectly displayed but the numerous flowers within had not opened. The Dogwood buttons were just beginning to open as the Redwood (or bud) blossom for though they had appeared several days the blossoms had not expanded. The Peach Trees were now full in bloom and the apples, Pears, and Cherries pretty full of young leaf.

Mr. John Lewis & his Brother Lawrence came down from Abingdon in my Barge before Dinner.

> *Parcel . . . from Philadelphia:* a parcel of grass seed sent by Clement Biddle (GW to Biddle, 16 May 1785, Columbia University), who probably had procured it from Elias Boudinot. In a letter of 31 Jan. 1785, GW thanked Boudinot for grass seed the latter had promised to send through Biddle but protested against Boudinot's depriving himself of the seed (*Papers, Confederation Series,* 2:300).
>
> John Lewis was the son of Fielding Lewis and his first wife. Lewis's illness (see entry of 12 Mar.) must have been severe, for he would remain at Mount Vernon recuperating for almost two more months before he returned home. Lawrence Lewis (1767–1839) was the son of Fielding Lewis and his second wife, Betty Washington Lewis, and half brother to John Lewis.

Sunday 24th. An Express arrived with the Acct. of the Deaths of Mrs. [Frances] Dandridge & Mr. B[artholomew] Dandridge, the Mother and Brother of Mrs. Washington.

Thursday 28th. To Dinner Mr. Pine a pretty eminent Portrait, & Historian Painter arrived in order to take my picture from the life & to place it in the Historical pieces he was about to draw. This Gentleman stands in good estimation as a Painter in England, comes recommended to me from Colo. [George William] Fairfax—Mr. [Robert] Morris Govr. [John] Dickenson—Mr. [Francis] Hopkinson & others.

> Robert Edge Pine (1730–1788), an English portrait painter well known for his historical works, was in the United States to complete a series of paintings of the Revolution. During his stay at Mount Vernon, Pine also painted portraits of Martha Washington, her four grandchildren, and her niece Fanny Bassett.

Friday 29th. I set off for the appointed meeting of the Dismal Swamp Company at Richmond. Dined at Dumfries, & lodged at My sister Lewis's (after visiting my Mother) in Fredericksburgh.

> The affairs of the Dismal Swamp Company were in abeyance during the years of the Revolution. GW wrote Hugh Williamson of North Carolina on 31 Mar. 1784 that he was "unacquainted with the opinions, & know as little of the Affairs & present management of the Swamp Company, in Virginia, (tho' a Member of it) as you do, perhaps less, as I have received nothing from thence nor have heard any thing of my interest therein, for more than nine years" (*Papers, Confederation Series,* 1:244–48). On 10 April 1785 GW wrote Dr. Thomas Walker: "I have requested a meeting of the Proprietors of the Dismal Swamp in Richmond on Monday the 2d. day of May next—at which time and place I should be glad to see you as it is indispensably necessary to

put the affairs of the Company under some better management—I hope every member will bring with him such papers as he is possessed of respecting this business" (ibid., 2:488–89).

May

Sunday—First. Took a late breakfast at Hanover C[our]t House. Went from *thence* to a Mr. Peter Lyon's where I intended to dine, but neither he nor Mrs. Lyon being at home, I proceeded to, & arrived at Richmond about 5 oclock in the afternn. Supped & lodged at the Governor's.

> Peter Lyons (d. 1801) was an Irish-born Virginia lawyer. In 1763 Lyons was attorney for the Rev. James Maury in the "Parson's Cause," and in 1779 he was made judge of the General Court; in 1789 he became a member of the Virginia Court of Appeals.
>
> Patrick Henry (1736–1799) served his fourth and fifth terms as governor of Virginia from Nov. 1784 to Nov. 1786.

Monday—2d. Received and accepted an invitation to dine with the Sons of Saint Taminy, at Mr. Andersons Tavern, and accordingly did so at 3 Oclock.

About Noon, having Assembled a sufficient number of the Proprietors of the Swamp, we proceeded to business in the Senate Chamber; & continued thereon till dinner, when we adjourned till nine Oclock next day.

> The Sons of St. Tammany, a democratic society opposing aristocracy and privilege, was named for a seventeenth-century Delaware chief supposed to have befriended the whites. The first society was formed in 1772 in Philadelphia as the Sons of King Tammany, a Loyalist group, but shortly afterwards, as political attitudes changed, the name was changed to the Sons of St. Tammany. After the Revolution the number of societies in various cities greatly increased.
>
> Anderson's tavern was commonly used for civic meetings until it burned in 1787. It may have been opened by Robert Anderson (d. 1784), who operated a tavern in Williamsburg in the 1770s.
>
> *Proceeded to business:* At this meeting of the proprietors of the Dismal Swamp Company, there was a discussion of proposals for procuring a large number of laborers from Holland or Germany and for obtaining a large foreign loan to aid in the work of draining the swamp (GW to Jean de Neufville, 8 Sept. 1785, GW to John Page, 3 Oct. 1785, *Papers, Confederation Series*, 3:238–40, 293–94).

Wednesday 4th. After doing a little business, & calling upon Judge Mercer and the Attorney General, I left Richmond about 11 Oclock.

Saturday 14th. My Nephew, George Augustine Washington arrived here from Charles Town after having been to Burmuda & the West Indies in pursuit of health which he had but imperfectly recovered.

George Augustine Washington sailed from Alexandria to the West Indies in the spring of 1784 in an effort to recover his health. He had suffered for some time from what may have been tuberculosis. After visits to several of the islands, he went to South Carolina and spent the winter with relatives in Charleston.

Monday 16th. Mr. Mazzai came here to breakfast and went away afterwds.

Philip Mazzei (1730–1816), born in Italy, had been a wine merchant in London for 18 years before coming to Virginia in 1773. He purchased an estate named Colle, adjoining Thomas Jefferson's Monticello in Albemarle County, where he carried on agricultural experiments, especially in wine making. In June 1779 Gov. Patrick Henry sent Mazzei to France to borrow money for the state. He returned in 1783 but sailed for Europe again in June 1785, shortly after his visit to Mount Vernon. In 1788 Mazzei published his history of America, *Recherches historiques et politiques sur les Etats-Unis de l'Amérique septentrionale* (Paris, 1788), based in part on notes given to him by Jefferson.

Tuesday 17th. I went to Alexandria to the appointed meeting of the Subscribers to the Potomack Navigation. Upon comparing, & examining the Books of the different Managers, it was found, including the Subscriptions in behalf of the two States, & the 50 Shares which the Assembly of Virginia had directed to be Subscribed for me, (& which I then declared I would only hold in trust for the State) that their were 403 Shares Subscribed, which being more than sufficient to constitute the Company under the Act—the Subscribers proceeded to the choice of a President & 4 Directors; the first of which fell upon me.

The law authorizing the creation of the Potomac Company provided for the subscription of 500 shares at 444 and ⅑ dollars (£100 sterling) each and stipulated that if at least half the shares were not subscribed by the end of the meeting set for this day, the company could not be organized (Hening, 11:512). The state governments of Virginia and Maryland each subscribed for 50 shares. In addition, the Virginia Assembly had voted 50 shares (plus 100 shares of James River navigation company stock) to GW as thanks from the state for his services in the Revolution.

Holding firm to his determination to accept no gifts or remuneration for his Revolutionary War services, GW agreed, as here stated, only to hold the shares in trust for the public benefit. By his will GW devised the Potomac Company shares to a national university, to be established in the District of Columbia (these shares depreciated and became worthless), and the James River shares to Liberty Hall Academy, Rockbridge County, Va., which later became Washington and Lee University.

Friday 20th. A Mr. Noah Webster came here in the Afternoon & stayed all Night. As did one Richd. Boulton a House joiner and Undertaker recommended to me by Colo. Wm. Fitzhugh of Maryld.

Noah Webster (1758–1843), of Massachusetts, had a short time before this published his *Grammatical Institute of the English Language.* The failure of Congress to enact copyright laws had led him to spend several years traveling through the states in an effort to encourage local legislation. During this year he had also published *Sketches of American Policy,* a plea for a strong federal government. He probably brought a copy to GW during this visit or during a return visit in November.

Richard Boulton of Charles County, Md., signed an agreement with GW on 21 May 1785 in which he agreed to finish the New Room "in a plain and elegant manner; either of Stucco, Wainscot, or partly of both." He was also, among other things, to make repairs to the roof of the mansion, wainscot the new piazza which had gone up under Lund Washington's supervision, and "do the necessary work of a Green House" (Washington Papers, Library of Congress). GW had been warned by William Fitzhugh, Boulton's former employer, that Boulton, his wife, and his daughter "had got such a Habit of Entertaining Idle Visitors, that I still found my work did not go on & that he had be[en] Led rather into Excess of Drinking." GW felt that Boulton could be rehabilitated and "will answer my purposes, as he has no one now to lead him into temptation, and will be far removed from improper associates unless he is at much pains to hunt them" (*Papers, Confederation Series,* 2:554–55, 3:7–8). Boulton signed the agreement but never returned to do the work.

June

Saturday 4th. In the Afternoon the celebrated Mrs. Macauly Graham & Mr. Graham her Husband, Colo. Fitzgerald & Mr. Lux of Baltimore arrived here.

Catherine Sawbridge Macaulay Graham (1731–1791), a prominent English author, wrote the much-lauded *History of England from the Accession of James I to That of the Brunswick Line,* published in London in eight volumes, 1763–83. Richard Henry Lee's letter of introduction to GW indicated that her only reason for venturing as far south as Virginia was to see GW (Lee to GW, 3 May 1785, *Papers, Confederation Series,* 2:532–34). GW thanked Lee for the introduction to Mrs. Macaulay Graham, "whose principles are so much, & so justly admired by the friends to liberty and of mankind. It gave me pleasure to find that her sentmts respecting the inadequacy of the powers of Congress . . . coincided with my own" (GW to Lee, 22 June 1785, ibid., 3:70–72). Mrs. Macaulay Graham's first husband, George Macaulay, had died in 1766, and her remarriage in 1778 to the 21-year-old William Graham, many years her junior, had caused her much ridicule.

Mr. Lux is George Lux (1753–1797), a merchant who lived at Chatsworth in Baltimore County, Md. Lux, who had met GW at Cambridge in 1775, later served in the Maryland militia and as clerk to the committee of observation in Baltimore.

Wednesday 8th. Placed my Military records in to the Hands of Mrs. Macauly Graham for her perusal & amusemt. (these indeed were placed there yesterday).

In 1783 GW ordered "six strong hair Trunks, well clasped and with good Locks" in which to transport his military papers (GW to Daniel Parker,

18 June 1783). On 9 Nov. of that year the papers were packed, loaded on wagons, and under military escort sent to Virginia. One bundle, containing GW's accounts as commander in chief, was left with the superintendent of finance at Philadelphia. The remaining manuscripts went to Mount Vernon. These were to form the nucleus of the Washington Papers eventually deposited at the Library of Congress.

Tuesday 14. About 7 Oclock Mr. Graham & Mrs. Macauly Graham left this on their return to New York. I accompanied them to Mr. Digges's to which place I had her Carriage & horses put over. Mr. Digges escorted her to Bladensburgh.

Sowed on each side of the Great Gate in front of the Ho[use] (between the Serpentine railing and the Orchard grass plats, & Ditches) Seeds of the Palmetto royal in Drills 15 Inches a part.

Wednesday 15th. Mr. John Lewis after a stay of almost 8 Weeks took his departure, very well recovered. My brother Charles also left this on his return home.

Rid to my Plantations at Muddy hole, Ferry, and Dogue run. Also to the Mill. Mr. Bushrod Washington came here before dinner.

Wednesday 22d. Just as we had done dinner Colo. Bassett & his two Sons, Burwell & John, arrived.

Burwell Bassett, Mrs. Washington's brother-in-law, was a member of the Virginia senate, serving there from 1777 until his death in 1793. Burwell Bassett, Jr. (1764–1841), eldest surviving son of Burwell Bassett, enjoyed a long career in the Virginia House of Delegates, the Virginia senate, and the United States House of Representatives. He resided at Eltham, which he inherited at his father's death in 1793. John Bassett (1766–1826), a lawyer, lived in Hanover County.

Thursday 23d. A Mr. Brisco, introduced by a letter from Colo. R.H. Harrison came here to offer himself to me as a Secretary.

Cut the grass in my Court yard and began to do the like in the river front of the House.

Mr. Brisco after dining went away. I took 8 or 10 days to give him a definitive answer in.

Robert Hanson Harrison introduced William Briscoe as a close relative of his wife (Harrison to GW, 20 June 1785, *Papers, Confederation Series*, 3:64–65). He may have been a son of Harrison's sister-in-law, Mary Hanson Briscoe and her husband, John Briscoe. Briscoe was not hired for the job. For further information on GW's search for a secretary, see note to the entry for 2 July 1785.

July

July 1st. Went to Alexandria to a meeting of the Board of Directors, who by Advertisement were to attend this day for the purpose of agreeing with a Manager and two Assistants to conduct the Undertaking of the Potomack Navigation—but no person applying with proper Credentials the Board gave the applicants until thursday the 14th. to provide these & for others to offer.

> The advertisement agreed to at the directors' first meeting on 31 May 1785 (see *Diaries,* 4:147) was printed in newspapers in Alexandria (*Va. Journal,* 9 June 1785), in Baltimore (*Md. Journal,* 10, 14, 17, 24 June 1785), and in Philadelphia (*Pa. Packet,* 22 June 1785). The company also printed handbills to be distributed about the Potomac Valley (GW to James Rumsey, 2 July 1785).

Saturday 2d. Doctr. Stuart, Wife & Sister, and Patcy & Nelly Custis came here to Dinner—As did Mr. McCrae & a Mr. Shaw whom Mr. Montgomerie recommended to me as a Clerk or Secretary. All of these stayed the Night.

> Robert McCrea (c.1765–c.1840), a native of Scotland, was a partner in the Alexandria firm of McCrea & Mease.
> GW had asked various friends to be on the lookout for someone to live at Mount Vernon and help him with the voluminous correspondence and bookkeeping which made increasing demands on his time. Thomas Montgomerie recommended William Shaw, newly arrived in the United States from Canada. Although Montgomerie knew Shaw only slightly, he knew his family, and the young man came with strong recommendations from Montgomerie's friends (Montgomerie to GW, 21 June 1785, *Papers, Confederation Series,* 3:67). GW wrote Montgomerie that besides writing letters and keeping books, Shaw would be required to "methodize my papers (which from hasty removals into the interior country [during the Revolution], are in great disorder); ride, at my expence, to do such business as I may have in different parts of this, or the other States . . . ; & occasionally to devote a *small* portion of time to inietate two little children (a Girl of six, & a boy of four years of age, descendants of the decd. Mr. Custis who live with me . . .) in the first rudiments of Education." Shaw would not agree to a definite term of service and demanded the large sum of £50 sterling per year, in addition to bed, board, and washing (GW to Montgomery, 25 June 1785, Shaw to GW, 4 July 1785, *Papers, Confederation Series,* 3:83–84, 103–4). GW agreed to these terms, and Shaw returned to Mount Vernon to begin his services on 26 July. He stayed only 13 months, leaving GW's service in Aug. 1786. GW was doubtless happy to see the last of Shaw, for the young man obviously spent too much time away from his duties. The diaries for the last months of 1785 and 1786 abound with the general's unhappy references to Shaw's absences from Mount Vernon.

Tuesday 5th. After dinner Mr. Gouvournr. Morris and Mr. Wm. Craik came in.

> Gouverneur Morris (1752–1816), formerly a member of the Continental Congress from New York and a longtime supporter of GW, was from 1781 to 1785 assistant to Robert Morris, superintendent of finance. Gouverneur Morris was involved in several business deals with Robert Morris and had come to Virginia in Jan. 1785 to attend to Robert Morris's tobacco shipments

Charles Willson Peale's portrait of business partners Gouverneur Morris and Robert Morris. (Pennsylvania Academy of the Fine Arts)

and to try to collect a debt from Carter Braxton of Virginia. The Braxton lawsuit was finally settled at the end of June, and at this time Morris was on his way from Williamsburg back to Philadelphia.

Wednesday 6th. General Lincoln & his Son; Mr. Porter, & a Doctr. Milne came to Dinner & returned afterwards.

Received from Genl. Lincoln 3 young trees of the Spruce Pine and two of the Fir or Hemlock in half Barrels which seemed to be healthy & vegitating.

Also received from Doctr. Craik by his Son a parcel of Chinese Seeds similar to those presented to me by Mr. Porter on the 2d Instt.

Benjamin Lincoln of Massachusetts and his son, Benjamin Lincoln, Jr. (d. 1788), probably were in Virginia on business. Their firm, Lincoln & Sons, conducted business with William Lyles & Co. and Porter & Ingraham, both of Alexandria. Thomas Porter, who appears here with them, was a close friend of both the Lincolns.

Saturday 9th. A Mr. Arnold Henry Dohrman, a Gentleman of Lisbon recommended by Govr. Henry to me as a Man of fortune & one who had been exceedingly attentive and kind to the American prisoners in captivity came here, dined, and continued his journey afterwards to New York with letters of Introduction from me to the Presidt. of Congress, and to Messrs. Wilson Grayson and Chase Members of it, from me.

> Arnold Henry Dohrman (1749–1813), a Portuguese merchant, aided American seamen captured during the Revolution by the English and set down penniless on the Portuguese coast. He not only gave them money and weapons but also helped them to reach home. In 1780 Congress made him United States agent in Portugal, with no pay but with his expenses to be paid by Congress. In 1785 he came to the United States to try to collect for the disbursements he had made. Congress finally settled Dohrman's accounts in 1787 (*JCC,* 33:587–88).

August

Monday 1st. Left home at 6 Oclock P.M. and after escorting Fanny Bassett to Alexandria I proceeded to Doctr. Stuarts where I breakfasted; and from thence went to George Town to the Annual Meeting of the Potomack Company appointed to be held at that place.

About Noon, a sufficient number of sharers having assembled to constitute a meeting, we proceeded to business—Mr. Danl. Carroll in the Chair—when the President & directors of the Company made a report of their transactions since their appointment, which was received & approved of.

The Board of Directors then sat, and after coming to some resolutions respecting rations to be allowed the Workmen—the mode of payment—manner of keeping an acct. of their work &ca. &ca. and to a determination of proceeding first to the Senneca Falls and next to those at the Mouth of Shannondoah for the purpose of investigation & to direct the operations thereat adjourned Sine Die. Dined at Shuters Tavern.

> *Shuters Tavern:* In 1783 John Suter (d. 1794) opened a tavern in Georgetown, Md., on the east side of Water Street (now Wisconsin Ave.) several doors south of Bridge (now M) Street.

Tuesday 2d. Left George Town about 10 Oclock, in Company with all the Directors except Govr. Lee. We dined at Mr. Bealls Mill 14 Miles from George Town and proceeded—that is the Directors and Colo. Johnson—to a Mr. Goldsboroughs, a decent Farmers House at the head of the Senneca falls—about 6 Miles and 20 from George Town.

Wednesday 3d. Having provided Canoes and being joined by Mr. Rumsay the principal Manager, & Mr. Stewart an Assistant to him, in carrying on the Works, we proceeded to examine the falls; and beginning at the head of them went through the whole by water, and continued from the foot of them to the Great fall. After which, returning back to a Spring on the Maryland Side between the Seneca & Great Falls, we partook (about 5 O'clock) of another cold Collation which a Colo. Orme, a Mr. Turner & others of the Neighbourhood, had provided and returned back by the way of Mr. Bealls Mill to our old Quarters at Mr. Goldsboroughs. The distance as estimated 8 Miles.

The Water through these Falls is of sufficient depth for good Navigation; and as formidable as I had conceived them to be; but by no means impracticable. The principal difficulties lye in rocks which occasion a crooked passage. These once removed, renders the passage safe without the aid of Locks. It appearing to me, and was so, unanimously determined by the Board of Directors, that a channel through the bed of the river in a strait direction, and as much in the course of the currant as may be, without a grt. increase of labour & expence, would be preferable to that through the Gut . . . a navigation through the bed of the river when once made will, in all probability, remain forever, as the currt. here will rather clear, than contribute to choak, the passage. It is true, no track path can be had in a navigation thus ordered, nor does there appear a necessity for it. Tracking, constitutes a large part of Mr. Ballendines estimate—The want of which, in the rapid parts of the river, (if Mr. Rumseys plan for working Boats against stream by the force of Mechanical powers should fail) may be supplied by chains buoyed up to haul by which would be equally easy, more certain, and less dangerous than setting up with Poles—whilst track paths, it is apprehended can not be made to stand, and may endanger the Banks if the Wood is stripped from them, which is their present security against washing.

The distance between the Seneca & Great Falls, is about 5 Miles; and except in one place within ¾ of a Mile of the latter, the navigation now is, or easily may be made, very good; and at this place, the obstruction arises from the shallowness of the Water. Boats may go almost to the Spout with safety. To the place where the water passes when the river is full it is quite easy & safe to descend to, being in a Cove of still Water.

Col. Archibald Orme (1730–1812), of the Rock Creek neighborhood in Montgomery County, Md., was an active surveyor in the area. Mr. Turner may be Samuel Turner, who was living in that neighborhood in 1790, or Hezekiah Turner (1739–c.1812), of Fauquier County, Va., who was active after the Revolution as a surveyor of lands in the upper Potomac Valley.

Track path: The problem GW is discussing is that of aiding boats to ascend the Seneca Falls (actually rapids). The track path was a towing path used to tow the boats through the rapid part of the river. GW disliked the cost of constructing and maintaining canals and locks and accepted the necessity of cutting a canal only when locks were clearly necessary, as at the Great Falls.

The Spout: The point in a river where the banks formed a narrow channel, thus creating rapids, was called a spout.

Saturday 6th. Breakfasted in Frederick Town [Md.], at Govr. Johnsons, and dined at Harpers ferry. Took a view of the River, from the Banks, as we road up the bottom from Pains falls to the ferry, as well as it could be done on Horse back. Sent a Canoe in a Waggon from the Ferry to Keeptriest Furnace in ordr. to descend the Falls therin tomorrow.

Thomas Johnson's house in Frederick Town was on Market Street; his country estate was about four miles northeast of the town.

The Keep Triste iron furnace was located on the right (Virginia) bank of the Potomac near the mouth of Elk's Run, about two miles above the confluence of the Potomac with the Shenandoah River. This area is now in Jefferson County, W.Va. GW left the Great Road to Frederick Town to follow the river road along the Potomac.

George Plater (1735–1792), of Sotterly, on the Patuxent River in St. Mary's County, Md., practiced law in Maryland and took a leading role in the Revolution, representing Maryland in the Second Continental Congress (1778–80).

Sunday 7th. About Sunrising, the Directors & myself rid up to Keeptrieste, where Canoes were provided, in which we crossed to the Maryland side of the river and examined a Gut, or swash through which it is supposed the Navigation must be conducted. This Swash is shallow at the entrance, but having sufficient fall, may easily (by removing some of the rocks) admit any quantity of water required. Having examined this passage, I returned to the head of the Falls, and in one of the Canoes with two skilful hands descended them with the common Currt. in its Natural bed—which I found greatly incommoded with rocks, shallows and a crooked Channel which left no doubt of the propriety of preferring a passage through the Swash. Here we breakfasted; after which we set out to explore the Falls below. At the foot of these falls the Directors & myself (Govr. Lee having joined us the Evening before) held a meeting—At which it was determined, as we conceived the Navigation could be made through these (commonly called the Shannondoah) Falls without the aid of Locks, and by opening them would give eclat to the undertaking and great ease to the upper Inhabitants as Water transportation would be immediately had to the Great Falls from Fort Cumberland to employ the upper hands in this work instead of removing the obstructions above, and gave Mr. Rumsey directions to do so accordingly—with general Instructions for his Governmt.

The Falls: Shenandoah Falls, running about two miles down the Potomac from Elk's Run to the mouth of the Shenandoah River. *His Governmt.:* In these instructions Rumsey was directed to hire as many workers as necessary to open the Shenandoah and Seneca Falls (Bacon-Foster, *Patomac Route,* 64).

Tuesday 9th. Having provided a light & convenient Boat—hired two hands to work her and laid in some Stores, Colonels Fitzgerald & Gilpin, and myself embarked in it, leaving Mr. Rumsey to engage more hds. & to set those he had to work about 6 Oclock P.M.

In this Boat we passed through the Spout, and all the other Falls and rapids, and breakfasted at a Captn. Smiths on the Maryland side; to which place our horses had been sent the Evening before—after which and dining on our prog at Knowlands Ferry (about 15 Miles from Harpers) we lodged at the House of a Mr. Tayler, about three Miles above the Mouth of Goose Creek and about 10 M. below Knowlands.

> *Captn. Smiths:* probably the home of Capt. John Smith, near the Smith's ferry. *Prog:* food, victuals, provender, especially provisions for a journey. *Knowlands Ferry:* Noland's Ferry crossed the Potomac downstream of Noland's Island from Loudoun County, Va., to the mouth of Tuscarora Creek in Montgomery County, Md. *Mr. Tayler:* possibly Thomas Taylor who lived in the vicinity of Harrison's Island.

Wednesday 10th. Before Sun rise we embarked and about Nine Oclock arrived at the head of the Seneca Falls and breakfasted with our old Landlord Mr. Goldsborough to which place our horses had proceeded the Over Night from Captn. Smiths.

After Breakfasting, and spending sometime with the labourers at their different works, of blowing, removing stone, getting Coal wood &ca.—we left the Seneca Falls about 2 Oclock A.M. & crossing the River about half a mile below them and a little above Captn. Trammels we got into the great Road from Leesburgh to Alexandria and about half after Nine O'clock in the Evening I reached home after an absence from it of 10 days.

> Smith's ferry, in Frederick County, Md., crossed the Potomac just below the mouth of Dutchman Creek in Loudoun County, Va.
> *Trammels:* John Trammell (d. 1794), of Frederick County, Md., owned several islands by Point of Rocks, the largest of which is now called Conoy. Lee's Island was possibly that island once owned by Thomas Lee, father of Gov. Thomas Sim Lee. It may be the Lee's Island at the mouth of Broad Run, Loudoun County, which was later renamed Seldon's Island.

Thursday 11th. The Drought, the effects of which were visible when I left home, had, by this (no rain having fallen in my absence) greatly affected vegetation. The grass was quite burnt & crisp under foot— Gardens parched and the young Trees in my Shrubberies, notwithstanding they had been watered (as it is said) according to my direction were much on the decline. In a word nature had put on a melancholy look—everything seeming to droop.

Wednesday 24th. Sowed some more of the Guinea Grass seed today in the manner of yesterday.

Measured round the ground which I intend to inclose for a Paddock, and find it to be abt. 1600 yards.

Receiv'd Seven hounds sent me from France by the Marqs. de la Fayette, by way of New York viz. 3 dogs and four Bitches.

My Boat went to Alexandria and brought home 100 Bushels of Salt, a hogshead of common rum, and a Cask of Nails 20d.

> GW had requested Lafayette to send him some French hounds. Lafayette wrote GW, 13 May 1785, that "French Hounds are not Now Very Easily got Because the King Makes use of English dogs, as Being more Swift than those of Normandy—I However Have got Seven from a Normand Gentleman Called *Monsieur le Comte doilliamson* the Handsomest Bitch Among them was a favourite with His lady who Makes a present of Her to You" (*Papers, Confederation Series,* 2:556–59). The dogs were accompanied from France to New York by young John Quincy Adams and were shipped from New York to Mount Vernon in Capt. S. Packard's ship *Dove.*

September

Monday 5th. Began to spade up the Lawn in front of the Court yard. And also began to prepare the Scaffolds for Cieling the Piazza.

> The lawn on the west front of the house was to be made into a bowling green.

Tuesday 6th. A Mr. Tayler, Clerk to the Secretary for Foreign Affairs came here whilst we were at Dinner, sent by Mr. Jay, by order of Congress, to take Copies of the report of the Commissioners who had been sent in by me to New York, to take an Acct. of the Slaves whch had been sent from that place (previous to the evacuation) by the British.

> George Taylor, Jr., in 1785 was appointed clerk to the secretary for foreign affairs, John Jay. Commissioners for embarkation had been appointed by GW in 1783 to go to New York to superintend the departure of the British troops and to try to enforce article seven of the provisional treaty of peace of Nov. 1782, which forbade British troops to carry off any American property, notably runaway slaves. There was, however, little the commissioners could do to enforce the provision, and so they withdrew. The report GW refers to is probably that of 30 May 1783, written by Egbert Benson and William Stephens Smith, two of the commissioners. On 23 June of that year GW sent a letter to Congress, enclosing copies of his entire correspondence with the commissioners (Washington Papers, Library of Congress).

Wednesday 7th. About Noon brought two Negro men from the River Plantation to assist in spading up the ground in front of the Court yard and Cornelius being Sick Tom Davis went to assist them.

At Night, a Man of the name of Purdie, came to offer himself to me as a Housekeeper, or Household Steward. He had some testimonials respecting his character—but being intoxicated, and in other respects appearing in an unfavorable light I informed him that he would not answer my purposes, but that he might stay all night.

Cornelius was undoubtedly the Irishman, Cornelius McDermott Roe, who signed an agreement with GW on 1 Aug. 1786 for one year as a "Stone Mason, Bricklayer, and (when not employed in either of these) in other jobs which he may be set about." McDermott Roe was to receive £32 in addition to board, washing, and lodging "as he has been usually accustomed to in the family; and will give him the same allowance of spirits with which he has been served" (Washington Papers, Library of Congress). Tom Davis, a dower slave, worked primarily as a bricklayer and stonemason. He also occasionally did painting and carpentry.

GW had advertised for a *"House-Keeper, or Household Steward,* who is competent to the charge of a large family, and attending on a good deal of company" (*Va. Journal,* 18 Aug. 1785). Because of the increasing number of visitors at Mount Vernon since the Revolution, GW felt it necessary to hire someone to help run the household.

Thursday 15th. Doctr. L'Moyer came in before Dinner.

Jean Pierre Le Mayeur (Lamayner, L'Moyer), a French dentist who came to New York during the Revolution, went to GW's headquarters in 1783 to do some work on his teeth. Le Mayeur visited Mount Vernon in the summer of 1784 and evidently became a favorite with little George Washington Parke Custis. He played games with the child and in August sent him a new red toy horse "just big Enough for the little house which master George and myself built upon the side of the hill" (Le Mayeur to GW, 14 Aug. 1784, *Papers, Confederation Series,* 2:38–39). After this visit to Mount Vernon, Le Mayeur went to Richmond where he advertised that he performed "operations on the teeth, hitherto performed in Europe, such as transplanting, &c., &c., &c." Le Mayeur also offered a payment of three guineas for good front teeth from anyone but slaves (*Va. Mag.,* 10 [1902–3], 325).

Monday 26th. Went up to Alexandria to meet Colonels Gilpin & Fitzgerald on business of the Potomack Compa. Doctr. La Moyer, Mr. B. Bassett and G.A. Washington accompanied me the first of whom remained there. Dined at the New Tavern, kept by Mr. Lyle.

Brought home Mr. Thomas McCarty, with whom I had agreed to serve me in the capicity of a Ho[use] keeper—or Household Steward at Thirty pounds pr. Ann.

GW and the directors of the Potomac Company ordered that 60 indentured servants be purchased in Philadelphia or Baltimore (Pickell, *Potomac Company,* 78). *New Tavern:* Capt. Henry Lyles (d. 1786) of Maryland had recently opened the commodious, three-story Alexandria Inn and Coffeehouse on the corner of Fairfax and Cameron streets.

Thomas McCarty was probably not related to GW's close neighbor Daniel McCarty. He worked for only a year at Mount Vernon and proved unsatisfactory as a steward.

Friday 30th. Mr. Hunter, and the right Honble. Fred. von Walden, Captn. in the Swedish Navy—introduced by Mr. Richd. Soderstroin came here to Dinner, and returned to Alexandria afterwards. In the Evening a Mr. Tarte—introduced by letter from a John Lowry of Back river came in to request my Sentiments respecting some Entrys they, in Partnership, had made in the Great Dismal Swamp, which I gave unreservedly, that they had no right to.

One of the Hound Bitches wch. was sent to me from France brought forth 15 puppies this day; 7 of which (the rest being as many as I thought she could rear) I had drowned.

> Capt. Frederick von Waldén on 28 July laid before Congress a plan of coinage of "copper to the amount of 100,000 £Stg." No action had yet been taken on his plan, and he may have been at Mount Vernon to try to enlist GW's support for the scheme (*LMCC*, 8:171; *JCC*, 29:587).
>
> Richard Soderstrom, the new Swedish consul at Boston, recently had been embroiled in a controversy with Congress because he had presented his credentials to the governor of Massachusetts before presenting them to Congress. Soderstrom's act was soon recognized not as a sign of disrespect but as an innocent blunder. See *LMCC*, 8:33, 51–52; *JCC*, 28:360–61, 393–94.
>
> John Lowry was probably the son of John Lowry (died c.1766) and Mary Lowry of Elizabeth City County. Back River runs through Elizabeth City County and empties into the Chesapeake Bay, midway between the James and York rivers. Several members of the Tarte (Tart) family lived in the Elizabeth City County–Norfolk County area.

October

Sunday 2d. Went with Fanny Bassett, Burwell Bassett, Doctr. Stuart, G.A. Washington, Mr. Shaw & Nelly Custis to Pohick Church; to hear a Mr. Thompson preach, who returned home with us to Dinner, where I found the Revd. Mr. Jones, formerly a Chaplin in one of the Pennsylvania Regiments.

After we were in Bed (about Eleven Oclock in the Evening) Mr. Houdon, sent from Paris by Doctr. Franklin and Mr. Jefferson to take my Bust, in behalf of the State of Virginia, with three young men assistants, introduced by a Mr. Perin a French Gentleman of Alexandria, arrived here by water from the latter place.

> James Thomson (1739–1812) was the minister of Leeds Parish, Fauquier County, from 1769 to 1812. David Jones (1736–1820), minister of the Great Valley Baptist Church, Chester County, Pa., had been a chaplain in the 3d and 4th Pennsylvania regiments during the Revolution.
>
> Virginia in 1784 adopted a resolution commissioning a statue of GW; and Thomas Jefferson and Benjamin Franklin, then United States representatives at the Court of France, agreed to locate and engage an outstanding sculptor for the commission. Jean Antoine Houdon (1741–1828) agreed to make the statue but insisted that he must come to America to make a life mask of GW and then return to France to complete the work. Jefferson's agreement with Houdon provided for a salary of 1,000 guineas plus expenses to America and the purchase of an insurance policy on the sculptor's life during the journey. Although the fee was much less than Houdon had asked, he was

eager to make a statue of GW and agreed to the terms, leaving such clients as Catherine the Great of Russia to await his return to Europe.

Joseph Marie Perrin, a merchant in Alexandria, had a store on Royal Street next to John Wise's tavern and opposite the courthouse. Perrin came to Mount Vernon as an interpreter for Houdon's party. In his diary entry for 10 Oct., GW gave a detailed account of the mixture of plaster of paris used by Houdon to make the life masks from which he produced the busts of GW. One of these busts he took back to France; the other remained at Mount Vernon (*Diaries,* 4:204).

Friday 14th. My Chariot which went up for, brought down Miss Sally Ramsay & Miss Kitty Washington, to be Bridesmaids tomorrow at the wedding of Miss Bassett.

Mr. George Washington, & Mr. Burwell Bassett went to the Clerks Office & thence to Colo. Masons for a license, & returned to Dinner; having accomplished their business.

> *For a license:* In order to obtain a marriage license for the wedding of his underage daughter, Fanny, to George Augustine Washington, Col. Burwell Bassett had to give his consent personally before the clerk of the court or in writing with two witnesses. His eldest son, Burwell, probably was taking this written permission with him to Alexandria at this time. George Mason, who was a Fairfax justice by 1749, probably was the oldest justice in point of service and had therefore to sign the license.

Saturday 15th. The Reverend Mr. Grayson, and Doctr. Griffith; Lund Washington, his wife, & Miss Stuart came to Dinner—All of whom remained the Evening except L.W.

After the Candles were lighted George Auge. Washington and Frances Bassett were married by Mr. Grayson.

> Spence Grayson (1734–1798) lived at Belle Air, two miles from Occoquan River, and had been for a number of years minister of Cameron Parish, Loudoun County.
>
> David Griffith was probably at Mount Vernon to deliver to GW some Cape of Good Hope wheat, which Samuel Powel of Philadelphia had sent (GW to Powel, 2 Nov. 1785).
>
> Miss Stuart is probably David Stuart's sister Nancy.
>
> Although he was still concerned about George Augustine's health (see entry for 14 May 1785), GW wrote Fanny's father on 23 May 1785, "It has ever been a maxim with me, through life, neither to promote, nor to prevent a matrimonial connection, unless there should be something indispensably requiring interference in the latter. I have always considered Marriage as the most interesting event of ones life . . . & therefore, neither directly nor indirectly have I ever said a syllable to Fanny, or George, upon the Subject of their intended connection: but as their attachment to each other seems of early growth, warm, & lasting, it bids fair for happiness. If therefore you have no objec⟨tion,⟩ I think, the sooner it is consummated the better." He added that he and Mrs. Washington wished the young couple to live at Mount Vernon (GW to Burwell Bassett, 23 May 1785, *Papers, Confederation Series,* 3:9–10).

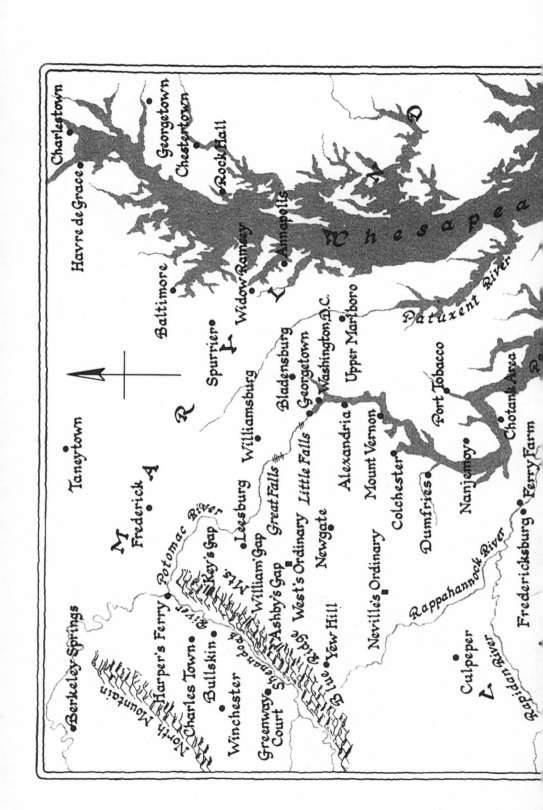

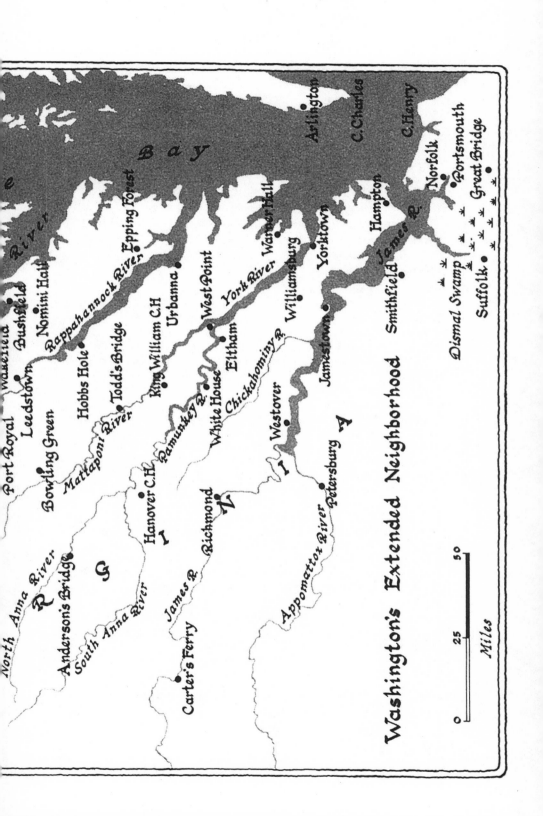

Washington's Extended Neighborhood

Miles

0   25   50

Wednesday 19th. Mr. Houdon having finished the business which brot. him hither, went up on Monday with his People, work, and impliments in my Barge, to Alexandria, to take a Passage in the Stage for Philadelphia the next Morning.

Wednesday 26th. Took the cover off my dry Well, to see if I could not fix it better for the purpose of an Ice House, by Arching the Top, and planking the sides.

Having received by the last Northern Mail advice of the arrival at Boston, of one of the Jack Asses presented to me by His Catholic Majesty, I sent my Overseer John Fairfax, to conduct him, and his Keeper, a Spaniard, home safe; addressing him to Lieutt. Governor Cushing, from whom I received the information. Finished the Shingling on the West front of the House.

> GW had decided not to build a new icehouse but to remodel his old one extensively along lines suggested by Robert Morris. The rebuilt icehouse had an inner well within the first, which was lined with wood for better insulation. Over the well was an arch, covered with soil and sodded. There was a tunnel in the face of the hill through which the ice could be carried from the river.
>
> *One of the Jack Asses:* Knowing that Spain produced excellent jackasses, GW made some inquiries about how he might obtain one for breeding purposes. Upon learning of this, Charles II, king of Spain, sent word that two Spanish jacks were being shipped to him as a gift (Thomas Jefferson to GW, 10 Dec. 1784, *Papers, Confederation Series,* 1:176–78). Early in October, GW was notified by Lt. Gov. Thomas Cushing of Massachusetts that one of the jacks had arrived at Beverly in the care of Pedro Tellez, and that another animal was expected soon. GW dispatched John Fairfax to Boston with instructions to escort the Spaniard and the two jacks. It later developed that the second jack had died at sea. Setting out from Boston on 10 Nov., Fairfax and Tellez reached Mount Vernon on 5 Dec. It soon appeared that while the jack itself was a gift, GW was expected to pay all charges except Tellez's wages. The jack, to be named Royal Gift, seemed a disappointment at first. GW wrote Lafayette, 10 May 1786, that although the animal was handsome, "his late royal master, tho' past his grand climacteric, cannot be less moved by female allurements than he is." He wrote William Fitzhugh, 15 May 1786, that he still hoped that when Royal Gift "becomes a little better acquainted with republican enjoyments, he will amend his manners, and fall into a better & more expeditious mode of doing business. If the case should be otherwise, I should have no disinclination to present his Catholic Majesty with as good a thing, as he gave me" (*Papers, Confederation Series,* 4:41–45, 52). Subsequent letters indicate that Royal Gift did learn to appreciate "republican enjoyments."

Thursday 27th. Mr. Battaile Muse came here before dinner but would not stay to it. After finishing some business with me respecting my Tenants and my agreeing to allow him Six pr. Ct. for Collecting my Rents, he went up to Alexandria.

Battaile Muse (1751–1803), son of Col. George Muse of Caroline County, had settled in Berkeley County. Muse was hired by GW as the rental agent for his tenant lands in Frederick, Fauquier, Berkeley, and Loudoun counties.

November

Friday 4th. Raised the heavy frame in my [Ice] House to day and planted 16 Pines in the avenues on my Serpentine Walks. In the Evening a Mr. Jno. Fitch came in, to propose a draft & Model of a Machine for promoting Navigation, by means of a Steam.

John Fitch (1743–1798), of Bucks County, Pa., had been experimenting with a steam-driven boat for the navigation of rivers, applying to the Continental Congress for financial assistance in Aug. 1785 and to the American Philosophical Society in September without success. On his way to Richmond to apply for aid from the Virginia legislature, Fitch stopped at former governor Thomas Johnson's in Frederick Town, Md., where he first heard of James Rumsey's boat. Concerned about the possibility that Rumsey too was experimenting with steam power, Fitch had, at Johnson's suggestion, stopped at Mount Vernon to ask GW whether Rumsey was experimenting with steam. According to Fitch, GW evaded a direct answer and gave him no encouragement (Westcott, *Life of John Fitch,* 127–47).

Saturday 5th. Went over the Creek to see how my people went on in raising mud from the bed of the Creek—their progress but slow. Mr. Robert Washington of Chotanck—Mr. Lund Washington & Mr. Lawrence Washington dined here, as did Colo. Gilpin and Mr. Noah Webster. The 4 first went away afterwards—the last stayed all Night. In the afternoon a Mr. Lee came here to sollicit Charity for his Mother who represented herself as having nine Children—a bad husband and no support. He also stayed the Evening.

Noah Webster, in his effort to get the state to enact a copyright law, had come to request letters of introduction from GW to officials in Richmond. Webster wrote GW, on 16 Dec. 1785, to inform him that the legislature had passed such an act. He also offered to come to Mount Vernon to act, without pay, as tutor for the Custis children, provided he would be given access to GW's papers. GW refused this offer, as he needed someone who could also act as secretary (GW to Webster, 18 Dec. 1785, *Papers, Confederation Series,* 3: 470–71).

Wednesday 9th. Having put in the heavy frame into my Ice House I began this day to Seal it with Boards, and to ram straw between these boards and the wall. All imaginable pains was taken to prevent the Straw from getting wet, or even damp, but the Moisture in the air is very unfavourable.

Thursday 10th. There having fallen so much rain in the Night as to convince me that the Straw which I had placed between the Cieling &

the Wall of my Ice House, must have got wet, and being in some doubt before of the propriety of the measure, lest it should get damp, heat, & rot; I had it all taken out, leaving the Space between unfilled with any thing.

Friday 18th. Began to take up a number of small Pines to replace the dead ones in my wilderness. Got them with much dirt about the Roots. Took an Account of the Horses, Cattle & Sheep at Home.

Began to take up my summer Turnips at the House. Got abt. half up to day.

Sent to Mr. Digges for Papaw Bushes to replace the dead ones in my Shrubberies. Coming late I had not time to plant them but put the Roots in the ground until tomorrow.

Planted the two duke Cherries—sent me by Major Jenifer in the two gardens—one under each Wall, abt. 30 feet from the Garden Houses—and planted the Bury & 2 St. Germain Pairs also sent me by him in the No. Garden—new part thereof—one of each kind on the circular Walk and the other two on the Strait walk.

Put the Box with the Magnolia, & other exotics from So. Carolina and that with the Kentucke Coffee tree under a bush cover in the open part of the Green Ho[use] and began to cover the Palmetto Royal at the Front gate with Brush with the leaf on—but got a small part only South of the gate & South part thereof done before night.

> The account of the horses included Magnolia, Nelson, and Blueskin. Magnolia, or Magnolio, was an Arabian horse which GW had bought for £500 from the estate of John Parke Custis (Ledger B, 224). He was a five-year-old, "a chestnut colour, near sixteen hands high, finely formed, and thought by all who have seen him to be perfect. He was got by the Ranger Arabian, his dam by Othello son of Crab, her dam by Morton's Traveller, and her dam was Selima by the Godolphin Arabian" (*Va. Journal,* 24 Mar. 1785).
>
> Nelson and Blueskin, two horses that had carried GW during the Revolution, were now in honorable retirement at Mount Vernon. Nelson was, according to George Washington Parke Custis, the chestnut that GW rode at Yorktown. He was named for Gov. Thomas Nelson, Jr., of Virginia, and was probably the horse that Governor Nelson sent GW as a gift in 1778 after hearing of GW's difficulties in finding a suitable animal to replace one he had been riding (Custis, *Recollections,* 166; Nelson to GW, 11 Aug. 1778, Washington Papers, Library of Congress). Blueskin seems to have been sold or given to GW by Benjamin Dulany or his wife.

Monday 21st. Colo. Harrison & Doctr. Craik left this after Breakfast, and I went up to Alexandria with G. Washington to meet the Directors of the Potomack Coma. and to a Turtle feast (the Turtle given by myself to the Gentlemen of Alexa.).

Returned in the Evening and found the Count Doradour recommended by, & related to the Marqs. de la Fayette here.

The directors of the Potomac Company met to approve some accounts receivable (Pickell, *Potomac Company,* 82).

The comte de Doradour, a Frenchman from Auvergne, was "Going to look for a settlement in America—His fortune Has Been partly deranged By a law Suit, and what Remains of it He intends to fix in some of the United States" (Lafayette to GW, 11 May 1785, *Papers, Confederation Series,* 2:551). Doradour carried letters of introduction to numerous Virginians from Thomas Jefferson, at this time United States minister to France, and eventually purchased a large tract of land west of the mountains.

Friday 25th. Mr. Shaw returned, having removed George & Lawe. Washington to the Alexandria Academy & fixed them at the Widow Dades.

Mrs. Dade was probably Parthenia Alexander Massey Dade, widow of Townshend Dade (d. 1781), and the aunt of GW's neighbor Robert Alexander. GW's two nephews boarded at Mrs. Dade's house in Alexandria until Jan. 1787, when they were moved to the home of Samuel Hanson of Samuel (Ledger B, 206, 229). Hanson had difficulties with the boys, and eventually they were removed to the care of GW's old friend Dr. Craik.

Tuesday 29th. Went out after Breakfast with my hounds from France, & two which were lent me, yesterday, by young Mr. Mason. Found a Fox which was run tolerably well by two of the Frh. Bitches & one of Mason's Dogs. The other French Dogs shewed but little disposition to follow and with the second Dog of Mason's got upon another Fox which was followed slow and indifferently by some & not at all by the rest until the sent became so cold that it cd. not be followed at all.

December

Sunday 4th. Last Night Jno. Alton, an Overseer of mine in the Neck—an old & faithful Servant who had lived with me 30 odd years died of an imposthume in his thigh after lingering for more than 4 Months with it, and being reduced to a mere skeleton—and this evening the wife of Thos. Bishop, another old Servant who had lived with me an equal number of years also died.

Thomas Bishop's wife, Susanna, had served as midwife for slaves and servants on the Mount Vernon plantations.

Monday 12th. After an early breakfast George [Augustine] Washington, Mr. Shaw & my self went into the woods back of Muddy hole Plantation a hunting and were joined by Mr. Lund Washington and Mr. William Peake. About half after ten Oclock (being first plagued with the Dogs running Hogs) We found a fox near Colo. Masons Plantation on little Hunting Creek (West fork) having followed on his Drag more than half a Mile; and run him with Eight Dogs (the other 4 get-

ting, as was supposed, after a second Fox) close and well for an hour—
When the Dogs came to a fault, and to cold Hunting until 20 Minutes
after 12 When being joined by the missing Dogs they put him up a
fresh and in about 50 Minutes killed [him] up in an open field of Colo.
Mason's—every rider & every Dog being present at the death.

Two Hounds which were lent, and sent to me yesterday by Mr.
Chichester—viz.—a Dog named Rattler, & a Bitch named Juno—be-
haved very well. My French Dogs also come on—all, except the Bitch
which raized Puppies, running constantly whilst the Scent was hot.

Saturday 17th. Went to Alexandria to meet the Trustees of the Academy in that place and offered to vest in the hands of the said Trustees,
when they are permanently established by Charter, the Sum of One
thousand pounds, the Interest of which only, to be applied towards
the establishment of a charity School for the education of Orphan and
other poor Children—which offer was accepted. Returned again in the
Evening—Roads remarkably wet & bad.

> GW wrote the trustees, 17 Dec. 1785: "It is not in my power at this time to
> advance the above sum; but that a measure which may be productive of good
> may not be delayed—I will until my death, or until it shall be more conve-
> nient for my Estate to advance the principal, pay the interest thereof (to wit,
> Fifty pounds) annually" (*Papers, Confederation Series,* 3:463–64). In his will,
> GW left 20 shares of stock in the Bank of Alexandria, valued at $4,000, to
> fulfill this promise. The charity school was incorporated as an integral part
> of the academy, to be governed by the same board of trustees. In 1786 there
> were 20 charity children attending the school.

Tuesday 20th. Dispatched at his own reqt. the Spaniard who had the
cha[rge] of my Jack from Spain. Sent him with Mr. Shaw to Alexandria
to go in the Stage to New York. Mr. Shaw returned in the evening accompanied by my Nephew Ferdinando Washington.

> *The Spaniard:* Pedro Tellez, who had accompanied the Spanish jackass to
> Mount Vernon (see entry for 26 Oct. 1785), had asked to return to Spain
> by way of New York, where he would see the Spanish minister, Don Diego
> de Gardoqui. He refused any payment from GW, asserting that he was being
> paid by the king, but GW did prevail upon him to take £21 "as an acknowl-
> edgment of the obligation I am under to him, for his care of the animal
> on which I set the highest value" (GW to Francisco Rendon, 19 Dec. 1785,
> *Papers, Confederation Series,* 3:473–74).
>
> Ferdinand, or Ferdinando, Washington (1767–1788) was the oldest son of
> GW's deceased brother Samuel and Anne Steptoe Washington. In 1783 GW
> had written his brother John Augustine about the possibility of a berth in the
> navy or on a merchant ship for their nephew, but nothing seems to have
> come of this inquiry. Ferdinand, by extravagance and bad conduct, incurred
> GW's displeasure, and GW later refused to assist in settling the young man's
> estate.

1786

February

Thursday 16th. Put one of Doctr. Gordons Subscription Papers (yesterday) in the hands of Doctr. Craik to offer to his acquaintance.

Dr. William Gordon (1728–1809), a dissenting minister in England, migrated to America in 1770 and settled in Roxbury, Mass., where he soon became active in the independence movement. As the Revolution progressed, Gordon began copying and collecting documents with which to write a history of the struggle, and in 1784 he visited at Mount Vernon for 2½ weeks while he copied and abstracted Revolutionary documents from among GW's papers. Before he returned to England (1786) to find a publisher, Gordon circulated subscription papers for his history, which was first published in four volumes as *The History of the Rise, Progress, and Establishment of Independence of the United States of America* (London, 1788). Besides this subscription paper given to Dr. Craik, GW forwarded copies to correspondents in Alexandria and Fredericksburg. GW subscribed to two sets himself, for a total of £2 (Ledger B, 223).

Saturday 18th. Began the yards back of the Green house designed for the Jack Ass & Magnolia.

The Bitch Stately was lined by the Dog Vulcan. Jupiter had been put to her and Venus but never seemed to take the least notice of them but whether he ever lined either of them is not certain. The contrary is supposed.

Rid to the Plantation in the Neck and returned home by Muddy hole and visited the sick men there whom I found better.

March

Friday 10th. Between breakfast and Dinner, a Mr. Rollins, who has undertaken to finish my new Room came here settled a plan with my joiners & returned before dinner.

John Rawlins, a stucco worker, or plasterer, was originally from England. Recommended by GW's former aide Tench Tilghman, now a Baltimore merchant, Rawlins had come to Mount Vernon in Sept. 1785 to make an estimate of the cost of decorating the New Room and in November sent GW a drawing of his design for the room and an estimate of £168 Maryland currency plus traveling expenses for "Ornaments in Ceiling, Cove, Cornice & moulding at top of cove, with pannels on the walls plaine" (Tilghman to GW, 31 Aug. 1785, GW to Tilghman, 14 Sept. 1785, Rawlins to GW, 15 Nov. 1785, *Papers, Confederation Series*, 3:213–14, 249, 359). Although GW declared this price to be exorbitant, he let Tilghman make an agreement with Rawlins for the work. GW was to provide food and lodging for Rawlins and his workers and transportation for them and for "such of the Stucco as it shall be necessary to mould at Baltimore."

Monday 13th. The ground being in order for it, I set the people to raising and forming the mounds of Earth by the gate in order to plant weeping willow thereon.

Sent my Boat to Alexanda. for Salt with the Overseer in it who by my order, engaged my Fishing landing at Johnsons ferry to Mr. Lomax in Alexandria—who is to put doors and windows to the house and pay Twenty five pounds for the use of it during the fishing Season.

> *Mounds of Earth:* GW's plan for the landscaping of the west front of Mount Vernon called for two artifical mounds, one on each side of the gate at the end of the bowling green. A weeping willow was to be planted on each mound.

Saturday 18th. Got the Mound on the left so far compleated as to plant the next largest of my weeping Willows thereon the buds of which were quite expanded, and the leaves appearing in their unfolded state— quaere, how much too far, in this state of the Sap, is the Season advanced? Also planted the cuttings from, or trimming, of these trees in a nursery they being in the same forward State.

Spaded up some of the ground in my botanical garden for the purpose of planting the scaly bark hiccory nut of Gloucester in.

Also a piece of ground No. West of the green House, adjoining thereto, the garden Wall, & Post & rail fencing lately erected as yards for my Stud horses in order to plant the Seed of the Honey locust &ca. &ca.

Sunday 19th. A Gentleman calling himself the Count de Cheiza D'arteignan Officer of the French Guards came here to dinner; but bringing no letters of introduction, nor any authentic testemonials of his being either; I was at a loss how to receive, or treat him. He stayed dinner and the evening.

> The comte de Cheiza d'Artaignan had just arrived in Alexandria from Cap Français in Saint Domingue (d'Artaignan to GW, 18 Mar. 1786, *Papers, Confederation Series,* 3:603).

Thursday 30th. Rid to the ferry, Dogue run, and Muddy hole plantations & to the Mill.

On my return home, found a Mr. Wallace, an Irish Gentlemen— some time since recommended to me by Mr. Edward Newenham, here.

Planted in the holly clumps, in my shrubberies, a number of small holly trees which some months ago Colo. Lee of Stratford sent me in a box with earth—also in the same shrubberies some of the slips of the Tree box. I also planted several holly trees which had been sent to me the day before by a Neighbour Mr. Thos. Allison.

> Sir Edward Newenham (1732–1814), the Irish politician who represented Dublin in Parliament at this time, had recommended Wallace to GW. GW

and Newenham corresponded from at least 1781 until a few years before GW's death. Wallace returned to Mount Vernon early in June and left soon after for Bordeaux.

Thomas Allison (Alliston) lived in the lower Accotink Creek area on the road leading to GW's mill.

April

Sunday 9th. Mr. Dalby of Alexandria came here to dinner, and returned afterwards. In the Afternoon Doctr. Stuart and his Sister arrived and stayed all night.

Philip Dalby came to enlist GW's support in recovering a slave. While visiting in Philadelphia, Dalby's servant had been lured away by a group of Quakers organized for the purpose of freeing slaves brought to that city. Dalby inserted a long notice in the Alexandria newspaper warning the general public of this "insidious" practice of the Quakers (*Va. Journal*, 30 Mar. 1786) and was at this time going to Philadelphia to petition the Pennsylvania assembly for the return of his property. GW wrote to Robert Morris, 12 April 1786: "If the practice of this Society of which Mr. Dalby speaks, is not discountenanced, none of those whose *misfortune* it is to have slaves as attendants, will visit the City if they can possibly avoid it." He added that although he deplored the institution of slavery, its abolition must come through legislative action (*Papers, Confederation Series*, 4:15–17. Dalby's suit was successful, and he recovered his slave.

Monday 10th. Began my brick work to day—first taking away the foundations of the Garden Houses as they were first placed, & repairing the damages in the Walls occasioned by their removal. And also began to put up my pallisades (on the Wall).

GW was in the process of enlarging his upper and lower gardens. The north and south walls of each garden were extended westward in an inward curve to a point where they converged. At this point in each garden, GW rebuilt an octagonal garden house.

Friday 21st. About Noon, one James Bloxham, an English Farmer from Gloucestershire arrived here with letters of recommendation from Colo. Fairfax (& others to him) consequent of my request to him to enquire after such a person.

Brought from England on the recommendation of George William Fairfax, James Bloxham signed an agreement with GW to serve as "Farmer and Manager" at 50 guineas a year, with house, provisions, and an extra 10 guineas to bring his family from England. Neither party to the agreement seemed entirely satisfied at first. GW wrote Arthur Young that Bloxham seemed to be a plain and honest farmer, but that his ability to manage a large farm was questionable. Bloxham wrote home that the plows were shocking, the farmhands disagreeable, and "it is impossible for any man to Do Bisness in any form" (Bloxham to William Peacey, 23 July 1786, in Abbott, "James Bloxham," 188–89).

May

Monday 8th. In the Evening a Captn. Whaley from Yohiogany came in on some business respecting the Affairs of the deceased Val. Crawford and Hugh Stephenson. He also promised to send in my Negros which had been hired to Gilbert Simpson or bring them in himself. In consequence of this assurance I gave him an order on Majr. Freeman to deliver them.

Thomas Freeman, GW's western agent, had been requested 16 Oct. 1785 to hire "a careful person" to bring the slaves at Washington's Bottom to Mount Vernon, "if the measure can be reconciled to them." Of the nine Negroes now there, three apparently were young children, and two, Simon and Nancy, had been among the four slaves sent by GW in 1773 to help start Simpson's plantation (Ledger B, 87). Despite an absence of nearly 13 years, these last two slaves had some reasons to return to Mount Vernon. "Simon's countrymen, & Nancy's relations," GW had explained to Freeman "are all here, & would be glad to see them; I would make a Carpenter of Simon, to work along with his shipmate Jambo." Nevertheless, none of the slaves, according to Freeman, could be persuaded to go to Mount Vernon "from any Argument I could use" (GW to Freeman, 16 Oct. 1785, Freeman to GW, 18 Dec. 1786, *Papers, Confederation Series*, 3:308–10, 4:463–65). All were sold to various purchasers 5 Oct. 1786, Simon bringing £100 and Nancy together with a young child bringing £80 15s. Total receipts amounted to £418 15s.

Monday 29th. About 9 Oclock, Mr. Tobias Lear, who had been previously engaged on a salary of 200 dollars, to live with me as a private Secretary & precepter for Washington Custis a year came here from New Hampshire, at which place his friends reside.

Agreed this day with James Bloxham, who arrived here the [21st] of April from England, to live with and superintend my farming business upon the terms mentioned in a specific agreement in writing.

Benjamin Lincoln recommended Tobias Lear (1762–1816), a Harvard graduate from New Hampshire, to GW for the position of secretary and tutor, describing him as having the "character of a Gentleman & a schollar" (Lincoln to GW, 4 Jan. 1786, *Papers, Confederation Series*, 3:492–93). Lear asked for $200 a year, and GW agreed to it in April. What started as only a one-year appointment developed into a close association and an enduring friendship. Lear served, with some intermissions, as secretary and executive assistant for much of the rest of GW's life.

June

Sunday 4th. Received from on board the Brig Ann, from Ireland, two Servant Men for whom I had agreed yesterday—viz.—Thomas Ryan a

Shoemaker, and Caven Bowe a Tayler redemptioners for 3 years Service by Indenture if they could not pay, each, the Sum of £12 Sterg. which sums I agreed to pay.

> On 8 June, William Deakins, Jr. (1742–1798), a Georgetown merchant, announced the arrival at Georgetown of "the brig Anne, Capt. Tolson, with one hundred and fifty very healthy indentured servants; among them are several valuable tradesmen—Their indentures will be disposed of on reasonable terms for cash or tobacco" (*Va. Journal,* 8 June 1786).

Monday 19th. A Monsr. Andri Michaux—A Botanest sent by the Court of France to America (after having been only 6 Weeks returned from India) came in a little before dinner with letters of Introduction & recommendation from the Duke de Lauzen, & Marqs. de la Fayette to me. He dined and returned afterwards to Alexandria on his way to New York, from whence he had come; and where he was about to establish a Botanical garden.

> André Michaux (1746–1802) was a French botanist whose work in America would later produce *Flora Boreali-Americana* (1803). He sent a note to GW the day after his visit, enclosing some seeds and promising to send live plants. In 1793 GW subscribed a small sum to assist the American Philosophical Society in financing an expedition Michaux planned to make to the Pacific. Thomas Jefferson collected the money on behalf of the society and wrote an elaborate set of instructions to guide Michaux in his research, just as he would do for Meriwether Lewis ten years later. While the objectives of the expedition were ostensibly scientific, Michaux was in reality acting as the agent of the French minister Edmond Genet in a scheme to mount an assault on Spanish possessions beyond the Mississippi. After Genet's recall Michaux's expedition was terminated by Genet's successor in Mar. 1794.

July

Wednesday 5th. I set out about sun rising, & taking my harvest fields at Muddy hole & the ferry in my way, got home to breakfast.

Found that my harvest had commenced as I directed, at Muddy hole & in the Neck on Monday last—with 6 Cradlers at the first—to wit, Isaac, Cowper Tom, Ben overseer Will, Adam, & Dogue run Jack who tho' newly entered, made a very good hand; and gave hopes of being an excellent Cradler. That Joe (Postilian) had taken the place of Sambo at the Ferry since Monday last, & the harvest there proceeded under the cutting of Caesar, Boatswain, & him. That in the Neck 6 cradles were constantly employed, & sometimes 7—viz. James, (who having cut himself in the meadow could not work constantly)—Davy, Overseer who having other matters to attend to, could not stick to it; Sambo, Essex, George (black smith) Will, Ned; and Tom Davis who had never cut before, and made rather an awkward hand of it. Tom Nokes was also there, but he cut only now & then, at other times shocking, repairing rakes &ca. That the gangs at Dogue Run & Muddy hole were united, & were assisted by Anthony, Myrtilla & Dolshy from the home house—That besides Tom Davis Ben from the Mill had gone into the Neck and that Sall brass (when not washing) & Majr. Washingtons Tom were assisting the ferry people—That Cowpers Jack & Da[v]y with some small boys & girls (wch. had never been taken out before) were assisting the Farmer in making Hay after two white men who had been hired to cut grass.

> GW had just returned from a meeting of the directors of the Potomac Company at Seneca Falls.
> The slaves named here can all be found in the entry for 18 Feb. 1786 of the unabridged *Diaries*. They were often shifted temporarily from one farm to another for special tasks.
> *The Farmer:* James Bloxham.

Monday 24th. After breakfast I accompanied Colo. [Theodorick] Bland to Mr. Lund Washington's where he entered the stage on his return home. Rid from hence to the Plantations at Dogue run & Muddy hole. On my return home, found colo. Humphreys here and soon after a Captn. Cannon came in with a letter from Colo. Marshall, from Kentucke.

> David Humphreys (1752–1818) of Connecticut was a graduate of Yale and a poet. He distinguished himself during the Revolution by his rapid promotions and his appointment as aide-de-camp to GW. A lifelong friendship developed between Humphreys and GW, and Humphreys often visited Mount Vernon. He went abroad in 1784 to negotiate commercial treaties and returned in the spring of 1786 to Connecticut where in September he was elected to the assembly. At this time he was at Mount Vernon attempting to gather information for a proposed biography of GW. He remained during the winter of 1787–88, served as one of GW's secretaries 1789–90, and in 1790 again went abroad on a series of diplomatic missions.
> John Cannon delivered to GW a letter from Thomas Marshall, 19 May 1786. Thomas Marshall, formerly of Fauquier County, Va., was now residing in Fayette County, Ky. GW had commissioned him to procure the seeds of trees requested by Lafayette for use at Versailles.

August

Tuesday 8th. In the evening Mr. Fitzhugh of Chatham and Mr. Robt. Randolph came here from Ravensworth.

> William Fitzhugh (1741–1809), of Chatham, owned Ravensworth in Fairfax County. He was married to Robert Randolph's sister Anne. Robert Randolph (1760–1825), of Fauquier County, served as a lieutenant in the 3d Continental Dragoons and was wounded and taken prisoner at Tappan, N.Y., in Sept. 1778.

Friday 11th. Rid to Muddy hole and Dogue run Plantations. At the first, Sowing wheat begun this Morning. At the latter I agreed with one James Lawson who was to provide another hand to ditch for me in my mill swamp upon the following terms—viz.—to allow them every day they work—each 1 lb. of salt or 1½ of fresh meat pr. day—1¼lb. of brown bread, 1 pint of spirits and a bottle of Milk—the bread to be baked at the House, & their Meat to be Cooked by Morris's wife—and to allow them 16 d. pr. rod for ditches of 4 feet wide at top, 1 foot wide at bottom, and 2 feet deep; with 12 or 15 Inches footing and 2/. for ditches of 6 feet wide at top, 2 feet at bottom, and two ft. deep with equal footing.

> GW and James Lawson of Fairfax County signed an agreement on 14 Aug. in which GW hired the latter on a temporary basis as a ditcher. In November Lawson agreed to a year's service at a salary of £31 10s. Virginia currency. Patrick Sheriden was probably the hand Lawson provided, as GW also engaged him in November, at eight dollars per month (agreements with Lawson, 14 Aug. and 18 Nov. 1786, Washington Papers, Library of Congress). GW discharged Sheriden in Dec. 1786, and Lawson left Mount Vernon because of ill health in Sept. 1787 prior to the termination of his contract.

Sunday 12th. Thomas McCarty left this yesterday—it being found that he was unfit for a Household Steward. Richard Burnet took his place on the wages of Thirty pounds pr. ann.

> Richard Burnet, whose tenure at Mount Vernon began in 1783, was a "House keeper," or steward. He lived in Benjamin Dulany's family before coming into GW's employ (Lund Washington to GW, 12 Mar. 1783, Mount Vernon Ladies' Association of the Union). Lund described him as "clever in his Way, he is a very good Natured Peacable inoffensive well behaved man, and so far as we have been able to judge, will answer the purpose for which he was got, he certainly is a good cook, he appears to be careful active & Industrious, with respect to preservg., Pickling &c.—he is at no loss, but does these things very Ready & Well" (Lund Washington to GW, 1 Oct. 1783, Mount Vernon Ladies' Association of the Union). Burnet seems to have left Mount Vernon briefly early in 1786 and returned in May. He is probably the same man who worked as butler or house steward at Mount Vernon from 1786 until 1789 under the name of Richard Burnet Walker (Ledger B, 234).

Sunday 13th. Mr. Shaw quitted this family to day.

> William Shaw resigned to go to the West Indies.

Monday 14th. Went by way of Muddy hole & Dogue run plantations to the Meadow, in my Mill Swamp, to set the Ditche[r]s to work, only one of whom appeared. I intended to have run a course or two of Fencing at Muddy hole but Meeting with Genl. Duplessis in the road who intended to Mt. Vernon but had lost his way I returned home with him where Colo. Humphreys had just arrived before us.

Thomas Antoine Mauduit du Plessis (1753–1791) came to America in 1777 and served in the Continental Army before France officially joined the war, distinguishing himself at Brandywine, Germantown, Red Bank, and Monmouth. He returned to France after the war but remained only temporarily. Writing to GW from New York on 20 July 1786, he reported that he had bought a large tract of land in Georgia and was looking forward to becoming an American citizen. In 1787, however, he returned to French service and was sent to Saint Domingue to command a regiment at Port-au-Prince, where he was killed in 1791 during the insurrection on the island.

Sunday 27. At home all day alone.

Monday 28th. Just after we had breakfasted, & my horse was at the door for me to ride, Colonel and Mrs. Rogers came in. When they sat down to breakfast which was prepared for them, I commenced my ride for Muddy hole, Dogue run & Ferry Plantations also to my meadow on Dogue run and the Mill.

Nicholas Rogers (1753–1822), the son of Nicholas Rogers III, was a prominent Baltimore merchant.

Tuesday 31st. Siezed with an ague before Six Oclock this morning after having laboured under a fever all night. Sent for Doctr. Craik who arrived just as we were setting down to dinner; who, when he thought my fever sufficiently abated, gave me a cathartick and directed the Bark to be applied in the Morning.

Bark: Quinine derived from the bark of various species of the cinchona tree was ground into a powder and taken to reduce fevers.

September

Friday 15th. Sent my Boat to Alexandria for Molasses & Coffee which had been sent to me from Surinam by a Mr. Branden of that place.

GW wished to breed Royal Gift, the jackass he had received from Spain in late 1785. Hearing that South America was noted for its jennies, GW, through William Lyles & Co. of Alexandria, got in touch with Samuel Branden, a merchant in Surinam (Netherlands Guiana), and asked him to purchase for him "one of the largest & best she asses that can be obtained in your country fit to breed from." Unsure how much such an animal would cost, GW had 25 barrels of superfine flour placed on board one of Lyles's ships bound for Surinam. If Branden could not procure an ass for him, GW asked that he send instead two hogsheads of molasses and some coffee. Branden sent GW an ass, and molasses and coffee as well, in exchange for the flour (GW to Branden, 10 Feb., 20 Nov. 1786, *Papers, Confederation Series*, 3:551).

Saturday 30th. Mr. McQuir came here to Dinner & to invite me to the Accadamical commencement in Alexandria on Thursday next.

Accadamical commencement: "On Friday the 6th instant was held in the Alexandria Academy, an Examination of the Classical School, under the Care of the Rev. William M'Whir" (*Va. Journal,* 19 Oct. 1786).

October

Wednesday 11th. Majr. Washington, his wife, and Nelly & Washington Custis went up to the race at Alexa. All but the Major returned to Dinner with Betcy & Patcy Custis along with them.

I rid to the Plantations, found most of my People had gone to the races. Those remaining in the Neck were cleaning rye which had been tread out the day before & preparing to continue their wheat sowing tomorrow.

Sunday 15th. Accompanied by Majr. Washington his wife Mr. Lear & the two Childn. Nelly & Washington Custis went to Pohick Church & returned to Dinner. Fell in with on the Road, Colo. Jno. Mercer, his Lady & child coming here and their nurse.

Col. John Francis and Sophia Sprigg Mercer of Maryland had a son, Richard, born 19 Nov. 1785.

Wednesday 18th. Monsr. Ouster, French Consul at Williamsburgh & Mr. Lacaze two French Gentlemen dined here & returned to Alexa. in the evening.

Martin Oster, who came to Philadelphia from France in 1778 as an officer in the French consular service, held the post of vice-consul of Philadelphia 1781–83 and of Norfolk and Williamsburg from 1783 until his recall in 1792. He was traveling to several port cities at the time of this visit to Mount Vernon. Mr. Lacaze was a French merchant active in the Franco-American trade during the 1780s.

Monday 23d. Mr. [John] Rumney went away directly after breakfast and Mrs. Washington with Nelly and Washington Custis for Abingdon about the same time. I remained home all day. In the evening Colo. Monroe, his Lady and Mr. Maddison came in.

James Monroe (1758–1831) had served as a delegate from Virginia to the Continental Congress since 1783 but had recently resigned because no delegate was eligible to serve more than three out of six years. Writing from New York on 7 Oct. 1786, Monroe had suggested to James Madison, who was in Philadelphia on personal business after attending the convention in Annapolis, that they travel to Virginia together and stop over at Mount Vernon to visit GW (Rutland, *Madison Papers,* 9:121–22, 143). Monroe and his wife, Elizabeth Kortright Monroe (d. 1830), were on their way to Fredericksburg, Va., where they intended to reside in a house belonging to Monroe's uncle, Joseph Jones. Madison was going to Richmond for the fall session of the Virginia General Assembly.

Sunday 29th. About noon Mrs. Stuart and one of her youngest Children left this for Mr. Lund Washingtons. At the same time I crossed the river with intention to view & Survey my land in Charles County Maryland. Went to and lodged at Govr. Smallwoods about 14 Miles from the Ferry.

> After his service as a major general during the Revolution, William Smallwood (1732–1792) was elected to the Confederation Congress in 1785 but before assuming office was chosen to succeed William Paca as governor of Maryland. After serving three one-year terms, Smallwood retired in 1788 to his home in southern Maryland.

Tuesday 31st. After breakfast I left Govr. Smallwoods & got home to dinner. Attempted to cross at the Widow Chapmans in order to pay Colo. Mason a visit but could not get over.

> Constantia Pearson Chapman (c.1714–c.1791) was the daughter of Capt. Simon Pearson (died c.1733) of Stafford County, Va., and the widow of Nathaniel Chapman of Charles County, Md.

November

Friday 3d. At home writing Letters.

Saturday 4th. Rid to all the Plantations. On my return home found Colo. Pinkney his Lady & 4 Childn., Mrs. Middleton her Child nurse &ca. here—also Mr. Robt. and Mr. Lawe. Washington and Mr. Thompson. The 3 last went away after dinner—the others stayed all Night.

> Charles Cotesworth Pinckney (1746–1825), the son of Charles and Elizabeth Lucas Pinckney of South Carolina, had a distinguished career in the public service of his state and country as a soldier, statesman, and diplomat. Pinckney's wife was Mary Stead Pinckney. The children GW mentioned here were Pinckney's by his first wife. Mrs. Middleton was probably Mary Izard Middleton, the daughter of Walter Izard of Cedar Grove, S.C., and the wife of Arthur Middleton (1742–1787), who was the brother of Sarah Pinckney. At this time Pinckney and his entourage were returning from a trip north.

Monday 6th. I rid to the Plantations at the Ferry, Dogue run & Muddy hole. On my return home found Colo. Lewis Morris and his Brother Major Jacob Morris here, who dined and returned to Alexandria afterwards where Mrs. Lewis Morris & her Mother Mrs. Elliot were on their way to Charleston.

> Lewis and Jacob Morris (1755–1844) were sons of Lewis Morris (1726–1798) and Mary Walton Morris of Morrisania, Westchester County, N.Y., and nephews of Gouverneur Morris. Both brothers served during the Revolution in the New York militia before becoming aides-de-camp.

Saturday 11th. Having received a letter from Baltimore, announcing the arrival of three Asses (a male and two females) from the Marquis de la Fayette for me together with some Pheasants and Pa[r]tridges from France, I sent my Overseer Jno. Fairfax and a servant to bring the former.

Monday 13th. Agreed to let the Widow Alton have the House used for a School by my Mill if the School should be discontinued and Told James Bloxham, my Farmer, who was about to write to England for his Wife & family, and who proposed the measure that he might write to one Caleb Hall a Neighbour of his in Gloucestershire (who had expressed a desire to come to this Country, and who he said was a compleat Wheel Wright, Waggon builder, and Plow & Hurdle maker) that I wd. give him 25 Guineas a year for his Services (if he paid his own passage to this Country) the first year, and if I found he answered my purposes, & we liked each other, that I might give him 30 guineas the next yr. and held out encouragemt. if he chose to work for himself, that I would provide him with some place to live at—Whilst with me that he should be found in Provisions, Washing & lodging.

> *Widow Alton:* Mrs. Elizabeth Alton was the widow of GW's old servant John Alton, who had died the previous year.
>
> James Bloxham had sent for his wife and two daughters to join him at Mount Vernon, while his two sons were to remain in England to obtain an education. Bloxham's former neighbor Caleb Hall eventually decided against emigrating (Peacey to GW, 2 Feb. 1787, and GW to Peacey, 16 Nov. 1786, 7 Jan. 1788, *Papers, Confederation Series,* 4:375–76, 5:6–7, 6:13–14).

Thursday 16. Rid into the Neck, and to Muddy hole plantations. On my return home, found Mons. Campoint sent by the Marqs. de la Fayette with the Jack and two She Asses which he had procured for me in the Island of Malta and which had arrived at Baltimore with the Chinese Pheasants &ca. had with my Overseer &ca. got there before me. These Asses are in good order and appear to be very fine. The Jack is two years old and the She Asses one three & the other two. The Pheasants and Pa[r]tridges will come round by Water.

> During his visit to Mount Vernon in 1784, Lafayette apparently had offered to obtain breeding stock from Malta. Because GW was unsure that his Spanish jacks were coming, he asked Lafayette to obtain "a male & female, or *one* of former & *two* of the latter" from the governor of Malta or some other person (GW to Lafayette, 15 Feb., 1 Sept. 1785, *Papers, Confederation Series,* 2: 363–67, 3:215–18). When they arrived, accompanied by caretaker Jacques Campion, GW was delighted. He wrote to Lafayette on 19 Nov. 1786: "On thursday last I received in very good order . . . the most valuable things you could have sent me, a Jack and two she Asses, all of which are very fine." He named the jack Knight of Malta. GW expected to pay for the animals, but Lafayette clearly intended them as a gift.

Saturday 25th. Bought the time of a Dutch family consisting of a Man by profession a Ditcher, Mower, &ca., a Woman his wife a Spinner,

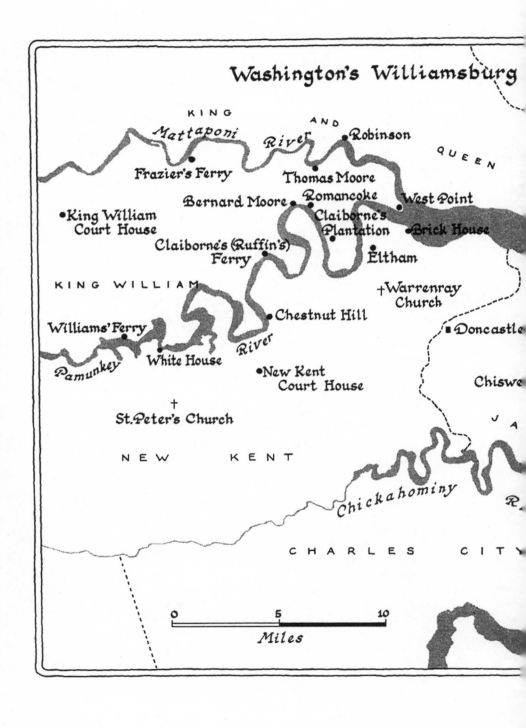

Washington's Williamsburg

KING

Mattaponi River AND Robinson

QUEEN

Frazier's Ferry Thomas Moore

Bernard Moore Romancoke West Point
Claiborne's
Plantation Brick House

•King William
Court House
Claiborne's (Ruffin's)
Ferry Eltham

KING WILLIAM
+Warrenray
Church

Chestnut Hill ∎Doncastle

Williams' Ferry

White House River Chiswe

Pamunkey •New Kent
Court House
J A

+
St.Peter's Church

N E W   K E N T

Chickahominy R.

C H A R L E S   C I T Y

0   5   10

Miles

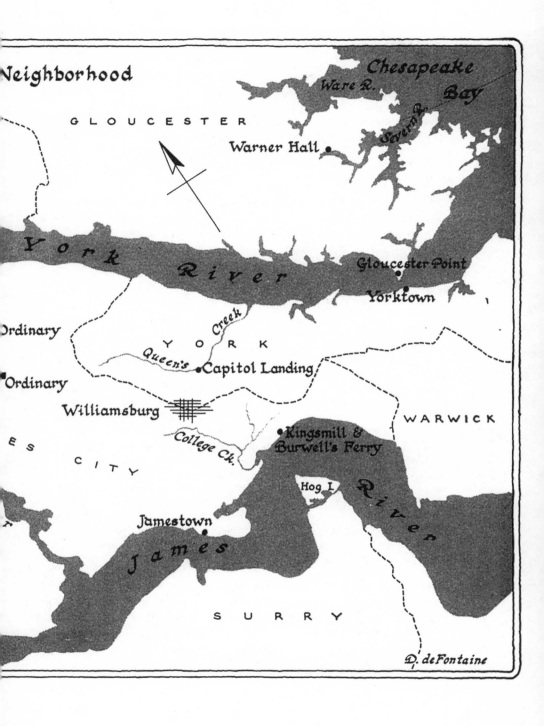

washer, Milker and their child—names. Daniel Overdunk Margarett
Overdunk Anna Overdunk. Dined at Colo. Hooes and returned home
in the evening.

> GW had secured the services of the Overdoncks, a German family—probably
> redemptioners—through the agency of Philip Marsteller, an Alexandria
> merchant. Today GW sent a barge to Alexandria to transport them to Mount
> Vernon and requested Marsteller "to impress upon them in strong terms
> the propriety of diligent attention to their duty" (GW to Marsteller, 27 Nov.
> 1786, and Marsteller to GW, 27 Nov. 1786, *Papers, Confederation Series,* 4:
> 402–4; Ledger B, 245).

Monday 27th. The Revd. Mr. Keith, and the Revd. Mr. Morse dined
here & returned to Alexandria in the Evening. Received my Chinese
Pheasents &ca. from Baltimore by the Packet—viz.—A Cock & Hen of
the Gold Pheast. A Cock & Hen of the Silver Pheat. A Cock & 2 Hens
of the French Pheat. and one French Patridge. The other French
Patridge died in coming round from Baltimore. The German Man, his
wife and Child came home last Night by water from Alexanda.

> Jedidiah Morse (1761–1826) was born in Woodstock, Conn., the son of
> Jedidiah and Sarah Child Morse. While studying theology at Yale in the early
> 1780s, Morse expanded an early interest in geography and in 1784 pub-
> lished the first school textbook on the subject, *Geography Made Easy,* a fore-
> runner of his more ambitious later works. The day after his ordination in
> the Congregational church on 9 Nov. 1786, Morse left his position as tutor
> at Yale and at this time was on his way to become pastor of a church in Mid-
> way, Ga.
>
> *My Chinese Pheasents:* The birds, from the royal aviary of France, were a gift
> from Lafayette. Charles Willson Peale wrote from Philadelphia that if any of
> the birds should die, he would like to obtain the bodies for display. GW re-
> plied on 9 Jan. 1787: "I cannot say that I shall be happy to have it in my
> power to comply with your request by sending you the bodies of my Pheas-
> ants; but I am afraid it will not be long before they will compose a part of
> your Museum as they all appear to be drooping" (*Papers, Confederation Series,*
> 4:506–7). In February GW sent Peale the body of a golden pheasant packed
> in wool and said he would like to free the others but feared they would be
> taken by hawks.

Tuesday 28th. A Hound bitch which like most of my other hounds appearing to be going Mad and had been shut up getting out, my Servant
Will in attempting to get her in again was snapped at by her at the arm.
The Teeth penetrated through his Coat and Shirt and contused the
Flesh but he says did not penetrate the skin nor draw any blood. This
happened on Monday forenoon. The part affected appeared to swell a
little to day.

1787

January

Wednesday 10th. Just before Dinner Mr. Brindley Manager of the Susquehanna Works & his Son in law came on their way to South Carolina.

About the sametime I recd. by express the acct. of the sudden death (by a fit of the Gout in the head) of my beloved Brother Colo. Jno. Auge. Washington. At home all day.

March

Saturday 3d. The Revd. Mr. Weems, and yg. Doctr. Craik who came here yesterday in the afternoon left this about Noon for Port Tobo. Doctr. Stuart came here in the evening.

> Mason Locke Weems (1759–1825), born in Anne Arundel County, Md., spent part of his youth in England, where in 1784 he was ordained a priest of the Anglican church, returning to Maryland to be rector (1784–89) of All Hallows Parish at South River in Anne Arundel County. Weems supported his wife and their ten children by traveling the east coast promoting and selling popular books, preaching in various sanctuaries (including Pohick Church), and writing moral essays and biographies of American heroes, including one of the earliest biographies of GW, which was published in 1800.

April

Tuesday 10th. Recd. from Mr. Jno. Lawson, Negro Neptune, on trial as a Brick layer.

> John Lawson (1754–1823), of Dumfries, had agreed to sell his newly acquired slave, Neptune, to GW. Upon the slave's arrival at Mount Vernon, GW wrote Lawson that Neptune, "although he does not profess to be a workman, yet as he has some little knowledge of Bricklaying, seems willing to learn, and is with a man who understands the business, I will keep him." Unfortunately, however, GW learned also that Neptune was unhappy at being sold so far from his wife. GW informed Lawson that he was "unwilling to hurt the feelings of anyone. I shall therefore if agreeable to you keep him a while to see if I can reconcile him to the separation (seeing her now and then) in which case I will purchase him, if not I will send him back." A short time later Neptune ran away and returned to Lawson's plantation. Lawson offered to hire him to GW by the month, an offer Neptune himself agreed to (Lawson to GW, 17 Mar., 2, 18, and 25 April 1787, and GW to Lawson, 10 April 1787, *Papers, Confederation Series,* 5:91–92, 121, 138, 150, 154–55).

GW had not attended the Annapolis Convention held in the fall of 1786 to discuss reform of commercial restrictions imposed on interstate commerce by various states. When the convention recommended that a convention dealing with the larger issues growing out of the weakness of the Articles of Confedera-

tion be held in Philadelphia the following May, GW's attendance became a matter of urgency. In spite of pressure from friends and political advisers, GW at first was reluctant to attend partly because he had already declined an invitation from the Society of the Cincinnati to preside over their meeting in May in Philadelphia, partly because he was uncertain of the legality of the meeting, and partly because he was concerned about the convention's prospects for success. Finally convinced of the necessity for his presence in Philadelphia, he set off for the city on 8 May 1787. Because he accidentally left the notebook in which he was currently recording his diary entries behind, his daily notations for the Constitutional Convention were entered in a new notebook and later recopied and expanded. For a description of the two diaries and their entries, see Diaries, 5:152–53. GW traveled to Philadelphia by way of Baltimore, where he dined at Daniel Grant's Fountain Inn and lodged with his former aide-de-camp James McHenry. On 12 May he crossed the Susquehanna River at Havre de Grace and proceeded to Wilmington, Del. On Sunday, 13 May, he reached Chester, Pa., where he was met by Pennsylvania and congressional dignitaries and escorted to Philadelphia. "On my arrival," he noted, "the Bells were chimed." During his stay in Philadelphia, GW lodged with Robert Morris and his wife Mary White Morris (Diaries, 5:153–56).

May

Tuesday. 8th. The Weather being squally with Showers I defer'd setting off till the Morning. Mr. Chas. Lee came in to dinner but left it afterwards.

A concise acct. of my Journey to Philadelphia, and the manner of spending my time there, and places where, will now follow—after whi[c]h. I shall return to the detail of Plantation occurrances as they respect my Crops & intended experiments agreeably to the reports which have been made to me by my Nephew Geo: Auge. Washington in my absence.

Monday 14th. This being the day appointed for the Convention to meet, such Members as were in town assembled at the State Ho[use]; but only two States being represented—viz.—Virginia & Pensylvania— agreed to attend at the same place at 11 'Oclock to morrow. Dined in a family way at Mr. Morris's.

> The convention met on 14 May for the first time but not enough states were present to hold sessions until 25 May when the arrival of the last member of the delegation from New Jersey gave the convention a quorum.

Tuesday 15th. Repaired, at the hour appointed to the State Ho[use], but no more States being represented than were yesterday (tho' several more members had come in) we agreed to meet again to morrow.

Govr. Randolph from Virginia came in to day. Dined with the Members, to the Genl. Meeting of the Society of the Cincinnati.

> Edmund Randolph, in his capacity as governor of Virginia, was the head of the Virginia delegation. *Cincinnati:* GW was dining with about 20 delegates of various state societies of the Cincinnati, in Philadelphia for the second general meeting of the society. The general meeting reelected GW president.

Wednesday 16th. No more than two States being yet represented, agreed till a quoram of them should be formed to alter the hour of Meeting at the State house to One oclock. Dined at the President Doctr. Franklins and drank Tea, and spent the evening at Mr. Jno. Penns.

> Benjamin Franklin later commented on this dinner: "We have here at present what the French call *une assemblée des notables* a convention composed of some of the principal people from the several States of our confederation. They did me the honor of dining with me last Wednesday" (Franklin to Thomas Jordan, 18 May 1787, Farrand, *Federal Convention,* 3:21). Franklin's dining room seated 24 comfortably, which was about the number of delegates in the city by this date.
> John Penn (1729–1795) of Lansdowne, a grandson of William Penn, was the last proprietary lieutenant governor of Pennsylvania. After 1776 he lived in political retirement, dividing his time between his country estate, Lansdowne, and his town house in Philadelphia.

Thursday 17th. Mr. [John] Rutledge from Charleston and Mr. Chs. Pinkney from Congress having arrived gave a representation to So: Carolina and Colo. Mason getting in this Evening placed all the Delegates from Virginia on the floor of Convention. Dined at Mr. Powells and dr[an]k Tea there.

> The Virginia General Assembly, through a joint ballot of both houses, elected a seven-man delegation (any three providing a minimum for a quorum), which could cast Virginia's vote in the convention by a majority vote within the delegation. The returns show GW first, followed by Patrick Henry, Edmund Randolph, John Blair, James Madison, George Mason, and George Wythe (Farrand, *Federal Convention,* 3:561). Of the seven originally chosen, GW vacillated for months before accepting; only Patrick Henry declined outright and was replaced by Dr. James McClurg.
> *Colo. Mason:* Three days after his arrival, George Mason wrote to his son, George Mason, Jr.: "the Virg[ini]a Deputies (who are all here) meet and confer together two or three Hours, every Day; in order to form a proper Correspondence of Sentiments" (Rutland, *Mason Papers,* 3:880).
> Samuel Powel's house was on the west side of Third Street between Spruce and Walnut streets.

Friday 18th. The representation from New York appeared on the floor to day.

Dined at Greys ferry, and drank Tea at Mr. Morris's—after which accompanied Mrs. [Morris] and some other Ladies to hear a Mrs.

O'Connell read (a charity affair). The lady being reduced in circumstances had had recourse to this expedient to obtain a little money. Her
performe. was tolerable—at the College-Hall.

> *Greys ferry:* The recently opened public gardens on the west bank of the
> Schuylkill at Gray's ferry were an innovation in public amusement gardens
> for Philadelphia. Patterned after the public gardens of London, the Gray's
> ferry gardens placed artificial grottoes and waterfalls among beds of flowers
> and exotic plants, set in several acres of the natural landscape along the
> Schuylkill River. Here concerts, illuminations, and fireworks were presented,
> especially on holidays. Refreshments and meals were served at the ferry inn,
> incorporated into the gardens.
>
> *Mrs. O'Connell:* On this day the *Pennsylvania Packet* reported: "The Lecture
> which was to have been read by a Lady in the University last evening was
> postponed until tonight, at the particular desire of several ladies and gentle-
> men of distinction. The Lecture to be read This Evening is a continuance of
> the Dissertation on Eloquence, which commenced in the first course."

Monday 21st. Delaware State was represented. Dined, and drank Tea
at Mr. Binghams in great Splender.

> William Bingham (1752–1804), scion of an old Pennsylvania family, was a
> British consul in Martinique before the Revolution and an American com-
> mercial agent in the West Indies during the war. In 1780 he returned to
> Philadelphia with a large fortune and married Anne Willing (1764–1801), a
> daughter of Thomas Willing and renowned as a great beauty and a brilliant
> hostess. After spending several years in Europe, the Willings returned to Phil-
> adelphia to build an elaborate town house on the west side of Third Street
> above Spruce Street, where they entertained extensively.

Wednesday 23d. No more States being represented I rid to Genl.
Mifflins to breakfast—after which in Company with him Mr. Madison,
Mr. Rutledge and others I crossed the Schuylkill above the Falls. Visited
Mr. Peters—Mr. Penns Seat, and Mr. Wm. Hamiltons.

Dined at Mr. Chews—with the Wedding guests (Colo. Howard of
Baltimore having married his daughter Peggy). Drank Tea there in a
very large Circle of Ladies.

> Thomas Mifflin's country seat overlooked the falls of the Schuylkill.
>
> Richard Peters (1744–1828), secretary of the Board of War (1776–81),
> was later appointed by GW a judge of the United States District Court for
> Pennsylvania. His country seat, Belmont, where he carried out large-scale
> agricultural experimentation, was on the west side of the Schuylkill below
> the falls. *Mr. Penns Seat:* Lansdowne, an Italianate house built c.1773 by lieu-
> tenant governor John Penn. Located on the west side of the Schuylkill about
> halfway between the falls and the Middle Ferry, Lansdowne was later incor-
> porated into Fairmount Park.
>
> William Hamilton (1745–1813), a wealthy Philadelphia patron of the arts,
> was particularly devoted to landscape gardening. Today GW is visiting Ham-
> ilton at Bush Hill, located just north of the city.
>
> Benjamin Chew's daughter Margaret (Peggy) Chew (1760–1824) married

John Eager Howard (1752–1827) on 18 May 1787. In 1788 Howard was elected governor of Maryland. This party was probably at the town house of Benjamin Chew, on Third Street between Walnut and Spruce streets. The house, built in the 1770s for William Byrd III of Westover, was later bought by Benjamin Chew, who was proscribed as a Tory during the Revolution. During the winter of 1781–82, GW made the Chew town house his headquarters.

Friday 25th. Another Delegate coming in from the State of New Jersey gave it a representation and encreased the number to Seven which forming a quorum of the 13 the Members present resolved to organize the body; when, by a unanimous vote I was called up to the Chair as President of the body. Majr. William Jackson was appointed Secretary and a Comee. was chosen consisting of 3 Members to prepare rules & regulations for conducting the business and after [ap]pointing door keepers the Convention adjourned till Monday, to give time to the Comee. to report the matters referred to them. Returned many visits to day. Dined at Mr. Thos. Willings and sp[en]t the evening at my lodgings.

A unanimous vote for GW as president had been generally expected by the delegates. Benjamin Franklin, the only other possible candidate for the honor, had planned to nominate GW, but he was unwell and Robert Morris made the nomination, seconded by John Rutledge. James Madison's notes described the scene: "General [Washington] was accordingly unanimously elected by ballot, and conducted to the chair by Mr. R. Morris and Mr. Rutlidge; from which in a very emphatic manner he thanked the Convention for the honor they had conferred on him, reminded them of the novelty of the scene of business in which he was to act, lamented his want of [better qualifications], and claimed the indulgence of the House towards the involuntary errors which his inexperience might occasion" (Farrand, *Federal Convention*, 1:3–4). Thomas Willing's three-story town house was on Third Street just below Walnut Street.

Saturday 26th. Returned all my visits this forenoon. Dined with a club at the City Tavern and spent the evening at my quarters writing letters.

My visits: In 1780 Chastellux remarked that following breakfast, "we went to visit the ladies, according to the Philadelphia custom, where the morning is the most proper hour for paying calls" (Chastellux, *Travels,* 1:135).

Sunday 27th. Went to the Romish Church—to high Mass. Dined, drank Tea, and spent the evening at my lodgings.

Romish Church: Of the two Roman Catholic chapels in Philadelphia at this time, GW probably attended the larger, St. Mary's, on Fourth below Spruce Street.

Monday 28th. Met in Convention at 10 Oclock. Two States more— viz.—Massachusetts, and Connecticut were on the floor to day.

Established Rules—agreeably to the plan brot. in by the Comee. for the governmt. of the Convention & adjourned. No com[municatio]ns without doors.

Dined at home, and drank Tea, in a large circle at Mr. Francis's.

No com[municatio]ns without doors: GW is referring to the secrecy rule that was proposed in the convention on this day. It was referred to the rules committee and adopted on the following day (Farrand, *Federal Convention,* 1:13, 15). This rule probably accounts for the fact that GW's diary entries for the convention reflect only his social activities with little mention of the work of the convention.

Tench Francis, Jr. (1730–1800), was the son of Tench Francis (d. 1758) and an uncle of Tench Tilghman, one of GW's aides during the Revolution. In 1787 he lived on Chestnut Street between Third and Fourth streets. He later became first cashier of the Bank of North America.

Tuesday 29th. Attended Convention and dined at home—after wch. accompanied Mrs. Morris to the benifit Concert of a Mr. Juhan.

Benifit Concert: Members of the local music community, made up of native Americans and post-Revolution musical migrants from England and the Continent, sometimes participated in benefit concerts in which the musician who benefited took the financial risks and received all the profits. Today's concert, which featured pieces by the contemporary European composers Haydn, Sarti, and Martini (Schwartzendorf), also included "A New Overture" by Alexander Reinagle, the local musical impresario, a flute concerto by the local composer and organist William Brown, a "Concerto Violoncello" by Henry (Henri) Capron, whom GW later hired as a music teacher for Nelly Custis, and several pieces for violin and piano by "Mr. Juhan" (*Pa. Packet,* 29 May 1787; GW Household Accounts, 1793–97).

In the spring of 1783 James Juhan (Joan, Juan), who advertised himself as a teacher of harpsichord, violin, flute, "Tenor Fiddle," violincello, and guitar, and also as a maker of harpsichords and "the great North American fortepianos," arrived in Philadelphia, and on 6 Aug. presented "a grand Concert of Music, Vocal and Instrumental" (*Pa. Gaz.,* 25 June, 6 Aug. 1783).

June

Friday 1st. June. Attending in Convention and nothing being suffered to transpire no minutes of the proceedings has been, or will be inserted in this diary.

Dined with Mr. John Penn, and spent the evening at a superb entertainment at Bush-hill given by Mr. Hamilton—at which were more than an hundred guests.

Saturday 2d. Majr. Jenifer coming in with sufficient powers for this purpose, gave a representation to Maryland; which brought all the States in Union into Convention except Rhode Island which had refused to send delegates thereto. Dined at the City Tavern with the Club & spent the evening at my own quarters.

Sunday. 3d. Dined at Mr. Clymers and drank Tea there also.

George Clymer (1739–1813) was a Philadelphia merchant and financier, an early advocate of independence, and a member of the Continental Congress (1776–78, 1780–83).

Monday 4th. Attended Convention. Representation as on Saturday. Reviewed (at the importunity of Genl. Mifflin and the officers) the Light Infantry—Cavalry—and part of the Artillery, of the City. Dined with Genl. Mifflin & drk. Tea with Miss Cadwallader.

Miss Cadwallader: probably either Rebecca Cadwalader (1746–1821) or Elizabeth Cadwalader (1760–1799), daughters of Dr. Thomas Cadwalader of Philadelphia.

Tuesday 5th. Dined at Mr. Morris's with a large Company, & Spent the Evening there. Attended in Convention the usual hours.

Wednesday 6th. In Convention as usual. Dined at the Presidents (Doctr. Franklins) & drank Tea there—after which returnd. to my lodgings and wrote letters for France.

Thursday 7th. Attended Convention as usual. Dined with a Club of Convention Members at the Indian Queen. Drank Tea & spent the evening at my lodgings.

The Indian Queen, on Fourth Street between Market and Chestnut streets, was the lodging house for a number of delegates to the convention.

Friday 8th. Attended the Convention. Dined, drank Tea, and spent the evening at my lodggs.

Saturday 9th. At Convention. Dined with the Club at the City Tavern. Drank Tea, & set till 10 oclock at Mr. Powells.

Sunday 10th. Breakfasted by agreement at Mr. Powell's, and in Company with him rid to see the Botanical garden of Mr. Bartram; which, tho' Stored with many curious plts. Shrubs & trees, many of which are exotics was not laid off with much taste, nor was it large.

From hence we rid to the Farm of one Jones, to see the effect of the plaister of Paris which appeared obviously great.

From hence we visited Mr. Powells own farm after which I went (by appointment) to the Hills & dined with Mr. & Mrs. Morris. Returned to the City abt. dark.

William Bartram (1739–1823) operated a botanical garden with his brother John, Jr. (1743–1812), on the west bank of the Schuylkill three miles from Philadelphia. William's reputation as a traveler-naturalist was enhanced by the publication in 1791 of his *Travels through North and South Carolina.* GW was a subscriber to the book but declined a request that it be dedicated to him. On 2 Oct. 1789 GW sent word to Clement Biddle, his agent in Philadelphia, that he wanted the Bartrams' list of plants plus a note about the care of each kind (*Papers, Presidential Series,* 4:124–25). In Mar. 1792 he obtained plants of 106 varieties, the surviving list bearing the heading "Catalogue of Trees, Shrubs & Plants, of Jno. Bartram." These plants were sent to George Augustine Washington, GW's manager at Mount Vernon, and a second shipment was sent down in November to replace the plants that had not flourished. While it is assumed that GW purchased the plants, it is quite possible that they were a gift from Bartram.

Samuel Powel (1739–1793) held a number of political offices in Philadelphia and was for many years mayor of the city. Powell was a member of the American Philosophical Society, a founder of the University of Pennsylvania, and president of the newly founded Philadelphia Society for Promoting Agriculture. He and his wife, Elizabeth Willing Powel, became intimate friends of the Washingtons during GW's presidential years. Today GW probably visited land Powel owned across the Schuylkill River southwest of Philadelphia.

Monday 11th. Attended in Convention. Dined, drank Tea, and spent the evening in my own room.

Tuesday 12th. Dined and drank Tea at Mr. Morris's. Went afterwards to a concert at the City Tavern.

This benefit concert, with tickets at 7s. 6d., was for Alexander Reinagle (1756–1809), an accomplished composer and a performer on several instruments, who immigrated to America in 1786 and soon became Philadelphia's leading musical impresario.

Wednesday 13th. In Convention. Dined at Mr. Clymers & drank Tea there. Spent the evening at Mr. Binghams.

Thursday 14th. Dined at Major Moores (after being in Convention) and spent the evening at my own lodgings.

Although there were several Major Moores in Philadelphia at this time, GW is probably visiting Maj. Thomas Lloyd Moore (d. 1819) on Pine Street between Second and Third streets.

Monday 18th. Attended the Convention. Dined at the Quarterly meeting of the Sons of St. Patrick—held at the City Tavn. Drank Tea at Doctr. Shippins with Mrs. Livingston.

Sons of St. Patrick: Founded in 1771 in Philadelphia by Irish-American merchants and their friends, the Society of the Friendly Sons of St. Patrick strongly supported the American Revolution, and several of its dinners were attended by GW, who was "adopted" by the society.

Tuesday 19th. Dined (after leaving Convention) in a family way at Mr. Morris's and spent the Evening there in a very large Company.

Wednesday. 20th. Attended Convention. Dined at Mr. Merediths & drank Tea there.

Samuel Meredith (1741–1817) had been a brigadier general under GW during the New Jersey campaigns (1777–78) and was now a Pennsylvania delegate to Congress. In 1789 GW appointed him first treasurer of the United States. His home was on Front Street between Arch and Race streets.

Thursday 21st. Attended Convention. Dined at Mr. Pragers, and spent the evening in my Chamber.

Mr. Prager is probably Mark Prager, Sr., a member of the Jewish mercantile family that came to Philadelphia shortly after the Revolution.

Friday 22d. Dined at Mr. Morris's & drank Tea with Mr. Frans. Hopkinson.

Francis Hopkinson, lawyer, musician, composer, and poet and, as a delegate from New Jersey, signer of the Declaration of Independence, was at this time a judge in the admiralty court of Pennsylvania.

Saturday 23d. In Convention. Dined at Doctr. Ruston's & drank Tea at Mr. Morris's.

Dr. Thomas Ruston, a native of Chester County, Pa., attended the College of New Jersey and received a medical degree from the University of Edinburgh in 1765. He practiced in England until after the Revolution. In 1785 Ruston returned to Philadelphia where he became an associate of Robert Morris in land speculations. He was jailed for debt in 1796.

Sunday 24th. Dined at Mr. Morris's & spent the evening at Mr. Meridiths—at Tea.

Monday 25th. Attended Convention. Dined at Mr. Morris's—drank Tea there—& spent the evening in my chamber.

Tuesday 26th. Attended Convention. Partook of a family dinner with Govr. Randolph and made one of a party to drink Tea at Grays ferry.

Saturday 30th. Attended Convention. Dined with a Club at Springsbury—consisting of several associated families of the City—the Gentlemen of which meet every Saturday accompanied by the females of the families every other Saturday. This was the ladies day.

Springsbury: One of the original manors set aside by William Penn for his family was named Springettsbury.

July

Monday. 2d. Attended Convention. Dined with some of the Members of Convention at the Indian Queen. Drank Tea at Mr. Binghams, and walked afterwards in the state house yard. Set this Morning for Mr. Pine who wanted to correct his portrt. of me.

For Robert Edge Pine's visit to Mount Vernon to paint this portrait, see entry for 28 April 1785.

Tuesday. 3d. Sat before the meeting of the Convention for Mr. Peale who wanted my picture to make a print or Metzotinto by. Dined at

Mr. Morris's and drank Tea at Mr. Powells—after which, in Company with him, I attended the Agricultural Society at Carpenters Hall.

> Charles Willson Peale, now living in Philadelphia, wrote GW of the "great desire I have to make a good mezzotinto print" of him, assuring GW he would "make the business as convenient to you as possible . . . by bringing my Pallette and Pensils to Mr. Morris's that you might sett at your leisure" (Diary, 29 May 1787, Charles Willson Peale Papers, American Philosophical Society). The Philadelphia Society for Promoting Agriculture, founded in Feb. 1785 to promote agriculture in the United States, consisted of active (resident) members living in or near Philadelphia and honorary (later corresponding) members. GW became one of the latter in 1785.

Wednesday 4th. Visited Doctr. Shovats Anatomical figures and (the Convention having adjourned for the purpose) went to hear an Oration on the anniversary of Independance delivered by a Mr. Mitchell, a student of Law—After which I dined with the State Society of the Cincinnati at Epplees Tavern and drank Tea at Mr. Powells.

> *Doctr. Shovats Anatomical figures:* The surgeon and anatomist Abraham Chovet (1704–1790) was born in England, studied in France, practiced in England and the West Indies, and in 1774 opened his "Anatomical Museum" of wax human figures on Vidal's Alley off Second Street in Philadelphia.

Tuesday. 10th. Attended Convention. Dined at Mr. Morris's. Drank Tea at Mr. Binghams & went to the Play.

> The play was performed at the Southwark Theater, located just south of the city boundary. Because of a state law (1779) prohibiting theatrical performances, the building was called an opera house by the American Company, which played there from 25 June to 4 Aug. To skirt this same law the plays presented were billed under false titles that could still be recognizable by the theatergoing public. Hence, in this evening's "concert" James Townley's *High Life below the Stairs* was billed as an "entertainment" called "the Servants Hall in an Uproar," while the farce *Love in a Camp, or Patrick in Prussia* was advertised as a "Comic Opera" (Scharf, *History of Philadelphia*, 2:965–67; Seilhamer, *American Theatre*, 2:217–21).

Saturday 21st. In Convention. Dined at Springsbury with the Club of Gentn. & Ladies. Went to the Play afterwards.

> The play was the tragedy *Edward and Eleanora* by the Scots poet James Thomson (Seilhamer, *American Theatre*, 2:221).

Sunday 22d. Left Town by 5 oclock A.M. Breakfasted at Genl. Mifflins. Rode up with him & others to the Spring Mills and returned to Genl. Mifflins by Dinner after which proceeded to the City.

> *Spring Mills:* Spring Mill was an old gristmill on the east side of the Schuylkill River, about two miles below Conshohocken in Montgomery County, Pa. It was powered by the combined waters from several springs in a small area.

*Miniature of George Washington. (Mount Vernon Ladies'
Association of the Union)*

Friday 27th. In Convention, which adjourned this day, to meet again
on Monday the 6th. of August that a Comee. which had been appointed (consisting of 5 Members) might have time to arrange, and
draw into method & form the several matters which had been agreed
to by the Convention as a Constitution for the United States. Dined at
Mr. Morris's, and drank Tea at Mr. Powells.

> Here GW was relying too much upon his memory, for his Philadelphia diary
> had no notation of the date of adjournment, which was actually 26 July (Far-
> rand, *Federal Convention,* 2:118, 128).

Tuesday 31st. Whilst Mr. Morris was fishing I rid over the old Canton-
ment of the American [army] of the Winter 1777, & 8. Visited all the
Works, wch. were in Ruins; and the Incampments in woods where the
ground had not been cultivated.

August

Friday 3d. In company with Mr. Robt. Morris and his Lady and Mr. Gouvr. Morris I went up to Trenton on another Fishing party. Lodged at Colo. Sam Ogdens at the Trenton Works. In the Evening fished, not very successfully.

> Samuel Ogden (1746–1810), an iron founder who had supplied iron products to GW's army during the Revolution, had also served as a colonel in the New Jersey militia.

Monday 6th. Met, according to adjournment in Convention, & received the rept. of the Committee. Dined at Mr. Morris's and drank Tea at Mr. Merediths.

Sunday 19th. In company with Mr. Powell rode up to the white Marsh. Traversed my old Incampment, and contemplated on the dangers which threatned the American Army at that place. Dined at German town.

> *White Marsh:* about 12 miles north and west of Philadelphia, the last camp of GW's army (Nov.–Dec. 1777) before he moved his men to Valley Forge for the winter.
> *German town:* the scene of a confused battle between the Continental Army and the British (3–4 Oct. 1777) a few miles north of Philadelphia on the east side of the Schuylkill River.

Monday 20th. In Convention. Dined, drank Tea and spent the evening at Mr. Morris['s].

Tuesday 21st. Did the like this day also.

> "We have lately made a rule to meet at ten and sit 'til four, which is punctually complied with" (David Brearley to William Paterson, 21 Aug. 1787, Farrand, *Federal Convention,* 3:73).

September

Monday 3d. In Convention. Visited a Machine at Doctr. Franklins (called a mangle) for pressing, in place of Ironing, clothes from the wash. Which Machine from the facility with which it dispatches business is well calculated for Table cloths & such Articles as have not pleats & irregular foldings and would be very useful in all large families. Dined, drank Tea, & spent the evening at Mr. Morris's.

Sunday 9th. Dined at Mr. Morris's after making a visit to Mr. Gardoqui who as he says came from New York on a visit to me.

> Today GW wrote George Augustine Washington that he thought the convention would adjourn within a week. "God grant I may not be disappointed in this expectation, as I am quite homesick."
> Diego de Gardoqui (1735–1798), Spanish representative in the United

States, was in the third year of frustrating negotiations regarding American rights to navigate the lower Mississippi River, which then ran through Spanish territory. GW's cryptic entry here may reflect his concern at being dragged into the emotional and nationally divisive debate of "the *Spanish negociation*," lately described as being "in a very *ticklish situation*" (James Madison to Thomas Jefferson, 23 April 1787, Rutland, *Madison Papers,* 9:400).

Friday 14th. Attended Convention. Dined at the City Tavern, at an entertainmt. given on my acct. by the City light Horse. Spent the evening at Mr. Meridiths.

Saturday 15th. Concluded the business of Convention, all to signing the proceedings; to effect which the House sat till 6 Oclock; and adjourned till Monday that the Constitution which it was proposed to offer to the People might be engrossed and a number of printed copies struck off. Dined at Mr. Morris's & spent the evening there. Mr. Gardoqui set off for his return to New York this forenoon.

Monday 17th. Met in Convention when the Constitution received the Unanimous assent of 11 States and Colo. Hamilton's from New York (the only delegate from thence in Convention) and was subscribed to by every Member present except Govr. [Edmund] Randolph and Colo. [George] Mason from Virginia & Mr. [Elbridge] Gerry from Massachusetts. The business being thus closed, the Members adjourned to the City Tavern, dined together and took a cordial leave of each other— after which I returned to my lodgings—did some business with, and received the papers from the secretary of the Convention, and retired to meditate on the momentous wk. which had been executed, after not less than five, for a large part of the time Six, and sometimes 7 hours sitting every day, sundays & the ten days adjournment to give a Comee. opportunity & time to arrange the business for more than four Months.

> The papers: "Major Jackson, after burning all the loose scraps of paper which belong to the Convention, will this evening wait upon the General with the Journals and other papers which their vote directs to be delivered to His Excellency" (William Jackson to GW, 17 Sept. 1787, *Papers, Confederation Series,* 5:329).

Tuesday 18th. Finished what private business I had to do in the City this forenoon. Took my leave of those families in wch. I had been most intimate. Dined early at Mr. Morris's with whom & Mr. Gouvr. Morris I parted at Grays ferry and reached Chester in Company with Mr. Blair who I invited to a seat in my Carriage 'till we should reach Mount Vernon.

> On his way back to Mount Vernon GW followed much the same route he had taken on his way to the convention, reaching home on Saturday, 22 Sept., "about Sunset after an absence of four Months and 14 days" (*Diaries,* 5:187).

October

Friday 5th. In the Afternoon Mr. Alexr. Donald came in.

On 12 Nov. 1787 Alexander Donald, a Richmond merchant, wrote to Thomas Jefferson of this visit: "I staid two days with General Washington at Mount Vernon about Six weeks ago. He is in perfect good health, and looks almost as well as he did Twenty years ago. I never saw him so keen for any thing in my life, as he is for the adoption of the new Form of Government. As the eyes of all America are turned towards this truly Great and Good Man, for the First President, I took the liberty of sounding him upon it. He appears to be greatly against going into Publick Life again, Pleads in Excuse for himself, His Love of Retirement, and his advanced Age, but Notwithstanding of these, I am fully of opinion he may be induced to appear once more on the Publick Stage of Life. I form my opinion from what passed between us in a very long and serious conversation as well as from what I could gather from Mrs. Washington on the same subject" (Boyd, *Jefferson Papers,* 12:345–48).

November

Thursday 1st. Rid by the way of Muddy hole where the people were taking up Turnips to transplant for Seed to Alexandria to attend a meeting of the Directors of the Potomack Company. Also the exhibition of the Boys of the Academy in this place. Dined at Leighs Tavern & lodged at Colo. Fitzgeralds after returning abt. 11 Oclock at Night from the performance which was well executed.

The exhibition of the Boys: part of "the public Examinations of the several Schools in the Alexandria Academy, antecedent to the autumnal Vacation.... In the Evening the Pupils of the Rev. Mr. M'Whir delivered public Orations before a large and respectable Audience, among whom were present General Washington, and the greater Part of the Principal Inhabitants, Ladies and Gentlemen, of the Town and the Neighbourhood: After which Prizes were distributed" (*Va. Journal,* 8 Nov. 1787). George Steptoe Washington, GW's nephew, won a prize in Latin and ancient geography. *Leighs Tavern:* George H. Leigh operated the Bunch of Grapes Tavern on the corner of Fairfax and Cameron streets.

1788

February

Saturday 2d. Visited my Ferry, Frenchs & Dogue run Plantations.

At all, the same work as usual, except that the Dogue run Women were employed in pulling up a cross fence in the Meadow by the Overseers house—

Set the home house gang to cording the Wood which had been cut for Bricks.

Began with a pair of Sawyers, this day, to cut the flooring planks for a Barn, proposed to be built between the Ferry & French's Plantations of 2 Inch Oak.

The barn was to be a two-story brick structure built according to a plan obtained from Arthur Young the previous year but with some changes by GW to adapt it to his particular needs. GW wrote Young 4 Dec. 1788 that he believed his barn to be "the largest and most convenient one in this Country" (*Papers, Presidential Series,* 1:159–63).

Tuesday 5th. The River, which had opened very much yesterday and promised a free Navigation was entirely closed again to day, in all the malignancy of the frost. I remained within all day.

"The Navigation of this river," GW today wrote Henry Knox, "has been stopped for near five weeks—at this moment we are locked fast by Ice—and the air of this day is amongst the keenest I ever recollect to have felt" (*Papers, Confederation Series,* 6:88).

Wednesday 13th. The Marqs. de Chappedelaine (introduced by letters from Genl. Knox, Mr. Bingham &ca.) Captn. Enys (a British Officer) Colo. Fitzgerald, Mr. Hunter, Mr. Nelson & Mr. Ingraham came here to Dinner—all of whom returned after it except the last. I remained at home all day.

The marquis de Chappedelaine, "a Captain in the first Regt of french Dragoons" who was touring the United States, had previously visited New York, Philadelphia, and Baltimore (Enys, *Journal,* 238–40). Chappedelaine may have been Jean René Chappedelaine (b. 1766), an officer in the Regiment de Barrois, who was said to have emigrated in 1792, or Jean Baptiste Marc de Chappedelaine, comte de Boslan (1741–1819), an officer in the Regiment de Soubise, who was said to have emigrated in 1791. Both men later returned to France (*Dict. Biog. Française,* 8:434).

John Enys (1757–1818) was commissioned an officer in the 29th Regiment of Foot in 1775 and served with that unit on garrison duty in Canada 1776–82 and 1784–87. Before returning to England, he made a tour of scenic and historical places in the United States. "We had no sooner alighted," Enys wrote of his visit to Mount Vernon, "than the Immortal General came to receive us at the door and conducted us into his Parlour." After some conversation about the new federal Constitution and a tour of the grounds, dinner was served. "It was a very good one," Enys reported, "but the part of the entertainment I liked best was the affable easy manners of the whole family. . . . The Ladies left the room soon after Dinner but the Gentlemen continued for some time longer. There were no public toasts of any kind given, the General himself introducing a round of Ladies as soon as the Cloath was removed, by saying he had always a very great esteem for the Ladies, and therefore drank them in preference to any thing else." The visitors did not leave until "it was near dark" (Enys, *Journal,* xviii–xxxv, 244–52).

March

Monday 17th. Went up (accompanied by Colo. Humphreys) to the Election of Delegates to the Convention of this State (for the purpose of considering the New form of Governmt. which has been recommended to the United States); When Doctr. Stuart and Colo. Simms were chosen without opposition. Dined at Colo. Fitzgeralds, and returned in the Evening.

> The Virginia Ratifying Convention was to meet in Richmond on 2 June. Election of delegates took place in each county on its appointed court day in March. The results, which were not fully known for several weeks, indicated a thin margin in favor of the friends of the Constitution.

Tuesday 18th. At the Mansion house, began the circular Post & rail fencing in front of the lawn yesterday Morning. Mr. Madison on his way from New York to Orange came in before dinner and stayed all Night.

> James Madison, Jr., who had been fulfilling his duties as a congressman in New York since the end of the Constitutional Convention, was going home to be present on 24 Mar. when Orange County was to elect its two delegates to the state ratifying convention. Madison was chosen as one of Orange's delegates and subsequently was one of the leaders in the fight for the Constitution in the convention.

Friday 21st. Rid to all the Plantations. On my return home, found a Mr. Rogers of New York here who dined and proceeded to Alexandria afterwds.

> John Rodgers (1727–1811), a renowned Presbyterian clergyman, served the Presbyterians of New York City as pastor from 1765 to 1810, except during the Revolution when he chose to live outside the British-occupied city.

April

Sunday 6th. Sent my two Jackasses to the Election at Marlborough in Maryld. that they might be seen.

> The Maryland General Assembly set 7 April as the day for electing all delegates to the state convention that was to meet in Annapolis two weeks later to consider ratification of the federal Constitution. It would, GW knew, be a good opportunity to display his two jackasses, Royal Gift and Knight of Malta, whose stud services had been advertised in the Annapolis and Baltimore newspapers for the past few weeks (*Md. Gaz.,* 13 and 20 Mar. and 3 April 1788).

Thursday 17th. Charles Hagan came to Brick making to day—set him to makg. a cover for the Bricks before he began to Mould. Gunner and Sam were sent to Work with him.

> Charles Hagan signed a contract with GW on 5 Jan. 1788, agreeing to begin work at Mount Vernon "as early in the spring as the state of the ground will

admit." His pay was set at a rate of £4 10s. a month, allowing 26 working days or nights to the month. In addition, he was to be given provisions and half a pint of rum a day (Washington Papers, Library of Congress). The slaves Gunner and Sam were laborers on the Home House plantation.

May

Saturday 17th. Mrs. Morris, Miss Morris and her two Sons (lately arrived from Europe) came here about 11 Oclk. and to Dinner came Mr. Hunter, a Mr. Braithwait, and Mr. McPherson who returned to Alexandria afterwards.

> Robert Morris, who had been on business in Richmond, had sent his servants and horses to Philadelphia a few weeks earlier to bring his wife, Mary White Morris, to Mount Vernon for a long-planned visit (Robert Morris to GW, 29 April 1788, *Papers, Confederation Series,* 6:248–49). Miss Morris is probably the Morrises' older daughter, Esther (Hetty) Morris (1774–1816). The two sons, Robert Morris (b. 1769) and Thomas Morris (1771–1849), had been studying in Geneva, Switzerland, 1781–86, and at the University of Leipzig, Germany, 1786–88. Both later became lawyers.
>
> Mr. McPherson is probably Daniel McPherson or Isaac McPherson, both merchants of Alexandria.

Wednesday 21st. Visited all the Plantations, and the Brick yard.

In my Botanical garden, I transplanted two roots of the Scarcity plant—but they were so dry & appeared to be so perished, as to leave little hope of their ever vegetating. Also (in the same place) from a Box which came by the Philadelphia Packet I set out a number of cuttings of what I took to be the Lombardy Poplar. These had been so long in moss as to have white sprouts issuing from many of the buds at least two or three Inches long.

> The Philadelphia packet boat, the sloop *Charming Polly* captained by John Ellwood (Elwood), Jr., sailed regularly between Alexandria and Philadelphia carrying freight and passengers. GW used Ellwood's freight service for many years, and Ellwood often did GW the favor of dropping off his goods at the Mount Vernon dock, saving a trip into Alexandria.

June

Monday 9th. Captn. Barney, in the Miniature Ship Federalist—as a present from the Merchants of Baltimore to me arrived here to Breakfast with her and stayed all day & Night. Remained at home all day.

> The *Federalist,* a fifteen-foot-long boat rigged as a ship, was a showpiece designed to represent Baltimore's maritime trades and to symbolize the proposed federal union. "Highly ornamented" and mounted on a horse-drawn carriage frame, the little ship had been pulled through the main streets of Baltimore on 1 May as part of a great procession of merchants, artisans, and professionals celebrating Maryland's ratification of the new Constitution five

days earlier. Miniature ships, named the *Federalist* or the *Union,* were features of many Federalist victory parades before and after Maryland's ratification. However, in Baltimore a group of Federalist merchants took the further step of launching their vessel after the celebration and dispatching it to Mount Vernon under the command of Joshua Barney (1759–1818), a naval hero of the Revolution and a staunch Federalist, for presentation to GW "as an Offering . . . expressive of their Veneration of his Services and Federalism" (*Md. Journal,* 6 May, 3 June 1788).

Saturday 28th. The Inhabitants of Alexandria having received the News of the ratification of the proposed Constitution by this State, and that of New Hampshire and having determined on public rejoicings, part of which to be in a dinner, to which this family was envited Colo. Humphreys my Nephew G.A. Washington & myself went up to it and returned in the afternoon. On my way up I visited all my Plantations.

The New Hampshire Convention ratified the Constitution 21 June by a vote of 57 to 46, and Virginia's Convention did the same four days later with a vote of 89 to 79. As the ninth and tenth states to ratify, they made it legally possible to implement the new Constitution.

A dinner held this day was at John Wise's tavern. GW "was met some miles out of town by a party of Gentlemen on horseback, and escorted to the tavern, having been saluted on his way by the light infantry company in a respectful manner. His arrival was announced by a discharge of ten cannon," and after dinner ten toasts were drunk, each punctuated by a cannon shot (GW to Charles Cotesworth Pinckney, 28 June 1788, *Papers, Confederation Series,* 6:360–62).

July

Thursday 24th. A very high No. Et. Wind all Night, which, this morning, being accompanied with Rain, became a hurricane—driving the Miniature Ship Federalist from her Moorings, and sinking her—blowing down some trees in the groves & about the houses—loosning the roots, & forcing many others to yield and dismantling most, in a greater or lesser degree of their Bows, & doing other and great mischief to the grain, grass &ca. & not a little to my Mill race. In aword it was violent and severe—more so than has happened for many years. About Noon the Wind suddenly shifted from No. Et. to So. Wt. and blew the remaining part of the day as violently from that quarter. The tide about this time rose near or quite 4 feet higher than it was ever known to do driving Boats &ca. into fields were no tide had ever been heard of before—And must it is to be apprehended have done infinite damage on their Wharves at Alexandria—Norfolk—Baltimore &ca. At home all day.

The sudden shift in wind direction indicated the passing of the eye of the storm. GW's apprehension about the damage done elsewhere was well founded. This hurricane ravaged Bermuda on 19 July, and after sinking many vessels on the North Carolina coast, it struck Norfolk about 5:00 P.M. on 23 July, lasting about nine hours and doing great damage (*Phila. Independent Gaz.,* 8 Aug. 1788). At Alexandria the storm was reported to have "brought in the highest tide that was ever known in this river, and the damage done to Tobacco, Sugar, Salt, &c. in the Warehouses in this town, is computed at five thousand pounds" (*Md. Journal,* 5 Aug. 1788). The center of the hurricane skirted Annapolis, causing little or no damage despite an unprecedented high tide (*Md. Gaz.,* 31 July 1788).

Tuesday 29th. A Mr. Vender Kemp—a Dutch Gentn. who had suffered by the troubles in Holland and who was introduced to me by the Marquis de la Fayette came here to Dinner.

> Francis Adrian Van der Kemp (1752–1829), Dutch soldier, scholar, and Mennonite minister, had been imprisoned in his homeland during a part of the previous year for revolutionary activities connected with the Patriot party, a group of Dutch liberals who wished to implement the republican ideals of the American Revolution in their country. Upon being freed, he sailed in Mar. 1788 with his wife and children for New York. To ease his way Dutch friends obtained for him several letters of introduction to prominent Americans, including a letter from Lafayette to GW. Van der Kemp found Mount Vernon, as did many visitors, to be a place "where simplicity, order, unadorned grandeur, and dignity, had taken up their abode," although he detected in his host "somewhat of a repulsive coldness . . . under a courteous demeanour" (Van der Kemp, *Autobiography,* 115–16). Van der Kemp became an American citizen in 1789 and lived the remainder of his life in upstate New York farming and pursuing his scholarly interests.

August

1st. A Mr. Obannon—D. Surveyer in the Western Country—came here with some executed Land warrants—dined & proceeded on to Richmond afterwards.

> John O'Bannon (d. 1813), a deputy surveyor of the Virginia Military Reserve lands northwest of the Ohio River, had surveyed for GW three tracts near present-day Cincinnati, Ohio, during the previous winter and spring. Totaling 3,051 acres, these tracts were surveyed on two military warrants purchased by GW.

Monday 4th. Went up to alexandria to a meeting of the Potomack Company; the business of which was finished about Sun down—but matters which came more properly before the Directors obliged me to stay in Town all Night. Dined at Wise's and lodged at Colo. Fitzgeralds.

> GW today delivered the annual report of the company's directors to the general members.

Tuesday 5th. The business before the Board of Directors detaining till near two Oclock (I dined at Colo. Fitzgeralds) and returned home in the Afternn.

At Mount Vernon this evening GW found his nephew Lawrence Augustine Washington, who had run away from Samuel Hanson's home apparently with the aid of his brother George Steptoe Washington. Lawrence complained of ill treatment by Hanson and "offered to shew . . . some bruises he had received." GW severely reprimanded the boy for running away, threatened to punish him with his own hands, and sent him back to Hanson the next day after obtaining a promise "that there should be no cause of complaint against him for the future" (GW to Samuel Hanson of Samuel, 6 Aug. 1788, GW to George Steptoe Washington, 6 Aug. 1788, and Hanson to GW, 7 Aug. 1788, *Papers, Confederation Series*, 429–32).

Saturday 23d. A Mr. George Thompson, from the Academy in Alexandria, with a letter to me from his father Doctr. Thompson respecting his Son in law Doctr. Spence; and Geo. Step. Washington came here to dinner & stayed all Night.

Dr. William Spence was the stepson of Dr. Thomas Thomson of Westmoreland County. As a boy Spence was sent to Great Britain for his education, which was culminated in 1780 by his taking a medical degree at Glasgow University. In Sept. 1781 he sailed for New York with a wife and child aboard the *Buckskin Hero,* but the vessel disappeared without a trace after having last been seen by another vessel two or three days' sail out of New York harbor. It was assumed that the *Buckskin Hero* had sunk with all aboard until a report in the spring of 1788 from a man claiming to be a former Algerian prisoner gave some hope that the vessel had been captured by Algerian pirates and the crew and passengers carried into slavery. That report prompted Dr. Thomson's letter, dated 12 Aug. 1788, to GW. For an account of the Algerian captives, see *Papers, Presidential Series,* 3:155–65, 246–47. Although Thomson did not know GW personally, he was confident that GW could assist the family by making inquiries about the fate of Dr. and Mrs. Spence and their child. Strongly doubting the truth of the report, GW wrote for further information to Thomas Barclay of Philadelphia, who had been involved with American affairs in North Africa. Barclay confirmed GW's suspicions. The *Buckskin Hero* was not among the vessels captured by the Algerians, a fact that was further substantiated later by Thomas Jefferson through James Madison.

George Thomson, a son of Dr. Thomson by his first wife, was apparently a schoolmate of George Steptoe Washington at the Alexandria Academy.

November

Sunday 2d. Mr. George Mason came here to dinner and returned in the Evening. After dinner word was brot. from Alexandria that the Minister of France was arrived there and intended down here to dinner. Accordingly, a little before Sun setting, he (the Count de Moustiers) his Sister the Marchioness de Brehan—the Marquis her Son— and Mr. du Ponts came in.

Mr. George Mason: probably George Mason, Jr., of Lexington (see entries for 17 Dec. 1773 and 29 Nov. 1785).

Eléanor François Elie, comte de Moustier (1751–1817), successor to the chevalier de La Luzerne as French minister to the United States, had ar-

This handsome miniature of Martha Washington was made by Charles Willson Peale in 1776. (Mount Vernon Ladies' Association of the Union)

rived at New York in January. Moustier spent most of his life in diplomatic service, but his mission to the United States was a failure almost from the start. "A very well informed man" sincerely desirous of promoting American-French commercial relations, he lacked the tact and insight needed to deal with American republicans (David Humphreys to Thomas Jefferson, 29 Nov. 1788, Boyd, *Jefferson Papers*, 14:300–304).

The marquise de Bréhan, an artist and much esteemed friend of Thomas Jefferson and variously described as Moustier's sister or sister-in-law, proved to be a further detriment to Moustier's reputation in America. "Appearances (whether well or ill founded is not important)," Jay told Jefferson, "have created and diffused an opinion that an improper Connection subsists between him [Moustier] and the Marchioness. You can easily conceive the Influence of such an opinion on the Minds and Feelings of such a People as ours" (Jay to Jefferson, 25 Nov. 1788, James Madison to Jefferson, 8 Dec. 1788, ibid., 290–91, 339–42).

For her part Madame de Bréhan was already "furiously displeased with America" (Jefferson to Maria Cosway, 14 Jan. 1789, ibid., 445–46). She came to America hoping to find a climate beneficial to her delicate health and a pastoral utopia where the simple virtues of rural life extolled by French intellectuals of the time really existed. The harshness of the American winters and the realities of American life both in towns and in the country soon gave the lie to those romantic preconceptions, leaving her with a feeling of betrayal (ibid., 14:300–304).

Madame de Bréhan's son, Armand Louis Fidèle de Bréhan (1770–1828), who later became the marquis de Bréhan, had been brought to America with the hope of giving him an education that would be "more masculine and less exposed to seduction" than in France (Jefferson to Abigail Adams, 30 Aug. 1787, ibid., 12:65–66).

Victor Marie du Pont (1767–1827), eldest son of the French economist and diplomat Pierre Samuel du Pont de Nemours (1739–1817), had recently become an attaché at the French legation.

Sunday 9th. At home all day. One of the Bucks in the Paddock having much wounded the Young woman Dolshy, Doctr. Craik was sent for who came and stayed all Night.

Dolshy, a dower slave, was listed in 1799 as a spinner. She was then the wife of the slave carpenter Joe.

Friday 14th. Mr. Wilming—the German Gentleman above mentioned having offered to engage a Gardener for me and to send him in a ship from Bremen; I requested that it might not exceed the following conditions for him and his Wife (if he brings one)—viz.—Ten pounds sterling for the 1st. year—Eleven for the 2d.—Twelve for the 3d. and so on, a pound encrease, till the sum should amt. to £15. beyond which not to go. That he would be found a comfortable House, or room in one, with bedding, victuals & drink; but no clothes; *these* for *self* and *wife* to be provided at his own expence—That he is to be a compleat Kitchen Gardener with a competent knowledge of Flowers and a Green House. And that he is to come under Articles and firmly bound. His, or their passages to be on as low terms as it can be obtained—The Wife if one comes is to be a Spinner, dairy Woman—or something of that usefulness.

Henrich Wilmans sent a gardener named John Christian Ehlers to GW in the summer of 1789. Ehlers began work at the rate of 12 guineas a year and received subsequent raises. In 1792 he was joined by his wife who engaged in making clothing and measuring the work of the spinners on the Mount Vernon plantation. At first GW was pleased with his services, always referring to him as "the Gardener," in the same way he did to James Bloxham as "the Farmer." Over the years several new contracts were negotiated but by the time Ehlers's contract expired in 1797, GW launched a search for a new gardener, since GW had "no inclination" to employ Ehlers any longer (*Papers, Presidential Series,* 3:64–65).

Saturday 15th. On my return home in the Evening I found Mr. Warville and a Mr. de Saint Tries here—brought down by Mr. Porter who returned again.

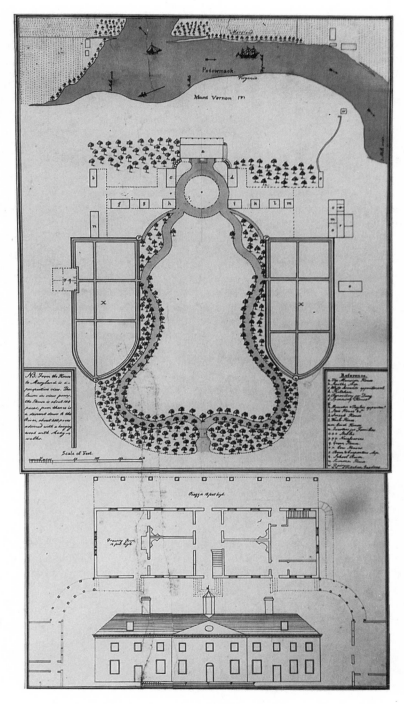

A reproduction of Samuel Vaughan's sketch of Mount Vernon, 1787. (Mount Vernon Ladies' Association of the Union)

Jacques (Jean) Pierre Brissot de Warville (1754–1793), French journalist and reformer, came to the United States in July of this year as an agent for three European financiers who were interested in investing in the American public debt and in public lands. Brissot also was thinking of settling in America, possibly in the Shenandoah Valley, and was planning to write a history of the new country (Brissot, *Travels*, xi–xxi). It was this last project that brought him to Mount Vernon in the hope of examining GW's papers.

December

Tuesday 9th. Concluded my exchange after dinner to day with Colo. Hy. Lee of Magnolio for 5000 acres of Kentucke Land.

GW was willing to part with Magnolia because the stallion was expensive to keep and had brought in little or no money for stud service during the past two and a half years despite frequent advertisement of that service (GW to Henry Lee, 30 Nov. 1788, *Papers, Presidential Series*, 139–40; Ledger B, 227).

Wednesday 10th. Remained at home all day. William Gardener—my New Overseer for the Neck, arrived (by Water) with his family to day.

William Garner, of Charles County, Md., today signed a contract with GW, agreeing to serve as overseer of River plantation "with the utmost Industry, Sobriety and Honesty" in return for £36 a year. He was employed until 1792 when he was dismissed for the neglectful way in which he conducted that year's harvest.

1789

January

Wednesday 7th. Went up to the Election of an Elector (for this district) of President & Vice President when the Candidates polled for being Doctr. Stuart and Colo. [Thomas] Blackburn the first recd. 216 votes from the Freeholders of this County and the second 16 Votes. Dined with a large company on venisen at Pages Tavn. and came home in the evening.

The Virginia General Assembly passed an act 17 Nov. 1788 authorizing election of the state's 12 presidential electors by districts. Fairfax County was in the district which also included Prince William, Loudoun, and Fauquier counties. Voting in all districts occurred on this day at the courthouses with all voters qualified to vote for General Assembly members eligible to participate (Hening, 12:648–53). David Stuart won his district by a margin of 347 votes (*Md. Journal*, 20 Jan. 1789). Virginia's electors met in Richmond on 4 Feb. and voted unanimously for GW for president as did electors of all the other ratifying states, who met that day also. GW was formally notified of his election on 14 April. See *Papers, Presidential Series*, 1:54–57.

William Page (d. 1790) ran a tavern in Alexandria.

February

Monday 2d. I went up to the Election of a Representative to Congress for this district. [V]oted for Richd. Bland Lee Esqr. Dined at Colo. Hooes & returned home in the afternoon.

All ten of Virginia's allotted representatives were elected today.

In the months after the Constitutional Convention, GW was inundated with letters from friends and supporters urging him to accept the office of president of the new republic, which would almost certainly be offered to him. GW's replies to these letters reflect his reluctance to leave the "vine & fig tree" he had so often stated he preferred to public life and his misgivings about his own abilities to fill the new office. See Papers, Presidential Series, *vol. 1. During the electoral campaign in the early spring of 1789 it was apparent that GW, as expected, would be the overwhelming choice to fill the first office, and he reluctantly began preparations to leave Mount Vernon, feeling, as he informed Henry Knox, not unlike "a culprit who is going to the place of his execution: so unwilling am I, in the evening of a life nearly consumed in public cares, to quit a peaceful abode for an Ocean of difficulties, without that competency of political skill—abilities & inclination which is necessary to manage the helm. I am sensible, that I am embarking the voice of my Countrymen and a good name of my own, on this voyage, but what returns will be made for them— Heaven alone can foretell. Integrity & firmness is all I can promise—these, be the voyage long or short; never shall forsake me although I may be deserted by all men"* (Papers, Presidential Series, *2:2–3*).

On 6 April the Senate and the House of Representatives, meeting in New York City, counted the electoral votes for president and vice-president. Out of the 138 ballots counted, GW received 69 and John Adams 34, and a committee was appointed consisting of members of both houses to inform GW of his election. Charles Thomson, long secretary of the old Confederation Congress, was instructed to take the notice of GW's election to Mount Vernon. Thomson left New York on Tuesday, 7 April, and "though much impeded by tempestuous weather, bad roads, and the many large rivers I had to cross," he reached Mount Vernon on 14 April and informed GW of his election. For Thomson's address to GW and GW's reply, see Papers, Presidential Series, *1:54–56.*

Although GW evidently kept a diary for at least part of the spring and summer of 1789, the diaries for this period have disappeared. Only two entries for these months are presently available, both in printed form. The entry for 16 April 1789 is taken from Marshall, Life of Washington, *5:154. The entry for 23 April is from Irving,* Life of George Washington, *4: 505–6. For the ceremonies attending GW's journey north and his reception in New York City, see* Papers, Presidential Series, *2:81–82, 107, 109– 10, 113–15. The diaries resume with the entries for October.*

April

[16 April] About ten o'clock I bade adieu to Mount Vernon, to private life, and to domestic felicity; and with a mind oppressed with more anxious and painful sensations than I have words to express, set out for New York in company with Mr. Thompson, and colonel Humphries, with the best dispositions to render service to my country in obedience to its call, but with less hope of answering its expectations.

[23 April] The display of boats which attended and joined us on this occasion, some with vocal and some with instrumental music on board; the decorations of the ships, the roar of cannon, and the loud acclamations of the people which rent the skies, as I passed along the wharves, filled my mind with sensations as painful (considering the reverse of this scene, which may be the case after all my labors to do good) as they are pleasing.

Today's diary entry is a fragmentary account of GW's reception in New York City. The New York *Daily Advertiser,* 24 April 1789, was more explicit: "Yesterday arrived the illustrious George Washington, President of the United States, amidst the joyful acclamation of every party and every description of citizens. . . . The President was received at Elizabeth-Town, by a deputation of three Senators, five Representatives of the Congress of the United States, and three officers of the State and Corporation; with whom he embarked in the barge, built . . . and rowed by thirteen pilots of this harbour, dressed in white uniform; Thomas Randall, Esq. acting as cockswain.

"No language can point the beautiful display made on his excellency's approach to the city. The shores were crouded with a vast concourse of citizens, waiting with exulting anxiety his arrival. His Catholic Majesty's sloop of war the *Galviston* (Mr. Dohrman's) ship North-Carolina, and the other vessels in port, were dressed and decorated in the most superb manner. His excellency's barge was accompanied by the barge of the Hon. Gen. Knox, and a great number of vessels and boats from Jersey and New-York, in his train. As he passed the Galviston, he received a salute of thirteen guns, and was welcomed by an equal number from the battery. . . .

"On his excellencys arrival at the stairs, prepared and ornamented, at Murray's wharf, for his landing; he was received and congratulated by his excellency, the Governor of this State, and the officers of the State and Corporation, and [a] . . . procession was formed . . . followed by an amazing concorse of citizens.

"The procession advanced through Queen street to the house fitted up for the reception of his Excellency, where it terminated, after which, he was conducted without form to the house of Governor Clinton, with whom his Excellency dined. In the evening the houses of the citizens were brilliantly illuminated."

October

Thursday 1st. Exercised in my Carriage in the forenoon.

The following company dined here to day. viz.—

Mr. Read of the Senate, Colo. Bland and Mr. Madison of the House of Representatives—Mr. Osgood and his Lady Colo. [William] Duer his Lady and Miss Brown Colo. Lewis Morris & Lady—Lady Christiana Griffin and her Daughter and Judge Duane & Mrs. Greene.

Mr. Thomas Nelson joined my Family this day.

Dispatched Many of the Comns. for the Judiciary Judges, Marshalls and Attorneys this day with the Acts.

George Read (1733–1798) was United States senator from Delaware.

Theodorick Bland had been elected to the House of Representatives from Virginia in 1789. James Madison had been elected to the House of Representatives from Virginia in 1789 with GW's quiet support. During the early months of his administration GW had frequently called upon Madison for advice on matters pertaining to appointments and protocol and requested his aid in drawing up such official papers as his first inaugural and other addresses and statements to Congress. In these months Madison assumed the role of an unofficial cabinet member and administration whip in the House of Representatives.

Samuel Osgood (1748–1813) had been a member of the Continental Congress 1781–84 and of the Board of Treasury 1785–89. Although he opposed ratification of the Constitution, GW appointed him postmaster general 26 Sept. 1789, a post he retained until the federal government moved to Philadelphia in 1790. In 1786 he married Maria Bowne Franklin, widow of Walter Franklin of New York. Upon GW's arrival in New York he occupied a house facing Franklin Square built by Walter Franklin and now owned by Osgood. The house, "square, five windows wide, and three stories high," had previously been occupied by the president of the Continental Congress (Decatur, *Private Affairs,* 117). Congress had ordered Osgood 15 April 1789 to "put the same, and the furniture therein, in proper condition for the residence and use of the President of the United States, to provide for his temporary accommodation" (*Annals of Congress,* 1:149–50).

English-born William Duer (1747–1799) was prominent in business and political circles in New York City. He was a member of the Continental Congress in 1777 and 1778 and in Mar. 1786 was appointed to the Board of Treasury. His appointment as assistant secretary of the treasury in 1789 was one of the Washington administration's more controversial appointments since Duer's speculative ventures had already excited the suspicions of the Antifederalists. In 1779 Duer married Catherine Alexander, usually called Lady Kitty, daughter of William Alexander, Lord Stirling.

Anne Brown (Browne; b. 1754) was a daughter of William and Mary French Browne of Salem, Mass. Lady Christiana Griffin (1751–1807) was the wife of Cyrus Griffin (1748–1810), a prominent Virginia jurist and the last president of the Continental Congress. In 1770 Griffin had married Lady Christiana Stuart, daughter of John Stuart, sixth earl of Traquair, in Edinburgh. James Duane (1733–1797), of New York City, was a member of the

Continental Congress from 1774 to 1783 where he was particularly active in financial and Indian affairs. He was mayor of New York City from 1784 to 1789 and a member of the New York Ratifying Convention where he strongly supported the Constitution.

Catherine Littlefield Greene (1755–1814) was the widow of Maj. Gen. Nathanael Greene. During the Revolution the Greenes became close friends of the Washingtons. Greene died in 1786, leaving a plantation in Georgia and a legacy of debt to his wife and five children. At this time Mrs. Greene was spending part of her time in Newport, R.I., and part in New York City, where she was attempting to settle Greene's Revolutionary War accounts with the new federal government.

Thomas Nelson, Jr., was the son of Gov. Thomas Nelson of Virginia. Governor Nelson had died in Jan. 1789 leaving his wife and children impoverished and with extensive debts. David Stuart wrote GW, 14 July 1789, suggesting that some government position might be found for young Thomas. Since the governor had been an "old friend and acquaintance," GW decided to appoint the young man as one of his secretaries, although "I must confess there are few persons of whom I have *no* personal knowledge or good information that I would take into my family, where many qualifications are necessary to fit them for the duty of it—to wit, a good address, abilities above mediocrity—secresy and prudence—attention and industry—good temper—and a capacity and disposition to write correctly and well, and to do it obligingly" (GW to Stuart, 26 July 1789, GW to Nelson, 27 July 1789, Nelson to GW, 13 Aug. 1789, *Papers, Presidential Series,* 3:321–27, 332–33, 425–26). Nelson resigned from GW's family in Nov. 1790. *Acts:* that is, the act of Congress creating the positions.

Friday 2d. Dispatching Commissions &ca. as yesterday for the Judiciary. The Visitors to Mrs. Washington this evening were not numerous.

Martha Washington held her levees, lasting about three hours, on Friday evenings at 8:00, and GW usually attended. "She gives Tea, Coffee, Cake, Lemonade & Ice Creams," Abigail Adams noted. "The form of Reception is this, the servants announce & Col. Humphries or Mr. Lear, receives every Lady at the door, & Hands her up to Mrs. Washington to whom she makes a most Respectfull courtesy and then is seated without noticeing any of the rest of the company. The President then comes up and speaks to the Lady, which he does with a grace dignity & ease, that leaves Royal George far behind him. The company are entertaind with Ice creems & Lemonade, and retire at their pleasure performing the same ceremony when they quit the Room." Frequently the receptions were "as much crowded as a Birth Night at St. James, and with company as Briliantly drest, diamonds & great Hoops excepted" (Abigail Adams to Mary Cranch, 9 Aug. 1789, 5 Jan. and 27 July 1790, Mitchell, *New Letters of Abigail Adams,* 18, 35, 55).

Saturday 3d. Sat for Mr. Rammage near two hours to day, who was drawing a miniature Picture of me for Mrs. Washington.

Walked in the Afternoon, and sat about two Oclock for Madam de Brehan to complete a Miniature profile of me which she had begun from Memory and which she had made exceedingly like the Original.

John Rammage (1763–1802) was a skilled miniature painter and silver-smith.

The marquise de Bréhan and the comte de Moustier, who had visited GW at Mount Vernon in 1788 (see entry for 2 Nov. 1788) now lived in the Macomb House on Broadway, soon to be occupied by GW. Both Moustier and his sister were widely unpopular in the United States. "We have a French minister now with us," John Armstrong complained, "and if France had wished to destroy the little remembrance that is left of her and her exer-tions in our behalf, she would have sent just such a minister: distant, haughty, penurius, and entirely governed by the caprices of a little singular, whimsical, hysterical old woman, whose delight is in playing with a negro child, and caressing a monkey" (Griswold, *Republican Court,* 93). The marquise had worked on a portrait of GW on her visit to Mount Vernon in 1788. "Her painting was in cameo-relief in blue, white, and black, and looks like carved reliefs, though painted profiles. She made a number of copies" (Eisen, *Por-traits of Washington,* 2:454–55, 591–92).

Sunday 4th. Went to St. Pauls Chappel in the forenoon. Spent the re-mainder of the day in writing private letters for tomorrows Post.

St. Paul's Chapel, opened in 1766, was one of two Protestant Episcopal chap-els in New York City. GW attended St. Paul's regularly in 1789 and early 1790.

Monday 5th. Exercised on horse back between the Hours of 9 and 11 in the forenoon and between 5 and 6 in the Afternn. on foot.

Had conversation with Colo. Hamilton on the propriety of my makg. a tour through the Eastern states during the recess of Congress to ac-quire knowledge of the face of the Country the growth and Agriculture there of and the temper and disposition of the Inhabitants towards the new government who thought it a very desirable plan and advised it accordingly.

GW had appointed Alexander Hamilton secretary of the treasury on 11 Sept. 1789.

Tuesday 6th. Exercised in a Carriage with Mrs. Washington in the forenoon.

Conversed with Genl. Knox (Secretary at War) on the above tour who also recommended it accordingly.

Henry Knox had been appointed secretary of war by GW 11 Sept. 1789.

Wednesday 7th. Exercised on horseback; & called on the Vice Presi-dent. In the afternoon walked an hour.

Upon consulting Mr. Jay on the propriety of my intended tour into the Eastern States, he highly approved of it—but observed, a similar visit wd. be expected by those of the Southern.

With the same Gentlemen I had conversation on the propriety of takg. informal means of ascertaining the views of the British Court with respect to our Western Posts in their possession and to a Commercial treaty. He thought steps of this sort advisable, and mentioned as a fit person for this purpose, a Doctr. Bancroft as a man in whom entire confidence might be placed.

Colo. Hamilton on the same subject highly approved of the Measure but thought Mr. Gouvr. Morris well qualified.

> Vice-President John Adams and his family were now living in a mansion on Richmond Hill, near Lispenard's Meadows at the corner of Varick and Van Dam streets.
>
> John Jay, secretary of foreign affairs under the Confederation, had been named chief justice of the Supreme Court by GW on 24 Sept. 1789. GW had appointed Thomas Jefferson secretary of state 25 Sept. 1789, but Jefferson was on his way to America from his post as United States minister to France before he could be notified and did not learn of his appointment until his arrival in Norfolk, Va., 23 Nov. 1789. Jay continued in charge of the State Department until Jefferson arrived in New York 21 Mar. 1790.
>
> Dr. Edward Bancroft (1744–1821), a native of Westfield, Mass., studied medicine in England and was living in London in 1776 when he became an unofficial agent for the American commissioners in Paris and remained a confidant of Benjamin Franklin and Silas Deane until the end of the war. At the same time he was pursuing a highly successful career as a spy for the British ministry. Although he was considered ill-mannered and indiscreet by such contemporaries as John Adams, only Arthur Lee seriously considered his activities treasonable. In 1789 Bancroft was living in London.
>
> Hamilton's suggestion was undoubtedly a welcome one to GW. In addition to his own frequent and pleasant contacts with Gouverneur Morris after the Revolution, Morris's abilities had been prominently displayed at the Constitutional Convention where he had led the fight for a strong and independent presidency. He was already in Europe, having arrived in Paris in early 1789 to attend to the problems arising out of business associate Robert Morris's tobacco contract with the French Farmers General and to engage in a highly speculative attempt to purchase the American debt to France. Since the mission to Britain was unofficial, the appointment would not have to run the gamut of the Senate where there was considerable suspicion of Morris's political principles and personal morality.

Thursday 8th. Mr. Gardoqui took leave, proposing to embark to morrow for Spain.

Mr. Madison took his leave to day. He saw no impropriety in my proposed trip to the Eastward; but with respect to the private agent to ascertain the disposition of the British Court with respect to the Western Posts & Commercial treaty he thought if the necessity did not press it would be better to wait the arrival of Mr. Jefferson who might be able to give the information wanted on this head—and with me thought, that if Mr. Gouvr. Morris was employed in this business it would be a commitment for his appointment as Minister if one should be sent to that Court or wanted at Versailles in place of Mr. Jefferson—and Moreover if either of these was his Wish whether his representations might not be made with an eye to it. He thought with Colo. Hamilton, and as Mr. Jay also does, that Mr. Morris is a man of superior talents—but with the latter that his imagination sometimes runs a head of his judgment—that his Manners before he is known—and where known are oftentimes disgusting—and from that, and immoral & loose expressions had created opinions of himself that were not favourable to him and which he did not merit.

Friday 9th. Exercised on horse-back between the hours of 9 and 11. Visited in my rout the Gardens of Mr. Perry and Mr. Williamson.

Received from the French Minister, in Person, official notice of his having recd. leave to return to his Court and intended embarkation—and the orders of his Court to make the following communication—viz.—That his Majesty was pleased at the Alteration which had taken place in our Government and congratulated this Country on the choice they had made of a Presidt.

> "Perry's garden was on the west side of the Bloomingdale road, west of the present Union Square. [David] Williamson's was a flower and nursery garden, and a place of public resort, on the east side of Greenwich Street, extending about three squares up from Harrison Street" (Baker, *Washington after the Revolution,* 149).

Saturday 10th. Pursuant to an engagement formed on Thursday last—I set off about 9 Oclock in my Barge to Visit Mr. Prince's fruit Gardens & shrubberies at Flushing on Long Island. The Vice President—Governor of the State, Mr. Izard, Colo. Smith and Majr. Jackson accompanied me.

These Gardens except in the number of young fruit Trees did not answer my expectations—The shrubs were trifling and the flowers not numerous.

The Inhabitants of this place shewed us what respect they could, by making the best use of one Cannon to salute.

On our return, we stopped at the Seats of General, and Mr. Gouvernr. Morris and viewed a Barn of which I have heard the latter speak much belonging to his farm—but it was not of a Construction to strike my fancy—nor did the conveniencies of it at all answer the cost.

From hence we proceeded to Harlaem where we were met by Mrs. Washington, Mrs. Adams and Mrs. Smith—Dined at the Tavern kept by a Captn. Mariner and came home in the evening.

> William Prince's Linnean Botanic Garden at Flushing, Long Island, had been established by his father, also William Prince, in 1737. Although Prince's extensive nurseries for plants and trees had been severely decimated by British depredations during the Revolution, the gardens and orchards had largely recovered by 1789, and GW often ordered fruit for his table from Prince (Decatur, *Private Affairs,* 62, 93).

Ralph Izard (1742–1804) was United States senator from South Carolina. *Seats of General, and Mr. Gouvernr. Morris:* Lewis Morris was now living on the portion of Morrisania, the Morris family estate, lying west of Mill Brook. Mrs. Smith was probably Abigail Adams Smith, the daughter of John and Abigail Adams.

Sunday 11th. At home all day—writing private Letters.

Tuesday 13th. At two Oclock received the Address from the People called Quakers. A good many Gentlemen attended the Levee to day.

The Address: presumably a statement of support for GW by "the Religious Society called Quakers, from their Yearly Meeting for Pennsylvania, New Jersey, and the western Parts of Virginia and Maryland" (*Papers, Presidential Series,* 3:265–69).

Thursday 15th. Commenced my Journey about 9 oclock for Boston and a tour through the Eastern States. The Chief Justice, Mr. Jay and the Secretaries of the Treasury and War Departments accompanied me some distance out of the City. About 10 Oclock it began to Rain, and continued to do so till 11, when we arrived at the house of one [Caleb] Hoyatt, who keeps a Tavern at Kings-bridge where we, that is Major Jackson, Mr. Lear and myself, with Six Servants which composed my Retinue, dined. After dinner through frequent light Showers we proceedd. to the Tavern of a Mrs. [Tamar] Haviland at Rye; who keeps a very neat and decent Inn.

Friday 16th. About 7 Oclock we left the Widow Havilands, and after passing Horse Neck [Greenwich] Six Miles distant from Rye, the Road through which is hilly and immensely stoney and trying to Wheels & Carriages, we breakfasted at Stamford which is 6 miles further (at one Webbs) a tolerable good house, but not equal in appearance or reality, to Mrs. Havilds. In this Town are an Episcopal Church and a Meeting house. At Norwalk which is ten miles further we made a halt to feed our Horses.

Webb's tavern was at the corner of Main and Bank streets in Stamford, Conn.

Saturday 17th. A little after Sun-rise we left Fairfield, & passing through Et. Fairfield breakfasted at Stratford, wch. is ten Miles from Fairfield, and is a pretty village on or near Stratford Rivr. The Road between these two places is not on the whole bad. There are two decent looking Churches in this place—though small—viz.—an Episcopal and Pres-beterian, or Congregationalist (as they call themselves). At Stratford there is the same. At this place I was received with an effort of Military parade; and was attended to the Ferry which is near a mile from the Center of the Town.

From Stratford the party traveled to Milford and reached New Haven about 2 o'clock on 17 Oct.

Sunday 18th. Went in the forenoon to the Episcopal Church and in the afternoon to one of the Congregational Meeting Houses—Drank Tea at the Mayors (Mr. [Roger] Sherman's). Upon further enquiry I find that there has been abt. [   ] yards of course Linnen manufactured at this place since it was established and that a Glass work is on foot here for the manufacture of Bottles. At 7 Oclock in the evening many Officers of this State, belonging to the late Continental Army, called to pay their respects to me.

Monday 19th. Left New haven at 6 oclock, and arrived at Wallingford (13 Miles) by half after 8 oclock, where we breakfasted and took a walk through the Town. At this place (Wallingford) we see the white Mulberry growing, raised from the Seed to feed the Silk worm. We also saw samples of lustring (exceeding good) which had been manufactured from the Cocoon raised in this Town, and silk thread very fine. This, except the weaving, is the work of private families without interference with other business, and is likely to turn out a benificial amusement. In the Township of Mansfield they are further advanced in this business. Walling ford has a Church & two meeting houses in it, which stands upon high and pleasant grd. About 10 Oclock we left this place and at the distance of 8 Miles passed through Durham. At one we arrived at Middletown on Connecticut River being met two or three Miles from it by the respectable Citizens of the place, and escorted in by them. While dinner was getting ready I took a walk round the Town, from the heights of which the prospect is beautiful. Belonging to this place I was informed (by a Genl. Sage) that there was about 20 Sea Vessels and to Weathersfield higher up 22 and to Hartford the like number. Other places on the River have their proportion, the whole amounting to about 10,000 Tonns. The Country hereabouts is beautiful and the Lands good. Having dined, we set out with the same Escort (who conducted us into town) about 3 Oclock for Hartford, and passing through a Parish of Middletown & Weathersfield, we arrived at Harfd. about Sun down. At Weathersfield we were met by a party of the Hartford light horse, and a Number of Gentlemen from the same place with Colo. Wadsworth at their head, and escorted to Bulls Tavern where we lodged.

Comfort Sage (1731–1799) was a native of Middletown Upper House in the area of present-day Cromwell, Conn. He had served in the Connecticut militia during the Revolution. Sage had applied for a post in the revenue service in the summer of 1789, but as GW regretfully informed him, the post was already filled. Since Sage's pretensions were supported by such prominent citizens of Connecticut as Gov. Samuel Huntington (Huntington to GW, 19 Dec. 1789), it is likely that GW's call was intended to soften his

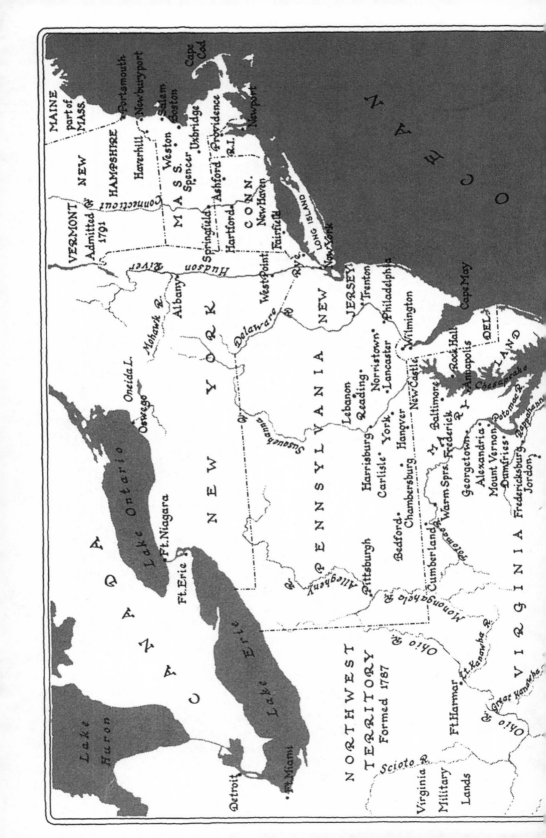

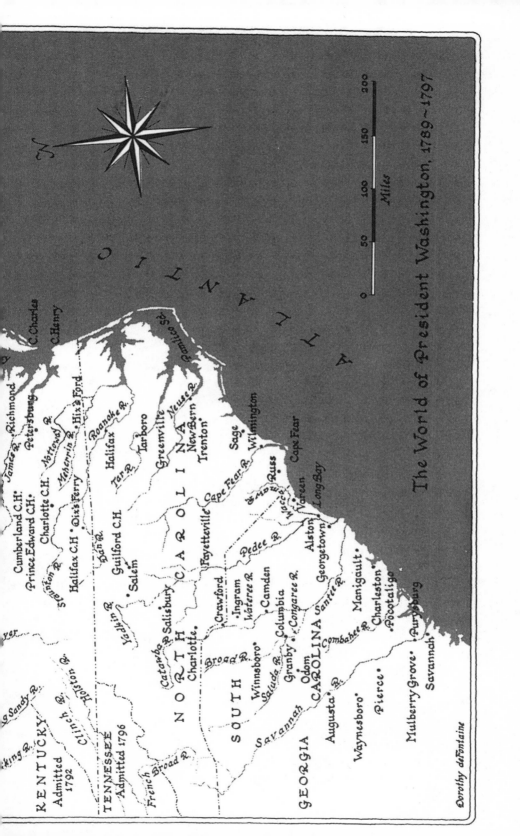

The World of President Washington, 1789~1797

Dorothy deFontaine

refusal. In Feb. 1790 the incumbent of the Middletown post resigned, and Sage received the appointment.

Tuesday 20th. After breakfast, accompanied by Colo. Wadsworth, Mr. Ellsworth and Colo. Jesse Root, I viewed the Woolen Manufactury at this place which seems to be going on with Spirit. There Broadcloths are not of the first quality, as yet, but they are good; as are their Coatings, Cassimers, Serges and everlastings. Of the first that is broad-cloth I ordered a suit to be sent to me at New York and of the latter a whole piece to make breeches for my servants. Dined and drank Tea at Colo. Wadsworth and about 7 Oclock received from, & answered the Address of the Town of Hartford.

> Oliver Ellsworth (1745–1807) was at this time Federalist senator from Connecticut. His home, Elmwood, was at South Windsor, Conn., where his wife, Abigail Wolcott Ellsworth, was a noted hostess. Jesse Root (1736–1822) was a Hartford lawyer.
>   The Hartford Woolen Manufactory began with a capital of £1,200 which by 1791 had been expanded to £2,800 and, although not incorporated, had received encouragement from the state of Connecticut in the form of tax exemptions and bounties. GW's examination of the new textile manufactory increased his interest in the possibility of introducing such a system of manufacturing in his own state or at least offering inducements to Virginia farmers to increase the number of sheep.

Wednesday 21st. By promise I was to have Breakfasted at Mr. Ellsworths at Windsor on my way to Springfield, but the Morning proving very wet and the rain not ceasing till past 10 Oclock I did not set out till half after that hour; Reached Springfield by 4 Oclock, and while dinner was getting, examined the Continental Stores at this place which I found in very good order at the buildings (on the hill above the Town) which belong to the United States. About 6 Miles before I came to Springfield I left the State of Connecticut and entered that of Massachusetts. There is a great equality in the People of this State—Few or no oppulent Men and no poor—great similatude in their buildings—the general fashion of which is a Chimney (always of Stone or Brick) and door in the middle, with a stair case fronting the latter, running up by the side of the latter [former]—two flush Stories with a very good shew of Sash & glass Windows. The size generally is from 30 to 50 feet in length and from 20 to 30 in width exclusive of a back shed which seems to be added as the family encreases. The farms by the contiguity of the Houses are small not averaging more than 100 Acres.

Thursday 22d. Set out about 7 Oclock; At Brookland [Brookfield] we fed the Horses and dispatched an Express which was sent to me by Govr. Hancock—giving notice of the measures he was about to pursue for my reception on the Road, and in Boston—With a request to lodge at his House. Continued on to Spencer 10 Miles further through pretty good roads, and lodged at the House of one Jenks who keeps a pretty good Tavern.

> On 22 Oct. GW replied, agreeing somewhat reluctantly to Hancock's plans for his reception. "But could my wish prevail I should desire to visit your Metropolis without any parade, or extraordinary ceremony. From a wish to avoid giving trouble to private families, I determined, on leaving New York, to decline the honor of any invitation to quarters which I might receive while on my journey—and with a view to observe this rule, I had requested a Gentleman to engage lodgings for me during my stay at Boston" (*Papers, Presidential Series*, 4:214).
>
> *One Jenks:* This is probably either Isaac or Lawrence Jenks, both listed in *Heads of Families, Mass.*, 236, as householders in Spencer.

Friday 23d. Commenced our course with the Sun, and passing through Leicester met some Gentlemen of the Town of Worcester on the line between it and the former to escort us. Arrived about 10 Oclock at the House of [   ] where we breakfasted—distant from Spencer 12 Miles. Here we were received by a handsome Company of Militia Artillery in Uniform who saluted 13 Guns on our entry & departure. At this place also we met a Committee from the Town of Boston, and an Aid of Majr. Genl. Brooke of the Middlesex Militia who had proceeded to this place in order to make some arrangements of Military & other Parade on my way to, and in the Town of, Boston; and to fix with me on the hours at which I should pass through Cambridge, and enter Boston. Finding this ceremony was not to be avoided though I had made every effort to do it, I named the hour of ten to pass the Militia of the above County at Cambridge and the hour of 12 for my entrance into Boston. On the Line between Worcester and Middlesex I was met by a Troop of light Horse belonging to the latter, who Escorted me to Marlborough (16 Miles) where we dined, and thence to Weston (14 More where we lodged).

> John Brooks (1752–1825) was a Reading, Mass., physician who had served in the Revolution, rising to the rank of lieutenant colonel. In 1786 Gov. James Bowdoin appointed him major general in the Middlesex militia where he served during Shays's Rebellion.

Saturday 24th. Dressed by Seven Oclock, and set out at eight. At ten we arrived in Cambridge According to appointment; but most of the Militia having a distance to come were not in line till after eleven; they made however an excellent appearance with Genl. Brook at their Head. At this place the Lieutt. Govr. Mr. Saml. Adams, with the Executive Council met me and preceeded my entrance into town—which was in every degree flattering & honorable. To pass over the Minutiae of the arrangement for this purpose it may suffice to say that at the entrance I was welcomed by the Select men in a body, Then following the Lieutt. Govr. & Council in the order we came from Cambridge (preceeded by the Town Corps very handsomely dressed) we passed through the Citizens classed in their different professions, and under their own banners, till we came to the State House; from which, across the Street, an Arch was thrown; in the front of which was this Inscription—"To the Man who unites all hearts" and on the other—"To Columbia's favourite Son" and on one side thereof next the State House, in a pannel decorated with a trophy, composed of the arms of the United States—of the Commonwealth of Massachusetts—and our French Allies, crowned with a wreath of Laurel was this Inscription—"Boston relieved March 17th. 1776." This arch was handsomely ornamented, and over the Center of it a Canopy was erected 20 feet high with the American Eagle perched on the top. After passing through the Arch, and entering the State House at the So. End & [as]cending to the upper floor & returning to a Balcony at the No. end—three cheers was given by a vast concourse of people who by this time had assembled at the Arch. Then followed an ode composed in honor of the President; and well sung by a band of select Singers—after this three Cheers—followed by the different Professions, and Mechanics in the order they were drawn up with their Colours through a lane of the People which had thronged abt. the Arch under which they passed. The Streets, the Doors, Windows & Tops of the Houses were crouded with well dressed Ladies and Gentlemen. The procession being over I was conducted to my lodgings at a Widow Ingersolls (which is a very decent & good house) by the Lieutt. Govr. and Council—accompanied by the Vice-President where they took leave of me. Having engaged yesterday to take an informal dinner with the Govr. to day (but under a full persuation that he would have waited upon me so soon as I should have arrived) I excused myself upon his not doing it, and informing me thro his Secretary that he was too much indisposed to do it, being resolved to receive the visit. Dined at my Lodgings, where the Vice-President favoured me with his Company.

The Revolutionary statesman Samuel Adams (1722–1803) served as lieutenant governor of Massachusetts 1789–93 and succeeded John Hancock as governor 1794–97. The *Pennsylvania Packet,* 18 Nov. 1789, observed that the "President's dress, on his arrival . . . was the American uniform, with two rich apaulets. His other dress is black velvet."

After GW had refused Hancock's offer of lodging while the president was in Boston (see entry for 22 Oct. 1789), the governor had replied, 23 Oct., extending an invitation to GW and "the Gentlemen of your suit" to dine with him *"en famille,* at any hour that the circumstances of the day will admit." On the same day GW replied from Weston accepting the invitation. The president had assumed, however, that the governor would call first on the president at his lodgings. When it became apparent that Hancock's illness, real or feigned, would not be an acceptable excuse to the president for the governor not making the first call, he sent GW a note stating that "the Governor will do himself the honor of paying his respects in half an hour. This would have been done much sooner had his health in any degree permitted. He now hazards every thing as it respects his health for the desirable purpose" (26 Oct. 1789, *Papers, Presidential Series,* 4:228–29). Hancock's illness was reported to be gout. For public furor over the incident, see *Boston Gaz.,* 26 Oct., 2 Nov. 1789, and *Mass. Centinel,* 28 Oct. 1789.

Sunday 25th. Attended Divine Service at the Episcopal Church whereof Doctor [Samuel] Parker is the Incumbent in the forenoon, and the Congregational Church of Mr. [Peter] Thatcher in the Afternoon. Dined at my Lodgings with the Vice President. Mr. [James] Bowdoin accompanied me to both Churches. Between the two I received a visit from the Govr., who assured me that Indisposition alone had prevented his doing it yesterday, and that he was still indisposed; but as it had been suggested that he expected to *receive* the visit from the President, which he knew was improper, he was resolved at all hazds. to pay his Compliments to day. The Lt. Govr. & two of the Council to wit [William] Heath & [Thomas] Russel were sent here last Night to express the Govrs. Concern that he had not been in a condition to call upon me so soon as I came to Town. I informed them in explicit terms that I should not see the Govr. unless it was at my own lodgings.

Monday 26th. The day being Rainy & Stormy—myself much disordered by a Cold and inflamation in the left eye, I was prevented from visiting Lexington (where the first blood in the dispute with G. Britn.) was drawn. Recd. the Complimts. of many visits to day.

GW was apparently one of the early victims of an epidemic of colds and influenza that followed his visit to Boston. Because it afflicted many of the spectators who stood in the bitterly cold wind during the festivities, the ailment was thereafter referred to as the "Washington influenza." In fact, it was part of a widespread epidemic of respiratory ailments which had already swept through the central and southern states and was now spreading into New England (*Pa. Packet,* 18 Nov. 1789; *Am. Mercury,* 9 Nov. 1789).

Tuesday 27th. At 10 Oclock in the Morning received the Visits of the Clergy of the Town—at 11 went to an Oratorio and between that and 3 Oclock recd. the Addresses of the Governor and Council—of the Town of Boston; of the President &ca. of Harvard College; and of the Cincinnati of the State; after wch., at 3 Oclock, I dined at a large & elegant dinner at Fanuiel Hall, given by the Govr. and Council, and spent the evening at my lodgings. When the Committee from the Town presented their Address it was accompanied with a request (in behalf they said of the Ladies) that I would set to have my Picture taken for

the Hall, that others might be copied from it for the use of their respective families. As all the next day was assigned to various purposes
and I was engaged to leave town on Thursday early, I informed them
of the impracticability of my doing this, but that I would have it drawn
when I returned to New York, if there was a good Painter there—or by
Mr. Trumbull when he should arrive; and would send it to them.

> The oratorio was held at King's Chapel (Stone Chapel) to raise money for an
> addition to the chapel (*Mass. Centinel,* 24 Oct. 1789).
> In spite of GW's refusal, Christian Gulager (1762–1827), a Danish artist
> living in Boston, apparently made some preliminary sketches in Boston
> which GW later approved. On 3 Nov., while in Portsmouth, N.H., he gave the
> artist a sitting for the Portsmouth Bust Portrait that Gulager probably com-
> pleted from memory and that was eventually presented to the Massachusetts
> Historical Society (Eisen, *Portraits of Washington,* 2:427–28). The painter
> John Trumbull (1756–1843) was in Europe at this time but planned to re-
> turn to the United States at the end of 1789.

Wednesday 28th. Went after an early breakfast to visit the duck Manufacture which appeared to be carrying on with spirit, and is in a pros-
perous way. This is a work of public utility & private advantage. From
hence I went to the Card Manufactury where I was informed about
900 hands of one kind and for one purpose or another. After my return I dined in a large Company at Mr. Bowdoins and went to the
Assembly in the evening where (it is said) there were upwards of
100 Ladies. There appearance was elegant and many of them very
handsome; the Room is small but neat, & well ornamented.

> The Boston Sailcloth Manufactory was established in 1788 by a group of
> Boston merchants and businessmen under the leadership of Samuel Breck
> and Thomas Alkers. By 1792 "there were four hundred employees, and the
> weekly product was not less than fifty pieces of duck" (Bagnall, *Textile Indus-
> tries,* 116). One observer noted that GW "made him self merry on this Occa-
> sion, telling the overseer he believed he collected the prettiest girls in Bos-
> ton" (Webb, *Correspondence,* 3:142–44).
> *Card Manufactory:* Presumably this was the cotton and wool card factory of
> Giles Richard and Co., on Hanover Square.

Thursday 29th. Left Boston about 8 Oclock. Passed over the Bridge at
Charles Town and went to see that at Malden, but proceeded to the
college at Cambridge, attended by the Vice President, Mr. Bowdoin,
and a great number of Gentlemen: at this place I was shewn by
Mr. [Joseph] Willard the President the Philosophical Aparatus and
amongst others Popes Orary (a curious piece of Mechanism for shewing the revolutions of the Sun, Earth and many other of the Planets)—
The library (containing 13,000 volumes) and a Museum. [*After leaving
Cambridge the party traveled to Lynn and then to Marblehead, which was four
miles out of the way but it was a town that GW wanted to see.*] The Chief

employmt. of the People of Marblehead (Males) is fishing—about 110 Vessels and 800 Men and boys are engaged in this business. Their chief export is fish. About 5000 Souls are said to be in this place which has the appearance of antiquity. The Houses are old—the streets dirty— and the common people not very clean. Before we entered the Town we were met, & attended by a Comee. till we were handed over to the Select Men who conducted us saluted by artily. in to the Town—to the House of a Mrs. Lee where there was a cold Collation prepared—after partaking of which we visited the Harbour—their fish brakes for cur- ing fish—&ca. and then proceeded (first receiving an Address from the Inhabitants) to Salem. At the Bridge, 2 Miles from this Town, we were also met by a Committee—who conducted us by a Brigade of the Militia, & one or two handsome Corps in Uniform, through several of the Streets to the Town or Court House—where an Ode in honor of the President was sung—an address presented to him amidst the accla- mations of the People—after which he was conducted to his Lodg- ings—recd. the compliments of many differt. Classes of People—and in the evening between 7 and 8 Oclock went to an assembly, where there was at least an hundred handsome and well dressed Ladies. Abt. Nine I returned to my Lodgings.

The orrery at Harvard was the work of Joseph Pope, Boston watchmaker, who had worked on it from 1776 to 1787. The instrument had been purchased for Harvard through a lottery sponsored by the Massachusetts legislature in Mar. 1789.

Mrs. Lee was Martha Swett Lee (d. 1791), wife of Col. Jeremiah Lee, a prominent Marblehead shipowner. The Lee house, on Washington Street, was an elegant mansion constructed in 1768, and Mrs. Lee was a noted hostess.

To one observer GW's progress to the courthouse seemed less than trium- phant: "His appearance as he passed thro' Court Street in Salem was far from gay, or making anyone else so. He looked oppressed by the attention that was paid him, and as he cast his eye around, I thought it seemed to sink at the notice he attracted. When he had got to the Court House, and had patiently listened to the ditty they sung at him, and heard the shouts of the multitudes he bowed very low, and as if he could bear no more turned hastily around and went into the house" (*Historical Collections of the Essex Institute*, 67 [1931], 299–300).

While in Salem, GW lodged at the imposing Ward house on Court (now Washington) Street, constructed between 1781 and 1785 by Samuel McIn- tire and presently owned by Joshua Ward.

Friday 30th. A Little after 8 Oclock I set out for Newbury-Port. After passing Beverley 2 Miles we come to the Cotton Manufactury which seems to be carrying on with Spirit by the Mr. Cabbots (principally). In this Manufactury they have the New Invented Carding and Spinning Machines—one of the first supplies the work; and four of the latter;

one of which spins 84 threads at a time by one person. From this place with escorts of Horse I passed on to Ipswich about 10 Miles—at the entrance of which I was met and welcomes by the Select Men and received by a Regemt. of Militia. At this place I was met by Mr. [Timothy] Dalton and some other Gentlemen from Newbury-port—partook of a Cold Collation, & proceeded on to the last-mentioned place where I was received with much respect & parade, about 4 Oclock. In the evening there were Rockets & some other fire-works and every other demonstration to welcome me to the Town. This place is pleasantly situated on Merimack River, and appears to have carried on (here & about) the Ship-building business to a grt. extent. The number of Souls is estimated at 5,000.

> The Beverly Cotton Manufactory was established in 1787–88 with John Cabot and Joshua Fisher as managers and George and Andrew Cabot as leading stockholders. In its early years the factory received considerable encouragement from the Massachusetts legislature—a grant of land in 1789 and a state lottery in 1791. It was incorporated 3 Feb. 1789 (Bagnall, *Textile Industries,* 93–94).

Saturday 31st. Left Newbury-port a little after 8 Oclock (first breakfasting with Mr. Dalton) and to avoid a wider ferry—more inconvenient boats—and a piece of heavy Sand, we crossed the River at Salisbury two Miles above; and near that further about—and in three Miles came to the Line wch. divides the State of Massachusetts from that of New Hampshire. Here I took leave of Mr. Dalton and many other private Gentlemen who accompanied me—And was recd. by the President of the State of New Hampshire—the Vice-President; some of the Council—Messrs. Langdon & Wingate of the Senate—Colo. Parker Marshall of the State, & many other respectable characters; besides several Troops of well cloathed Horse in handsome Uniforms, and many Officers of the Militia also in handsome (white & red) uniforms of the Manufacture of the State. With this Cavalcade we proceeded and arrived before 3 Oclock at Portsmouth, where we were received with every token of respect and appearance of Cordiallity under a discharge of Artillery. The Streets—doors and windows were Crouded here, as at all the other Places—and, alighting at the Town House, odes were Sung & played in honor of the President. The same happened yesterday at my entrance into New-buryport—Being stopped at my entrance to hear it. From the Town House I went to Colonel Brewsters Ta[ver]n the place provided for my residence.

> On his way from Newburyport to Portsmouth, GW "passed through the towns of Amesbury and Salisbury where several companies of Militia were paraded which saluted as he passed. The Marine Society of this town pre-

pared and decorated a handsome Barge, for the purpose of carrying the President across Merrimack River, which was previously sent . . . opposite to Amesbury Ferry, where it waited his arrival. The Barge men were all dressed in white" (*Essex Jl. and New Hampshire Packet,* 4 Nov. 1789). John Sullivan (1740–1795) had been president of New Hampshire in 1786 and 1787 and was reelected in 1789. John Pickering (c.1738–1805), one of New Hampshire's leading jurists, was now vice-president of the state. John Langdon (1741–1819) and Paine Wingate (1739–1838) were New Hampshire's two United States senators. In Sept. 1789 GW had appointed John Parker United States marshal for the district of New Hampshire.

The tavern was kept by William Brewster.

November

November 1st. Attended by the President of the State (Genl. Sullivan) Mr. Langdon, & the Marshall; I went in the fore Noon to the Episcopal Church under the incumbency of a Mr. Ogden and in the Afternoon to one of the Presbeterian or Congregational Churches in which a Mr. Buckminster Preached. Dined at home with the Marshall and spent the afternoon in my own room writing letters.

> Rev. John Cosens Ogden was pastor of St. John's Episcopal Church from 1786 to 1793. The Rev. Joseph Buckminster became pastor of the North Congregational Church in Portsmouth in 1779 and held the post for thirty-three years.

Monday 2d. Having made previous preparations for it—About 8 Oclock attended by the President, Mr. Langden & some other Gentlemen, I went in a boat to view the harbour of Portsmouth; which is well secured against all Winds; and from its narrow entrance from the Sea, and passage up to the Town, may be perfectly guarded against any approach by water. The anchorage is also good & the Shipping may lay close to the Docks &ca. when at the Town. In my way to the Mouth of the Harbour, I stopped at a place called Kittery in the Provence of Main, the River Piscataqua being the boundary between New Hampshire and it. From hence I went by the Old Fort (formerly built while under the English government) on an Island which is at the Entrance of the Harbour and where the Light House stands. As we passed this Fort we were saluted by 13 Guns. Having Lines we proceeded to the Fishing banks a little with out the Harbour and fished for Cod—but it not being a proper time of tide we only caught two—with wch. about 1 Oclock we returned to Town. Dined at Col. Langdons, and drank Tea there with a large Circle of Ladies and retired a little after Seven O'clock. Before dinner I recd. an address from the Town—presented by the Vice-President and returned an answer in the Evening to one I had recd. from Marblehead and an other from the Presbiterian Clergy of the

State of Massachusetts & New Hampshire delivered at Newbury Port; both of which I had been unable to answer before.

> *Old Fort:* Fort William and Mary, later called Fort Constitution, was on New-castle Island in Portsmouth harbor.
>
> GW's first attempt at deep-sea fishing apparently was even less successful than he intimates. One of the two cod "was hooked by a fisherman named Zebulon Willey, who was trying his luck in a neighboring boat. Getting a bite, he handed his line to the President, who landed the fish and rewarded Zebulon with a silver dollar. When returning to town, the President saw an old acquaintance. This was Captain John Blunt, the helmsman of the boat during the famous crossing of the Delaware" (Decatur, *Private Affairs,* 84).

Tuesday 3d. About 2 Oclock I recd. an Address from the Executive of the State of New Hampshire; and in half an hour after dined with them and a large Company at their Assembly room which is one of the best I have seen any where in the United States. At half after Seven I went to the Assembly where there were about 75 well dressed, and many of them very handsome Ladies—among whom (as was also the case at the Salem & Boston Assemblies) were a greater proportion with much blacker hair than are usually seen in the Southern States. About 9 I returned to my Quarters.

> After visiting New Hampshire, GW apparently had originally intended to continue into Vermont and return to New York City by way of Albany. However, on 3 Nov. a heavy fall of snow blanketed Albany and the surrounding area, and GW decided to return to the capital by the most direct route (*Gaz. of the U.S.,* 11 Nov. 1789; *Pa. Packet,* 20 Nov. 1789).

Wednesday 4th. About half after seven I left Portsmouth, quietly & without any attendance, having earnestly entreated that all parade & ceremony might be avoided on my return. Before ten I reached Exeter 14 Miles distance. From hence passing through Kingstown (6 Miles from Exeter) I arrived at Haverhill about half past two & stayed all Night. Walked through the Town which stands at the head of the Tide of Merrimack River and in a beautiful part of the Country.

Thursday 5th. About Sun rise I set out, crossing the Merimack River at the Town over to the Township of Bradford and in nine Miles came to Abbots Tavern in Andover where we breakfasted, and met with much attention from Mr. [Samuel] Philips President of the Senate of Massachusetts, who accompanied us thro' Bellarika [Billerica] to Lexington, where I dined, and viewed the Spot on which the first blood was spilt in the dispute with great Britain on the 19th. of April 1775.

> From Lexington GW proceeded to Watertown where the party spent the night at the house of the widow of one Nathaniel Coolidge.

Friday 6th. A little after Seven oclock, under great appearances of Rain or Snow, we left Watertown, and Passing through Needham (five Miles therefrom) breakfasted at Sherburn which is 14 Miles from the former. Then passing through Holliston 5 Miles, Milford 6 More, Menden 4 More, and Uxbridge 6 More, we lodged at one Tafts 1 Miles further; the whole distance of this days travel being 36 Miles. The Roads in every part of this State are amazingly crooked, to suit the convenience of every Mans fields; & the directions you receive from the People equally blind & ignorant; for instead of going to Watertown from Lexington, if we had proceeded to Waltham we should in 13 Miles have saved at least Six; The House in Uxbridge had a good external appearance (for a Tavern) but the owner of it being from home, and the wife sick, we could not gain admittance which was the reason of my coming on to Tafts; where, though the people were obliging, the entertainment was not very inviting.

GW apparently found Taft's accommodations adequate. On 8 Nov. he wrote Samuel Taft: "Being informed that you have given my name to one of your Sons, and called another after Mrs. Washington's family—and being moreover very much pleased with the modest and innocent looks of your two daughters Patty and Polly I do, for these reasons, send each of these Girls a piece of chintz—and to Patty, who bears the name of Mrs. Washington, and who waited more upon us than Polly did, I sent five guineas, with which she may buy herself any little ornaments she may want, or she may dispose of them in any other manner more agreeable to herself. As I do not give these things with a view to have it talked of, or even to its being known, the less there is said about the matter the better you will please me; but that I may be sure the chintz and money have got safe to hand, let Patty, who I dare say is equal to it, write me a line informing me thereof directed to 'The President of the United States at New York.'" Taft's daughter, whose name was Mercy rather than Martha, acknowledged the gifts in a letter to GW, 28 Dec. 1789 (*Papers, Presidential Series,* 4:281–82).

Saturday 7th. Left Tafts before Sunrise, and passing through Douglas wood breakfasted at one Jacobs in Thompson 12 Miles' distant—not a good House. Bated the Horses in Pomfret at Colo. Grosveners, distant 11 Miles from Jacobs and Lodged at Squire Perkins in Ashford (called 10 Miles, but must be 12).

The tavern in Thompson, just off the main road between Hartford and Boston, was kept by John Jacobs. Thomas Grosvenor (1744–1825) was a Pomfret, Conn., attorney and a 1765 graduate of Yale. The tavern in Ashford was kept by Isaac Perkins.

Sunday 8th. It being contrary to Law & disagreeable to the People of this State (Connecticut) to travel on the Sabbath day and my horses after passing through such intolerable Roads wanting rest, I stayed

at Perkins's Tavern (which by the bye is not a good one) all day—
and a meeting House being with in a few rod of the Door, I attended
Morning & evening Service, and heard very lame discourses from a
Mr. Pond.

> The Rev. Enoch Pond (1756–1807) had been ordained only the year before.

Monday 9th. Set out about 7 Oclock and for the first 24 Miles had hilly,
rocky and disagreeable Roads. Arrived at Hartford a little before four.

Tuesday 10th. Left Hartford about 7 Oclock & took the Middle Road
(instead of the one through Middleton which I went). Breakfasted at
Worthington in the Township of Berlin, at the House of one Fuller.
Bated at Smiths on the plains of Wallingford 13 Miles from Fullers,
which is the distance Fullers is from Hartford—and got into New
Haven which is 13 Miles more, about half an hour before Sun-down.
At this place I met Mr. Gerry in the Stage from New York who gave me
the first certn. acct. of the health of Mrs. Washington.

> The Fuller with whom GW breakfasted is probably Ephraim Fuller, listed in
> the 1790 census as a resident of Berlin, Conn. Elbridge Gerry, United States
> congressman from Massachusetts, was probably on his way to his home, Elm-
> wood, in Cambridge, where he had lived since 1787.

Wednesday 11th. Set out about Sunrise, and took the upper Road
to Milford, it being shorter than the lower one through West haven.
Breakfasted at the former—Bated at Fairfield and dined and lodged at
a Majr. Marvins 9 Miles further; which is not a good House, though the
People of it were disposed to do all they cou'd to accomodate me.

> Ozias Marvin's tavern was located "on the Westport-Norwalk road, at the
> intersection of the King's Highway with the turnpike. Washington is said to
> have eaten only bread and milk" (Crofut, *Connecticut*, 1 : 162).

Thursday 12th. A little before Sunrise we left Marvins and breakfasting
at Stamford 13 Miles distant, reached the Widow Havilands 12 Miles
further; where, on acct. of some lame horses, we remained all Night.

Friday 13th. Left Mrs. Havilands as soon as we could see the Road and
breakfasted at Hoyets Tavern this side Kings-bridge and between two
and three Oclock arrived at my House at New York where I found Mrs.
Washington and the rest of the family all well. And its being Mrs. Washington's Night to receive visits a pretty large Company of Ladies and
Gentlemen were present.

Saturday 14th. At home all day—except taking a Walk round the Battery in the Afternoon.

Sunday 15th. Went to St. Pauls Chapel in the forenoon and after returning from thence was visited by Majr. Butler Majr. Meridith and

Mr. Smith So. Cara. Received an Invitation to attend the Funeral of Mrs. Roosevelt (the wife of a Senator of this State) but declined complying with it—first because the propriety of accepting any invitation of this sort appeared very questionable and secondly (though to do it in this instance might not be improper) because it might be difficult to discriminate in cases wch. might thereafter happen.

> Pierce Butler (1744–1822) was a United States senator from South Carolina. Samuel Meredith (1741–1817) was appointed surveyor of the Port of Philadelphia in 1788. William Loughton Smith (1758–1812) was a congressman from South Carolina. Isaac Roosevelt's wife was Cornelia Hoffman Roosevelt (1734–1789), daughter of Martinus Hoffman of Dutchess County, N.Y.

Monday 16th. The Commissioners, who had returned from the proposed Treaty with the Creek Indians before me, to this City dined with me today, as did their Secretary Colo. Franks and young Mr. Lincoln who accompanied them.

> During the summer of 1789 an increasing stream of reports came from state officials and frontier settlers telling of Indian attacks by war parties from southern tribes, urged on by the Creek chief Alexander McGillivray. The administration in Aug. 1789 appointed Benjamin Lincoln, Cyrus Griffin, and David Humphreys United States commissioners to open negotiations with the southern tribes on behalf of the government and "establish peace between the State of Georgia and the Creeks" (*ASP, Indian Affairs,* 1:65–68). The commissioners arrived in Savannah 10 Sept. and conducted negotiations with state officials and such Indian leaders as Creek chief Alexander McGillivray over the next three weeks. By 10 Nov. they were back in New York. On 17 and 20 Nov. they reported to Knox that the Creek were determined not to make a treaty. See *Papers, Presidential Series,* 3:551–65.
> David Salisbury Franks (c.1740–1793) of Philadelphia had acted as secretary to the commissioners. *Young Mr. Lincoln:* one of Benjamin Lincoln's sons.

Sunday 22d. Went to St. Pauls Chappel in the forenoon—heard a charity Sermon for the benefit of the Orphans School of this City.

Had a good deal of conversation in the Evening with the above Commissioners on the more minute part of their transactions at the Treaty with the Creek Indians and their opinion with respect to the real views of Mr. McGilivry.

> This benefit was conducted to aid the Charity School operated by Trinity Church. The sermon was preached by Rev. Dr. Benjamin Moore, and £80 8s. 10d. was collected for the Charity School (*N.Y. Daily Advertiser,* 16 and 23 Nov. 1789).

Monday 23d. Rid five or Six miles between Breakfast & dinner. Called upon Mr. Vanberkel & Mrs. Adams.

> Franco Petrus Van Berckel had succeeded his father as minister to the United States from the Netherlands in Aug. 1788 and presented his credentials in

May 1789. He was generally popular in New York, although Sen. William Maclay termed him "gaudy as a peacock" (Maclay, *Diary*, 46).

Tuesday 24th. A good deal of Company at the Levee to day. Went to the Play in the Evening.

The play GW attended was a performance of a comedy *The Toy; or A Trip to Hampton Court* which, with several shorter pieces, was performed by the Old American Company at the John Street Theatre. The *Gazette of the United States,* 28 Nov. 1789, noted that "On the appearance of The President, the audience rose, and received him with the warmest acclamations."

Thursday 26th. Being the day appointed for a thanksgiving I went to St. Pauls Chapel though it was most inclement and stormy—but few people at Church.

On 25 Sept. 1789 the House of Representatives resolved that the president should recommend a day of thanksgiving and prayer to the people of the United States acknowledging divine favor and especially the "opportunity peaceably to establish a Constitution of government for their safety and happiness." The Senate concurred on 26 Sept. The wording of the resolution did not escape comment. Rep. Aedanus Burke of South Carolina objected to the "mimicking of European customs." Thomas Tudor Tucker of South Carolina felt that Congress had no right to ask for a day of thanksgiving. Citizens "may not be inclined to return thanks for a Constitution until they have experienced that it promotes their safety and happiness. We do not yet know but they may have reason to be dissatisfied with the effects it has already produced; but whether this be so or not, it is a business with which Congress have nothing to do. . . . If a day of thanksgiving must take place, let it be done by the authority of the several States; they know best what reason their constituents have to be pleased with the establishment of this Constitution" (*Annals of Congress*, 1:949–50). GW issued the proclamation on 3 Oct., assigning 26 Nov. as the first Thanksgiving Day under the Constitution. In celebration of the day the president contributed £7 10s. 4d. for "provisions & beer" to prisoners confined for debt in the New York City jail (Decatur, *Private Affairs,* 91; *N.Y. Journal,* 3 Dec. 1789).

Monday 30th. Went to the Play in the Evening and presented Tickets to the following persons—viz.—Doctr. Johnson and Lady—Mr. Dalton & Lady—The Chief Justice of the United States and Lady—Secretary of War & Lady—Baron de Steuben and Mrs. Green.

On 30 Nov. 1789 the Old American Company gave a benefit performance of *Cymon and Sylvia,* an "Opera or Dramatic Romance," at the John Street Theatre (Ford, *Washington and the Theatre,* 40–43). GW noted in his letter of invitation to the Jays that "this is the last night the President proposes visiting the theatre for the season." Sarah Livingston Jay, the lovely and vivacious daughter of Gov. William Livingston of New Jersey, had become one of New York's leading hostesses while her husband was secretary for foreign affairs during the Confederation. Lucy Flucker Knox was the daughter of Thomas Flucker, who had been royal secretary of the Province of Massachusetts Bay.

Mrs. Knox's social ambitions occasionally were noted derisively by her contemporaries. Abigail Adams Smith wrote her mother, 15 June 1788, that
Mrs. Knox is "neat in her dress, attentive to her family, and very fond of
her children. But her size is enormous; I am frightened when I look at her"
(Griswold, *Republican Court,* 95).

December

Tuesday Decr. 1st. A pretty full Levee to day—among the Visitors was
the Vice President and all the Senators in Town.

Exercised on Horseback betwn. 10 and 12.

Read the Papers relative to our Affairs with the Emperer of Morocco
and sent them to Mr. Jay to prepare answers to them.

> Presumably GW is referring to papers submitted by Jay 1 Dec. concerning
> United States relations with the emperor of Morocco. In 1788 the emperor
> had granted special privileges to American vessels and from time to time he
> had used his good offices to aid American shipping in the area. With his
> letter to GW, Jay submitted letters of 25 April and 18 July 1789 from Giuseppe
> Chiappe, United States agent at Mogadore, intimating that the emperor felt
> that his concessions had not received sufficient recognition from the United
> States.

Sunday 6th. Went to St. Pauls Chapel in the Forenoon.

Monday 7th. Walked round the Battery in the afternoon.

Tuesday 8th. Finished by Extracts from the Commissioners Report of
their proceedings at the Treaty with the Creek Indians and from many
other Papers respecting Indian matters and the Western Territory. A
full Levee today.

> GW had received the report of the commissioners appointed to negotiate
> with the southern Indians on 21 Nov.

Saturday 12th. Exercised in the Coach with Mrs. Washington and the
two Children (Master & Miss Custis) between Breakfast & Dinner—
went the 14 Miles round.

> *The 14 Miles round:* A favorite excursion for New Yorkers was the ride
> around a portion of Manhattan Island, covering a distance of approximately
> 14 miles. Although the route varied somewhat, the path frequently taken led
> up the Bloomingdale Road along the Hudson River on the west side of Man-
> hattan to the vicinity of present-day 94th Street and then east by a crossroad
> as far as Kingsbridge. The return journey to the city was south by the Old
> Boston Post Road.

Friday 18th. Read over, and digested my thoughts upon the subject of
a National Militia, from the Plans of the Militia of Europe—those of
the Secretary at War & the Baron de Steuben.

Monday 21st. Framed the above thoughts on the subject of a National Militia into the form of a Letter and sent it to the Secretary for the Department of War.

Sat from ten to one Oclock for a Mr. Savage to draw my Portrait for the University of Cambridge in the State of Massachusetts at the request of the President and Governors of the said University.

> The portrait begun today by Edward Savage (1761–1817) was commissioned by the trustees of Harvard to be hung at the college. At today's sitting and at those of 28 Dec. and 6 Jan. 1790, Savage may also have made preliminary sketches for his Washington family portrait although the latter was interrupted by his sojourn in England 1791–94 and was not finished until 1796 (Eisen, *Portraits of Washington*, 2:457, 462–63).

Tuesday 22d. A pretty full & respectable Levee to day—at which several Members of Congress, newly arrived, attended.

Wednesday 23d. Exercised in the Post-Chaise with Mrs. Washington to day. Sent the dispatches which came to me from the Assembly of Virginia and from the Representatives of several Counties therein respecting the State of the Frontiers and depredations of the Indians to the Secretary for the Department of War requesting his attendance tomorrow at 9 Oclock that I might converse more fully with him on the subject of these communications.

> These dispatches included an undated "Address of the General Assembly of Virginia to the President of the United States," expressing the assembly's concern about Indian depredations in the state's western counties and assuring GW of Virginia's financial support if the administration should find it necessary to mount an expedition against the western tribes. A second letter, 12 Dec. 1789, signed by the representatives of the frontier counties of Ohio, Monongalia, Harrison, and Randolph, warned the president of the vulnerability of the counties to Indian attack (*ASP, Indian Affairs*, 1:85–86).

Thursday 24th. The Secretary at War coming according to appointment, he was instructed, after conversing fully on the matter, what answers to return to the Executive of Virginia and to the Representatives of the Frontier Counties.

Friday 25th. Christmas day. Went to St. Pauls Chapel in the forenoon. The Visitors to Mrs. Washington this afternoon were not numerous but respectable.

1790

January

Friday first. The Vice-President, the Governor—the Senators, Members of the House of Representatives in Town—Foreign public characters and all the respectable Citizens came between the hours of 1 2 & 3 Oclock to pay the complimts. of the Season to me—and in the Afternoon a great number of Gentlemen & Ladies visited Mrs. Washington on the same occasion.

Thursday 7th. About One Oclock recd. a Committee from both Houses of Congress informing me that each had made a House and would be ready at any time I should appoint to receive the Communications I had to make in the Senate Chamber. Named to morrow 1 1 oclock for this purpose.

Friday 8th. According to appointment, at 1 1 Oclock I set out for the City Hall in my Coach—preceeded by Colonel Humphreys and Majr. Jackson in Uniform (on my two White Horses) & followed by Mesr. Lear & Nelson in my Chariot & Mr. Lewis on Horse back following them. In their rear was the Chief Justice of the United States & Secretaries of the Treasury and War Departments in their respective Carriages and in the order they are named. At the outer door of the Hall I was met by the Doorkeepers of the Senate and House and conducted to the Door of the Senate Chamber; and passing from thence to the Chair through the Senate on the right, & House of representatives on the left, I took my Seat. The Gentlemen who attended me followed & took their stand behind the Senators; the whole rising as I entered. After being seated, at which time the members of both Houses also sat, I rose (as they also did) and made my Speech; delivering one Copy to the President of the Senate & another to the Speaker of the House of Representatives—after which, and being a few moments seated, I retired, bowing on each side to the Assembly (who stood) as I passed, and dessending to the lower Hall attended as before, I returned with them to my House.

In the Evening a *great* number of Ladies, and many Gentlemen visited Mrs. Washington.

On this occasion I was dressed in a suit of Clothes made at the Woolen Manufactury at Hartford as the Buttons also were.

GW today delivered his first annual address to Congress. William Maclay, who was present in the Senate chamber, noted: "all this Morning nothing but Bustle about the Senate Chamber in hauling Chairs and removing Tables. . . . The President was dressed in a second Mourning, and . . . read his speech well" (Maclay, *Diary,* 179–80). The *Pennsylvania Packet,* 1 3 Jan. 1790, noted that "the doors of the Senate Chamber were open, and many citizens admitted." *Suit of Clothes:* The *Pennsylvania Packet* for 1 4 Jan. noted: "The President of the United States when he addressed the two Houses of Congress yesterday, was dressed in a crow-coloured suit of clothes of American manufacture: The cloth appeared to be of the finest texture—the colour of that beautiful changeable blue, remarked in shades not quite black. This elegant fabric was from the manufactory in Hartford." GW was wearing mourning for his mother Mary Ball Washington, who had died at Fredericksburg, Va., in Aug. 1789. GW had last visited her shortly before he left for New York to assume the presidency. Knowing that she was seriously ill, he had assumed that this would be their last meeting. Upon receiving word of his mother's death, GW ordered "mourning Cockades & Ribbons" for his household, and official New York adopted the modified or American mourning prescribed by the Continental Congress in 1774—"black crape or ribbon on the arm or hat, for gentlemen, and a black ribbonand necklace for ladies" (Household Accounts, 15, Yale University; *Gazette of the United States,* [New York], 9 Sept. 1789; *JCC,* 1:78).

Robert Lewis, the son of Fielding Lewis and GW's sister Betty Washington Lewis, came to New York in May 1789 to serve as one of GW's secretaries.

Tuesday 12th. Exercised on Horse-back between 10 and 12, the riding bad.

Previous to this, I sent written Messages to both Houses of Congress informing them, that the Secretary at War would lay before them a full & complete Statement of the business as it respected the Negotiation with the Creek Indians—My Instructions to, and the Commissioners report of their proceedings with those People. The letters and other papers respecting depredations on the Western Frontiers of Virginia, & District of Kentucky All of which was for their *full* information, but communicated in confidence & under injunction that no Copies be taken, or communications made of such parts as ought to be kept secret.

Thursday 14th. At the hours appointed, the Senate & House of representatives presented their respective Addresses—The Members of both coming in Carriages and the latter with the Mace preceeding the Speaker. The Address of the Senate was presented by the Vice-President and that of the House by the Speaker thereof.

Friday 22d. Exercised on Horse back in the forenoon. Called in my ride on the Baron de Polnitz, to see the operation of his (Winlaws) threshing Machine.

Friedrich, Baron von Poellnitz, occupied a farm of about 21 acres in the vicinity of Murray Hill on Manhattan, where he carried on a number of agricultural experiments.

Saturday 23d. Went with Mrs. Washington in the Forenoon to see the Paintings of Mr. Jno. Trumbull.

Sunday 24th. Went to St. Pauls Chapel in the forenoon. Writing private letters in the afternoon.

Wednesday 27th. Did business with the Secretaries of the Treasury & War—With the first respecting the appointment of Superintendants of the Light Houses, Buoys &ca. and for building one at Cape Henry—With the latter for nominating persons (named in a list submitted to me) for paying the Military Pensionrs. of the United States and the policy and advantages (which might be derived from the measure) of bringing Mr. Alexr. McGillivray Chief of the Creek Nation here being submitted to me for consideration I requested that a plan might be reported by which Governmt. might not appear to be the Agent in it, or suffer in its dignity if the attempt to get him here should not succeed.

Thursday 28th. Sent a letter (with an Act of the Legislature of the State of Rhode Island, for calling a Convention of that State to decide on the Constitution of the Union) from Governor Collins, to both Houses of Congress—to do which, was requested by the Act, of the President.

> *Rhode Island:* Gov. John Collins's letter to GW, enclosing the act of the Rhode Island legislature authorizing a state ratifying convention, is dated 18 Jan. 1790.

February

Monday 1st. Agreed on Saturday last to take Mr. McCombs House, lately occupied by the Minister of France for one year, from and after the first day of May next; and wd. go into it immediately, if Mr. Otto the present possesser could be accomodated and this day sent My Secretary to examine the rooms to see how my furniture cd. be adapted to the respective Apartments.

> By the beginning of 1790 GW concluded that the house owned by Samuel Osgood which he had occupied since his arrival in New York City was no longer commodious enough to accommodate his family and staff and to maintain the dignity of the presidential office. In spite of the fact that it was expected that Congress might move the capital from New York City, GW decided to lease Alexander Macomb's mansion at numbers 39–41 Broadway. The Macomb house had been occupied by the comte de Moustier and, after his departure for France, by Louis Guillaume Otto, chargé d'affaires of the French embassy. Preparations continued throughout the month, and the presidential household moved to the new residence on 23 Feb.

Saturday 6th. Walked to my newly engaged lodgings to fix on a spot for a New Stable which I was about to build. Agreed with [ ] to erect one 30 feet sqr., 16 feet pitch, to contain 12 single stalls; a hay loft, Racks, mangers &ca.—Planked floor and underpinned with Stone with Windows between each stall for 65£.

Tuesday 16th. The Levee to day was thin. Received some papers from the Secretary at War respecting a corrispondence to be opened betwn. Colo. Hawkins of the Senate, and Mr. McGillivray of the Creek Nation for the purpose of getting the latter, with some other Chiefs of that Nation to this place as an expedient to avert a War with them. But, the Commissioning a Person to Negotiate this business with McGillivray without laying the matter before the Senate and the expence of the business appearing to bring in question the *Powers* of the President I requested to see & converse with the Secretary of War, tomorrow, on this Subject.

Wednesday 17th. The Secretary attending; and reference being had to the Act constituting the Department of War, and the Act appropriating 20,000 dollrs. for the expence of Treating with the Southern Indians, seeming to remove (at least in a degree) the above doubts but not in an unequivocal manner, I desired him to take the opinion of the Chief Justice of the United States and that of the Secretary of the Treasury on these points and let me know the result.

Wednesday 24th. Employed in arranging matters about the House & fixing matters.

Thursday 25th. In the afternoon a Committee of Congress presented an Act for enumerating the Inhabitts. of the United States.

An Act: This act provided for the taking of the first federal census.

March

Tuesday 9th. A good many Gentlemen attended the Levy to day; among whom were many members of Congress.

Wednesday 10th. Exercised on Horse-back between 9 and 11 oclock. On my return had a long conversation with Colo. Willet, who was engaged to go as a private Agent, but for public purposes, to Mr. McGillivray principal chief of the Creek Nation. In this conversation he was impressed with the critical situation of our Affairs with that Nation— the importance of getting him & some other Chiefs to this City—the arguments justifiable for him to use to effect this—with such lures as respected McGillivray personally & might be held out to him.

In a letter to GW, 15 Feb. 1790, concerning the government's plan to bring Creek chief Alexander McGillivray to New York, Knox had suggested that a person be appointed to carry a letter of invitation to McGillivray. The choice as emissary fell on Marinus Willett (1740–1830), an Antifederalist New York merchant and veteran of the French and Indian War and the Revolution. Willett's mission proved successful. McGillivray agreed to accompany him to New York (McGillivray to William Panton, 8 May 1790, Caughey, *McGillivray of the Creeks,* 259–62).

Tuesday 16th. Exercised on horseback between 10 & 12 Oclock. Previous to this, I was visited (having given permisn.) by a Mr. Warner

Mifflin, one of the People called Quakers; active in pursuit of the Measures laid before Congress for emancipating the Slaves. After much general conversation, and an endeavor to remove the prejudices which he said had been entertained of the motives by which the attending deputation from their Society were actuated, he used Arguments to shew the immoralty—injustice and impolicy of keeping these people in a state of Slavery; with declarations, however, that he did not wish for more than a graduel abolition, or to see any infraction of the Constitution to effect it. To these I replied, that as it was a matter which might come before me for official decision I was not inclined to express any sentimts. on the merits of the question before this should happen.

Warner Mifflin (1745–1798) was a prominent Quaker abolitionist.

Wednesday 17th. Gave Mr. Few Notice that I would receive the Address of the Legislature of Georgia tomorrow at half after ten oclock. Sent to both House[s] of Congress the Ratification of the State of Pennsylvania of the amendments proposed by Congress to the Constitution of the Union.

Thursday 18th. In the Evening (about 8 Oclk.) I went with Mrs. Washington to the assembly where there were betwn. 60 & 70 Ladies & many Gentlemen.

Sunday 21st. Went to St. Pauls Chappel in the forenoon. Wrote private letters in the afternoon. Received Mr. Jefferson, Minister of State about one Oclock.

Shortly after his return to the United States in 1789, Jefferson received GW's letter of 13 Oct. 1789 offering him the post of secretary of state. Jefferson, who preferred to return to Paris, somewhat reluctantly indicated he was willing to serve. He left Virginia early in March and arrived in New York today.

Monday 22d. Sat for Mr. Trumbell for my Picture in his Historical pieces—after which conversed for more than an hour with Mr. Jefferson on business relative to the duties of his office.

Tuesday 23d. A full, & very respectable Levee to day—previous to which I had a conversation with the Secretary of State on the following points, viz—

First, with respect to our Captives in Algiers, in which, after detailing their situation—the measures he had taken for their relief and the train in which the business was in by means of a Genl. [   ] who is at the head of a religious society in France whose practice it is to sollicit aids for the relief of the unfortunate Christians in captivity among the Barbarians, it was concluded betwn. us, that it had better remain in that train a while longer. This person had been authorised to go as far as about £150 Sterlg. each, for the ransom of our Captives; but the

Algerines demanding a much larger sum it was conceived that acceding to it might establish a precedent which would always operate and be very burthensome if yielded to; and become a much stronger inducement to captivate our People than they now have, as it is more for the sake of the ransom than for the labour, that they make Slaves of the Prisoners. Mr. Short was to be written to on this Subject, and directed to make enquiry of this General [   ] what his expectations of redemption are at present.

Second—He is of opinion, that excepting the Court of France, there is no occasion to employ higher grades in the Diplomatic line than Chargé des affaires; and that these, by the respectibility of their appointments, had better be at the head of their grade, than Ministers Plenipotentiaries by low Salaries at the foot of theirs. The reason of the distinction, in favor of a Minister Plenipo at Versailles, is, that there are more Ambassadors at that Court than any other and therefore that we ought in some measure to approximate our Representative and besides, its being a Court with which we have much to do.

Third—With respect to the appointment of Consels he refers to a letter on the nature of this business—the places where necessary—and the characters best entitled to appointmts. which he had written on the Subject, while in France, to the Secretary of Foreign affairs.

Fourth—That it might be advisable to direct Mr. Charmichael to Sound the Spanish Ministry with respect to the obstacles which had hitherto impeded a Commercial Treaty to see if there was any disposition in them to relax in their Territorial claims & exclusive right to the Navigation of the River Missisipi.

First: The Algerian captives were the 21 officers and men of two American ships—the *Maria* out of Boston and the *Dauphin* out of Philadelphia—that had been captured by Algerian corsairs off the coast of Africa in 1785. Fearing that the seamen, already held as slaves in Algiers, might be sold south into the interior of Africa, the United States government made several unsuccessful attempts to ransom them during the Confederation. By Dec. 1788 six of the captives were dead (Thomas Jefferson to Père Chauvier, 27 Dec. 1788, Boyd, *Jefferson Papers,* 14:395–97). Père Chauvier was the head of the Order de La Sainte Trinité de la Redemption des Captifs, usually called the Mathurins. In 1786–88, while he was United States minister to France, Jefferson had discussed with members of the order the possibility that they might assist in redeeming the prisoners, and in Dec. 1788 he opened negotiations with Père Chauvier (ibid., 14:401–2). See also *Papers, Presidential Series,* 3: 155–65.

William Short (1759–1849), a 1779 graduate of the College of William and Mary, accompanied Thomas Jefferson to Paris in 1784 where he served as his secretary and later as secretary of legation. When Jefferson returned to the United States, Short was left to represent the United States in France with the rank of chargé d'affaires.

Second: GW was undoubtedly concerned with Jefferson's opinion on diplomatic appointments because of discussion aroused by a bill for "providing the means of intercourse between the United States and foreign nations" (*DHFC,* 3:269). Introduced in Jan. 1790, the bill had engendered extensive and sometimes acrimonious debate on the appointment of American diplomats abroad and the manner in which they were to be paid. The bill involved constitutional questions as to whether the president should determine the rank and emoluments for diplomatic appointments or whether this was to be a function of Congress as had been the case during the Confederation (*Annals of Congress,* 1:1004–5, 1113, 1118–30, 2:1526). On 31 Mar. 1790 "the committee to whom was re-committed the bill 'providing the means of intercourse between the United States and foreign nations,' presented an amendatory bill to the same effect, which was received and read the first time." See *DHFC,* 3:351. Debates in the House and Senate on the amended bill dragged on until the passage of "An Act providing the means of intercourse between the United States and foreign nations" (1 *Stat* 128 [1 July 1790]).

Third: Jefferson's letter to John Jay, 14 Nov. 1788, detailed Jefferson's views on a consular establishment and suggested individuals who might fill consular posts in France (Boyd, *Jefferson Papers,* 14:56–66).

William Carmichael (c.1738–1795), of Queen's County, Md., served in the Continental Congress 1778–79 and as John Jay's secretary in Spain in 1779. In Sept. 1789 GW appointed him chargé d'affaires in Madrid.

Thursday 25th. Went in the forenoon to the Consecration of Trinity Church, where a Pew was constructed, and set apart for the President of the United Sts.

Received from the Senate their opinion and advice on the Papers which had been submitted to them respecting the Incroachments on the Eastern boundary of the United States, and the disputes consequent thereof.

And from a Com[mitt]ee. of Congress two Acts—one for establishing the mode for uniformity in Naturalization of Foreigners—the other Making appropriations for the support of Government for the year 1790.

The following Company dined here to day—viz—

The Chief Justice Jay & his Lady Genl. [Philip] Schuyler & his Lady, the Secretary of the Treasury & his Lady, the Secretary of War & his Lady & Mrs. [Catharine] Greene The Secretary of State (Mr. Jefferson) Mr. [Charles] Carroll & Mr. [John] Henry of the Senate Judge [James] Wilson, Messrs. Madison & [John] Page of the Ho. of Representatives, and Colo. Smith Marshall of the District.

Friday 26th. Had a further Conversation with the Secretary of State on the subject of Foreign appointments, and on the Provision which was necessary for Congress to make for them—the result of which was that under all circumstances it might be best to have Ministers

Plenip[otentiar]y. at the Courts of France and England (if any advances from the latter should be made) And Chargés des Affaires in Spain & Portugal—Whether it might be necessary to send a Person in this character to Holland—one in the character of Resident—or simply a person well Skilled in commercial matters in any other character being questionable; nothing finally was decided—but it was concluded that the Secretary's information to a Committee of Congress with whom he was to converse on the subject of the Provision to be made, that the Salaries allowed to our Diplomatic characters was too low—that the Grades which wd. be fixed on, to transact our Affairs abroad would be as low as they cd. be made without giving umbrage that therefore, about 36,000 dollrs. might answer as a provision for the characters to the Courts before named—or that it might take forty nine or 50,000 dollars if it should be found that the lower grades will not answer. The company this evening was thin, especially of Ladies.

April

Tuesday 6th. Sat for Mr. Savage, at the request of the Vice-President, to have my Portrait drawn for him.

> The portrait for which GW sat today was painted by Edward Savage for John Adams and hung by the Adamses in their home in Quincy, Mass.

Saturday 10th. Exercised in the Coach with Mrs. Washington and the Children. Walked in the afternoon around the Battery and through some of the principal Streets of the City.

In the Afternoon the Secretary of State submitted for my approbation Letters of credence for Mr. Short as Charges de affaires at the Court of Versailles, & his own Letter to Monsr. Montmorin taking leave of that Court both directed to that Minister—also to Mr. Short on the Subject of our Prisoners at Algiers. And at Night he submitted the Copy of a letter he had drafted to Mr. Carmichael respecting the Governor of the Island of Juan Fernandez who had been disgraced & recalled from his government of that Island for having permitted the ship Washington which had suffered in a storm to put into that Port to repair the damages she had sustained in it, & to recruit her wood & water. This Ship belonged to Barrel & Co. of Boston.

> Jefferson's letter to William Carmichael, 11 April 1790, is in Boyd, *Jefferson Papers,* 16:329–30. The letter concerned the *Columbia,* commanded by Capt. John Kendrick, and the *Lady Washington,* commanded by Capt. Robert Gray, both of which left Boston in 1787 on their way to the west coast of North America to open a fur trade with Russian settlements there. The *Lady Washington,* damaged in a storm in the vicinity of the Juan Fernandez Islands off the west coast of Chile, had been permitted by Gov. Don Blas Gonzalez to

put into one of the islands' ports for repairs. "For this act of common hospitality," Jefferson informed Carmichael, "he was immediately deprived of his government unheard, by superior order, and remains still under disgrace."

Sunday 11th. Went to Trinity Church in the forenoon and [wrote] several private letters in the afternoon.

Sunday 25th. Went to Trinity Church, and wrote letters home after dinner.

Monday 26th. Did business with the Secretaries of State, Treasury, and War, & appointed a quarter before three tomorrow to receive from the Senators of the State of Virga. an Address from the Legislature thereof.

Tuesday 27th. Had some conversation with Mr. Madison on the propriety of consulting the Senate on the places to which it would be necessary to send persons in the Diplomatic line, and Consuls; and with respect to the grade of the first. His opinion coincides with Mr. Jays and Mr. Jeffersons—to wit—that they have no Constitutional right to interfere with either, & that it might be impolitic to draw it into a precedent their powers extending no farther than to an approbation or disapprobation of the person nominated by the President all the rest being Executive and vested in the President by the Constitution.

At the time appointed, Messrs. [Richard Henry] Lee & [John] Walker (the Senators from Virginia) attended, & presented the Address as mentioned yesterday & received an answer to it.

A good deal of respectable Company was at the Levee to day.

Wednesday 28th. Fixed with the Secretary of State on places & characters for the Consulate but as some of the latter were unknown to us both he was directed to make enquiry respecting them.

Sent the nominations of two Officers in the Customs of North Carolina, and one in the place of Mr. Jacob Wray of Hampton in Virginia—who has requested to resign his appointment to the Senate for their advice & consent thereon.

Received from the Secretary for the Department of War a report respecting the Sale of certain Lands by the State of Georgia; and the consequent disputes in which the United States may be involved with the Chicasaws & Choctaw Nations; part, if not the whole of whose Countries, are included within the limits of the said Sale. This report refers to the Act of the Legislature of Georgia, by which this sale is authorized and to the opinion of the Attorney General respecting the Constitutionality of the Proceeding—submitting at the same time certain opinions for the consideration of the Presidt.

Today's consultation with Jefferson on consular appointments was in preparation for the list of nominations sent by GW to the Senate on 4 June 1790, when 14 names were submitted for confirmation (*DHFC*, 1:74–78). Knox's report concerned the sale in 1789 by the state of Georgia of over 15 million acres of land in western Georgia to three land companies, the South Carolina Yazoo Company, the Virginia Yazoo Company, and the Tennessee Yazoo Company, at a projected cost to the companies of approximately $200,000. The federal government took as strong action as possible during the summer of 1790 to prevent the companies, which were heavily involved in land speculation, from implementing their claims.

Thursday 29th. Fixed with the Secretary of State on the present which (according to the custom of other Nations) should be made to Diplomatic characters when they return from that employment in this Country and this was a gold Medal, suspended to a gold Chain—in ordinary to be of the value of about 120 or 130 Guineas.

Friday 30th. Conversed with the Secretary of the Treasury, on the Report of the Secretary at War's propositions respecting the Conduct of the State of Georgia in selling to certain Compa[nies] large tracts of their Western territory & a proclamation which he conceived expedient to issue in consequence of it. But as he had doubts of the clearness of the ground on which it was proposed to build this proclamation and do the other acts which were also submitted in the report. I placed it in the hands of the Secretary of State to consider & give me his opinion thereon.

May

May 1st. Mr. Alexr. White, representative from Virginia, communicated his apprehensions that a disposition prevailed among the Eastern & northern States (discoverable from many circumstances, as well as from some late expressions which had fallen from some of their members in the Ho[use]) to pay little attention to the Western Country because they were of opinion it would soon shake of its dependence on this; and in the meantime, would be burthensome to it. He gave some information also of the temper of the Western Settlers, of their dissatisfactions, and among other things that few of the Magestrates had taken the Oaths to the New Government not inclining in the present state of things and under their ideas of neglect to bind themselves to it by an Oath.

Tuesday 4th. Exercised in the forenoon on Horse back. A respectable Company at the Levee to day.

Wednesday 5th. Requested General Rufus Putnam—lately appointed a Judge in the Western Government and who was on the eve of his departure for that Country to give me the best discription he could

obtain of the proximity of the Waters of the Ohio & Lake Erie—
the nature of their Navigations—Portages—&ca.—Also of the occurrences in the Country—the population of it—Temper of the people
&ca. &ca.

Sunday 9th. Indisposed with a bad cold, and at home all day writing
letters on private business.

> GW's cold rapidly developed into pneumonia. Local physicians Dr. Samuel
> Bard, Dr. Charles McKnight, and Dr. John Charlton were summoned to the
> president's bedside, but in spite of their efforts GW grew steadily worse. To
> avoid public concern, the president's illness was kept as quiet as possible. On
> 12 May, William Jackson, one of GW's secretaries, wrote to Clement Biddle
> in Philadelphia enclosing a letter to Dr. John Jones, a prominent Philadel-
> phia physician, requesting him to attend the president in New York. "The
> Doctor's prudence will suggest the propriety of setting out as privately as pos-
> sible; perhaps it may be well to assign a personal reason for visiting New York,
> or going into the Country." By 15 May, however, the seriousness of GW's
> condition was widely known. "Called to see the President," William Maclay
> noted in his diary, "every Eye full of Tears. his life despaired of. Doctor Mac-
> knight told me he would trifle neither with his own Character nor the public
> Expectation; his danger was imminent, and every reason to expect That the
> Event of his disorder would be unfortunate" (Maclay, *Diary*, 269). By the
> next day, however, the outlook was more hopeful. On 16 May Jefferson wrote
> his daughter Martha Jefferson Randolph "that from a total despair we are
> now in good hopes of him" (Boyd, *Jefferson Papers*, 16:429). Although he was
> able to resume most of his duties by the end of May, GW did not recover fully
> from his illness for several more weeks. He wrote to Lafayette on 3 June that
> he had recovered "except in point of strength," and in mid-June he was still
> experiencing chest pains, coughing, and shortness of breath. For a detailed
> account of GW's illness, see *Papers, Presidential Series*, 5:393–400).

Monday 10th. A severe illness with which I was seized the 10th. of this
Month and which left me in a convalescent state for several weeks after
the violence of it had passed; & little inclination to do more than what
duty to the public required at my hands occasioned the suspension of
this Diary.

June

Sunday 27th. Went to Trinity Church in the forenoon and employed
myself in writing business in the afternoon.

Monday 28th. Exercised between 5 & 7 Oclock in the Morning & drank
Tea with Mrs. Clinton (the Governors Lady) in the Afternoon.

> Gov. George Clinton's residence was at 10 Queen Street, near the end of
> Cedar Street. It was presumably this residence rather than the Clintons' farm
> on the Hudson outside the city which GW visited today. GW and Mrs. Wash-
> ington had frequent social contacts with Clinton and his wife, Cornelia Tap-

pan Clinton, during the Revolution, and after the war a friendly correspondence had been maintained, Clinton sending GW trees and various plants for Mount Vernon. In spite of political differences between Clinton and GW after the new government was established, social relations between the two families remained warm. As a rule, partly because of Mrs. Clinton's ill health, the Clintons did little entertaining. Abigail Adams Smith found Mrs. Clinton "not a showy, but a kind, friendly woman" (Roof, *William Smith,* 197).

July

Thursday July 1st. Having put into the hands of the Vice President of the U: States the communications of Mr. Gouvr. Morris, who had been empowerd to make informal enquiries how well disposed the British Ministry might be to enter into Commercial regulations with the United States, and to fulfil the Articles of Peace respecting our Western Posts, and the Slaves which had been carried from this Country, he expressed his approbation that this step had been taken; and added that the disinclination of the British Cabinet to comply with the two latter, & to evade the former, as evidently appears from the Corrispondence of Mr. Morris with the Duke of Leeds (the British Minister for Foreign Affairs) was of a piece with their conduct towds. him whilst Minister at that Court; & just what he expected; & that to have it ascertained was necessary. He thought as a rupture betwn. England & Spain was almost inevitable, that it would be our policy & interest to take part with the latter as he was very apprehensive that New Orleans was an object with the former; their possessing which would be very injurious to us; but he observed, at the sametime, that the situation of our affairs would not Justify the measure unless the People themselves (of the United States) should take the lead in the business.

Received about three Oclock, official information from Colo. Willet, that he was on the return from the Creek Nation (whither he had been sent with design to bring Colo. McGillivray, and some of the Chiefs of these people to the City of New York for the purpose of treating) that he, with the said McGillivray and many of the head Men, were advanced as far as Hopewell in So. Carolina on their way hither and that they should proceed by the way of Richmond with as much expedition as the nature of the case wd. admit.

In the fall of 1789 GW had requested Gouverneur Morris to open unofficial discussions with the British ministry on outstanding differences between the United States and Great Britain (see entry for 7 Oct. 1789). Among the letters that GW showed to Adams today was probably Morris to GW, 7 April 1790, describing in detail his polite but unsatisfactory interview with the duke of Leeds, British minister for foreign affairs (*Papers, Presidential Series,* 5:319–23).

McGillivary, Marinus Willett, and their party apparently started north in mid-May, arriving in New York City on 20 July. The negotiations with the Creek continued in July and early August, and the Treaty of New York was signed on 7 Aug. 1790.

Sunday 4th. Went to Trinity Church in the forenoon. This day being the Anniversary of the declaration of Independency the celebration of it was put of until to morrow.

Monday 5th. The Members of Senate, House of Representatives, Public Officers, Foreign Characters &ca. The Members of the Cincinnati, Officers of the Militia, &ca., came with the compliments of the day to me. About One Oclk. a sensible Oration was delivered in St. Pauls Chapel by Mr. Brockholst Levingston on the occasion of the day—the tendency of which was, to shew the different situation we are now in, under an excellent government of our own choice, to what it would have been if we had not succeeded in our opposition to the attempts of Great Britain to enslave us; and how much we ought to cherish the blessings which are within our reach, & to cultivate the seeds of harmony & unanimity in all our public Councils. There were several other points touched upon in a sensible manner.

In the afternoon many Gentlemen & ladies visited Mrs. Washington.

I was informed this day by General Irvine (who recd. the acct. from Pittsburgh) that the Traitor Arnold was at Detroit & had viewed the Militia in the Neighbourhood of it twice. This had occasioned much Speculation in those parts—and with many other circumstances—though trifling in themselves led strongly to a conjecture that the British had some design on the Spanish settlements on the Mississipi and of course to surround these United States.

After the Revolution, Benedict Arnold lived in England with his family until 1785. In that year, finding his inflated claims for compensation for his services to the British government during the Revolution were not successful, he sailed for the Loyalist settlement of St. John, New Brunswick, where he established a mercantile and shipping business.

Wednesday 7th. Exercised between 5 & 7 this Morning on Horse-back.

Saturday 10th. Having formed a Party, consisting of the Vice-President, his lady, Son & Miss Smith; the Secretaries of State, Treasury & War, and the ladies of the two latter; with all the Gentlemen of my family, Mrs. Lear & the two Children we visited the old position of Fort Washington and afterwards dined on a dinner provided by Mr. Mariner at the House lately Colo. Roger Morris but confiscated and in the occupation of a common Farmer.

Gentlemen of my Family: GW's secretaries, Tobias Lear, William Jackson, Bartholomew Dandridge, Jr., David Humphreys, and Robert Lewis. Dandridge (d. 1802) was the son of Mrs. Washington's brother Bartholomew Dandridge.

Mrs. Lear, Tobias Lear's wife, was Mary (Polly) Long Lear of Portsmouth, N.H. The Lears were married in April 1790 in Portsmouth, and upon their return to New York they were invited to make their home with the Washingtons. Mrs. Washington in particular apparently became very fond of young Mrs. Lear, who made herself useful to the presidential household in a number of ways. The living arrangements continued after the household moved to Philadelphia. Polly Lear died, at the age of 23, in Philadelphia, 28 July 1793. The two children were Mrs. Washington's grandchildren George Washington Parke Custis and Eleanor Parke Custis.

Fort Washington, in the vicinity of present W. 183d Street in Manhattan, had fallen to the British in Nov. 1776. Later Fort Knyphausen had been constructed by the British on the site of the American works. The Morris Mansion (Jumel Mansion), constructed by Lt. Col. Roger Morris in 1765, was confiscated at the end of the Revolution as Loyalist property and was advertised in Mar. 1790 for sale at public auction. The house was to be sold on 3 May 1790.

Monday 12th. Exercised on Horse back between 5 & 6 in the Morning. Sat for Mr. Trumbull from 9 until half after ten.

And about Noon had two Bills presented to me by the joint Committee of Congress—The one "An Act for Establishing the Temporary & permanent Seat of the Government of the United States"—The other "An Act further to provide for the payment of the Invalid Pensioners of the United States."

Bills: The Residence Bill, establishing a new federal district on the banks of the Potomac River for the permanent capital of the United States, had been under debate in Congress since 31 May, but the struggle over the location for the capital long preceded the bill's advent in Congress. GW's close personal involvement in the matter is fully treated in the correspondence volumes of the *Papers.* Under the terms of the Residence Act the president was authorized to appoint three commissioners who would "under the direction of the President" oversee the surveying and construction of the new city, a provision which guaranteed GW's continued close involvement with the Federal City for the rest of his administration. The act also provided that the capital would move from New York to Philadelphia by Dec. 1790 and remain there until Dec. 1800 when the new Federal City presumably would be finished. (1 *Stat.* 130 [16 July 1790]).

Wednesday 14th. Exercised on horseback from 5 until near 7 Oclock.

Had some further conversation to day with the Chief Justice and Secretary of the Treasury with respect to the business on which Majr. Beckwith was come on. The result—To treat his communications very civilly—to intimate, delicately, that they carried no marks, official or authentic; nor, in speaking of Alliance, did they convey any definite meaning by which the precise objects of the British Cabinet could be discovered. In a word, that the Secretary of the Treasury was to extract as much as he could from Major Beckwith & to report it to me, without committing, by any assurances whatever, the Government of the U States, leaving it entirely free to pursue, unreproached, such a line of conduct in the dispute as her interest (& honour) shall dictate.

Southern Tour
March–July 1791

From the first days of his presidency, GW was determined "to visit every part of the United States" during his term of office if "health and other circumstances would admit of it" (GW to Edward Rutledge, 16 Jan. 1791). A month after he returned from his New England tour, Gov. Charles Pinckney of South Carolina wrote him suggesting a tour of the southern states (14 Dec. 1789), and GW replied (11 Jan. 1790) that nothing would give him more pleasure although his time was not his own.

By the following summer rumors were circulating in the South that GW would visit the region in the autumn, but when William Blount of North Carolina called on GW at Mount Vernon in September, he learned that the southern tour would be delayed until spring. When Congress adjourned 3 Mar. 1791, GW was free to leave the capital, but bad roads delayed his departure from Philadelphia for a time. However, the need to traverse the route before "the warm and sickly months" were upon the South prompted him to leave New York on 21 Mar.

Before setting off, GW prepared a careful itinerary describing the dates, places, and mileages for his proposed "line of march." His route south was to be an eastern one through Richmond and Petersburg, Va., New Bern and Wilmington, N.C., and Georgetown and Charleston, S.C., to Savannah, and his return by "an upper road" from Augusta, Ga., through Columbia and Camden, S.C., Charlotte and Salem, N.C., and Fredericksburg, Va. In all he was to be gone more than three months and would travel an estimated 1,816 miles.

As on the New England tour, GW planned to lodge only at public houses and to refuse all offers to stay in private homes. "I am persuaded you will readily see the necessity of this resolution both as it respects myself and others," GW wrote his relative William Washington of South Carolina, 8 Jan. 1791. "It leaves me unembarrassed by engagements, and by a uniform adherence to it I shall avoid giving umbrage to any by declining all invitations of residence." Nevertheless, lack of suitable ordinaries along several parts of his route was to oblige him to make exceptions to this rule on more than one occasion.

1791

March

Monday 21st. Left Philadelphia about 11 O'clock to make a tour through the Southern States. In this tour I was accompanied by Majr. Jackson. My equipage & attendance consisted of a Chariet & four horses drove in hand—a light baggage Waggon & two horses—four Saddle horses besides a led one for myself—and five Servants including to wit my Valet de Chambre, two footmen, Coach man & Postilion.

Thursday 24d. Left Chester town about 6 Oclock. Before nine I arrivd at Rock-Hall where we breakfasted and immediately; after which we began to embark—The doing of which employed us (for want of contrivance) until near 3 Oclock and then one of my Servants (Paris) & two horses were left, notwithstanding two Boats in aid of The two Ferry Boats were procured. Unluckily, embarking on board of a borrowed Boat because She was the largest, I was in imminent danger, from the unskilfulness of the hands, and the dulness of her sailing, added to the darkness and storminess of the night. For two hours after we hoisted Sail the Wind was light and a head. The next hour was a stark calm after which the wind sprung up at So. Et. and encreased until it blew a gale—about which time, and after 8 Oclock P.M. we made the mouth of Severn River (leading up to Annapolis) but the ignorance of the People on board, with respect to the navigation of it run us aground first on Greenbury point from whence with much exertion and difficulty we got off; & then, having no knowledge of the Channel and the night being immensely dark with heavy and variable squals of wind—constant lightning & tremendous thunder—we soon grounded again on what is called Hornes point where, finding all efforts in vain, & not knowing where we were we remained, not knowing what might happen, 'till morning.

Friday 25th. Having lain all night in my Great Coat & Boots, in a birth not long enough for me by the head, & much cramped; we found ourselves in the morning with in about one mile of Annapolis & still fast aground. Whilst we were preparing our small Boat in order to land in it, a sailing Boat came of to our assistance in wch. with the Baggage I had on board I landed, & requested Mr. Man at whose Inn I intended lodging, to send off a Boat to take off two of my Horses & Chariot which I had left on board and with it my Coachman to see that it was properly done—but by mistake the latter not having notice of this order & attempting to get on board afterwards in a small Sailing Boat was overset and narrowly escaped drowning.

Was informed upon my arrival (when 15 Guns were fired) that all my other horses arrived safe, that embarked at the same time I did, about 8 Oclock last night.

Was waited upon by the Governor [John Eager Howard] (who came off in a Boat as soon as he heard I was on my passage from Rock hall to meet us, but turned back when it grew dark and squally) as soon as I arrived at Mans tavern, & was engaged by him to dine with the Citizens of Annapolis this day at Manns tavern and at his House tomorrow— the first I accordingly did.

GW stayed at George Mann's tavern, sometimes called the City Hotel.

Monday 28th. A few miles out of Town I was met by the principal Citizen[s] of the place, & escorted in by them; and dined at Suters tavern (where I also lodged) at a public dinner given by the Mayor & Corporation—previous to which I examined the Surveys of Mr. Ellicot who had been sent on to lay out the district of ten miles square for the federal seat; and also the works of Majr. L'Enfant who had been engaged to examine, & make a draught of the grds. in the vicinity of George town and Carrollsburg on the Eastern branch making arrangements for examining the ground myself tomorrow with the Commissioners.

The Residence law, which authorized the establishing of a new capital, also provided for the president to appoint three commissioners to supervise the land surveying, the layout of the Federal City (later Washington, D.C.) in the district, and the construction of public buildings (see entry for 12 July 1790). The three commissioners, appointed by GW in 1791, were Thomas Johnson of Fredericktown, Md., Dr. David Stuart, of Hope Park in Fairfax County, and Daniel Carroll (1730–1796).

Andrew Ellicott (1754–1820) was appointed by GW to survey the district lines, which he began in the late winter of 1791. Pierre Charles L'Enfant (1754–1825), born and trained in engineering and artistic design in France, volunteered as an officer of engineers in the Revolution. In 1791 GW appointed L'Enfant to design a Federal City to be built within the district. Carrollsburg, still only a paper town in 1791, was laid out c.1770 on the neck between James Creek and the Anacostia River for Charles Carroll, father of Daniel Carroll of Duddington.

Tuesday 29th. In a thick mist, and under strong appearances of a settled rain (which however did not happen) I set out about 7 Oclock for the purpose abovementioned—but from the unfavorableness of the day, I derived no great satisfaction from the review.

Finding the interests of the Landholders about George town and those about Carrollsburgh much at varience and that their fears & jealousies of each were counteracting the public purposes & might prove injurious to its best interests whilst if properly managed they might be made to subserve it—I requested them to meet me at Six oclock this afternoon at my lodgings, which they accordingly did.

To this meeting I represented, that the contention in which they seemed engaged, did not in my opinion, comport either with the public interest or that of their own; that while each party was aiming to obtain the public buildings, they might, by placing the matter on a contracted scale, defeat the measure altogether; not only by procrastination but for want of the means necessary to effect the work; That neither the offer from George town, or Carrollsburgh, seperately, was adequate to the end of insuring the object—That both together did not comprehend more ground nor would afford greater means than was required for the federal City; and that, instead of contending which of the two should have it they had better, by combining there offers make a common cause of it and thereby secure it to the district. Other arguments were used to shew the danger which might result from delay and the good effects that might proceed from a Union.

> Landowners in Georgetown and Carrollsburg were at odds over where the public buildings in the new capital were to be located. At today's meeting GW made the first official public pronouncement on the size of the new capital: it would encompass the sites promoted by both the Georgetown and Carrollsburg interests, making the city a project far more ambitious than either group of landholders originally conceived.

Wednesday 30th. The parties to whom I addressed myself yesterday evening, having taken the matter into consideration saw the propriety of my observations; and that whilst they were contending for the shadow they might loose the substance; and therefore mutually agreed, and entered into articles to surrender for public purposes, one half of the land they severally possessed with in bounds which were designated as necessary for the City to stand with some other stipulations which were inserted in the instrument which they respectively subscribed.

This business being thus happily finished & some directions given to the Commissioners, the Surveyor and Engineer with respect to the mode of laying out the district—Surveying the grounds for the City & forming them into lots—I left Georgetown—dined in Alexandria & reached Mount Vernon in the evening.

> GW's directions for laying out the district were based upon his proclamation dated Georgetown, 30 Mar. 1791, establishing a district ten miles square beginning at Jones Point at the mouth of Hunting Creek on the south side of Alexandria. The survey was done by "the Surveyor" Andrew Ellicott, with the assistance of Benjamin Banneker. The "Engineer" was Pierre L'Enfant. For further information on GW's role in the formation of the new Federal City, see *Papers, Presidential Series*, 7:161–68.

Thursday 31st. From this time, until the 7th. of April, I remained at Mount Vernon—visiting my Plantations every day.

From hence I also wrote letters to the Secretaries of State—Treasury and War in answer to those received from [them] on interesting subjects—desiring in case of important occurrances they would hold a consultation and if they were of such a nature as to make my return necessary to give me notice & I would return immediately. My rout was given to them & the time I should be at the particular places therein mentioned.

April

Thursday 7th. April. Recommenced my journey with Horses apparently well refreshed and in good spirits.

In attempting to cross the ferry at Colchester with the four Horses hitched to the Chariot by the neglect of the person who stood before them, one of the leaders got overboard when the boat was in swimming water and 50 yards from the Shore—with much difficulty he escaped drowning before he could be disengaged. His struggling frightned the others in such a manner that one after another and in quick succession they all got over board harnessed & fastened as they were and with the utmost difficulty they were saved & the Carriage escaped been dragged after them as the whole of it happened in swimming water & at a distance from the shore. Providentially—indeed miraculously—by the exertions of people who went off in Boats & jumped into the River as soon as the Batteau was forced into wading water—no damage was sustained by the horses, Carriage or harness.

Proceeded to Dumfries where I dined—after which I visited & drank Tea with my Niece Mrs. Thos. Lee.

> GW's niece at Dumfries was Mildred Washington Lee, daughter of John Augustine Washington. Her husband Thomas Lee (1758–1805), a son of Richard Henry Lee, was practicing law in the town at this time.

Friday 8th. Set out about 6 oclock—breakfasted at Stafford Court House and dined and lodged at my Sister Lewis's in Fredericksburgh.

Tuesday 12th. In company with the Governor, The Directors of the James River Navigation Company—the Manager & many other Gentlemen. I viewed the Canal, Sluces, Locks & other Works between the City of Richmond & Westham. The Canal is of Sufficient depth every where but in places not brought to its proper width; it seems to be perfectly secure against Ice, Freshes & drift Wood. The locks at the head of these works are simple—altogether of hewn stone, except the gates & Cills

Washington's brother John Augustine Washington. (Mount Vernon Ladies'
Association of the Union)

and very easy & convenient to work. There are two of them, each calculated to raise & lower 6 feet. They cost, according to the Manager's,
Mr. Harris acct. about £3,000 but I could see nothing in them to require such a sum to erect them. The sluces in the River, between these
locks and the mouth of the Canal are well graduated and easy of assent.
To complete the Canal from the point to which it is now opened, and
the Locks at the foot of them Mr. Harris thinks will require 3 years.

Received an Address from the Mayor [George Nicholson], Aldermen & Common Council of the City of Richmond at Three oclock, & dined with the Governor at four Oclock.

In the course of my enquiries—chiefly from Colo. Carrington—I cannot discover that any discontents prevail among the people at large, at the proceedings of Congress.

GW had arrived in Richmond on 11 April to attend a meeting of the James River Company of which he was president 1785–95. GW's involvement was largely in name only since he took little part in the company's affairs.

Edward Carrington, having been appointed United States marshal for Virginia 26 Sept. 1789 and supervisor of the federal revenue for the state 4 Mar. 1791, was now undertaking to perform the duties of both offices.

GW left Richmond on 14 April, traveled to Petersburg, then to Halifax and Tarboro, N.C., reaching Greenville by the 19th where he spent the night at Shadrach Allen's tavern.

Wednesday 20th. Left Allans before breakfast, & under a misapprehension went to a Colo. [John] Allans, supposing it to be a public house; where we were very kindly & well entertained without knowing it was at his expence until it was too late to rectify the mistake. After breakfasting, & feeding our horses here, we proceeded on & crossing the River Nuse 11 miles further, arrived in Newbern to dinner.

At this ferry which is 10 miles from Newbern, we were met by a small party of Horse; the district Judge (Mr. [John] Sitgreave[s]) and many of the principal Inhabitts. of Newbern, who conducted us into town to exceeding good lodgings. It ought to have been mentioned that another small party of horse under one Simpson, met us at Greensville, and in spite of every endeavor which could comport with decent civility, to excuse myself from it, they would attend me to Newburn. Colo. Allan did the same.

Thursday 21st. Dined with the Citizens at a public dinner given by them; & went to a dancing assembly in the evening—both of which was at what they call the Pallace—formerly the government House & a good brick building but now hastening to ruins. The company at both was numerous—at the latter there were abt. 70 ladies.

GW sat down to dinner with the citizens at 4:00 P.M.; he remained at the ball until 11:00 P.M. Earlier in the day he walked around New Bern and during the afternoon received an address from a committee of local Freemasons representing St. John's Lodge No. 2. A general address from the town's inhabitants also was given to him apparently at West's ferry the previous day. (*Dunlap's American Daily Adv.*, 13 May 1791).

The palace, built in 1767–70 at the urging of Gov. William Tryon (1729–1788), served as residence for North Carolina's governors until 1780 and as an occasional meeting place for the General Assembly until 1794.

GW left New Bern on 21 April.

Sunday 24th. Breakfasted at an indifferent House about 13 miles from Sages and three Miles further met a party of Light Horse from Wilmington; and after them a Commee. & other Gentlemen of the Town; who came out to escort me into it, and at which I arrived under a federal salute at very good lodgings prepared for me, about two O'clock. At these I dined with the Commee. whose company I asked.

The New Hanover County tavern at which GW breakfasted was probably Jennett's. The Wilmington Troop of Horse, commanded by Capt. Henry Toomer, met GW about 12 miles from town, and the gentlemen of the town, all on horseback, greeted him about six miles farther down the road. Stepping out of his chariot, GW mounted one of his horses and rode the remaining distance to Wilmington, preceded by four dragoons with a trumpet and followed by the rest of his escort. His servants and baggage brought up the rear of the procession.

The federal salute which GW received on reaching the town was a "triple" one—three rounds of fifteen shots each—fired by a battery of four guns under the command of Capt. John Huske. GW then, according to a newspaper account, was escorted to his lodgings "through an astonishing concorse of people of the town and country, whom, as well as the ladies that filled the windows and balconies of the houses, he saluted with his usual affability and condencension. Upon his alighting, the acclamations were loud and universal. The Ships in the harbour, all ornamented with their colours, added much to the beauty of the scene" (*Columbian Centinel,* 11 June 1791; Henderson, *Washington's Southern Tour,* 104–7, 115).

Monday 25th. Dined with the Citizens of the place at a public dinner given by them. Went to a Ball in the evening, at which there were 62 ladies—illuminations, Bonfires &ca.

Tuesday 26th. Having sent my Carriage across the day before, I left Wilmington about 6 oclock accompanied by most of the Gentlemen of the Town, and breakfasting at Mr. Ben. Smiths lodged at one Russ' 25 Miles from Wilmington—an indifferent House.

GW crossed the Cape Fear River in a "Revenue-barge, manned by six American Captains of ships, in which the standard of the United States was displayed." As previously arranged, the gentlemen of the town attended him in "boats from the shipping in the harbour, under their national colours," while in the background could be heard "the firing of cannon, accompanied by the acclamations of the people, from the wharves and shipping" (*Columbian Centinel,* 11 June 1791).

The presidential party reached Georgetown, S.C., on 30 April. GW, who estimated the population of the town at not more than "5 or 600," found it "to be in the shade of Charleston," although the president was "introduced to upwards of 50 ladies who had assembled (at a Tea party) on the occasion."

May

Sunday—May first. Left Georgetown about 6 Oclock, and crossing the Santee Creek [Sampit River] at the Town, and the Santee River 12 miles from it, at Lynchs Island, we breakfasted and dined at Mrs. [Harriott Pinckney] Horry's about 15 Miles from George town & lodged at the Plantation of Mr. Manigold [Joseph Manigault] about 19 miles farther.

Monday 2d. Breakfasted at the Country Seat of Govr. [Charles] Pinckney about 18 miles from our lodging place, & then came to the ferry at Haddrels point, 6 miles further, where I was met by the Recorder of the City [of Charleston], Genl. [Charles Cotesworth] Pinckney & Edward Rutledge Esqr. in a 12 oared barge rowed by 12 American Captains of Ships, most elegantly dressed. There were a great number of other Boats with Gentlemen and ladies in them; and two Boats with Music; all of whom attended me across and on the passage were met by a number of others. As we approached the town a salute with Artillery commenced, and at the wharf I was met by the Governor, the Lt. Governor [Isaac Holmes], the Intendt. of the City [Arnoldus Vanderholst]; The two Senators of the State [Pierce Butler and Ralph Izard], Wardens of the City—Cincinnati &ca. &ca. and conducted to the Exchange where they passed by in procession. From thence I was conducted in like manner to my lodgings—after which I dined at the Governers (in what I called a private way) with 15 or 18 Gentlemen.

Tuesday 3d. Breakfasted with Mrs. [Elizabeth Grimké] Rutledge (the Lady of the Chief justice of the State [John Rutledge] who was on the Circuits) and dined with the Citizens at a public dinr. given by them at the Exchange.

Was visited about 2 oclock, by a great number of the most respectable ladies of Charleston—the first honor of the kind I had ever experienced and it was as flattering as it was singular.

Wednesday 4th. Dined with the Members of the Cincinnati, and in the evening went to a very elegant dancing Assembly at the Exchange—At which were 256 elegantly dressed & handsome ladies.

In the forenoon (indeed before breakfast to day) I visited and examined the lines of Attack & defence of the City and was satisfied that the defence was noble & honorable altho the measure was undertaken upon wrong principles and impolitic.

Thursday 5th. Dined with a very large Company at the Governors, & in the evening went to a Concert at the Exchange at wch. there were at least 400 lad[ie]s—the Number & appearances of wch. exceeded any thing of the kind I had ever seen.

Saturday 7th. Before break I visited the Orphan House at which there were one hund. & Seven boys & girls. This appears to be a charitable institution and under good management. I also viewed the City from the balcony of [   ] Church from whence the whole is seen in one view and to advantage. The Gardens & green trees which are interspersed adding much to the beauty of the prospect.

Monday 9th. At Six oclock I recommenced my journey for Savanna; attended by a Corps of the Cincinnati, and most of the principal Gentlemen of the City as far as the bridge over Ashly river, where we breakfasted and proceeded to Colo. W[illiam] Washington's at Sandyhill with a select party of particular friends—distant from Charleston 28 Miles.

Thursday 12th. In my way down the River I called upon Mrs. Green[e] the Widow of the decreased [deceased] Genl. [Nathanael] Green[e] (at a place called Mulberry grove) & asked her how she did. At this place (12 Miles from Purisburgh) my horses and Carriages were landed, and had 12 Miles farther by Land to Savanna. The wind & tide being both agt. us, it was 6 oclock before we reached the City where we were recd. under every demonstration that could be given of joy & respect. We were Seven hours making the passage which is often performed in 4, tho the computed distance is 25 Miles. Illumns. at night.
    I was conducted by the Mayor & Wardens to very good lodgings which had been provided for the occasion, and partook of a public dinner given by the Citizens at the Coffee room.

> Purrysburg, S.C., a village first settled by Swiss colonists in 1732, is on the Savannah River about 25 miles upstream from the city of Savannah.

Friday 13th. Dined with the Members of the Cincinnati at a public dinner given at the same place and in the evening went to a dancing Assembly at which there was about 100 well dressed & handsome Ladies.

Saturday 14th. A little after 6 Oclock, in Company with Genl. [Lachlan] McIntosh Genl. [Anthony] Wayne the Mayor and many others (principal Gentlemen of the City) I visited the City, and the attack & defence of it in the year 1779, under the combined forces of France and the United States, commanded by the Count de Estaing & Genl. [Benjamin] Lincoln. To form an opinion of the attack at this distance of time, and the change which has taken place in the appearance of the ground by the cutting away of the woods, &ca., is hardly to be done with justice to the subject; especially as there is remaining scarcely any of the defences.

Dined to day with a number of the Citizens (not less than 200) in an elegant Bower erected for the occasion on the Bank of the River below the Town. In the evening there was a tolerable good display of fireworks.

Sunday 15th. After morning Service, and receiving a number of visits from the most respectable ladies of the place (as was the case yesterday) I set out for Savanna [Augusta], Escorted beyd. the limits of the City by most of the Gentlemen in it and dining at Mulberry grove—the Seat of Mrs. Green—lodged at one Spencers—distant 15 Miles.

> Writing to Tobias Lear in the midst of his Savannah visit, GW observed that at Charleston "the continual hurry into which I was thrown by entertainments—visits—and cermonies of one kind of another, scarcely allowed me a moment I could call my own—nor is the case much otherwise here" (Maine Historical Society). On 17 May GW lodged at Waynesboro and reached Augusta on 18 May.

Thursday 19th. Received & answered an Address from the Citizens of Augusta; dined with a large Company of them at their Court Ho.; and went to an Assembly in the evening at the Accadamy; at which there were between 60 & 70 well dressed ladies.

Friday 20th. Viewed the ruins, or rather small remns. of the Works which had been erected by the British during the War and taken by the Americans—also the falls, which are about 2 Miles above the Town; and the Town itself.

Dined at a private dinner with Govr. [Edward] Telfair to day; and gave him dispatches for the Spanish Govr. of East Florida, respecting the Countenance given by that Governt. to the fugitive Slaves of the Union—wch. dispatches were to be forwarded to Mr. [James] Seagrove, Collector of St. Mary's, who was requested to be the bearer of them, and instructed to make arrangements for the prevention of these evils and, if possible, for the restoration of the property—especially of those Slaves wch. had gone off since the orders of the Spanish Court to discountenance this practice of recg. them.

> GW left Augusta on 21 May, accompanied by a number of dignitaries. He was met on the road by a delegation from Columbia and reached that town on 22 May.

Monday 23d. Dined at a public dinner in the State house with a number of Gentlemen & Ladies of the Town of Columbia, & Country round about to the amt. of more than 150, of which 50 or 60 were of the latter.

Wednesday 25th. Set out at 4 'Oclock for Cambden (the foundered horse being led slowly on). Breakfasted at an indifferent house 22 miles from the town (the first we came to) and reached Cambden about two oclock, 14 miles further where an address was recd. & answered. Dined late with a number of Gentlemen & Ladies at a public dinner.

> An address from the citizens of Columbia, Granby, and vicinity, bearing today's date, was presented to GW before he left town by Alexander Gillon (1741–1794), a wealthy merchant and early Revolutionary leader who had been embroiled in much controversy as a commodore in the South Carolina navy during the war.
>
> The welcoming address from the citizens of Camden and vicinity apparently was presented to GW by the town's intendant and patriarch, Col. Joseph Kershaw (c.1723–1791), a militia veteran of the Revolution.
>
> GW, according to local tradition, lodged in Camden at the house of Adam Fowler Brisbane (1754–1797), a Lancaster County justice, and the public dinner was probably at the house of Col. John Chesnut (1743–1813), a veteran of the South Carolina line and prominent indigo planter, who discussed agriculture at some length with GW during his stay in town. A month later GW sent Chesnut a drill plow from Mount Vernon to try in sowing indigo seed. At the dinner GW "was introduced to the ladies individually. The ladies rose after the 2d or 3d toast, and the President sat till near twelve o'clock" (*Md. Journal*, 17 June 1791). In all there were 17 toasts, including 2 given after GW retired for the night.

Thursday 26th. After viewing the british works about Cambden I set out for Charlotte. On my way—two miles from Town—I examined the ground on wch. Genl. Green & Lord Rawden had their Action. The ground had but just been taken by the former—was well chosen—but he not well established in it before he was attacked; which by capturing a Videt was, in some measure by surprize. Six miles further on I came to the ground where Genl. Gates & Lord Cornwallis had their Engagement wch. terminated so unfavourably for the former. As this was a night Meeting of both Armies on their March, & altogether unexpected each formed on the ground they met without any advantage in it on either side it being level & open. Had Genl. Gates been ½ a mile further advanced, an impenitrable Swamp would have prevented the attack which was made on him by the British Army, and afforded him time to have formed his own plans; but having no information of Lord Cornwallis's designs, and perhaps not being apprised of this advantage it was not siezed by him.

> GW is describing the battle at Hobkirk's Hill, 25 April 1781, and Camden, 16 Aug. 1780.

Sunday 29th. Left Charlotte about 7 Oclock, dined at a Colo. Smiths 15 Miles off, and lodged at a Majr. Fifers 7 Miles farther.

GW had arrived at Charlotte on 28 May and found it "a very trifling place." Martin Phifer, Jr. (1756–1837), of Mecklenburg County lived at Red Hill plantation on Irish Buffalo Creek, now in Cabarrus County, a short distance west of present-day Concord.

Monday 30th. At 4 Oclock I was out from Major Fifers; and in about 10 Miles at the line which divides Mecklenburgh from Rowan Counties, I met a party of horse belonging to the latter, who came from Salisbury to escort me on.

I was also met 5 Miles from Salisbury by the Mayor of the Corporation, Judge McKoy [Spruce McCoy], & many others; Mr. [John] Steel[e], Representative for the district, was so polite as to come all the way to Charlotte to meet me. We arrived at Salisbury about 8 Oclock, to breakfast, 20 miles from Captn. Fifers.

This day I foundered another of my horses.

Dined at a public dinner givn. by the Citizens of Salisbury; & in the afternoon drank Tea at the same place with about 20 ladies, who had been assembled for the occasion.

Tuesday 31st. Left Salisbury about 4 Oclock; at 5 Miles crossed the Yadkin, the principal stream of the Pedee, and breakfasted on the No. Bank (while my Carriages & horses were crossing) at a Mr. Youngs; fed my horses 10 miles farther, at one Reeds; and about 3 Oclock (after another halt) arrived at Salem; one of the Moraviann towns 20 miles farther—In all 35 from Salisbury.

Salem is a small but neat Village; & like all the rest of the Moravian settlements, is governed by an excellent police—having within itself all kinds of artizans. The number of Souls does not exceed 200.

June

Wednesday June 1st. Having received information that Governor Martin was on his way to meet me; and would be at Salem this evening, I resolved to await his arrival at this place instead of halting a day at Guilford as I had intended.

Spent the forenoon in visiting the Shops of the different Trades Men—The houses of accomodation for the single men & Sisters of the Fraternity & their place of worship. Invited Six of their principal people to dine with me—and in the evening went to hear them Sing, & perform on a variety of instruments Church music.

In the Afternoon Governor Martin as was expected (with his Secretary) arrived.

Alexander Martin (1740–1807), governor of North Carolina 1782–85 and 1789–92, was a bachelor who lived at Danbury plantation on the Dan River in Rockingham County about 40 miles northeast of Salem.

Governor Martin accompanied GW to the "singstunde [song service of the Moravian congregation] in the evening, the singing being interspersed with instrumental selections, and they expressed their pleasure in it. In the evening the wind instruments were heard again, playing sweetly near the tavern." Music was also furnished for the dinner with the six Brethren (Salem Diary, 1791, Fries, *Moravian Records,* 5:2325).

Many people from the neighborhood and the other Moravian congregations came to Salem to see GW during his stay in town, and according to the Salem diary, "the President gladly gave them opportunity to gratify their wish" (ibid.).

Thursday 2d. In company with the Govr. I set out by 4 Oclock for Guilford.

On my way I examined the ground on which the Action between Generals Green and Lord Cornwallis commenced and after dinner rode over that where their lines were formed and the scene closed in the retreat of the American forces—The first line of which was advantageously drawn up, and had the Troops done their duty properly, the British must have been sorely galded in their advance, if not defeated.

Ground: GW is referring to the battle at Guilford Court House on 15 Mar. 1781. When the British advanced on Nathanael Greene's forces, which had taken a stand on favorable terrain on the road south of the courthouse, the North Carolina militia in the American front line fired one volley and fled. Although the remainder of his troops fought well, Greene was forced to order a withdrawal later in the day. Two days after the battle, Cornwallis, having won the field but at the cost of 532 dead and wounded out of a force of about 1,900 men, was obliged to begin retreating toward the coast.

Friday 3d. In conversing with the Governor on the State of Politics in No. Carolina I learnt with pleasure that opposition to the Genl. Government, & the discontents of the people were subsiding fast and that he should, so soon as he received the Laws which he had written to the Secretary of State for, issue his proclamation requiring all Officers & members of the Governmt. to take the Oaths prescribed by Law. He seems to condemn the Speculators in Lands and the purchases from the State of Georgia, & thinks as every sensible & disinterested man must that schemes of that sort must involve the Country in trouble—perhaps in blood.

On 4 June GW crossed the North Carolina–Virginia border on his return journey, having "finished my tour thro' the three Southernmost States." In his entry for this date he described in detail the terrain through which he had traveled and continued his entry with observations on the life of the people.

Saturday 4th. Excepting the Towns, (and some Gentlemens Seats along the road from Charleston to Savanna) there is not, within view of the whole road I travelled from Petersburgh to this place, a single house which has anythg. of an elegant appearance. They are altogether of Wood & chiefly of logs—some indd. have brick chimneys but generally the chimnies are of Split sticks filled with dirt between them.

The accomadations on the whole Road (except in the Towns, and even there, as I was informed for I had no opportunity of Judging, lodgings having been provided for me in them at my own expence) we found extremely indifferent—the houses being small and badly provided either for man or horse; though extra exertions when it was known I was coming, wch. was generally the case, were made to receive me. It is not easy to say on which road—the one I went or the one I came—the entertainment is most indifferent—but with truth it may be added, that both are bad, and to be accounted for from the kind of travellers which use them; which with a few exceptions only on the uppr. Rd. are no other than Waggoners & families removing; who, generally, take their provisions along with them. The people however appear to have abundant means to live well the grounds where they are settled yielding grain in abundance and the natural herbage a multitude of meat with little or no labr. to provide food for the support of their Stock—especially in Georgia where it is said the Cattle live through the winter without any support from the owners of them.

The manners of the people, are far as my observations, and means of information extended, were orderly and Civil. And they appeared to be happy, contented and satisfied with the genl. governmt. under which they were placed. Where the case was otherwise, it was not difficult to trace the cause to some demago[g]ue, or speculating character. In Georgia the dissatisfied part of them at the late treaty with the C[ree]k Indians were evidently Land Jobbers, who, Maugre every principle of Justice to the Indians & policy to their Country would, for their own immediate emolument, strip the Indns. of all their territory if they could obtain the least countenance to the measure. But it is to be hoped the good sense of the State will set its face against such diabolical attempts: And it is also to be wished and by many it was said it might be excepted—that the Sales by that State to what are called the Yazoo Companies would fall through.

The discontents which it was supposed the last Revenue Act (commonly known by the Excise Law) would create subside as fast as the law is explained and little was said of the Banking Act.

Friday 10th. Left Mrs. Jordans early, & breakfasting at one Johnstons 7 Miles off reached Fredericksburgh after another (short) halt about 3 Oclock & dined and lodged at my Sister Lewis's.

On 9 May GW had lodged at Jerdone Castle with Sarah Macon Jerdone of Louisa County, Va., whose husband Francis Jerdone had been a prominent merchant.

GW reported to Tobias Lear that he arrived at Fredericksburg "in good health, but with horses much worn down" (GW to Lear, 12 June 1791).

Saturday 11th. After a dinner with several Gentlemen whom my Sister had envited to dine with me I crossed the Rappahannock & proceeded to Stafford Ct. House where I lodged.

Sunday 12th. About Sun rise we were off—breakfasted at Dumfries and arrived at Mt. Vn. to D[inner].

No Washington diaries have been found for the period from GW's return from his southern tour and the fall of 1794 when he accompanied federal forces to put down the Whiskey Insurrection in western Pennsylvania.

The Whiskey Insurrection
1794

GW's brief journal for 30 Sept.—20 Oct. 1794 records his journey from Philadelphia to western Pennsylvania with the militia raised to suppress the insurrection that erupted in the fall of 1794 in the western Pennsylvania counties of Westmoreland, Fayette, Washington, and Allegheny. The Excise Act, passed by Congress 3 Mar. 1791, had imposed substantial duties on domestically distilled spirits and provided an elaborate system for efficient collection. Popular enough with affluent easterners, the laws evoked only sullen compliance in western counties of the southern and middle states where small distilleries abounded and there were large numbers of individually operated stills. Already disenchanted with the course of events under the new government—the drain of specie to the east, an Indian policy considered ineffectual by frontier areas, the operation of the militia laws, failure to open the Mississippi to western trade—westerners made the excise law the focus for dissatisfaction. Opposition continued to grow, with much of the agitation centered in the four western counties of Pennsylvania, constituting the state's federal Survey No. 4. Beginning peacefully enough with petitions and memorials requesting repeal of the excise, in July 1794 the situation suddenly erupted into violence. The immediate cause of the outbreak was the attempt by federal revenue officers to serve processes issued by the United States District Court at Philadelphia against distillers who had not registered the previous year. United States Marshal David Lenox was sent to western Pennsylvania to serve the processes. He presented the documents without incident in Fayette, Cumberland, and Bedford counties, but in Westmoreland on 15 July 1794 while he was accompanied on his rounds by Col. John Neville, inspector of the revenue for Survey No. 4, he met armed opposition. Quickly serving as many of his processes as possible, he retreated to Pittsburgh. Somewhat later in the day, Neville's house on Bower Hill was attacked by a group of armed men, and Neville appealed for state militia to put down the rioters. On 17 July the house was again attacked and this time burned.

Word of the violence quickly reached Philadelphia, and on 2 Aug. GW and members of the cabinet met with Gov. Thomas Mifflin and state officials to consider whether the situation warranted calling out the Pennsylvania militia, a step the state officials plainly opposed. On 7 Aug. GW issued a proclamation recapitulating the events in Pennsylvania's western counties and, citing as his authority the 2 May 1792 Militia Act, stated his determination "under the circumstances of the case, to take measures for calling forth the Militia . . . and I have accordingly determined to do so, feeling the deepest regret for the occasion, but withal, the most solemn conviction, that the essential interests of the Union demand it." All persons "being insurgents" were commanded "on or before the first day of September next, to disperse and retire peaceably to their respective abodes." Gov. Thomas Mifflin of Pennsylvania issued a similar proclamation on the same day, promising full support of the state government, and Secretary of War Henry Knox sent a circular letter, also dated 7 Aug., to the governors of Pennsylvania, New Jersey, and Virginia, requesting those states to supply a total of 12,950 militia. In spite of conciliatory efforts by the federal government, incidents of violence increased, and it appeared that resistance was spreading to western Virginia and Maryland and even eastward in Pennsylvania. On 25 Sept. GW issued a proclamation stating that militia had been called out from New Jersey, Pennsylvania, Virginia, and Maryland, "and I do, moreover, exhort all individuals, officers, and bodies of men, to contemplate with abhorrence the measures leading directly or indirectly to those crimes, which produce this resort to military coercion. . . . And lastly, I again warn all persons, whomsoever and wheresoever, not to abet, aid, or comfort the Insurgents aforesaid, as they will answer the contrary at their peril."

GW decided to accompany the troops at least as far as Carlisle and to decide later whether to continue farther on the march.

1794

September

Tuesday 30th. Having determined from the Report of the Commissioners, who were appointed to meet the Insurgents in the Western Counties in the State of Pennsylvania, and from other circumstances— to repair to the places appointed for the Rendezvous, of the Militia of New Jersey Pennsylvania Maryland & Virginia; I left the City of Philadelphia about half past ten oclock this forenoon accompanied by Colo.

Hamilton (Secretary of the Treasury) & my private Secretary. Dined at Norris Town and lodged at a place called the Trap—the first 17, and the latter 25 Miles from Philadelphia.

At Norris Town we passed a detachment of Militia who were preparing to march for the rendezvous at Carlisle—and at the Trap, late in the evening, we were overtaken by Major Stagg principal Clerk in the Department of War with letters from Genl. Wayne & the Western Army containing official & pleasing accounts of his engagement with the Indians near the British Post at the Rapids of the Miami of the Lake and of his having destroyed all the Indian Settlements on that River in the vicinity of the said Post quite up to the grand Glaize—the quantity not less than 5000 acres—and the Stores &ca. of Colo. McGee the British Agent of Indian Affairs a mile or two from the Garrison.

> *Private Secretary:* Bartholomew Dandridge, Jr., Mrs. Washington's nephew, had succeeded Tobias Lear as GW's chief secretary in mid-1793.
>
> The Trappe was the name given to a small German settlement and to the area surrounding it. It was on the Germantown Road about nine miles from Pottsgrove.
>
> The message John Stagg brought GW was a letter of 28 Aug. 1794 from Maj. Gen. Anthony Wayne to Secretary of War Henry Knox describing Wayne's decisive victory over some 2,000 Indians at Fallen Timbers near the Maumee Rapids on 20 Aug. *McGee:* Alexander McKee (c.1742–1799) was a British agent at Fort Pitt from 1755 to 1775. During the Revolution he remained loyal to the crown, was held prisoner for a time at Pittsburgh, and then fled to Detroit. He was now British deputy agent for Indian affairs in the area. McKee was with the Indians during their retreat from Wayne's victorious army.

October

1st. Left the Trap early, and breakfasting at Potts grove 11 Miles we reach Reading to Dinner 19 Miles farther where we found several detachmts. of Infantry & Cavalry preparing for their March to Carlisle.

2d. An accident happening to one of my horses occasiond. my setting out, later than was intended. I got off in time, however, to make a halt (to bait my horses) at Womeldorfs 14 miles and to view the Canal from Myers town towards Lebanon—and the Locks between the two places; which (four adjoining each other, in the dissent from the Summit ground along the Tulpihockin; built of Brick;) appeared admirably constructed. Reached Lebanon at Night 28 miles.

> Womelsdorf (Middletown) was in Berks County, Pa. Myerstown, Dauphin County, Pa., was about 77 miles from Philadelphia. Lebanon, in Dauphin County, at this time consisted of 2 churches and about 40 houses, mostly built of log (Clunn, "March on Pittsburgh," 48).

3d. Breakfasted at Humels T. 14 M. and dined and lodged at Harrisburgh on the Banks of the Susquehanna 23 miles from Lebanon.

At Harrisburgh we found the first Regiment of New Jersey (about 560 strong) commd. by Colo. Turner drawn out to receive me. Passed along the line, to my Quarters—and after dinner walked through and round the Town which is considerable for its age (of about 8 or 9 years).

Hummelstown, Dauphin County, was ten miles east of Harrisburg.

Turner: The 1st New Jersey Regiment was under the command of Lt. Col. Francis Davenport. Apparently no Colonel Turner accompanied the New Jersey troops. GW may have meant to write "Forman." Lt. Col. Jonathan Forman was in command of the 3d New Jersey Regiment, infantry, and New Jersey militia (Clunn, "March on Pittsburgh," 58, n.80). Captain William Gould notes this day that he, Colonel Forman, and another militia officer "accepted an invitation from the President to take a glass of wine with him" (Gould, "Journal," 178).

After his arrival in Harrisburg, a group of the town's citizens presented GW with an address supporting the government. GW replied before his departure early on 4 Oct.

4th. Forded the Susquehanna; nearly a mile wide, including the Island—at the lower end of wch. the road crosses it.

On the Cumberland Side I found a detachment of the Philadelphia light horse ready to receive, and escort me to Carlisle 17 miles; where I arrived at about 11 Oclock. Two miles short of it, I met the Governors of Pennsylvania & New Jersey with all the Cavalry that had rendezvouzed at that place drawn up—passed them—and the Infantry of Pennsylvania before I alighted at my quarters.

Captain Gould noted today that the troops "suffered much with the cold in crossing [the Susquehanna], it being a very cold morning. The President, General Washington, forded the river in a coach—drove it himself, &c." (Gould, "Journal," 179).

The detachment of the Philadelphia Light Horse had left Carlisle at 3:00 A.M. and met GW just after he crossed the river (*Dunlap's American Daily Adv.*, 17 Oct. 1794).

At Carlisle, GW found a town "regularly laid out, consisting of several parallel streets, crossed by others at right angles. It contains upwards of 400 dwellings, chiefly of stone and brick. The public buildings are, a college, a jail, a handsome brick court-house, which stands in the centre of the town; and four houses for public worship" (Scott, *Gazetteer*). During the Revolution, Carlisle Barracks had been an ordnance depot, and in 1791 it had been designated as a general rendezvous for federal troops and supplies. It is estimated that during the insurrection between 10,000 and 15,000 troops encamped on the common (Tousey, *Military History*, 164–65).

There was "the greatest vieing between the New Jersey and Pennsylvania horse," Captain Ford of the New Jersey troops noted, as to "who should be first on the ground to receive the President. At ten o'clock, the signal for mounting came, and away went the horse" (Ford, "Journal," 85). At 12 o'clock it was announced that the president was approaching. "Immediately the 3 troops from Philadelphia, Gurney's and Macpherson's battalions, and the artillery paraded. The horse marched down the road about two miles, followed by the Jersey cavalry. . . . We were drawn up on the right of the road when our beloved Washington approached on horseback in a traveling dress, attended by his Secretary, &c." (*Pa. Archives,* 2d ser., 4:361).

5th.—Sunday. Went to the Presbiterian Meeting and heard Doctr. Davidson Preach a political Sermon, recommendatory of order & good government; and the excellence of that of the United States.

6th. to the 12th. Employed in Organizing the several detachments, which had come in from different Counties of this State, in a very disjointed & loose manner; or rather I ought to have said in urging & assisting Genl. Mifflin to do it; as I no otherwise took the command of the Troops than to press them forward, and to provide them with necessaries for their March, as well, & as far, as our means would admit.

On the 9th. William Findley and David Redick—deputed by the Committee of Safety (as it is designated) which met on the 2d of this month at Parkinson Ferry arrived in Camp with the Resolutions of the said Committee; and to give information of the State of things in the four Western Counties of Pennsylvania to wit—Washington Fayette Westd. & Alligany in order to see if it would prevent the March of the Army into them.

After hearing what both had to say, I briefly told them—That it had been the earnest wish of governmt. to bring the people of those counties to a sense of their duty, by mild, & lenient means; That for the purpose of representing to their sober reflection the fatal consequences of such conduct Commissioners had been sent amongst them that they might be warned, in time, of what must follow, if they persevered in their opposition to the laws; but that coercion wou'd not be resorted to except in the dernier resort: but, that the season of the year made it indispensible that preparation for it should keep pace with the propositions that had been made; That it was unnecessary for me to enumerate the transactions of those people (as they related to the proceedings of government) forasmuch as they knew them as well as I did; That the measure which they were not witness to the adoption of was not less painful than expensive—Was inconvenient, & distressing—in every point of view; but as I considered the support of the Laws as an object of the first magnitude, and the greatest part of the expense had already been incurred, that nothing Short of the most unequivocal *proofs* of absolute Submission should retard the March of the army into the Western counties, in order to convince them that the government could, & would enforce obedience to the laws—not suffering them to be insulted with impunity. Being asked again what proofs would be required, I answered, they knew as well as I did, what was due to justice & example. They understood my meaning—and asked if they might have another interview. I appointed five oclock in the After noon for it. At this second Meeting there was little more than a repeti[ti]on of what had passed in the forenoon; and it being again mentioned that all the *principal* characters, except one, in the Western counties who had been in the opposition, had submitted to the propositions—I was induced, seeing them in the Street the next day, to ask Mr. Redick who that one was?—telling him at the same time I required no disclosure that he did not feel himself entirely free to make. He requested a little time to think of it, and asked for another meeting—which was appointed at 5 oclock that afternoon—which took place accordingly when he said David Bradford was the person he had alluded to in his former conversations.

He requested to know if a Meeting of the people, by their deputies, would be permitted by the Army at any given point, on their March into that Country (with fresh evidence of the sincerity of their disposition to acquiesce in whatever might be required). I replied I saw no objection to it, provided they came unarmed; but to be cautious that not a gun was fired, as there could be no answering for consequences in this case. I assured them that every possible care should be taken to keep the Troops from offering them any insult or damage and that those who had always had been subordinate to the Laws, & such as had availed themselves of the amnesty, should not be injured in their persons or property; and that the treatment of the rest would depend upon their own conduct. That the Army, unless opposed, did not mean to act as executioners, or bring offenders to a Military Tribunal; but merely to aid the civil Magistrates, with whom offences would lye. Thus endd. the matter.

On 6th Oct. GW wrote Secretary of State Edmund Randolph from Carlisle: "As I reached this place Saturday only, & have no very precise information from the Insurgent counties I cannot decide definitely at this moment whether I shall proceed into them with the Troops, or return in time for the meeting of Congress. As soon as I can ascertain the true state of the Troops & other matters at this place I intend to proceed to Williamsport, & probably from thence to Fort Cumberland and Bedford" (Cornell University). By 9 Oct. he had decided to go with the army at least as far as Bedford and ordered Bartholomew Dandridge to request that Henry Knox send on "sundry Articles such as tents, &ca.&ca." Knox was to forward only such articles "as you conceive to be *absolutely necessary* for the President's accommodation. . . . As the President will be going, if he proceeds, into the Country of Whiskey he proposed to make use of that liquor for his drink, and presuming that beef and bread will be furnished by the contractors he requires no supply of these Articles from you" (Dandridge to Knox, 9 Oct. 1794, and GW to Daniel Morgan, 8 Oct. 1794, Washington Papers, Library of Congress).

12th. Octr. Having settled these Matters, seen the Troops off, as before mentioned; given them their rout & days Marching; and left Majr. Genl. [William] Irvine to organise the remainder of the Pennsylvania detachments as they might come in, & to March them & the Jersey Troops on when refreshed, I set out from Carlisle about 7 Oclock this Morning—dined at Shippensburgh 21 miles further & lodged at Chambersburgh 11 M. farther where I was joined by the Adjt. Genl. [Edward] Hand.

16th. [At Oldtown, Md.] After an early breakfast we set out for Cumberland—and about 11 Oclock arrived there.

Three miles from the Town I was met by a party of Horse under the command of Major [George] Lewis (my Nephew) and by Brigr. Genl. [Samuel] Smith of the Maryland line, who Escorted me to the Camp; where, finding all the Troops under Arms, I passed along the line of the Army; & was conducted to a house the residence of Major [David] Lynn of the Maryland line (an old Continental Officer) where I was well lodged, & civily entertained.

17th. & 18th. Remained at Cumberland, in order to acquire a true knowledge of the strength—condition—&ca. of the Troops; and to see how they were provided, and when they could be got in readiness to proceed.

I found upwards of 3200 Men (Officers included) in this Encampment; Understood that about 500 more were at a little Village on the Virginia side, 11 Miles distant, called Frankfort, under the command of Majr. Genl. [Daniel] Morgan; that 700 more had arrived at that place the evening of the 18th. undr. Brigr. Mathews and 500 more were expected in the course of a few days under Colo. Page and That the whole were well supplied with Provns., Forage & Straw.

Having requested that every thing might be speedily arranged for a forward movement, and a light Corps to be organized for the advance under the command of Major Genl. Morgan, I resolved to proceed to Bedford next Morng.

From Colo. Mason (who has been a uniform friend to Government) and from a variety of concurrant accounts, it appears evident that the people in the Western Counties of this State have got very much alarmed at the approach of the Army; but though Submission is professed, their principles remain the same; and that nothing but coercion, & example will reclaim & bring them to a due & unequivocal submission to the Laws.

Washington Reviewing the Western Army at Fort Cumberland, Maryland, *attributed to James Peale.* *(Metro-politan Museum of Art, Gift of Col. and Mrs. Edgar William Garbisch)*

General Henry ("Light Horse Harry") Lee. (The Society of the Lees of Virginia)

19th. In company with Genl. Lee, who I requested to attend me, that all the arrangements necessary for the Army's crossing the Mountns. in two columns might be made; Their routs, & days Marches fixed, that the whole might move in Unison—and accompanied by the Adjutant General and my own family we set out, abt. eight oclock, for Bedford, and making one halt at the distance of 12 Miles, reached it a little after 4 oclock in the afternoon being met a little out of the Encampment by Govr. Mifflin—Govr. [Richard] Howell—& several other Officers of distinction.

Quarters were provided for me at the House of a Mr. Espy. Prothonotary of the County of Bedford—to which I was carried & lodged very comfortably.

20th. Called the Quarter Master General, Adjutant General, Contractor, & others of the Staff departmt. before me, & the Commander in chief, at 9 Oclock this morning, in order to fix on the Routs of the two Columns & their Stages; and to know what the situation of matters were in their respective departments—and when they wd. be able to put the Army in motion. Also to obtain a correct return of the strength—and to press the commanding Officers of Corps to prepare with all the Celerity in their power for a forward movement.

Matters being thus arranged I wrote a farewell address to the Army through the Commander in Chief—Govr. Lee—to be published in orders—and having prepared his Instructions and made every arrangement that occurred, as necessary I prepared for my return to Philadelphia in order to meet Congress, and to attend to the Civil duties of my Office.

I found also, which appeared to me to be an unlucky measure—that the former had issued his warrants against, and a party of light horse had actually siez'd, one Harman Husband & one Filson as Insurgents or abetters of the Insurrection. I call it unlucky because my intention was to have suspended all proceedings of a Civil Nature until the Army had united its columns in the Center of the Insurgent Counties & then to have ciezed at one & the same all the leaders and principals of the Insurrection and because it is to be feared that the proceeding above mentioned will have given the alarm and those who are most obnoxious to punishment will flee from the Country.

Herman Husbands (1724–1795), one of the leaders of the insurrection, and Robert Philson, a storekeeper in Berlin, Bedford County, were sent to Philadelphia for trial. On 19 Oct. Dr. Robert Wellford, who had accompanied the army, noted in his diary that "this morning the President of the United States set out for Bedford on his return to the right wing of the Army, & from there to the seal of Government" (Wellford, "Diary," 8–9). On his return to Philadelphia, GW apparently followed a route from Bedford to Chambersburg, from Chambersburg to York, and then to Lancaster, from which place he proceeded to Philadelphia, arriving on 28 Oct. After GW's departure from Bedford, the army, unruly and poorly disciplined, continued on the march to the Pittsburgh area and to Washington County, reaching the disaffected counties early in November. By 17 Nov., Alexander Hamilton, who had remained with the army, wrote GW that "the list of prisoners has been very considerably increased, probably to the amount of 150. . . . Subsequent intelligence shews that there is no regular assemblage of the fugitives where it is supposed—there are only small vagrant parties in that quarter affording no point of Attack. Every thing is urging on for the return of the troops." On 19 Nov. Hamilton wrote that "the army is generally in motion homeward" (Washington Papers, Library of Congress). A regiment of infantry, with nine months' enlistment, was raised by Henry Lee to maintain order in the counties involved in the insurrection. The insurgents' trials dragged on through much of 1795, and most of the accused were acquitted for lack of evidence,

GW issuing a proclamation 10 July pardoning most of those who were not already sentenced or under indictment.

Only a few diaries for 1795 and 1796 apparently survive, and most contain only routine entries and weather.

1796

January

1. Remarkably mild and pleasant—perfectly clear. Received the National Colours from Mr. Adet the Minister Plenipo. to day. Much company visited.

Pierre Auguste Adet, French minister plenipotentiary, had arrived in the United States on 13 June 1795 to replace Jean-Antoine-Joseph Fauchet, the former minister. Adet brought with him a French flag, a gift of the French Committee of Public Safety, and an accompanying speech of warm friendship for the United States. His awareness of the anti-French bias in the American government, however, caused him to delay presenting the flag. In Dec. 1795 he finally notified GW that he desired to make the presentation, and GW chose New Year's Day for the ceremony. GW answered the French address in a friendly manner, but he included the statement that the French flag would be placed in the archives. Adet took violent exception to this. An American flag presented earlier by James Monroe to the French National Convention was on prominent display in the French chamber, and Adet had expected the French flag to be accorded a conspicuous place in the halls of Congress. The Federalists, however, felt that Adet's presentation was a flagrant attempt to sway American feeling during the discussion of the Jay Treaty.

1797

January

7. Wind at No. West and cold with clouds. Road to German Town with Mrs. Washington to see Mr. Stuarts paintings.[14]

Gilbert Stuart (1755–1828) had recently returned to America after a long stay in England and Ireland, first as a student and then as a successful painter of portraits. He painted three portraits of GW from life between 1794 and 1796. From each of these life portraits he made numerous copies to answer the great demand from both Americans and foreigners for likenesses of the first president. In the summer of 1796 Stuart had moved his studio from Philadelphia to a stone barn in Germantown.

9. Went to the Theatre, for the first time this Season. The Child of Nature & The Lock & Key were performed.

Went: GW inadvertently wrote "Wind" in the MS. The New Theatre on Chestnut Street above Sixth Street had opened in 1794 and was said to be the finest theater in America at this time. It was copied after the theater at Bath,

Eng., and seated 2,000 people. A stock company had been formed by theater managers Hugh Reinagle and Thomas Wignall, and they spent money lavishly to procure costumes and scenery and to obtain a supply of good actors, many from England. *The Child of Nature* was a comedy in four acts, and *The Lock and Key,* a comic opera in two acts.

24. Went to the Pantheon in the evening.

The following advertisement appeared in a Philadelphia newspaper on 23 Jan.: "Pantheon, *and Ricketts's, Amphitheatre. Mr. Ricketts* takes the liberty of announcing to his friends and the public, that to-morrow evening there will be a variety of performances, at the Pantheon *By Desire of the President of the United States*" (*Gaz. of the U.S.* [Philadelphia], 23 Jan. 1797). Ricketts's Amphitheatre, or Circus, was devoted principally to equestrian performances and slack and tightrope walking. John Bill Ricketts, a Scotsman, had come to Philadelphia in 1792 and shortly afterwards had built his large, circular amphitheater at the corner of Chestnut and Sixth streets. Ricketts and his son were the two main equestrians, performing dangerous feats of riding and acrobatics on horseback. The amphitheater burned in 1799, and Ricketts, bankrupt, returned to England (Scharf, *History of Philadelphia*, 2:952–53).

February

6. Went to the Play of Columbus in the evening.

Columbus; or A World Discovered, a historical play, was presented at the New Theatre at six o'clock this evening. Also on the bill was a farce called *Barnaby Brittle; or A Wife at Her Wit's End.* The production of *Columbus* was an unusually ambitious one. The theater had been closed for several days before the first performance on 30 Jan., "on account of the extensive preparations" necessary for the new scenery, machinery, and decorations. Included in the production were a representation of a storm, an earthquake, a volcano eruption, and "a procession of Indians and the first Landing of Columbus" (*Gaz. of the U.S.* [Philadelphia], 23 Jan., 6 Feb. 1797).

17. A very crouded drawing Room.

That the drawing room, or levee, was particularly crowded on this day was undoubtedly the result of a rumor that this was to be Mrs. Washington's last levee before the Washingtons retired to Mount Vernon. John Adams was to be inaugurated as the new president on 4 Mar., and GW's last weeks in office were marked by a hectic round of visits and addresses from various groups including congressmen, merchants, the Pennsylvania governor and legislature, the Society of the Cincinnati, and army officers. There were also elaborate dinners and entertainments given in his honor. The Washingtons themselves on 3 Mar. gave a farewell dinner followed by Mrs. Washington's last drawing room. On 4 Mar. at noon GW attended the inauguration of the new president.

18. One third of the Pennsylvania Ho. of Representatives dined here.

22. Went in the evening to an elegant entertainmt. given on my birth night. Mery. 38.

The "elegant entertainment" took place at Ricketts's Amphitheatre and was followed by dinner and a ball "which for Splendour, Taste and Elegance, was, perhaps, never excelled by any similar Entertainment in the United States." This entertainment was the culmination of a whole day of celebration which had begun by the ringing of bells and the firing of cannon (*Claypoole's Advertiser* [Philadelphia], 23 Feb. 1797).

March

9. Left Phila. on my return to Mt. Vernon—dined at Chester & lodged at Wilmington.

Accompanying GW and Mrs. Washington on the trip home to Mount Vernon were Nelly Custis and the marquis de Lafayette's son, George Washington Motier Lafayette (1779–1849), accompanied by his tutor, Felix Frestal. George Washington Parke Custis was in school at Princeton, and Tobias Lear and Bartholomew Dandridge, Jr., had been left in Philadelphia to supervise the packing and moving of the Washingtons' belongings and the cleaning of the presidential house. Young Lafayette had fled France with his tutor in 1795, three years after his father's arrest and imprisonment. The young man's arrival in America had been an embarrassment to GW. As much as he wished to have the only son of his close friend come to live in his family, he wanted to do nothing to offend the French government or the French partisans in this country. He therefore arranged for the boy and Frestal to live in New York under his family name, Motier. Finally, in April 1796, in spite of warnings by some members of the government, GW invited young Lafayette and Frestal to Philadelphia for a visit with his family. The visit lengthened into a permanent residency.

15. Recd. the Compliments of the Citizens of George Town as I had done the day before of those of the City of Washington. Stopped in Alexa. & got to Mt. V. to dinner.

The party arrived at Mount Vernon at 4:00 P.M. (Eleanor Parke Custis to Elizabeth Bordley, 18 Mar. 1797, manuscript owned by Mount Vernon Ladies' Association of the Union). Of the journey from Philadelphia and the conditions prevailing at Mount Vernon when he arrived, GW wrote: "We got home without accident, & found the Roads drier, & better than I ever travelled them at that Season of the year. The attentions we met with on our journey were very flattering, and to some whose minds are differently formed from mine would have been highly relished, but I avoided in every instance where I had any previous knowledge of the intention, and c[oul]d by the earnest entreaties prevail, all parade, or escorts. . . . I find myself in the situation, nearly, of a new beginner; for although I have no houses to build (except one, which I must erect for the accommodation & security of my Military, Civil & private Papers . . .) yet I have not one or scarcely any thing else about me that does not require considerable repairs. In a word I am already surrounded by Joiners, Masons, Painters & ca." (GW to James McHenry, 3 April 1797, Washington Collection, New York Public Library).

George Washington Motier Lafayette, by a member of the Sharples family. (Mount Vernon Ladies' Association of the Union, Robert E. Lee IV and Mrs. A. Smith Bowman Collection)

August

7. I went to the annual Meeting of the Potk. Co. at George town. Dined at the Union tavern & lodged at Mr. Thos. Peter's.

Potk. Co.: Work on building locks and clearing the Potomac River and its tributaries for navigation had been under way for more than a decade. When money was plentiful, the work progressed rapidly, with the employment of many Irish and German indentured servants and hired laborers; but from 1788 until the present year, funds for the work on the river gradually became harder to procure. Efforts were largely bent on obtaining enough money to complete the locks at Great Falls, the only part of the Potomac River at which a portage was still necessary. There were repeated calls on shareholders for additional contributions; the legislatures of Maryland and Virginia were petitioned at various times for the sale of more shares to be added to the capital stock; attempts were made to force delinquent subscribers to pay their quotas. Despite all efforts to raise money, funds were at this time entirely exhausted. At the 1797 annual meeting in Georgetown, the shareholders of the Potomac Company found it necessary to agree to sell the indentures of the servants and discharge the company's laborers.

10. Miss Fanny Henley came.

Frances (Fanny) Henley (b. 1779) was the eldest child of Martha Washington's sister Elizabeth and her second husband, Leonard Henley, of James City County. Fanny later became the third wife of Tobias Lear.

12. Genl. Lee, Lady & daughter came.

Genl. Lee: Henry (Light Horse Harry) Lee's first wife, Matilda, died in 1790, and in 1793 Lee married Anne Hill Carter (1773–1829), daughter of Charles Carter of Shirley and his second wife, Anne Butler Moore Carter. The daughter who accompanied the Lees was Lucy Grymes Lee (1786–1860), a child of Lee's first marriage.

13. General ⟨L.⟩ & ca. went away & Mr. Bourne and Mr. Lear came.

Mr. Bourne may be Sylvanus Bourne, who was vice-consul in Amsterdam about 1794 and in June 1797 was appointed consul general to the Batavian Republic.

Tobias Lear, whose second wife, Fanny Bassett Washington Lear, had died in late Mar. 1796, seems to have been living in Washington City. Lear, now a merchant in the Federal City, was also president of the Potomac Company and was on his way to the Great Falls on company business.

31. Mr. Lawe. Lewis in the evening.

Lawrence Lewis, son of GW's sister Betty, had been invited by GW to reside at Mount Vernon to help with the entertainment of the many guests. GW informed Lewis, however, that he would "expect no Services from you for which pecuniary compensation will be made. I have already as many on wages as are sufficient to carry on my business and more indeed than I can find means to pay, conveniently. As both your Aunt and I are in the decline of life, and regular in our habits, especially in our hours of rising & going to bed; I require some person (fit & proper) to ease me of the trouble

A primitive painting depicting Mount Vernon around 1797. (Mount Vernon Ladies' Association of the Union)

of entertaining company; particularly of Nights, as it is my inclination to retire (and unless prevented by very particular company, always do retire) either to bed, or to my study, soon after candle light. In taking these duties (which hospitality obliges one to bestow on company) off my hands, it would render me a very acceptable service, and for a little time *only*, to come, an hour in the day, now and then, devoted to the recording of some Papers which time would not allow me to complete before I left Philadelphia, would also be acceptable" (4 Aug. 1797, Mount Vernon Ladies' Association of the Union).

September

12. Col. Otway Byrd, Doctr. Barraud came to Dinr. & Mr. Saml. Washington in the Afternoon.

Francis Otway Byrd (1756–1800), son of William Byrd III (1729–1777) and his first wife, Elizabeth Hill Carter Byrd, resigned his post in the British navy at the beginning of the Revolution to take the position of aide to Maj. Gen. Charles Lee. After the Revolution, Byrd was sheriff and clerk of the court of Charles City County.

Dr. Philip Barraud (1757–1830) practiced medicine in Williamsburg.

Samuel Washington (c.1765–1832), the younger son of GW's brother Charles and Mildred Thornton Washington, lived in or near Charles Town, Berkeley County. Samuel, who had become responsible for his ailing father's debts and had suffered two disastrous years in which he lost his crops, wrote GW on 7 July requesting a loan. GW was short of money himself but agreed to let his nephew have $1,000 in order to prevent him from having to sell his land; at the same time he gave him a stern lecture on the evils of borrowing (Samuel Washington to GW, 7 July 1797, David Library of the American Revolution, Washington Crossing, Pa.).

October

3. Doctr. Stuart came hear to Dinner. Washington Custis came home.

George Washington Parke Custis was home after an unsuccessful year at the College of New Jersey at Princeton. His academic career was distinctly checkered and caused GW much concern. During the early years of the presidency, GW had sent the boy to a small private school in New York run by Patrick Murdoc. When the seat of government was moved to Philadelphia, he enrolled young Custis at the "College, Academy and Charitable School" associated with the University of Pennsylvania. Even at this early date there was dissatisfaction with his progress. In 1796 young Custis matriculated at Princeton and, armed with much good advice from his grandfather, seemed for a time to be doing well. GW's letters to him during the fall and early winter are full of admonitions to exert himself in his studies and avoid bad habits; Custis's replies give repeated assurances of his good intentions and progress. Soon after Custis's return to Princeton from his spring vacation, however, GW received a letter from the president of the college, Samuel Stanhope Smith (1750–1819), which, GW wrote Smith, "filled my mind (as you naturally supposed it would) with extreme disquietude. From his infancy I have discovered an almost unconquerable disposition to indolence in everything that did not tend to his amusements; and have exhorted him in the most parental and friendly manner often, to devote his time to more useful pursuits" (GW to Smith, 24 May 1797, Custis, *Recollections,* 83–84). Custis himself a few days later wrote GW a letter full of apologies and promises for improved conduct, and GW replied that he would "not only heartily forgive, but will forget also, and bury in oblivion all that has passed" (Custis to GW, 29 May 1797, and GW to Custis, 4 June 1797, ibid., 84–87). However, despite much good advice from GW and frequent assurances of good conduct from Custis during the next few months, Washington Custis's homecoming on 3 Oct. marked, to GW's dismay, the end of young Custis's schooling at Princeton.

12. Mr. G. W. La Fayette & Mr. Frestal left this for Geo. Town to take the stage for New York to embark for France. I accompanied them to the Fedl. City.

Young George Washington Motier Lafayette had received reports from correspondents in Hamburg that his father, together with his mother and sisters who had voluntarily joined him in prison at Olmütz, had been released and were on their way to Paris. GW was unable to persuade him to wait until the reports were confirmed. He and his tutor, Felix Frestal, sailed from New York for Le Havre on 25 Oct. on the brig *Clio*. Definite word of the release of the Lafayette family reached GW several weeks later. There followed two years of exile for the Lafayette family in Hamburg, Holstein, and Holland.

14. Mr. McDonald & Mr. Rich Brith. Com. came to dinner. Christopher set out for Lebanon.

Thomas Macdonald and Henry Pye Rich were British commissioners sent to the United States to settle claims under the terms of the Jay Treaty.

GW's body servant, Christopher (sometimes called Christopher Sheels), was "on Monday last . . . Bit by a Small Dog belonging to a Lady in my house, then as was supposed a little diseased. And Yesternight died (I do think) in a State of madness. As soon as the Boy . . . was Bit application was made to a medical Gentleman in Alexandria who has cut out so far as He could, the place Bit, applyed Ointment to keep it open, And put the Boy under a Course of Mercury" (GW to William Henry Stoy, 14 Oct. 1797, *Writings,* 37: 581). GW, upon hearing of the miraculous cures performed in such cases by Dr. William Henry Stoy (1726–1801) of Lebanon, Pa., sent Christopher to him for further treatment. Stoy wrote GW on 19 Oct. that the servant was in no further danger since he had taken his medicine. Stoy's remedy consisted of "one ounce of the herb, red chickweed, four ounces of theriac and one quart of beer, all well digested, the dose being a wine glassful" (Kelly, *Medical Biography,* 1177). Christopher survived Dr. Stoy's treatment and lived to attend GW during his final illness and death.

24. Spanish Minister & Mr. Barry came to dinner.

Don Carlos Martinez de Yrujo y Tacon (1763–1834) had come to America as Spanish minister in 1797, succeeding Don José de Jáudenes. In a previous visit, in 1796, Yrujo had spent two days at Mount Vernon at GW's invitation, and GW described him at that time as "a young man, very free and easy in his manners; professes to be well disposed towards the United States; and as far as a judgment can be formed on so short an acquaintance, appears to be well informed" (GW to Timothy Pickering, 4 July 1796, Pickering Papers, Massachusetts Historical Society). In 1798 Yrujo married Sally McKean, daughter of the chief justice of the Pennsylvania Supreme Court.

Mr. Barry was James Barry, an Irishman, a merchant in the East India trade, and a heavy investor in lots in the new Federal City.

30. Doctr. Stuart went away after breakfast. Mr. Cottineau & Lady, Mr. Rosseau & Lady, the Visct. D'Orleans, & Mr. De Colbert came to Dinner & returned to Alexa. afterwards.

> *Mr. Cottineau & Lady:* Denis Nicholas Cottineau de Kerloguen (c.1745–1808) was a Breton officer who had served with the Continental navy during the Revolution. He had commanded the United States frigate *Pallas,* serving under John Paul Jones's command during the fight between the *Bonhomme Richard* and the *Serapis,* and had himself fought and captured the *Countess of Scarborough* in the same battle. After the Revolution, Cottineau returned to his plantations in Saint Domingue but was forced to flee because of the insurrection there. He settled in Philadelphia and for a time became a shareholder and settler at the French Royalist colony of Azilum on the Susquehanna River. Later he moved to Savannah. *Mr. Rosseau & Lady:* Possibly Jean Rosseau, a volunteer on the *Bonhomme Richard* (*Diaries,* 4:263). *Visct. D'Orleans:* GW may mean Louis Philippe, duc d'Orleans (1773–1850), or one of his brothers, Antoine Philippe d'Orleans, duc de Montpensier (1775–1807), or Louis Charles d'Orleans, comte de Beaujolais (1779–1808). The three Princes of the Blood were in exile in America and had visited GW at Mount Vernon for four days in April 1797 before starting on a three-month tour through the wilderness of Tennessee, Kentucky, western Virginia, and Pennsylvania. GW at that time had given them letters of introduction and a map of the roads they were to follow on their journey. The duc d'Orleans in 1830 became King Louis Philippe of France. *Mr. De Colbert:* This is probably Edouard Charles Victurnin, chevalier Colbert de Maulevrier (1758–1820). Colbert later became comte de Colbert de Maulevrier. At the beginning of the French Revolution he commanded a French vessel, but he lost his command and eventually was forced to flee France. He spent a part of his exile in America, returning to France in 1814 at the restoration of the Bourbons.

November

13. The British Envoy Mr. Liston & his Lady—Mr. Marchant & his lady & her Son Mr. Brown and Mr. Athill Speaker of the Assembly of Antigua came to Dinner as did a Doctr. Pinckard. The last went afterwards.

> Robert Liston (1743–1836) served as British minister and ambassador at several important posts before being appointed in 1796 as envoy extraordinary and minister plenipotentiary to the United States. He served in this capacity until 1802. In Feb. 1796, just before coming to this country, he married Henrietta Merchant, "daughter of the late Nathaniel M. esq. of Antigua" (*Gentleman's Mag.,* 66 [1796], 254). Nelly Custis characterized Mrs. Liston as having "kind & friendly manners" and seemed fond of her, but she refused an invi-

tation to spend part of the winter with the Listons in Philadelphia because of her reluctance to leave Mount Vernon and especially her grandmother (Eleanor Parke Custis to Elizabeth Bordley, 23 Nov. 1797, owned by Mount Vernon). *Mr. Marchant:* undoubtedly a relative of Mrs. Liston's. According to Nelly Custis, Mrs. Merchant was "a sweet beautiful engaging Woman, her husband very pleasing & entertaining. I am really sorry that his health is so very precarious. . . . Mr. Brown is a very genteel young man, I am sorry he has left Philadelphia, as I am sure the Belles will feel his loss—he was in my opinion one of the most elegant & pleasing young men last Winter" (Eleanor Parke Custis to Elizabeth Bordley, 23 Nov. 1797, owned by Mount Vernon). Mr. Athill may be John Athill. Nelly Custis thought him "a sensible agreeable man." The Listons were to accompany the Merchant family and Mr. Athill by water as far as Norfolk, from whence the Merchants, Brown, and Athill were to embark for Antigua.

24. A Mr. Welch from Greenbrier dined here.

James Welch of Rockingham County, now living in Greenbrier County, arrived at Mount Vernon armed with a cautious letter of introduction from Daniel Morgan. He had no money but had a grandiose scheme for leasing GW's 23,000 acres of land on the Kanawha River and dividing it into small farms for sublease. On 29 Nov., Welch submitted a definite proposition for leasing the land with an option to buy. GW wrote Dr. James Craik in Alexandria to try to find out more about him before carrying negotiations any further.

25. Mr. Russel came here abt. 9 Oclock A.M.

Mr. Russel: probably William Russell (1740–1818), a merchant and reformer of Birmingham, Eng., who engaged in an export trade from Birmingham and Sheffield to Russia, Spain, and the United States.

December

6. Mrs. Forbes our House keeper arrived here this day.

The steady stream of visitors to Mount Vernon put quite a strain on Mrs. Washington. There was no steward or housekeeper at Mount Vernon, and to make matters worse, their slave cook, Hercules, had run away sometime in the early fall. GW wrote several friends requesting them to help him find either a housekeeper or a steward and a cook, either slave or for hire. He also inserted an advertisement in the newspaper for a housekeeper "competent to all the duties of that office in a large family—for such, one hundred and fifty dollars per annum will be allowed. Or In place of a House-keeper, a Household Steward, well acquainted with the duties of a Butler, and skilled in the art of cookery (the manual part of which would not be required of him) would be employed at the above, or greater wages, if his qualifications entitled him to them" (*Columbian Mirror*, 12 Aug. 1797). The choice fell upon Mrs. Eleanor Forbes, a 50-year-old English widow who had served as housekeeper for Robert Brooke during his term as governor of Virginia. Mrs. Forbes was, according to Brooke, "active & Spirited in the execution of her business—sober & honest—well acquainted with Cookery & . . . capable of ordering & setting out a table . . . her appearance is decent & respectable

& such is her general deportment" (Bushrod Washington to GW, 8 Nov. 1797, owned by Mount Vernon). Mrs. Forbes was due to come to Mount Vernon immediately but was unable to come until December (GW to Bushrod Washington, 22 Nov. 1797, Washington Papers, Library of Congress). She proved satisfactory and remained at Mount Vernon until after GW's death.

7. Doctr. Fendall went away, & Docr. Stuart came.

Dr. Benjamin Fendall of Cedar Hill in Charles County, Md., was a dentist. He probably came to see Mrs. Washington, who was to have some new teeth made.

9. Mr. Law & family & Doc. Stuart went away after breakfast & Mr. Welch came to Dinner & returned afterwards.

James Welch had come to Mount Vernon to deliver his final proposal for GW's lands on the Kanawha River in what is now W.Va. There had been correspondence back and forth since his original proposal on 29 Nov., and GW had received some rather disquieting reports about Welch. However, Welch's offer of his 99,995-acre tract on Elk River in Randolph County (now W.Va.) to be held in trust by GW as security for payment induced GW to agree to Welch's latest proposal. Welch was to have a 30-year-lease on GW's four tracts of land on the Kanawha River.

25. Mr. W. Dandridge came.

William Dandridge was a son of Martha Washington's brother Bartholomew Dandridge (1737–1785) and Mary Burbidge Dandridge (d. 1809).

30. Mrs. Washington came here and Mr. Wm. Dandridge to do business for me in the way of writing.

William Dandridge probably did not stay long at Mount Vernon. The only mentions of him in the accounts after this date are an entry for $25 on 3 Feb. 1798, "By Cash *given* to Mr. Wm. Dandridge," and a similar entry on 11 April (GW's Cash Memorandum, 1 Sept. 1797–20 Feb. 1799, owned by the John Carter Brown Library, Providence). GW probably did not approve of the young man's requests for such sizable sums of money in so short a time after his employment.

1798

January

2. A Mr. Elliot came to dinnr. and stayed all Night.

Mr. Elliot: Barnard Elliott, Jr. (c.1777–1806), was the only son of Lt. Col. Barnard Elliott (d. 1778), a former member of the king's council in South Carolina and an officer of the South Carolina Regiment of Artillery in the Revolution. Young Elliott was at Mount Vernon to solicit GW's aid in securing a claim against the government for land for his father's service in the war. GW wrote a letter to Secretary of War James McHenry on this day asking him to aid the young man if possible in pressing his petition. A claim for seven years' half pay was finally approved in 1810.

8. A Mr. Marshall Music Master came here—Tuned Nelly Custis's Harpsicord & returned after din⟨ner⟩.

15. I went to Alexandria to a meeting of the Stockholders of that Bank to an Election of Directors.

> GW attended a meeting to elect nine directors of the Bank of Alexandria for one-year terms under the charter granted by the Commonwealth of Virginia in 1792 (*Columbian Mirror*, 4 Jan. 1798).

February

1. A Mr. Lad & a Mr. Gibbes from Rhode Island dined here & returned to Alexandria.

> John G. Ladd was a merchant in Alexandria. Of Mr. Gibbes from Rhode Island, Nelly Custis later remarked: "I do not know what subjects he discusses with *gentlemen* . . . as I have seen too little of him, to fathom his *scull*, yet his conversation to Ladies is composed of . . . *Hearts, darts, hopes, fears, heart achs,* & all the etcetera superfluous of the *tender passion*" (Eleanor Parke Custis to Elizabeth Bordley, 20 Mar. 1798, owned by Mount Vernon).

3. A Mr. Adamson from Hamburgh & Doctr. Stuart came to Dinner.

> William Adamson wrote GW a letter on 5 Feb. 1798 thanking him for "the polite & kind reception" that he had received at Mount Vernon.
>
> Dr. David Stuart was at Mount Vernon to discuss with GW what was to be done with his young stepson George Washington Parke Custis. After young Custis's return from Princeton in October (see entry for 3 Oct. 1797), GW made out a schedule of study with the intention of having the boy pursue his education at Mount Vernon. The results, as may have been expected, were not satisfactory. GW wrote to Stuart on 22 Jan. to see if he and Custis's mother could find out what the boy wanted to do. Stuart replied on 26 Jan. that Custis himself "found his habits of indolence and inattention so unconquerable, that he did not expect to derive any benefit from the plans pursued in [a college]." Stuart promised GW that he would be at Mount Vernon soon to talk over the situation (Washington Papers, Library of Congress). He came again on 18 Feb.

8. Visited the Public buildgs. in the Morng. Met the Compy. at the Union Tavern & dined there—lodged as before.

> GW went to a meeting of the Potomac Company at Georgetown on 7 Feb. Visitors to the Capitol and the president's residence in the new Federal City in Feb. 1798 found the buildings well along. At the Capitol the superintendent reported "the freestone work on the outside is raised as high as the top of the Corinthian capitals all round the building. . . . The brickwork is also raised as high as the roof, and the naked flooring of the building is almost entirely laid." At the "President's House" the stonework was almost finished,

the chimneys were up to the roof, which was finished except for the laying of the slate, and the doors "of the two principal stories" were all framed, "and some of them are panelled" (*Columbian Mirror,* 27 Feb. 1798).

12. Went with the family to a Ball in Alexa. given by the Citzen[s] of it & its vicinity in commemoration of the Anniversary of my birth day.

Feb. 11 was GW's birthday according to the Julian (Old Style) calendar, but in 1752 the corrections of the Gregorian (New Style) calendar were adopted by England, Ireland, and the colonies, and GW's birthday became 22 Feb. The citizens of Alexandria chose to celebrate GW's birthday on the Old Style date, but it fell on a Sunday in 1798, and consequently the ball was held on Monday, 12 Feb. Nelly Custis accompanied GW's party to the ball, where she found her old music "master for singing" from Philadelphia who "performed with the band . . . and his clarinet sounds as sweetly as ever." She also found "the room . . . crouded, there were twenty five or thirty couples in the first two setts . . . we danced until two o'clock" (Eleanor Parke Custis to Elizabeth Bordley, 20 Mar. 1798, owned by Mount Vernon).

March

5. Doctr. Stuart left this, to accompany Washington Custis to St. Johns College at Annapolis.

After much thought GW had finally decided to enroll George Washington Parke Custis in St. John's College, a small nondenominational school opened in 1789 in Annapolis. Custis's uncle George Calvert had recommended the college. GW thought the boy might like it better than a school farther from home, and also he felt "there is *less* of that class of people which are baneful to youth, in that City, than in any other" (GW to David Stuart, 26 Feb. 1798). In a letter of 5 Mar. to Samuel McDowell, president of the college, GW warned of young Custis's indolence. He added, however, that he knew of no vice in the boy. "From drinking and gaming he is perfectly free and if he has a propensity to any other impropriety, it is hidden from me. He is generous, and regardful of truth" (Washington Collection, New York Public Library).

18. Mr. Steer Senr. & Junr. Miss Steer & Mrs. Vanhaver dined here & returned to Alexa. afterwards. Mr. Peter came in the afternoon.

Henri Joseph Stier (1743–1821), member of the States General of the Province of Antwerp, Belgium, fled the wars of the French Revolution in 1794 and brought his family to America, settling in Annapolis, Md. With him at Mount Vernon today were his son, Jean Charles Stier, his daughter Rosalie Eugenia Stier, and another daughter, Isabel, wife of Jean Michel Van Havre.

20. Albin Rawlins came to live with me as Clerk.

GW, upon "finding it impracticable to use the exercise on horse back which my health business and inclination requires, and at the same time to keep my acots., and perform all the writing, which my late Public Occupations have been the means of involving me in, I resolved to employ a clerk," preferably "a single man . . . on very moderate wages . . . [to] be content to eat with, and live in the same manner the Housekeeper does, having a room to himself to write in, and another to lodge in, over the same" (GW to William Augustine Washington, 27 Feb. 1798, Washington Papers, Library of Congress). The clerk's "principle employment" would be "to copy and record letters and other Papers, to keep Books (if required) and an account of articles received from and delivered to the Farms . . . to go . . . to such places as my business may require, to receive grain, and attend to the measurement of it, and other things when it is necessary to send a trustworthy person to see it done" (GW to Albin Rawlins, 12 Feb. 1798, Washington Papers, Library of Congress). After some dickering GW hired Albin Rawlins, of Hanover County, for $150 per year.

27. Mr. Charles Carroll Jun. & Mr. Willm. Lee came to dinner.

Charles Carroll, Jr. (b. 1775), of Homewood, was the son of Charles Carroll of Carrollton. His attentions to Nelly Custis at an Alexandria ball the previous spring set off rumors of romance that were discounted by Nelly, who, although finding Carroll "a pleasing young man," was left with the impression that he "unfortunately has been told too often of his merit and accomplishments, and it has given him more affectation than is by any means agreeable" (Eleanor Parke Custis to Elizabeth Bordley, 30 May 1797, owned by Mount Vernon). With this visit by Carroll the romantic rumors resumed, and to Nelly's brother, George Washington Parke Custis, GW wrote: "Young Mr. C[arroll] came . . . to dinner, and left us next morning after breakfast. If his object was such as you say has been reported, it was not declared here; and therefore, the less is said upon the subject, particularly by your sister's friends, the more prudent it will be until the subject develops itself more" (Custis, *Recollections,* 102).

Willm. Lee: probably William Lee (1775–1845), of Frederick County, Md.

31. A Mr. Fevot—a French Gentleman recomd. by Count de Rochambeau dined here & a Mr. Freeman Member in Congress from N. Hamps. came in the afternoon & returned.

Paul Ferdinand Fevot (b. 1756) was born in Lausanne, Switzerland. He was in ill favor with the French whose influence was strong in his country at this time and had come to the United States with a cautious, unsigned letter of introduction from the comte de Rochambeau, whose own position in France was extremely precarious. Fevot wrote GW a long, rambling letter a few days after this visit expressing disillusionment in general with people and conditions in America, and particularly dissatisfaction with GW's reception and entertainment at Mount Vernon. "I was not surprised in beholding your reserved Countenance at first meeting, but I entertained a chearfull hope that it would clear up when I should have made myself better Known. I respectfully presented to You my note of recomandation, & Your Excellency told me You did not read French; upon which I took the Liberty to Express my hope that You Knew the hand writing; & Your answer was You *rather* thought it was! If I am still acquainted with the English language this expression is to carry with it if not a thourough doubt of an allegation at least a strong shade of it injurious in this instance to any honest man, and very ungenerous, very cruel indeed to a Stranger of a genteel appearance & behaviour; 1200 leagues distant from his native Country, who having exposed himself to run 400 more at a grievous expence for him, relying on a recomandation, does not

get by it the least token of interest or protection but not even a Kind word!"
He continued, "If to obtain in life a high Situation, if the worship of the
Multitude is to be captivated by divesting oneself of humanity & generosity
there is much more comfort in my [lowly] position than I thought." Fevot
added, however, that he found Mrs. Washington a civil and polite lady. GW
was nonplussed by Fevot's letter and replied on 15 April: "Not perceiving
what has been your object in addressing such sentiments as your letter of the
4th inst. contained—and not being conscious of having merited the repre-
hension you have judged it expedient to inflict on me, I shall not give you
the trouble of reading an answer in detail. I can not forbear observing however that as it is not usual with me, to treat any Gentleman with incivility or
even with indifference (especially under my own Roof) I am unable to recollect any part of my behaviour which could give rise to such misconception
of my motives" (Fevot to GW, 16 Oct. 1797 and 4 April 1798, and GW to
Fevot, 15 April 1798, Washington Papers, Library of Congress).

Jonathan Freeman (1745–1808) lived in Hanover, N.H., where he farmed
and served as treasurer of Dartmouth College for over 40 years.

May

19. About 8 Oclock in the forenoon Mrs. Washington & Myself sat out
on a visit to Hope Park & the Federal City. Got to the former to Dinner
and remained there until Morning when we proceeded to the City.
Dined at Mr. Thos. Peter's & remained there until Wednesday, and
then went to Mr. Laws & remained there until friday when we sat out
on our return home & called at Mount Eagle to take our leave of the
Revd. Mr. Fairfax who was on the point of Embarking for England.

Thomas Law and Thomas Peter were married, respectively, to Mrs. Washington's granddaughters Elizabeth Parke Custis and Martha Parke Custis.
Another guest of Thomas Law today was Julian Ursyn Niemcewicz (1758–
1841) who visited Mount Vernon on 2 June. Niemcewicz was a Polish literary
and political figure who came to America in 1797 as the companion of
Tadeusz Kociuszko, leader of the Polish insurrection against Russia. Upon
their release from a Russian prison, the two Poles had come to America
where Kociuszko had earlier gained fame as a colonel of engineers in the
Revolution. GW and Mrs. Washington came to the Law home on 23 May for
a two-day stay while Niemcewicz was still there. "The whole time he [GW]
was courteous, polite, even attentive; he talked very little, now and then on
agriculture, on natural history, on all that one would wish, except politics,
on which he maintains an absolute silence and reserve." During this visit
GW renewed his interest in billiards. "He plays with a mace and although it
is 25 years since he has played, his attention and skill made up for the lack
of practice" (Niemcewicz, *Vine and Fig Tree*, 86–87). A billiard mace is a cue
with a knob on the end.

Revd. Mr. Fairfax: GW wrote the earl of Buchan that "ill health and advice
of Physicians have induced him [Bryan Fairfax] to try the effect of Sea Air,
& his inclinations have led him to give a voyage to England the preference"
(15 May 1798, Washington Papers, Library of Congress).

30. Colo. Morris, Lady & 4 children came here after dinner.

Colonel Morris is probably Lewis Morris (d. 1829), who had visited Mount Vernon with his brother Jacob Morris on 6 Nov. 1786. Morris had settled in South Carolina after the Revolution and was an original member of the South Carolina Society of the Cincinnati.

June

2. Mr. Law & a Polish Gentleman, the Companion of General Kosciaski came here to dinner, as did Miss [Portia] Lee of Greenspring with Nelly Custis who returnd to day.

A Polish Gentleman: See entry for 19 May 1798. Neimcewicz made a full report of his Mount Vernon visit in his journal, including a detailed description of the Mansion House, farms, gardens, and something about the daily lives of the Washingtons. He immediately became infatuated with Nelly Custis: "This was one of those celestial figures that nature produces only rarely, that the inspiration of painters has sometimes divined and that one cannot see without ecstacy . . . she plays the harpsichord, sings, and draws better than any woman in America or even in Europe" (Niemcewicz, *Vine and Fig Tree,* 97).

26. Mr. Law & two French Gentn.—viz. Mr. La Guin & Mr. Clarmont.

Anna Maria Brodeau Thornton wrote in her diary on 27 June 1798 that "Mr. La Guin & Mr. Flamand two French Gentlemen from New York came" (William Thornton Papers, Library of Congress). Nelly Custis recorded that they were "old friends" of Thomas Law's (Eleanor Parke Custis to Elizabeth Bordley, 1 July 1798, owned by Mount Vernon).

July

1. Mr. Fitzhugh of Chatham & Doctr. Welford dined here—as did Dr. Fld.

Dr. Robert Wellford (1753–1823), originally of Hertfordshire, Eng., came to America as a surgeon with the British army under Gen. William Howe in 1776. While stationed in Philadelphia, Wellford distinguished himself for his treatment of sick and wounded American prisoners, and in 1781, after resigning his commission, he established a practice in Fredericksburg. In 1794 GW chose him as surgeon general of the army called out to put down the Whiskey Rebellion. *Dr. Fld.:* GW probably means William Pinckard Flood.

4. Went up to the Celebration of the anniversary of Independance and dined in the Spring Gardens near Alexa. with a large Compa. of the Civil & Military of Fairfax County.

The Celebration: "The auspicious morning was ushered in by a discharge of sixteen guns . . . Gen. Washington was escorted into town by a detachment from the troop of Dragoons. He was dressed in full uniform, and appeared in good health and spirits. At 10 o'clock . . . uniform companies paraded . . . the different corps were reviewed in King street by General Washington, and Col. Little, who expressed the highest satisfaction at their appearance and manoeuvering; after which they proceeded to the Episcopal Church, where a suitable discourse was delivered by the Rev. Dr. Davis.

"A dinner was prepared at Spring Gardens by Mr. John Stavely; which, considering the number of citizens and military that partook of it (between 4 and 500) was conducted with the greatest propriety and decorum" (*Claypoole's American Daily Advertiser*, 19 July 1798). Spring Gardens, a modest building surrounded by gardens set in the fields south of Alexandria, was a popular setting for large gatherings.

11. Mr. McHenry—Secy. of war came in the evening.

James McHenry, the secretary of war in John Adams's cabinet, brought GW's commission as "Lieutenant General and Commander in Chief" of the provisional army then being raised in expectation that the current undeclared naval war with France would develop into open hostilities. GW's commission is dated 4 July 1798. GW accepted the commission with the proviso that he would not enter active service until the army was in the field, an event which never occurred. During the course of the next year and a half, however, GW became rather heavily involved in the politics and appointments of the new army. After differences between the United States and France were settled, the army was disbanded in 1800.

August

2. Mr. Lear dined here & Mrs. Washington of Bushfield & her G. daughter Ann Washn. came in the Afternn.

Ann Aylett Washington (1783–1804), daughter of Jane Washington (1759–1791) and William Augustine Washington (d. 1810), was the granddaughter of Jane's mother, Hannah Bushrod Washington of Bushfield, widow of GW's brother John Augustine Washington (1736–1787).

5. Custis came home fm. College.

Washington Custis had been at St. John's College just over four months when GW received a letter from him, 21 July 1798, asking whether he should pack only for the coming vacation or to come home to stay. GW was astonished and outraged and wrote young Custis, 24 July, that "it would seem as if *nothing* I could say to you made more than a *momentary* impression" (Dreer Collection, Pennsylvania Historical Sociey). It was by this time evident, however, that sending the boy back to school would serve no useful purpose. After some correspondence with David Stuart on the subject, GW decided to keep Custis at home and have him tutored by Tobias Lear, who had returned to GW's service as his military secretary. GW's final attempt to solve the problem of what to do with Washington Custis was made in December of this year; he had the young man appointed a cornet in a troop of horse.

14. Mr. Booker came in the afternn.

William Booker erected a threshing machine of his own design for GW at the Union Farm in July 1797. The machine's performance had been disappointing, and Booker was back at Mount Vernon to make repairs.

George Washington Parke Custis wearing a uniform in a miniature painted for Lafayette c.1799. (Virginia Historical Society)

20. No acct. kept of the Weather &ca. from hence [19 Sept.] to the end of the Month—on acct. of my sickness which commenced with a fever on the 19th. & lasted until the 24th. which left me debilitated.

> *My sickness:* GW suffered a severe fever for about a week, for which he received quinine treatments but lost about 20 pounds. On 14 Sept. he was still "recovering my flesh fast—nearly a pound, & half a day" (GW to Alexander Spotswood, 14 Sept. 1798, David Library of the American Revolution). .

September

3. In the Morning to breakfast came Genl. Marshall & Mr. Bushrod Washington.

> John Marshall, after serving as one of three American peace commissioners to France in 1797, had recently returned home to Virginia. GW had invited Marshall to Mount Vernon to urge him to run for Congress as a Federalist for the district around Richmond.

4. In the Afternoon Mr. & Mrs. Parks of Fredericksbg. came here.

> Mr. and Mrs. Parks were Andrew Parks, a merchant in Fredericksburg, and his wife, Harriot Washington Parks (1776–1822), youngest child of GW's brother Samuel Washington and his fourth wife, Anne Steptoe Allerton Washington. When the topic of their marriage arose in 1796, GW, acting in place of Harriot's deceased father, assured Parks that if he were "a gentleman of respectable connexions; and of good dispositions" and able to support her decently, he would assent to the marriage, declaring: "my wish is to see my niece happy" (GW to Parks, 7 April 1796, Washington Papers, Library of Congress; Betty Washington Lewis to GW, 27 Mar. 1796, owned by Mount Vernon). GW sent his niece "a great deal of good advice which," Harriot replied, "I am extremely obliged to you for." The wedding took place in July 1796.

20. Went up to the Federal City. Dined & lodgd at Mr. Thos. Peters.

21. Examined in company with the Comrs. some of the Lots in the vicinity of the Capital & fixed upon No. 16 in [square] 634 to build on. Dined & lodged at Mr. Laws.

> Lot 16, square 634, was on the west side of North Capitol Street between B and C streets, about the middle of the block. GW was to pay $535.71 for it in three annual installments, the first of which was paid in 1798. The construction of a double town house on the lot, which GW hoped would "promote the necessary improvements in the City," was begun that fall.

25. Mr. Geo. Steptoe Washington who came to dinner yesterday returned to day.

> George Steptoe Washington was now living at Harewood with his wife, Lucy Payne Washington, sister of Dolley Madison.

October

31. Doctr. Craik visited Patients at Union farm & dined here.

November

5. I set out on a journey to Phila. about 9 Oclock with Mr. Lear my Secretary—was met at the Turnpike by a party of horse & escorted to the Ferry at George Town where I was recd. with Military honors. Lodged at Mr. T. Peters.

GW was going to Philadelphia to make plans for the provisional army then being raised in case of an invasion by the French. The "military honors" began as he entered Alexandria where, at about 11 o'clock, "his Excellency Lieutenant-General George Washington, accompanied by his Secretary Colonel Lear . . . was met at West End and escorted into town by Colonel Fitzgerald's and Captain Young's troops of cavalry, and the company of Alexandria blues" (*Claypoole's American Daily Advertiser,* 10 Nov. 1798).

9. Breakfasted in Wilmington & dined & lodged at Chester—waitg. at the latter the return of an Exps. At this place was met by sevl. Troops of Phila. horse.

10. With this Escort I arrived in the City about 9 Oclock & was recd. by Genl. McPhersons Blues & was escorted to my lodgings in 8th. Street (Mrs. Whites) by them & the Horse.

McPhersons Blues: William MacPherson's battalion, largely Federalist in its composition, had been reorganized and enlarged in June 1798 to include units of cavalry, infantry, and artillery. *Lodgings in 8th. Street:* Mrs. Rosannah White, a widow, kept a boardinghouse at 9 North Eighth Street.

11, 12, & 13. Dined at my Lodgings receiving many Visits.

26. Dined at the Presidents of the U. States.

27. Dined in a family with Mr. Morris.

Robert Morris was at this time confined to the Prune Street Prison, the section of the Walnut Street Prison used for debtors. Morris had overextended himself in land speculation so that with the financial problems caused by the war in Europe he could not meet taxes on his lands or interest on loans. He was to remain in prison until 1801, when he obtained his release under the federal bankruptcy law.

December

14. After dinner set out on my journey home. Reached Chester.

GW reached Mount Vernon on 19 December.

1799

February

8. Mr. Thos. Digges dined here & returned. Mr. Tracy came to dinner.

Thomas Atwood Digges (1742–1821) was the sole surviving son of William Digges of Warburton. Thomas and his brother George (d. 1792) had been in school in England when the Revolution broke out, and although George soon returned home to Maryland, Thomas remained in England. There he followed a controversial and frequently discreditable career. During the Revolution he undoubtedly worked to alleviate the sufferings of American prisoners of war in Britain, but he also seems to have pocketed a large por-

*Eleanor ("Nelly") Parke Custis in her wedding gown, by James Sharples.
(National Trust for Historic Preservation)*

tion of the money sent him for this purpose and was accused of being both
a double agent and a thief (*William and Mary Quarterly*, 3d ser., 22 (1965),
486–92; *Pa. Mag.*, 77 (1953), 381–438). Thomas Digges arrived back in
America in 1799 and took up residence at Warburton.

11. Went up to Alexandria to the celebration of my birth day. Many
Manœuvres were performed by the Uniform Corps and an elegant Ball
& Supper at Night.

> Participating in the maneuvers in honor of the Old Style date of GW's birth-
> day were the Alexandria Silver Grays, the "Volunteer Troop of Light Dra-
> goons," and the Alexandria Dragoons (*Columbian Mirror*, 9 Feb. 1799). The
> ball was held at Gadsby's tavern, which was located on Royal Street at the
> corner of Cameron.

22. The Revd. Mr. Davis & Mr. Geo. Calvert came to dinner & Miss
Custis was married abt. Candle light to Mr. Lawe Lewis.

Revd. Mr. Davis: Thomas Davis, Episcopalian clergyman of Charles City County, was an usher at the College of William and Mary 1768 and was ordained in London 1773. Davis later this year presided at GW's funeral.

April

3. Went up to four mile run to run round my land there. Got on the grd. about 10 Oclock and in Company with Captn. Terret and Mr. Luke commenced the Survey on 4 mile run & ran agreeably to the Notes taken. In the evening went to Alexa. & lodged myself at Mr. Fitzhughs.

> *My land there:* This plot of about 1,200 acres on Four Mile Run, bought by GW in 1775, lay about four miles north of Alexandria on the road to Leesburg. It had been losing timber to trespassers for years, and GW particularly suspected the owners of adjoining lands, among whom were Capt. William Henry Terrett, Jr. (d. 1826), and John Luke.

12. Doctr. Wade came this Aftn. Spread Plaster of Paris this Morning on the circle & sides before the door & on the Lawn to the Cross Path betwn. the Garden gates & on the Clover by the Stable.

> Dr. Robert H. Wade had been to Mount Vernon three times during March and April to attend sick slaves.

17. Jno. Tayloe Esqr. & Mr. Jno. Herbert came here to dinner.

> John Tayloe (1771–1828) was one of the most notable owners of racehorses in Virginia at the turn of the century. He divided his time between his family home, Mount Airy, in Richmond County and his town house—the Octagon House—built for him in the Federal City.

21. A B. Heppesley Coxe Esqr. recomd. by Mr. [William] Bingham came here to dinnr.

> *B. Heppesley Coxe:* probably John Francis Buller Hippisley Coxe of Stone Easton, Somerset, Eng. He was the son of James Buller of Devon and his wife, Mary Hippisley Coxe Buller, of Somerset. In 1793 young Buller by royal license had assumed the surnames of Hippisley Coxe.

24. Gentlemen who came yesterday went away after breakfast and I went up to Alexa. to an Election of a Representative from the District to Congress & from the County to the State Legisla[tur]e.

> *From the District:* GW voted for Henry (Light Horse Harry) Lee, who won election to the United States House of Representatives for the Sixth Congress, which was the only term he served. Three weeks after the first session opened, on 26 Dec. 1799, Lee spoke for the whole Congress on the death of GW and reminded his fellow Americans that while GW was "First in war— first in peace—and first in the hearts of his countrymen, he was second to none in the humble and endearing scenes of private life" (*Annals of Congress,* 10:1310). *From the County:* Richard Bland Lee and Thomas Swann were elected to the Virginia House of Delegates from Fairfax County.

29. Went up to run round my land on 4 Mile run. Lodged at Colo. Littles.

30. Engaged in the same business as yesterday & returned home in the afternoon.

May

6. Mr. & Mrs. Lewis set out on their journey.

> Nelly and Lawrence Lewis left Mount Vernon on a prolonged round of visits to the homes of various members of Lawrence's family. They were away from Mount Vernon most of the time until late October or early November (Eleanor Parke Custis Lewis to Elizabeth Bordley, 14 Nov. 1799, owned by Mount Vernon).

10th. Mr. Thos. Digges & Mr. Jas. Welch dined here & retd.

> The due date for Welch's first payment on the Kanawha lands (31 Dec. 1798) had gone by without GW receiving any word from Welch. GW wrote several times requesting the money due him. He not only needed the money, but as he finally wrote Welch on 7 April 1799, "I have heard too much of your character lately, not to expect tale after tale, and relation after relation, of your numerous disappointments, by way of excuses for the noncompliance of your agreement with me . . . however you may have succeeded in imposing upon and deceiving others, you shall not practice the like game with me, with impunity" (Washington Papers, Library of Congress). Welch protested his good intentions and promised to come to Mount Vernon in May. Welch was still unable at this time to come up with the money, and although GW gave him a further extension until November, he never received a penny from Welch for the lands. After GW's death, his executors seem to have canceled the contract and permitted Welch to keep his Elk River lands.

14. Majr. Wm. Harrison came here to dinner.

> GW, who believed Harrison's tenants were stealing timber and livestock from Mount Vernon, wished to lease or buy Harrison's land to rid himself of those particular neighbors. On 10 April 1799 GW wrote to Harrison: "if you will come & take a bed at my house, I have a Clerk (living with me) who Surveys very well & shall do it for you without cost, the next day" (Washington Papers, Library of Congress).

23. Mr. Thos. Adams, third son to the President & Mr. Joshua Johnson, Lady & son came to dinr.

> Thomas Boylston Adams (1772–1832) was the third son of Pres. John Adams. Joshua Johnson (b. 1742), a brother of Gov. Thomas Johnson of Maryland, served as an American agent in France during the American Revolution and was later appointed by GW as the first American consul at London.

June

11. Bishop Carroll, Mr. Digges & his Sister Carroll—Mr. Pye & Doctr. Craik all dined here.

Bishop John Carroll (1735–1815), son of Daniel Carroll (1696-1750/51) of Upper Marlboro, was born in Upper Marlboro, Md., studied for the priesthood at the Jesuit College at Liege, and returned to Maryland in 1774. While sympathetic to the American Revolutionaries, his only major activity in the Revolution was in accompanying the American mission to Canada in 1776. After the Revolution, Carroll became the first Roman Catholic bishop in the United States. *His sister Carroll:* Although GW may have meant Bishop Carroll's unmarried sister Elizabeth Carroll, he probably meant Thomas Digges's sister Elizabeth Digges Carroll (1743–1845), widow of Bishop Carroll's nephew Daniel Carroll, Jr., of Rock Creek (d. 1790).

Mr. Pye is probably one of the members of the Pye family of Charles County, Md. A Mr. Charles Pye had been entrusted by Thomas Atwood Digges with a box of seeds sent GW by a London seedsman during the previous year.

20. The following company dined here—Chief Justice of the U.S. Ellsworth Mr. & Mrs. Steer Senr.—Mr. & Mrs. Steer Junr. Mr. Van Havre— Mr. & Mrs. Ludwell Lee—Mrs. Corbin Washington Mr. & Mrs. Hodgson & Miss Cora. Lee Mr. & Mrs. Geo. Calvert and a Captn. Hamilton & Lady from the Bahama Islands.

GW's dinner guests today included: Oliver Ellsworth, whom GW appointed in 1796 to the United States Supreme Court as chief justice of the United States; Henri Joseph Stier and his wife, Marie Louise Peeters Stier; their son Jean Charles Stier and his wife, Marie Van Havre Stier; Marie's brother Jean Michel Van Havre, an émigré from Belgium; Ludwell Lee and his second wife, Elizabeth Armistead Lee; William Hodgson and his bride, Portia Lee Hodgson; Portia's younger sister Cornelia; and George Calvert and his bride of nine days, Rosalie Eugenia Stier (1778–1821), daughter of Henri and Marie Stier. *Mrs. Corbin Washington:* Hannah Lee (1766–c.1801), second daughter of Richard Henry Lee, married Corbin Washington in 1787.

July

3. Doctr. Stuart, & a Parson Lattum from Pennsylvania dined here & left it in the afternoon.

Parson Lattum: probably Rev. James Latta (1732–1801), Presbyterian minister of Chestnut Level, Lancaster County, Pa., or one of his sons.

4. Went up to Alexa. and dined with a number of the Citizens there in celebration of the anniversary of the declaration of American Independe. at Kemps Tavern.

Kemps Tavern: Peter Kemp ran the Globe Tavern at the northeast corner of Cameron and Fairfax streets.

23. Mr. Needham Washington came in the afternoon.

> Needham (Nedham) Langhorne Washington (d. 1833), eldest son of Law-
> rence Washington (b. 1728) of Chotank and Elizabeth Dade Washington, in-
> herited his father's plantation in the Chotank neighborhood of King George
> County.

August

5. Went up to George Town, to a general Meeting of the Potomac Company—dined at the Union Tavern & lodged at Mr. Law's.

> In July 1799 a letter had been sent to each shareholder in the Potomac
> Company, outlining the financial plight of the company and soliciting assis-
> tance. The president (James Keith) reported that tolls were down from the
> previous year and work had been at a standstill for the past two seasons. How-
> ever, a new machine for hoisting cargo over the Great Falls had been in-
> stalled, replacing an earlier one, and there was still hope that the state of
> Maryland would lend further assistance. This was the last meeting GW was
> to attend. The Potomac Company survived until 1828, when it was incorpo-
> rated into the Chesapeake and Ohio Canal Company.

September

6. Mr. B[ushrod] W[ashington] & wife went after breakfast. Doctr.
Craik who was sent for in the Night to Mrs. Washington came early this
Morning.

> *Doctr. Craik who was sent for in the night:* GW wrote Thomas Peter on 7 Sept.
> that "Mrs. Washington has been exceedingly unwell for more than eight
> days. Yesterday she was so ill as to keep her bed all day, and to occasion my
> sending for Doctr. Craik the night before, at Midnight. She is now better,
> and taking the Bark; but low, weak and fatiegued—under his direction. Her's
> has been a kind of Ague & fever—the latter never, entirely, intermitting until
> now. I sent for the Doctor to her on Sunday last, but she could not, until he
> came the second time—yesterday morning—be prevailed upon to take any-
> thing to arrest them." After sealing the letter, GW added a postscript saying
> that the fever had returned "with uneasy & restless symptoms." He requested
> that Mrs. Eliza Law also be informed (manuscript owned by Mount Vernon).
> Mrs. Washington's illness persisted for several weeks, and not until late Octo-
> ber did GW write that she was "tolerably well" (GW to William Augustine
> Washington, 22 Sept. 1799, manuscript owned by Mount Vernon).

12. Cap: Truxton came to dinner.

> Thomas Truxton (1755–1822) was owner and master of several privateers
> during the Revolution and later was a merchant trading with the Orient. In
> 1794 he was appointed captain in the United States Navy. In Feb. 1799 Trux-
> ton, commanding the frigate *Constellation,* met and captured the French frig-
> ate *L'Insurgent* in a battle in the West Indies; he returned to America to find
> himself acclaimed a hero. Truxton was at Mount Vernon by GW's invitation.

October

15. A Mr. Bourdieu of the House of Bourdieu, Chollet & Bordieu of London (accompanied by a Mr. Gardner)—Mr. Gill & Mr. B. Bassett dined here. The three first went away afterwards.

> Mr. Bourdieu is either James Bourdieu or his son James, both partners in the important London firm of Bourdieu, Chollet & Bourdieu which remained in business at the same address in London from the 1740s to the 1840s. John Gill, whom GW termed "late of Alexandria," came to Mount Vernon to discuss his rental payments for GW's land on Difficult Run.

29. Colo. Griffen Mr. Law and a Mr. Valangin (an Engh. Gentleman introduced by Mr. Barthw. Dandridge). The latter went away afterwards.

> Charles W. Valangin, the son of Dr. de Valangin of London, came to the United States with the intention of making it his permanent residence. He was especially interested in agriculture. Dandridge had written him a letter of introduction to GW because he knew of GW's desire "to encourage improvement of our husbandry by the introduction of farmers of good character" and felt Valangin's information on modern English farming methods would make him a welcome visitor to Mount Vernon. Dandridge wrote that Valangin brought with him samples of many varieties of English seed which Dandridge "advised him in the first instance to entrust to yr. care & which he will do with pleasure" (Bartholomew Dandridge, Jr., to GW, 1 July 1799, Washington Papers, Library of Congress).

November

2. Mr. Jno. Fairfax (formerly an overseer of mine) came here before dinner and stayed all Night.

> John Fairfax resigned from GW's employ in Dec. 1790 and settled in Monongalia County, where he became a justice of the peace in 1794 and later represented that county in the Virginia House of Delegates (1809–10, 1814–15).

5th. Set out on a trip to Difficult-run to view some Land I had there & some belonging to Mr. Jno. Gill who had offered it to me in discharge of Rent which he was owing me. Dined at Mr. Nicholas Fitzhughs and lodged at Mr. Corbin Washingtons.

> *Difficult-run:* On his 15 Oct. visit John Gill offered to sign over some of his own land on Difficult Run to pay back rents he owed to GW.

7. Finished Surveying my own Tract & the Land belonging to Gill— returning, as the Night before to Wileys Tavern.

> John Gill's land lay on both sides of Difficult Run near the bridge. For this surveying GW brought along a surveyor and several local residents to help find old boundary markers (GW to John Gill, 12 Nov. 1799). GW was unimpressed by Gill's land, since the 85 acres Gill was offering GW were "not only

extremely hilly & broken, but much worn and gullied" (GW to Gill, 12 Nov. 1799, DLC:GW). He made a counterproposal to Gill but died before any agreement was reached.

8. I returned to Wiley's Tavern & stayed there the remainder of the day.

15. Rode to visit Mr. now Lord Fairfax who has just got home from a Trip to England. Retd. to dinner.

While in England, Bryan Fairfax applied for certification as eighth Baron Fairfax of Cameron, succeeding his deceased cousin Robert Fairfax (d. 1793), seventh Baron Fairfax of Cameron. In May 1800 his claim was accepted by the House of Lords.

27. Doctr. Craik who was sent for to Mrs. Lewis (& who was delivered of a daughter abt. [   ] oclock in the forenoon) came to Breakfast & stayed [to] dinner.

Eleanor Parke (Nelly) Custis Lewis's daughter was named Frances Parke Lewis (d. 1875).

December

12. Morning Cloudy—Wind at No. Et. & Mer. 33. A large circle round the Moon last Night. About 1 oclock it began to snow—soon after to Hail and then turned to a settled cold Rain. Mer. 28 at Night.

13. Morning Snowing & abt. 3 Inches deep. Wind at No. Et. & Mer. at 30. Contg. Snowing till 1 Oclock and abt. 4 it became perfectly clear. Wind in the same place but not hard. Mer. 28 at Night.

On Thursday, 12 Dec., in the midst of the day's severe weather, GW rode out to supervise winter activities at the various farms, becoming wet and chilled in the course of his ride. On Friday, the 13th, in spite of a developing cold and sore throat, he went out on the front lawn late in the day to mark some trees for cutting. During the night he awoke with a severe inflammation of the throat. The best account of GW's final hours are contained in the diary of Tobias Lear, who had returned to GW's service in the summer of 1798 and resumed his previous role as secretary and executive assistant. "Between two & three o'clock on Saturday Morning, he awoke Mrs. Washington, and told her he was very unwell, and had had an ague. She observed that he could scarcely speak and breathed with difficulty; and would have got up to call a Servant; but he would not permit her lest she should take cold. As soon as the day appeared, the Woman (Caroline) went into the Room to make a fire, and Mrs. Washington sent her immediately to call me. I got up, put on my clothes as quickly as possible and went to his Chamber. Mrs. Washington was then up, and related to me his being taken ill as before stated. I found the General breathing with difficulty, and hardly able to utter a word intelligibly. He desired that Mr. (One of the Overseers) might be sent for to bleed him before the

Doctors could arrive. I dispatched a Servant instantly for Rawlins, and another for Dr. Craik, and returned again to the General's Chamber, where I found him in the same situation as I had left him. A mixture of Molasses, Vinegar & butter was prepared to try its effects in the throat; but he could not swallow a drop; whenever he attempted it he appeared to be distressed, convulsed and almost suffocated. Rawlins came in soon after sun rise, and prepared to bleed him. When the Arm was ready the General observing that Rawlins appeared to be agitated—said, as well as he could speak 'Don't be afraid.' And after the incision was made, he observed 'The orifice is not large enough.' However the blood ran pretty freely. Mrs. Washington not knowing whether bleeding was proper or not in the General's situation, begged that much might not be taken from him, lest it should be injurious, and desired me to stop it; but when I was about to untie the string, the General put up his hand to prevent it, and as soon as he could speak, said—'more, more!' Mrs. Washington being still very uneasy lest too much blood should be taken, it was stop'd after taking about half a pint. Finding that no relief was obtained from bleeding, and that nothing would go down the throat, I proposed bathing it externally with Salvilatila, which was done; and in the operation, which was with the hand, and in the gentlest manner, he observed "'tis very sore.' A piece of flannel dip'd in salvilatila was put round his neck, and his feet bathed in warm water; but without affording any relief.

"In the mean time; before Dr. Craik arrived, Mrs. Washington desired me to send for Dr. [Gustavus Richard] Brown of Port Tobacco whom Dr. Craik had recommended to be called, if any case should ever occur that was seriously alarming. I dispatched a messenger (Cyrus) immediately for Dr. Brown (between 8 & 9 o'clock). Dr. Craik came in soon after, and upon examining the General, he put a blister of Cantharides on the Throat, took some more blood from him, and had a gargle of Vinegar & sage tea and ordered some Vinegar & hot water for him to inhale the steam, which he did; but in attempting to use the gargle he was almost suffocated. When the gargle came from the throat some phegm followed it. And he attempted to cough, which the Doctor encouraged him to do as much as possible, but he could only attempt it. About eleven o'clock Dr. Craik requested that Dr. [Elisha Cullen] Dick might be sent for, as he feared Dr. Brown would not come in time. A messenger was accordingly dispatched for him. About this time the General was bled again. No effect, however, was produced by it, and he remained in the same state, unable to swallow anything. A glister was administered about 12 o'clock, which produced an evacuation; but caused no aleration in his complaint.

"Dr. Dick came in about 3 o'clock, and Dr. Brown arrived soon after. Upon Dr. Dick's seeing the General, and consulting a few minutes with Dr. Craik, he was bled again; the blood came very slow, was thick, and did not produce any symptoms of fainting. Dr. Brown came into the chamber soon after; and upon feeling the general's pulse &c. the Physicians went out together.

Dr. Craik returned soon after. The Genl. Could now swallow a little. Calomil & tarter em. were administered; but without any effect.

"About half past 4 O'clk. He desired me to call Mrs. Washington to his bed side, when he requested her to go down into his room, and take from his desk two Wills which she would find there, and bring them to him; which she did. Upon looking at them he gave her one, which he observed was useless, as being superseded by the other, and desired her to burn it, which she did, and took the other and put it into her closet.

"After this was done, *I returned to his bed side and took his hand. He said to me,* 'I find I am going, my breath cannot last long; I believed from the first that the disorder would prove fatal. Do you arrange & record all my late military letters and papers. Arrange my accounts and settle my books, as you know more about them than any one else, and let Mr. Rawlins finish recording my other letters which he has begun.' *I told him this should be done. He then asked if I recollected anything which it was essential for him to do, as he had but a very short time to continue among us. I told him I could recollect nothing; but that I hoped he was not so near his end; he observed, smiling, that he certainly was, and that as it was the debt which must all pay, he looked to the event with perfect resignation.*

"In the course of the afternoon he appeared to be in great pain & distress, from the difficulty of breathing, and frequently changed his position in the bed. On these occasions I lay upon the bed & endeavoured to raise him, & turn him with as much care as possible. He appeared penetrated with gratitude for my attentions, & often said, I am afraid I shall fatigue you too much; and upon my assuring him that I could feel nothing but a wish to give him ease; he replied *'Well! It is a debt we must pay to each other, and I hope when you want aid of this kind you will find it.'* . . .

"About 5 O'clk Dr. Craik came again into the Room & upon going to the bed side, the Genl. Said to him, [']Doctor, I die hard; but I am not afraid to go, I believed from my first attack, that I should not survive it; my breath cannot last long.['] *The Doctor pressed his hand; but could not utter a word. He retired from the bed side & sat by the fire absorbed in grief.*

"Between 5 & 6 o'clk Dr. Dick & Dr. Brown came into the room, and with Dr. Craik went to the bed; when Dr. Craik asked him if he could sit up in the bed. He held out his hand & I raised him up. He then said to the Physicians, 'I feel myself going, I thank you for your attentions; but I pray you to take no more trouble about me, let me go off quietly; I cannot last long.' *They found that all which had been done was without effect, he laid down again, and all retired, exceptg Dr. Craik. He continued in the same situation, uneasy & restless; but without complaining; frequently asking what hour it was. When I helped him to move at this time he did not speak; but looked at me with strong expressions of gratitude.*

"About 8 oclk the Physicians came again into the room & applied blisters *and cataplasms of wheat bran to his legs & feet; after which they went out (except Dr. Craik) without a ray of hope.*

I went out about this time and wrote a line to Mr. Law & Mr. Peter, requesting them to come with their wives (Mrs. Washingtons granddaughters) as soon as possible to Mt. Vernon.

"About ten o'clk he made several attempts to speak to me before he could effect it; at length he said, 'I am just going! Have me decently buried; and do not let my body be put into the vault in less than three days after I am dead.' *I bowed assent, for I could not speak. He then looked at me again and said,* 'Do you understand me? ['] *I replied yes;* ['] 'Tis well' *said he.*

"About ten minutes before he expired (which was between ten & eleven o'clk) his breathing became easier; he lay quietly; he withdrew his hand from mine, and felt his own pulse. I saw his countenance change—I spoke to Dr. Craik, who sat by the fire; he came to the bedside. The general's hand fell from his wrist—I took it in mine and put it into my bosom. Dr. Craik put his hands over his Eyes and he expired without a struggle or a sigh!

"While we were fixed in silent grief, Mrs. Washington (who was sitting at the foot of the bed) asked, with a firm & collected voice, Is he gone? I could not speak; but held up my hand as a signal that he was no more. 'Tis well, said she in the same voice, 'All is now over, I shall soon follow him! I have no more trials to pass through!'" *(Tobias Lear Diary, Historical Society of Pennsylvania).*

Washington was buried in the family vault at Mount Vernon on Wednesday, 18 Dec. 1799.

Index